8/09 UC

The Price of DEFIANCE

The Price of

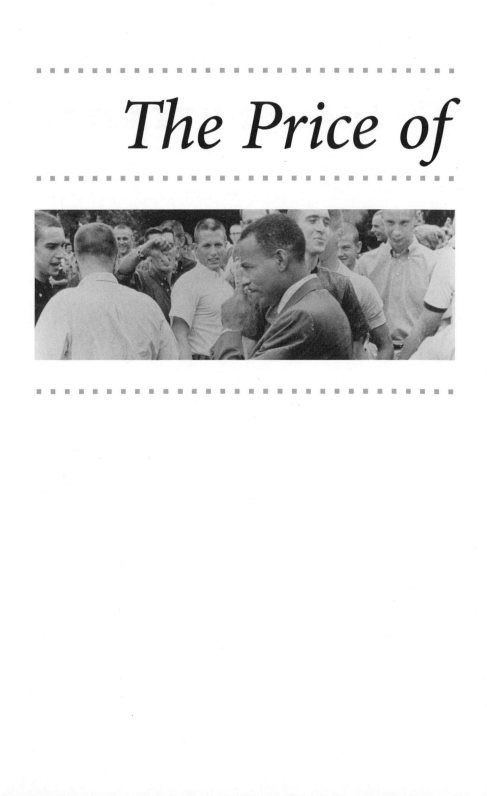

DEFIANCE

James Meredith and the Integration of Ole Miss

CHARLES W. EAGLES

The University of North Carolina Press

CHAPEL HILL

The publication of this book was supported by a
generous grant from the Watson-Brown Foundation, Inc.

The following song lyrics have been reprinted with permission: "Alma Mater," words and
music by Michael McWhinney and Jerry Powell, © 1963, 1964 by Alley Music Corp. and
Trio Music Company, copyright renewed, international copyright secured, all rights reserved;
"Oxford Town," by Bob Dylan, © 1963, renewed 1991 Special Rider Music, all rights reserved,
international copyright secured.

Parts of this book have been reprinted with permission in revised form from the following
works: "The Closing of Mississippi Society: Will Campbell, 'The $64,000 Question,' and Reli-
gious Emphasis Week at the University of Mississippi," *Journal of Southern History* 67 (May
2001): 331–72; " 'Thought Control' in Mississippi: The Case of Professor William P. Murphy,"
Journal of Mississippi History 66 (Summer 2004): 151–99; and " 'The Fight for Men's Minds':
The Aftermath of the Ole Miss Riot of 1962," *Journal of Mississippi History* (forthcoming).

Set in Minion by Keystone Typesetting, Inc.

The paper in this book meets the guidelines for permanence and durability of the Committee
on Production Guidelines for Book Longevity of the Council on Library Resources.

The University of North Carolina Press has been a member of the Green Press Initiative since 2003.

Library of Congress Cataloging-in-Publication Data
Eagles, Charles W.
The price of defiance : James Meredith and the integration of Ole Miss / Charles W. Eagles.
    p. cm.
Includes bibliographical references and index.
ISBN 978-0-8078-3273-8 (cloth : alk. paper)
1. University of Mississippi—History. 2. Meredith, James, 1933– 3. College integration—
Mississippi—Oxford—History. 4. African Americans—Civil rights. 5. Civil rights—
Mississippi—Oxford—History. I. Title.
    LD3413.E24 2009
    378.762'83—dc22   2008047142

13 12 11 10 09   5 4 3 2 1

For Brenda, Daniel, and Benjamin

Toast to Ole Miss

*Here's to Ole Miss who fluttered and flared and
cussed and sweared and tried to keep colored folks
out by hook or by crook, and loopholes they took in
the law, and indignations and proclamations and
brickbats to the jaw, showing off their bravery like in
slavery when white folks was the law and they could
knock a colored man down, right to the ground, and
he dare not fight back because he was black. But in
this day and time, things is not that way. A toast to
Ole Miss on Integration Day.*

LANGSTON HUGHES, *Chicago Defender,*
October 27–November 12, 1962

Contents

A section of photographs appears after page 198.

The Price of DEFIANCE

Introduction

■ ■

After his first night in his dormitory room, James Meredith rode in a riot-battered border patrol car to the Lyceum building at the center of the University of Mississippi campus. Escorted by agents of the U.S. Justice Department, he observed the debris from the previous evening's conflagration as he entered the Lyceum at 8:15 A.M. to register for classes. His enrollment on Monday, October 1, 1962, made him the first black student formally admitted to the school popularly known as Ole Miss, and indeed the first to breach racial segregation in the state's system of higher education. The story of his struggle for admission to the all-white university also involves white Mississippi's long defiance of racial change at Ole Miss.

Meredith's venture at Ole Miss exhibited several characteristics atypical of other desegregation efforts. In his initial overture to the university, Meredith acted alone, not as part of any organized movement; only later did he receive assistance from the National Association for the Advancement of Colored People (NAACP). The evening before Meredith registered, his challenge precipitated a deadly riot on the university campus. The president of the United States deployed the army to restore order. The resistance to integration was so intense because Meredith waged his crusade in Mississippi, perhaps the most intransigently segregationist southern state, and because he targeted Ole Miss, an especially powerful symbol for white Mississippians. The most violent confrontation over school integration evolved from many complex historical factors, and it occurred at the University of Mississippi in 1962 for reasons peculiar to that time and place.

Meredith's enrollment at the University of Mississippi completed a campaign that he initiated with his first letter to the university in January 1961. Though not at first sponsored by any civil rights group, Meredith's quest became an important event in the wider black freedom struggle. During his service in the air force from 1951 to 1959, Meredith missed the emergence of the civil rights movement and its increasing momentum after the *Brown v. Board of Education of Topeka* Supreme Court decision and the Montgomery bus boycott. The movement that revolutionized race relations occurred unevenly across the South, and though Mississippi had a majority-black population as late as 1930 and the largest black population percentage of any state in 1960, the freedom struggle came late to his rural, recalcitrant home state.

NAACP branches had existed in Mississippi since the 1910s, but only after World War II did they begin to prove effective. In the late 1940s the state NAACP fought for equal pay for black teachers and for the right to vote for all blacks. Voter registration increased after the war, and NAACP branches developed in many towns across the state. Black indigenous activism increased, and after the *Brown* decision blacks took tentative steps toward school integration. Whites quickly retaliated. Started by Mississippi whites in the summer of 1954, the Citizens' Councils waged a campaign of repression against any challenge to white supremacy and racial segregation. In 1955 the notorious lynching of Emmett Till evidenced the dominant power of whites. Between 1956 and 1959 ten blacks were killed by whites, and in 1959 Mack Charles Parker, charged with raping a white woman, was lynched in southwestern Mississippi. The violent, repressive tactics of white segregationists blunted the efforts of the NAACP, the Regional Council of Negro Leadership, and other black activist groups and delayed the emergence of the Mississippi movement. In her memoirs, Myrlie Evers, the widow of murdered NAACP leader Medgar Evers, maintained that the movement had "stagnated" in the "backwater" of Mississippi until the spring of 1961. In April of that year Tougaloo College students staged a sit-in at the Jackson Public Library, and the next month the Freedom Rides arrived in Jackson.[1] The previous January, James Meredith had contacted the university and begun his assault on white supremacy.

By the time of Meredith's application to Ole Miss, the long process of desegregating southern higher education had been underway for more than two decades. Begun in the 1930s, it had progressed slowly. Although nearly all southern colleges remained segregated at the time of the *Brown* decision, a few colleges in twelve of the seventeen southern and border states had desegregated. The admission of blacks occurred initially in graduate and professional programs, and first in the border and peripheral southern states. The University of Maryland law school enrolled a black student in 1936, and state universities in Oklahoma, Arkansas, and Kentucky desegregated in the 1940s. In 1950 the law schools at the University of Virginia and Louisiana State University admitted their first black students, and in 1952 the University of Tennessee's graduate and professional program started to admit blacks. After the *Brown* decision in 1954, desegregation of higher education continued. The District of Columbia's colleges ended segregation in 1954, followed a year later by the University of North Carolina. In 1956 Autherine Lucy attended classes at the University of Alabama for only a few days before being expelled. As late as

1960, however, South Carolina, Georgia, Alabama, and Mississippi still maintained completely segregated public universities.[2]

When Meredith applied to Ole Miss, pressures on all-white colleges were escalating. On January 3, 1961, the first three black undergraduates enrolled at the University of Tennessee in Knoxville; at the same time, the university medical school in Memphis admitted its first black student. Also, early in January, just two weeks before Meredith made his original inquiry, a federal judge ordered the University of Georgia to enroll its first two black undergraduates. After some disturbances and last-ditch attempts to block their enrollment, Hamilton E. Holmes and Charlayne Hunter began attending classes in Athens on January 11.[3] By the end of the month James Meredith had applied to Ole Miss.

Some aspects of the story of James Meredith and the integration of the University of Mississippi have previously been told. Three books appeared within a few years of the riot. Drawing on a quarter-century of experience as a history professor at the university, James W. Silver's *Mississippi: The Closed Society* (1964) presented a fervent, impressionistic analysis of the state's repressive culture and a brief description of "the great confrontation and its aftermath." Though it reproduced nearly one hundred pages of his personal correspondence, Silver's book drew on no archival research and contained no footnotes. Two significant books appeared in 1965. Popular nonfiction writer Walter Lord interviewed more than one hundred people and delved into court records to write *The Past That Would Not Die* about the riot and its causes, but his journalistic account slighted both the university's past and Meredith the man. Drawing extensively on newspaper coverage, Russell Barrett, a political scientist at the university, compiled *Integration at Ole Miss*, a factual narrative of Meredith's case from his first application to his graduation. The following year in *Three Years in Mississippi*, James Meredith provided his own firsthand account of his experiences back home after leaving the air force in 1960.[4]

Three decades later three accounts by journalists offered competing perspectives. Nadine Cohodas's sprawling story in *The Band Played Dixie: Race and the Liberal Conscience at Ole Miss* reported on integration from some early attempts through the 1962 riot and the state of race relations on campus in the late 1990s. She relied mainly on interviews, published sources, and newspapers. Narrowing his focus to "the Battle of Oxford," documentary producer William Doyle wrote a detailed, dramatic account of the military's involvement in 1962 that drew on many interviews and some government documents. In *An American Insurrection: The Battle of Oxford, Mississippi, 1962*, Doyle paid little attention to the historical context and to larger questions involving race, the university, and state politics. Paul Hendrickson's *Sons of Mississippi: A Story of Race and Its Legacy* used the 1962 riot as the background for an examination of how race subsequently affected several families involved in the violence at Ole Miss.[5] Histories of the civil rights movement and of the Kennedy administration also have included brief discussions of the crisis at the University of Mississippi as part of their larger subjects.[6]

The Price of Defiance examines events within the broader context of the confluence of race, politics, and higher education in postwar Mississippi. It analyzes the culture of racial segregation, the politics of white supremacy, and the history of Ole Miss. A dissection of what James Silver called the "closed society" probes the local, institutional, and personal backgrounds of the violent clash and the obsession of many Mississippi whites with preserving segregation, particularly at Ole Miss. Examination of a variety of episodes and events involving early attempts at integration, life on the segregated campus, religion, intercollegiate athletics, state politics, and academic freedom reveals a multifaceted portrait of the institution and its complex race relations. More than two decades before 1962, overlapping and escalating events reinforced the importance of race at Ole Miss, made clear the meaning and power of the "closed society," and created the hostile environment in which James Meredith found himself in the early 1960s.

James Meredith was the essential actor, the proximate cause of the 1962 crisis. When examined in detail, he emerges as far more complicated than a stereotypical movement crusader or hero. Born in Attala County, Mississippi, and raised on his parents' farm, he benefited from their strength and independence. His unusual family background, his personal values, and his air force service helped to prepare him for his assault on white supremacy. Dedicated to his cause, Meredith quietly persisted despite all the obstacles he confronted. The account of his extended fight through the federal courts to gain admission to the university demonstrates his character and exposes the unsavory tactics of the state's segregationist leaders to delay, if not completely prevent, desegregation.

Even after the federal courts ordered Meredith's admission, Mississippi remained defiant. As a result Meredith, assisted by the U.S. Department of Justice, clashed repeatedly with inflexible state leaders when he tried to register. The story of the skirmishes and confrontations provides a neglected prelude to the violent deaths and destruction of September 30–October 1, 1962, when the state and the university finally paid the price for their defiance. For Meredith, however, his mission continued for another tumultuous and stressful year as an Ole Miss student. He graduated in August 1963, and after his experience, other blacks matriculated more easily. As black enrollment grew in succeeding decades, the university periodically experienced other, comparatively minor, racial controversies. One measure of Ole Miss's adjustment to racial change came in 2006 with the dedication of a campus civil rights memorial that included a statue of James Meredith, but even it sparked controversy and proved that issues involving race had not finally been settled.

PART ONE *Ole Miss and Race*

■ ■

1. "Welcome to Ole Miss, Where Everybody Speaks"

■ ■

At the start of the 1960 football season, *Sports Illustrated* featured a full-page color photograph of a beautiful young woman and a handsome football player strolling hand in hand across the University of Mississippi campus.[1] Although many colleges had pretty women and good-looking male athletes, the article's title, "Babes, Brutes, and Ole Miss," seemed more applicable to Ole Miss than to its competitors. *Sports Illustrated* had captured in a single image the university's national reputation: it was, as the caption suggested, home to "the best of both worlds," beauty queens and winning football teams.[2]

The university's renown received powerful confirmation in September 1958 when senior Mary Ann Mobley became the first Mississippian to win the Miss America beauty pageant. She had the year before finished second in the Miss Mississippi contest and earlier had been selected as National Football Queen, State Forestry Queen, and State Travel Queen. Mobley, an excellent student, came to the university in 1955 in the first group of prestigious Carrier Scholars, and she served as an officer in student government and had been selected for Mortar Board, an honorary leadership group. A trained singer, dancer, and model, the "brown-haired Southern belle" sang a medley of operatic and popular songs and performed a modern jazz dance for the Miss America judges and a national television audience. Her selection thrilled Mississippi. After a spontaneous street party by three thousand people that lasted past midnight in her small hometown of Brandon, Mayor John McLaurin said being Miss America's mayor was a special honor, and he praised the little girl he had watched grow up. One Mississippian declared her selection "the best thing that had happened to Mississippi since the South won the first Battle of Bull Run."[3]

One year later, the day after the Miss America pageant, the *Jackson Clarion-Ledger*'s front page proudly announced, "The Miss America crown stays in Mississippi." Outgoing queen Mary Ann Mobley crowned Lynda Lee Mead of Natchez as Miss America for 1960. For the first time in more than twenty years, the crown remained in the same state, and for the fifth time in ten years a southern girl was named Miss America. Not only were Mobley and Mead fellow students, they also were sorority sisters in Chi Omega. Once again the campus, as well as the rest of the state, went "wild over Lynda's victory," with perhaps the biggest celebration at the Chi Omega house. The chapter president said her sorority sisters were "overjoyed and just happy." Mead's selection particularly pleased the campus because she had started out as Miss University. Two weeks after her crowning, the proud student newspaper ran four extra pages of stories and pictures of the school's second Miss America. A Jackson newspaper columnist boasted, "Mississippi may be last in a lot of things, but we can cite to the world that we are first in womanhood!"[4]

Although the university had gained national fame for its beautiful women, the emphasis on female beauty ran deeper than two Miss Americas. Each year after World War II, dozens competed in the Miss University pageant and others entered contests in towns across the state and the South. Eight times between 1948 and 1961, a student had been crowned Miss Mississippi, and twice in the late 1940s the university had hosted the state contest. In 1961, for the fourth consecutive year, an Ole Miss student went to Atlantic City as Miss Mississippi, and for the first time women from Ole Miss also represented Missouri and Tennessee.[5]

Beauty and beauty contests had long formed an integral part of student life at the university. In 1909 students first elected the most beautiful woman, and in 1918 the yearbook began including a "Parade of Beauties." The yearbook also perennially displayed dozens of photographs of pretty girls chosen by various groups as queens, favorites, and sponsors. The competition could be keen: a month after the second Chi Omega was crowned Miss America, the student newspaper carried a lengthy article about beauty titles held by the new pledges of Delta Delta Delta to prove that their sorority "isn't short on beauty either." One Tri-Delt was Mississippi's Miss Hospitality, Miss Franklin County, and Forestry Queen for 1957, while another reportedly, and importantly, had "probably won more beauty crowns than any girl on the Ole Miss campus." Photographs of the young women accompanied the story.[6]

Other female students, not just the official beauty queens, also routinely impressed visitors to the campus. One concluded that "beauty here is no legend." Enjoying watching the women, another male guest did not find "one unattractive" woman or one "lacking in taste, in dress or grooming. At least half," he concluded, were "actually pretty and an astonishing number beautiful." The "fetching girl students with voices like pearls floating in a dish of cornmeal mush" nearly overwhelmed a reporter from outside Mississippi.[7]

As the *Sports Illustrated* photograph suggested, the university's football teams matched its beauty queens in stimulating school pride and in garnering national recognition for the school. The phenomena of athletes and beauty often intertwined at Ole Miss. The woman in the picture was the daughter of the baseball coach, and she would marry the man in the photograph who was a baseball and football player and who would later serve as the university's athletic director. One young man who had dated both of the university's Miss Americas was an Academic All-American football player who would decades later become chancellor of the university.[8] Athletics, and particularly football, played an important role at the university.

The Ole Miss Rebels under coach John Vaught established a reputation as a big-time football program. After becoming the Rebels' head coach in 1947, Vaught compiled the second-best coaching record in major college football. In the late 1950s and early 1960s, the Rebels' golden age, Vaught's teams reached the pinnacle of collegiate football and, according to one expert, "set a national standard for excellence." Ole Miss won two Southeastern Conference (SEC) championships and went to five postseason bowl games in the 1950s, and in 1960 they became the national champions with a record of 10–0–1. The Rebels' achievement was particularly impressive because the teams played relatively few games in Oxford, with "home" games often before larger crowds in Memphis and Jackson.[9]

Ole Miss football was, however, more than a game on Saturday. One alumnus recalled that, in the late 1950s and early 1960s, "Football transcended almost all else." For the entire state, college football seemed to dominate each autumn. In 1960 *Time* described the effects of Rebel football: "Inspired by Ole Miss, the whole state vibrates in a constant football flap. No high school would think of scheduling a game for the time that Vaught's team is playing; anyone who cannot get over to Oxford for the Ole Miss game listens to it over his radio." On the Saturdays of home football games, thirty thousand fans descended on the remote small town. Each game was a major social event for the state's white elite—part reunion, part celebration of their football powerhouse, and part fancy party. In 1961 Ole Miss was the quintessential football school.[10]

Though Vaught's teams had great success, Ole Miss athletics included more than gridiron heroics. The Rebel baseball team won SEC championships in 1959 and 1960. Four Rebels made the all-SEC first team. In terms of national renown and popularity within the state, however, football was still king.[11]

Ole Miss's national image accurately reflected student life. According to one study of college environments in 1961, the university was "a freewheeling sort of place that fits very well with its newspaper reputation as a home for beauty queens and bowl teams."[12] The national survey confirmed many impressions of observers of the university. For example, the study found that Ole Miss students were generally very friendly and concerned about the welfare of others in their group. The university did, after all, encourage students to meet and speak to each other. At the beginning of the fall semester, special signs greeting students announced, "Welcome to Ole Miss, Where Everybody Speaks," and the campus paper promoted the school's reputation as "the friendly University." The official student handbook claimed Ole Miss's friendliness made it "unique in the system of great universities." One observer remarked that "even if they didn't say much the students spoke politely when spoken to." In most campus activities, "proper social forms and manners" were important, but the report found "a surface mannerliness" more than a thoroughgoing concern for others.[13]

Within such a friendly environment of only four thousand on a compact campus, students found teachers approachable and helpful outside of class, and most professors called students by their first names. Group activities, ranging from student government to intramural sports, played a significant role in the students' daily lives. In all activities, students displayed considerable school spirit and enthusiasm for their campus. The Ole Miss atmosphere probably differed little from that at other state institutions across the nation, while much smaller church-related liberal arts colleges had even friendlier campuses that supported meaningful group activities for their students.[14]

Compared to other college students, Ole Miss students demonstrated a remarkable lack of interest in intellectual, aesthetic, and humanistic concerns. A New York Times correspondent found few Ole Miss undergraduates had heard of Flaubert, Kierkegaard, Pushkin, Camus, or J. D. Salinger. To defend the university's intellectual climate, George M. Street, an assistant in public relations, polled a number of full professors and reported that none of them could identify all of the authors, which only proved the students were not so ignorant as the New York writer claimed. Street himself confessed that he had heard of only Camus, Pushkin, and Salinger and had never read any of their works. Similarly, although the Department of Modern Languages regularly screened foreign films with subtitles, few students reported having seen the movies. Describing the university's cultural life as "barren," one critic deplored the unavailability, even in Oxford, of a decent bookstore or any magazines other than the most popular. Students showed relatively little interest in serious art, drama, and music, and the campus did not include any examples of stimulating art and architecture among its mostly classical revival–style buildings.[15]

Despite an apparent lack of emphasis on academics, the university did produce some stellar students in science, business, and the professions. In addition to the designation of several as Woodrow Wilson fellows and Fulbright scholars, the selection of five students as Rhodes scholars between 1950 and 1961 pointed to the institution's academic strengths.[16]

In general the academic performance of the student body, however, remained mediocre. In the 1950s one university committee concluded, "The general level of ability of students in the College of Liberal Arts is not high, being at the 45th percentile on national norms for college aptitudes." The university accepted all white Mississippi high school graduates who had passed the required courses and had the necessary recommendations. Though it warned students from the bottom quartile of their high school classes that college-level work might be challenging, many came anyway only to fail later. One anonymous professor maintained, "We have a lot of students here who are incredibly dumb," but, he added, "It's pretty hard to flunk out of this university." As evidence he cited the belief among some students that "the Lord created the world in six days." Only lax academic standards allowed the university to retain a sizable enrollment.[17]

The practical aspects of education and status-oriented activities primarily concerned Ole Miss students. Popular majors in business, education, and the sciences typically focused on specialized learning rather than on a broad liberal education. The prevailing climate valued tangible, concrete information rather than abstractions and theories. Even in the arts and sciences, students often limited their studying to the textbook and, like students elsewhere, avoided rigorous and demanding classes.[18]

Once on the campus, students learned that grades and serious intellectual activities were not accorded priority and that the university tolerated barely adequate academic performance. Academic rigor simply was not a hallmark of Ole Miss. According to one assessment, the policy of accepting many marginal students "tended to brake the progress of abler students." Limited state appropriations, a dependence on tuition, and an emphasis on increasing enrollment of less able students retarded any inclination to push for academic excellence. As historian James W. Silver commented, "In a sophomore class of 30, before the end of the first month I'm talking to only five. If the rest don't bother me, I don't bother them."[19]

Instead, Ole Miss stressed social life, encouraged conformity, and emphasized institutional traditions. The student handbook claimed that "Ole Miss is not only a school of many traditions, but also a tradition itself." An Ole Miss Rebel became part of "this living tradition" connecting the past with the present. Traditions involved many social activities ranging from fervent support for the athletic teams to party times called Rebelee and Dixie Week. Freshmen had to learn the alma mater, football cheers, and "Dixie." Hazing of male freshmen included shaving their heads, making them wear blue "Ole Miss" beanies, and compelling basic conformity to Rebel values.[20]

Belonging to a fraternity or sorority often defined an individual on campus; the first question asked upon meeting a student commonly dealt with his or her Greek affiliation. The *Mississippian*, the weekly student newspaper, covered the campus social scene, which revolved around the fraternity and sorority parties. Even the popular intramural program depended on sports teams representing Greek organizations. One national study compared the university itself to a large club, and alumnus and journalist Curtis Wilkie (class of 1963) concurred when he recalled that "Ole Miss had the aura of an exclusive club for the planter class." A visiting journalist offered a similar analysis: "More social than academic, Ole Miss is in essence an avenue to status in the state." Agreeing, Wilkie explained, "Ole Miss functioned as a . . . finishing school for the young women [and men] who would marry the elite and preside over their mansions." It was, according to a *New York Times* reporter, a school "for the middle and upper classes, for posting 'gentleman C's,' making 'contacts' and finding a suitable wife or husband." The *Mississippian*'s regular announcements of engagements and marriages in a "To the Altar" column evidenced the importance of finding a mate at Ole Miss.[21]

A focus on personal appearance also suggested the significance of social affairs. The two Miss Americas were only the best-known examples of a student culture that celebrated female beauty. Ole Miss exalted physical attractiveness of women even before they enrolled in college by regularly hosting summer cheerleader camps for a thousand high school students and a camp for six hundred baton twirlers. In 1961 the university also sponsored a "Young and Beautiful Charm Camp" where more than two hundred "pretty" teenagers learned, among other skills, "how to use makeup effectively." The stress on appearance did not stop with physical beauty but included clothing as well. Ole Miss coeds dressed up, but in ways too flashy for people accustomed to the more relaxed styles of northern colleges. For men the standard dress, which some outsiders considered several years behind national trends, included khaki pants, a white shirt, and scuffed loafers. More than other state colleges, and far more than many liberal arts colleges, the university exemplified the important social function performed by higher education. It served as a social and cultural institution even more than an academic one.[22]

Resembling their students, Ole Miss professors generally lacked a scholarly research drive, especially when compared to faculty at more highly regarded institutions. In 1947 the chancellor observed that, outside of education, medicine, and public administration, research was "all but non-existent" at the university, which provided minimal support for research. Only half of the slightly more than two hundred full-time faculty members held doctoral degrees, so many of them had little experience, or preparation for, conducting research. One claimed that many of his colleagues suffered from "associate professor syndrome": all they wanted was an easy, undemanding job that resembled retirement. "Unless a man has a social conscience," he observed, "there is nothing here to bother him." As a bonus, the Oxford area boasted great fishing and hunting and a golf course for a professor's enjoyment.[23]

Despite a lack of peer support, meager institutional funding, and few professional incentives for research, some faculty did serious scholarly work. In 1950, for example, the chairman of the classics department hailed archaeologist David M. Robinson's "phenomenally active program of research, writing, and publication," and during the 1950s historians James W. Silver, Sanford Higginbotham, Harris Warren, Allen Cabaniss, and George Carbone published many books and essays. Several professors in English, philosophy, and the sciences also pursued active research agendas. In the mid-1950s a biology professor secured a major grant from the Atomic Energy Commission and published his results in the prominent journal *Genetics*.[24] Productive scholars remained, however, the exception.

If many professors lacked motivation, they also presented few intellectual challenges to their students. Most professors apparently did not provoke or promote individual creativity. Except in math and science classes, professors did not introduce their students to research methods and scholarship in their disciplines. Just as classes sparked few intense academic debates, articles in the student newspaper provoked few philosophical or political discussions among students, who seemed uninterested in national and world events. With a few notable exceptions, such as history professor Silver, the campus, according to a visiting journalist, lacked "any tradition of dissent or any rallying point of liberal thought. This reflects a state of mind in which, with minor exceptions, the range of political and social opinion is from Y to Z." In the 1950s the regular screening of visiting speakers revealed a fear of open expression of controversial ideas and confirmed the general dearth of serious intellectual activity.[25]

Though the intellectual and cultural climate might not have been the richest, it did provide significant rewards for the intellectually active. Omicron Delta Kappa and Mortar Board, honorary leadership organizations, annually sponsored a speakers' series on the campus. Other groups also brought speakers to the campus. In one week in 1954, for example, both Paul Tillich and Felix Frankfurter spoke in Oxford.[26] Although the university presented students with artistic, cultural, and intellectual opportunities, the social aspects of campus life had a greater appeal. For most students the *Sports Illustrated* photograph captured the essence of their years at Ole Miss.

Even if by 1960 the university had not achieved any general academic distinction, it had in many other ways fulfilled the goals of its founders. Ole Miss self-consciously and proudly defended southern traditions and customs while it protected white Mississippi's sons and daughters from dangerous outside influences. For the children of the elite, the campus provided a home where they formed powerful loyalties to each other and to the institution and its values. As a result, Ole Miss played a persistent and prominent role in the lives of its alumni and, because they filled positions of power in the state, in the lives of all Mississippians.

When the legislature decided in 1841 to establish a state university in Oxford, the state's leaders hoped to provide a quality education for their sons so they would not have to travel to the North where they risked conflict over and contamination by abolitionist ideas. Chartered three years later, the university opened in 1848 with the Lyceum building at the center of the campus, and the law school opened in 1854. The sons of the slave-owning gentry would receive a southern education at a self-consciously southern university. About 1840, for example, Gov. Alexander G. McNutt supported the establishment of the university because, as he said, "Those opposed to us in principle can not safely be entrusted with the education of our sons and daughters." His successor, Albert Gallatin Brown, concurred that white Mississippians needed to stop "sending our youth abroad, where they sometimes contract bad habits [and] false prejudices against our home institutions and laws." The governors had in mind slavery and states' rights. The university's founders and early supporters believed, therefore, that it ought to inculcate and perpetuate the political and cultural values of the dominant slave-owning whites.[27]

From the beginning Mississippi's wealthy planters and elite lawyers dominated the board of trustees and imposed their values on the institution. The central purpose of their university was not to introduce students to new and exciting ideas but to perpetuate conformity to established ones. For example, the antebellum board barred textbooks that criticized slavery. Faculty and administrators, particularly Chancellor F. A. P. Barnard, tried to make the new university a creditable academic institution, but political interference and financial limitations hamstrung their efforts. Northern-born administrators like Barnard had to prove to the trustees their soundness on slavery and states' rights. Antebellum students, according to the university's historian, consisted of the "pampered sons of the Southern gentry," who retained slaves to work as their servants on campus. Accepting the ideology promulgated by the university, students in early 1861 confiscated and burned all library books espousing antislavery.[28]

Late in 1860, before the state seceded, students organized a military company called the University Greys; when the war started, the Greys joined the Confederate army, and the university closed for the duration. The Greys fought in many of the war's major battles, and none of the few surviving student soldiers ever returned to the university. The mostly empty campus also did not escape the Civil War. After the battle of Shiloh in the spring of 1862, Confederates sent casualties to a military hospital established on the campus, but in the fall Union forces under General U. S. Grant returned and occupied the campus and Oxford for several months.[29]

The university reopened in October of 1865, but it did not forget the war, the University Greys, or the southern cause. A "key foundation of the Civil War memory" at the university, according to one scholar, was racial segregation. A tutor reported "a strong undercurrent of nervous apprehension" in 1870 because of a worry that a Negro would apply, and the result, he thought, would certainly have been "an explosion." Reacting to questions about the university's response to a black applicant, Chancellor John Newton Waddell reassured whites that the faculty would "instantly resign should the trustees require them to receive negro students."[30] After the war the university continued to stand as a defender of white supremacy.

Vestiges of the war also existed on campus. Confederate and Union armies had buried more than 700 soldiers in a cemetery created on the campus's southwestern edge, and it served as a reminder of the war's devastating effects. A quarter-century after the war, alumni and members of Delta Gamma sorority raised funds to honor the more than 130 students who had died in the fighting. In the lobby of the university's new library building, they dedicated a three-panel Tiffany stained glass window depicting the University Greys. Seventeen years later, in 1906, to memorialize "Our Confederate Dead, 1861–1865," the Oxford chapter of the United Daughters of the Confederacy erected at a central point on campus a twenty-nine-foot-tall marble depiction of a soldier holding his rifle.[31] The cemetery, the library window, and the statue all tied Ole Miss to its southern past.

Friends of the university also perpetuated the Lost Cause at the school. In 1906, for example, a Confederate veteran created the John W. Odum Confederate Memorial Prize for the best student essay or speech defending the South's right to secede in 1861 or the South's leaders and their actions. Chapters of the United Daughters of the Confederacy also reinforced connections with its past by establishing memorial scholarships.[32]

When students in 1897 named their new yearbook *Ole Miss*, they began the university's long association with the term. According to tradition, the name had two possible derivations. One suggested that *Miss* was simply the diminutive name for Mississippi, while *Ole* referred to the antebellum and Confederate periods. A more likely explanation claimed that it came "from darkey dialect." Previously, the shortened phrase referred to the "Old Mistress," the name slaves used for the wife of the antebellum southern planter. It captured the "beauty of the tender affection of the slaves for the gracious ministrations of their owners" and "the glamorous days when the lovely lady . . . within the sphere of her domain reigned supreme. Therefore, the term 'Ole Miss' is one which is redolent of the romance, the chivalry, the beauty, the culture, the graciousness and the finest traditions of the Southland." It again conjured up "the love and all the wonderful incidents thereof inspired in the hearts of those to whom 'Ole Miss' ministered in the slave days."[33]

For alumni the term "Ole Miss" signified their strong emotional attachment to their alma mater, similar to the slaves' presumed dedication to their mistresses. Years later, alumnus Frank Everett Jr. distinguished between the university and Ole Miss: "The University is buildings, trees and people. Ole Miss is mood, emotion and personality. One is physical, and the other is spiritual. One is tangible, and the other intangible. The University is respected, but Ole Miss is loved." The commitment of white Mississippians to Ole Miss had many implications and meanings. Whites ironically employed the language of black slaves, whom they considered their inferiors, to identify their beloved all-white institution. Based on the plantation mistress, the name "Ole Miss" reinforced the university's aristocratic image and worked against greater popular support for the school in some parts of the state. The term's connotations also suggested the institution's commitment to upholding the reigning racial status quo of black inferiority, racial segregation, and disfranchisement. By giving their university a female image, whites also proposed that they had to protect and defend it just as they did southern white women: the main threat to the school's virtue came from blacks, especially black men.[34]

While Ole Miss linked the institution to its southern heritage, the university also tried to adapt to change. Toward the turn of the twentieth century, it was, according to one historian, "in a state of transition from an old-time liberal arts college to modern secular university," a shift common in higher education. It accepted its first female students in 1882 and a few years later employed its first woman faculty member. By the end of the century more than half of the three hundred students belonged to the fraternities and sororities that soon dominated campus life. In 1893, the formation of a football team began a program of intercollegiate athletics. Within the next decade the university also added schools of engineering, education, and medicine, but the transition to a modern university was neither quick nor complete.[35]

At the turn of the century, Chancellor Robert Fulton tried to advance the university by improving its physical facilities and expanding its academic programs. The aristocratic Fulton lost his job, however, when Gov. James K. Vardaman fought to end the wealthy elite's hold on the university. In 1907, a new chancellor, Andrew Armstrong Kincannon, declared his intention to create a "greater University of Mississippi" by making it more democratic. Despite the best efforts of Fulton, Vardaman, Kincannon, and others, the institution continued to languish. Persistent political interference, inadequate state support, financial and sexual scandals, and the state's conservatism and complacency stalled the transformation into a modern university.[36]

In the 1920s Chancellor Alfred Hume turned Ole Miss into what some jokingly called "Hume's Presbyterian University" that served the interests of conservative whites. Under Hume's leadership it became "a lonely outpost amid the splendors of the old regime" and "whispered the last enchantments of an earlier age." Hume, who did not support original thinking even among the faculty, criticized the principle of academic freedom and believed that "pernicious doctrines, teachings that are subversive of the best in our Christian civilization, should not be tolerated." Hume gave one example: "A history professor in this section believes that Robert E. Lee was a traitor and teaches men so. Ought not that chair of history to become instantly vacant? Should it avail anything if the professor argues that 'academic freedom' has been invaded and that he conscientiously believes that Lee was guilty of treason? The emphatic answer, coming quick and hot, is 'Sir, . . . You may not trample under foot what we regard as sacred as long as you hold a position in our institution.' "[37]

Hume's conservatism put him at odds with Gov. Theodore G. Bilbo. Supported by a major study of the state's public colleges, the populist governor wanted to reform and reorganize higher education by moving the university to the state capital, replacing the chancellor, and reorganizing the faculties of the state schools. In the summer of 1930, the governor attempted to end the gentry's dominance of the university, eliminate "dry rot," and upgrade the faculty. To transform the university, Bilbo replaced more than a dozen faculty and removed Chancellor Hume. Though his intentions may have been good, his methods backfired. The Bilbo "purge" provoked damning criticism within the state and resulted in a loss of accreditation by the Southern Association of Colleges and Schools (SACS). Two years later, Alfred Hume resumed the chancellorship. Instead of propelling the university forward, Bilbo had set it back; instead of breaking the gentry's grip, he had returned it more tightly to the hands of Hume and the conservatives. After two years, SACS provisionally restored accreditation, but severe damage had been done to the university and its reputation at a time of financial distress.[38]

While the university suffered from political interference, its popular image became even more intimately associated with the Confederacy and the Lost Cause. The school's sports teams, after being called the "Red and Blue" for years, had in 1929 become known as the "Mississippi Flood," probably a ramification of the great Mississippi flood of 1927. Other names considered in a contest run by the student newspaper included "Rebels," "Democrats," and

"Old Marsters," which would have balanced "Ole Miss." When the "Flood" failed to gain acceptance, another contest in 1936 resulted in the selection of "Rebels," which beat out "Stonewalls" and "Confederates." A new mascot, "Colonel Rebel," emerged to personify the Rebels, and he appeared in the yearbooks and on the uniforms of the cheerleaders. In 1948, the centennial of the university and the year of the Dixiecrat political party, the Confederate battle flag became closely, if unofficially, identified with Ole Miss school spirit. Cheerleaders waved it at ball games, and the marching band displayed a sixty- by ninety-foot version in its halftime performances. At the same time, the band, the student body, and Ole Miss also informally adopted the anthem "Dixie."[39]

As the university became more tightly bound to the Confederacy, it struggled through the Great Depression and World War II. Prewar enrollment had peaked in 1939–40 at fifteen hundred students, but wartime mobilization caused it to plunge. By the fall of 1943 an "acute enrollment shortage" left only about five hundred enrolled and the future uncertain. Eighty years after Union troops had occupied the empty campus, federal military forces returned with the introduction of various manpower training programs, and quickly more than half the student population was in uniform. The student newspaper reported that the campus had taken on a "military air." Soldiers staged dances for students in the gym where a "khaki-clad rebel orchestra performed." After the cancellation of intercollegiate athletics for one year during the war, army personnel played several football games to entertain fans on campus.[40]

One apparently typical student in the Navy V-12 program in September 1945 was Harry S. Murphy Jr. He grew up in Atlanta, where his father owned a printing business known as "The House of Murphy." After graduating from English High School in Boston, Murphy enlisted in the U.S. Navy, was assigned with the V-12 program to the University of Mississippi, and lived in Leavell Hall. In addition to naval sciences classes, he followed the usual liberal arts program in history, English, Spanish, mathematics, and economics. Except for Spanish, Murphy maintained nearly a "B" average. He participated on the track team, and the handsome and friendly freshman enjoyed a social life of dating and dancing with the female students, going to movies, and eating in Oxford restaurants with friends. With the end of the V-12 program and his discharge from the navy, Murphy returned to Georgia to continue his education.[41] His year in Oxford had been unremarkable, except for one crucial fact— Harry Murphy was a Negro.

At the university Murphy had not caused a stir because none had realized that he was, as he would have been called at the time, "colored." His naval and university records had erroneously listed him as white or Caucasian. In 1945 when Murphy realized the mistake, he initially thought about trying to correct it but decided to avoid controversy by not mentioning it. As long as Murphy had not been perceived as African American, nobody objected to him. Despite rigid segregation in the state, his light complexion had allowed him to pass for white and to complete a year of study at the all-white school. Although university records remain silent, blacks before Murphy may also have passed for white. Ironically, with his prosperous Atlanta background and his elite Boston secondary education, Murphy, though a Negro, had in many ways fit the image of the ideal Ole Miss student.[42]

Harry Murphy's "integration" of the university became known only in September of 1962, shortly before James Meredith finally, officially desegregated the institution. Newspapers ran a photograph of Murphy holding his Ole Miss identification card and explained that the New York resident had studied at the university during World War II.[43]

After the war, the university enhanced its academic programs. Under the leadership of Chancellor J. D. Williams, who arrived in 1946, it placed new emphasis on graduate education and faculty research. The chancellor oversaw a dramatic development of its physical facilities and the enhancement of its academic reputation. Even with the improvements, however, the inadequacy of the academic facilities surprised one visitor, who concluded, "The equipment is that of an undernourished junior college." The only exception to the poor conditions on campus that he found was the enormous football stadium. Nevertheless, Williams took pride in the transformation from what he called a "finishing school for the children of the gentry" to a more reputable university. It nonetheless maintained its reputation as a school for the sons of wealthy aristocrats, as the "country club of the South." In 1947 the student newspaper acknowledged Ole Miss's country club reputation and declared that the students were "proud of the accusations." Many parents also considered it decadent and too "amoral in its social standards." The chancellor maintained such charges were "ridiculous," but he conceded that the stigma was a real and constant problem. Trying to persuade Mississippians otherwise, he noted that many students had need-based scholarships and even more worked to pay for their educations.[44]

In the early 1960s, an alumnus reinforced his alma mater's traditional image when he humorously compared Ole Miss to Mississippi State in a "Treatise on Higher Education." Offering advice to high school graduates, Stanley Dearman suggested a student go to Mississippi State if "you want to learn the latest scientific method of diggin' a ditch; the proper procedure for attaching a milking machine to the underside of a cow; . . . how to make a pipe from the cob when you done chawed the corn off." On the other hand, Ole Miss should be selected if the student wanted "to learn the medicinal value of good bour-bon, suh; to see a lot of pretty babes lolling about the campus; at which angle it's most appropriate to carry yo' nose in the air; the evils of work; how to relax at all times under undue stress and strain; the history of the plantation aristoc-racy in Mississippi, and which families to marry into."[45]

The image might not have inclined some legislators, especially the alumni of other colleges, to appropriate money for Ole Miss, but the institution's reputation continued to distinguish it and to attract students. In the postwar years it was still the largest and strongest of the state's five institutions of higher learning that served whites. While the university in the 1950s became a much better institution, its position atop Mississippi's higher education hierarchy had weakened. By authorizing the expansion of curricula and graduate pro-grams at the state's other schools, officials had undermined the university's unique status. Mississippi State had become a university and greatly expanded its offerings in the humanities and social sciences, but in 1960 it remained primarily an agricultural college still struggling for recognition as a com-prehensive university. Though the white Mississippi Southern College had experienced remarkable postwar growth and an expansion of its mission to include the liberal arts, it still emphasized teacher education. The other two white colleges, Delta State College and Mississippi State College for Women, were even smaller than Mississippi Southern.[46]

Regardless of the changes at the other schools, the University of Mississippi retained its academic superiority within the parochial world of Mississippi higher education. By the provincial standards of many white Mississippians, it was still, as one university official insisted, "a real bright spot in Mississippi," and a Mississippi editor called it the state's "mecca of social life, culture, and intellectualism." By regional and national standards, however, Ole Miss re-mained overall an undistinguished state university. As Chancellor Barnard had realized a century earlier, "universal laudation" by the state's press misled Mississippians by convincing them of the university's high quality when its excellence was actually "more imaginary than real." In the 1850s Barnard had believed that such local praise effectively inoculated the university from "that outside pressure which is the most effectual stimulus to internal improve-ment." Mississippians, therefore, paid little attention when *Time* magazine in the early 1960s called Ole Miss "a cheerfully unintellectual institution."[47]

At the same time, as its founders had hoped, Ole Miss still held special importance for the state's powerful lawyers, doctors, politicos, and business leaders. For the rural, premodern society of mid-twentieth century Missis-sippi, it functioned as a preparatory school for entrance into the legal, corporate, and political elite, or, as Curtis Wilkie wrote, it served as a "clearinghouse for the state's political power structure." With the only law school in the state, for example, the university played a vital role for the legal and governmental communities. One astute student of the South concluded, "It would be difficult to overestimate the importance of the Ole Miss Law School in the legal and political scheme of things in Mississippi." Any graduate of the law school automatically gained admission to the bar without having to take the exam required of all other prospective attorneys, and most of the state's lawyers were Ole Miss alumni. As a result, graduates of the law school dominated state government and the judicial system. As *Time* magazine observed, the law school was "the prep school for political power in Mississippi." Who trained the lawyers and what they were taught, therefore, held crucial significance for the state's leaders.[48] The same held true for doctors: the vast majority of physicians had begun their medical education at the state's only two-year medical school in Oxford. Much of the college-educated business and financial leadership had also studied at the university. The loyalty of Mississippi's upper crust to Ole Miss greatly enhanced the university's significance in the state.

Even beyond the elite, the university held great importance. It drew students from scores of communities, mostly small and rural ones, across Mississippi, and fans, alumni, and the families of students all developed a special relationship with Ole Miss. They wanted to keep up with what was going on at the university. Their interest derived in part from the university's leadership role, but also from the dearth of other social activities and cultural diversions, in the largely rural state. Without a major metropolitan area, Mississippi lacked the entertainment attractions of New Orleans and Atlanta, or even Memphis and Birmingham. The university in Oxford provided a bit of excitement and sophistication in an otherwise undeveloped state.

The state's newspapers regularly provided extensive coverage of university events. In one month in the spring of 1962 the state's major daily newspaper reported on the selection of Colonel Rebel and Miss Ole Miss, who reigned over the annual Dixie Week celebration at Ole Miss, but it also covered a Law Day speech at the law school by the president of the state bar association. The *Jackson Clarion-Ledger* also announced a recital of contemporary music presented by the music department and told of a graduate student's band that had "hit the big time." One story even featured twins, a boy and a girl, from Ackerman. In March 1962, the major story involved student government elections; several stories reported the backgrounds of the candidates, their stands on the issues, the inconclusive election results, and the runoff election.[49] All aspects of the university, but especially its nonacademic elements, seemed to fascinate white Mississippians. Ole Miss provided a point of contact and cohesion for a dispersed elite, a touchstone for an uneducated rural population, and a symbolic link to the powerful Lost Cause.

In 1960 the university represented for whites one of the few remaining redoubts of the glories of the Old South. Ole Miss stood for the nobility of the Lost Cause, the honor of Confederate veterans, and the gentility of the state's landed aristocracy. The introduction to the 1961 student yearbook portrayed Ole Miss as "down here among the spreading magnolias, where the hint of honeysuckle and azaleas fill the warm air. It's the land of mint juleps and antebellum columns. . . . only here you can lean back after the sun sets on the levee, cast away all those earthly cares, and listen as darkies sing softly in the moonlight." It beckoned "you lovely belles . . . you sons of the Ole South" to experience Ole Miss. While some American intellectuals believed that the "point of a university is that it should be a subculture where the hysterias of the larger culture are subjected to reason and criticism," Mississippi whites expected Ole Miss to uphold and perpetuate their traditions and defend the values of the old regime, including, of course, white supremacy.[50] In the view of whites steeped in the Lost Cause traditions, the university should instill the old verities into each successive generation. In 1960, just as before the Civil War, whites expected their university to serve as a bulwark for the racial orthodoxy that stressed the continuation of racial segregation. Not only should Ole Miss itself remain segregated, but its teachings should reinforce the ideology of white supremacy; the university should indoctrinate, not educate, its students. Despite the best efforts of some faculty and administrators, the university had become a key component of the "closed society" as described by Jim Silver. Any challenge to Ole Miss, whether internal or external, posed a direct threat to the values and stability of the dominant white culture.

In his challenge to the closed society, prospective student James Meredith understood the university's complex, prominent place in the lives of whites. When anyone asked him why he wanted to attend the University of Mississippi, Meredith did not mention football championships or beauty queens, but he simply explained that it was the best, most prestigious institution in his home state. Dissatisfied with the educational opportunities for blacks at Jackson State College, he thought that he and other members of his race should have equal access to the best education, and in 1961 Ole Miss was the state's premier institution of higher learning. Probably none of the segregated black colleges would have merited accreditation even if SACS had considered them. Among white institutions, the University of Mississippi was the best. As a political science major who might go to law school, Meredith naturally selected the state's major liberal arts university, which also had a law school.

Aware also of the university's key role in white culture, Meredith believed that if he could breach the racial barriers at Ole Miss, the remaining white state colleges and other segregated institutions in Mississippi would fall as well. Meredith's decision to challenge racial segregation and white supremacy at the University of Mississippi derived, therefore, from his appreciation for the relative importance, both academically and especially symbolically, of all of the state's educational institutions. As one New Yorker observed in September 1962, "Ole Miss is the physical and emotional center of Mississippi's struggle" over race and civil rights.[51]

2. Following Community Mores: J. D. Williams and Postwar Race Relations

■ ■

In 1951, Chancellor J. D. Williams counseled a Kentucky colleague on the race question by recommending that he "follow the mores of the community in which you are located." Acknowledging that no blacks attended Ole Miss, Williams explained that his university followed the will of the people: "We feel that as long as the people of Mississippi have indicated their desires by state law, there is no point in our taking a stand" on the question of racial integration. Throughout his twenty-two years as chancellor (1946–68), Williams worked to enhance the university within a context increasingly dominated by race. He wanted to transform the university, as he described it, "from a small and in some ways almost proprietary institution into a full-grown large university," and he realized that any agitation of the race question would imperil his primary objective by provoking retaliation by the state's segregationist leadership. After the momentous *Brown* decision in 1954, stiffening segregationist sentiment made the chancellor's task of protecting Ole Miss even more difficult. As the civil rights movement strengthened, both in the nation and eventually in Mississippi, the dangers for the university posed by race only intensified.[1]

When John Davis Williams came to Oxford in 1946, he knew very little about Mississippi, its history, Ole Miss, or southern race relations. A native of Campbell County, Kentucky, just across the Ohio River from Cincinnati, he was a southerner but not from the Deep South. Williams entered the University of Kentucky in 1921 and married while a college student. In 1924, he accepted a job as an elementary school principal in a small Kentucky town but continued his education at the University of Cincinnati. After a year, he returned to the University of Kentucky, where he graduated with an education major in 1926. Continuing his career in rural and small-town Kentucky as a principal and school superintendent, he also received in 1930 a master's degree in education from Kentucky, where his thesis examined one-teacher rural schools. Williams returned again to the University of Kentucky in 1935 to teach and direct its laboratory school. In 1940 he finished a doctorate at Columbia University's Teachers College.[2]

In 1942 Marshall College in Huntington, West Virginia, tapped the thirty-nine-year-old Williams as its president. During the war years, Marshall suffered the enrollment declines and financial difficulties common to higher education. As a result, Williams had virtually no opportunity to expand its curriculum or to improve its physical facilities. According to Marshall's historian, however, the young president did, despite the wartime stringencies, achieve notable "success in exalting the professional standing of the faculty." Earlier, before he arrived at Marshall, the college administration and state board of education had "for personal, partisan, or ideological reasons arbitrarily discharged faculty without benefit of a hearing." Williams led in the creation of rules and procedures for faculty employment, promotion, and tenure.[3] His experience proved valuable in Mississippi, where higher education still suffered the effects of the Bilbo purge.

When the trustees in 1946 considered Williams for the job as chancellor of Ole Miss, they recognized that, although not an accomplished scholar, he had considerable experience as an administrator and understood how a university operated. In the interview Williams evidently proved skillful in handling difficult situations and effectively conveyed his vision for the university. His attitudes and experiences regarding race would certainly have concerned the trustees, but his explanations must have reassured them that he would not agitate the racial status quo and satisfied them that he was safe. He later said that his views had been "thoroughly explored" and were "consistent and in harmony with" the views of the trustees and with their policies. On other occasions when the board and the chancellor discussed segregation, his stated views did not conflict with their policies. He undoubtedly told the board that he supported segregation and the laws of Mississippi.[4]

Although Williams had never attended or taught in an integrated school in Kentucky, and one Negro in a class at Columbia University had been the extent of his contact, his Kentucky background gave him a perspective on race relations at variance with the dominant white Mississippi view, but as chancellor he kept his attitudes private. He thought that the state's demography and history made it different from his home state. "I know little about the deep resentment of Mississippians toward integration of their schools," he confided to a friend in West Virginia, "because . . . I came from the part of the country where the percentage is much less, where we were never governed by Negroes in the Legislature, or Negroes as governors, or Negroes as justices in the courts as this part of the country experienced during the Reconstruction period." He had learned in Mississippi that "these experiences burned themselves into the souls and blood streams, not only of that generation, but of the second and third generation to follow."[5]

Williams had not always been so reticent about race relations. At Marshall

College he had taken a much more openly liberal position. In the spring of 1945 he spoke at the annual meeting of the National Association of Collegiate Deans and Registrars in Negro Schools that met at historically black Wilberforce University in Ohio. In 1945 he also affiliated Marshall with the American Council of Education's College Study in Intergroup Relations, funded by the National Conference of Christians and Jews. One of eight colleges in the study group, Marshall agreed to emphasize "current social problems involving race, creed, immigrant cultures, and socio-economic class levels" in its teacher preparation curriculum. The purposes of the voluntary program included studying intergroup relations, particularly in the local community, with the goal "to democratize human relations in classrooms and outside, going as fast as we can and as slow as we must." The program was the first at Marshall to stress interracial cooperation and involved students, faculty, and local citizens in seminars and discussions.[6]

According to Marshall College's historian, "Williams' social attitudes were a light year ahead of the lay citizenry of Huntington, and as a matter of fact he was even more open-minded than most members of the college faculty." The program in intergroup relations probably helped create the more tolerant atmosphere at the college that later allowed Marshall to abide more comfortably with requirements for racial desegregation. Certainly J. D. Williams convinced the Marshall community in the early 1940s that he had "liberal social views."[7]

After being in Mississippi only a couple of years, Williams conceded that a racial problem existed that needed attention. He commented that race relations resulted from "many complex forces and will not be changed peacefully by legislative fiat but must first find its solution in the hearts of men." Unlike most southern whites who refused to acknowledge serious racial problems, Williams maintained that "time, patience, understanding, education and the church are on the side of improved relations between the races in the South." In view of Mississippi's policy of segregation, especially after the *Brown* decision, Williams saw "no point in our taking a stand on a question of this kind." Just as the university stayed out of politics, he thought it should not take official positions on controversial public issues or "become a propaganda agency" for any cause. On occasion he even declined invitations to participate in regional meetings dealing with race relations because he feared news of his involvement would not help the situation in Mississippi.[8]

Except for his routine endorsement of segregation, Williams rarely spoke about race. By 1956, after living in Mississippi for a decade, he realized that of all the southern states, it would "have the most difficulty in satisfactorily meeting its problem of race relations." Hoping for a long-term peaceful solution, he regretted the "inflammatory talk and speech making" that dominated public discussion and prevented "more intelligent thinking and statesmanlike leadership" in the state. He could discern in at least a cursory way the ultimate goal of such leadership. In a confidential note to J. Oliver Emmerich, the moderate editor of the McComb newspaper and perhaps his closest friend on the board of trustees, Williams alluded "to what must be recognized as the inevitable if we are to practice the Christian ideals to which we profess."[9] As an active and devout Methodist, Williams seemed to realize that his faith led directly, if not immediately, to racial equality. After the *Brown* decision, however, he became more cautious, and his ritual defense of segregation reflected his desire to protect Ole Miss, not any personal commitment.

Williams's reticence about race relations distinguished him from his counterparts at Mississippi State and Southern Mississippi. Benjamin Franklin Hilbun and William D. McCain, native Mississippians, each openly endorsed segregation. In one racial crisis in the 1950s, for example, President Hilbun proclaimed that "the white race can serve the world best by remaining pure" and argued that "if we believe in segregation we had better act that way." Even more outspoken, President McCain eagerly defended Mississippi's segregated way of life to northern audiences. In 1960 he told a group in Chicago "how whites and Negroes in our State work together, plan together, and make mutual progress together under segregation." According to McCain, Mississippi Negroes supported school segregation, and outsiders had fomented any dissent. McCain, a staunch segregationist and a member of and adviser to segregationist organizations, maintained that "the Negroes prefer that control of the government remain in the white man's hands."[10]

When compared to the outspoken defenses provided by Hilbun and McCain, Williams's reserve on race undoubtedly caused questions about his loyalty to the Mississippi way of life. As the first person in decades brought from outside Mississippi to head a state college, he already had aroused wariness. His rather polished urbanity, affinity for the fine arts, and gentle scholarly demeanor further set him apart in a state not far removed from its frontier heritage. His willingness to seek advice and assistance not only from non-Mississippians but from nonsoutherners also made him different. Williams's participation in many regional and national organizations, such as the American Council on Education, the State Universities Association, the National Education Association, and the Southern Regional Education Board, also made him distinctive.[11]

Williams did not dare articulate in public his private opinions on civil rights because to do so would have embroiled Ole Miss in a debilitating controversy. As chancellor he felt caught between the NAACP and the Citizens' Council. He discreetly assured his counterparts at black colleges that "I cannot find it in my heart to hate" and that he hoped "time, patience, understanding, education, and the church" would lead to changes "in the hearts of men." When pressed by segregationists, however, he claimed that Ole Miss had "supported and defended" racial segregation and "the precious heritage which is ours." Nothing could have been gained by antagonizing segregationists, especially the politicians in the legislature.[12] Instead, he struggled throughout his tenure to avoid public conflicts, to protect his students and faculty from outside pressures, and to preserve academic freedom. Williams's role in racial disputes varied. On some occasions he was a central participant, but in other instances directly involving the university, state officials excluded him, either because they wanted to protect him or because they did not trust him. Williams preferred to operate behind the scenes as a quiet negotiator and conciliator.

Modernizing the university within the state's volatile racial context required all of Williams's academic training, administrative experience, and political skills. On his first day at work, he saw groundskeepers using a mule to pull a grass mower. The long-term process of change would, he could see, cause "some discomforture, some embarrassment, and some disillusionment to the former proprietors," but it had to be his objective. To revive, redirect, and reform the university, Williams reorganized the administrative structure, streamlined accounting and purchasing procedures, started an academic council of deans, created a department of public relations and an alumni association, and contracted with a Massachusetts firm to institute long-range planning. At each step, the board of trustees approved Williams's efforts in spite of his frequent reliance on expertise from outside Mississippi.[13]

The university first needed additional physical facilities. From the spring of 1945 to the fall of 1947, the student body nearly quintupled to thirty-five hundred, many of them veterans. With the additional students straining resources, the new chancellor inaugurated a major building program. By the summer of 1947, more than twenty construction projects had begun on the campus, and by the end of Williams's first decade, the university had added an education building, a library, an engineering building, new residence halls, a continuing studies center, and an alumni building. Also by 1956, the university had expanded the medical school to a full four years and moved it to Jackson, constructed an airport, and renovated many buildings.[14]

Williams expanded the academic and research missions because he realized that the university "is falling further behind rapidly." He created a faculty research fund and declared scholarly publications one proof of a faculty's strength. New academic programs included nursing at the medical school, criminology, and art; he also enhanced the music department. Graduate programs also expanded, with the first doctoral work in anatomy in 1947, then in education and English, and, by the mid-1950s, in a dozen disciplines.[15]

Limited resources often stymied Williams. Some relief came in the spring of 1952 with two major external grants: $500,000 from the Carrier family for a new engineering building, and a five-year challenge grant of $250,000 from the General Education Board (GEB) of New York. The trustees of the Institutions of Higher Learning (IHL) pledged to supplement the challenge grant with $100,000 a year for five years. The fate of the GEB matching grant exemplified the continuing problems faced by the university. As the chancellor reported in 1956, "Much to the embarrassment of the Board of Trustees and to the chagrin and distress of the University less than one tenth of the matching funds has been allocated by the Board of Trustees." In the end, not all of the matching funds were made available to the university.[16] Financial distress was the norm. The demands of improving the curriculum, expanding research, enlarging the physical plant, and raising faculty salaries must have seemed insurmountable. Williams may have gained some consolation by realizing that many other state universities shared the same financial woes, but he also recognized that his institution faced an additional difficulty—the problem of race—that in some ways surpassed all the others as an ominous threat to Ole Miss.

In the postwar years, black activism in Mississippi gradually increased, with more attempts at voter registration, a more activist NAACP chapter, and lawsuits seeking equality in public schools, especially in teacher salaries. In Washington, President Harry S. Truman's Civil Rights Commission called for a national program, and the president submitted proposals to Congress for action on voting discrimination, poll taxes, lynching, and segregation in interstate transportation. And the NAACP's work preliminary to the *Brown* decision continued.[17]

Despite the portents of change, white Mississippians remained confident of the racial status quo but also maintained a constant vigilance. Any violation of the prevailing racial patterns required correction, and any challenge to white supremacy necessitated a response. A strong anti-intellectualism among Mississippi's powerful elite made whites particularly alert to any hint of racial dissent at the university they loved, and they held the chancellor responsible for making sure Ole Miss continued to conform in all matters related to race.

In the late 1940s and early 1950s, the university experienced several mild and temporary racial controversies. Most involved only students, while another embroiled a faculty member and spilled out into the state. Each illuminated racial attitudes at Ole Miss and anticipated more serious eruptions after the state mobilized to protect segregation in the wake of the *Brown* decision.

In 1946 and 1947, *Mississippian* editor Tom Bourdeaux stirred student debate by questioning the racial status quo. Echoing Mark Ethridge, the Kentucky journalist who had spoken on campus, Bourdeaux declared, "The South must realize her civilization cannot exist upon low wages and the economic subjugation of a race—that her standard of living will always be low as long as she insists upon keeping the negro standard of living low." To avoid northern interference, the editor suggested, responsibility for the South's plight rested not entirely with exploitative Yankees but also with southerners who "have willfully and maliciously economically oppressed another race." Denying that he advocated a social revolution or social equality between the races, Bourdeaux argued that for the South to prosper, southerners had to get "out of the gutter" together. He referred his opponents to the Bill of Rights and to the Pledge of Allegiance: "one nation, indivisible, with liberty and justice for ALL."[18]

Conservative campus critics battered Bourdeaux. Elmore D. Greaves Jr. denied that the South was somehow sick because of the whites' oppression of Negroes. He asked if the editor meant to suggest that Washington, Jefferson, Calhoun, Davis, and Lee also had been sick. According to Greaves, "the only sick part of Southern society are those pseudo-enlightened crusaders, who advocate rash and unsound social change." The managing editor of the newspaper also disagreed with Bourdeaux's views. Without claiming expertise in race relations, Paul Newton objected to dangerous theoretical approaches because they lacked the stability he found in common sense. In fact, theoretical appeals based on equality, justice, and democracy often were used "falsely to cover underlying motives aimed at reaching diabolical objectives." Cognizant of Americans' sympathy for the underdog, subversive propagandists cleverly appealed for Negro rights in an effort to attract followers and gain power. They wanted "almost immediate equalities for the negro race" and "fostered radical legislation, the passage of which would cause nothing short of a southern revolution." Southern progressives "must of necessity be throttled," Newton argued, because their radical program would have a "disastrous effect" on the region. Instead, he and his fellow conservatives believed that the South "must refrain from any views of social equality." Improved race relations would only result from a practical, commonsense program directed by white southerners; it would have to be "an extremely gradual and controlled process of the state government without federal interference."[19]

One student tried to reconcile the apparent conflicts between the editor and his opponents. Both sides, observed Robert Leavell, "carefully skirt the nucleus, the very core, of the problem, which is the matter of social equality." Proposing "to face the basic issue down, now," he maintained that neither the South within the nation nor Negroes within the South could be isolated.

Prosperity required integration of the region in both senses. Integration did not worry Leavell because he believed that the Negro and the white "will instinctively cleave to the people of his own race. Such is human nature." He saw no threat of "mongrelization" because, like other whites, he would "instill in my own son an inherent interest in his own race."[20]

With the student debate over racial change opened but unresolved in the spring of 1947, the Ole Miss student government considered joining the new National Student Association (NSA). Growing out of an international student congress in Czechoslovakia in 1946, the NSA sought to organize college students to give them a voice within the United States and internationally. The University of Mississippi student body president, James Barnett, attended a meeting at Louisiana State University where students from many states discussed joining the NSA. When the meeting considered a part of the proposed constitution dealing with equal educational opportunities regardless of race, Barnett led the fight for segregated educational opportunities. Back in Oxford, the *Mississippian* supported him and called "foolhardy" anyone advocating anything but segregated education. To eliminate the barrier between the races "would be to loose upon the Southland a maelstrom of riots and criminal acts, the mind of the Negro being what it is."[21]

Even though opposed to NSA's racial stance, an Ole Miss delegation attended NSA's founding convention that summer at Madison, Wisconsin. Later student leaders formed a special committee to consider ratifying the NSA constitution. The committee believed that "there can be no compromise with segregation," considered the NSA objectives "distasteful and unsavory" and "alien to Mississippi," and advised against joining NSA. In January 1948, the student government voted unanimously not to affiliate with the NSA, and the *Mississippian* agreed. Though some objected to the lack of a referendum, students generally supported the determination not to join the NSA. Undoubtedly affected by the increasing discussion of civil rights on a national level, especially the recommendations of President Truman's Committee on Civil Rights, Ole Miss students resisted outsiders who tried to change their way of life.[22]

Ole Miss students showed commitment to segregation later in 1948 by supporting the States' Rights Democratic, or Dixiecrat, Party that endorsed states' rights as the crucial means for maintaining segregation and white supremacy. In July more than fifty Oxford students attended the Dixiecrat convention in Birmingham that nominated Governor Fielding Wright of Mississippi for vice president and Governor Strom Thurmond of South Carolina for president. Walter Sillers, the longtime speaker of the state house of representatives, congratulated the students: "Never have I been prouder of Ole Miss than . . . at Birmingham when I saw the splendid group representing our great University." When they returned, the students formed an Ole Miss States' Rights Association to stand "for the segregation of the races and racial integrity of both races." It condemned the Democrats' calling for "social equality" that "would be utterly destructive of the social, economic, and political life of the Southern people."[23]

Some students stood loyal with the national Democratic Party, but speakers on campus generally sided with the Dixiecrats. A poll of the students revealed that more than 90 percent backed the idea of states' rights. Their reasons varied little. One explained that states' rights was "a defense of white supremacy," while to another it was "to prevent the Negro's having the right to sit next to you in the picture shows, schools, and buses." One premedical student simply said, "It's to prevent racial equality when you come down to the root of it all."[24]

In the 1948 presidential election, the Dixiecrat ticket swept Mississippi, with the Thurmond-Wright ticket garnering 87 percent of the vote.[25] Because Ole Miss student opinion mirrored sentiment in the state, student actions in the campaign elicited no negative reaction from political or educational leaders. As long as the university was not involved in public controversy, the administration only watched silently, content that politics had not affected the university.

The question of NSA membership arose again in 1952 when the NSA president came to Oxford and urged the student senate to join. NSA's Ole Miss supporters maintained that it had eliminated subversive elements and had taken a more responsible stand on segregation. Regretting the rejection in 1948, the *Mississippian* endorsed joining the national organization because it opposed communism, supported academic freedom, and could provide services to students. The editor argued that NSA opposed all discrimination but realized that ending racial discrimination in the South would take time. If NSA policy changed in a way unacceptable to Mississippians, the paper pointed out, the university could withdraw.[26]

The decision whether to join NSA threatened to split the student body. In a two-hour meeting in April, the student senate argued over participating. The student body president considered the segregation issue of minor importance. Another supporter pleaded with senators to disregard opinion in the state: "We are walking on eggshells; we are afraid of what people think. I ask you to vote by your conscience not by your constituents." Opponents claimed NSA stood for principles and programs opposed by Ole Miss students, and they stressed that NSA's stand against segregation violated the state constitution.

Finally the senators voted 22–12 not to join, but then decided to submit the question to a student referendum.[27]

Before the referendum, the debate intensified, with each side claiming the other exaggerated its position. A flood of letters and articles in the student newspaper tried to clarify the issue, and each side sent representatives to speak in fraternity and sorority houses and in dorms. The night before the vote, a meeting of the student body gave each side one last chance to appeal for support. Proponents of membership pointed to advantages deriving from membership, said that no national organization endorsed segregation, and urged the university to end its isolation from national groups. Opponents alleged that NSA had "the shadow of communism over it" and that its opposition to all segregation violated Mississippi law. A leader of the anti-NSA forces also cautioned of dire repercussions from the legislature, egged on by reactionaries like the *Jackson Daily News*, if the students voted to join NSA. "We must be practical enough to realize," Hunter Gholson warned, "that this could ruin the University of Mississippi."[28]

Shortly before the students voted, Chancellor Williams issued a brief statement: "I have never and do not now intend to interfere in any way with the free expression of the student body when it is directed through orderly processes of student government. I have not expressed myself on this issue and do not intend to. As Chancellor of the University it is my responsibility to see to it that the freedom to learn, freedom to think, freedom to express one's self as provided by the Constitution and the law are properly safeguarded." Williams's stand pleased many faculty. In the referendum students voted 640–124 not to join NSA. Gholson hailed the result as "a conscientious effort to save the University."[29] The vote must have relieved the chancellor because support for the NSA could have brought a storm of criticism upon Ole Miss. In addition to supporting segregation and opposing outside interference in racial matters, the voters had shown their concern for their university's fate if it stirred up powerful segregationists. Not all controversies ended so easily.

A more inflammatory dispute involved a professor of criminology, Alfred C. Schnur. Hired in 1948 with a doctorate from the University of Wisconsin, the thirty-year-old Pennsylvanian taught criminology and penology halftime in the sociology department; his appointment also called for "research in the Mississippi correctional system" and assistance "in the development of a professionally oriented correctional system in Mississippi." The IHL board had proposed the split appointment, which the Mississippi Association on Crime and Delinquency supported. Williams seemed pleased that Schnur would work with state officials to provide "better and more effective treatment" of convicts. Within a month, Schnur began to work at Parchman State Penitentiary, the parole division of the Department of Public Welfare, and the Mississippi Association on Crime and Delinquency. He also spoke to civic groups, delivered papers at conferences, and published in professional journals. Schnur included his graduate students in his work at Parchman.[30]

Schnur's most controversial research involved the administration of the state penal system, especially Parchman. Founded at the turn of the century in Sunflower County, it incarcerated about two thousand inmates and had a reputation for brutal and abusive treatment. On the twenty-thousand-acre prison farm, inmates produced twice as much food as they consumed and thousands of bales of cotton. Supt. Marvin Wiggins had instituted many changes in pursuit of both profitable farming and convict rehabilitation, and he permitted Schnur to gather data from prison records. While at Parchman, Schnur stayed at the Wiggins's home and became a personal friend; Mrs. Wiggins even introduced him to his future wife. Schnur systematically and scientifically pursued his research about the inmates' backgrounds, education, and skill levels.[31]

The use at Parchman of a leather lash known as "Black Annie" especially offended Schnur. He, like other critics of Parchman, wanted use of the lash stopped, but any call for change elicited charges of undermining the traditional racial patterns because the overwhelming majority of the inmates were Negro. Prison reform smacked of racial reform. As the civil rights movement began to emerge in the early 1950s, pressure for reform at Parchman increased. In January 1952, the chairman of the senate's penitentiary committee advocated a parole system, more rehabilitation programs, a department of corrections, and better professional training for the prison staff. The state bar association and liberal editors also supported reform, but legislative efforts failed.[32]

In the midst of growing criticism of Parchman came Schnur's first brush with controversy. In February he addressed the North Jackson Lions Club on "Crime in Mississippi." Although state officials had recently reported that Parchman was in excellent condition, he declared that it "has a long way to go before it becomes a correctional institution guaranteeing maximum protection from the criminal at minimum cost to the people." Schnur acknowledged that Wiggins had "made remarkable improvements considering what he has been allowed to work with." Instead of listing his accomplishments, Schnur pointed out what needed to be done. Only with major improvements in personnel and facilities, he declared, could the prison "operate on a diagnosis and therapy basis rather than a blame, punishment and financial recovery basis that tends to confirm criminals in crime." The university penologist suggested that the prison personnel's expertise was either "absent or too embryonic," but Schnur confessed that "we are all victims of that unintentional ignorance which leads to complacency and indifference about crime control and corrections."[33]

Frederick Sullens of the *Jackson Daily News* reacted swiftly to the criticism. Translating Schnur's remarks into "plain English," Sullens said, "Dr. Schnur thinks we need some convict coddling at Parchman. We don't. We don't need any of his 'diagnosis and therapy basis,' whatever that is." The trial court, he went on to say, made any necessary diagnosis and decided the remedies. Entitled "Poof-Poof and Bah-Bah," the editorial found in Schnur and his field "a helluva lot of plain and unadorned ignorance."[34] Unstated, but powerful, racial bigotry underlay the *Daily News*'s response: the overwhelmingly black prison population did not deserve efforts at rehabilitation, and, as inferior beings, Negroes would be unaffected by Schnur's reform efforts. To follow Schnur's advice would have been to recognize that deep social problems, more than alleged black inferiority, were responsible for crime.

The only public reaction at the university came when an editorial in the *Mississippian* wondered if Sullens wanted to lead the state "back to the dark ages" and to "the rack and the iron maiden, torture instruments of a bygone day." Supporting Schnur, the editorial argued that prisons had to try "to prepare men and women [in prison] to resume their roles in society" because 95 percent eventually got out of prison. The *Mississippian* labeled Sullens's criticism of the study of criminology and penology as "Poof-Poof and Bah-Bah, indeed!"[35]

The 1952 tempest soon passed but controversy over Parchman persisted. In his defense, Wiggins marshaled his allies, including the governor, many state politicos, and Delta planters. He invited journalists to visit the prison, and the governor even led several reporters on a tour of the facility. Changes at Parchman impressed some visitors. The McComb and Greenville newspapers, however, renewed their indictments of Parchman, and Schnur repeated his assessment in speeches to civic groups across the state.[36] As a state employee and as an individual without a network of supporters among state leaders, Schnur made an easy target.

In March 1954, the Penitentiary Committee of the Mississippi House of Representatives objected to Schnur's statements on factual, ethical, and political grounds. Referring to his "sustained, vicious and seemingly unwarranted attacks," the committee protested to Chancellor Williams. Offended that Schnur referred to Parchman as "a wonderful training school for criminals," the representatives argued that Parchman's rehabilitation programs did work, and they praised Wiggins's "revolutionary changes" to help "better prisoners become better free men." The committee also attacked Schnur on ethical

grounds. Wiggins, who had under his good-old-boy exterior "the tempera-
ment of a rattlesnake," undoubtedly had complained about Schnur's treachery:
he had allowed the professor full access to Parchman files in exchange for an
agreement that Schnur would clear any material with him before he used it
publicly. The committee claimed that Schnur had violated his trust with Wiggins by attacking the penal system. "It seems to us," the committee complained
to Chancellor Williams, "highly unbecoming behavior and poor returns for
the trust, assistance and hospitality accorded Doctor Schnur during his long
stay at Parchman." The legislators believed that Schnur put "the University of
Mississippi in the highly embarrassing position of publicly attacking another
state owned institution."[37]

The representatives reminded the chancellor that he would not appreciate
Marvin Wiggins's attacking "drunkenness and immorality" at Ole Miss. They
warned, "Doctor Schnur's attacks may reflect unjustly on the University. . . .
We sincerely believe this will hurt the University if it is not stopped." In effect,
the committee warned that Schnur's "unethical behavior" might cause a cut in
university appropriations, as had occurred in earlier times of social and political unrest. The representatives proposed that Schnur restrict his comments to
the classroom or resign.[38]

When the committee made its letter to the chancellor public, Williams and
Schnur responded. Williams defended Schnur's professional expertise, called
him a "respected member of the faculty," and reiterated the university's policy
of cooperating with the legislature in solving the state's problems. The chancellor expressed regret and pledged to repair relationships. Williams thought his
statement was "a strong fist and a velvet glove," but it struck some observers as
"bland" and "guarded." In scholarly prose, Schnur stressed that he had criticized the penal system and not Superintendent Wiggins and emphasized his
academic responsibility to "prevent first crimes and render convicted law
violators into useful, law abiding and self-sufficient citizens." Schnur hoped
that the interest he had inadvertently stimulated would lead to reforms.[39]

At the same time, Governor Hugh White in a Jackson press conference
declared that Schnur "ought to be fired." A strong supporter of Wiggins, the
governor thought it "unbecoming for a professor at the University to criticize
another institution or department." In response to newsmen, White questioned "the wisdom of even teaching students to criticize another state department." He denied that academic freedom played any role in Schnur's comments and acknowledged that he had warned several members of the IHL
board that Schnur's actions "could hurt the university and colleges in the
state." The following day, the governor finally asked the chancellor about
Schnur, his background, and the university's criminology program.[40]

The next week, Chancellor Williams replied to the governor, to the legislative committee, and to other critics. In more discreet private correspondence, he explained Schnur's appointment and his high professional reputation. Williams vouched for Schnur's "fine professional attitude" and for his fulfillment of his agreement with Parchman's superintendent. To the legislators, Williams quoted the definition of "embryonic" ("in the early stages, undeveloped, rudimentary") to prove that Schnur did not mean to be derogatory or insulting. Reminding the representatives that Schnur's ideas essentially repeated the proposals made by a legislative committee two years earlier, Williams argued that Schnur's position was "based upon the facts which he has at his disposal, many of which are confidential, and upon his professional knowledge as a criminologist." Williams made no claim for academic freedom, because he knew that nobody at the university or on the IHL board questioned Schnur's right to criticize the penitentiary. He did, however, recognize the importance of academic freedom, and in letters to friends he claimed to "stand solidly behind Doctor Schnur" and "his right to express his views without being subjected to the threat of economic intimidation." But Williams attempted to guard academic freedom without debating it in the press and "getting people's emotions involved." To worried supporters of the university, he pledged "an atmosphere and attitude of freedom" on the campus; otherwise, "we cease to be an educational institution and a university in the truest definition of those terms."[41]

Others also defended Schnur. At an Ole Miss alumni meeting in Meridian, law dean Robert J. Farley also supported Schnur's right to make "constructive criticism" of any state agency and condemned the "veiled threat" to cut the university's funds. At the same meeting, IHL board member Dr. H. M. Ivy of Meridian endorsed Dean Farley's comments. Some professors in the state argued that, if Schnur were fired, professors would become political appointees to be fired when the powerful politicians did not like what they said.[42]

More outspoken than the academics, Hodding Carter led the defense in his Greenville newspaper. Calling the legislative committee's stand "an outrageous attack," he accused it "of an arrogant and contemptible assault upon academic and individual freedom." And the governor was "just as guilty." McComb, Memphis, and Millsaps College editorialists echoed Carter. Worried by the "danger of gag rule at the university," J. Oliver Emmerich, the McComb newspaper editor, for example, warned that if politicians gagged faculty through "threat, intimidation, innuendo or law enactment . . . the harm, the hurt, to Mississippi and her future" would be great."[43]

A strong rebuttal attack on Schnur came from the *Jackson Daily News*, the state capital's afternoon newspaper. It called him "a self-styled criminologist" and dismissed his criticism of Parchman as "proof conclusive that he doesn't know what he is talking about and that he is no more capable of planning prison management than he would be in flying a stratosphere plane to Jupiter. No matter how many college degrees he has trailing behind his name, Dr. Schnur is not qualified to sit in judgment on the Parchman penal farm." The diatribe charged that professors like Schnur were needed "just like the average man needs seven more holes in his head."[44]

The controversy over Schnur soon receded as attention shifted to other issues. The legislature debated capital punishment. The governor and other officials, anticipating the Supreme Court's segregation decision later in May, worried about financing a dual school system to foil desegregation. The chancellor and Schnur welcomed the subsiding of the uproar. Even though he survived the strife, the next year Schnur resigned and moved to Ohio State University.[45]

Although the Schnur case faded in the spring of 1954, it served as a warning of what the university could face if its faculty and students appeared to challenge the state's entrenched racial mores; it also served as a reminder of what one historian has called the "nightmare" that had happened to the university during the Bilbo administration twenty-five years earlier. The *Memphis Commercial Appeal*, for example, referred in March 1954 to the earlier political interference and hoped the university could avoid similar consequences. At the height of the Schnur imbroglio, J. D. Williams declared that he wanted "to keep the University out of partisan politics and to keep partisan politics out of the University."[46] While Alfred Schnur's unusual experience with an issue that had obvious, if not explicit, racial content demonstrated the threat of renewed political interference, daily life at Ole Miss presented few worries because it largely reflected the state's prevailing racial practices.

3. "I Love Colored People, but in Their Place":
Segregation at Ole Miss

■ ■

Ole Miss had no black students in the 1940s and 1950s, but black workers on the campus nonetheless interacted in limited ways with white students, faculty, and staff. A complicated combination of customs, habits, rules, and laws regulated their contacts. Written rules and laws governed many aspects of race relations in post–World War II Mississippi, as they had for generations. Beginning in the late nineteenth century, the state enacted laws to control relations between whites and Negroes. A series of statutes starting in 1888, for example, required racial segregation in transportation, and in 1922 a new law forbade taxis from carrying blacks and whites at the same time. An 1878 law and the 1890 state constitution barred integrated public education, and other statutes kept the races apart in hospitals and jails. The legislature in 1920 also formally prohibited anyone from writing anything in support of racial intermarriage or social equality between the races. One historian has suggested, however, that Mississippi may have had fewer laws mandating segregation than did other southern states because Mississippi whites had more confidence that "the forces of social habit and white opinion were in themselves usually sufficient to ensure that the races knew their places."[1]

Among Mississippians and other southerners, black and white, a sometimes subtle and informal code continually confirmed the superiority of whites and enforced Negroes' deference. The etiquette included customs and habits that did not have legal sanction but nonetheless governed racial relationships. Intricate, informal standards forced blacks to concede their inferiority, and whites constantly monitored the actions and demeanor of blacks to detect deviations from the accepted order. Whites also watched each other for any breach in the established relationship with Negroes. Mississippians did not openly discuss, much less debate, most racial conventions because whites generally assumed, and even some Negroes acknowledged, their importance. In the 1930s sociologist Bertram Doyle suggested that blacks willingly accepted the etiquette as a way to accommodate whites and smooth black-white relations, but Gunnar Myrdal argued that "the majority of blacks are at bottom embittered by the performance of these actions and keep it up only to avoid violence and greater humiliation."[2] Although attitudes toward the customs undoubtedly varied among Negroes, depending on the situation and the issue, blacks generally conformed.

Mississippi's racial practices applied to Ole Miss, but they had a limited impact at the all-white university because whites and blacks had so few contacts. Race did not affect relations among the students and between students and faculty because all were assumed to be white. Racial standards applied only to people identified as African American. Other persons who might have been suspected of being racially different coexisted with white students without incident. In the spring of 1962, for example, the front page of the student newspaper ran a photograph of several Iranian students who participated in a beard-growing contest. Later that year, Peter, Paul, and Mary performed on campus, and their group included a bass player who was "a light-skinned Dutch Negro"; not only did he play without incident, but he ate dinner in the Phi Mu sorority house and spent the night in the Alumni House because nobody recognized his African origins. The student body also included "dark-skinned Hindu students from Bombay" who reported a friendly reception at Ole Miss. Foreign students also came from Taiwan and other Asian nations, but the prevailing racial customs did not apply to them. As one northerner observed, "It is not dark-skinned people but dark-skinned citizens of Mississippi who are objected to."[3] The etiquette did, however, govern how white professors and students interacted with black university employees and with black visitors to the campus, especially black entertainers who performed on campus. It also influenced white attitudes toward blacks.

Black workers on campus filled only menial positions and always under the supervision of whites. Black men and women performed the physically arduous, dirty, or unpleasant tasks that whites did not want to do. They cooked and served meals to the white students in the university cafeteria, and they washed the dishes after they ate. The cooks, servers, and dishwashers, however, could not eat in the cafeteria where they worked. Others tended the campus grounds by cutting grass, raking leaves, and trimming shrubbery, but they did not later enjoy strolls across the campus. They moved furniture, mopped and swept floors, emptied trash cans, washed windows, and cleaned bathrooms, but they could not use the restrooms or water fountains reserved for whites; they had their own segregated toilet facilities, usually in the basements. (Fraternities and sororities employed blacks for similar tasks in the Greek houses.) At the same time, no black held any white-collar position as secretary, clerk, supervisor of any kind, professor, or professional staff member. Subordinate jobs reinforced their inferiority in the segregated southern society of which Ole Miss was definitely a part. The system's oppressive work environment did not provide for or encourage black occupational development but instead kept workers in low-paying positions without any chance of advancement. Like the rest of the white South in the postwar era, Ole Miss endorsed black inferiority and capitalized on it.

Although relations between white supervisors and black workers varied, whites customarily treated them disrespectfully and sometimes malevolently. For example, in the mid-1950s one black worker, frustrated with his low wage and the general treatment of the university's black employees, wrote officials in Washington to protest. When the man's superior learned of his impertinent letter, he fired him. The example had a debilitating effect on other blacks. After a warning from a boss that the same thing would happen to him if he made any protest, one of the fired man's coworkers quit and escaped to work in a fraternity house. Even when blacks more innocently breached the racial rules, the repercussions could be rough. One summer while cleaning and repairing dormitory rooms, a black maintenance worker sought relief from the heat by taking a drink from a dormitory water fountain. When his white supervisor realized what he had done, he berated him and threatened to fire him. Black employees continually experienced such indignities. Despite such outrages, black workers endured because university jobs were nonetheless good compared to other work available in Oxford and Lafayette County, and the other employment opportunities would have involved similar treatment.[4]

Three exceptional stories in the 1950s demonstrated the complex and contradictory nature, the benefits and limitations, of everyday race relations at Ole Miss. Even within the strict limitations of segregation, white paternalism did sometimes help blacks. One janitor developed as an artist under the informal tutelage of an art professor. A dean befriended another custodian and helped him further his education. The third even more unusual example of a black person who benefited from white indulgences involved a man who was not actually a university employee. The three cases' remarkable and atypical characteristics reveal the narrow options open to blacks and whites under the constraints of segregation.

The most persistent presence on campus during the first half of the twentieth century was James E. Ivy. An Ole Miss institution by the 1920s, Jim Ivy became known to thousands of students and alumni, but his true personal story became partly shrouded in myth. Born to a former slave in 1872, Jim Ivy grew up in Alabama and moved to Mississippi as a young man. He worked on river boats and picked cotton in the Delta before settling in Oxford. While working in 1894 painting a bridge over the Tallahatchie River, Ivy got paint or creosote in his eyes and completely lost his sight. For a short time he tried to support himself by singing for pennies on the streets of Oxford, but by 1896 he began selling candy and peanuts to students on the campus. Ivy later recalled,

"They didn't like me much when I first came here," and, according to another account, he initially "met much sarcasm and ill-treatment from the boys as a result of their not accepting him." In the spring of 1896, however, Jim Ivy won acceptance among the students.[5]

In a baseball game against the University of Texas, Mississippi fell far behind and seemed sure to lose when Jim Ivy emerged from behind the stands and began cheering for the home team. Cheering louder than anyone else, he stirred the crowd, the students bought all of his peanuts, and together they inspired the team to a comeback victory. In succeeding months and years, the tall and mustachioed Jim Ivy and his cry of "Come on, Miss'ippi" became increasingly popular, and college students began affectionately to call him "Blind Jim." A few years later Blind Jim designated himself the "Dean of Freshmen."[6]

As unofficial adviser and counselor to freshmen, Blind Jim often spoke to them at pep rallies and at the welcoming party at the beginning of the year. "I'se the dean and about the first thing I'se going to do is to make my speech to the freshmen Thursday night," he explained. "I'se going to tell them just exactly what's expected of them, so they won't get in any trouble." More informally the ordained Baptist minister regaled freshmen and other students with stories about Ole Miss, shared his own life's experiences with them, and made regular predictions about the athletic teams. Wearing a one-foot-square sign around his neck identifying himself as "Blind Jim, Dean of Freshmen," he attended football, basketball, and baseball games with the first-year students. In return for his support, freshmen took turns guiding him around campus, escorted him to the games, and bought him a new suit of clothes each year. Students also helped him navigate the changing campus when the university constructed buildings and added sidewalks.[7]

Blind Jim became known as the Rebels' most devoted supporter and traveled to many away games. In 1942, for example, the *Mississippian* announced that "Blind Jim Ivy will lead the freshmen of Ole Miss in a counter-attack against all Georgia cheers at the Rebel-Bulldog encounter at Crump Stadium in Memphis tomorrow." For fifty-nine years he never missed a homecoming game, and he boasted, "I've been to more Ole Miss games than anybody else, and I've never seen the Rebels lose yet!" He often sat on the sidelines and, just as at his first baseball game, led the fans in cheers. He reportedly invented a popular cheer used at Alabama games—"Ramma Tamma, Yellow Hammer, Down with Alabama."[8]

To support himself, Blind Jim initially sold peanuts and candy around campus. He parched the peanuts himself at his home and brought them to campus to vend. By the late 1940s he had set up a stand inside the Lyceum building not far from the chancellor's office where he sold candy and other refreshments. Such employment for the blind was not unusual; in fact, a federal law passed in the 1930s promoted concession stands operated by the blind in federal office buildings. By the early 1950s, Blind Jim had transferred his operation to the foyer of the campus cafeteria.[9]

Students helped Blind Jim when he had problems. During the 1930s, like so many other Americans, Jim Ivy encountered financial difficulties. In the fall of 1936, he could not repay the five-hundred-dollar debt he had incurred two years earlier when he purchased his one-room shanty just south of the campus. The student newspaper appealed for students, alumni, and others to help Blind Jim. In the midst of the Great Depression, students pitched in but could not raise the money alone. After articles appeared in Jackson and Memphis papers, alumni sent donations. Seventeen years after graduating, one alumnus sent a note with his check: "I shall not forget the joy I had in knowing you Blind Jim." After several weeks, Blind Jim was able to keep his small home largely because well-to-do alumni in New York sent enough to help him meet his obligation.[10]

During World War II, Ivy's modest business suffered from the shortages and high prices common in the national economy. Wartime restrictions made it impossible for him to buy candy to sell, and the price of peanuts was so high that he could not afford them. In October 1942, the *Mississippian* announced, "So bad as Jim hates it, he has had to place himself open for donations in order to keep his usually thriving enterprise from going into receivership."[11] With the help of Ole Miss students and alumni, Ivy did survive his wartime economic crisis.

In the early 1950s, the white-haired and elderly Blind Jim slowed down but continued to hold the students' respect and affection. For example, the student body in the spring of 1950 honored him during Rebelee party weekend by staging a "Blind Jim Parade." He rode on the student body float in the parade that also included bands, student government officers, and candidates for Miss University. When able, he continued to attend Rebel sporting events, and his home was painted Rebel red and blue. By the summer of 1954, however, he visited campus less frequently because his doctor had ordered him to avoid the overexertion of yelling or getting into large crowds. At the opening of the fall term, he predicted the football team would win the Sugar Bowl but indicated that he would not be traveling with the team to games. A year later, an adopted son took Jim Ivy to his home in Chicago where he could take better care of his aging father. A special university committee announced it would raise funds at the Arkansas game to help pay Ivy's medical and living expenses. During a brief hospitalization, Blind Jim died of tuberculosis on October 20, 1955, at the age of eighty-three.[12]

Two days later his beloved Rebels defeated Arkansas in the annual home-coming game in Oxford, and his friends collected donations to help with his funeral. Flags at Ole Miss flew at half-staff in his honor. On the day of the game, the alumni association's regular meeting adopted a resolution honoring Blind Jim, who, of course, would never have been allowed to come to one of the meetings. In sorrow, the resolution recognized him as "a colorful figure" who had "won the love and affection of generations of Ole Miss students since 1896." The alumni praised Blind Jim's "spirit of cheerfulness, good humor, dignity, and independence" and the courage with which he lived a life in blindness. In thanking Jim Ivy for his "substantial and valuable contribution to school spirit," the alumni never mentioned that he was a Negro.[13]

Immediately after Ivy's death, an ad hoc committee, including Athletic Director Tad Smith, Provost Alton Bryant, and Financial Secretary W. C. "Chuck" Trotter, continued to raise money. Organized to solicit contributions to provide for Ivy's final needs, it announced after his death that it would continue to seek donations to pay Jim Ivy's remaining bills but also to erect a memorial to him on the campus. In Jackson, meanwhile, the *Daily News* and WJTV launched a campaign to establish in honor of Blind Jim a college scholar-ship for Mississippi Negroes at one of the state's black colleges. The IHL board unanimously and enthusiastically endorsed the effort to raise funds for both a memorial and a scholarship. In supporting the plan, J. Oliver Emmerich claimed that Blind Jim "was as well known in Mississippi as either candidate for the presidency in the last election." Another trustee insisted that the univer-sity memorial "should be a life size statue just as 10,000 Ole Miss students remember him." The chancellor commented blandly, "We think the plan is just fine and will cooperate fully in the matter."[14]

Ten days after Jim Ivy's death, Ole Miss students, faculty, alumni, and staff filled the Second Baptist Church in Oxford for a thirty-minute memorial service. George Street, university director of placement and an alumnus, con-ducted the service. Calling Blind Jim "an integral part of the life of the Univer-sity of Mississippi," Street remembered that "Jim's life was marked by per-severance, optimism, and humor (how many have heard him say 'I've never seen the Rebels lose a game'), loyalty, and finally by a deep religious faith." Ole Miss and Blind Jim had had, according to Street, an "astonishing association" for sixty years, and he suggested that Blind Jim had embodied the sentiments in the alma mater. After a minute of silent prayer the memorial service ended. Later in the same church, Ivy's Negro friends and family gathered for his fun-eral. He was buried in the Negro section of St. Peter's Cemetery in Oxford.[15]

At the time of Jim Ivy's death, a *Jackson Clarion-Ledger* editorial summed up his importance for Ole Miss and, perhaps unintentionally, explained how the racial etiquette functioned in the early postwar period. "The aged Negro," according to the newspaper, "could well serve as an inspiration to his own people as well as to the multitude of whites who knew and loved him." Not only had he "earned the affection and respect of untold thousands over the state of Mississippi and elsewhere," but he "never had cause to resent the fact he was a Negro." According to the Jackson editor, "He showed the students and faculty how a Negro can live as a Negro without resentment or jealousy or inferiority or loss of self-respect."[16]

For whites in segregated Mississippi, Blind Jim had seemed the model Negro—content, humble, and friendly in his assigned place of inferiority. Students had often described him as "this lovable old Negro" or "darkey" and an "ever-lovable" and "faithful Negro." Two decades before his death, one observer had described Jim Ivy as "a harmless, inoffensive, lovable old darkey" and as the "perfect proto-type" of a southern Negro. At the time white Mississippians were raising money to help Ivy save his home, a Jackson journalist declared, "Listen all ye white folks who dwell above the Mason and Dixon Line: Down here we love our negroes and our negroes love us. We are willing and ready to go to the limit for them and they are ready and willing to do the same thing for us. . . . Yankees can't understand that. No use for any Yankee trying to understand."[17] Nonsoutherners could not appreciate fully the wonders of southern race relations as represented by Blind Jim and as celebrated by Mississippi whites.

Jim Ivy personified the Negroes' acquiescence in racial segregation and in their own inferiority. While others, especially outside the South, denounced the southern way of life, Blind Jim's day-to-day pursuits seemed to validate and justify the white defense of southern racial mores because he showed that race relations could be peaceful and harmonious. In Ivy's case, southern paternalism simply seemed to work. In exchange for his acceptance of a subservient role, the superior whites took care of him by supporting his business, providing him clothes, taking him to the Rebels' games, and helping him in personal financial emergencies. But whites also controlled him and their interactions. Even within Ivy's close relationship with whites, he did not breach or even challenge the racial barriers. He ate his noon meal, after all, not with students in the cafeteria, but in the back with the black cafeteria workers. When he went to out-of-town football games with students, he had to stay in the black section of town, not with the students.[18]

For some observers, the happy Blind Jim embodied Uncle Remus. The *Oxford Eagle* once claimed that "Joel Chandler Harris' 'Uncle Remus' practically comes to life in Blind Jim. He not only tells tales equally as well as 'Uncle Remus,' but he actually resembles the character created by Harris." Like Uncle

Remus, Blind Jim passed his wisdom on to young whites by telling them stories. In Jim Ivy's case, his stories helped the new freshmen adjust to Ole Miss. Unlike Uncle Remus, however, Blind Jim's tales never had any underlying message even slightly subversive of the racial status quo. His stories instead confirmed his white listeners' racial stereotypes and reinforced the prevailing racial mores. On one occasion, for instance, Blind Jim shared some "nigger-ology" with his freshmen. He asked, "Did you ever see a tub full of crabs? You don't have to put a top on to keep 'em in. No, sir—when one climbs nearly to the top the others will yank him back. Niggers just that way."[19] His story verified the whites' view that blacks could not see their own best interest, that they could not make progress on their own.

Ivy's blindness strengthened and softened his role as a black racial pro-totype, though few whites probably ever considered the effects of his blindness on their relationship with him. Sighted people typically respond to blind individuals such as Blind Jim with pity. "The blind are forever preoccupied with pity," according to two scholars of blindness, because "the environment of the blind is so saturated with pity." People fear the misfortune of blindness, but instead of striking out against the blind, sighted people out of a sense of guilt react with pity that marks the blind as inferior to themselves and works to keep them isolated, even while coming in contact with them. Hector Chevigny and Sydell Braverman have argued that "pity is the perfect excuse, for it cloaks its purpose in what seem the highest of social sanctions."[20]

Visual differences, therefore, reinforced the relationship between the Negro Blind Jim and his sighted, white Ole Miss friends. Blindness buttressed race. The treatment of both the blind and racial minorities involved ostracism, inferiority, stereotypes, and the fear of integration.[21] Blind Jim was, therefore, doubly inferior because of his color and his handicap. The pity of the sighted for the blind reinforced the paternalism of whites toward the black man, and pity combined with paternalism to prompt whites to take care of the depen-dent Blind Jim. The barrier between the blind and the sighted became greater when compounded by Blind Jim's race at the same time that pity brought the white students closer to him.

Jim Ivy's blindness also made him less of a threat to whites than other sighted black males. Whites had long feared black men as sexual aggressors. Just months before Blind Jim died, the lynching of Emmett Till in Mississippi demonstrated the white fear of black males; the Chicago youth had not actu-ally raped a white woman but ostensibly had only made inappropriate sexual remarks to her, and angry whites responded by killing him in the name of protecting white womanhood. Sighted people commonly perceived the blind as less sexually powerful, perhaps unsexed, even castrated. Jim Ivy had twice been married, once to a blind woman and once when he was nearly eighty to a sixty-four-year-old woman, but he had no children. Unlike Emmett Till and Mack Charles Parker, who was later lynched for allegedly raping a white woman, Blind Jim seemed to pose no sexual threat to white female students and could be trusted on the Ole Miss campus. He could not even look at a white woman. As a blind man, Blind Jim was safe, especially in his later years.[22]

If any death can be considered timely, Blind Jim's death in the fall of 1955 may have been. The civil rights movement's challenge to white supremacy, segregation, and discrimination had begun. Barely six weeks after his demise the Montgomery bus boycott accelerated the movement. The role of a lovable darkey who confirmed the prejudices of whites would become increasingly untenable and anachronistic, even in Mississippi. By the spring of 1955, the white segregationist reaction against *Brown* and the civil rights movement may have even affected the relationship between students and Blind Jim. Paul Baccaro, a student, complained about "sadistic tendencies" of some students who persecuted Blind Jim. After seeing the elderly Jim Ivy on campus for the first time in months, Baccaro inquired about his recent absence, and Blind Jim told him that he thought students did not want him around because they had been verbally abusing him and harassing him when he did come to the university. Blind Jim's increasing irrelevance in the 1950s became even more apparent after his death in the fate of plans to honor him. After paying for Ivy's funeral and gravestone, the fund in his honor had a balance of less than ten dollars, which was turned over to the Mississippi Vocational College in Itta Bena. The funds raised by the Jackson newspaper and television station amounted to slightly more than one thousand dollars, and that also went to the vocational college. No scholarship was ever named in honor of Blind Jim, and no memorial was ever constructed on the Oxford campus in his memory.[23]

The story of another Negro revealed how, even under strict segregation and the prevailing paternalism before the civil rights movement, whites and blacks could interact in a meaningful and significant way at the university. In 1949, Stuart R. Purser moved to Oxford to found an art department. As he drove through rural Pontotoc County that summer, Purser noticed some impressive artwork on a front porch. Intrigued, he stopped at the farm house in the small community of Ecru, about thirty miles east of Oxford, and inquired about the creator of the two striking busts on display. An older black woman told the professor that her son had made them, and she introduced Purser to a young man named M. B. Mayfield.[24]

One of the busts that Purser saw on the porch was a self-portrait that Mayfield sculpted by looking in a mirror. He based the other, of boxer Joe Louis, on a newspaper picture of the Brown Bomber. Mayfield had made his own bust out of clay, but it kept cracking, so he fashioned the boxing champion out of cement; he shined both of the busts with brown shoe polish. "I had never seen a real statue," Mayfield later confessed, "until I made the ones of Joe Louis and myself." Purser admired Mayfield's accomplishments, especially because he had made them without any artistic training. Before leaving Ecru, Purser gave Mayfield some art supplies and then made him an astounding offer: he would arrange a job for Mayfield as custodian in the art department.

Forty-two-year-old Stuart Purser had long had a keen interest in blacks and southern race relations. He had grown up in mill towns in Arkansas and Louisiana where his father worked as a skilled foreman in sawmills. From a young age Purser had learned the complexity of southern race relations, in part because his parents frequently disagreed about it. Purser's father, who came from the Tennessee hills and once served as the head of a local Ku Klux Klan, usually treated individual blacks decently but was prejudiced against the race. On the other hand, Purser's mother was a devout Christian who discreetly opposed the KKK and supported instead duly constituted law and order; she believed that whites should help and encourage blacks through love and understanding. Stuart Purser's closest boyhood friend in Good Pine, Louisiana, had been a Negro his own age named James Jackson, called "Applehead" or just "Ap." Together Stuart and Ap played sports, roamed the creeks and woods, and hunted and fished, at least until Ap in 1927 had to flee after accidentally injuring a white boy with a baseball bat.

After graduating from Louisiana College in 1928, Stuart Purser studied at the Art Institute of Chicago and received a master's degree in 1933. After one year at Washington State University and a decade at his alma mater, he taught for four years at the University of Chattanooga, where he stayed until moving to Oxford. In his art Purser sought to depict "the existing conditions and the social and economic conditions that are taking place in the South." He painted the world he knew, especially southern biracial communities. One critic noted that "central to the artist's vocabulary is the visual metaphor of rural Black America."[25] That a white artist such as Purser painted blacks at all demonstrated his sincere interest in them, and his works reveal a genuine respect and affection for them as fellow human beings.

M. B. Mayfield and a twin brother, L. D., were born in Ecru in 1923. By 1949 M. B. had lived all his life in the small rural community where his father had grown cotton. The family of twelve suffered many losses early in Mayfield's life: his father died when M. B. was not quite three years old, and five siblings died of tuberculosis before he was grown. After his mother married a man with five children from his first marriage, M. B. Mayfield grew up in a large family. Issues of the *Memphis Commercial Appeal* covered the walls of his house, and the young M. B. spent many hours copying the colorful comics. The introverted and antisocial Mayfield avoided farmwork whenever he could and hid in the house and drew. At school he began to draw and color with crayons, but he never went to the local Negro high school.[26]

While farming in Ecru in 1941, Mayfield suffered a bout of fatigue. A local physician found a spot on one of his lungs, suspected tuberculosis, and prescribed extended rest. While self-treating the dreaded disease at home, Mayfield suffered a nervous breakdown. For several years he fought to regain his physical and mental health. Throughout the 1940s, he passed the time by drawing, writing, and listening to music on the radio. He also developed several pen pals through the *Pittsburgh Courier*. During his convalescence, Mayfield began to take his art more seriously. When he met Purser toward the end of his recuperation, his life took a dramatic change.

After settling into the university, Purser sent Mayfield the promised bus ticket to Oxford. After riding behind a curtain at the back of a segregated bus, the young black man arrived at the campus on October 3, 1949, to begin working as a janitor. He divided his duties between the art department's classrooms and studios on campus and the department's off-campus art gallery, where he also had a small apartment. Though frightened by being away from Ecru for the first time, Mayfield found a warm reception at the university and quickly felt at home.[27] His job involved more than cleaning and sweeping because Purser and his art students took an active interest in Mayfield's development as an artist.

In addition to his janitorial duties, Mayfield set up art materials for the students and operated the art gallery. In his activities Mayfield had an opportunity to learn by watching; for example, he learned art history when he operated a slide projector for Purser's art history and art appreciation classes. His custodian's closet, located just off an art classroom, permitted him to sit and observe everything in the class: he, in effect, took art classes at a distance in his own cramped studio. Neither professors nor students objected to his passive participation in their classes. On occasion, Purser, who helped local blacks by hiring them to model for his classes, also asked Mayfield to pose for his students.[28]

More important than Mayfield's peripheral involvement in the art classes was Purser's nurturing of the black janitor's artistic talent in individual lessons in drawing and painting. Mayfield had his own private tutor. Many art students also took an interest in his development by giving him their leftover art supplies, encouraging his artwork, and inviting him to display his work at their Christmas auction. Others also knew of Purser's tutelage of the janitor, especially after a positive article on Mayfield appeared in the student newspaper in the spring of 1950. The dean of liberal arts approved of Mayfield's unusual relationship with the art department, and an education professor and his wife provided Mayfield with art supplies. As a result of his art "lessons," Mayfield later claimed that he became "Ole Miss' first black student."[29]

Purser believed that "with the proper training he [Mayfield] could become one of the outstanding colored artists in the South," but his concern for Mayfield extended beyond his development as an artist and included his growth as an individual. Purser frequently asked Mayfield to accompany him on short trips. From the lectures he overheard and from their conversations in the car, Mayfield was always learning from his mentor. When Purser made art presentations in other Mississippi towns, for example, Mayfield went along. Once they arrived at their destination, Mayfield helped set up the art displays and then sat behind the curtain to listen to the presentation. On their overnight trips, Purser always arranged for Mayfield's accommodation at black hotels and paid all of his expenses. One afternoon Mayfield visited Tennessee for the first time when he went with Purser to Memphis to pick up office and art supplies. From radio and newspapers when he was growing up and from conversations at Ole Miss, he had heard about the city and its Brooks Art Gallery, and for years his family had ordered out of the Sears catalog by using a mail order form that had a Memphis address. After they got their supplies, Purser took Mayfield sightseeing. They drove by the Peabody Hotel and the Sears store, and then to the Brooks Art Gallery. Though closed to blacks except for one day a week, Purser prevailed on the director to give Mayfield a special tour, his first visit to an art gallery.[30]

In the spring of 1951, Purser again surprised Mayfield by sending him to Jackson to take the GED exam at Jackson College for Negro Teachers. Both men, but especially Purser, must have known that passing the high school equivalency test would help Mayfield obtain a better job and follow his artistic talent. Purser made all the arrangements, including the bus ticket, a hotel room on Pearl Street, and an appointment to take the test. Mayfield apparently passed.[31]

The highlight of Mayfield's time in Oxford came in the late spring of 1951. Again at Purser's instigation, professors, students, and friends, including William Faulkner, raised the money and made the arrangements to send Mayfield to Chicago to see a Van Gogh exhibit. Mayfield rode a bus from Oxford to Batesville, where for the first time he boarded a train. In several days in Chicago, he saw the spectacular exhibit and toured the city. From his YMCA hotel, he wrote to his mother in Ecru, "I am having a WONDERFUL time here in Chicago. Wish I could stay." Chicago even more than Jackson or Memphis, and Van Gogh more than the Brooks, opened the world and the world of art to Mayfield.[32]

M. B. Mayfield worked at Ole Miss for another year and a half, but for the last six months life around the art department was not the same, because his mentor had left. In 1951, after two years in Oxford, Stuart Purser moved to the University of Florida. At the end of the same year, Mayfield also decided to leave his job and to return to Ecru to care for his sick mother. When she recovered, he returned to the university for several months in the spring of 1954 but again found the situation different without Purser; when his mother had a stroke he moved back to Ecru to care for her. After she died, Mayfield moved to Wisconsin for half a dozen years before returning to the South. From 1967 to 1979 he worked at the Brooks Art Gallery as a custodian and later as a security guard. After other jobs in Memphis, he returned to live and paint in Ecru. In the forty years after he left Oxford, Mayfield exhibited his artwork in galleries from Texas to Massachusetts; his first show appeared in Starkville, Mississippi, in 1955. He attributed much of his success, personal as well as artistic, to Stuart Purser, his "long-standing friend and art instructor."[33]

Purser indeed had a profound impact on Mayfield. The art professor could work with the black janitor because he did it so casually and subtly that many did not even notice and few would have objected to their exceptional relationship. As an experienced observer of southern racial practices, Purser knew better than to challenge segregation overtly, so he worked for tolerance and equality by nurturing the career of his black employee. For all of his thoughtful deeds on behalf of Mayfield and other blacks, Purser never discussed race with him and was always careful that Mayfield never violate racial taboos; Mayfield may have always ridden in the front seat of a car on trips, but Purser insisted that he ride in the back seat on errands in town with the department secretary. Instead of launching a futile assault on racial prejudice and discrimination that would have jeopardized Mayfield's position as an unconventional student, Purser and Mayfield worked within the prevailing system of segregation to undermine the racial status quo.

The Purser-Mayfield relationship differed significantly from Jim Ivy's association with Ole Miss. Though each man worked within a tightly segregated university, Blind Jim humbly benefited from the kindness and generosity of whites while never threatening white superiority. Ivy apparently accepted his subservient status and did not expect his situation to improve, but he cultivated white sympathy for his own benefit. Mayfield also did not question Mississippi's racial mores and used the opportunities presented to him. The development of his artistic talents under Purser, however, confused accepted racial distinctions more than Blind Jim ever could. By demonstrating a black man's talent, Mayfield defied white condescension toward blacks. Whites had long recognized black achievements in the arts and explained them as a function of the emotional and nonintellectual character of blacks, so Mayfield's accomplishments only slightly jeopardized white confidence. Granting M. B. Mayfield's artistic achievement also involved only one individual, not an appreciation for the entire race.[34] If Ivy and Mayfield found space under white supremacy to eke out limited personal success, a third African American university employee in the 1950s followed a different route toward achievement in Jim Crow Mississippi.

In the early 1950s, Ernest McEwen Jr. worked as a janitor in the Lyceum. Born in Lafayette County in 1931, McEwen grew up just west of Oxford in the Spring Hill community where he went to school. Each of his parents had only an eighth-grade education. His father was a sharecropper but in 1944 bought land from a friendly white man and became an independent farmer; his mother taught school for a few years. The family was a mixture of white, black, and Native American. The elder Ernest McEwen had such light skin that he could have passed for white, but his son had very dark skin like his mother's. Though the McEwens went to Oxford frequently on weekends, they never attended a Rebel football game but from their farm could see cars going to Oxford for games. In the eleventh grade, McEwen married and began working at the university. On a night crew that started a daily eight-hour shift at 3:00 P.M.., McEwen cleaned the Lyceum. The popular, well-spoken, and handsome young black man's enthusiasm and ability impressed people. An Ole Miss student who learned that McEwen wanted to go to college introduced him to L. L. Love, the dean of student personnel who had an office in the building.[35]

Though Love was a native of Oregon, his parents' families came from Tennessee and Kentucky, and he thought of himself as partly a southerner. He joined the university in 1949 after teaching in Oregon, serving in the navy, and working as a dean at Ohio State University, where he had received his doctorate in 1932. The father of four grown children, Love took an interest in Ernest McEwen. He appreciated McEwen's intelligence and his interest in college. The dean and the janitor got to know each other when McEwen visited in Love's campus home. As a result of conversations over coffee and Cokes, Love concluded that McEwen was not a member of the NAACP, did not advocate integration, and had the potential to become the kind of black leader Mississippi needed.[36]

When McEwen told Love he wanted to study engineering at a northern college, Love initially tried to help him gain admission to Howard University in Washington. The dean did not consider suggesting Ole Miss, but after corresponding with officials at Mississippi's black colleges, Love proposed that McEwen consider staying in the state. The dean persuaded him to attend

Alcorn A&M College, and he arranged for a scholarship, a job as foreman on a custodial crew, and a married-student apartment. In the fall of 1953, the twenty-two-year-old McEwen moved to Alcorn with his wife and their three children. McEwen and Love maintained contact; on visits to Oxford, McEwen sometimes called on his mentor, and Love and others at Ole Miss occasionally gave him clothing and money. In McEwen's third year at Alcorn, he was elected president of the student body. Love's interest in and concern for one of the Lyceum's custodians had paid impressive dividends.[37]

Racial customs at Ole Miss extended beyond Ivy, Mayfield, and McEwen to include campus visitors. After World War II no blacks came with visiting athletic teams or as speakers to university audiences; such appearances would have suggested equality with or even superiority to Ole Miss audiences. Black entertainers, however, did frequently perform at concerts and at fraternity parties.[38] In the antebellum South, slave singers and musicians often performed for whites, and Ole Miss continued the tradition after World War II when black performers remained common. Without causing any controversy, fraternities often hired African American musical groups for their parties and dances. In the 1950s the university also featured concerts by jazz musicians Lionel Hampton, Louis Armstrong, and Duke Ellington.

In February 1952, the student body hosted the renowned vibraharpist Lionel Hampton. With the state's general assembly in its biennial session, the chairman of Ole Miss's social committee advised the student government sponsors not to use photographs of Hampton in their concert publicity and suggested that they tear the pictures from already printed posters. Earlier the committee had bowed to administration pressure and canceled an appearance by Count Basie and Billy Eckstein at the students' major winter dance, but it decided to proceed with Hampton's visit. Paul Pittman, the editor of the *Mississippian*, suggested that the university administration feared "repercussions" if the legislators knew "a Negro band would play for Ole Miss students." According to Pittman, "The result: Supreme Idiocy."[39]

Despite the concerns about embarrassing publicity, "The Hamp" and his eighteen-piece group presented, according to the student newspaper, a "sensational performance" that the "audience loved." The band "blew and blew, played and played, and the audience loved it" for three and a half hours; students "stood and yelled, clapped and stomped, and crowded to the front" of the auditorium. "Stupendous," declared the *Mississippian*. One student called it the most powerful performance in the twenty-five years of the Fulton Chapel auditorium. A letter to the editor condemned the "perverted" "blockheads" who had opposed the black artist's appearance and claimed that even "racial prejudice" cannot "crush art." Despite the concerns of the Ole Miss administration, the event stirred no controversy, and two weeks later the legislature increased appropriations for the state's institutions of higher education.[40]

Hampton returned in April 1954 for a repeat performance, but without many of the worries about publicity. Coming later in the year, his concert posed less of a threat to legislative appropriations, and the lack of attention in the state's press reduced the fears of administrators. On a Thursday evening more than one thousand students crowded into Fulton Chapel and turned into a "mass of feverish, screaming humanity, waving their arms and stomping their feet" in response to the jazz. The orchestra included a white pianist, a Japanese saxophonist, and several musicians from Europe, but the hysterical all-white audience paid no attention to the racial mixture. Overly enthusiastic students in the standing-room-only crowd climbed on stage to dance with the band, and only an intermission calmed the students. After three encores, the concert ended, and Hampton declared Ole Miss audiences among his more enthusiastic from all over the world, and he intimated he might write a song and call it "Ole Miss." Hampton later fondly recalled drinking and dancing with the students after the show and remembered that fifty cars of Ole Miss students drove to his concert the next evening in Nashville.[41]

When Louis Armstrong came to Ole Miss the following spring, engineers feared that a reception similar to Hampton's would threaten the safety of the Fulton Chapel audience. A special notice warned that "structural engineers have advised us that demonstrations, such as jumping up and down and unnecessary stomping of feet, are not to be permitted in the interest of safety." When the great trumpeter and his All-Stars performed, engineers enforced the decree. Though the spectators were "unusually reserved," perhaps because of the warning, the auditorium "rocked in the spring heat to the hot music." Like Hampton's earlier concerts, Satchmo's appearance at Ole Miss gained little attention outside Oxford and caused no controversy. With the general assembly not in session, the March 1955 appearance worried administrators far less than concerts when the legislators were meeting in Jackson.[42]

Duke Ellington, the third major African American musician to appear at the university in the 1950s, played for the students' major spring dance in 1956. Though acclaimed as a composer, pianist, and bandleader, Ellington in the mid-1950s had reached a fallow period and struggled professionally. Trying to keep the band together, they played at places that would not be able to afford them after Ellington's renaissance at the Newport Jazz Festival in July 1956, which came soon after his appearance at Ole Miss. Coming in May, his orchestra's performance fell safely after the close of the legislature, and it too attracted little statewide publicity and elicited no criticism from the state's white segregationists.[43]

As the experiences of Hampton, Armstrong, and Ellington testified, Mississippi whites in the postwar era accepted blacks as entertainers. They could appreciate the unique gifts of individual blacks without undermining their basic belief in the superiority of the white race. Black performers on stage remained removed from whites, and their presence before whites did not imply social equality. Blacks may have succeeded more in the music industry than in any other because whites, even in the South, accepted them more as singers, musicians, dancers, and actors than as any other professionals. Blacks also routinely performed before all-white audiences in both the South and the North without challenging segregation. Hampton, Armstrong, and Ellington had roots in the South, understood the region's racial mores, and did not crusade for integration. More than two years after Armstrong's appearance at Ole Miss, he caused a public controversy during the crisis over integrating the schools in Little Rock by criticizing the Eisenhower administration's actions. His comments in the fall of 1957 startled people because he had been so quiet on civil rights. According to a biographer, even after Satchmo's outburst, "if Louis had any policy on race, it was still, basically, not to rock the boat." Economic and professional needs forced black performers' acquiescence, which made them more acceptable to white segregationists.[44]

Unknown to many at the university, Armstrong's concert attracted one unusual observer, Robert Patterson, the founder of the Citizens' Council. He observed with "pleasure(?)" Satchmo's "inter-racial orchestra consisting of two blacks, two whites, and two yellows." The next day he reported to Edwin White of Holmes County and half a dozen other business and political leaders, "You should have heard the co-eds shriek when the yellow boy soloed on his slide trombone." He expressed dismay that Armstrong used first names to address his white colleagues and "hugged them affectionately." Even in the wake of the Supreme Court's decision in *Brown v. Board of Education*, however, Armstrong's behavior did not trigger in Patterson any fear for the southern way of life; he did not sound the alarm for retaliation against Ole Miss or for a tightening of racial segregation. Though he disliked aspects of Armstrong's behavior, even Patterson apparently accepted black musicians' performances before white audiences.[45]

While students cheered black performers and befriended Blind Jim, they retained a powerful commitment to white supremacy and the southern way of life. Two polls of student opinion in the mid-1950s revealed overwhelming support for segregation. A small minority supported admission of blacks, but most favored integration. One compared the inevitability of integration to the cooling of the sun: "Both of those events are a long way off." Among the small minority favoring immediate integration, realism forced one student to concede, "It is impossible to believe that the University can buck the Supreme Court." A majority opposed any integration at Ole Miss, and nearly half were certain that blacks would never attend the university. As one student commented, "I love colored people, but in their place." And their place did not include Ole Miss, unless they worked in menial capacities, because, as one freshman declared, "Negroes have been out of the jungle and have worn clothes instead of loin cloths for only 200 years." Segregation's defenders agreed that separate but equal educational facilities for the two races provided the only solution to the problem.[46]

Student social activities more indirectly revealed racial attitudes. In November 1950, Ole Miss students initiated an annual Dixie Week that celebrated the Old South and the Civil War. It sought to "please the whims of every Southern Belle and Confederate Gentleman." Culminating with a home football game, often against archrival Mississippi State, the festivities included replacing the U.S. flag with the Confederate flag, reading the state's Ordinance of Secession, honoring a surviving Confederate veteran from Alabama, a memorial service for Confederate soldiers, and the chancellor's wreath-laying at the Confederate monument. With no concern for the feelings of Jim Ivy or M. B. Mayfield, students made clear their political preferences and racial values with the assassination of Lincoln in the student grill, the sale of cheerleaders in a "slave" auction, and the appearance of the Ku Klux Klan. In 1953 the student senate endorsed the "doctrines of the Southern Confederacy," particularly "the principles of States' rights," and it deplored "the impositions, arrogancy and abominations" of the federal government that had committed "unbearable transgressions of our sacred rights" and "despoiled our traditions." The racial mores allowed the white students to be outspoken and insensitive toward an entire race. When Dixie Week moved to the spring, it continued to celebrate white supremacy, slavery, and the Lost Cause. Fondness for Blind Jim and an appreciation for Louis Armstrong's jazz did not mitigate the students' love for the Old South and their disdain for blacks in general.[47]

Fraternities and sororities frequently demonstrated racial prejudice in their party themes. Identified closely with the Old South, Kappa Alpha typically had social affairs that emphasized the antebellum South, plantation life, and the Confederacy; at a 1948 dance, two KAS dressed as "happy, cheerful slave servants" of Robert E. Lee to greet the guests. Using similar themes, Kappa Sigma fraternity staged a Plantation Ball in 1946 and Phi Kappa Psi an Old South party in 1954. Delta Psi's men had a jungle party in 1952, and the next year a voodoo party. Though perhaps thoughtlessly, the students endorsed the prevailing racial stereotypes of African Americans.[48]

The most prevalent racial theme at Greek events in the postwar years involved blackface worn in minstrel shows. Sigma Alpha Epsilon, for example, had a minstrel party in 1947 that featured an interpretation of Al Jolson's "Mammy." The next year in a charity stunt, Delta Gamma sorority contributed a "Musical Minstrel of Magnitude" in which young women appeared in blackface to sing songs and tell jokes. At the same fund-raiser, the men of Sigma Nu parodied Harriet Beecher Stowe's *Uncle Tom's Cabin*, and Phi Delta Psi fraternity presented "life in a colored beauty salon" in "The Beale Street Beauty Salon." Three years later in another stunt night, Delta Delta Delta acted out "Coal Black and the Seven Spades," a takeoff on "Snow White," and women from Chi Omega wore blackface in another minstrel act. Tri-Delta in 1955 and Sigma Alpha Epsilon fraternity in 1956 featured minstrel shows.[49]

Minstrelsy extended beyond the Ole Miss students. In 1951 the Oxford Lions Club presented a minstrel show at the local grammar school, and the blackface performers included several Ole Miss professors and Robert B. Ellis, the university registrar. The following year, the Lions staged another minstrel show that featured a "Negro Zuzu Zuzu Dance."[50] Rather than being atypical, the Ole Miss students' actions reflected the larger culture.

For whites, the minstrel shows confirmed everyone's status in the segregated South. By donning blackface, students could assume the role of blacks and act as they expected and wanted blacks to behave; the "black" performers personified the white stereotypes of blacks. The characters reminded the students of the inherent inferiority of blacks but also reassured whites that blacks were happy and contented, that they willingly conformed to the southern way of life. What troublesome outsiders interpreted as discrimination and oppression was, according to the minstrel shows, the natural and accepted order. Exceptions such as M. B. Mayfield and Ernest McEwen confirmed the larger rule of black inferiority as exemplified by Blind Jim and the minstrel show characters. Whites could, therefore, believe that blacks did not want integration or equality and, indeed, that they knew their proper place, which did not include being students at Ole Miss.

4. "Negroes Who Didn't Know Their Place": Early Attempts at Integration

■ ■

I n October 1950, the editor of the *Mississippian* endorsed racial integration. Though two hundred Negroes attended previously all-white southern colleges and universities, Ole Miss remained completely white. Defying the state's rigid policy of segregation in higher education, Albin Krebs declared, "We believe that qualified Negroes should be allowed to enter the School of Law and any other professional schools." Pointing to recent events in other southern states, Krebs predicted that Negroes would eventually apply to Ole Miss, and, although Mississippi might be the last state to have its segregation practices in higher education challenged, Krebs believed that the U.S. Supreme Court would order the admission of Negroes. The "professional schools will have to open their doors to qualified applicants of that race," concluded the editor, because the Supreme Court had "ruled that in the field of education, the pigment of a man's skin must have nothing to do with the measurement of his ability." The *Jackson Daily News* proclaimed Krebs's editorial "the first open statement advocating admission of Negroes to the University of Mississippi."[1]

For Krebs, the end of segregation in graduate programs provided "the only answer to our age-old problem of 'the Negro.'" He invoked the "principles of justice for all, of fair play, of dignity of the individual," as well as the Constitution and Christian values. More practically, he argued that better education would enable blacks to elevate themselves and thereby help the entire state progress.[2]

Anticipating criticism, Krebs denied that his proposal had anything to do with racial segregation. "That's another question," he suggested, "but we think it poses no real problem here. Segregation is simply a matter of choice. Southerners will continue to pick their own associates, no doubt until the end of time." Fully expecting that the "'professional Southerner,' who mourns the death of [Senator Theodore G.] Bilbo and believes in an Aryan philosophy of race, will rant and shout and scream" against the admission of Negroes, Krebs dismissed their objections and pointed out that "a democratic majority of the people in this country want justice and a better democracy extended everywhere, and their will will be done. And rightly so."[3]

Krebs's heretical stance derived from many complicated sources that included his family background, his religion, his personal racial experiences, his general editorial policy, and his sexuality. Raised a Roman Catholic in the predominantly Protestant coastal town of Pascagoula, Krebs may have been particularly alert to religious prejudice. Once a friend admitted that he did not expect Krebs to understand the religious themes in a movie because Krebs was not a Christian but a Catholic. More often indirect and subtle, the anti-Catholic attitudes sensitized Krebs to the feelings of other minorities and prepared him to defend the oppressed.[4]

One of Krebs's editorials defended a religious minority at Ole Miss. A professor had badgered a student who arrived late to class with a series of questions: "Your initials are S. A., aren't they? What's the 'S' for, Samuel? . . . How about the 'A'? What does it stand for? Abraham? . . . I notice you came in late today. Who are you, anyway, the lost child of Jerusalem?" Krebs blasted the remarks as a "stupid, vicious attack." Although the student apparently made no objection, Krebs protested the "bigoted remarks" and "anti-Semitic jibes." The professor was, according to Krebs, "obviously too stupid and narrow-minded to be teaching in a state university."[5]

A racial incident after his freshman year made quite an impression on Krebs. During the summer, he and a couple of friends journeyed by bus to New York City. On their return trip, an older man boarded and proceeded toward the back of the bus where custom dictated that Negroes should ride. When the bus driver told him he could not sit back there with the "niggers," the dignified man simply replied, "I belong back here." Even though the man could have passed for white and sat in the front of the bus, he chose to sit with his fellow Negroes in the rear. The cruelty embarrassed Krebs. Privileged by his skin color, he had witnessed the meanness of segregation and the indignity of discrimination.[6]

Initially uninvolved in fraternities, Krebs joined the staff of the *Mississippian* in his first semester, and it became a major part of his life. As editor he declared a bold editorial policy: "We intend to wield that sword and wield it often. We intend to use it to cut down anything that stands in the way of progress or freedom of thought and expression." He expected that "this sword, this voice, will be used to criticize, to cut into and expose to view good and bad, despite the fact that some will suffer for it." Disparaging the "lily-livered editor who has a spine like that of a jelly-fish," Krebs promised not to straddle fences or hug the middle of the road.[7]

Before calling for integration, Krebs wrote nonconformist editorials on related racial issues, though without much controversy. Standing for First Amendment rights of free expression, for example, he criticized the University of California student bookstore for banning *Little Black Sambo* because it caricatured Negroes. Krebs could not imagine "anyone forming hate patterns by reading" the childhood classic. He also lauded Dr. Ralph Bunche for winning the Nobel Peace Prize and declared, "We Americans should feel a great deal of pride in the knowledge that Dr. Bunche is *one of us.*" Claiming the selection committee "could not have chosen a more deserving man," he noted that Bunche "rose from very modest circumstances, against almost insurmountable odds. He is the son of a barber. He is also the grandson of a slave."[8]

At a time when the state and the nation were in the throes of an intense campaign against disloyal Americans, Krebs editorialized against loyalty oaths and attempts to control communists. He denounced the McCarran Internal Security Act because it "in effect made lawful the very storm-trooper tactics we fought against in World War II. . . . [and] forbids Americans to exercise some of their basic rights." A required loyalty oath for state employees struck Krebs as innocuous, but he claimed that "free men ought not to be forced to say they are loyal." Krebs concluded, "We've become so war-hysterical, so Red-scared, that we're hunting witches and burning innocent people in the process."[9] Even in the home of ardent anticommunists Senator James Eastland and Representative John Rankin, Krebs's pointed pronouncements provoked little critical reaction.

Although the young Krebs did not discuss his opinions much even with his parents, he did find support for his dissenting views. During his high school years, he worked as a stringer for the weekly *Pascagoula Chronicle,* where Easton King and Ira Harkey mentored him. In the 1950s Harkey gained a reputation as a liberal on racial matters; in 1963 he would win a Pulitzer Prize for his editorials. Krebs found their progressive outlook compatible with his own emerging ideas.[10]

Krebs's unorthodox views may also have been affected by his uncertainty about his own sexuality. Although as an adult Krebs became openly homosexual, his commentaries in college demonstrated his inability or unwillingness to recognize or accept his sexual orientation and his resulting discomfort. For a student journalist of 1950, he wrote inordinately about women and sex. His newspaper humor, for example, usually involved sexually suggestive, but aggressively heterosexual, comments. Women's breasts seemed especially to fascinate Krebs.[11]

The writer's preoccupation with sex proved that he had, as he admitted, "given the matter a lot of thought." His compulsive commentary revealed his intention to appear thoroughly masculine, to avoid drawing attention to his sexuality, and to hide his own ambivalence. Ole Miss in the early 1950s did not tolerate homosexuality. In the spring of 1950, when Krebs became editor of the newspaper, university discipline forced three homosexual students and one faculty member to leave the university. Even if he had wanted to, Krebs could not have publicly discussed his homosexuality, but his own sexual repression may have made him sensitive to the oppression of excluded or persecuted groups, particularly black Americans.[12]

His startling editorial on integration in the fall of 1950, like his other uses of the editorial sword, presented a reasoned, even cautious position. He did not expect any reaction to comments on well-known current events. For more than a decade the NAACP had waged a legal battle against segregation in higher education, particularly in graduate and professional programs. In its legal challenges, the NAACP argued that states had not fulfilled the "separate but equal" requirements of *Plessy v. Ferguson*. In June 1950, four months before Krebs's editorial, the Supreme Court further explicated the *Plessy* standard in two NAACP cases. Holding that a separate law school in Houston was not equal to the University of Texas law school, the Court directed the University of Texas to admit Heman Marion Sweatt, the black applicant. On the same day, it held that segregating a black graduate student within the University of Oklahoma— at cafeteria tables, in classrooms, and in the library—violated the Fourteenth Amendment's mandate of equal protection of the law for all citizens. In the two cases, the Court did not overrule *Plessy*'s separate-but-equal principle but made the standard nearly impossible to achieve.[13]

The court decisions did not escape the attention of southerners. In 1948 the *Mississippian* surveyed students about admitting Negro graduate and professional students to Ole Miss. Though one law student conceded that the Supreme Court would probably compel the university to accept Negroes, most students insisted on segregation. Opinions ranged from a curt "Hell no!" to a more dispassionate "No, but equal opportunity should be offered to the Negroes." One senior from Duck Hill demanded, "Keep them separated," while another replied, "Hell no! I'm a confirmed Rebel." A more restrained law student opposed admitting blacks because "it would be the beginning toward a deplorable end."[14]

Mississippi newspapers also followed the Supreme Court. In addition to carrying news stories, the Oxford and Tupelo newspapers, for example, commented on the 1950 decisions. Like other editors, Albin Krebs followed the developing story. The *Mississippian* repeated a report from the *Jackson Daily News* that originally ran in the *Jackson Advocate*, a conservative black weekly newspaper: a Negro would soon apply to the university's law school. Frustrated by repeatedly failing the state bar exam, blacks wanted to go to the Ole Miss law school to gain automatic admission to the bar.[15] The subject of Krebs's editorial, therefore, did not surprise his readers.

The day following Krebs's October 27 editorial, the state's newspapers reacted vehemently with front-page stories. In the evening of the day Krebs's editorial appeared, Chancellor J. D. Williams issued a brief statement that Krebs "does not represent the University. He cannot speak for the university, and he does not. State law requires segregation, and that's our position." Except for his cool and measured recognition of state policy, the chancellor did his best to avoid taking a position on racial segregation.[16] Once again, Williams hoped the controversy would, if left alone, quickly disappear. But it did not.

Three days later, on a Monday evening, a crowd demonstrated outside Krebs's dormitory. A few dozen students sang, "We'll hang Albin Krebs from a sour apple tree," and shouted, "We want Krebs." Hearing the disturbance, other students poured out of the dorms. Chanting "Hotty Toddy," the Ole Miss cheer, about forty students signed a petition to remove Krebs from office. Someone stuck in the lawn between two dorms a five-foot-tall cross with an oil-soaked sheet wrapped around it. Set afire, it blazed in the night, and when the fire subsided a student threw a can of gasoline on it, and flames shot twenty feet upwards. In the light of the burning cross, one student read Krebs's editorial to the crowd. When Krebs walked from the *Mississippian* office toward his dorm, a football player from Pascagoula told him to go to his room where he and his friends would protect him. Fearing physical danger, Krebs complied. One observer considered the event more of a pep rally than a serious protest, and a demonstrator reportedly told Krebs, "We want to burn a cross. . . . We're just having some fun." In the wake of the cross-burning, Krebs hoped people in other parts of the nation "will not seize on this as an opportunity to cry: 'There has been another cross-burning in Mississippi,' and point a finger at us."[17]

Newspapers reported that two thousand students had demonstrated, and the editor got calls of support from other parts of the nation. In another statement about the "unfortunate incident" prompted by Krebs's "unfortunate" editorial, Chancellor Williams maintained that the "students were exercising the same prerogative in voicing their opinion as Mr. Krebs was in writing the editorial." Williams refused to be drawn into the effort to remove the editor because it was "the province of the students, and not of the University administration." Upon investigation, the administration learned that the demonstration involved only about two hundred students and was "nothing more than a 'bubbling over of animal spirits,' and that this was a chance to have fun." According to one report, the hilarity "stemmed from a lack of something else to do."[18]

Student reaction continued throughout the next week. The participation of some of his new fraternity brothers in the protests particularly hurt Krebs. Even more troubling, his roommate, who worked on the newspaper, moved out.

Students made occasional derogatory comments directly to Krebs, but most voiced their opposition in letters to the editor. Elmore D. Greaves Jr. committed to Negro inferiority and racial inequality, denied that the Negro was capable of "sustaining modern civilization and culture." He also dismissed Krebs's appeals to Christianity and reminded him of nineteenth-century Christian defenses of slavery. Greaves called on the South to "defend her civilization —preferably by reason, but if necessary by force." One student denied any contradiction in being a Christian and believing in racial segregation. Another called the editorial "a masterpiece of stupidity." Opposed to "tearing down of any social barriers" between the races, Robert Hedges, a sophomore from Choctaw County, contended, "Anyone who tells you that allowing Negroes to enter our schools is not a step toward the mixture of our races is lying or very shortsighted indeed." Racial purity required racial segregation, even at Ole Miss.[19]

Endorsements of Krebs's position came from Ole Miss and other schools. Student newspapers at Arkansas, Miami (Florida), Auburn, and North Carolina endorsed Krebs. At Ole Miss one student applauded Krebs's courage. Though a loyal southerner, she thought "fighting for a lost cause" was pointless. Another local student warned Krebs that he would probably elicit "indignant howls" from the "sewer sheets" like the Jackson newspapers, but he hailed Krebs for his courage to take an unpopular stand in the land of archsegregationists like Bilbo and Rankin. Declaring that "ALL men are equal, whether they be blue, black, white, yellow, or orange," Krebs's defender called on white Mississippians to educate Negroes instead of exploiting them. The strongest public defense of Krebs came from the *Delta Democrat Times*, where Hodding Carter liked Krebs's courage and urged him to persist in spite of the assaults. Although Carter doubted Krebs's stand would have any effect on desegregating the university, he appreciated the young editor's advocacy of Christian values and democratic principles.[20]

Krebs also came in for caustic criticism from outside Oxford by defenders of white supremacy. An alumnus from Newton called him "a low down, nigger-lovin', small town hick" and declared he should be run out of the state. A Jackson man referred to Krebs and liberals in general as "a contemptible and bastard kind of cultural and psychological paederasts and petunias . . . little intellectual snobs and poseurs." Another segregationist decreed, "Segregation *must* be maintained, no matter what the Supreme Court says. If it is necessary to die on our feet, man, woman, and child, then we must die!" He hoped that Ole Miss had not become "a gelding institution where we send our children to have them castrated of their racial virility." A Memphis man argued that Krebs's position would lead to "miscegenation and intermixture of the races."

From nearby Sardis, one man disregarded the state's large Negro population in declaring that "99.9 per cent of all Mississippians" disagreed with Krebs's editorial. He explained why Krebs's statement was particularly noxious: "I like to think of Ole Miss as the last line of defense for the Confederate States of America—the last stronghold of Southern sentiments and our way of life."[21]

Representative John Rankin, whom Ira Harkey called "perhaps the vilest hater ever to disgrace the halls of Congress," charged in a speech to the Tupelo Rotary Club, "That was a Communist editorial in the University newspaper," and "the Communists are trying to ruin the South by forcing equality with the Negro." Krebs could not avoid Rankin's attack. "I am honored to be placed in the same category as professor Albert Einstein, whom Rankin also once called a Communist because he would not agree with him," said Krebs. "I'd like to see Mr. Rankin reconcile my religion with Communism." With legal representation by Karl Wiesenburg, Krebs threatened a libel suit unless Rankin apologized; later Rankin settled the matter with a letter of apology and payment of one dollar. Many Mississippians, however, agreed with Rankin.[22]

While one alumnus complimented Chancellor Williams for denying Krebs publicity by paying him as little attention as possible, L. B. Porter from Union charged the chancellor with "gross negligence of your official position" for allowing the "unequivocal catastrophe" of Krebs's editorial. He advocated some form of censorship of the student newspaper to prevent such a "deplorable" event. Another correspondent urged Williams to "KICK Krebs out." Charles Hills, a political columnist for the *Jackson Clarion-Ledger*, chided Williams's wavering in the equivocal middle. Also from Jackson, a supporter of Ole Miss criticized Williams's "policy of silence and indifference. If you don't know how to defend the sacred principle of segregation," he warned Williams, "then you have no business being the chancellor of a Southern University."[23]

Despite the pleas for action, J. D. Williams hoped the rumpus would go away. Honoring the *Mississippian*'s long tradition of editorial independence, he did not attempt to muzzle the paper because he believed that any administrative interference would be undesirable, even if the students did on occasion use their freedom unwisely. He continued to maintain that Krebs did not speak for the university, whose policy was racial segregation. Though Williams thought that Krebs reveled in the attention, he refused to reprimand him. He also dismissed worries about the cross-burning as the result of a student "lark," but he did regret the publicity given the event.[24] The chancellor simply waited and allowed the students to deal with their editor.

Krebs said little to his critics, but in the next issue of the *Mississippian*, he apologized. Intending to speak only for himself, Krebs regretted that some readers misinterpreted "we" to mean he thought he spoke for everyone at Ole

Miss. Also "unfortunate," according to the editor, was the negative publicity for the university. Out of respect for other views, he published many letters, both supportive and critical, but he did not retract his call for admitting Negroes. With the November 3 issue, he announced that further discussion "only adds fuel to the fire" and that the staff had "decided to end the discussion."[25]

The controversy refused to die so easily. Three days after Krebs's second editorial, students presented to the student body president a petition calling for the editor's ouster. With chants of "Get rid of Krebs," the peaceful demonstration evolved into an old-fashioned pep rally. At a meeting the next evening, the student senate's executive council considered the petition from forty students and decided to turn the matter over to the full senate, which decided the next evening to hold a special meeting the next week to consider the petition.[26]

On November 8, the senators received the executive council's recommendation to drop the case against Krebs. Before voting, however, the senators debated freedom of the press, the editor's responsibilities, censorship, and the reaction to Krebs's editorial. Maurice Dantin, student government president, tried to separate Krebs's views from his rights as an editor, and he reported that the executive council thought Krebs was within his rights. "It is a question of whether we want censorship even of a student newspaper," declared Dantin. While others spoke in support of Krebs's rights and against censorship, one student urged the senate to act against the editor to satisfy offended Mississippians. "It is not a question of freedom of the press," opined another. "The students own the paper. If Krebs can't follow the policy of the student body, he should not be allowed to continue as editor." Tom Roberts further argued that his fellow students had to oppose integration because students at other southern schools had allowed desegregation to occur by not mounting stiff opposition to the admission of blacks. Finally the senate voted 43–21 to ignore the petition to remove Krebs and to approve a resolution endorsing freedom of the press and recommending "that this case be considered closed."[27]

The chancellor and the student senate got their wish, as the brouhaha soon subsided. An armed attack on President Harry S Truman, the awarding of the Nobel Prize in literature to William Faulkner, and congressional elections helped overshadow the controversy, but it abated largely because of a lack of interest among segregationists. Although Krebs's editorial had been "foolish" and "in bad taste," the *Jackson Daily News* considered it merely "untimely" and not particularly threatening; no Negro had seriously sought admission to a white school, so his position was irrelevant. Referring to the whole affair as "that mess at Ole Miss," the capital's evening paper dismissed Krebs's opinion even though it had been "violative of Mississippi's fundamental policy—segregation in education."[28] Segregation seemed secure.

Krebs finished his term as editor without further incident, yet the controversial editorial continued to have ramifications. At his graduation in the spring of 1951, none of Krebs's family attended, partly due to financial limitations but also probably because of embarrassment at his notoriety. When he received his diploma, many booed and hissed. When in full uniform he received his army commission, he heard only silence. Within weeks of his graduation, Krebs traveled to Atlanta to speak to the first national convention of the NAACP to meet in the South. Aaron Henry, the Clarksdale pharmacist and longtime leader of the state NAACP, had invited him to speak. Sharing the dais with Thurgood Marshall, Roy Wilkins, and other dignitaries, Krebs told of his experiences. Afterward, he met many people, including a light-skinned Negro from Atlanta who introduced himself and his parents: he was, Krebs learned a decade later, Harry Murphy.[29]

The question broached by Krebs's editorial and discussed by the former editor at the NAACP convention—integration of the university—had confronted chancellors since the NAACP began its legal campaign in the 1930s. J. D. Williams and his two predecessors had conformed to the state's segregation policy, avoided integration, and escaped publicity or controversy. In 1939, even after the Supreme Court had ruled in *State of Missouri ex rel. Gaines v. Canada* (1938) that states with limited educational facilities must admit blacks as well as whites, Chancellor A. B. Butts believed integration was "not a question that will immediately confront us." If and when it did arise, Butts had a simple answer: "No negro will enter the University of Mississippi." He believed that the state would accommodate any black applicant while maintaining segregation in higher education; it would probably make some "special provision" to offer more courses at Alcorn A&M College, the state's only black college. The chancellor, of course, kept the IHL board fully informed of all matters relating to integration, and he knew his position had the trustees' support. On one occasion, expressing his approval of Butts's stance, W. C. Wells, the chairman of the board, agreed that Negroes "will not be admitted. We will litigate 'until the cows come home.'" More ominously, he told Butts that, even if the courts did order a Negro enrolled, "I would feel sorry about what would happen to them in 24 hours after they got there."[30]

With Chancellor Butts on active army duty during World War II, Acting Chancellor Alfred Hume continued the policy of segregation, which he personally endorsed. Confessing great affection and sympathy for his "good many friends among the colored people," Hume wanted better education for Negroes, but not at the University of Mississippi. Negroes, according to Hume, had special needs already being provided at the separate Alcorn A&M College, and he could not foresee any reason for change.[31]

The first bona fide application from a Negro arrived at the university in the summer of 1948, after J. D. Williams had assumed the chancellorship and a few months after the Supreme Court's decision in favor of admitting Ada Sipuel to a whites-only law school (*Sipuel v. Board of Regents of the University of Oklahoma*, 1948). The university registrar thought Charles H. Gray's application for graduate study was questionable, so he sent a copy of the papers to E. R. Jobe, the executive secretary of the IHL board. After inquiries, Jobe determined that Gray was in fact a Negro and that he wanted a scholarship to further his education. Williams, therefore, directed the registrar to inform Gray that the university did not offer graduate scholarships but to assure him that "Mr. Jobe will give any assistance possible." In his initial consideration of a black applicant, Williams refrained from invoking the state's segregation policy; instead he relied on the peripheral question of financial assistance to dismiss Gray's application.[32]

Two years later, after the Court's key decisions in 1950 but before Krebs's editorial, Williams could no longer evade the integration question. The university received applications from two Mississippi Negroes: Pauline Y. Weathersby, a graduate of Tuskegee Institute, and Robert C. Leathers, a student at Tougaloo College. The registrar first took each case to the chancellor and the dean of the faculty. Aware of the recent court decisions, Williams knew the applications from blacks had to "be screened carefully." The officials next consulted with Jobe. They concluded, of course, that the university would not admit Negroes. With his superiors' approval, Robert B. Ellis, the registrar, sent a blunt form letter to all Negroes, who were automatically deemed "applicants ineligible for admission": "Provisions in the constitution and also in the general laws of the State of Mississippi make it impossible to grant admission to applicants other than those who are members of the Caucasian race. It is suggested that ineligible applicants who reside in Mississippi write to the Board of Trustees of Institutions of Higher Learning and determine the possibility of securing a scholarship for advanced study at another institution." One month later, the trustees in effect endorsed the chancellor's action when they authorized Williams and the presidents of the other state schools "to accept or reject any such application, if in his judgment, such an acceptance or rejection is for the best interest of the institution."[33]

As in the Gray case in 1948, the university denied Weathersby and Leathers admission, but in two years the justification had changed from a narrow consideration of financial aid to a far broader one based on state racial policies. Unable to circumvent the race question any longer, Chancellor Williams authorized an explanation that relied on the state constitution. The university's response lacked the passionate, determined commitment to segregation that white supremacists would later demand, but in 1950 it sufficed. Even though the state constitutional requirement for segregation applied specifically only to public schools and had not been tested in court, the chancellor recognized that the white consensus in the state supported its application to higher education as well, and he had no interest in challenging community mores.[34] As he demonstrated in the Krebs controversy, Williams preferred to minimize conflict in the hope that it would go away without forcing him to take a stand. Although his practice worked in the early 1950s, after the 1954 *Brown* decision, it would become more problematic.

Mississippi's political leaders understood some of the ramifications of the Supreme Court's early decisions on school segregation and, as a result, began even before *Brown* to equalize spending for public education for the two races as one way to maintain segregation. Pressured by an NAACP lawsuit on teacher salaries, the legislature appropriated funds to address pay inequities. Any effort to meet the demands of separate-but-equal education also meant more money for the woefully inferior black schools. Elected in 1951, Governor Hugh L. White faced increasing insistence from the state NAACP, the Mississippi Negro Teachers Association, and individual blacks, so he proposed a major program to equalize black and white schools.[35]

At the same time, Mississippi blacks followed progress in higher education in other southern states. The *Jackson Advocate*, for example, ran several articles on the admission of blacks into other public universities. In the fall of 1950 the conservative black newspaper reported predictions that blacks would seek to enroll in the Ole Miss law school. The entire state had only two Negro lawyers, and blacks who graduated from law schools outside the state often failed the Mississippi bar exam. The previous summer an honor graduate of Howard University's law school had failed the exam. One way for blacks to gain admission to the bar was to graduate from the state's only law school. The importance of black lawyers was clear: they would have great opportunities in the state, and they could represent blacks in civil rights cases.[36]

In 1952 the law school received its first black applicant. He had graduated from an unaccredited college, and the University of Iowa had refused him admission. The law school may have had to consult with the board of trustees before taking action because sometime in the early 1950s, the trustees required that any "unusual applications" had to be sent to the board for its consideration. It may then have routinely submitted the questionable application to the state's attorney general for his review and advice. Whatever process the authorities followed in 1952, the result was that the application was rejected.[37]

The next year, the law school received an application from Charles Herbert Thomas Dubra, the Negro pastor of St. Mark's Methodist Episcopal Church in

Gulfport.[38] Born in 1905 in Moss Point, the light-skinned Dubra studied at Haven Institute in Meridian and Claflin College in South Carolina, where he graduated in the 1920s. In 1932 he received a divinity degree from Gammon Theological Seminary in Atlanta and then served several Methodist churches in Mississippi.

Reverend Dubra volunteered for military service in the fall of 1941 and served during World War II as an army chaplain in the Pacific, where he saw combat with an army engineer unit. Lieutenant Dubra was the first American chaplain in New Guinea, and the short, stocky clergyman remained in the southwest Pacific for two and a half years. For his distinguished military service, he was promoted to captain and received the Legion of Merit and three Bronze Stars. After the war, he earned a master's degree in religion at Boston University in 1946 before resuming his pastoral work in southern Mississippi. After returning to his home state, Dubra became a prominent and popular leader in the black community—pastor of leading black congregations such as St. Mark's, a scoutmaster, one of the founders of an alumni chapter of his fraternity, owner of a popular soda fountain, and president of the Gammon Seminary alumni association. Dissatisfied with the treatment of blacks, Reverend Dubra joined the local NAACP chapter, served a term as its president, and worked in local efforts to register blacks to vote. His civil rights activity may have given him an increased awareness of the power and importance of the law and led him to consider studying law.

On November 1, 1953, Dubra filed his application with the university. He declared that he would do everything possible to achieve admission except file a lawsuit against the university. Given the experience of earlier black applicants, his chances of success seemed negligible, especially if he forswore legal action. Soon after he applied, some observers speculated that his admission to the law school would be denied because he was not really a student. Dubra had, they reasoned, already chosen his profession when he became a minister, so legal training would be unnecessary and even superfluous.[39]

Many blacks supported the fifty-year-old minister's effort to enter the law school. In addition to the NAACP, members of the influential Mississippi Negro Teachers Association wanted to back Dubra's attempt to enter Ole Miss, but a proposal to use the organization's resources to help fund his effort split the membership. J. D. Boyd, the association's president and principal of the Utica Institute and the Hinds County Agricultural High School, opposed having the group assist in any attempt to integrate the university. Although the conservative Boyd blocked the move to support Dubra, the Alpha Phi Alpha fraternity's chapter in southern Mississippi did contribute one thousand dollars to Dubra's effort.[40]

When Dean Robert J. Farley of the law school received Dubra's application, he wanted to know more about the minister and his objectives. Questioned by the dean, Dubra declared that he was not an agitator or an integrationist and did not want to cause trouble. If necessary he volunteered to forgo dormitory life and live with blacks in Oxford. Though impressed with Dubra and inclined to admit him, Farley conferred with the chancellor about how to handle the unusual application. Following the customary practice, Williams knew the matter had to be referred to the IHL board, but in Dubra's case he also suggested that Dean Farley present the entire matter and his recommendation to the trustees at their next meeting.[41]

Farley was well known and respected in the state. His father had been dean of the law school from 1913 to 1921, and he had served as dean since 1946. A graduate of the university and its law school, Farley had received a doctorate from Yale and had taught at Tulane before returning to Oxford. The dean's presentation of the Dubra case to the board of trustees and particularly his recommendation that the law school admit him sparked intense debate among the trustees. The chairman endorsed Farley's recommendation, but the majority could not accept integration and turned down Dubra's application.[42]

The board's ostensible reason for rejecting Dubra—that Claflin College was not accredited—ignored two significant points. First, SACS, the major accrediting agency in the South, did not in 1953 grant membership to any black colleges. Second, Dubra had a graduate degree from Boston University, a fully accredited institution. The board's decision nevertheless stood, and Dubra accepted it and dropped his attempt to enter the law school. He lacked both the personal resources and the willingness to wage a court battle, but the NAACP soon found a more likely applicant to support.[43]

Late in 1953, within weeks of Dubra's failed application, Medgar Evers decided to apply to the law school. The NAACP's State Legal Redress Committee had worked on a plan to challenge segregation at the university and had sought a potential applicant. In a speech to an NAACP meeting in Indianola, Dr. E. J. Stringer, a Columbus dentist and the new president of the state NAACP, stressed the need to desegregate the university and implied that the NAACP would support an applicant. Prompted by Stringer, Evers finally decided that evening to apply to the law school. Evers, a member of the state NAACP board of directors, announced his decision at the board's meeting on January 10, 1954, and the gathering burst into applause. The day after the meeting, following weeks of discussion and consultation, Evers submitted his application; he retained the NAACP attorney Thurgood Marshall to represent him.[44]

Born in 1925 in Decatur in east central Mississippi, Evers served in Europe during World War II and graduated from Alcorn A&M College in 1952. He sold insurance in the Delta for Magnolia Mutual Insurance Company, owned by T. R. M. Howard, a prominent black physician, businessman, and leader of the Regional Council of Negro Leadership. Encouraged by Howard, Evers became active in the organization in addition to the NAACP and started recruiting for it in 1952. Attracted by reports of the Kenyan freedom fighter Jomo Kenyatta, Evers, according to his wife, "flirted intellectually with the idea of fighting back in the Mississippi Delta" because "he was an angry young man, grasping for any solution that might bring an end to the degradation he saw around him." Despite his frustration, Evers found greater promise in the NAACP, and he joined its state board. His activism led him in 1952 to participate in a boycott of gas stations that had restrooms only for whites. Two years later, prompted by Howard and the NAACP, Evers's activism took aim at segregation in education.[45]

On January 11, 1954, Evers submitted his application to the University of Mississippi. The registrar who received Evers's application referred it to Chancellor Williams, who in turn sent it to Jackson for the IHL board to consider. Nearly two weeks after Evers applied, his application became known publicly when E. J. Stringer announced it and the *Jackson Daily News* gave it front-page coverage. In response to reporters' questions, E. R. Jobe, the IHL board's executive secretary, testily said, "We don't think applications for entrance into state schools by Negroes is news at all." Increasingly sensitive about applications by Negroes to attend white colleges, Jobe probably disliked the publicity because it could politicize the issue; like the chancellor, he hoped to dispose of integration attempts discreetly. Jobe's criticism of the press may have led the *Jackson Clarion-Ledger* and other state papers to omit mention of Evers's application.[46]

In the meantime, the IHL board did not consider Evers's application at its January 21 meeting. Initially, Jobe said that Ole Miss officials would decide the fate of Evers's application, but the next day the procedure had changed, perhaps because of the volatility of the issue. Instead Jobe turned Evers's file over to J. P. Coleman, the state's attorney general, for a ruling. Some expected Coleman to make a recommendation to the board by the time of its next meeting on February 18, but no such prompt action would occur.[47]

Even though Evers's application to the law school became well known in the state, no word came out of either the university or the board of trustees about any actions under consideration. Except for a simple acknowledgment that his application had been received, Evers himself heard nothing for several months. Ole Miss students meanwhile debated the possible integration of their school. An informal survey of law students revealed few objections to going to class with a qualified Negro, but some did object to integration outside the classroom; one complained, "I would be opposed to a Negro here if it meant association in the dorm, cafeteria, grill, dances." Another worried that racial mixing would not stop at higher education but "will spread to the educational levels of secondary and elementary schools, and this would be bad." Many recognized that the courts would order the school to admit a Negro, so they seemed resigned to integration.[48]

Black Mississippians overwhelmingly supported Evers. An increasingly assertive state NAACP declared itself "unalterably opposed to segregation" in education and supported "a direct attack on segregation" at all educational levels. The president of the Mississippi Negro Teachers Association, J. D. Boyd, however, continued to oppose the use of any of the association's money to support a lawsuit. After a "stormy all-day session" of its executive committee, Boyd still refused to convey funds raised through a special assessment of members for the sole purpose of assisting Evers. The editor of the *Jackson Advocate* pointed out the difficulty in equalizing public schools and concluded "no sane person in Mississippi" could advocate the even more difficult task of establishing separate but truly equal higher educational facilities. It, therefore, supported Evers's attempt at integration and called on President Boyd to resign.[49]

Evers's wife, however, was "frightened and angered" by his sudden decision to return to school. In repeated arguments, she tried to convince him not to go to law school. Worried by all the press attention to Evers and his application, his parents also tried to dissuade him. The family needed his regular income to survive, especially after Myrlie Evers discovered she was pregnant with their second child. For Medgar, however, a second child just provided added incentive to fight for the rights of blacks and against racial segregation. His commitment also intensified as a result of his father's hospitalization and death. Not only did his father receive inferior treatment in the hospital's basement, but his last days were disturbed when an angry mob of whites tried to get at a black man who had been brought to the hospital after being wounded in a row with police. Medgar Evers realized then that blacks could not live or die peacefully as long as segregation and white supremacy ruled. The system had to change.[50]

While Mississippians waited for a conclusion to the Evers case, the U.S. Supreme Court on May 17, 1954, increased the tension surrounding the case and aroused white racial passions when it handed down its decision in *Brown v. Board of Education of Topeka*. By ruling separate-but-equal schools unconstitutional, the Court knocked out a major support for segregation and white supremacy. White Mississippians immediately rallied to defend their way of life. The *Clarion-Ledger*, for example, called May 17 a "black day of tragedy." Politicians such as Senator Eastland railed against the Court and its verdict. Contending that the "institutions, the culture and the civilization of the South are built" upon racial segregation, Eastland proclaimed that the "future greatness of America depends upon racial purity and the maintenance of Anglo-

Saxon institutions." He believed the Court's "campaign against segregation is based upon illegality" and called on whites to fight it.[51]

Other whites agreed with Eastland. Edwin White, a state senator from Holmes County and an Ole Miss alumnus, explained in apocalyptic terms that whites opposed integration because there "is only one thing in the whole [racial] situation which the white man asks for, and that is, the privilege of his children, and his children's children, continuing to be white people." He believed that the implementation of the *Brown* decision would mean that "in a few centuries the races would become amalgamated. Thus to put the Supreme Court's decision into effect would operate to violate God's creation and Law, and when any court decision violates His Law it is sinful, unholy and unworthy of obedience."[52]

White Mississippians, however, did more than revile the Court and its decision. In July 1954, a group in Indianola formed the first Citizens' Council, and it quickly grew into a grassroots movement across the South in opposition to desegregation. And later in the summer Governor White, who had initially hoped blacks would agree to voluntary segregation in the schools, called a special session of the legislature to convene on September 7 to consider state action to prevent desegregation of the public schools. His proposals included a constitutional amendment to allow the legislature to close the public schools.[53]

Behind the scenes, state officials tried to decide how to handle Medgar Evers's application. Months elapsed without a word. In June, in response to Evers's inquiry about his application, Dean Farley agreed with the frustrated applicant that he was "entitled to a decision" but explained the policy of sending "unusual applications" to the IHL board. Finally, on August 23, E. R. Jobe informed Evers that his application was being considered "by the authorities of the University" and that he "would be informed at a later date as to the disposition of the application." In an abrupt shift three days later, Jobe invited Evers to come to his Jackson office "to discuss your application" on August 31. Evers quickly arranged with the NAACP to have a lawyer accompany him to the meeting. A. P. Tureaud, an experienced black civil rights lawyer from New Orleans and the legal counsel for the NAACP in Louisiana, agreed to go to Jackson for the Evers-Jobe conference.[54]

On the afternoon of August 31, Evers and Tureaud met briefly with Jobe before going with him to Attorney General J. P. Coleman's office. Although a segregationist, Coleman had a reputation as a moderate on racial questions because, as one observer noted, he "did not espouse racial terrorism, but he *did* espouse Massive Resistance" to integration.[55] Archsegregationists in Mississippi often found Coleman unreliable on segregation. The IHL board, however, wanted to protect itself by securing his legal advice before it acted.

Having examined Evers's application and other relevant papers from the IHL files, Coleman interrogated him. Coleman wanted to know if Evers was serious in his application, why he had waited until he was twenty-nine to go to law school, and why he did not instead continue in business administration. Believing that some black teachers had used fraudulent transcripts from Alcorn A&M to receive raises, he questioned the validity of Evers's transcript. Coleman, concerned about Evers's "radical" brother Charles, quizzed him about any connection between his application and Charles's civil rights agitation in Philadelphia, Mississippi. Coleman wanted an alternative to integration, so he asked Evers if he would accept a state scholarship to a law school in another state. Finally, the attorney general wanted to know whether Evers would want to live in a dorm and eat in the cafeteria.[56]

Evers answered each of Coleman's questions. He was serious about going to law school, and he had decided to pursue a law degree because he now more fully appreciated the importance of the law and the utility of a law degree. His application, of course, had no link to his brother's work, and he would not accept attending an out-of-state law school. On Coleman's query about his expected accommodations, Evers replied, "Yes, I plan to live on campus in a dormitory and to do all the things any other student of the law school might do: use the library, eat in the dining hall, attend classes. But I can assure you that I wear clean clothes, and that none of the brown of my skin will rub off. I won't contaminate the dormitory or the food."[57]

As the interview with Evers wound down, Coleman conveyed that he would recommend against admitting Evers, even though he conceded that no law prevented a Negro from attending any state college. The attorney general apparently would base his decision on doubts about Evers's academic background and about his good faith in seeking to enter the law school. At the end of the interview, Coleman informed Evers and Tureaud that he would transmit his recommendation to the dean in Oxford, but instead he sent his advice to the IHL board, which would rule on Evers's application.[58] Ole Miss officials remained silent on the case and apparently had no involvement with it after they sent Evers's files to Jackson.

The IHL board governed all the four-year state colleges and the university. The legislature had originally established the board in 1910 to protect the schools from political influence and to give some central direction to higher education in the state. The board had authority over the university in Oxford and Alcorn A&M and over the predecessors of Mississippi State and Mississippi State College for Women, but not over the teachers colleges. After Governor Bilbo's intrusion into higher education, the legislature in 1932 combined the IHL board with two that governed the teachers colleges. The twelve members of the new board served staggered twelve-year terms. Each one-term governor named four members, so the board got four new members every four years. Two trustees came from the state at large, but the others were distributed by congressional and supreme court districts across the state. The 1932 law also created an executive secretary to direct the board's permanent staff. During World War II, the board gained further insulation when a constitutional amendment re-created the board; the change from a basis in law to one in the constitution made tampering with the board's structure or authority more difficult.[59]

Governors Thomas L. Bailey, Fielding L. Wright, and Hugh L. White had appointed the trustees who in 1954 considered Medgar Evers's application. Businessmen, farmers, and lawyers who were friends or political allies of the governors dominated the board. At their September 16 meeting, the trustees discussed the Evers matter and easily came to a conclusion. On a motion by David Cottrell, an Ole Miss alumnus and Gulfport lawyer, the board unanimously declared Evers "had not complied with the rules and regulations of the University Law School." Specifically, the board found that he had not submitted the required letters of recommendation from prominent citizens in his community who had known him for ten years. Evers had told Coleman that he had lived in all-black Mound Bayou for the last two years, yet his recommendations came from two white men, A. C. Mackell in Natchez and J. M. Thames in Decatur, "neither of the places named being the community in which the applicant has lived for the past two years."[60]

The board did not, however, outright reject Evers's application. To give Evers "an opportunity to comply with the regulations as to letters of recommendation," the trustees voted to continue their consideration of the matter and to reconsider the application when Evers had submitted additional letters of recommendation.[61] The board gave no reason why it had delayed so long in its appraisal of Evers's application or why it had waited until days before fall semester classes started at the law school to tell Evers his letters of recommendation were unacceptable. In effect the late action prevented Evers's registration and attendance.

Later in the same meeting, the trustees followed Coleman's recommendation and changed the entrance requirements for the state's university and colleges by creating an even more formidable barrier against black applicants. To ensure the "moral qualifications of all people applying for admission," the board unanimously directed that after the beginning of the fall 1954 semester all applications from Mississippians "shall be supported by at least five (5) letters of recommendations to the good moral character from alumni of the institution to which the application is made." In addition, the letters had to come from alumni in the county where the applicant had lived for two years (if less than two years of residence, then letters from the previous county of residence would be considered). Without the required letters, an application could not be considered.[62]

Although the board announced its decision regarding Medgar Evers, it kept secret the new requirement of five alumni references. After the meeting, the trustees refused to comment and withheld the minutes of their meetings from the press. The next day, persistent reporters learned about the rule change when "leaks" revealed what had happened. Observers immediately recognized that the new regulations were designed to prevent blacks from attending Ole Miss and the other white colleges. According to John Herbers, a reporter for United Press International, the board's "new segregation policy" only aimed to continue the well-established practice of complete segregation.[63]

Myrlie Evers later maintained that everyone knew how to interpret the trustees' action: "No one in the state of Mississippi, black or white, misunderstood the sophistry of the board's explanation. It was precisely the sort of explanation Mississippians, black and white, had been trained to expect. It accomplished two important goals at one and the same time: it informed white people that it was really quite simple to outwit ignorant Negroes who didn't know their place and it let the Negroes know there wasn't a chance that such an application would ever be considered on its merits."[64] The board of trustees did not, however, indicate definitively whether it expected Evers to submit more appropriate recommendations or what it would do if it later did receive acceptable letters. In Mississippi in 1954 the ultimate admission of Medgar Evers seemed extraordinarily unlikely, yet the trustees must have known, as the attorney general knew, that no basis existed in state law to reject any applicant to the university solely on the basis of race. The board's unclear, if unequivocal, stand may therefore have been intended to delay a final resolution of the case and thereby avoid a lawsuit by the NAACP to integrate the university, a lawsuit that would probably have succeeded.

In the days after Medgar Evers learned of the trustees' action, he conferred with NAACP representatives and lawyers. Evers's decision was related to a change in his occupation. In the fall of 1954 he decided not to pursue his application for law school and instead accepted appointment as Mississippi field secretary for the NAACP. In the process of making the shift from potential plaintiff to organizer, Evers may have submitted additional letters to the IHL board, because the trustees at their December meeting did again briefly consider his application but took no action.[65]

With the end of Evers's effort to enroll in the Ole Miss law school, the board of trustees and the university had parried the most serious threat so far to segregation. Other attempts to desegregate Ole Miss would follow, but as the civil rights movement built momentum, white resistance became even more determined. In 1958 a more aggressive challenge to segregation at Ole Miss would cause a sensational clash.

5. Integration and Insanity: Clennon King in 1958

■ ■

On June 5, 1958, Clennon Washington King arrived at Ole Miss to regis-ter for the first session of summer school. Weeks earlier, the black minister and college professor had announced his intention to break the color barrier, but unlike other blacks interested in attending the university, King actually went to Oxford. His family background and his experiences in Mississippi encouraged him to believe that he would be allowed to enroll, that he was prepared for such an intrepid move, and that conservative whites would support him. The results of his quixotic action surprised and dis-appointed King. Once again Mississippi demonstrated its intransigent opposi-tion to integration at Ole Miss.

Born in 1920 in Georgia, Clennon W. King Jr. was the oldest child of Clennon and Margaret King, founders of a large, prominent, and activist Albany, Georgia, family. Clennon King's great-grandfather was the son of a white woman and a black man, and his great-grandfather's well-to-do white grandparents raised him in Florida and left him some property. Originally named Blackshear, King's great-grandfather took the name King. His son Allen King worked in the Florida Panhandle around the turn of the century as a drayman and blacksmith, and he acquired land. When, about 1915, local whites tried to take his property, Allen King shot and killed one of them; as a result, he and his family fled Florida and eventually settled in Albany. At the time of the escape, Allen King's son Clennon was away studying at Tuskegee Institute. Born about 1891, Clinton Washington King changed his name to Clennon.[1]

At Tuskegee, Clennon King Sr. served as a carriage driver for Booker T. Washington and became a follower of the "Wizard of Tuskegee." After graduat-ing in 1916, he taught at Utica College near Jackson before serving in the army during World War I. In 1919 he married Margaret Slater, a Tuskegee student. Light enough to be mistaken for white, she was the daughter of a prosperous builder in Milledgeville, Georgia, and the niece of Tuskegee's comptroller. The young couple settled in Albany. Clennon King worked twenty-five years with the post office, opened the town's first black restaurant, and operated various other businesses, while also accumulating considerable real estate.[2] The Kings became the leading black family in Albany.

Clennon King Jr. had an extraordinary experience growing up. Enjoying the services of both a maid and a cook, the cultured and sophisticated Kings read widely and listened to and performed classical music in their home. King's father organized the town's Boy's Club, started the NAACP branch, and attended at least one national NAACP meeting. In addition to the family ties to Booker T. Washington, the Kings knew W. E. B. Du Bois, who had married Maggie King's cousin. The brilliant, popular younger King served as class president and valedictorian; he liked being a leader and the center of attention, and others enjoyed the company of the eccentric and impatient young man. He founded Albany's NAACP Youth Council and as a boy regularly read the NAACP's *The Crisis*. He met prominent blacks such as Du Bois and Channing Tobias and important whites such as Mary White Ovington when they visited the King home.[3]

At his parents' insistence, Clennon King attended Tuskegee, where he became an advocate of Washington's teachings. At Tuskegee he also met a young woman from Oklahoma, and they soon married. After graduating in 1940, King sought admission to the University of Georgia law school, but the chancellor informed King that "there is no provision for aiding negroes in graduate or professional study" and rejected his inquiry. King appealed to the NAACP for help, but it apparently decided not to pursue King's challenge to segregation at the university.[4]

Rebuffed by his state's university, King in the late 1940s and early 1950s took an erratic path as he bounced among half a dozen jobs and schools; his intolerance and feeling of superiority often caused conflicts with his employers and made keeping a job difficult. He worked as a Baptist pastor, as a newspaper editor-publisher, as a radio announcer, and as a life insurance agent. At various times he attended the Oberlin Graduate School of Theology, Adelbert College, the University of Chicago, and Florida A&M University. In 1945 he received a master's degree in European history from Ohio State University, where he became a doctoral candidate in 1955. In Columbus he tried in early 1956 to organize the International African Progress Brotherhood to help "lost Africans" find Africa "in thought and deed."[5]

In 1956 Clennon King moved to Mississippi, where he pastored Hazlehurst's Wesley Chapel Methodist Church and taught history at Alcorn A&M College. Founded in 1871 on the site of the defunct white Oakland College, Alcorn was the nation's first land grant college for Negroes and the state's second oldest college. Located in the state's southwestern corner, Alcorn was, according to one observer, "so far off the beaten track few Mississippians have seen it. . . . At Alcorn you can walk over a hill from the campus and feel like you are a thousand miles from civilization." For decades it suffered from legislative neglect. After the state acquired Jackson College in 1940 (later Jackson State University), many supporters of Alcorn believed their school received even less support. Competition for funds increased with the creation of Mississippi Vocational College (later Mississippi Valley State University) in 1950. Early in the post–World War II era, Alcorn was, according to a state official, "in shambles . . . and virtually uninhabitable." It stressed the liberal arts for its five hundred students rather than engineering and agriculture, but its library had fewer than fifteen thousand books, and only one professor held a doctorate.[6]

Clennon King had an eventful stay at Alcorn. According to one report, he demonstrated "a wonderful ability to stay in the headlines." During his first fall semester, King wrote two letters to the *Jackson State Times*. One criticized the NAACP's policies as "unrealistic" and blamed the failures on "Northern whites" who controlled the civil rights organization. His second letter asked, "What is the objection to colored American ambassadors to colored nations?" As a proud Negro "with unapologetic African ties," King sought respect, not pity or sympathy, and he wanted "a colored population that is so cohesive, proud and strong that . . . Afro-Americans can effectively influence policies of the older mother country." Afro-American ambassadors could have helped solve the Suez crisis in northern Africa, he argued, but the United States sent a Negro as ambassador only to Liberia.[7]

After King's second letter, Jesse R. Otis, the Alcorn president, asked him to stop writing to the editor, but King invoked academic freedom to protect his right to speak. Otis argued that it had to be "properly exercised" and directed King "to adhere strictly to the business of education and to avoid controversial issues." According to the president, the professor's "independent and personal" actions could imperil his job. In December 1956, Otis believed King had promised to stop his controversial contributions to local newspapers. Continuing his writing campaign, King in January 1957 sent some essays to the Mississippi State Sovereignty Commission. The commission did not use his work but found it interesting and paid close attention to him.[8]

King incited his first major controversy when the *Jackson State Times* published eight of his articles on race relations. Though a lifelong member of the NAACP, King in his first article on Sunday, March 3, attacked the organization as "a tool for conniving whites" that did little to solve southern racial problems. Charging that it "didn't adequately reflect our [ordinary Negroes'] thinking," he alleged that it "deliberately ignored" chances to help Negroes by easing racial tensions, by combating Negro crime, by attacking discrimination in the Congress of Industrial Organizations, and by seeking industrial jobs for southern Negroes. The essay sparked a peaceful boycott of his classes the next day, and succeeding installments further antagonized Alcorn students. On Monday, he belittled Representative Adam Clayton Powell for his "double standard" in opposing federal aid to segregated schools while preaching at a black church and representing a Negro congressional district. To worries about separate but unequal education, King observed that "Negroes segregate themselves, even in voluntary situations," that "Negroes can be discriminated against just as effectively in unified school systems," and that integrated school systems "can more easily hide discriminatory situations."[9]

By Wednesday the boycott involved nearly all of Alcorn's five hundred students. Ernest McEwen, the student council president, said that they objected not to King's views but to his involving the college in controversy. Signs branded King an "Uncle Tom" and called for his removal. After conferring with the IHL board's head, President Otis said that he would take no action until the students returned to class and that the trustees would decide whether to fire King.[10]

On Thursday, the fourth day of the strike, the trustees' Committee on Negro Education visited the campus to hear complaints from McEwen and others but refused to consider charges against King until the students returned to classes. If students did not return, the board ordered that all buildings be locked down on Saturday. It refused to consider any appeals from students or professors until normal operations resumed. On the same day, Gov. J. P. Coleman announced that he had fired Otis, even though the governor had no authority to remove a college president. Otis actually had already resigned for health reasons effective April 1. Thursday evening at a vesper service in the college chapel, Otis urged students to return to class because otherwise the IHL board might close the college. One student shouted, "Let's go home," and most students agreed to go unless King left first, so they returned to their rooms to pack.[11]

King held firm. The *Jackson State Times* continued to publish his essays. The third celebrated the lot of Negroes in America compared to that in other countries. "The glorious thing about America is," King exulted, "America gives all of us a chance!" Instead of complaining about segregation and discrimination, he believed that a Negro could be elected president. More than injustice, King's fourth article criticized American race relations for the "dearth of choices" for Negroes. To offer an option and to stimulate interest in their historical background, he proposed migration back to Africa.[12] His iconoclastic ideas failed to soothe Alcorn's students.

During the crisis, King reportedly would have resigned only if the college president sought his resignation. Instead Otis recommended his dismissal to the trustees. King did not want to work where he was not wanted, but he knew also that he had to have a job to support his family. Admittedly "very disturbed" by the student protests, King thought, "It's a shame the students are so undemocratic that they would rather leave school than be under a professor who expressed his freedom of speech." He believed, "The students are destroying what they are trying to build."[13]

On Friday morning students gathered again in the college chapel, and a dean told them to expect King to announce his resignation. King, near tears and carrying a handkerchief, instead asked for their understanding. "I'm a Negro just like you are. I sit in a Jim Crow car just like you do," he told the students. "I don't enjoy people dishonoring me and disrespecting me any more than you do." When King said that his life had been threatened and that the threat might be carried out right then at the meeting, student body president McEwen disputed the allegation. King pled for them to reconsider his statements. After half an hour, the students calmly exited the chapel and left the town of Lorman. Ernest McEwen declared, "The oldest Negro land grant college in America died today at 11:55 A.M. As far as the students are concerned the institution is dead."[14]

With his family, a distraught King left their campus apartment for their home in Hazlehurst. Although King denied he was an Uncle Tom, he recognized that "if any Negro raises any question about the NAACP . . . they slap the 'Uncle Tom' tag on him." He began to doubt if anyone could question the NAACP without being destroyed. King thought his articles had raised important questions, but they also revealed his preference for the ideas of Washington and his appreciation of the African past of American blacks. He told a reporter, "They misunderstood me and they felt I was a traitor." He explained: "What I was trying to say was that it's not just one race in America that needs to learn tolerance—but all of us. Negroes included. We aren't getting the best of deals, but we seem to take the attitude that we are spotless little lambs." King believed that the students based their protests on a few misinterpreted newspaper headlines, and he suspected that the faculty started the protests and the Jackson NAACP kept them going.[15]

In the midst of the crisis, King complained to *Time* magazine about its coverage. He defended his behavior and claimed students continued to like him. His efforts to "understand white Southerners" caused the "persecution" by the students. King recognized that he had also provoked a reaction by questioning blacks who were "slavishly strapped to Northern white thinking" in the NAACP. He objected to the "incongruous" control of the NAACP by whites who "create its policies [but] don't have to pay the price for its errors." More important, however, was his analysis of the NAACP's assimilationist approach to race. He charged, "if we become absorbed into the white race—like Negroes in Europe—what noble purpose will have been served by Africans ever having been here?" King refused to trim his iconoclastic views.[16]

On Saturday, at the end of the tumultuous week, the IHL board met in a special session in Jackson. President Otis and J. D. Boyd, his designated successor as of April 1, waited outside the boardroom. After a lengthy discussion, the trustees concluded that the Alcorn administration had "wholly failed" and that Otis had acquiesced in, if not approved, the student protest. The board made his departure from Alcorn effective that day and gave J. D. Boyd authority as president. The trustees considered the conservative Boyd a safe appointment because he did not support the NAACP and had blocked the state's black teachers' association from backing lawsuits to integrate the university. The trustees ruled that the protesting students who did not comply with the orders to return to class were expelled and that the college would continue its normal operation without them. Regarding Clennon King, the board made no announcement. In response to reporters' questions, the board chairman stated, "He's still a member of the faculty. Professor King's name was not brought up. There was no reason to bring it up."[17]

The next day, Sunday, a despondent King explained to the *Pittsburgh Courier*, "Negroes everywhere say I hate my race. Everyone knows me as Mississippi's biggest fool because they say I turned against my own people." He announced that he would go to "Jackson to stand until I fall, without food, in front of the State Capitol, or until they arrest me, and after I am released, I will return again and stand until they arrest me or until I fall." King declared, "I will not kill myself like Judas. I want a white person to do it for me because it was the white people who caused me to do what I did. The Governor of Mississippi said on TV I was right," he explained. "The State Board of Education said they backed me and the biggest newspaper in the state said so, too." By late Sunday, however, King had abandoned martyrdom. As he told the *Courier*, "I thought that I had lost all of my friends until today," when friends had convinced him to drop his plans.[18]

King's fate at the college nevertheless remained unclear. The new Alcorn president denied firing him and said the IHL board would settle King's employment. King then issued a statement: "If I'm not fired, I will resign voluntarily, because I think it would be the best thing for the school. . . . The new president can then be assured of the students' returning." The next day, however, he learned that the trustees wanted to meet with him. After a two-hour meeting, board executive secretary E. R. Jobe announced that King would retain his job but would not be teaching. "He's been through a trying experience," said Jobe. "Prof. King is subject to recall when we need him. . . . he is still a member of the faculty and can return any time he wants to."[19]

On Sunday and Monday, March 10 and 11, the final installments of King's series appeared in the *Jackson State Times*. Suggesting that most blacks did not follow Martin Luther King Jr. and were without a leader, Clennon King warned that a "leaderless people fall quick prey to charlatans and demagogs." Instead he hoped that Negroes would return to the leadership model of Booker T. Washington. "He successfully stood for orderly inter-racial relations," explained King. "He asked whites to be fair. He asked Negroes to be realistic. . . . He preached respect for all men." King appreciated Washington's emphasis on learning skills, saving money, building families, and "group pride and independence," and he believed that Washington's example provided a better example for blacks than did either the NAACP or Martin Luther King.[20]

Despite Clennon King's last two essays, Alcorn calmed down and the boycott ended. By Monday perhaps a hundred and fifty students had returned to classes, and by Thursday three hundred had returned. President Boyd ejected Ernest McEwen and a handful of other students "on the basis of their individual attitudes and actions," which in McEwen's case struck Boyd as insulting. By the middle of April, all but a dozen had returned and Alcorn functioned in a nearly normal fashion.[21]

An editorial in the NAACP's *The Crisis* alleged that King sought publicity, and it denied his "farrago of misinformation and lies" about the NAACP. It sought to combat the "racial barbarism in Mississippi" that King seemed to ignore. It aligned King, "a genuine Uncle Tom," with southern white opponents of the NAACP and used King's own words to describe him as "a low, inconsistent, sneaking, double talking character that neither white nor Negro can trust." In response King called the editorial "libelous" and questioned whether the organization allowed dissent. He wanted to renew his membership but could not accept the NAACP's objective of "complete integration."[22]

After the boycott, King received support from unlikely sources. Some whites liked his challenge to the NAACP and, from their perspective, his support of racial segregation. The chairman of the board of trustees spoke favorably of King. Charles M. Hills of the *Jackson Clarion-Ledger* applauded the professor as "a man who had the guts to say what he thought." Robert Webb, the *Jackson State Times* associate editor, claimed that King's articles "broke through the halo around" the NAACP and "put his race on guard against many other fallacies surrounding the integration-segregation issue." The *State Times* received so many requests for King's series that it reprinted it as a pamphlet entitled "The Clennon King Story." Later in the summer the Sovereignty Commission paid nearly three hundred dollars for twenty-five hundred copies of "The Clennon King Story" and envelopes to distribute them. Clennon King must have found heartening the support of the IHL board, the positive interest of the Sovereignty Commission, and the favorable comments from white journalists. They liked his ideas because he said what they wished blacks thought.

Their interest gave King confidence that he had strong and wide support among whites, and, as a result, his plans grew bolder.[23]

In the spring of 1957 King remained on the Alcorn faculty even though he did not return to the campus. He told the head of the IHL that he could not return to work because of a death threat and what he considered the "degrading circumstances" at the college. Calling King "a publicity seeker who has done nothing but agitate," President Boyd said that King could not count on a job beyond May 31, but the IHL board announced in the summer that King had been given a contract for the coming academic year.[24]

In July 1957, another unrelated controversy briefly embroiled King. Wesley Chapel Methodist Church in Hazlehurst fired King as its pastor on charges that he had misused church money. King denied the charges. When he found the church door locked and was warned that he would be arrested if he removed the lock, he broke the lock and was arrested for breaking and entering. He refused to post bond and spent one night in the Copiah County jail. Authorities released him after church officials dropped the charges in exchange for King's agreeing to leave. He obtained another job with the St. Andrew African Methodist Episcopal Church in Gulfport.[25]

King continued to speak out on the volatile race question. In the summer after the student boycott, he went to Washington, D.C., to testify before a subcommittee of the Senate Foreign Relations Committee for a bill authorizing loans to African Americans who wanted to migrate to Liberia. King declared that voluntary migration to Africa would "mean more to our people's civil rights than anything which has happened since the emancipation proclamation of 1863." Recognizing that the bill was not "the answer" to the nation's racial problems, he argued that "if wisely handled [it] could be an answer." It could provide the possibility of "real security in the home of his ancestors" instead of in the United States, where they "try to get it by imitating whites." In Washington, King objected that the NAACP promoted racial integration that would necessarily include racial intermarriage. Like many southern whites, King opposed the creation of "a different stock of people" through assimilation; he did not want blacks "to try to be white" and believed the proposed legislation offered a real alternative. Despite his efforts, the bill failed.[26]

Six months later, in January 1958, the *American Mercury* published King's "I Speak as a Southern Negro." Repetitious of his *Jackson State Times* articles, it reiterated that the NAACP was "a *white organization*" that deceived blacks into thinking they were real participants. The NAACP "has done more harm to the long-range interests of the American Negro than good," according to King, because it "is interested in power over the Negro mass." From its beginnings, the NAACP had mistakenly stressed social equality for Negroes instead of solving the concrete problems of Negroes involving "the basic necessities of life." Risking being branded "a liar, a coward or a nitwit," King advocated Booker T. Washington's program. The contrast was clear: the NAACP advocated forced change, was not opposed to communism, used propaganda to achieve equality, and encouraged "mass regimentation," while Washington's philosophy stressed peaceful change, was strongly anticommunist, wanted to demonstrate equality, and promoted individualism. Even on integration, King disagreed with the NAACP. He "questioned the wisdom of 'advancement' based on forcing complete grade-school desegregation." In his experience, white southerners had "been ready for some time to give up *forced* segregation." In any case, King argued that Negroes' greatest need was *good* schools, regardless of who attended them. King also contended that integration—being "absorbed into whiteness"—meant Negroes would lose the freedom to be black, which he wanted to preserve because he considered it an honor to be a Negro.[27]

Early in May 1958, Alcorn's President Boyd informed Clennon King that he would not renew his contract. The IHL board issued a similar announcement because King "had chosen not to cooperate with the administration of the College in the orderly development of the instructional program of the institution, but has chosen to disregard the policies of the College and to disrupt its orderly operation." Anticipating criticism, the board contended it "has protected King's right to academic freedom and owes him no further obligation." King responded that his actions and the student walkout had caused his dismissal, but authorities had just waited "until those who are interested in what I stand for forget why I was finally dismissed." He claimed that he had been sacrificed to the NAACP because of his criticism of it and because of his support for segregation.[28]

Elaborating on his theme in "The Real Reason I Was Fired," King's next sermon blamed "a misguided clique of big time white Mississippi hypocrites" and Negroes who supported them. The whites wanted him to quit talking about racial matters, even if he seemed to agree with them by questioning integration and criticizing the NAACP, and the blacks misunderstood what he said. "It is wrong," King told his congregation, "to label a Negro as pro-segregation because he believes we should have something of our own. It is wrong to label a Negro as a white man's stooge because he believes in reasonable diplomacy and negotiation." King reminded his listeners of the "very real race problem for black and white Christians to solve in Mississippi" and maintained it could not be settled "by intimidating school teachers and preachers to keep quiet."[29]

Revealing an inconsistent view of integration, King announced to his congregation that he had that morning applied for graduate study in American history at the University of Mississippi beginning in June. "I seriously expect to attend," he declared. In an abrupt shift from his position of the previous year, he regretted the end of the Alcorn protest because the students "could have initiated the opening of the University of Mississippi to deserving Negroes quicker than any other action" if they had closed Alcorn. Instead they followed President Boyd and returned to classes. "Ole Miss was saved," said King.[30] The task of desegregating Ole Miss remained.

On Sunday, May 11, 1958, King requested from the Ole Miss registrar admission forms for both the summer school and the following academic year. Two days later Robert B. Ellis sent the forms for graduate school, even though the university did not offer a doctorate in history. Ellis pledged to handle King's letter routinely, but he believed King sought publicity more than an education. Admission requirements included the names of six alumni living in the applicant's county who had known the applicant for two years and would recommend admission. The applicant did not have to contact the alumni, only submit their names.[31]

To solicit alumni assistance, King wrote to alumni in Harrison County to explain why he wanted to attend Ole Miss, and he placed a quarter-page advertisement in the *Gulfport Daily Herald*. He implored alumni to understand his real motives in applying—he needed to further his education to qualify for a job. The better jobs required a doctorate, but in Mississippi no black college offered a doctorate. To avoid disrupting his family and incurring moving expenses to attend a northern university, King concluded, "this means *we must* attend white universities." He also assured alumni that he did not want to humiliate anyone or "break down segregation at the University of Mississippi." He suggested that racial integration was not the issue involved in his application. Reminding alumni that he had never counseled any black applicant to the university, he stated, "personally, *I would prefer to attend a Negro university*." In a further bid for support, he said that his admission would confirm his "loudly claimed" belief that the Negro's best friends were southerners.[32]

King's views on segregation and integration may have seemed ambivalent, contradictory, or confused, but he had a generally consistent position. He did not want to force the integration of the university, and he would have preferred to go to a black university. In the absence of alternatives in the state, he had faith that reasonable whites would judge him deserving because of his academic qualifications and his racial attitudes and, therefore, admit him to Ole Miss. His experiences the previous year led him to believe, mistakenly, that many whites considered him unusually intelligent and trustworthy. With their support, he expected to enroll at Ole Miss.[33]

Because he knew few Mississippi whites, King worried that he would be unable to obtain the necessary references before registration began on June 5.

After discussing alternatives with Jobe on May 23, King had the impression that the lack of recommendations might not foreclose his admission. At Jobe's suggestion he asked registrar Ellis to treat him as an applicant from a county with few alumni. He had already consulted David Cottrell, a Gulfport lawyer, alumnus, and former member of the board of trustees, and Cottrell had not encouraged King about receiving an exception to the regulations. When King asked Ellis if his failure to obtain the alumni references would "seriously block" admission, the registrar avoided the question by telling King to deal with Jobe and the board directly and by stating publicly that the matter "is in the hands of the Board."[34]

Ellis's response resulted from consultations among Jobe of the IHL board, Joseph T. Patterson and Dugas Shands in the Mississippi Attorney General's office, and Hugh Clegg, assistant to Chancellor Williams. In addition to the recommendations, questions arose about "the discontinuance of the services of King" at Alcorn, his trouble with his church (including the accusation that he had broken into the church), and King's avowed NAACP membership in spite of his failure to list the NAACP on his loyalty affidavit when employed at Alcorn. Assistant Attorney General Shands persuaded the others not to mention the discrepancy over the NAACP membership for fear of a controversy. He also advised that the chancellor stay as far removed from the matter as possible and that two individuals always attend any meeting with King.[35]

All along, King made his intentions clear. His advertisement in the Gulfport paper declared he would try to enroll in the June summer session, and he told the registrar and Jobe the same thing. He informed Ellis that he wanted to take Jim Silver's course on the rise of southern nationalism and Clare Marquette's "Historical Criticism and Historiography," and he indicated that he might want to change to a doctoral program in education with a history minor. King did not want to live on campus but preferred staying with a Negro family close to the campus, if that could be arranged. In return, King received little cooperation. He could not even get anyone to send him a college catalog. As he later explained, the lack of a definitive rejection of his application suggested to him that state officials "were possibly sincere" in their statements that his application would be handled routinely, that race would not be a factor.[36]

In his attempt to enter Ole Miss, King appealed for the support of the NAACP, the Congress of Racial Equality (CORE), and Martin Luther King's Southern Christian Leadership Conference (SCLC). As one King explained to another, "Every hypocritical ruse is being used to keep my application from being recognized solely because of my black African background." A few days later he met Martin Luther King Jr. at an SCLC meeting in Clarksdale, and he followed up with another letter, but he received no response. To his request for help, the national NAACP passed the matter on to its state affiliate with the warning that King might just be trying to "cause trouble" for the NAACP. Without a Mississippi presence, CORE could not offer legal assistance and referred him to the NAACP, SCLC, and the American Civil Liberties Union (ACLU).[37]

Frustrated by the lack of support, King pressed on by calling Jobe. According to King, Jobe only made "clear that my presence was not preferred at the University on June 5 and that cowardly subterfuge would be used to keep me out." Undeterred, King wrote Ellis that, if he were not allowed to register (even provisionally, which he would accept), he would appeal to the governor and the president. "I do not intend to leave the campus voluntarily except I am given some decent satisfaction. I do not mind being killed, beaten or imprisoned," he told the registrar. If Ole Miss did not want him, he vowed to "demand that our government immediately return me to Africa from which white Americans took my ancestors against their wills and blot my name from a hopeless 'citizenship.'" He released a similar statement to the press.[38]

Realizing King's determination, Ole Miss and state officials plotted strategy. Privately Governor Coleman conferred extensively with Jobe and the board chairman, and Hugh Clegg made detailed plans with Dugas Shands, Joe Patterson, and the board chairman. Specifics included who would interview King at the university, how newsmen would be treated, and where King could use a restroom (King would "be informed of the rest rooms in the cafeteria which are used by colored help or in other buildings where such facilities are provided"). The attorney general also wanted a background check of King by the state patrol and the Sovereignty Commission, and the university police chief asked the FBI and the police of Albany, Georgia, for information on King. During the state holiday for Jefferson Davis's birthday, the governor worked in a closed state capitol to prepare for King's announced arrival in Oxford the next day.[39]

At 8:00 P.M. on June 4, Clennon King boarded a bus in Gulfport for the trip to Oxford. Under the governor's direction, a plainclothes highway patrolman also rode on the bus, while an unmarked patrol car followed. In Grenada another officer boarded the bus. On campus the state's plans were activated. At the direction of the governor, waiting twenty miles away in Batesville, and under the personal supervision of Public Safety Commissioner Tom Scarbrough, about fifty uniformed highway patrolmen and plainclothes policemen took positions at the campus entrances and around the Lyceum before seven o'clock on the morning summer registration began. Referring to disorder at the University of Alabama in 1956 when a black student enrolled, Scarbrough explained their presence: "We don't want another Autherine Lucy case here."[40]

At about 6:20 A.M.. on Thursday, King arrived in Oxford and went to a private residence. In a light rain about nine o'clock, he took a taxi to the education building for summer school registration. Registrar Ellis met him and took him in his personal car a couple of blocks to the Lyceum at 9:32. No newsmen were allowed into the administration building. For two hours and fifteen minutes as many as two hundred reporters and onlookers waited outside. Other than a few scattered jeers and one person who hollered, "Bring the nigger out," the wait was uneventful.

Inside the Lyceum, King met for about fifteen minutes with Ellis, Clegg, and Tom S. Hines, director of student activities, in the registrar's office. Ellis asked King if he had come to present papers for admission, and King said he had and offered a completed application form and a list of five references. For a permanent address, King listed his home in Gulfport, but for his current address he put a residence on Jackson Avenue in Oxford, where he had never lived. King's five alumni references were T. G. James of Mississippi City, William L. Power and Bowman Clarke of Biloxi, and Joe Buckley and David Cottrell Jr. of Gulfport. Power, a recent university graduate and a seminary student at Emory University, simply said that he had spoken with King, and, based on King's qualifications and his interest in education, Power recommended King's admittance. More forcefully, James (B.A., 1932, and M.A., 1935) declared, "I see no reason other than basically unChristian racial pride to deny him consideration as a student—so long as he remains convinced that the University is the right place for him." In a telephone call that day, Cottrell told Hugh Clegg that he had not authorized King to use him as a reference.[41]

After receiving the papers, Ellis told King he would be notified of the university's decision. When King indicated that he wanted to return to the registration line, Ellis said an application had to be received in advance of registration to allow consideration according to the admission procedures, even if it came from an individual within the state's higher education system. Ellis also pointed out that King had not supplied transcripts of his other college work. King's application also lacked the required student health record and photograph. Moreover, the university did not have the "transient" student status King requested. Clegg then inquired if King had other documents to offer, and when King replied that he did not, Clegg said the brief discussion was over. King, however, refused to leave.

Clegg left the office to ask Public Safety director Tom Scarbrough to talk with King. Scarbrough also failed to persuade him to leave. Officials left King alone for more than an hour while they discussed what to do. In the meantime, Hines offered King a Coca-Cola, which he refused. Coleman finally authorized the Highway Patrol to remove King. Apparently feeling trapped in the unfamiliar office and not knowing what to do, King panicked and called for help; state officials reported that he "went berserk." Within seconds patrolmen seized the screaming King, took him downstairs and out a side basement door, forced him into an unmarked patrol car, and drove from the campus at about 11:45. Governor Coleman at first ordered that King be put out of the car outside Oxford, but when he learned that the officers suspected King would return to the campus, Coleman figured King was insane and ordered him taken to Jackson.

Later in the afternoon of June 5, Lafayette County officials charged King with disturbing the peace and resisting arrest, and the sheriff, probably after consulting with state officials, secured a lunacy warrant against King from J. B. Howell, the local chancery judge. Under Mississippi law, the warrant required that King be given a lunacy hearing either in the county of residence or in the county where he was taken into custody. The hearing would occur after King had been examined by two medical authorities who would explain their findings to the judge.[42]

When asked by reporters, Scarbrough said he did not know where King had been taken, and for the rest of the day King's whereabouts remained unknown. That evening reporters found King in a windowless, eight-by-ten cell on the top floor of the Highway Patrol headquarters in Jackson. Reporters talked with King briefly before they were expelled from the facility. King told them, "I just want to get out of here. . . . I don't know what they are going to do." He said he had not been mistreated at the university, but he did not want to go back. At the Jackson headquarters, Scarbrough observed that King appeared to be "mentally unbalanced."[43]

In a statement the next day, the governor and the attorney general offered their explanation of events. They claimed that King was "interested in personal publicity for himself and was trying to stir up riots or other public disorders calculated to harm the reputation of the good people of Mississippi." More specifically, he sought revenge for having been released from his position at Alcorn. Coleman and Patterson also claimed that the alumni references that King offered had been fraudulently written by King himself. Though Ole Miss officials had exercised great patience and courtesy in counseling King, he had gone "berserk" and tried to "start a demonstration" in the Lyceum; the police had no alternative but to arrest him for disturbing the peace and for resisting arrest. King, however, "was not placed in jail on those charges, because his behavior indicated, as had been suspected for at least a year, that he is mentally unbalanced and is not legally responsible for his actions." The two lawyers stressed, "It is illegal for any man to be prosecuted for any offense if he is not sane and does not understand the import of his actions."[44]

At a noon news conference, Governor Coleman announced a lunacy hearing for King. A deposition from Sam R. Ivy of the state Highway Patrol maintained that King "is not mentally responsible and until treated properly is a menace to the general public and needs treatment for his own best interest." The hearing would be held in Jackson because the sheriff of Harrison County (where King lived) had come to Jackson and believed it could more easily be held in the capital, which had doctors, psychiatrists, and a state hospital. Earlier Coleman had arranged for the doctors to examine King. The governor refused to divulge King's whereabouts but said, "We're being very careful to see that his civil rights are not being violated." Coleman said he had asked that the warrant for King's arrest not be served until after the lunacy hearing. Although claiming to have "nothing to conceal about this case," the governor denied that newsmen had interviewed King.[45]

At 12:45 P.M., with Stokes V. Robertson presiding, the lunacy hearing began on the third floor of the heavily guarded Hinds County Chancery Court building "amid an atmosphere of mysterious secrecy," according to Charles Dunagin, the only reporter inside the courtroom. Highway patrolmen refused entrance to other reporters. Escorted by law enforcement officers into the courtroom, King called to Dunagin, "Please help me!" The judge, however, expelled Dunagin because he did not want to make "a public show" out of the hearing. After examining King, Dr. Mary Lee, a physician with the Hinds County Health Department, and Dr. Beverly E. Smith, a neuropsychiatrist, reported that King "is suffering from a mental or nervous disorder, condition or affliction" and "is in need of treatment, supervision and control at a mental institution of the State of Mississippi." When Sidney Tharp, a black Mississippi lawyer called the night before by Mrs. King to represent her husband, asked, "Why do you think a man is crazy just because he wants to go to the University of Mississippi?" the judge threw him out for "interfering with an examination by reputable physicians." As he left, Tharp threatened to take his plea to federal court because the judge had no right to kick a member of the bar out. Later Robertson said, "Sidney appears to be under the influence of alcohol or goof balls." In fact, Robertson learned later that he had recently been released from a local hospital and was still under medication. At the end of the hearing, the judge "ordered, adjudged and decreed that the said Clennon King be committed to the Mississippi State Hospital at Whitfield, Mississippi for observation and treatment." As the sheriff took him away, a weeping King said, "They aren't doing me right."[46]

Established in Jackson in 1855, the state mental hospital moved in 1935 to Whitfield, in Rankin County, ten miles east of the capital. Its director was Dr. William Lawrence Jaquith, a native of Vicksburg, who ran Whitfield according to high professional standards. When King arrived, Jaquith announced that his staff would examine King "as soon as practicable" and "if Clennon King is not insane, he's got to go." He pledged that the staff would treat their new patient "just like anyone else, whether they be black or white. We have no axe to grind."[47]

R. Jess Brown, a Negro lawyer from Vicksburg, and C. B. King, from Albany, tried to obtain King's release. A petition filed for King's wife on June 10 in Hinds County Circuit Court claimed that the circumstances of King's arrest were "illegal, confusing, abusive and indefinite," that King had committed no crime, that the officers had no authority to arrest him, that his right to consult an attorney had been violated, that King had been denied the right of counsel at his lunacy hearing, and that he was being "deprived of his liberty" and was "illegally restrained" at the state hospital. In an amended petition, King's lawyers argued that the state had "acted so arbitrarily and capriciously against him that such acts resulted in the denial of due process." They also suggested that the entire sequence of events had been planned solely in an effort to "frustrate efforts of petitioner to enter the University of Mississippi." The attorney general denied all the allegations. Five days after the petition was filed, arch-segregationist Judge M. M. McGowan held a hearing in Jackson. Claiming the petition should have been filed in Rankin County where Whitfield was located, he dismissed it because he lacked jurisdiction. King's lawyers transferred their petition to Rankin County, where a hearing was scheduled for June 19.[48]

Others also protested the state's treatment of King. Medgar Evers, head of the state NAACP, called Ole Miss's rejection of King "un-American." "Committing a man to the insane asylum," the state NAACP declared, "because he gave a challenge to the Mississippi way of life is immoral, un-Christian, unconstitutional," and it pointed out that "no other state has ruled a man crazy because he wanted to get an education." Roy Wilkins objected to the "obvious injustice" in trying to find King mentally incompetent and called for King's admission to the university, and he remarked on the irony that no whites had questioned "King's mentality when he advocated segregation and attacked this association and the Supreme Court of the United States." Responding to King's overtures, Martin Luther King Jr. also pointed out the hypocrisy of King's white critics and lodged with Governor Coleman "the strongest possible protest against the inhumane and unchristian treatment," and he "shudder[ed] at the prospects of what might follow."[49]

Concerned that the state of Mississippi had violated King's civil liberties, the national office of the ACLU contacted one of its few Mississippi members, William P. Murphy, a law professor at the university. In a telephone conversation with the ACLU executive director, Murphy reported that no lawyer in the state would represent the ACLU in the King case, but he did agree to try to determine the facts in the case. Murphy then wrote to a former student practicing law in Jackson and asked about the case. In reply, Scott Tennyson made clear that he was not a member of the ACLU and did not want to get involved in the King case. Using his long personal relationship with Stokes Robertson, Tennyson nevertheless asked the judge about the treatment of King. Based on his conversation with Robertson, Tennyson reported that King's rights had not been violated. Murphy relayed Tennyson's findings to the ACLU, and the national group intervened no further.[50]

The Murphy-Tennyson correspondence revealed the heightened fear affecting well-educated and well-intentioned white Mississippians. Tennyson's first letter had a very formal tone and opened with caveats about his lack of interest in both the ACLU and King's situation. As a precaution against accusations of involvement with King, Tennyson copied his letter to Judge Robertson. Even Murphy stressed that he did not represent the ACLU "legally or officially in any way." Saying that he had typed his original letter to Tennyson, Murphy admitted that he had failed to keep a carbon copy and asked him to return it so he could make a copy. Murphy either wanted to retain a copy to substantiate his limited role or did not want to risk wider circulation of his letter. In their final exchange, Tennyson's more personal letter explained that as a new lawyer trying to establish his practice he had "to be exceedingly circumspect . . . not only . . . orthodox, but extremely politic and provident as well." Though opposed to outside meddling in southern race relations, Tennyson explained how expediency really shaped his actions: "It appears to me that I can best keep my creditors at bay by not playing hide-and-seek with an organization which— at least on some occasions—inevitably must make a frontal assault on social institutions which the majority of the people among whom I am chosen to live support and defend."[51]

A few Mississippi whites risked opprobrium by criticizing the treatment afforded King. In his *Delta Democrat Times*, Hodding Carter proclaimed the secrecy surrounding King "inexcusable" and labeled the Coleman administration's handling of the episode its "biggest blunder." The allegations of King's bizarre behavior at the university sounded to the editor "more like a manufactured excuse than the truth." In a startling admission, even the *Jackson Clarion-Ledger* conceded the administration might have followed a different course, but then quickly added, "The essential thing is that the situation called for action, and the governor acted."[52]

In the late afternoon of June 18, twelve days after being committed, King walked out of the state mental hospital with his wife and brother. Dr. Jaquith refused to make public the confidential results of tests on King but pointed out that state law forbade the release of an insane individual. In his official report to Judge Robertson, Jaquith declared, "It was the unanimous opinion of the Medical Staff that he [Clennon King] is without psychosis. By this, we mean that we could find no evidence of mental disorder. He is competent and reasonable." Although medical ethics prevented the doctors from discussing King's motivations, Jaquith observed, "His participation in the Alcorn College and Oxford disturbances have been looked on by people of both races as denoting a mental illness; but the patient feels he was well-motivated in both cases, and our examination shows that he is not mentally ill. His judgment in several instances has been poor, but this in itself does not mean that he is mentally ill."[53]

King still faced charges of disturbing the peace and resisting arrest, but Lafayette County officials made no effort to arrest him. The day after his release from Whitfield, he flew to Georgia for a visit with his family in Albany. He said that he feared state officials more than the so-called crackpots and extremists. Though he had no more interest in attending a white university in Mississippi, he threatened to sue Ole Miss if it did not apologize for his treatment. When he returned to Mississippi, he asked Chancellor Williams to have the warrant for his arrest dismissed. King declared, "As long as the University of Mississippi, through its agents, has warrants for my arrest, I am not free. . . . This anxiety is worse than being out of prison on parole because this is legal intimidation." King also wanted his suitcase that he had left at the home of an Oxford Negro and his papers that he had accidentally dropped in the Lyceum.[54]

King never sued, and Lafayette County never pursued its warrants. Instead King returned to his church in Gulfport, waged a brief attempt to integrate the public schools there, and within a few months left Mississippi. In subsequent years he moved along a path even more erratic than the one that had led him to Alcorn; his volatile career offered little proof of mental stability. He went to Africa, then to California and Mexico, and at various times he was arrested in Georgia, California, and New Orleans. He ran unsuccessfully for public office many times: in 1960 for president of the United States, in 1970 for governor of Georgia, and in 1974 and 1976 for a seat in the Georgia legislature. Just before the 1976 presidential election, King caused a sensation when he tried to integrate Jimmy Carter's church in Plains, Georgia. He was certainly a bizarre, unpredictable, independent individual. In 1976, after the incident in Plains, C. B. King seemed to suggest that the Whitfield doctors had been wrong after all; he acknowledged that his brother was "emotionally and mentally disturbed."[55]

Regardless of King's mental condition, white Mississippi's response to him demonstrated its own collective emotional and mental instability in its alarm over integration after the *Brown* decision. The politically appointed IHL board, the attorney general, and the governor—not Ole Miss officials—plotted strategy and made the major decisions in the King case. Only people of proven loyalty to the Mississippi way of life could be trusted to protect racial segregation. Chancellor Williams had been insufficiently resolute in earlier crises to convince the state's politicians he would stand fast against Clennon King. The reasons used to reject King—an incomplete application, a lack of alumni references, a minor violation of the law, and mental instability—were only a transparent mask for the real reason that everyone recognized: his race.

6. They Will "Want to Dance with Our Girls": Unwritten Rules and Rebel Athletics

■ ■

In the wake of the 1954 *Brown* decision, white Mississippians mobilized to defy desegregation, not just in public schools but in all areas of life. They interpreted *Brown* as a harbinger of greater threats to segregation and white supremacy. As one student of the Mississippi civil rights movement has observed, for segregationists "preserving the southern way of life soon assumed all the trappings of a holy crusade."[1] Though before 1954 few could have doubted Mississippi whites' commitment to segregation, after the court decision whites wasted no time in organizing their defense of the status quo. Initially they rallied private support, but soon the power of the state also moved behind the resistance effort.

Within weeks of *Brown*, state judge Thomas P. Brady of Brookhaven denounced the decision in a speech before the Sons of the American Revolution in Greenwood. He expanded his critique into a booklet published in June 1954 as *Black Monday*. In addition to damning the *Brown* verdict as a violation of the Constitution and legal precedent, he harangued about Negro inferiority and warned of the imminent dangers of racial amalgamation if whites allowed segregation to end. Based on his belief that ad hoc, individual protest would not suffice, Brady proposed creating in each southern state a group of whites dedicated to resisting integration with a regional organization to coordinate the state units.[2]

Black Monday had a special impact on Robert B. "Tut" Patterson, a former Mississippi State football star, a World War II paratrooper, and the manager of a Delta plantation. For many months he had worried about the effects of the school desegregation cases. On July 11, 1954, he convened a dozen leaders of his town, Indianola in Sunflower County, to plan organized opposition to *Brown*. A week later nearly one hundred whites met at the town hall and formed the first Citizens' Council. At Patterson's instigation, similar groups developed in other Mississippi communities, and in October, representatives from councils in twenty counties met to form the Association of Citizens' Councils in Mississippi. Within two years, the Citizens' Councils claimed eighty thousand members in Mississippi.[3]

The Citizens' Council established its headquarters in the state capital, across the street from the governor's mansion and a couple of blocks from the capitol. Its influence involved more than proximity to power; it exerted political muscle across the state, especially in areas with large black populations. Many political leaders endorsed the Citizens' Council and its program of total opposition to desegregation, and the *Jackson Clarion-Ledger* and *Jackson Daily News* also supported it. By February 1956, one observer declared that it had "in fact become the government in Mississippi" and it "controls the legislative, executive and judicial arms of government."[4]

The Citizens' Council's sway extended beyond state government. Among high school students it promoted an essay contest on one of four topics: "Why I Believe in Social Separation of the Races of Mankind," "Subversion in Racial Unrest," "Why the Preservation of States' Rights Is Important to Every American," or "Why Separate Schools Should Be Maintained for the White and Negro Races." The state Citizens' Council propaganda for segregation also included *The Citizens' Council*, its monthly newspaper, and a weekly "Forum" for radio and television.[5]

At the same time, the state enhanced official resistance to integration. In February 1956, the legislature unanimously adopted a "Resolution of Interposition" that declared Mississippi had never "delegated to the federal government its right to educate and nurture its youth and its power and right of control over its schools, colleges, education and other public facilities, and to prescribe the rules, regulations, and conditions under which they shall be conducted." According to the resolution, when the state and the federal government contested for power, as it did over school desegregation, Mississippi claimed the right to decide where the power ultimately resided.[6]

To implement interposition and to maintain segregation, Speaker of the House Walter Sillers and more than fifty other representatives proposed on March 20, 1956, to create the Mississippi State Sovereignty Commission. The house overwhelmingly approved the bill, and within ten days the senate unanimously also passed it. It gave the twelve-member commission the responsibility "to do and perform any and all acts and things deemed necessary and proper to protect the sovereignty of the State of Mississippi . . . from encroachment thereon by the Federal Government . . . and to resist the usurpation of the rights and powers reserved to this state." Governor J. P. Coleman claimed it "will enable us during the next two years to maintain a successful fight for preserving the separation of the races in this state." The commission promoted the southern way of life, investigated subversive activities, and countered the NAACP. The governor, lieutenant governor, attorney general, and speaker of the house served on the commission, along with two senators, three representatives, and three civilians. It soon employed a director, a public relations official, and investigators.[7]

In its first years, the Sovereignty Commission employed public relations to promote Mississippi's segregated way of life. In an early effort to counter the negative image of the state's race relations, twenty journalists from small-town newspapers in New England were invited for a weeklong tour of the state to convince them that blacks and whites lived peacefully and harmoniously under segregation. Though the tour failed to persuade the editors to change their opinions that racial segregation could not last, commission officials considered it a great success because it generated favorable publicity in New England papers. In another public relations campaign, the commission distributed hundreds of thousands of newsletters, brochures, pamphlets, and other forms of propaganda "to educate the rest of the country . . . on Mississippi's problem with reference to segregation and the progress the negro is making in this State."[8]

Interest in the attitudes of Mississippi blacks complemented the commission's concern for nonsouthern opinion. To encourage conservative blacks, it provided financial support to friendly black journalists, ministers, and teachers; in return they were expected to support both the commission's work and racial segregation. The commission also confidentially enlisted cooperative blacks to act as its agents. While some informants volunteered their services, the commission paid others.[9]

Though the tax-supported Sovereignty Commission often competed and feuded with the private Citizens' Council, their efforts overlapped and reinforced each other.[10] Neither had law enforcement responsibilities, but each worked to keep Mississippi closed to dissent and subversion. They relied on exposure, harassment, and intimidation to coerce a united front among whites. Once sealed, the closed society would perpetuate itself, and the council, the commission, and their accomplices would only have to maintain vigilance over the state.

One of the Citizens' Council's earliest actions involved a baseball game. In September 1954 a Memphis promoter arranged for two minor league all-star teams to play a Sunday afternoon exhibition game in Greenville, just as they had in other southern cities. A sports reporter for the *Delta Democrat Times* called it historic because it "will be the first time that an all white baseball club will be meeting an all Negro aggregation here." The white Cotton States League all-stars would play the Negro Big League all-stars at the local park used in the 1950s by the Greenville Bucks in the Cotton States League. The Bucks' board of directors, who still leased the park, reached an agreement for the game. "They have been playing all over the country including the South," said the promoter, "and we never before have had any trouble."[11]

As soon as the integrated game was announced, the five local Greenville directors heard objections from whites. Hodding Carter believed the new Citizens' Council orchestrated the protests. According to one report, citizens identifying themselves as members of the council "threatened a sit-down strike on the field" to prevent the game and to protect the Mississippi way of life. As tensions grew, protests escalated. On Saturday, handbills thrown from an airplane asked, "Are you proud of Greenville?" and threatened economic retaliation against the town if the integrated game were played. Local leaders quickly decided against an integrated game. Instead, the promoter at the last minute scheduled an exhibition between two black all-star teams. To mollify local segregationists, Carter's paper announced in a front-page article that "a special section will be reserved for white persons."[12]

Carter denounced the cancellation and reminded readers of all the integrated baseball played on television, in Greenville backyards, and in the Cotton States League. Recognizing the tension created by the *Brown* verdict, Carter asked, "If we object to legal compulsory integration of the schools, how can we endorse the threat of illegal compulsion to prevent the playing of a game of baseball?"[13] His rhetorical question went for naught. The Citizens' Council had preserved segregation in athletics. Though no statute applied, white opinion in Greenville would not even allow whites and blacks to play catch together.

Similar unwritten regulations supplemented and reinforced the legal regulations of race relations in the state. The rules applied to Mississippi colleges that had contact with integrated institutions mostly through intercollegiate sports. A controversial aspect of racial relations in the 1950s and early 1960s, therefore, involved intercollegiate athletics. Whether teams would compete in integrated contests had great significance because for white Mississippians college athletics was much more than a game. According to longtime Rebel football coach John Vaught, sports provided "an outlet, a gateway to recognition for a people" in a poor state denigrated and scorned by others.[14] Football, especially, held significance in the 1950s and 1960s—the very time of the civil rights movement—because whites could take great pride in Ole Miss's successes. The importance of the university's athletic teams caused Mississippi's leaders to pay close attention to the teams' opponents, particularly when racial tensions escalated after 1954.

Prior to 1954, white Mississippi collegians had competed against blacks in track meets, and in the 1930s a white Mississippi State boxer on his way to a national heavyweight championship had defeated a black opponent. Mississippi State and Delta State basketball teams had played in integrated tournaments since World War II. In 1950 an integrated Evansville College football team defeated Delta State College in Indiana, and Mississippi Southern's football team had lost the 1953 Sun Bowl game to an integrated team from the College of the Pacific.[15] In their effort to enforce a strict line between the races, segregationists conveniently forgot earlier integrated athletic encounters.

Most other southern states also fought to preserve segregated intercollegiate athletics. Throughout the 1950s and early 1960s, the South's major athletic conferences—the Atlantic Coast Conference, the Southwest Conference, and the Southeastern Conference—remained completely segregated.[16] The racial problem arose, nevertheless, when southern teams competed against teams from the North and West that allowed blacks on their rosters.

Outside the South after World War II, changing race relations meant that blacks increasingly participated in sports, both collegiate and professional. In the postwar decades, northern schools often acquiesced to southern mores and kept black players out of competition against segregated southern schools. As the civil rights movement accelerated in the 1950s, however, northern institutions became less willing to comply with southern racial standards. By 1956 two developments signaled a change in northern attitudes. Protesting southern racial segregation, Harvard's all-white basketball team refused to play four games in the South. Also in 1956, Indiana University and several other midwestern colleges declared that they would no longer play southern colleges if they had to withhold their black players. At the same time that northern colleges became less cooperative, the southern commitment to segregation intensified.[17]

The hardening of attitudes in Mississippi became apparent in 1955. The winning Rebel football team had a chance to go to the Sugar Bowl in New Orleans on New Year's Day, 1956. Before Thanksgiving, the Mid-Winter Sports Association announced that the University of Pittsburgh would play in the Sugar Bowl against a Southeastern Conference team. The Pittsburgh Panthers team, however, included a black reserve fullback. Opposed to playing black players, some Ole Miss alumni threatened, as the chancellor privately explained, to "ride us out of town on a rail" if the Rebels played Pittsburgh. When the predicament became known, Williams publicly declared that Ole Miss had not asked the Sugar Bowl to invite another SEC team. He disingenuously said the university was "eager to go to a bowl game and is not opposed to any of the bowls." A Sugar Bowl spokesman told reporters, "There is no truth in any rumor that Ole Miss has asked us not to invite them to the Sugar Bowl."[18]

The mere public discussion of the effect of Pittsburgh's Negro player on Ole

Miss's reaction to a Sugar Bowl invitation may have killed the Rebels' chance to play in New Orleans. Even though Ole Miss beat archrival Mississippi State 26–0, the Sugar Bowl selected Georgia Tech, while Ole Miss accepted an invitation to play Texas Christian University in the less prestigious Cotton Bowl. Chancellor Williams confided to a friend that the Cotton Bowl was "where we wanted to go in the first place."[19] Without taking a stand on integration, Williams had avoided getting the university embroiled in a controversy.

Georgia Tech's agreement to play Pittsburgh caused an uproar. Leading the opposition, Governor Marvin Griffin proclaimed, "The South stands at Armageddon. . . . We cannot make the slightest concession to the enemy in this dark and lamentable hour of struggle." He called for a special meeting of the state board of regents to enact a rule to prevent Tech from playing in the Sugar Bowl if Pittsburgh brought Negro players. A Pittsburgh sports writer responded, "We'd rather see the University of Pittsburgh pull out of the Sugar Bowl than submit to the wishes of narrow-minded, bigoted and vicious groups who are hundreds of years behind the times." Protesting Tech students and fans hung the governor in effigy. The equivocal regents allowed Tech to play but voted to prevent any future integrated contest. Tech won the game. Six months later, the Louisiana legislature prohibited integrated athletic contests, including the Sugar Bowl.[20]

Days after Ole Miss dodged the Sugar Bowl controversy, Chancellor Williams watched another flare up after the all-white Jones County Junior College (JCJC) football team accepted an invitation to play in the tenth annual Little Rose Bowl. Lieutenant Governor Carroll Gartin, a JCJC alumnus, announced that he would attend the game, and local businessmen and civic leaders worked to raise fifteen thousand dollars to send the college band to the bowl game. About the first of December, however, Mississippians learned that the undefeated Bobcats' opponent would be California's Compton Junior College team that included eight Negro players.[21]

The year before in the Little Rose Bowl, the Hinds County Junior College team had without controversy defeated an integrated team from El Camino, California. By 1955, however, many whites had grown more intolerant of any apparent breach in segregation. Aware of possible criticism, the JCJC president nonetheless said, "We accepted the bid and that's it as far as I know," and the president of the school's board of trustees declared "it's too late to do anything about it." Even though the JCJC players did not object to playing against blacks, the prospect of integrated athletics upset many whites. William J. Simmons claimed it would be "interpreted by the NAACP and other 'mixiecrats' as furthering the cause of integration." A Natchez legislator thought the planned game would be "a real blow to the entire South," and the wary lieutenant governor canceled his plans to attend the game. A Jackson radio station and the Mississippi Power and Light Company scratched the broadcast of the game because "it is too controversial," and the Covington County Board of Supervisors withdrew its financial support for the team's trip.[22]

On December 10, 1955, the JCJC Bobcats lost, 22–13, to the Compton Tartars, but the controversy did not end then. Representative Ralph H. Herrin of Covington County promised to introduce in the next legislature a measure to prevent integrated sports: "This policy should be short and to the point—We play no College that plays Negroes." Under his proposal, the coach and president of an offending school would be fired. "You cannot straddle the fence on this issue," Herrin argued. "You must get right or get out!"[23]

Despite strong public support, the legislature never enacted the proposal. Instead, a group of legislators met privately with the presidents of more than twelve of the state's junior colleges. To avoid a cut in appropriations, the presidents agreed that their teams would engage in no integrated athletic contests. According to John Herbers, a United Press International (UPI) reporter in Mississippi, the unwritten agreement "can be found in no public record, but it is branded in the minds of college officials." Adopted after the 1955 Little Rose Bowl affair, the unwritten law became part of the state's racial etiquette. The following December, for example, the undefeated Pearl River Junior College (PRJC) football team refused an invitation to the Little Rose Bowl because its probable opponent had black players.[24] Within a year or two, whites referred to the unwritten law as if it had been policy for generations. Repeatedly in the 1950s and early 1960s, it prevented schools from competing in tournaments and bowls.

Shortly after PRJC refused to play in an integrated bowl game, the basketball teams from Ole Miss and Mississippi State traveled to holiday tournaments in Kentucky and Indiana. On December 29, 1956, Mississippi State defeated the University of Denver to advance to a championship game against the University of Evansville. When State's athletic director, C. R. "Dudy" Noble, heard that Denver had black players, he ordered the team home. "If we had known the Denver team had Negroes our team would not have been there to play the game," President Ben F. Hilbun explained. "It's not our policy to play teams with Negro members and I'm sorry it developed. It won't happen again." Going further, Noble claimed, "it's always been our policy that our teams would not compete against Negroes. That's traditional with our institution."[25]

At the same time, after losing its initial contest in the All-America City tournament in Owensboro, Kentucky, the Rebels discovered that their consolation opponent, Iona College from New York, had a black player. Aware of Mississippi State's action the previous day, after the Rebels' coach conferred with Ole Miss administrators, the team withdrew. A tournament spokesman regretted the withdrawal but asserted that it had "never denied any player the right to play because of race or color." Athletic director Tad Smith claimed, "The tournament chairman was told last summer we would have to abide by state policies." The next day J. D. Williams and Smith issued a defensive statement: "When we accepted the invitation to that tournament, it was with an understanding that there would be no Negroes in it." A tournament official disagreed: "The question of Negroes was never discussed with University of Mississippi officials, and absolutely no guarantee was made that there would be no Negro players in the tournament." Whereas Hilbun looked forceful in adhering to the unwritten rule, an embarrassed Chancellor Williams scrambled for an excuse for his team's unfortunate plight.[26]

Legislators nonetheless rushed to praise both schools. The president pro tem of the state senate thought Hilbun and Williams "took the only honorable course they could, in good conscience, follow" and demonstrated "that Mississippi is not going to tolerate integration in any phase of education." Representative Russell Fox insisted, "We can compromise on method and manner, but never on principle." Agreeing with his mentor, Speaker Walter Sillers, C. B. "Buddie" Newman congratulated Hilbun and Williams because they had "acted properly to help preserve Mississippi traditions and customs."[27]

While many whites agreed with their state's leaders, a few dissented. A Clinton resident thought the withdrawals made each team look "like a little sulking boy picking up his marbles and going home." From Hazlehurst came the sarcastic suggestion that the state not stop at barring teams from playing in integrated athletic contests but extend the ban to watching them on television and even to prohibiting watching "Ed Sullivan shake hands with Sammy Davis." Critical editorials appeared in the moderate *Jackson State Times*, in Hodding Carter's newspaper, and in the university's student newspaper. The *Mississippian*'s editor worried that the teams' withdrawals only proved the "small-minded prejudices of Mississippi and the South" and did not win friends for the cause of racial segregation.[28]

Despite some criticism, the new policy quickly became a respected custom and soon also applied to all-black Jackson State College. In March 1957, the Jackson State basketball team won its conference championship and advanced to the NCAA small college tournament. It won its first-round game and prepared to play in the regional contests in South Dakota. Four days before its next game against one of three all-white teams also in the tournament, Jacob L. Reddix, the college president, announced that the IHL board had advised him that playing a team with white players violated established policy. He telegraphed the head of the NCAA: "Regret circumstances beyond our control force us to withdraw our basketball team from further competition in the playoffs of the NCAA basketball tournament." Jackson State players expressed their disappointment, and students staged a brief protest, but the unwritten law prevailed.[29]

In the spring of 1958, the unwritten rule affected a girls' basketball team. For the fourteenth time, a team from Lumberton traveled to St. Joseph, Missouri, to participate in an Amateur Athletic Union tournament. After a defeat, the team was scheduled to play a consolation game against an integrated Ohio team, even though the coach had been assured the team would not compete against blacks. To preserve the color line, even outside the state, a team not sponsored by a public institution quit and returned home rather than play an opponent with three black players.[30]

The well-known informal regulation against integrated athletics even affected postseason football bowl games in the Rebels' glory days. Through the first half of the 1958 season, the Ole Miss team won all of its games and was a possibility for several major bowls. In what some considered the South's "game of the year," the Rebels faced Louisiana State in Baton Rouge; experts thought that the winner would go to the Sugar Bowl and the loser to the Orange Bowl. The Colorado-Oklahoma game the same day would determine the champion of the Big Eight and, therefore, the other Orange Bowl team. After the Rebels lost and Oklahoma won, they seemed the likely Orange Bowl opponents, directed by the nation's two most successful coaches, Johnny Vaught and Bud Wilkinson. The *Mississippian* hoped for a Rebels-Sooners game because it "would provide the top game of the day as far as thrills go," but the sports editor acknowledged the Oklahoma team had black players. Jimmie McDowell, sports editor of the *Jackson State Times*, revealed that Ole Miss had spurned an overture from the Orange Bowl because Oklahoma had Negro players. The Rebels instead played Florida in the less important Gator Bowl.[31]

In the late 1950s and early 1960s, Jimmie McDowell was perhaps the leading critic of the unwritten law. Born in Brookhaven in 1926, McDowell was the son of a professional baseball player and grew up a sports participant, fan, and writer. After service during World War II, he attended a junior college before going to Millsaps College. When he and his father went to Memphis to see the Rebels play in the Delta Bowl on New Year's Day, 1948, they ran into Tad Smith, an admirer of the senior McDowell. Smith convinced Jimmie McDowell to transfer to Ole Miss, where he covered sports for the *Mississippian*. In the half-dozen years following his graduation in 1949, McDowell wrote for several Mississippi newspapers and worked as director of public relations and sports publicity at Southern Mississippi College before joining the new *Jackson State Times* as sports editor. During his nearly seven years with the *State Times*,

McDowell also had a regular sports show on Jackson's WLBT television station. While just in his thirties, McDowell had extensive state contacts, wide journalistic experience, and influential platforms in Jackson from which to oppose the unwritten law. He spoke out against it because he thought athletes should always compete against the best possible opponents. Race was not an issue for him. Playing against blacks never bothered him, and as a sportswriter he wanted Mississippi teams to compete for national championships regardless of their opponents.[32]

In the spring of 1959, following the Rebels' failure to play in the Orange Bowl, the unwritten law continued to plague Mississippi athletics. In the hottest controversy, it first affected Mississippi State's basketball team; later it hit the Rebels baseball squad. According to a local commentator, the 1958–59 Mississippi State basketball team was the best in the state's history and may have been the best in the nation that year. After it defeated perennial national power Kentucky, the State team seemed poised to win the SEC championship and an automatic invitation to the NCAA tournament. Two of the country's best players were Negroes—Oscar Robertson of Cincinnati and Tom Hawkins of Notre Dame—so the tourney would certainly include blacks.[33]

As the Maroons continued winning, McDowell observed, "Sooner or later it had to come: will State be allowed to go?" In a state election year, politicians refused to discuss it. An informal poll by McDowell found a six-to-one majority in favor of allowing State to play in the NCAA tournament, even against Negroes. Some whites who otherwise supported segregation wanted State to bring home the national championship. Dudley S. Bridgforth, a member of the IHL board, stated the position clearly when he said, "I am a segregationist. If our team competes, I think they'll probably have to play teams with Negroes on them. I hate to do it, but it looks like if we're ever going to compete in these national bowls and tournaments, we'll have to face it. I guess I'll have to say I'm in favor of the team playing in the tournament." To strict segregationists, however, no exception could be granted without imperiling the entire southern way of life.[34]

McDowell argued for a "when in Rome do as the Romans do" policy that would have allowed teams to play integrated opponents outside the state but conform to segregation practices in the state. Alabama, Georgia, Tennessee, and Louisiana had already adopted such a policy. Predicting that SEC competitors would soon have black players, he warned that Mississippi teams could be left with few acceptable opponents. He thought the teams could be good ambassadors for the state, just as Ole Miss's recent Miss America had brought invaluable favorable publicity. If the State basketball team could not compete against blacks, McDowell proposed the state's congressmen quit the integrated

Congress, the state American Legion refuse to participate in its integrated national convention, and State students stop competing in integrated agricultural contests. McDowell clearly wanted to see State play for the national championship, and he decried the "utter lack of courage and the sickening fear of a biased political whip hover[ing] like a menacing shadow over Mississippi State's shoulder."[35]

If the politicians dodged the issue, the *Mississippian* spoke out against the unwritten law. Though not directly affected, Ole Miss students realized the implications—what could happen to State's basketball team in the spring could happen to the Rebels football team in the fall with bowl games. The *Mississippian* objected to the treatment of the State team and referred to the practices of other southern states in allowing out-of-state integrated competition. The newspaper hoped that the trustees would "not be swayed by any group of bigoted politicians" and would "trust the men of Mississippi State to uphold the customs and traditions of this great state" by playing in the tournament. Sports columnist Jimmie Robertson thought the resolution of the issue would be the "most fateful decision" in the history of collegiate sports in Mississippi. It would determine if athletics were going to be restricted to "intrastate (perhaps that should read intra-'white'-state) competition." The "principle involved is whether Mississippi should be allowed to compete against Negroes and not whether NEGROES SHOULD GO TO SCHOOL WITH WHITES." The question, however, had "been twisted and distorted by stubborn and . . . ignorant" Mississippians who implied that anyone who supported State's playing in the NCAA tournament also advocated complete racial integration.[36]

From the other side, the editor of the *Prentiss Headlight* asked, "Is there enough glory in winning a championship . . . to compensate jeopardizing the winning of the greatest battle ever to be fought in this nation—that of segregation of the races? We say not!" Similarly the *Houston Times Post* declared, "There is no middle ground where segregation is concerned." The prime opposition to State's playing in the NCAA came from the Citizens' Council; its executive committee announced it was "unalterably opposed to integration of the races, whatever may be the disguise. . . . This includes basketball games." Its founder, Robert Patterson ominously suggested, "They will want to play the girls next." The maintenance of the Mississippi way of life simply required a rigid line between the races, even on the collegiate playing fields.[37]

Other influential whites were reluctant to take a stand. Though a steadfast segregationist, political columnist Tom Ethridge equivocated. He saw the issue "as brutal logic vs. deeply rooted sentiment" and could appreciate both sides. While he recognized the likely charge of hypocrisy if teams competed against blacks outside the state but not at home, he realized schools might eventually have no worthy opponents if they refused to play integrated teams. "Shall we 'hold the line'—or compromise in the interest of expediency?" he asked. "Personally, if this decision was ours to make we would say, 'Hold the line'— regretfully but nonetheless positively. The question is not for us to decide, thank the Lord." Candidates for governor refused to take a stand. In what McDowell called "buck-passing at its finest cornpone hour," Governor Coleman said the IHL board had authority over intercollegiate athletics, and the trustees turned the matter over to the head of Mississippi State.[38]

The answer, therefore, had to come from Mississippi State's president. Ben Hilbun, recovering from surgery, waited until after the final game against Ole Miss in Oxford to announce his "tough" decision. Meanwhile, pressure on him grew as a student poll at State revealed that 85 percent wanted their team to go to the NCAA tournament, even as rumors circulated that the basketball coach would quit if the president vetoed participation. Hilbun heard from white Mississippians who wanted State to play in the tournament. Claiming most Mississippians agreed with him, comedian Jerry Clower, a former State player, telegraphed Hilbun to urge him to pray and then to "let them go." Dick Sanders, a Jackson journalist and member of the state's Agricultural and Industrial Board, told Hilbun that preventing the team from going to the tournament would only offer proof that "Mississippians are unreasonable and backward."[39]

Finally, after State beat Ole Miss, 21–16, Hilbun referred to "long-standing policies and customs" barring integrated competition and declared State would not go to the tournament. He maintained that "in this situation there are great issues involved which transcend mere athletic competition." Privately, he explained that a "gamble on winning a ball game at the expense of our heritage isn't worth taking." He believed that "the white race can serve the world best by remaining pure" and that "if we believe in segregation we had better act that way." Hilbun was discouraged, however, that "a lot of our people are willing to surrender on great issues in order to experience the thrill that may come from fleeting fickly sports."[40]

Unlike most observers, the *Mississippian* excoriated President Hilbun. Jimmie Robertson concluded that Hilbun's judgment amounted to a "death warrant for this state's athletic program" because the teams could not compete nationally, and soon even some SEC games would be banned because several SEC universities would have black players. Frustrated by the unwritten rule, Robertson urged the legislature either to enact the informal policy into law or do away with it entirely. His editor agreed. "They are laughing at poor, backward Mississippi," Travis Stallworth editorialized. He pointed out the hypocrisy of rabid segregationist John Bell Williams debating Adam Clayton Powell and using the same toilet and cafeteria facilities as the Negro congressman while the State basketball team could not play against a few Negroes. The editor opined, "If we are not going to play under national rules, I say we should resign from the NCAA and all other groups which have national integrated affiliations," including the Boy Scouts, the Methodist Church, 4-H clubs, the American Legion, the YMCA, and the Army Reserves.[41]

Just weeks later, the Ole Miss baseball team contended for the SEC title and a trip to the NCAA World Series. Two years before, the Rebels had gone to the World Series and finished third in the nation. In May of 1959, the Rebels won the SEC western division and faced Georgia Tech in a best-of-three playoff series to determine the SEC season champion. Before the series began, university officials discreetly notified the SEC commissioner that the state's unwritten law would prevent the Rebels from going to the NCAA championship competition.[42]

Once again Jimmie McDowell used his sports column to object to the unwritten rule as illogical, impractical, and counterproductive. For example, he pointed out that, in spite of the protests over the 1955 Sugar Bowl, Georgia policy permitted Tech to play in the 1959 World Series against integrated teams, even though integrated games could not be played within the state. Recalling the Rebels' 1956 World Series play, McDowell reminded his readers that the very same state officials who had permitted that team to compete now stood aside and let the unwritten rule block the Rebels. He thought that "battling for national honors" could only bring favorable publicity to a state that had recently received plenty of criticism, especially after the notorious Mack Charles Parker lynching in Pearl River County. According to McDowell, the state's sports programs would continue to suffer under the unwritten law because the state's colleges would have to play Hardin-Simmons and Arkansas State instead of the integrated teams of Notre Dame, Southern California, and Michigan State.[43] But his lone protests, like the *Mississippian*'s logical argument, had no effect.

By the end of 1959, the application of the unwritten law had gained several precedents. In the spring of 1960, Mississippi again won the SEC baseball championship and had an overall record of 20–3. Athletic director Smith announced that the Ole Miss baseball team would not participate in the NCAA playoffs. Referring to "a number" of reasons, Smith mentioned the beginning of final exams and the players' lack of interest in the World Series—"the majority of them had rather not go." When asked whether the unwritten law had anything to do with the decision, Smith replied, "Not too much." McDowell thought Smith's comments "a shade weak." A conflict with exams as an excuse was preposterous, and the ostensible lack of interest among the players was "a far cry" from reality. "When the day comes," he wrote in his column, "that Ole

Miss athletes are not interested in winning national acclaim, you can mark the Rebels down as a second rate sports power."[44]

The next year, the football team finished the season undefeated and, except for a tie, had a perfect record. As late as the middle of November, Ole Miss apparently still had a chance to play Washington in the Rose Bowl. The unwritten rule, however, posed a major obstacle because Washington's team included several Negro players. Tad Smith appealed directly to Governor Barnett. Elected in 1959 as an avowed segregationist, Barnett might have swayed the board of trustees and calmed any public resistance to allowing one of the state's teams to play against an integrated team, but he refused to consider any breach in the policy of segregation. After defeating Mississippi State, the Rebels therefore accepted a Sugar Bowl invitation to play the unranked Owls of Rice University.[45]

Once again the unwritten rule had penalized the Rebels by preventing their participation in an integrated game. It may also have hurt Mississippi teams by limiting their regular season opponents. At the end of the season, Ole Miss students had protested the national rankings of the Rebels. From the student union they hanged dummies labeled "AP" and "UPI" and later burned them on a bonfire while they chanted, "Go to Hell, AP" and "Go to Hell, UPI." The unbeaten Rebels had been ranked third in the nation after Minnesota and Iowa in one poll and second behind Minnesota in the other, even though each of the other teams had one loss. A sports editor at the University of Florida pointed out, however, that the Rebels played an easy schedule that included Houston, Memphis, Chattanooga, Tulane, and Vanderbilt. A *Mississippian* sports columnist tried to excuse the schedule by claiming that other schools did not want to play the powerful Rebels, but the unwritten rule probably played a role in limiting the schedule.[46]

In 1961 enforcement of the unwritten law continued. When Mississippi State won the SEC basketball title and received an automatic invitation to the NCAA tournament, Barnett objected to all integrated sports. "If integrated teams played in Mississippi," he asked, "where would they eat? Are they going to want to go to the dance later and want to dance with our girls?" McDowell ridiculed Barnett by commenting that athletes "aren't interested in playing footsie with anyone." Hodding Carter derided the "unwritten law" that "makes us look silly over and over again" and charged that "in the long run, by its very absurdity, it serves to undermine the same status quo the men who formulated it are straining at gnats to preserve." Nevertheless, the 1961 Maroons declined the NCAA invitation. Later that year the PRJC football team received an invitation to play in the junior colleges' Little Rose Bowl against a California opponent, either Bakersfield or Santa Monica. Both California squads, however, included Negro players. After the final game, the PRJC president sent a telegram to the bowl officials declining the invitation.[47]

During the same fall, the Ole Miss football team compiled a 9–1 record. The Rebels' schedule, however, again included Houston, Tulane, Vanderbilt, and Chattanooga, and McDowell remarked that a "snickering sports world would view with distaste" a game against the lowly Chattanooga Moccasins. Ranked fifth in the nation in spite of their schedule, the Rebels expected to play in a bowl game. Although the Cotton Bowl against Texas was most likely, a Rose Bowl encounter with an integrated UCLA squad remained possible after Ohio State rejected an invitation to Pasadena. Cotton Bowl officials apparently had little concern about losing the Rebels to the Rose Bowl because, as the *Jackson State Times* reported, "Mississippi does not play integrated teams. UCLA, host team for the Rose Bowl, has Negroes on its team." On New Year's Day, Ole Miss played Texas in the Cotton Bowl.[48]

By the early 1960s, the unwritten law seemed entrenched, but in the first months of 1962 it came under increasing attack. After the *Jackson State Times*'s demise in January of 1962 silenced Jimmie McDowell, Jimmie Robertson took up the assault. The *Mississippian* editor grew up in Greenville, where he learned that "the measure of a man's character was how far he could hit a baseball," not his race. His accountant father had Hodding Carter's *Delta Democrat Times* as a client, and in high school he worked for the paper part-time as a sports-writer. Robertson's schoolteacher mother had been class valedictorian in 1926 at the University of Mississippi, so her son naturally gravitated to Oxford for college.[49]

As a freshman Robertson joined Kappa Alpha, the fraternity most closely identified with traditional southern mores, and began covering sports for the *Mississippian*. For two years he worked in the press box, keeping statistics for the athletic department. He became acquainted with Jimmie McDowell, Tad Smith, and Johnny Vaught but knew little about their racial or political views. As sports editor, Robertson used his weekly column to discuss the unwritten law; later, as editor, he spoke out more strongly against the law. He seldom received any comment from university officials about his commentary. George Street, an Ole Miss public relations employee, did regularly discuss the re-actions of state political figures to his editorials but never told him what to write. Tad Smith once summoned Robertson to his office. When Robertson arrived, he found Smith smiling and happy because he liked his skewering of the Jackson politicos over the unwritten law. Confident that the rule was a creation of public officials rather than university administrators, Robertson was encouraged to keep up his attack.[50]

In a probing editorial in February 1962, Robertson listed "eight reasons against the state's unwritten law." After pointing out that other southern states did not consider such a policy essential to maintaining segregation, Robertson stressed that playing games against Negroes was not the same as advocating integration or going to school with them. As others had, the editor reminded Mississippians that the rule had been adopted only a few years earlier and was routinely violated by citizens who participated in integrated activities such as the national Congress and Miss America beauty pageants. In regard to sports, the policy would "eventually destroy Mississippi intercollegiate athletics" because the state's teams would find fewer acceptable opponents. He also argued that it was unfair to athletes because it deprived them of "deserved national recognition." It also cost the state millions of dollars of free advertising and allowed other states to get the recognition that Mississippi deserved.[51]

Two other Mississippians also openly spoke out against the rule. One elected public official, Representative A. C. "Butch" Lambert, said, "There's nothing wrong with five white boys winning the national championship." Although Lambert did not favor scheduling games with integrated teams, the Tupelo legislator thought the restriction should not apply to tournaments to decide national championships. Lambert did say that he believed that many other legislators agreed with him but refused to speak because of fear of retaliation by constituents. Immediately after State's final basketball game in Oxford, the Maroons' coach said, "I think the boys should be allowed to play against integrated teams away from home." Babe McCarthy announced that he favored a relaxation of the rule so that teams could play integrated squads only outside the state, and his team could, therefore, play in the tournament. He would nevertheless abide by the law and the directions of his superiors but, refusing further comment, referred all questioners to the SEC office.[52]

For the third time in four years, Mississippi State won the SEC championship. The new college president, Dean Colvard, wanted the team to play in the national tournament, but he felt a "conflict between my desire and my judgment." He opposed the rule but felt unable to do anything about it; like some others, he realized that brutal logic could not yet defeat deeply rooted sentiment. He thought at the time that "it will be far better for the pressure for change to be felt by political leaders than for me to attempt to change the longstanding custom without the help of public opinion." Believing he "lacked the prestige to upset this longstanding unwritten policy," Colvard decided the Maroons should stay home. The unwritten law continued to stand in the Maroons' way.[53]

The student editors in Oxford and Starkville regretted Colvard's decision and called on the politicians to change the law. If they refused to act, Robertson wanted the schools to withdraw from the SEC as the "only honorable recourse," because the Rebels and the Maroons should not compete for the championship if they could not represent the conference. The *Mississippian* editor conceded, however, that the law "is not likely to be altered." His counterpart at State thought it should be eliminated but suspected that the "unwritten law grows in stature each time it becomes necessary for its enforcement."[54]

Robertson's editorial against the unwritten law elicited some support. One Rebel athlete endorsed the policy of playing integrated teams outside the state. According to Bennett Alport, such competition could not hurt. "I have had the opportunity to compete with and against Negro athletes on many occasions," Alport declared, "and I have found that no matter how many times a heavily perspiring Negro brushed up against me, the color didn't rub off."[55]

Other students defended segregation in the *Rebel Underground*, an anonymous alternative paper that began appearing on the campus in February 1962. It denounced Robertson's "warped thinking and his misplaced sense of values" in trying to justify an end to the unwritten rule. "If Mississippi is to remain segregated, it must do so not only in athletics, but in every walk of life," it declared. Though others may be "willing to sacrifice their principles, tradition, and prestige for the sake of athletics, Mississippi is not!" The *Rebel Underground* conceded that total segregation in every situation may not always be possible, but it stressed that it must be enforced "in circumstances over which we do have control." In a challenge to Robertson, it declared that "if you are truly for segregation and the preservation of our way of life, then you will realize that there is no middle road—either you have segregation or you do not have it." Claiming one could not "compromise integrity and tradition," the paper rejected the idea of enforcing the unwritten rule within the state while allowing teams to play against integrated opponents outside Mississippi—"it is not where you play that is important, but whom you play." An inconsistent policy would, according to the *Rebel Underground*, give the NAACP a logical claim that the state discriminated in its athletic endeavors. A change in the rule would also diminish the state's right to determine its own policies and would play into the hands of communists who wanted to subvert states' rights.[56]

By 1962 the informal, unwritten athletic policy still had significant public support and seemed a permanent component of Mississippi's racial etiquette. It enforced a rigid pattern of segregation that would not even allow blacks and whites to meet on the basketball court or the football field. Many white Mississippians feared that any approved interracial contact in sports would be interpreted as yielding on the larger question of segregation, which could never be compromised. They believed that any breach of segregation would lead, as Governor Barnett so forthrightly suggested, to interracial dancing, interracial marriage, and mongrelization of the white race. The unwritten law was, however, just one small element of a complicated system of customs, rules, and traditions that governed racial matters. Complementing the more formal laws and rules that operated at Ole Miss, the racial etiquette applied not just to athletics but to many aspects of campus life, including religion and freedom of expression.

7. "Mississippi Madness": Will Campbell and Religious Emphasis Week

■ ■

Barely three months after the *Brown* decision, Reverend Will Campbell became director of religious life at Ole Miss. During the next two years, the Baptist minister helped coordinate a provocative religious program related to civil rights. His activities ran afoul of the state's white supremacist orthodoxy and embroiled Ole Miss in controversy at the very time that violent resistance to racial change pervaded the state. In 1954 a special legislative session changed the conspiracy law to include attempts "to overthrow or violate segregation laws of this state."[1] By 1955 segregationists had little tolerance for dissent. A controversy at Mississippi Southern College and reactions by the IHL board and by the legislature revealed the increasing sensitivity.

In March 1955, at Mississippi Southern College in Hattiesburg, Reverend Henry H. Crane, a pacifist Methodist minister from Detroit, told a Religious Emphasis Week (REW) audience, "This country needs small groups in every town and community in the land who are willing to defy the government and refuse to go to war, refuse to sail ships, refuse to man the factories producing war materials." The local paper called it "dangerous talk," more appropriate for Moscow than Mississippi. It urged Crane to "stick to your Bible (not the Revised Standard Version) and leave the wars and fighting up to the Joint Chiefs of Staff."[2]

A week after Crane spoke, and before his comments could cause a controversy, the IHL board resolved that every speaker invited to a state-supported college "must first be investigated and approved by the head of the institution" and that the speaker's name had to be filed with the board. A week later, a representative proposed screening speakers to prevent one with an "anti-American way of life philosophy" from addressing students, and the house agreed by a vote of 109–10. The Ole Miss newspaper called the new policy "disastrous" and the "beginning of thought control." "Courage in seeking the truth has given way to expediency," charged the *Mississippian*, and the result would be that "bright people will not tolerate suppression of freedom of thought and they will go where they may have peace of mind." Campus groups called for repeal of the new policy. The Mississippi Southern College's *Student Printz* termed the policy "a violation of America's freedom of speech." When other newspapers criticized the policy, the board's executive secretary claimed, "Nobody's freedom is going to be suppressed." Hodding Carter called the response "double talk" that meant the board would not use the term "screening" but would in fact bar anyone "who might broach some controversial topic from an angle that differs from the prevailing Neanderthal attitude of the Legislature."[3]

Throughout the discord over Crane and speakers in general, nobody mentioned blacks or civil rights, but in the mid-1950s, fear of dissent always rested on white opposition to criticism of the racial status quo. The IHL board and the legislature demonstrated increasing intolerance of unorthodox ideas and a hardening of the segregationist position. More ominous evidence came later in 1955 with an outbreak of violence against blacks seeking to exercise their citizenship rights. In May the first Negro registered voter in Humphreys County in the Delta was shot to death as he drove in Belzoni. The sheriff ruled Reverend George Washington Lee's shotgun slaying resulted from an argument with another black man over a woman. Three months later in Brookhaven in southern Mississippi, a black activist was murdered in the middle of the day in front of the courthouse; the sheriff could find no witnesses and made no arrest. Later in the same month, the murder of Emmett Till occurred in the Delta. Shocked by the brazen violence against blacks, the NAACP publicized the horror in a pamphlet titled *M Is for Murder and Mississippi*. In the violent cauldron of an intolerant society seeking to extinguish all heresy, Reverend Campbell attempted his Christian witness.[4]

Will Davis Campbell was born in 1924 in Amite County, where one of his great-grandfathers settled in 1816. Campbell grew up on his father's small cotton farm in the southwestern corner of the state. Baptized at the age of seven, "Dave" Campbell was at seventeen ordained a Baptist minister. After studying from 1941 to 1943 at Louisiana College, he enlisted in the army and served as a medic in the South Pacific. He graduated from Wake Forest College in 1948 with a heightened social conscience. Four years later, with a Bachelor of Divinity degree from Yale University, he began his ministerial career at a small Baptist church in Taylor, Louisiana. Many in his congregation found his social activism unpalatable. He preached on workers' rights, Negro rights, and the danger of the far right in politics, but he also walked the picket line with strikers, paid his black maid the minimum wage, and visited black friends at Grambling College. One woman complained, "One Sunday you preach about [Senator Joseph] McCarthy and the next about Negroes." After a year and a half, Campbell decided the parish ministry was not for him.[5]

In August 1954, Campbell became the university's director of religious life. He wanted to live in his home state and to continue his ministry without a church. As chaplain, he served "as a co-ordinator, counselor, leader of group activities, [and] advisor on religious matters to the university administrative officials." In addition to being the executive secretary of the campus YMCA, he worked with student denominational groups. After an uneventful first year, Campbell in the fall of 1955 became embroiled in two controversies related to race.[6]

Both difficulties involved religious speakers Campbell brought to the campus through the auspices of the Committee of One Hundred. Consisting of students, faculty, and Oxford citizens, it invited to campus religious leaders for monthly lectures. Once a year in an intensive four-day period called Religious Emphasis Week, speakers addressed assemblies, spoke to classes, conducted seminars, and led discussions in dormitories and fraternity and sorority houses "to have their presence felt in every area of campus life." Each year after REW, the Committee of One Hundred designated a smaller committee to meet during the summer to select a theme and invite speakers for the next year. The director of religious life, as the primary official involved and as the experienced authority in the field, played a major role in advising the summer group.[7]

Campbell decided that the next REW should deal with Christianity and race relations. Realizing that open discussion would be provocative, he guided the summer committee to ensure that the individuals invited for the 1956 REW would be sympathetic to racial justice; though the assigned topics would not be explicitly racial, he believed questions dealing with segregation and discrimination would emerge from discussions. In effect, he tried to manipulate the committee to achieve his desired result. During the summer of 1955, the committee prepared to invite speakers for a February 20–22 REW. The topics would deal with religion and love, modern drama, foreign affairs, and politics. Instead of "religion and race relations," the committee took a euphemistic approach with "religion and human affairs." For speakers it selected a former director of the Methodist Wesley Foundation at Ole Miss, a Jesuit sociologist from New Orleans, a Presbyterian minister from Arkansas, an Episcopal rector from Ohio, and two laymen.[8]

As plans proceeded, one of the committee's monthly speakers visited in October. G. McLeod Bryan, a Baptist minister and professor of Christian ethics at Mercer University, gave a talk titled "Facing the Cultural Crisis." When he expressed an interest in visiting his friend Gene Cox, who lived on Providence Farm in Holmes County, Campbell agreed to take him. Though Campbell had never been to the county or met Cox, he had read newspaper accounts of a controversy involving Cox and Providence Farm and was interested in learning more about it.[9]

Before the trip, however, Bryan explained to a campus convocation that religion played a dual role as a conserver that "blesses the local mores" and as a "pioneering element" that "initiates social change." The "religion of the status quo" was in tension with the "religion of the inspired prophets." Pointing out that religion too often served only the conservative function, he said that the "culture which remains 'closed,' fighting all foreign ideas and killing off its prophets, all because it cannot stand change, is sure not to stand. It is doomed." Bryan reminded Christians that they had to be both "critical and redemptive," and he used segregation as his provocative illustration.[10]

White southerners, according to Bryan, "grievously separated preaching from politics," but in 1955 they had to reemphasize Christian ethics and turn the pulpit into an agent for change. Suggesting that southerners expand their idea of sin and redemption to include race relations, because "in the matter of civil rights we botch the Golden Rule," he warned that the "bigger the definition of sin, the more toes are stepped on." To encourage his audience, Bryan quoted Hodding Carter's response to his wife's caution: "Mama, somebody's got to do it." Bryan exhorted, "Somebody's got to do the dirty work. Christians responding to the Almighty God, seeking to convert and transform their culture, can say that with more force and meaning. We must say it!"[11]

Bryan's call for redeeming the white South by practicing the Golden Rule in its race relations pleased Will Campbell. That afternoon, the chancellor dropped Campbell a note saying he thought Bryan's speech was "splendid" and only regretted more had not heard it.[12]

After the convocation, Campbell and Bryan drove south to Providence Farm. Christian socialists established it in the late 1930s as an experiment in biracial living. By the 1950s, Dr. David Minter and A. Eugene Cox and their wives led the farm. Earlier, in October 1955, just weeks after the lynching of Emmett Till, Providence became embroiled in a dispute when several black boys allegedly frightened a white girl waiting for her school bus and another young Negro cursed a white woman. On edge after the Till lynching, whites found the young blacks, and leaders of the local Citizens' Council—including state senator Edwin White—grilled them for two hours about Providence Farm, where they sometimes played. The fearful youngsters' reports of interracial activities angered the whites. Three nights later at a mass meeting at a high school, Holmes County whites interrogated Cox and Minter. At the end of the meeting, five hundred voted that Providence Farm must dissolve and the residents leave the county.[13]

A week after the ultimatum, Bryan and Campbell spent several hours visiting the interracial community. When they left about midnight, the sheriff and the makings of a posse waited down the road. Pretending to go to his clinic,

Minter drove Campbell's car through a roadblock while the menacing whites took down the car's license number. Later, Minter got out of the car, and Campbell and Bryan drove back to Oxford. The next morning Chancellor Williams told Campbell that Representative Wilburn Hooker had come to campus and demanded to know what an Ole Miss employee had been doing the night before at Providence.[14] Although Campbell explained his trip, he took the call as a warning that the watching Citizens' Council would not tolerate any dissent on race. A more serious uproar over REW soon eclipsed Campbell's visit to Providence Farm.

Speakers for the 1956 REW included Reverend Alvin Kershaw on religion and modern drama. A native of Louisville, Kentucky, Kershaw graduated from the University of the South and went to seminary at Sewanee and the University of Chicago; he later did graduate work at Harvard and became a disciple of theologian Paul Tillich. After a pastorate in Bowling Green, Kentucky, Kershaw taught philosophy at Miami University in the late 1940s and 1950s while serving as rector at the Episcopal church. He met Will Campbell in 1954 at a meeting in Wisconsin where Kershaw spoke on theological implications of modern drama. Active in civil rights causes in Ohio, Kershaw and his wife had raised money for the NAACP's Legal Defense and Education Fund, Kershaw had served as vice president of the local NAACP chapter, and they had entertained blacks in their home.[15] Kershaw would, Campbell knew, voice liberal views if questions about race arose.

Between the invitation and his planned visit for REW, Kershaw gained national publicity on television. In 1955 he did a series of shows on religion and jazz for the Sunday network religious program *Look Up and Live*. As a youth in Louisville, Kershaw had heard many great jazz musicians on the riverboats and developed a keen interest in jazz. An Episcopal minister with expertise in jazz intrigued the staff of *The $64,000 Question*, and the new quiz show recruited him. For several weeks in the summer and fall of 1955, he flew to New York twice weekly—on Sunday for *Look Up and Live* and on Tuesday for the quiz show. After winning $32,000 in four appearances, Kershaw on November 1 decided not to continue for a chance to win $64,000. When asked about his plans for the money, Kershaw said he supposed he and his wife would give to the causes they supported. "One is a parish project for the resettlement of homeless and refugee people," he said. "The other is to help support the NAACP litigation in desegregation issues."[16]

Unaware of Kershaw's comments regarding the NAACP, Ole Miss's public relations office tried to capitalize on his fame by issuing a news release about his forthcoming REW appearance. In the state's newspapers, Kershaw's comments next to the university press release caused a storm of protest. Many white Mississippians could not believe that Ole Miss would invite an NAACP supporter to speak. The Citizens' Council demanded that his invitation be withdrawn. Will Campbell's careful plans had taken a wild and unexpected turn; REW appeared to flout the segregationist status quo. Within days the chancellor received many letters of protest. One alumnus objected that contributing to the NAACP "was a far worse offense than murder" and constituted "an accessory before the fact . . . in an act of treason . . . to destroy our public institutions." A Mississippi lumberman blasted the "poisonous tongues of heretics and the vile babblings of those opposed to our system of free enterprise" such as Kershaw. Another alumnus explained that Kershaw and other integrationist preachers had been duped by the communists and warned the chancellor that the affair might jeopardize state funding for the university.[17]

With a new legislature in January 1956, financial retribution must have seemed a real possibility to Chancellor Williams and other friends of Ole Miss. One Mississippian threatened to have his representatives "cut every penny off the budget of Ole Miss" if Kershaw spoke at REW. The mother of Walter Sillers, the powerful Speaker of the house, asked that Kershaw "never speak" at the university, and the Speaker's cousin, Florence Sillers Ogden, contended that to allow Kershaw to speak would be "a repudiation of all our State stands for." A Humphreys County representative objected to letting "an advocate of mongrelization" speak at the university. With unintended irony, Representative Lamar Moss argued that the citizens of a state who were "bleeding ourselves white financially" to support a dual school system would be "committing suicide" by inviting a friend of the NAACP to speak at Ole Miss. Even a legislator who thought Kershaw's speaking would cause no great harm still urged Williams to maintain a united front by withdrawing his invitation.[18]

James A. Morrow, a forty-two-year-old lawyer and state legislator from Rankin County, led the protests. Two days after Kershaw's statements, Morrow assured Williams that the members of his Brandon Episcopal church did not agree with Reverend Kershaw. "I do and will continue to believe in segregation, no matter what my religion or any preacher may say to the contrary," wrote Morrow, "and I know every other redblooded Mississippian feels the same." He called for revoking Kershaw's invitation but excused the persons responsible for inviting him because they must not have known of his attitudes. In the same letter in the *Jackson Clarion-Ledger*, Morrow suggested that Ole Miss "publicly rebuke him [Kershaw] as he publicly, on a national TV show, rebuked our way of life in the South by his intention to aid in the fight to desegregate the races."[19]

When the Kershaw story broke, Chancellor Williams was in Europe. In his absence, Vice Chancellor W. Alton Bryant explained that, when Kershaw was invited, university officials knew he was a southerner, had graduated from Sewanee, had worked with young people, and had expertise in music and drama. When the chancellor returned ten days later, he avoided dealing publicly with the matter by waiting until after the IHL board had considered the question.[20]

As John Herbers of the United Press International pointed out, "The University of Mississippi, through no fault of its own, has found itself squarely in the middle of the touchy segregation issue." Academic freedom clashed with the wishes of segregationist legislators who controlled the university's funding. Canceling Kershaw's appearance would, Herbers recognized, be seen as censorship, but permitting him to speak would invite retaliation by powerful forces in the state. Hodding Carter concurred. Admittedly disagreeing with Kershaw and the NAACP, the Greenville editor saw that the university was "torn between financial support on the one hand and intellectual honesty on the other." Defending Kershaw's right to speak, he argued that if the university submitted to the "obvious censorship of ideas, it would begin to lose its intellectual freedom, its ability to teach objectively, and its attraction to students who want to learn, and not be spoon-fed." Williams, caught in the bind, dodged questions of free speech, academic freedom, and the importance of a free exchange of ideas. He did remark, "This is when I wish I were a professor."[21]

While the chancellor refused comment, the university garnered some backing among Mississippians. Support came from two young lawyers and alumni, Maurice Dantin and Tom Bourdeaux. Although Dantin disagreed with Kershaw on the NAACP, he wanted to protect the university's reputation by letting Kershaw participate in REW. Bourdeaux recalled the chancellor's statement in 1948 that he would leave if unpopular beliefs could not be espoused on the campus, and he urged Williams to resist intimidation. Kershaw's fellow Episcopal priests provided the widest approval for him. From Meridian, Reverend Duncan M. Hobart denied that Morrow spoke for the diocese. According to Oxford's A. Emile Joffrion, the "infantile and petty measures" used by Kershaw's opponents to keep him from the campus would cause an "irreparable loss of prestige" for the university. Duncan M. Gray Jr., a minister in Cleveland, hoped that Ole Miss would "refuse to knuckle under to the implied threats of fearful little men," because if it did, Mississippi could have a "repetition of what happened in Germany under Hitler."[22]

In a survey nearly three-fourths of the students thought Kershaw should be allowed to speak. Opposing any censoring of Kershaw even if he did support the NAACP, the *Mississippian* opined, "The citizens councils have failed to grasp the meaning of a university." Critics claimed he "opposed our way of life" and might "lead some immature student astray." Others suggested inviting Kershaw and then either pelting him with eggs or totally ignoring him. A law student was more adamant: "We have to take a strong stand on this. You can't be a little bit pregnant: either you are or you aren't." Without endorsing the NAACP or Kershaw, the student senate on November 16 overwhelmingly asked Chancellor Williams not to cancel Kershaw's appearance.[23]

The IHL board met in Jackson two days later to consider the Kershaw commotion, and two weeks after the dispute started it moved rapidly toward a resolution. In the chancellor's absence, Vice Chancellor Bryant, an alumnus and a longtime English professor married to the niece of former chancellor Alfred Hume, represented the university. After relating the history of Kershaw's invitation, Bryant argued that no legal basis existed for denying Kershaw's visit and explained that withdrawing the invitation would suggest a new policy of barring anyone who supported any organization, including many religious ones, that opposed segregation. Apparently uncertain what to do, the board delayed action until its December meeting.[24]

The board's inaction did not calm the storm over Kershaw. While unyielding segregationists pummeled Ole Miss and the chancellor, other events fueled racial tensions. The sensational Emmett Till case continued into November as a grand jury considered indicting on kidnapping charges the two men acquitted in Till's death. Also in November the Supreme Court ordered an end to segregation in public recreational facilities, and early in December the Montgomery bus boycott began. Perhaps the most inflammatory incident occurred when William Faulkner spoke on race relations at a historical convention in Memphis. He raised the ire of some Mississippi white supremacists when he declared, "To live anywhere in the world of A.D. 1955 and be against equality because of race or color, is like living in Alaska and being against snow."[25]

In reaction to Faulkner's comments, Senator Edwin White of Lexington reiterated the fears of many whites and their worries about Kershaw. The segregationist said that "the South's true reason for insistence upon the continuation of segregation is to preserve the racial integrity of its people" because "racial amalgamation is against the will of God." Support for integration came not from the masses of Negroes but from a "blatant group of white writers, politicians, *educators and clergymen.*" Fearing the apocalypse of "a mixed breed population," White believed that "the white parenthood of the South will not agree to the death of their race by sending their children to integrated schools."[26] Kershaw's invitation had, therefore, not just symbolic importance but also posed a literal threat to their way of life.

Most of the state's newspapers opposed Kershaw. From the state's northeast corner, the *Itawamba County Times* suggested that Chancellor Williams should instead invite one of the many "ministers who have a knowledge of God and His Son, Jesus Christ, and who know that segregation is of God." The *Kosciusko Star* thought that inviting a supporter of the NAACP to speak was "too much like coddling a viper in your own bosom." Alumnus Elmore D. Greaves discounted academic questions involving rights and instead argued for the paramount importance of avoiding "annihilation" of the white race and maintaining its "racial hegemony."[27]

Segregationists did not go unchallenged. In the Ole Miss newspaper, one reader logically replied to Greaves: "If the hegemony of the white race is destined or ordained, there is no need for suppression, regression, intimidation, and violence." A former *Mississippian* editor, Navy ensign Paul Pittman, wondering if politicians "fear the light of honest inquiry into the foundations of our 'southern way of life,'" contended that the "policy of ignoring a problem, in order to solve it" was unwise, so he supported allowing Kershaw to speak. Newspapers at Mississippi State College and Mississippi Southern College agreed, and the moderate *Jackson State Times* thought the whole Kershaw question had been "magnified . . . out of all proportions to its real importance," and it hoped Kershaw would be allowed to speak."[28]

While the debate continued, Campbell covertly worked to make sure that REW would have the desired impact. Initially he had hoped that the participants would, if questioned during REW, speak as Christians against racial segregation and discrimination. Once the Kershaw controversy began, however, Campbell's indirect challenge changed into a more open attack on racial orthodoxy; he hastily devised a new plan with three simple parts. First, in his discussions with the administration, Campbell refused to be a conciliator or compromiser and made clear that he would not be a party to withdrawing Kershaw's invitation. In every other way, however, he tried to keep anyone from detecting his involvement. Second, he wanted Kershaw not to withdraw voluntarily from REW. Third, Campbell encouraged the other participants to remain committed to REW and, if Kershaw's invitation were canceled, to withdraw from the program.[29] Campbell's plan would yield one of two results. In the better outcome, REW would proceed with Kershaw and the other invited participants and would include discussion of the role of Christianity in achieving racial justice. The second, less desirable outcome would involve a cancellation of Kershaw's invitation and the withdrawal of all the others as well in a major public showdown with the Citizens' Councils over race and freedom of speech and religion.

Campbell involved the participants in his schemes. Reverend Joe Earl Elmore, the Methodist minister to Ole Miss students from 1952 to 1954 and in

1955 a pastor in New York City, cooperated with Campbell. Accomplices also included Reverend Emile Joffrion of St. Peter's Episcopal Church in Oxford. A Laurel native, a graduate of the University of the South, and a World War II veteran, Joffrion came to Oxford about the same time Campbell did, and they had become friends. Joffrion helped by communicating with the scheduled speakers. Immediately after the controversy began in early November, for example, Joffrion tried to explain the gravity of the situation to Kershaw. He and Campbell described the opposition as "part of a death struggle of desperate men" and said the clergymen could "not back up one inch and still live with ourselves." Campbell compared the "fantastic" situation to a "mental ward." Though aware of the administration's hope that the storm would quietly pass with Kershaw's withdrawal, the two clergy prepared for battle with the "monstrously evil power" of legislators led by the Citizens' Councils. Even threats of economic reprisals aimed at the university did not dissuade Campbell. He told Kershaw that the Citizens' Council "is threatening to close the university if you come. Can you imagine! I say let them close it!! If we can't have a university the doors might as well be closed."[30]

In Ohio, Reverend Kershaw received letters urging him not to come to Ole Miss. They questioned his faith, suggested he was a communist ally, and challenged him to consider that his work would lead to racial mongrelization. "God created and SEGREGATED the races," a man from Long Beach, Mississippi, declared, "and no individual, executive, court, or Congress has either the moral or spiritual right to defy his will by ordering or allowing racial integration." A New Orleans man hoped that Kershaw's children would marry Negroes "so that your grand children will be the mongrels you wish to make out of the white people of this country."[31]

The fight had more importance for Campbell than for Kershaw. Worried that Kershaw might succumb to the pressures, Campbell traveled to Cincinnati to urge him to continue. Joined by officials from the Southern Regional Council and the national YMCA, as well as a professor from Miami University, the two ministers discussed the developing battle. After a few hours, all knew they would continue the fight.[32] Despite the pressures and embarrassing publicity, Kershaw did not retreat, and the dispute continued.

On December 15, the day of the IHL board's scheduled meeting, the *Jackson Daily News* weighed in to deny that withdrawal of Kershaw's invitation would violate his right to free speech. It agreed with the Citizens' Council that any NAACP supporter was an enemy of the southern way of life and should be barred from speaking. Kershaw had a "poisonous" mind "impregnated with the teaching of the NAACP—integration, social equality, miscegenation, mixed marriages and mongrelization of the white race." Moreover, communism had infiltrated the NAACP. "To invite the serving of that kind of mental food," declared the *Daily News*, "is akin to asking that your breakfast be served from the slop and swill of the garbage can."[33]

The trustees' agenda did not include the Kershaw question, but they discussed it informally and took no action. Though in attendance, the chancellor remained silent. In response a frustrated and disappointed Morrow announced that in January he would introduce a resolution to ban Kershaw's visit. He could not risk waiting until the trustees met again in January because Kershaw was scheduled to come in February. At Ole Miss, students supported Morrow's position by circulating a petition opposing Kershaw's visit. Nearly three hundred students expressed their "desire to link ourselves with the great mass of [white] Mississippians desiring to uphold segregation in this State of Mississippi" and called on the chancellor to cancel Kershaw's invitation.[34] Chancellor Williams silently temporized, hoped the commotion would naturally subside, and waited for possible board action in January.

The chancellor's strategy seemed to succeed. Passions appeared to cool as the press, politicians, and public paid greater attention to the inauguration of a new governor and to the upcoming legislative session. In December of 1955, Senator James Eastland, Representative John Bell Williams, and Judge Tom P. Brady called for their state to endorse interposition, the theory that a state can place itself between a court order and its people and thereby block the effect of the court ruling. The desired result would be to nullify the *Brown* decision in Mississippi. Although Governor-elect J. P. Coleman opposed interposition, he did not waver in his opposition to integration, and Mississippians waited anxiously to hear his program for dealing with the racial problem. At the same time, legislators prepared several bills to effectively outlaw the NAACP, to establish a committee to monitor subversive organizations, and to create an agency to preserve segregation.[35] As 1955 yielded to 1956, racial discord intensified.

At its regular meeting on January 19, the IHL board finally considered the Kershaw case. With Chancellor Williams present, the trustees received the petition from Ole Miss students. More important, the board learned that Kershaw had cleared the screening process required of all speakers. In the middle of the discussion, one trustee, J. Oliver Emmerich, editor of the *McComb Enterprise-Journal*, left the room and telephoned Kershaw directly. To clarify the issues, Emmerich asked Kershaw if the press had misquoted him about his financial support for the NAACP. Kershaw explained that he had been misquoted and that in the press conference after his final appearance on *The $64,000 Question* he had not made a definite commitment to the civil rights organization; he had only indicated that he and his wife would probably use the money to support causes promoting justice and understanding, and one of them was the NAACP's legal effort to end segregation. Kershaw explained that he did not try to correct the misunderstanding because he did not want to appear to be disagreeing with the NAACP's work. He also reminded Emmerich that his topic for REW was not integration but religion and drama.[36]

Emmerich reported back to his fellow trustees that Kershaw had been misquoted in the press about his commitment to the NAACP. After they heard James Morrow's objections to Kershaw, the trustees adopted a resolution to end the matter. The board acknowledged that Kershaw was not a member of any group blacklisted by the FBI or of any un-American organization. It praised him as an "outstanding" minister of growing "national recognition in using drama to emphasize, demonstrate, and portray Christian principles," and it characterized the accusations against the southern clergyman as "vague and apparently unfounded" because "none of these accusations could be substantiated."[37]

Regarding Kershaw's racial views, the board justified its position in three ways. First, it stressed that Kershaw would talk on drama and Christianity and "not on any other subject." Second, it rationalized that withdrawing his invitation "would be just what the NAACP would covet most and would be used as propaganda against our state." Third, the board did not want to prolong the "sideline incident" because it "divert[ed] national attention away from the primary goal which is the maintenance of segregated schools in Mississippi." In conclusion, the board declared the disposition of Kershaw's invitation an administrative matter left to Ole Miss officials.[38]

Within hours of the decision, and after speaking with Kershaw, Morrow publicly apologized to the Ohio Episcopalian, to the university, and to the Committee of One Hundred "for any embarrassment I may have caused." Without changing his views on the NAACP in the slightest, Morrow expressed his "exhilaration" that Reverend Kershaw had been misquoted and misled into giving inaccurate statements to the press. The Brandon lawyer and representative also voiced relief that nothing implied that his Episcopal church supported integration.[39]

The IHL board's action and Morrow's apology pleased and relieved Chancellor Williams. He told Morrow, "Nothing that has occurred to me for a long time has been as encouraging, as inspiring, or as soul satisfying as your statement." The chancellor also appreciated Emmerich's call to Kershaw because his report constituted the turning point in the deliberations. As a result of the board's decision, Williams notified Kershaw that he had decided to let his invitation stand without further public comment. The "Kershaw incident had been laid to rest," he hoped. "The University has been saved great embarrassment. Its prestige has been maintained."[40] He rejoiced too soon.

When Will Campbell met with the chancellor, he learned that Emmerich had apparently not told the IHL board that Kershaw belonged to the NAACP— or perhaps Emmerich did not even understand it from his conversation with Kershaw. Even Chancellor Williams may not have comprehended that Kershaw was an active member of the civil rights organization. Campbell told Kershaw that Williams and some trustees "would prefer not to know that you [Kershaw] are active in the NAACP. If they don't know it they are covered." In the confusion, Campbell worried that a clarification by Kershaw would bring charges of trying to restart the controversy, yet if he refused to come to the university, critics would claim that all he had ever wanted was a fight over the NAACP. Admitting "it is difficult to know what to say or do at this point," Campbell counseled Kershaw to tell of his direct involvement with the NAACP. Kershaw soon got his chance.[41]

Four days after the board of trustees tried to settle the matter, the *Mississippian* editor wrote Kershaw for his side of the controversy. In response Kershaw on January 28 sent a lengthy letter to the *Mississippian* and a similar letter to the chancellor. Chagrined that his comments embarrassed Mississippi, he regretted that he had not quickly clarified his position, but he had assumed that people would understand that "a true university is the matrix of open academic discussion and free inquiry, of responsible consideration of alternative positions on any issue." Kershaw also expressed to Williams his distress that both the board's statement and Morrow's apology seemed unaware of important facts that he had stressed to Emmerich in their telephone conversation. Regarding his statement about contributing his winnings to the NAACP, Kershaw emphasized that he had been misquoted about his specific plans but not about his "convictions and concerns." He also declared that he planned to speak on modern drama but could not conceive that "discussion and questions on segregation would not be a natural and inevitable part of student interest," and he would answer from his own convictions.[42]

To make sure the chancellor and others at Ole Miss understood his position and to take his stand without any deceit, Kershaw spelled out his "spiritual and organizational whereabouts." As a Christian who believed the "core of the Faith is love of God and neighbor," he affirmed that all men were "of equal worth as children of God." As an active, contributing member of the NAACP, he supported its efforts "to bring to realization what in ideal and in principle is consistent with democratic tradition." As a southerner, he found distressing the Mississippi atmosphere that "smothered the freedom necessary to all democratic thought."[43]

At a hasty meeting at the chancellor's home, Williams and several key advisers discussed what to do. Enmeshed in what he saw as a "tangled . . . clouded, distorted" mess, Williams wanted most to avoid any incident that could become a "spark to ignite an explosive situation." After the group summoned Campbell, the chancellor pressed for the chaplain to withdraw Kershaw's invitation, but Campbell refused. Williams then decided to contact Kershaw personally. Unable to reach him by telephone on February 2, he notified Kershaw by telegram that he was withdrawing his invitation. Claiming that Kershaw withheld information from Emmerich and implicitly had deceived him as well, Williams maintained that Kershaw's letter to the *Mississippian* "will provoke additional controversy inconsistent" with the purposes of REW. As a result Williams had decided that his appearance would be "unwise."[44]

The *Jackson Clarion-Ledger* judged that the chancellor had acted "wisely" because "Kershaw has nothing to emphasize that is worth listening to." Suspicious of the "Communist infiltrated" NAACP, it did not believe that Kershaw had been misquoted about giving part of his winnings to the NAACP, and it ridiculed Kershaw's area of expertise—jazz. "Jazz is not music, from the spiritual viewpoint. Jazz music was born among savages in the dark jungles of Africa," the editor claimed. " 'Jazz' is a slang word which originally meant illicit sexual intercourse," in which Africans engaged in public orgies, including "every manner of revolting vice." According to the editor, "The mumbo jumbo of jazz can never replace the 'Rock of Ages,' and 'Jesus, Lover of My Soul.' " The attack ended by dismissing Kershaw for being "as ignorant as a Hottentot concerning that sublime and inextinguishable thing known as the Southern way of life. Mister Kershaw! Oh, pshaw! Likewise, fiddlesticks!" The *Jackson Daily News* said "good riddance" to the speakers: "There is not time or place on a platform in Mississippi for men . . . who are so shallow-minded that they cannot see what integration, miscegenation, mixed marriages and mongrelization of the white race would mean in the South—or anywhere else, for that matter."[45]

On the evening of February 7, before the regular monthly meeting of the Men's Faculty Club, the chancellor defended his decision. "If Rev. Kershaw had come here it would have wrecked the entire Religious Emphasis Week program," an emotional Williams declared. "Everybody would have gone to hear him. The campus would have been full of newspaper, radio and television reporters. There would have been a student demonstration of some kind." Showing the strain of recent events, he maintained that he had averted an incident "similar to the tragedy at the University of Alabama," where a mob of white segregationists had earlier in the week so disrupted the campus that the board of trustees had expelled Autherine Lucy, the first Negro to enroll at the university. Williams conceded that the Kershaw incident would damage the university's prestige but not as much as the convulsion his appearance would have caused.[46]

Before most Mississippians could react, Morton B. King resigned as professor of sociology, effective at the end of the school year. A member of the faculty since 1939, except for the war years, King served as chairman of his department and of the Friends of the Library. A native of Tennessee, he had studied at Vanderbilt University and the University of Wisconsin. In December he had warned the provost that he would resign if the chancellor withdrew Kershaw's invitation, and eight weeks later he did. King declared that Williams's cancellation of the invitation was "the immediate and precipitating reason" for his resignation. Without specifics, King referred also to an "accumulation" of grievances involving "such essential prerequisites of higher education as freedom of thought, inquiry, and speech."[47]

Though King believed that many faculty took his side but repressive forces kept them silent, he never claimed that the university had literally violated his academic freedom in the classroom or in his scholarship. On the other hand, the local chapter of the American Association of University Professors (AAUP) concluded that academic freedom was not involved in the Kershaw case and that the faculty "overwhelmingly" sided with Chancellor Williams because they thought Kershaw had not been forthcoming with the board about his ties to the NAACP. The AAUP chapter also decided that Morton King's resignation did not result from any abridgement of his academic freedom. Acknowledging that "the *threat* to academic freedom is very real in Mississippi," the local AAUP president believed that the "general climate of opinion in the State is extremely discouraging," and he contended that the "entire question [surrounding Kershaw] is inextricably involved with the segregation issue."[48]

In a joint statement on February 7, J. D. Williams and Morton King announced King's resignation. Elaborating on his reasons, King granted that the chancellor had acted in good faith but maintained that recent events had demonstrated that the "administration and the Board are no longer able to defend, here and on other campuses of the state, the freedom of thought, inquiry, and speech which are essential for higher education to flourish." A member of the Committee of One Hundred, King also thought the state had "unnecessarily infringed upon the freedom of voluntary religious activities" that he cherished. As a result, he could not be happy or a good scholar or teacher at Ole Miss. Williams repeated his earlier written statement to King that he accepted his resignation with "sincere regret" because his departure would be "a distinct loss" to the institution.[49]

Many legislators proved less understanding. Senator George Yarbrough of Red Banks introduced a resolution to prevent King from finishing his contract because of his "actions against the welfare and best interests of the people of the state of Mississippi" and called for the chancellor to pay him the remainder of his salary but order him to leave the campus. Fifteen other senators joined in sponsoring an amended resolution that urged King to leave "at his convenience."[50] Before the legislature could act, the crisis expanded.

On February 8 at Mississippi State College, William Buchanan resigned as assistant professor of government. As he explained to President Ben F. Hilbun, "When ministers are prevented from speaking to students, and editors [e.g. Hodding Carter] from speaking to faculty members, and when trustees feel they must screen not only our speakers but our thoughts, it appears to me that a college cannot perform its functions as an institution of higher learning." He wanted to resign "*before* the law is passed which might make the expression of these sentiments a criminal act." Buchanan, a Virginian with a Princeton doctorate who married a Mississippi woman, regretted leaving but saw no alternative. Hilbun reacted differently than Williams had to King. Denying Buchanan's charges, Hilbun argued that he would "yield to no man in cherishing academic freedom." Hilbun accepted his resignation effective immediately because his statements had severely damaged his usefulness at the college; he did, however, continue Buchanan's salary at the discretion of the president and the trustees.[51]

After the tumultuous week, pundits, politicians, and partisans of Ole Miss praised Chancellor Williams. The house of representatives overwhelmingly lauded Williams and Hilbun for their handling of the dissident professors. Branding Buchanan and King "moral derelicts," one representative declared, "We need to weed the likes of them out of our colleges. There will never be a white man who favors integration who is not a sex degenerate, whether he be in the pulpit or the classroom," he seethed. "I thank God I am a white man." Representative Russell Fox agreed: "We have the right to make sure our children's minds are not taught things contrary to our views, just as we have the right to refuse to have our daughters taught the profits of prostitution."[52]

More temperately the *Jackson Clarion-Ledger* expressed "greatest confidence" in Williams and Hilbun and suggested King and Buchanan had only brought attention to themselves, put their interests above their students, abandoned a ship when under fire, and not helped their ostensible cause of academic freedom by resigning. Political columnist Charles M. Hills dismissed the professors as "pink fringed professors" who had been "filling the young minds of our youth with things contrary to our way of life." The *Mississippian* editor "wholeheartedly back[ed]" Williams's decision regarding Kershaw. Other friends of Ole Miss also supported Williams's stands. Stokes V. Robertson Jr., a Hinds County chancery judge, thought that Williams had been "100% right" in his handling of Kershaw and that professors should not be allowed to teach against the state's constitution and policies. Segregationist Tom Brady thought canceling Kershaw's engagement would help allay fears that Ole Miss contained a "hotbed of left-wing socialists." Governor Coleman strongly endorsed the college leaders. Although he had initially preferred that Reverend Kershaw be allowed to speak, he changed his mind after Kershaw wrote "the silliest three-page letter I've ever read explaining his activities for racial integration." Coleman denied that thought control existed at the institutions. "They belong to the people," Coleman explained, "and the people of Mississippi have the right to demand that teachers expounding against our way of life be ousted," and he insisted that closing the state colleges to prevent integration would be "as inevitable as the sunrise" because Mississippians "would not support integrated schools."[53]

More privately, people reproached Williams, especially when compared to Hilbun. Senator White of Lexington, for example, expressed keen disappointment that the Ole Miss chancellor had regretted King's resignation because White had for several years heard reports that sociologists at the university endorsed integration. Unlike Williams, Hilbun received a telegram from several members of the legislature—including George Yarbrough, Buddy Newman, and Russell Fox—complimenting him on his quick, decisive treatment of Buchanan. Wilburn Hooker and Jim Morrow, two of J. D. Williams's strongest critics, also congratulated Hilbun. A Natchez resident implored Hilbun, "Please don't let Miss. State fall to the depths of Ole Miss," while the mayor of Forest admitted he wanted Williams to do exactly what Hilbun had done "instead of letting [King] hang around until May."[54]

The most telling criticism of Williams's revocation of Kershaw's invitation came from the other speakers invited to REW. Will Campbell called Joe Elmore in New York, and Elmore then told the other participants what had happened to Kershaw. After further conversations, each one of them withdrew, just as Campbell had designed. Joseph H. Fichter, a Catholic priest and sociologist at Loyola University in New Orleans, considered the action toward Kershaw "intolerant and irresponsible." An Arkansas Presbyterian minister, George Chauncey, objected to the cancellation of the invitation as "unjust because it implies that his stand against racial segregation disqualifies him as a suitable religious leader." Francis Pickens Miller was the last to withdraw. The Virginia layman, "distressed beyond measure" at what had happened to Kershaw, notified Campbell that the "Christian cause would be better served" by his not participating in REW.[55]

The nondenominational *Christian Century* hit the university especially hard, when it observed that "there will be no Religious Emphasis Week at the University of Mississippi because religion was emphasized." Seeing real Christian faith in action, it praised the "humbling courage" of Kershaw and the other invited speakers who stuck to their principles and withdrew. "Even more courageous" were Morton King and William Buchanan for resigning their secure positions in protest. At the same time, it pointed to the "humiliating cowardice" of the state and university leaders; it especially criticized Williams for readily accepting King's resignation.[56]

Perhaps the most damning criticism of Ole Miss and Williams came from Joe Elmore, who knew both well from his years in Oxford. Elmore withdrew because "to do anything else would make a mockery of the Christian, democratic and educational convictions I hold." He expressed his "shock that an academic institution dedicated to the search for truth would carefully screen all prospective speakers to its campus towards the end of excluding anyone whose views might be controversial. The action of the University of Mississippi is an affront to the maturity and intelligence of its students, faculty, and staff and it is a disservice to education, democracy, and the Christian faith." To J. D. Williams, Elmore defended the essential freedom to speak, even if wrong, and declared his belief, "on pragmatic, democratic, and indeed Christian grounds, that the university must be kept as a primary locus of this freedom. . . . It cannot simply reflect the ideas and attitudes of its area . . . else it is no longer a university." Unwilling to dodge the issue of segregation, Elmore stated his position: "I can only come to the simple conclusion that it is fundamentally wrong—irrational, unAmerican, and unChristian." He concluded with a plea for that "redemptive love that will heal our collective sickness and make us whole."[57]

The withdrawal of the out-of-state participants left REW with virtually no program. Some students began moves to invite leading segregationists such as Judge Brady, author of *Black Monday*, and Reverend G. T. Gillespie, president emeritus of Belhaven College, who in 1954 had written "The Christian View of Segregation." For Will Campbell, such speakers would be the antithesis of what he had wanted for REW, and if the original team could not be involved, he preferred to dramatize the conflict with the Citizens' Councils by canceling the entire program. The final decision rested with the Committee of One Hundred and its executive committee. In what one observer called a "stormy session" and what Campbell called "quite a fight," the executive committee on February 13 discussed plans for REW. Before considering new participants, it debated whether to explain to Reverend Kershaw that the university's action did not necessarily reflect the committee's views; after heated exchanges, the committee decided only to express its regret to Kershaw and the others who had pulled out. In its main discussion, Campbell managed to get the committee to reject inviting segregationists in favor of a compromise to invite the Oxford clergy to lead REW. Campbell had been tempted to go along with invitations to the segregationists just to see if the chancellor would accept them after rejecting Kershaw, but he decided he did not want to put the Committee of One Hundred on record as having invited them and did not want to run the risk that Williams would approve them.[58]

Though Campbell feared the local ministers might participate, his friend Emile Joffrion persuaded them to decline. The five ministers worried that their participation or nonparticipation would be misinterpreted. They also believed that the whole "controversy would make it difficult to maintain an atmosphere in which real religious values could be given proper consideration." They recommended that REW "be suspended this year."[59]

The next afternoon the executive committee met again. To solve the problem over REW, Will Campbell offered a solution—a period of prayer and meditation. To "salvage what it could of this REW," the committee unanimously approved Campbell's recommendation that came in his first public statement throughout the entire controversy: "On each of the three days . . . I shall walk into Fulton Chapel at 10 o'clock and sit for thirty minutes in silent meditation and prayer. The organ will play suitable religious music. I extend a most sincere and cordial invitation to all students, faculty, staff and townspeople to join me. This call to prayer is not a display of superficial piety. It is rather the recognition that we have gone as far as we can go and perhaps it is upon such admission that God chooses to order human history."[60] The administration and Oxford clergy agreed with the new plan, and it worked. Each morning several hundred people joined Campbell for a quiet time. The auditorium stage had only a drawn curtain and two empty chairs. REW had finally come to a peaceful end.

For Will Campbell the long controversy had been a personal ordeal. At first he worked behind the scenes, was willing to "play dumb" when necessary, and hoped to deceive the administration. In the fall as the crisis began, he relished the fight and even signed a letter to Kershaw, "On with the revolution." He had tried to follow "a moderate course" but by Thanksgiving found "no longer any room for the least amount of dissent." He began to see the opposition as "dangerous and evil," but he had not given up hope and instead called on friends to support the chancellor.[61]

By the time Kershaw's invitation was withdrawn, however, Campbell realized that the whole controversy threatened his position at Ole Miss, but also more than ever he believed that he had been right. He tired of the generally unknown "little manipulations, the pressures, the innuendos" from the administration and others in the state. Although he granted that the chancellor and others involved thought they were right, he feared that the "truth is that which fits, which saves someone or protects an idea." He found the circumstances "frightening to the point that I no longer know what to do personally." He wanted to stay in Mississippi as part of an "underground movement" testifying to "the greater truth of the Gospel even to the point of subterfuge and what some would call dishonesty," but increasingly he knew that his foe was dangerous. All around him he saw "Mississippi madness" that he described as "the madness of black folks and white folks hating one another." Campbell considered departing the state and leaving it all to the Citizens' Council. At the height of the crisis in early February, worried that his surreptitious role would be discovered, he realized that the choice might not be his, that he might be forced out of his job and Mississippi. A month later he thought his chances of remaining had decreased, and he seemed more committed than ever to the overt promotion of racial change. In his last letter to Al Kershaw, he again closed, "On with the revolution!"[62] The exclamation point marked a change from his almost teasing use of the same line four months earlier—the events had had a radicalizing effect on Will Campbell.

Campbell's decision regarding his employment became easier when the National Council of Churches decided to hire someone to work in the South on race relations. In early May 1956 Campbell accepted the position and submitted his resignation to the university. He was not fired; in fact, he had for the next year received a raise, though less than that awarded other department heads. The dean of student personnel told Campbell of his deep regret that he had decided to leave. "You have done an excellent job and I had great hopes for the program under your administration," he declared. "I have particularly admired your level-headedness and cooperation under difficult circumstances, yet, I am sure without compromise of your principles." J. D. Williams expressed his distress: "I cannot imagine anyone that we can get to take your place who will be able to do as well as if you had stayed. You and your family have been a source of strength to students and faculty in our community." Later the chancellor and several other administrators sent Will Campbell some luggage as a present, and Campbell responded in a handwritten note thanking the chancellor for "the fine job you're doing for the old home state."[63]

Two final events in the early summer of 1956 illustrated Campbell's precarious place at Ole Miss. At the opening of summer school in June, Campbell's office of religious life held a party at the YMCA building for students. Refreshments included punch in a large bowl. A minister who worked with one of the campus religious groups suggested Campbell examine the punch. He discovered floating in the icy fruit punch a piece of human feces apparently powdered with sugar. When Campbell complained to Hugh Clegg, an assistant to the chancellor and a former FBI agent, Clegg said it would be impossible to figure out who put it there.[64] The perpetrator's identity really did not matter because Campbell understood its message.

Another incident at the YMCA building in June caused a bit more commotion. Campbell had befriended John E. Cameron, a young black Oxford minister and encouraged him to apply for a university correspondence course. Because no black student had ever enrolled at Ole Miss, Campbell thought the easiest way to break the racial barrier might be through a correspondence course. One evening after visiting the Negro pastor, Campbell suggested they drop by his YMCA office to check the regulations. After consulting the university catalog, Campbell's friend spied a Ping-Pong table and suggested they play a game.[65]

Before their Ping-Pong game really got started, W. M. "Chubby" Ellis, an acting registrar for summer school and an assistant in the registrar's office, spotted the two men playing. After their game, Campbell gave his friend a ride home. When he returned to the YMCA building, he found Ellis and another man waiting. After a short confrontation over whether the minister playing Ping-Pong with Campbell was a Negro, the two observers left. When the dean of student personnel learned of the incident, he called both Campbell and Ellis to his office that night for an emergency meeting. Campbell and Ellis each interpreted the meeting as a reprimand. Ellis thought the administration was worried that he would take some reprisal against the Negro minister or turn the incident into a public brouhaha. Campbell, on the other hand, believed the administration was expressing its displeasure with his agitating the race question by publicly associating with a Negro and, worse yet, playing a game with him.[66]

Soon after the Ping-Pong game, Will Campbell left Ole Miss, but the race issue continued to haunt the university. To maintain the institution's integrity, Williams had engaged in what he conceded were "compromises and rationalizations" as he dealt with the Citizens' Council, alumni, politicians, and his faculty over academic freedom and race relations. He recognized the dangers of compromise but concluded, "I haven't compromised too far." In many ways like Will Campbell, he struggled over whether he should "leave or stay and do the best that can be done." In the spring of 1956, after the Kershaw episode, Williams concluded that he had "been able to do the latter in all good conscience."[67]

The chancellor's penchant for a safe middle position often satisfied nobody. As a result of the crisis over Kershaw and King, doubts increased about Williams's resolve in the face of pressures for racial change. At the peak of the uproar, Edwin White had chided him "because you have never publicly stated your position on segregation." If he could not support the state segregation policy, White maintained, "then it does seem that your remaining on as Chancellor will not be in the best interest of the institution or of the State."[68]

At the same time, faculty such as Morton King found that Williams's inclination toward compromise meant that "expediency may become administrative policy. And expediency usually compromises away that integrity of purpose, of ends and principles, without which both the scholarship of faculty and the learning of students lacks moral as well as intellectual fiber." He thought Williams and his administration had been ineffective in coping with the "moral and intellectual climate in the state which threatens" the university. King concluded that political interference and funding shortages were strangling the university.[69] The civil rights movement's increasing momentum and the stiffening resistance to change caught Ole Miss and its chancellor in the middle.

8. Nemesis of the Southern Way of Life—Jim Silver

Many alumni of Ole Miss and leaders in Mississippi knew Chancellor Williams because he spoke to alumni groups and worked with the political and economic elite, but few ordinary citizens would have recognized his name. Similarly, Dean Robert Farley of the law school had a strong reputation limited largely to the legal community. The best-known Ole Miss personality and a genuine hero to many was, of course, football coach Johnny Vaught. Another well-known representative of the university in the 1950s was James W. Silver, a history professor.

Silver, who had taught American history at the university since 1936, was anything but a hero to most white Mississippians. Beginning in the late 1930s, he acquired a reputation as a radical because of his unconventional positions on controversial issues. His speeches and letters to editors made him a target for conservatives and a negative symbol of Ole Miss. Early on, his views on the New Deal and labor unions made him notorious. Accusations that he was a communist fellow traveler primed his opponents for attacks when around 1950 he began to address racial issues. Gradually growing to advocate black civil rights and to criticize white supremacists, he became the nemesis of the "southern way of life." Because conservatives often conflated support for unions and for civil rights, Silver's stands on class and race compounded his vulnerability. Legislators and editors regularly damned his apostasy. Following his exploration of the pathological "closed society" in Mississippi, Silver became, according to one observer, "the most hated man in Mississippi."[1]

Part of the animosity toward Silver derived from his Yankee origins and his suspected Jewish background. James Wesley Silver was a native of New York, but he was not a Jew. His ancestors—the Silvers and the Squiers—had come from England and had settled first on farms in New Hampshire before moving in the 1820s to western New York. In Rochester, Henry Dayton Silver, Jim Silver's father, owned a thriving grocery business and was a staunch capitalist and conservative Republican. For years Henry Silver wanted to retire and move away from the terrible winters, and he worked hard to finance the move. In 1920, the Silver family finally moved to Southern Pines, North Carolina, a small resort town on a New York-to-Florida railroad line where northerners escaped during the winter to enjoy golf and tennis.[2]

After graduating as high school valedictorian, Jim Silver enrolled at the University of North Carolina. Though a good enough student to qualify for Phi Beta Kappa, the "inveterate loner" remained largely unaffected by the university's intellectual life, which he recalled "did little to expand my horizons." In his senior year, the student council expelled Silver and a dozen other students for violating the honor code by lying to student officials about gambling, but Silver had already accumulated enough credits to graduate.[3]

Silver moved to Nashville in 1928 to study education at George Peabody College for Teachers and spent seven years in the Tennessee capital. He received a master's degree from Peabody in 1929 and then switched to Vanderbilt University for graduate work in history. A self-described "dilettante," Silver honed his poker skills, played tennis, practiced his romantic charms, supported himself with odd jobs, and was a desultory student. Unpersuaded by Vanderbilt's Agrarians, he remembered that the "Vanderbilt academic community . . . seldom seemed to reach the heart of social questions" and usually paid little attention to racial issues.[4]

In 1935 he received his doctorate in U.S. history, accepted a job at Southwestern College, a Methodist school in Winfield, Kansas, and married Margaret "Dutch" Thompson, a Vanderbilt freshman from Montgomery. The next year they moved to Oxford. She resumed her college study and in 1941 received a bachelor's degree. Their family grew with the births of a son and two daughters, as the Silvers readily adapted to the community. Silver, for example, joined the local Rotary Club, and his wife tutored Ole Miss athletes and advised a sorority. Despite serious allergies and skin rashes, Silver played golf, participated in intramural basketball and tennis, and fished at Sardis Lake near Oxford. He joined friends weekly for drinks and poker. The tall, handsome professor was a notorious ladies' man and his philandering was legendary.[5] He was an unusually passionate and indomitable individual.

Silver quickly made a place for himself at Ole Miss. He coached the men's tennis team and filmed football games for the athletic department. He also advised Omicron Delta Kappa, the major honorary organization. Jim and Dutch Silver befriended many students and often entertained them in their home. In 1938, he successfully organized the first High School Day for more than two thousand students. At the same time, he joined a strong history department. When he arrived in the fall of 1936, David Potter and Joseph Mathews had also just joined the department. Each of the three would later serve as president of the Southern Historical Association, as would the next department chair, Bell I. Wiley, who moved to Oxford two years later. In 1940

Chairman Wiley recommended Silver for promotion to associate professor, because he "is unusually adept at getting along with his students and at inspiring them to an improvement in scholarly performance . . . [and has] rendered exceedingly valuable service to the school and to the department through his extracurricular activities." In 1946 Silver commenced a decade as chair of the history department.[6]

Silver also embarked on a career as a scholar. During the 1940s he focused on revising his dissertation on Edmund Pendleton Gaines (1777–1849), who had spent most of his adult life in the U.S. Army on the western frontier, some of it in what would become Mississippi.[7] While he worked on General Gaines, Silver and his subject seemed to grow remarkably alike. Perhaps Gaines attracted the historian because of an affinity he felt for the frontier general's life. The scholar may have identified with his subject and modeled his own career after Gaines's, or perhaps he molded his biography of Gaines to reflect his own predilections. By the time Silver wrote the foreword to his book on Gaines, any differences between them had blurred almost beyond recognition.[8]

According to Silver, Gaines, a "colorful individual" with a "commanding personality," knew that on the frontier "the individual had to be a *man* to survive," capable of demonstrating "personal courage approaching rashness, hospitality, idealism, a pride in achievement, and an abundance of hope." Gaines had "arrogance and braggadocio . . . [that] often led him into grave, useless disputes, at times threatening the disruption of the morale and efficiency of the entire" military organization. He "risk[ed] the wrath" of his superiors and engaged in "violent denunciation" of his opponents, and he had "charm and wit that tended toward sarcasm." For Gaines, "ideals assumed the form of passions." His "imagination often kindled in him the enthusiasm of the visionary; this was surely because he looked a little further into the future than his contemporaries." Race relations marked him as a dissenter; his opposition to the exploitation of the less-powerful racial group and his offer of fair treatment was "directly in contravention" of the actions of elected leaders. Preferring reconciliation rather than continued suppression, Gaines found himself "diametrically opposed" to the government programs. At the same time, he believed the people on the frontier most needed the assistance of the federal government and the constitutional protections guaranteed all citizens. Despite his sometimes strong dissent, however, Gaines remained steadfastly loyal to his country.[9]

In 1936, when Silver began working at Ole Miss, he was not exactly like Gaines, but by 1949 the resemblance between their personalities had become unmistakable as Silver's actions in the intervening years demonstrated his affinity for his subject. In 1940 he helped to start an annual series of speakers under the auspices of Omicron Delta Kappa and Mortar Board, another honorary society. A speaker's topic, Silver explained, "must be a controversial one, because we will want to ask questions from the floor." For fifteen years, Silver chaired the ODK committee that annually invited a half-dozen prominent individuals to speak in an open forum and answer questions from the audience. He balanced speakers according to political views, occupations, and geography. The community appreciated his commitment to the series; the chancellor in 1949 congratulated him on his "fine job" and praised the "excellent speakers." The series gave Silver great satisfaction and reflected his teaching style of exposing students to many different viewpoints, instilling in them an appreciation for intellectual inquiry and allowing them to reach their own conclusions. It also contributed to Silver's image as a fomenter of dissent.[10]

Though Silver did not seek to indoctrinate students, he developed increasingly strong ideas. Some of his values he learned from his parents, but many others developed through his own experiences. As a youngster, for instance, Silver accepted his Baptist mother's "primitive church," but he gradually grew away from it; as an adult his attitude resembled that of his father, who later in life thought churchgoers were hypocrites.[11] By his twenties, Silver had also rejected his parents' puritanism and emotional reserve for a more libertine lifestyle. In politics, he did not share his father's Republican views but instead became an ardent supporter of the New Deal and of organized labor. His father's business activities may, however, have contributed to the son's recognition of economic forces in history. Jim Silver had also learned from his parents to value learning and hard work, and he applied his energy to a wide range of professional obligations.

Silver's extracurricular involvements also contributed to his radical reputation. Far more than most faculty, the charming and gregarious professor spoke to civic clubs, historical associations, and other groups, and he wrote numerous letters to editors. His heretical public statements often embroiled him in controversy and made him a target for conservatives suspicious of the university and its faculty.

Incidents during his first decade at Ole Miss marked him as a threat to the status quo. Under the auspices of the state Department of Education, he spoke in Clarksdale on the 1938 Wages and Hours Act. Though he presented arguments for and against the law, as a supporter of the New Deal and organized labor he endorsed the minimum wage. Whites in the conservative Delta believed that any minimum wage requirement, even one that did not apply to farm workers, violated states' rights, threatened the power of employers, and smacked of communism. The next day the *Clarksdale Register and Daily News* attacked his stance, and soon thereafter one of the paper's columnists wrote directly to Silver to tell him that the trustees would soon fire him.[12]

Two years later, when newspapers carried stories on strikes in defense industries, Silver again spoke in Clarksdale on labor's right to strike during wartime. Pointing to the unequal power between employers and employees, he warned that workers, who supplied more sons for war than did their bosses, would be most productive only when proud of their work. The next day a local columnist attacked Silver. Claiming the historian had no practical experience and knew only the New Deal side of the issue, his Clarksdale critic contended that a wartime striker was like a disobedient soldier, and neither could be tolerated.[13] The criticism contributed to Silver's emerging reputation as a radical.

Shortly before Pearl Harbor, Silver got involved in another scrape when he spoke in neighboring Pontotoc County. Sharing the platform with Luther A. Smith, the grand master of the state's Masons, Silver discussed the war from a historian's perspective. For a balanced view, he presented both interventionist and isolationist arguments. Silver proposed that the war amounted to an extension of previous economic struggles and that American values were not at issue in the conflict. Smith found his discussion so "reprehensible" that he complained to the chancellor; he thought that Silver had called for Americans not to be swayed by idealism but instead to recognize the self-interest, the flaws, and the errors of all sides, including the United States. Silver's stress on economic factors instead of patriotism especially rankled Smith, who argued that Silver's philosophy would not produce proud and patriotic students.[14]

Silver's letters to editors also stirred up the public. In the winter of 1943, he challenged George Morris, Washington columnist for the *Memphis Commercial Appeal*, over his criticism of the Roosevelt administration. He called on Morris to help to create harmony and to quit using his patriotism to brand his opponents as communists and racketeers. Silver specifically defended the controversial Farm Security Administration and Eleanor Roosevelt. When Morris refused to back down, the professor decried Morris's "distorted" reporting and his "unrivaled capacity for innuendo and perversion." Claiming to support the American system and to "abhor Communism," Silver declared his complete confidence that the nation "is neither going Communist with Mr. [Earl] Browder nor Fascist with Mr. Morris." The *Commercial Appeal*'s Mississippi readers quickly rallied to Morris's defense and denounced Silver. One indicated that some state officials believed that Silver was "a very dangerous man to have in our colleges."[15]

A year later Silver risked renewed attack when he spoke to an Ole Miss group as part of a YMCA series on race relations and the Negro. He stressed the lack of scientific evidence to support the common belief in the innate in-feriority of blacks and denied that any "race" was superior to another. When Silver claimed that blacks had advanced more in the previous twenty-five years than any other race had in a similar period in history, however, he seemed to grant their current inferiority. Optimistic about black progress, he supported further advancement in part because he believed that whites could prosper only if blacks did too. The progress envisioned by Silver did not include social equality, but he did endorse black voting rights by speaking out strongly against poll taxes as "un-American and undemocratic." Progress would come only when southerners themselves, white and black, worked to solve the Negro question. Silver's comments veered far from racial orthodoxy and left him open to counterattacks by white supremacists, segregationists, and other de-fenders of the racial status quo. His remarks, however, apparently passed nearly unnoticed; only a three-paragraph article appeared in the *Mississippian*. Someone did send him unsigned note that said, "Keep your views on the Negro to *yourself*."[16]

Silver survived the sniping during his first decade at Ole Miss, but oppo-sition intensified after the war. Combined concerns about communism and civil rights created a fearful climate in the Deep South. As part of the growing "red scare," President Harry S Truman instituted a program to investigate the loyalty of all federal employees, and he submitted to Congress a set of major civil rights proposals. The president's actions seemed to confirm the fears of white southerners about communist influences at home and threats to racial segregation.[17]

In February 1948, the *Jackson Clarion-Ledger* reported a "flaming reaction" against Truman and "murmers [*sic*] of rebellion" among white southerners because they believed their entire way of life was threatened. The paper ap-pealed for "determined, courageous, drastic action by Southern Democrats, real Democrats, cherishing our social and political systems and determined to prevent their destruction." It saw the president's civil rights plan as a "desper-ate bid" for the support of "the pink and black vote." Representative John Bell Williams told Congress that the minority groups behind the administration's civil rights program were either communist fronts or communist-infiltrated organizations, and he denounced the "Communistic barnacles which have attached themselves to our party."[18] Mobilization had begun in the South that would lead to the creation of the States' Rights, or Dixiecrat, Party later that year.

During the legislature's biennial session that began in January 1948, legisla-tors were caught up in the reactionary spirit. One representative introduced a bill that called for people who made false charges of racial discrimination and prejudice to be given ten dollars and a train ticket out of the state and for a state agency to remove all of their personal possessions. In response to worries about loyalty at the state's colleges, legislators introduced measures to establish committees to investigate them. Doubting Silver's loyalty, legislators and others began what the professor described as a "whispering campaign (a stage whisper, that is)" against him. In February 1948, he personally encountered the hostility in the lobby of Jackson's King Edward Hotel. Witnessing an argument over President Truman, the professor commented, "If Truman's whole program goes through, it won't make much difference in Mississippi, because we won't pay any attention to it anyway." When a legislator accused him of supporting Truman, Silver said his views were unimportant and refused to discuss the matter. In response to a question about how long he had been at Ole Miss, he responded thirteen years, and the legislator replied, "Too damn long." In retaliation for his notorious views, Silver's legislative opponents later caused his ouster from the Mississippi Historical Commission, but more important their animus toward Silver contributed to several bills aimed at purging dissidents from the state's colleges.[19]

In April 1948, as the rumors and innuendos against Silver and the university spread and intensified, he struck back in a speech to a District Rotary Conference in Biloxi. Biting and bold, funny and forthright, Silver made his case for "freedom of discussion and freedom of expression." He then admitted that many Mississippians still considered him "a Yankee and an outsider" even though he had lived in the South for nearly three decades, had married an Alabamian, had written on southern topics, and had been at Ole Miss for years. He employed the pronouns "we" and "our" to include himself among the Mississippians he analyzed to make himself seem less threatening. He reassured the Rotarians that he was "a firm believer in and teacher of capitalism and the idea that you can't change a section's habits by passing an expedient law in Washington." Taking on the question of radicals at Ole Miss, he claimed he could not even find a supporter of Henry Wallace. "The Ole Miss Faculty is about as radical as the Biloxi Rotary Club." Instead of communists, the university had scholars who disagreed about nearly everything because they could see four or five sides to every question.[20]

After confessing his own role in several controversies, Silver admitted responsibility for the ODK forums but denied any imbalance in the series. Anyway, students, especially the older veterans, had the "funny habit of taking very little on faith or because it's written in a book or because someone said so." He argued that charges of communism on the campus sometimes came from speakers who "had been asked to back up some antiquated generalizations with facts." The professor declared, "I hope the day will come in Mississippi when the irresponsible trick of branding a political opponent or someone who disagrees with you as a communist will be frowned into the contempt it deserves." He deplored the "supposedly normal mental straight-jacket way of community thinking." Challenging the ideas of laissez-faire and states' rights, he proposed, "It is highly possible that much economic thinking, handed down from a frontier economy when it made sense, no longer applies to a modern, complicated inter-dependent society." Laissez-faire had become a "holy doctrine" and states' rights a "fetish."[21]

Urging the Rotarians "to do some thinking of their own," Silver concluded with the controversial example of federal aid to education. A few years earlier he had defended such a program before a Tupelo civic club, only to be accused later of advocating racial equality. In Biloxi he contended that the question of federal aid should be decided "solely on the basis of whether it is good or bad for our children and our society! Let us not confuse, in our thinking, this inherited ideology in regard to states' rights with the crying needs of our children." Referring to his son, he jested, "As far as I have been able to discover, he has not imbibed any federal or Muscovite indoctrination along with his hot dogs and cabbage" in his federally supported elementary school lunch. Silver believed that "progress comes only when there is freedom of discussion and freedom of expression, even for college professors. It implies further that the people of Mississippi have a perfect right to go through life head first or tail first."[22]

Silver's speech did not quell the controversy in part because inaccurate coverage in the Biloxi newspaper did not make clear that Silver had denied ever seeing a communist at Ole Miss, either among professors or invited speakers. He worried that the misreporting could lead to further controversy when his intent had been to clear it up. When Chancellor Williams heard from the coast about Silver's speech, he endorsed him as an individual, a professor, a historian, and "an absolutely honest scholar."[23]

Armed with an advance copy of Silver's Rotary talk, his friend Hodding Carter prepared a two-part defense. An editorial in the *Delta Democrat Times* praised an unnamed "Professor X" for his "intellectual honesty" even though critics considered him "a dangerous man, who is corrupting the minds of their young." Agreeing that ideas should be presented and discussed at a university, Carter contended that "a historian should teach history and not myths," even if misunderstanding Mississippians concluded that Professor X was a "subversive." Carter also encouraged dissent in an address to the Southern Literary Festival at Delta State College. Again without naming the professor, the Pulitzer prizewinning editor endorsed "a spirit of intellectual protest against re-action in any of its many guises." Echoing Silver, Carter argued, "Things will improve only when they are challenged." And Carter, like Silver, saw the need to alleviate "economic insecurity, discrimination, lack of job opportunity, educational lags and sub-human living conditions" in Mississippi. By that summer Silver had the support of a growing number of loyal, appreciative former students.[24]

Perhaps Silver's most valuable supporter was Martin Van Buren Miller, chair of the IHL board and an avid fan of Ole Miss sports. Miller had likely first gotten to know Silver through the athletic department because of the professor's role in filming the football games and his wife's work tutoring athletes. Beginning in the spring of 1948, Silver also advised Miller's son. After the 1948 legislative session, where Miller heard gossip about Silver, Miller suggested that the chancellor arrange for Silver to speak to the state bar association to answer the "absurd" charges about communism. Miller's support would have deflected criticism that came before the trustees. In his memoirs Silver suggested that once, probably during the 1948 attacks, Miller as chairman of the board did dismiss allegations that Silver was a communist by commenting, "Jim Silver is no more of a Communist than I am. Next order of business."[25]

Even knowing that observers kept an eye on him, the professor refused to compromise. After Virginia editor Virginius Dabney spoke in 1949 at an ODK forum on the future of the Dixiecrat movement, Speaker of the House Walter Sillers asked Silver for a copy of Dabney's talk. Silver sent a copy and told the Dixiecrat supporter it was the best argument for states' rights that he had heard recently. Silver added, "I am not implying that I, myself, am a states' righter, which is beside the point." Unwilling to let the comment pass, Sillers inquired if Silver supported states' rights and, "If not, do you mind telling me why?" Undaunted, Silver wrote a three-page reply. Feigning reluctance in writing to the experienced and powerful Speaker, the professor nevertheless sought to teach him some history. He affirmed his belief in capitalism and otherwise claimed "no particular beliefs about society" except for his support for opportunity for all, but he set out his views on states' rights and the contemporary role of government. Silver primarily objected to states' rights because its logical conclusion was unworkable. "I believe as firmly as Jefferson did in the local community taking care of its own problems," he maintained. "But modern society has brought with it many problems which simply can't be solved at the local level."[26]

Silver explained that states had proven incapable of controlling wealthy corporations; only the federal government protected the consuming public from the "excesses of concentrated power." Interested in "individual freedom," he feared "concentrated wealth" more than federal bureaucracy. The professor recognized that the Speaker disagreed, but Silver suggested that states' rights advocates opposed governmental power when they were out of office but willingly used federal authority when they controlled it.[27] Silver's letter convinced Sillers that he could not be trusted because he did not support states' rights and the Mississippi way of life.

A few months later, while Silver was on a Fulbright scholarship at the University of Aberdeen in Scotland, the charges of communism resurfaced among legislators. Probably as an aftereffect of the 1948 rumors, a legislative committee investigated charges of communism. Established in 1946, the General Legislative Investigating Committee (GLIC) had sweeping powers. When the legislature was not in session, the committee of three representatives and three senators had "full, complete and plenary authority and power to conduct an investigation of all state (a) offices, (b) departments, (c) agencies, (d) institutions and instrumentalities" funded by the state. It could subpoena and question witnesses, who were subject to perjury and contempt charges.[28]

In 1949 the GLIC investigated Jim Silver and Hodding Carter. The committee operated in secret, but one witness, Hugh H. Clegg, played the key role. Governor Fielding L. Wright had become acquainted with Clegg, a native Mississippian, an assistant director of the FBI, a dependable source on domestic communism, and a future assistant to the chancellor. While Clegg vacationed in Mississippi, the governor asked him to come to Jackson. When Clegg arrived at the capitol, he was taken upstairs to a GLIC meeting. The chairman explained its investigation of communism and asked Clegg what he could tell them. Bound by FBI confidentiality, Clegg could speak only in general terms. When asked about the two individuals under investigation, Clegg referred to information made public by J. Edgar Hoover about the number of communists in each state, and Mississippi had the lowest number—one. Clegg assured GLIC that the communist was neither a newspaperman nor a university employee. In effect, he vouched for Silver and Carter.[29]

During the 1950 legislative session, professors came under legislative attack, probably condoned by the Speaker. Hamer McKenzie, a young legislator and an Ole Miss law student, charged that fellow travelers, including Silver, taught communism in their classes. In the legislature, one of McKenzie's fellow law students defended Jim Silver and the ODK speakers series. William F. Winter, a former student of Silver, declared that in six years at the university he had "never detected anything communistic, subversive or un-American" and denounced the "irresponsible witch hunt" because it could harm the university. Other Ole Miss supporters defended Silver and other alleged radicals. The crisis subsided, but not before the legislature mandated a loyalty oath by professors and all other state employees.[30]

In Scotland, Silver remained removed from the controversy. A university friend playfully addressed him as "Dr. Stalin" and told him he "would have been amazed at the number of friends you had on the floor [of the legislature] who are caring for your interests." Unable to participate in a debate that he would have relished, Silver could only respond to the charges in a "Report from Britain," one of his essays written for several dozen newspapers during his year in Scotland. His contact at the university planned to release it only if McKenzie renewed his assault.[31]

Writing from a "British university where for a long, long time academic freedom has prevailed," Silver blasted the "silly antics of a small minority of red baiters and professional patriots." He believed that he had never met McKenzie, so the representative could have had no personal knowledge of Silver. According to Silver, "the youngster has confused presentation of all sides of an issue with un-Americanism." The column reported earlier challenges by legislators seeking information from his own students threatening to have him fired, by an Ole Miss administrator who kept a file on him for a congressman, and by a campus visitor who reported to the governor that he was a communist. Though his personal feelings had been hurt and his constitutional rights violated, Silver never complained of the abuses of his academic freedom because he had no official proof, did not want to harm the university, tried to shield his family from "nasty disputation," and trusted the intelligence and fairness of the educational and political leaders, particularly at the university. He wondered, however, if Ole Miss could ever become "more than a trade school" if professors had to worry about "the whims and prejudices of the nearest legislator" and "adolescent and irresponsible outbursts" in "an atmosphere of suspicion and distrust."[32]

To people back home who assumed that he agreed with or at least had sympathy for any idea he discussed, the professor pointed out in another "Report from Britain" that he taught about feminism, anarchism, fascism, pacifism, vegetarianism, agrarianism, and other ideologies "without ever having the slightest desire to embrace the faith." As for communism, Silver believed Americans knew too little about its tenets and propaganda methods. To educate himself, he had gone to a communist rally, where he discovered a "warped interpretation" of America, "nonsense," and "the burning zeal of religious fanatics." He came away convinced that "our controlled free enterprise and democratic society affords the smoothest road to peace and prosperity."[33]

The brouhaha in 1950 over communism and political and economic radicalism scarcely affected Silver directly, except that he had to sign the new loyalty oath when he returned. At midcentury his controversial views stressed economics, and his classes emphasized economic forces. Even when Silver applied for grants for further study, he focused on government-business relations, labor, economic theory, and business history. His economic thinking always advocated capitalism, but he argued that capitalism had not been allowed to operate in the United States during the modern industrial era. In the American capitalist system either genuine competition had to be restored or the country had to accept that the current trend of greater government regulation would likely result in socialism. Preferring free enterprise, the prospect of socialism did not please him, but he saw few viable options because business continued its short-sighted pursuit of profits. He predicted that the continued excesses of big business would force change.[34]

Among southern whites anticommunism took priority over race. They may have suspected communists of fomenting unrest among blacks, but civil rights had yet to become the public issue it would be later in the 1950s. Whites usually assumed Negro inferiority and believed segregation was immutable. Even Silver rarely focused on racial matters, especially publicly, but he was not unaware of southern race relations. He had quite limited personal contacts with Negroes. The Silvers depended on a black mechanic to maintain their automobiles and a Negro handyman to work on their plumbing, electrical appliances, and furnace. Shortly after they moved to Oxford, Jim and Dutch Silver also employed a black domestic worker, Thera Jones, who worked for them for a quarter-century and was like a member of the family. At least once she accompanied them on a vacation to North Carolina, and frequently she stayed with the Silver children when their parents went out of town. Like most whites, particularly during the Depression, the Silvers did not pay Jones much, but they did what they could for her. Jim Silver, for example, arranged surgery for Jones to remove a life-threatening goiter. Except for black workers at Ole Miss, Silver knew few other blacks. One exception was his "limited friendship" with the principal of the Oxford Industrial School, the local public school for black children. The professor visited the principal at the school and, as adviser to the ODK forum, often took visitors to speak to the student body. Silver also visited the school annually as a member of the Rotary Club. He later recalled, "For twenty-five years I was forbidden to have any meaningful intellectual relationship with a Mississippi Negro." In the mid-1950s, Silver could not even have Carl Rowan, a black journalist from Minnesota, speak to his class or eat and sleep in his home on campus during a visit to Oxford.[35]

Though restricted in his contacts with blacks, Silver "read *everything* that [he] could find on race." He consumed scholarly studies by Franz Boas and Margaret Mead, the Chapel Hill Regionalists, John Dollard, Hortense Powdermaker, and Gunnar Myrdal, as well as Richard Wright's *Native Son* and W. J. Cash's *The Mind of the South*. His study did not yet compel him to much activism. In his first decade at Ole Miss, racial issues apparently stirred the campus only in 1937 when some students attended an interracial meeting at a North Carolina YMCA. In 1939 Silver did attend a few interracial meetings in Oxford to discuss the lack of restrooms for blacks on the town square, but the short-lived effort came to an inconclusive end. During his service with the Red Cross during World War II, Silver also witnessed racial discrimination in the military.[36]

Prior to the *Brown v. Board of Education of Topeka* decision, Silver began to pay more attention to racial questions and was optimistic about their solution. For example, he did not dodge the race issue in his response to Walter Sillers's inquiry about states' rights. After averring his resentment of northern interference in civil rights, Silver proposed that the best way to ward off northern meddling would be for Mississippi to eliminate its poll tax and to enact a law against extralegal violence. Five years later, on a campus panel dealing with the question, "What Is Mississippi's Future in Race Relations?" Silver and his colleagues unremarkably and hopefully concluded that the solution to the racial problem involved better education and improved economic conditions.[37]

Silver may have been sanguine but he was not naive about racial change. By the early 1950s, he detected progress in Mississippi and claimed that "the race issue down here is gradually being taken care of. . . . White supremacy is a thing of the past." He later recalled "the great optimism and excitement among those who sought to civilize Mississippi" in the years before *Brown*. Silver sensed that a revolution had begun in the state. He reported slow advances toward black economic security. Balancing hope and realism, he insisted that the revolution had to proceed slowly because the state "goes almost berserk at the thought of social equality being imposed on them from the outside, by the federal government." Silver's awareness of the perils of pushing progress caused him to continue to subordinate racial equality to economic equality, but he thought economic equality could eventually provide the only basis for racial equality.[38]

Though Silver had battled states' rights advocates and called for improvements in black life, he acknowledged in 1952 that he would have seemed to northerners more like a moderate than a radical. For his efforts, however, Silver had endured numerous attacks from conservative whites, but he did not want to leave or become a martyr. When asked by the leftist Southern Conference Education Fund (SCEF) to participate in a conference on discrimination in education, Silver demurred. Though he admired SCEF's work, he acknowledged that he probably "would last just about ten minutes here at the University of Mississippi" if he publicly supported SCEF. He conceded that he had to be careful or he would lose his job.[39]

As Silver began to pay more attention to race, one individual and several significant events played important roles. Silver initially met William Faulkner because his stepdaughter, Victoria, was in Silver's first Ole Miss class; only later did the novelist and the historian became friends. About the time *Intruder in the Dust* was filming in Oxford in 1949, they, according to Silver, "began an interminable discussion of the race question." As southern moderates criticized by extremists on all sides of the race question, they understood the imminent change facing their region's policy of segregation. They wanted to prepare the South for the impending transformation and hoped Mississippi would accept change without violence. In 1955, at Silver's suggestion as the program chairman for the Southern Historical Association convention, Faulkner participated in a panel on the *Brown* decision at which he appeared to advocate racial equality. Silver later acknowledged that, in grappling with the race question in the 1950s, "Faulkner without question, sustained me in what I suppose was my own slow radicalization" on race.[40]

In the spring of 1949, at about the time Silver was getting to know Faulkner, a rape case in Oxford forced the professor to confront the severity of racial prejudice. Nathan Cohran, a black university employee, was charged with raping a local white woman. Silver and Cohran had become friends in the late 1930s because the Silvers depended on him for help with plumbing, electrical, and other problems around their home. Later, with a white partner, Cohran established a private plumbing business in Oxford. His partner's wife charged that Cohran raped her one weekend while her husband was out of town. On the day of his trial, prosecutors convinced Cohran that his family might be subjected to mob violence if the white woman had to testify, and they gave him the option of pleading guilty to avoid possible harm to his family. Silver believed Cohran was innocent of rape and hoped he would not yield, but he realized the fearful possibilities for Cohran's wife and children if the trial occurred. In exchange for a sentence of three years and then a pardon by the governor after the uproar passed, Cohran agreed to confess. Cohran served three years in Parchman and then immediately left the state.[41]

The incident troubled Silver because he recognized Cohran's "horrible dilemma." Silver could not ignore the mob's racial prejudice that made law enforcement officers unwilling to guarantee the safety of Cohran's family. After Cohran pled guilty, Silver never saw him again, but for thirty years he continually "agonized" over Cohran's fate and what it said about life in Mississippi. The experience contributed to Silver's growing awareness of racial injustice.[42]

The *Brown* decision had an even greater impact on Silver. Less than two weeks later, the white historian went the couple of blocks from his campus home to give the commencement address at the black Oxford Training School.

He declared that the court decision would probably be the greatest single event in the graduates' lives because it marked a watershed between restrictions based solely on the color of their skin and complete freedom. The nation would no longer tolerate second-class citizenship. He urged the graduates to pay their poll taxes and vote. Despite his apparent hopefulness, Silver predicted that few present that evening would see dramatic differences because real change in race relations would take decades.[43]

Within a few weeks of Silver's speech, two events changed his outlook. Hoping to avoid integration of the public schools, Governor Hugh White conferred on July 1 with eight prominent conservative blacks about his plan to maintain voluntary segregation in the public schools by undertaking a massive program to equalize schools. After getting a favorable response, White assembled a larger group of black leaders late in July, but they told White that they supported the *Brown* decision and wanted it enforced. If the blacks' unwillingness to accept the status quo stunned White, it also "proved the greatest shock of [Silver's] entire life."[44]

On July 11, between Governor White's two meetings, the Citizens' Council emerged as a reflection of what Silver later called "the militant desperation of whites." He realized that, just as segregationists had to defend their beliefs, he too would soon have to stand up for what he thought was right. In Silver's case, the heightened racial tensions contributed to his "faltering radicalization," which led him to take stands against the Citizens' Councils.[45]

Silver's scholarly research on public opinion and propaganda during the nineteenth-century sectional crisis, especially in the Confederacy, had relevance for the South's contemporary problems. His *Confederate Morale and Church Propaganda* described "thirty years of emotional agitation [that] had developed in the South by 1860 an orthodox and perhaps a closed mind. Result: the most colossal blunder in American history." As he wrote in the middle 1950s, "In view of the heated agitation of this day it might be well for Southerners to ponder the course of action of their section a century ago."[46]

In speeches to the Tupelo Kiwanis Club in December 1954 and to the Rotary Club a few months later, Silver made the analogy explicit. Comparing the South's situation in the 1950s to its predicament a century earlier, he argued "that abolition of segregation in public schools in Mississippi is just as inevitable now as was the abolition of slavery in 1860." Acknowledging the South's "tragic fate" as a minority in the nation, he maintained that "the South had the right to secede, but the results of its trying to do so were disastrous." By implication, the contemporary South should not pursue a similarly radical course. He did not advocate immediate integration; instead he wanted desegregation, but not too quickly. Silver's Tupelo proclamation apparently caused little stir, perhaps because his colleague, law professor William P. Murphy, had six months earlier made a similar public argument.[47]

In the spring of 1955, during the segregation crisis, Silver stood for freedom of speech when the IHL trustees required screening and prior approval for all speakers invited to state college campuses. The new rule reflected the conviction that the educational institutions should support segregation and white supremacy. As the director of the Ole Miss speakers series, Silver opposed it because the forums sought to rattle the status quo. In a speech to the Greenville Rotary Club, he said the situation resembled the South's position a century earlier when doctrinaire positions had led to secession, defeat, reconstruction, and economic subservience. If Mississippi tried a new secession, he believed the results would be worse than after the Civil War. The policy could not work because "ideas cannot be kept out of a state" and neither can people be refused entrance. For Silver, the policy of screening speakers typified a larger movement to impede change and progress in the South. Though not explicitly tied to race, the speaker ban served for both sides as a proxy for loyalty to the Mississippi way of life, for the racial status quo. Silver's attack on the policy did not draw fire, perhaps because the *Jackson State Times*, the *Mississippian*, Hodding Carter, and others had also spoken out against the rule and because other issues intruded. Within a year the controversy over Religious Emphasis Week erupted, and Silver soon relinquished his role with the forum series.[48]

While the *Brown* decision provoked what came to be called "massive resistance," it spurred Silver to more vigorous dissent. In his unsigned occasional contributions to *The Economist*, the weekly British magazine, he provided a context for the developing racial crisis that could only be understood in relation to other social and economic changes sweeping across the state. Silver suggested that older whites desperately held on to segregation because of changes in so many other parts of their lives, but he hoped younger people would worry less about preserving the southern way of life. After the state approved a constitutional amendment for the abolition of public schools to avoid integration, he still claimed that the state would try to persuade Negroes to accept segregation by equalizing black and white schools, but he thought the federal courts would likely rule against the plans to equalize or abolish the schools. In the meantime, he worried about the "definite danger of extra-legal action and even the possibility that whites will be goaded and stampeded into such a frenzied state of mind that they will accept abolition of the schools altogether rather than integrate them."[49]

By 1956, Silver seemed far more troubled by events in Mississippi. After the murders of several Mississippi Negroes, the creation of the Sovereignty Com-

mission, and the REW controversy, he concluded that the battle over segregation had so permeated the state and that public opinion had so hardened that
every white person had to either endorse segregation or remain silent. Everywhere he observed "the belligerent determination of Mississippi whites to
maintain their traditional way of life." The state's political leadership, including Governor J. P. Coleman, supported almost any means to thwart integration, and most white Mississippians resented outside agitators trying to
force changes. White supremacists "equated support for racial integration
with communism" and threatened not only "those who would uphold laws
banning segregation, but also . . . who entertain any but the most conservative
views of race, politics, economics, and religion." Deteriorating race relations
particularly concerned him. "Fear and hatred," he declared, "have gripped
both races to a degree unknown since the bloody days after the Civil War."
Though Silver suspected relatively few whites actually believed that segregation
could be permanent, he thought the vast majority would work hard to preserve it. The key factor would be the federal government's efforts for racial
justice. The prospect of a clash between the federal government and organized
segregationists prompted the pessimistic professor to predict Mississippians
would "be engulfed in a maelstrom completely beyond their control." Under
the frightening and deplorable circumstances, Silver regretted he could only
participate in the "rearguard action of a few clergymen, teachers, and editors
in defense of freedom of thought."[50]

On October 17, 1956, Silver addressed the Rotary Club in Jackson, Tennessee, with a speech titled "The Lunatic Fringe and the Moderates—A Hundred Years Ago and Now." Secession had been "a tragic blunder . . . based on
certain beliefs of the people that turned out to be illusions." It had not been
peaceful, the North did fight, abolitionists controlled the federal government,
cotton did not pull Britain and France into the war, and the South lacked unity.
To explain the misperceptions in 1861, Silver reviewed the last thirty antebellum years and found that the South had moved from Thomas Jefferson's
ideas on freedom of thought to the enforced orthodoxy of thought before the
Civil War. As a minority, the South "had increasingly stifled dissent within its
own region to make its power stronger in national councils." By the 1850s, after
accelerating indoctrination in the antebellum period, the South lacked other
points of view. For Silver, "the danger of enforced orthodox thinking" meant
the South made the wrong decisions. Comparing antebellum attitudes toward
abolitionists to contemporary feelings about the NAACP, he implied that the
state and the region in the 1950s were repeating many of their earlier errors
and were moving toward another "tragic blunder." Although the South was
not ideologically a part of the nation because it held to a different southern

creed based on segregation and states' rights, Silver believed that eventually the American creed would prevail in the South also and the Union would be whole.[51]

The Associated Press's distorted account of Silver's talk the next day in the *Jackson Daily News* shocked Silver. It accurately quoted his comments about the blunder of secession, the South's illusions, his comparison of the abolitionists and the NAACP, and his belief that the South would intellectually join the Union, but it did not mention his central arguments about the dangers of enforced orthodoxy and the need for freedom of thought. The inaccurate coverage contributed to the outraged calls for action against him. Citizens demanded that the trustees fire Silver. In the *Jackson Clarion-Ledger*, Tom Ethridge suggested Ole Miss apologize for his "asinine" remarks, and an editorial on the "professor's crackpot talk" fueled the controversy. The *Daily News* alleged that Silver was "not in sympathy with the South, or Southern causes" and called for a new chairman for the history department, and it demanded Silver's firing because he had disrespected the Confederacy and displayed tremendous ignorance of the South and its history.[52]

Spurred by the criticism, the IHL board directed its executive secretary to obtain a copy of the speech. Silver explained that he spoke from notes, but he then laid out for the trustees the essential parts of his talk. He described his talk as "simply a plea for freedom of thought, backed up by sound historical fact." Although he admitted the subject's controversial nature, Silver assured the board that most southern historians would agree with his main contentions.[53] He also shared his letter with a number of friends and acquaintances, who provided some vital support.

Important aid came from Governor Coleman. Silver had first become acquainted with him four years earlier when he spoke at the university, and in succeeding years the professor twice provided him with historical research. After Coleman read Silver's letter to the trustees, he told Silver, "You and I are in general agreement on this whole situation." The governor also wrote to the IHL secretary: "His speech is very much along the same lines as speeches I have made for a number of years." Though "unalterably opposed to integration," Coleman said that "the great problem confronting Mississippi right now is to keep the hotheads from repeating the mistakes of the 1850's and 1860's." William Winter, in 1956 the state tax collector, reassured his old mentor that he thought the controversy was over but pledged to defend Silver just as he had helped fend off attacks in the 1950 legislature.[54]

The IHL board began to think better of pursuing the matter. J. O. Emmerich, editor of newspapers in McComb and Jackson and a trustee, assured Silver that he had not said anything objectionable. Other trustees felt pressure from Silver's supporters. One businessman reported to Silver that in extended conversations with two trustees he had convinced one to support the historian and had begun to persuade the other one too. As a result, the storm surrounding Silver's speech soon subsided.[55]

During the controversy over his Tennessee talk, Silver did not debate his critics because he realized the dangers involved in public controversies, especially one involving the trustees and possibly his position at Ole Miss. After so many public squabbles, he understood how any response usually proved futile and often incendiary. In 1956, though, he did consult a lawyer about the possibility of suing the Jackson papers for their distorted coverage of his speech. By the late 1950s, Silver had become, as he later characterized himself, much more a "quiet reformer" than he had been.[56]

The professor's opponents remained poised to pounce at any provocation. In January 1959, for instance, an article in the *Memphis Commercial Appeal* charged that John Ben Nelson's recent master's thesis reflected Silver's teaching in its criticism of Mississippi's Confederate government. Amazed that it had been approved, a Macon lawyer complained to the governor: "This vicious and scurrilous attack . . . is trash!" Criticism of the Confederacy amounted to disloyalty to white supremacy, states' rights, and all of southern orthodoxy. After Coleman suggested that some of Nelson's ideas could be found in other historical studies, the governor passed the complaint on to Chancellor Williams, who in turn requested a reply from Silver. The thesis, the professor pointed out, had been written in the summer of 1957 while he taught at Emory, so he had not closely supervised it. He disliked it because it contained nothing original; southern historians, including many native southerners and Mississippians, had long ago established every statement in the thesis. Far from shocking, Silver found it conventional. The thesis tempest quickly yielded to more contentious matters.[57]

Two other controversies that proved the state's growing intolerance ensnared Silver at the end of the 1950s. One involved an invitation to a former colleague to speak at Ole Miss. In the spring of 1958, the College of Liberal Arts authorized the history department to invite two special lecturers the following year, one in American history and one in European. After one Europeanist declined, the department turned to Joseph J. Mathews, a Kentuckian educated at Duke University and the University of Pennsylvania in European diplomatic history. Mathews had taught at Ole Miss for a decade before moving after World War II to Emory University. Insufficient funds caused the department to postpone the invitation for a year, but Mathews went through the required speaker screening, and the chancellor approved the invitation to speak in the spring of 1960.[58]

In January 1960, the *Saturday Evening Post* contained an article by Mat-hews's wife about her experience as a college professor at Morehouse College, a black men's college in Atlanta. In addition to supplementing her husband's salary, she took the job "to see for myself what it was that made integrated schools so distasteful." As a result of her Morehouse experiences, she began to identify with her black students and her colleagues who experienced racial discrimination. Along with his wife, Joe Matthews became involved in inter-racial work in Atlanta and even became something of a "crusader." As he explained to his friend Jim Silver, "I think it is the utter, blind stupidity of it all that gets me the most, especially when I confront it in people who have no right to be blindly stupid." After a year and a half at Morehouse, Marcia Mathews concluded, "I have learned the difference between black and white. It is the difference that exists between black and black or white and white. The difference, basically, between man and man."[59]

On January 11, immediately after the article appeared, William T. Doherty, the chairman of the history department, conferred with Provost Bryant, and they agreed that the article would not affect Mathews's visit. Later that day, however, Bryant told Doherty that he had decided that Mathews's invitation should be rescinded. Doherty and Silver then met with Bryant to try to per-suade him to allow Mathews to speak, but Bryant insisted that he not appear. After Mrs. Mathews's article, the provost believed, many white Mississippians would object to her husband's visit and embroil the university in a controversy reminiscent of the Kershaw affair four years earlier. At the provost's direction, Silver told his friend that his invitation had been withdrawn, and Mathews, after first resisting, agreed not to come to Oxford.[60]

The provost's decision outraged some history professors. After debating their options, they condemned the cancellation as "an alarming curtailment" of academic freedom and declared that the action "emphatically endangered" the department's new doctoral program because of the "present academic climate in the State of Mississippi." Ten days later J. D. Williams told Doherty that he would not change the decision. The administration agreed to pay Mathews the scheduled honorarium; Silver later speculated that the admin-istration's payment to Mathews for services not rendered probably violated state law, but the law mattered little in the fight over segregation.[61]

Silver's complicity in denying Mathews's invitation must have chagrined him because he later called the affair the "most outrageous incident that occurred during these years that I spent at the University of Mississippi." It and many similar incidents and the general atmosphere of the "intellectual jungle" of Mississippi caused him to think about leaving. Although he did not con-sider himself a latter-day abolitionist, a radical, or a crusader, he knew that if he stayed he would have to work with others "to pull Mississippi out of the morass it has been in for a hell of a long time." Silver refused, as one of his friends put it in 1959, to quit "fighting sin in Mississippi" or to "face the fact that you aren't going to save the soul of the South in your time." He decided he had to try, even if it cost him his job, and his experience with a second serious controversy in the late fifties—a Red Scare at the University of Mississippi—let him know that his job and the positions of many other faculty members were truly imperiled.[62]

9. "On the Brink of Disaster": Defending States' Rights, Anticommunism, and Segregation

■ ■

"**I** know that communism is being taught by some professors at Ole Miss, and I believe the same is true for Mississippi State [College] and other state institutions," charged Representative Hamer McKenzie of Benton County in January 1950. His allegations came at the height of a national furor over communist subversion. Branding the unnamed professors as fellow travelers, the twenty-six-year-old veteran and law student advocated a special committee to investigate the colleges and universities and to "take a broom and sweep our own backsteps while we are calling on the government to purge our enemies in Washington."[1]

During the national red scare, anticommunists often focused on public schools where, they believed, academics could instill subversive values. Legislators and school boards used loyalty oaths to weed out "subversive" teachers and banned the teaching of "un-American" ideas. In the South, the hunt for subversives coincided with the start of the civil rights movement, and for whites threats to the racial status quo overlapped and reinforced the fear of communists. Charges of communism were used to discredit potential challenges to white supremacy. Conservatives also saw communism as just one step beyond the welfare state created by New Deal liberalism.[2] Segregationists often blurred distinctions among communists, subversives, and integrationists.

McKenzie's charges drew quick responses. The president of Mississippi State College replied, "I don't believe we have any Communists at all." Ole Miss's J. D. Williams defended his faculty: "I know them individually and cannot believe there is a single Communist among them." During a two-hour closed legislative session, McKenzie replied that the colleges were "infested with communist fellow travelers and socialists" and accused five Ole Miss professors of "molding the minds of Mississippi students along socialistic lines." The accused included Jim Silver.[3]

The university and its friends in the legislature and the press decried the "witch hunt." Hodding Carter chastised the "irresponsible" McKenzie for thinking anyone with "a political or economic stand somewhere to the left of the Stock Exchange" was a Red. Before a Delta civic group, Dean Robert Farley called the charges "groundless and without fact." One professor said, "They are accusing some professors of molding students' minds when I can't even teach some of them enough to pass a course." *Mississippian* editor Albin Krebs declared, "A country becomes a police state when its citizens, be they college professors or ditchdiggers, are forced by the state government to knuckle under to what a few politicians call 'the proper attitude.' "[4]

Support for McKenzie quickly faded. The *Jackson Daily News* suggested that the legislators "promptly drop that subject and waste no time on an investigation." McKenzie then backed off and denied accusing anyone of being a communist. The legislature did, however, adopt the Subversive Activities Act that required a loyalty oath for state employees. As of July 1, every university employee had to sign a statement affirming that he or she was not a subversive.[5]

As the chancellor recognized, the allegations in 1950 were not the first, nor would they be the last, about Ole Miss. Though rumors circulated about Alfred Schnur, Will Campbell, Jim Silver, and others, the university had generally avoided upheavals tied explicitly to the larger Red Scare. The state's anticommunist hysteria trailed that of the nation as a whole and peaked after it. When *Brown* intensified racial fears, several prominent alumni, a few recent graduates, and a couple of former employees, many with Citizens' Council ties, began to orchestrate complaints about Ole Miss.

In June 1955 the Madison Citizens' Council sponsored the first meeting of five gubernatorial candidates. Before they spoke, the gathering heard from the cosmopolitan, intellectual, and reserved William J. Simmons. Though a political novice and an inexperienced public speaker better suited as a behind-the-scenes political operator, he rose rapidly to become the executive director of the Citizens' Council movement. In Madison the thirty-eight-year-old mustachioed son of a prominent businessman alleged that Ole Miss and Millsaps College, a Methodist school in Jackson, had liberals sabotaging the state's defense of segregation. He accused them of indoctrinating public school teachers, who then spread integrationist ideas. Newspapers picked up Simmons's comments, but the heads of the institutions rebuffed the charges. "We are not in the propaganda business," J. D. Williams declared. "We don't exercise thought control." He denied any leftist orientation at Ole Miss. Although none of the gubernatorial candidates followed up on Simmons's accusations, the questions continued to roil under the surface.[6]

Later in June, in a letter to the university, Robert B. Patterson of the Citizens' Council repeated recent charges. Criticizing the chancellor's "beguiling charm" and "completely dishonest" reply to Simmons, Patterson objected to "anti-segregation professors from the North." Specifically he protested the use of an education textbook that presented ideas "adverse to the best interests of white people in Mississippi" and two labor union pamphlets distributed at a workshop for teachers; the materials convinced him that the faculty taught from a prointegration and prolabor perspective. He also worried about the student newspaper's liberal policies and warned of "repercussions" if any of the "ugly rumors" proved to be true.[7]

Hugh Clegg, an assistant to the chancellor, received Patterson's complaint. A fifty-eight-year-old Mathiston native and a Millsaps College graduate, he had earned a law degree from George Washington University before starting to work for the FBI in 1926. For his last twenty years with the bureau, he served as assistant director in charge of training and inspection. In 1954 the chancellor recruited him. Ole Miss attracted him because his wife, an alumna, wanted to return to Oxford after he retired. The tough, bald, roly-poly bureaucrat complemented the tall, academic, urbane chancellor. Clegg brought knowledge of Washington, close ties to the congressional delegation, unimpeachable patriotism, connections in the state, and an ability to work with conservatives. In the 1950s, he handled many difficult tasks for the chancellor: he screened campus speakers with the help of his Washington sources, served on the advisory board of the right-wing Patriotic American Youth, and functioned as a contact for segregationists like Patterson.[8]

After consulting with colleagues, Clegg suggested, "Let's examine the facts," and then he declared that the facts were "sufficient to discard the premise on which all the various allegations" rested. Regarding Patterson's broader claims, Clegg suggested that they rested on an "assumption that a conspiracy existed," and he denied, for instance, that Yankee deans hired northerners to teach contrary values. Regarding the School of Education, Clegg pointed out that the dean hailed from Indiana but had taught in Kentucky and Louisiana before coming to Mississippi. Prior to his appointment by Chancellor A. B. Butts, he had married a Mississippian and taught in the state for a quarter-century. Clegg also defended the independence of the *Mississippian* and opposed any censorship as long as it operated "within the bounds of decency and morality." As liaison to segregationists, he allayed Patterson's concerns.[9]

Though not an issue in the 1955 gubernatorial election, the university did not escape controversy. The uproar in the fall of 1955 over REW brought Ole Miss back into the spotlight, and during the winter of 1955–56, the sudden withdrawal of the Rebels from an integrated basketball tournament sparked adverse comment about the university's racial policies. Unknown to Ole Miss officials, however, a more serious problem developed in the summer of 1956 because Patterson and his Citizens' Council colleagues quietly collected information about Ole Miss.

Malcolm Mabry Jr., a 1955 Delta State College graduate and a teacher in Marks, attended Ole Miss in the summer of 1956 to work on a master's degree in social studies. He found Silver's Civil War and Reconstruction class offensive because the "anti-Southern" Silver criticized the legislature, disparaged John Bell Williams and Jim Eastland, and compared the Citizens' Council to the NAACP. Worse, he subtly espoused socialism and integration. Mabry concluded that he could not return to Ole Miss as long as the "dangerous" Silver taught there. He complained to Patterson and pledged to "do anything to help rid the University and our state of this man."[10]

A key ally in building a case against the university was William Chamberlain "Chuck" Trotter. Born in 1890 in Winona, he played football and baseball at Ole Miss, where he earned both undergraduate and law degrees. After he worked in state government a few years, his political friend Theodore Bilbo appointed him university financial secretary during the 1930 purge of higher education. Except for four years at Mississippi College for Women, he served Ole Miss from 1930 until his retirement in 1956. Much of his influence derived from his popularity among students and alumni and his extensive contacts. When J. D. Williams became chancellor, Trotter introduced him to many of his friends. At the university Chuck Trotter was known as a segregationist and a defender of the Mississippi way of life. In retirement on a plantation near Indianola, he became active in the Citizens' Council. Just months after leaving Ole Miss he complained to the chancellor after Silver's talk in Jackson, Tennessee. Williams did not want to alienate Trotter, but he understood his malignant influence. Privately Williams acknowledged that he believed Trotter responsible for much of the "poison" spread about Ole Miss. Dean Farley agreed that Trotter was "the cause of most of our bad publicity."[11]

Through the Citizens' Council, Trotter knew Patterson, Simmons, and Mabry. In two closed sessions in February 1957, Trotter, Mabry, and three others took their concerns about Ole Miss to the General Legislative Investigating Committee (GLIC). At the first hearing, Trotter declared that he would not send a child to Ole Miss because the faculty "brainwash[ed]" students. In addition to REW, controversial literature at the YMCA, and education professor Harley F. Garrett's classes, he pointed to a chemistry professor's helping a black cafeteria worker donate blood and a faculty spouse's referring to a black waiter as a "gentleman." The alleged liberal dominance so alienated Trotter that he refused to join the Alumni Association's athletics committee: he believed that attention paid to football so excited people about the games that they paid little attention to the liberal takeover.[12]

Joseph Jeffreys, a 1924 an alumnus of Baylor University, also testified. A former farmer, teacher, and justice of the peace in the Delta, he studied for a master's degree in education. According to him, Harley Garrett, adviser to the Ole Miss chapter of Phi Delta Kappa, an educators' association, denounced segregation and discussed admitting blacks to Ole Miss. Jeffreys realized that Phi Delta Kappa "has embarked upon a program of tearing away segregation in southern colleges and universities." He contended that integrationists dominated Ole Miss; even a library display of Richard Wright's *Black Boy* reflected antisegregation attitudes. According to him, Ole Miss "now is not a southern school" because "radicals" had taken over.[13]

George Milton Case from Canton, a recent law school graduate, repeated stories about Garrett, Campbell, and Silver. For Case nearly thirty new library books on race, none of which supported segregation, represented "a dangerous method of brainwashing." He also reported that in the spring of 1956 students incorporated the Conservative Club to "relentlessly resist by all peaceful, legal and constitutional means any indoctrination . . . by any left-wing, socialistic or communistic advocate," to uphold state laws, "particularly related to racial issues," and to defend states' rights. But he believed the administration worked behind the scenes to prevent its success, and as a result no professor would affiliate with the club. Its failure demonstrated that integrationists hostile to Mississippi's way of life dominated Ole Miss.[14]

In a second secret session, GLIC heard from Roman Lee Thorn Jr. and Malcolm Mabry. They became friends during the 1956 summer school when they discovered that each belonged to the Citizens' Council. Since 1951 Thorn had taught in the Shaw schools where the people shared his values of "Americanism, free enterprise, segregation, and the southern way of life." He found Ole Miss people "afraid to speak out for segregation," and he worried that professors used spies to identify segregationists. Thorn charged that the director of University High School indoctrinated students with socialist and integrationist views. He reported a class discussion in which a professor reacted positively to school integration in Tennessee. Mabry echoed his earlier complaints.[15] After the two days of testimony, GLIC apparently made no report to the legislature.

In 1957 and 1958, leadership of the critics shifted to Hillery Edwin White and Edwin Wilburn Hooker Sr. of Holmes County. Its residents were predominantly black sharecroppers or tenant farmers for the white elite, of which White and Hooker were leaders. Born in the county seat of Lexington in 1907, White graduated from Southwestern College (now Rhodes College) in Memphis and the Ole Miss law school, and he practiced in Holmes County. Before and after wartime army service, he was elected to the legislature. White lived next door to Hooker. A half-dozen years younger, he was born in New Orleans but descended from old Holmes County families. Hooker, his father, and his grandfather all graduated from Ole Miss, and Hooker met his wife there. He managed the family's four-thousand-acre plantation. In 1958, Wilburn Hooker Jr. studied at Ole Miss.[16]

White and Hooker were not close friends or colleagues. White was a quiet, scholarly attorney; Hooker was a gregarious businessman and politician who had been elected to the state house of representatives in 1955. White was a Presbyterian and Hooker a Methodist. Despite their dissimilarities, the two worked together to purge Ole Miss of undesirables. They believed in segregation, participated in the Citizens' Council, opposed socialism and communism, and were loyal alumni. They knew many people at Ole Miss; Hooker especially knew the chancellor and was close to Trotter. They felt compelled to act because nobody "was willing to do what is necessary to correct" a threatening situation where professors taught "foreign" ideas to students.[17]

Hooker became concerned during the 1950 legislative session and again in 1955 when Will Campbell visited Providence Farm. The previous year, Justice Felix Frankfurter's visit to the law school had startled him. Appearances on campus by Hodding Carter and a Yale University dean with alleged communist-front connections troubled White. As a result, he and Hooker in 1955 shared their frustrations and gradually expanded their conversations to include several legislators and others fearful for the university. Trotter encouraged them. As White and Hooker heard from more people, they became the center of a loosely organized effort to purify Ole Miss.[18]

In the summer of 1958, White and Hooker revealed their information to a score of alumni. The group appointed a committee—Hooker, Webb Overstreet of Jackson, and Hugh S. Potts of Kosciusko—that met with the IHL board chairman and in September with the board. A board committee asked them to submit their concerns in writing. In a lawyerly twenty-six pages, White with regret and dismay presented the principles perverted at Ole Miss: "Belief in one omnipotent God; that the Bible is true; that we have souls which are immortal"; private property and private enterprise; states' rights, specifically the control of public schools and the supremacy of the Constitution; "belief in the ethnological truth that where races of different color mix with each other socially that intermarriage inevitably results and that we have the obligation, and the inalienable right, to preserve the identity of the white race."[19]

Allegations also came from W. M. "Chubby" Ellis, a Columbus native, veteran, and Citizens' Council member. After playing on the Rebels' 1947 championship football team, he coached high school football before returning to Ole Miss as assistant registrar. He had reported Will Campbell's Ping-Pong game with a black man and had witnessed Clennon King's attempt to register. Through coaching he befriended Robert Patterson, and through Rebel athletics booster meetings he met Wilburn Hooker. He also developed a relationship with Chuck Trotter, and Milton Case had worked for Ellis in the registrar's office.[20]

In October 1958, about a year after he left Ole Miss, Ellis told the board, "You could not [in 1955] find a segregationist on the faculty or staff." Trotter was the only visible defender of segregation, and one official warned Ellis not to let people know where he stood on the race question because it might cost him his job. Behind professors' pushing students to favor integration he detected "something on the order of a Communist Cell" at Ole Miss. When Ellis began an informal investigation of the communists, Dean L. L. Love and the provost, according to Ellis, threatened to fire him. Soon after, Ellis communicated with Hooker, White, Trotter, and others. Among many details, he reported that Love had invited Negroes into his home through the front door and served them tea or coffee in his living room. Though he believed he lost his job because of his segregationist opinions, Ellis denied any spite or revenge behind his charges.[21]

The trustees accumulated allegations ranging from indictments of the administration to more than one hundred charges about individual professors, the schools of education and law, the student body, and campus religious life. When the board relayed the allegations to the chancellor, Williams turned to Clegg and Alton Bryant to answer. Clegg's FBI credentials made him a logical choice to rebut the charges of disloyalty and communism, and Bryant's Mississippi background and his experiences as an Ole Miss student, professor, and administrator gave him formidable qualifications.[22]

From the beginning, university officials took the charges seriously and worked quietly to build support around the state, especially among alumni. In a reassuring letter to Walter Sillers, for example, Clegg warned of possible damage by further smears and allegations. Worried also about a legislative investigation, he suggested that the state should rely on the trustees to act "with quiet dignity as befits an educational institution" instead of the recent "bombast" and "fanfare." Ole Miss officials repeatedly met with alumni to allay concerns. With one hundred alumni in Jackson, Clegg discussed academic freedom, some of the charges, and the risk to accreditation. A second alumni group formed a committee of lawyers to advise university officials. Alumni also formed a larger auxiliary committee to defend Ole Miss in their communities.[23]

During the winter and early spring of 1959, the university prepared its defense. Though many complaints seemed trivial and even ridiculous, the chancellor recognized the need for a calm, comprehensive, factual rebuttal of each point. At his behest, Clegg and Bryant asked the implicated faculty to reply to the specific charges. As the two administrators conducted their own research and formulated a response, the university's case emerged.[24]

The hard-hitting draft reply challenged the "assumptions underlying the allegations." It admitted that faculty tried to change the "Mississippi way of life," and it pointed to "poverty, ignorance, and absentee ownership of her [the state's] economic system" as examples of what had to change for the state to rise "out of the economic doldrums in which she has wallowed since the Civil War." Economic progress required "new ideas, new methods, new attitudes, and changing habits." The draft argued that a professor's place of birth had little to do with success as a teacher or scholar and that the university "must recognize . . . the genius of the individual regardless of his origin," because in the "Nuclear Age, Mississippi cannot exist as a closed society." It supported academic freedom: "Otherwise . . . the University becomes a tool for the perpetuation of a closed and static society characterized by the thought control so familiar to us in the teachings of the Nazis and the Communists." If the chancellor did not protect professors and students from public opinion and political pressure, the university would violate tenure, cause good faculty to leave and others to stay away, endanger accreditation, and depreciate the value of an Ole Miss degree.[25]

The first draft revealed an understanding that attacks on Ole Miss came in reaction to strains caused by modernization and the civil rights movement.[26] Political reality, however, required a less combative, more conciliatory strategy. Clegg and Bryant, therefore, edited the faculty responses into a calm, neutral document resembling a legal brief, although some professors' combative tone remained. By softening or dropping entirely the earlier bold arguments and analyses, the university ceded some of the high ground in the fight.

In the spring of 1959, the university offered a comprehensive rebuttal of most of the charges. It accepted indisputable contentions, defused other criticisms by explaining them in layman's terms, brushed aside as irrelevant the allegations that would have been difficult to explain, and, when possible, essentially ignored some of the more complicated issues. In general, it pointed to increased alumni support, new construction, student academic and athletic success, strong faculty research, and reaccreditation. To charges of subversion of sacred principles, the chancellor affirmed his beliefs in God, the Bible, and the immortality of the soul; in state sovereignty; in private property; and in the deleterious effects of racial intermarriage and the importance of racial integrity. The report argued that no person committed to such values could subvert them. It then shifted to more than one hundred specific allegations, which with a few exceptions, involved religion, communism, race, or some combination of them.[27]

Regarding the 1954 REW appearance of Dean Luther A. Weigle of Yale Divinity School, the report dismissed complaints by pointing out that he was the father-in-law of Dr. Arthur Guyton of the medical school and that Weigle had not discussed integration. After nearly four years, the university again defended its handling of the 1955 REW controversy. The report denied that student religious organizations were hotbeds of integrationist sentiment. The church affiliation of every professor disproved charges of atheism in the psychology department. To more than twenty charges about professor Quinter M. Lyon's treatment of Christianity, the report explained modern academic theories and interpretations and conceded nothing.[28]

The university also responded to claims of communist subversion. According to the report, no evidence substantiated the charge of a communist cell. Dean Love claimed that Ole Miss "would be just as ruthless in stamping out a communist cell as it would be a dope ring."[29]

The accusations overwhelmingly concerned race, especially segregation. In confronting them, J. D. Williams maintained that the institution did not take a stand on issues, worked within state law, and did not try to make or change the law. Policy questions, including segregation, fell under the purview of state officials, not professors. Dismissing the idea of a plan to subvert southern traditions, the university argued that it did not try to monitor, control, or censor the faculty. The report declared that the administration never lobbied for any candidate or issue and that no university bloc vote existed. Though Williams took no official position on segregation or integration, he said that he personally supported segregation. His statement attempted to defend him against charges of disloyalty and to deflect attacks on Ole Miss. One observer thought he had "sort of sold his soul to the devil" to protect Ole Miss momentarily.[30] The risky maneuver locked Williams into publicly supporting segregation.

Hooker, White, and their allies also challenged the racial views of Dean Robert J. Farley. He replied that he neither supported integration nor opposed segregation, that he had advocated keeping the public schools open, that Justice Frankfurter had spoken at the law school *before* the *Brown* decision, and that Farley had signed a petition defending the integrity of the Supreme Court and its justices. As proof of the absence of subversion at the law school, the report pointed to its graduates' success in defending southern values as politicians, judges, and other public leaders.[31]

The university's report went to the board's special committee for review. The slow answer frustrated Hooker and White, but the board may have wanted to prevent Ole Miss from becoming an issue in the 1955 gubernatorial election. Avoiding any reply in June and July, the trustees invited complainants to their

August meeting. During the second week of July newspapers began to discuss the controversy, and initial commentary backed J. D. Williams and Ole Miss. As a result of the publicity, the board chairman said that the chancellor's views on segregation had satisfied the trustees when they hired him, and in the meantime he had never equivocated on segregation. As a result, he had "the full confidence of the members of the Board."[32]

Surprised by the board's preemptive judgment, Hooker and White released their accusations in a series of press releases designed for maximum publicity. Beginning on July 13, their half-dozen installments ran in newspapers during the last two weeks of July.[33]

In response the university marshaled its defenses. On June 28, sixty alumni met in Jackson at the invitation of the head of the alumni association. They voted full confidence in the chancellor and organized a campaign to protect him and their alma mater. Within weeks alumni in Hinds, Grenada, Coahoma, and Pike Counties and the Washington County Bar Association backed Williams and Ole Miss. Meridian alumnus Martin V. B. Miller said Hooker and White "evidently believe in the technique of Hitler, that accusations often repeated, even if false, will be accepted as true." The *Tupelo Daily Journal* vouched for Williams as "a Christian gentleman, a scholar and one who believes in the Southern way of life." One student leader dispatched the charges as "absurd and a bit silly." Two weeks after the charges became public, Alton Bryant observed that "nobody is paying much attention to the charges." Hooker and White believed the attacks on them "just go to prove we are right" and contributed to the "whitewash."[34]

The crisis climaxed on August 27 when the trustees cleared the university and its faculty of the "sensational charges of teaching and conspiring to accomplish apostasy, subversion, and the violation of Mississippi law and tradition." The trustees "unanimously and unreservedly" expressed confidence in the chancellor and his beliefs, actions, and loyalty to the state. As for subversion and communism, the board decided they were "without foundation in fact." The board also endorsed academic freedom. Among the hundreds of university employees, the trustees acknowledged the inevitability of "some sign of human frailty or some unwise action or statement," and they acknowledged "some tactlessness and imprudence" on the part of a few faculty. The problems were, however, negligible.[35]

Public discussion of the Hooker-White charges soon dwindled, but the chancellor feared an extensive legislative investigation. His fears were justified. As the controversy reached its peak during the summer, Hooker contacted the GLIC chairman and asked that the committee postpone its scheduled routine visit to the university until after he and White received a response to their charges; the committee thought his suggestion wise. After the board's response, Hooker and White refused to relent and again charged that the "universities are hotbeds of disbelief" and renewed their demand for specific answers to each of their accusations. In the fall of 1959 GLIC held a one-day hearing in which Hooker and White repeated their accusations. The committee called no other witnesses and did not to pursue the matter. In the next legislative session Representative Hooker tried unsuccessfully to revive interest in the issue.[36]

In November, IHL executive secretary Jobe sent Hooker and White a copy of the trustees' statement and declared that their charges had been investigated and the people involved had provided the board with full and satisfactory explanations. Jobe said that the board stood ready for the governor or the legislature to check its performance but wanted and expected no further inquiry. Chancellor Williams concluded that Ole Miss had, through the efforts of alumni, faculty, staff, and the board, escaped "what could have been a popular witch hunt by a mob."[37]

Wilburn Hooker, however, proved unyielding. During the spring 1960 legislative session, he repeated his indictment and dismissed the trustees' assessment as nothing but a "whitewash." Rejecting the renewed assault, the chairman of the IHL board declared the case closed. A final, devastating blast at Hooker came from Hodding Carter. Addressing "Poor Wilburn Hooker," he poked fun at his "Neanderthal ideas" about "thought control." What Hooker saw as the influence of communists, integrationists, and atheists merely amounted, according to Carter, to the working of common sense. "But common sense is something that Wilburn Hooker would not recognize. To do so you need to be relatively intelligent, and no one ever accused Wilburn of that."[38] The specific charges finally disappeared.

By the spring of 1960, Ole Miss had survived a serious attack. Conservatives failed to cleanse it of traitors to the southern way of life, but they persisted in their concerns about communism, subversion, and integration. Though the emphasis on the university declined, the preservation of state sovereignty and segregation remained top priorities. In the following two years, several more episodes involving the volatile mix of communism, states' rights, and segregation in Mississippi demonstrated segregationists' escalating fears about any change in race relations. Local media, especially radio and television, exacerbated tensions.

Early in 1961 the law school invited U.S. Supreme Court Justice Tom C. Clark to address a banquet honoring the Mississippi Supreme Court. Dean Farley felt honored to host his old acquaintance. Inviting anyone associated with the *Brown* decision would likely cause an uproar, but Farley supported the law of the land, and Clark seemed the least objectionable member of the Court. A Texan, Clark had deep roots in the South and in Mississippi. His paternal grandfather had been a Mississippi slave owner, and his father had graduated from Ole Miss before moving to Texas. In 1949 Clark's nomination to the Supreme Court aroused objections from liberals who considered him too conservative, too hostile to unions, and unfriendly to civil rights.[39]

For Mississippi segregationists, Clark's most notorious act had been his support of the *Brown* decision. As a result, Governor Barnett objected to his invitation and refused to attend the dinner in Oxford. Others agreed. Speaker Sillers privately called the invitation "abhorrent" and damned the justice as "a member of the 'Dark Court' which plunged the dagger of integration and mongrelization into the backs of the white people of America and the South." Although the chancellor made no official defense of academic freedom, indeed did not reply to the critics, Dean Farley countered that Clark's "talk will have nothing to do with the segregation question." A few days before Clark's appearance, an anonymous memorandum mailed in Sovereignty Commission envelopes asked each member of the IHL board if Clark would be allowed to speak. The commission director denied knowing anything about it and refused to comment on any possible investigation. The chairman of the trustees acknowledged receiving the letter but suggested that the board would take no action.[40]

Clark's visit proved uneventful. Four hundred people, including a "blue ribbon roster of the state's bar and judiciary," attended the banquet. During his visit, Clark avoided issues that might come before the Supreme Court and instead talked generally about how the Court worked. His national stature, conservative constitutional views, southern origins, and Mississippi ties undoubtedly made stirring up segregationists unlikely, but a reporter offered a different explanation. The Sovereignty Commission deployed Mississippians to explain the southern way of life to northerners, so, "how could Mississippians refuse to accept speakers who were integrationists while expecting audiences in other areas to accept the Sovereignty Commission speakers?"[41]

Mississippi accepted Clark with relative equanimity but would not tolerate protests against a visiting evangelist of segregation and anticommunism. Four days after Clark departed, the Sovereignty Commission sponsored Myers G. Lowman, a Methodist layman and reputed expert anticommunist. The fifty-seven-year-old businessman and native of Pennsylvania served in Cincinnati as executive secretary of the Circuit Riders, a group dedicated to eliminating socialist and communist influences in their church. In 1956 the national Methodist Church censured the Circuit Riders and in 1960 expressed dismay at their tactics. Lowman claimed that nine thousand ministers and six thousand teachers "wittingly or unwittingly" supported communism.[42]

In January, the Paul Revere Ladies, an outgrowth of the Citizens' Councils, hosted Lowman at meetings in McComb, Vicksburg, and Yazoo City. A second visit in February sponsored by the Sovereignty Commission included stops at Greenwood, the Mississippi Vocational and Industrial College for Negroes, Ole Miss, and several other colleges, to raise awareness of the threats by communists, civil rights activists, and other subversives. The chief danger, Lowman said, came from communists who used racial discord to weaken the nation. They already had considerable success controlling the NAACP. Lowman implored Mississippians "to resist to the fullest" the efforts of communist "front organizations" to subvert their way of life.[43]

In Ole Miss's Fulton Chapel, the balding and bespectacled Lowman repeated his warnings and claimed to have evidence of communist infiltration. Though he cleared Ole Miss of communist contamination, he claimed to have documentary proof of Hodding Carter's communist connection and branded him a communist sympathizer. As a friend of Carter, Jim Silver found the charges unbelievable. In the question-and-answer session, Silver challenged Lowman, accused him of slandering Carter, and demanded Lowman produce his evidence. In a heated exchange, neither convinced the other. When Lowman finally regained control of the proceedings, he refused to recognize Silver for further questions, but students continued the questioning.[44]

Less than two weeks later, Silver, scheduled to speak to the Mississippi Historical Society on "Mississippi in the Confederacy," renewed his attack on Lowman. According to Silver, when Lowman spoke to the Daughters of the American Revolution a few days after his engagement at the university, he included Silver on his list of suspected communists. Lowman also accused Silver of leading a demonstration when he spoke at Ole Miss. Silver said, "There was no demonstration. Nobody interrupted Lowman." He conceded that he may not have treated Lowman politely, but he simply wanted proof of the allegations.[45]

The campus confrontation captured little attention, but the *Jackson State Times* reported Silver's remarks, and letters to the editor briefly continued the controversy. Lowman wrote the *State Times* to welcome criticism and to accuse Silver, Carter, and others of "socialistic, pro-Communistic and other forms of un-American activities." Trying to have the last, winning word, Silver quoted J. Edgar Hoover's *Masters of Deceit* that condemned people who "slap the label of 'Red' or 'Communist' on anybody who happened to be different from them or to have an idea with which they do not agree." According to the FBI director,

"Smears, character assassination, and the scattering of irresponsible charges have no place in this nation."[46] Despite Silver's efforts, Lowman's crusade and Justice Clark's earlier visit reinforced the defense of segregation and state sovereignty against subversive influences.

Later in 1961 the Jackson Citizens' Council brought Carleton Putnam to Mississippi as part of its campaign to promote the southern way of life. A native of New York, Putnam graduated from Princeton University and the Columbia University law school before entering the airline business in the 1930s. After his airline merged with Delta Air Lines in 1953, he served as chairman of the new company for a year before turning his attention to writing a multivolume biography of Theodore Roosevelt. In September 1958, Putnam became embroiled in debates over race. When *Life* magazine would not publish his reply to an editorial on school desegregation, the editor of the *Memphis Commercial Appeal*, who had become a friend of Putnam when as an airline executive he had lived in Memphis, did publish it. In October 1958, Putnam wrote a similar letter to President Eisenhower, and newspapers reprinted it. In 1961 he wrote *Race and Reason: A Yankee View* largely in the form of a "point by point" reply to his critics.[47]

Putnam objected to the attempt by one section unaffected by racial problems to tell another how to deal with its race relations, and he defended segregation as the will of the southern white majority. For him school segregation remained the key: integrated schools promoted social contacts and led to intermarriage. Even more he decried the "equalitarian virus" in social science that almost eliminated considerations of racial differences and that helped communists who "have made the integration movement a part of their conspiracy." Putnam stressed the biological inequality of the races and rejected as "total error" the anthropological stress on the environment's determinative effects. At the same time, he disagreed with the southern white emphasis on states' rights because arguments over states' rights simply did not deal with the essential "hidden issue" of the black race's lack of adaptability due to serious limitations in "character and intelligence."[48]

Soon after publication of *Race and Reason* early in 1961, the *Jackson Clarion-Ledger* endorsed it, the Citizens' Council recommended it, and columnist Florence Sillers Ogden praised its defense of "the integrity of the white race." Governor Barnett sent copies to other governors because he believed that many critics of the South failed to understand segregation. He thought that Putnam's analysis contained "a brief, forceful, and understandable presentation of the reasons why integration" would "destroy the white race." By late summer, Putnam's work was, except for the Bible, the all-time best seller at one Jackson bookstore.[49]

The Jackson Citizens' Council invited Putnam to speak to a fund-raising banquet in late October 1961. Each diner received an autographed copy of *Race and Reason*. Representative John Bell Williams chaired the Carleton Putnam Dinner Committee of 174 leading citizens. Urging attendance, Williams warned, "Our enemies are marshaling their forces for an all-out assault against our people and institutions." The governor declared October 26 "Race and Reason Day" and exhorted citizens to attend the banquet. On the same day, Myers Lowman and Fulton Lewis III spoke to the Paul Revere Ladies. A former researcher for the House Un-American Activities Committee, Lewis alerted them to communism's internal threat, especially among American young people. Lowman again linked communists to the civil rights movement.[50]

Five hundred people attended the Citizens' Council banquet. In introducing the speaker, President W. D. McCain of Mississippi Southern College praised Putnam for providing "abundant food for thought" for northerners and giving "a clear presentation of the South's position in terms the North can understand." Putnam's speech repeated the book's themes about pseudoscience, racial differences, racial integrity, and states' rights. He received a standing ovation.[51]

Although some of Putnam's comments about states' rights may have surprised his audience, the *Jackson Clarion-Ledger* and the Citizens' Council's magazine *The Citizen* both praised his address. Not only did he defend segregation, but he supported the ideas of white supremacy and Negro inferiority "when white civilized society as free people know it is already on the brink of disaster." Even Putnam's disagreement with southern segregationists over states' rights was a difference over tactics in the defense of segregation; on the constitutional merits of states' rights, he fully agreed with his audience. Far from contradicting white Mississippians, Putnam's speech in Jackson, as well as his book, validated them and encouraged them to fight on.[52]

Soon after Putnam departed, one hundred whites called the Group of Mississippi Friends of General Edwin A. Walker prepared an appearance by the general. A West Point graduate and veteran of World War II and Korea, Walker in 1957 commanded the federal forces in Little Rock during the school desegregation crisis. Early in 1961 he gained national attention when the army relieved him of his command in Germany because he had indoctrinated soldiers with the ideas of the John Birch Society. For Walker, "communism is the enemy," and he believed Americans "are at war. We are infiltrated. We are losing that war." Unable to serve under the restrictions placed on him by "little men, who in the name of my country, punish loyal service to it," he ended his thirty-year military career, but he continued his fight against communism.[53]

Mississippians invited Walker to Jackson on December 29. When he arrived for just his third public appearance since leaving the army, Governor Ross Barnett, Representative John Bell Williams, the Jackson mayor, and fifty others greeted him at the airport. At a press conference Walker reassured his southern friends that the president, not the military, decided to employ troops in Little Rock and that as a soldier he could not have avoided carrying out the order. Walker considered such a use of troops without a request from the state's governor to be contrary to the Constitution.[54]

Later he devoted most of his ninety-minute address to attacking communism, the United Nations, and the Kennedys, but he also hit on many other important themes. He praised Mississippi as "a great state—greatest in its stand for freedom" and lauded its defense of state sovereignty. "The Communists are afraid of you," he declared. "They distrust you and the power of your state sovereignty and your great unity of purpose." He praised "men armed with the Bible and Christianity." To the audience's delight, Walker blasted the media's treatment of Mississippi and called it "the most lied-about state in the Union." More than three thousand people interrupted the speech ninety-seven times with cheers and applause, including a final standing ovation.[55]

If Walker's address did not explicitly tie states' rights and anticommunism to segregation, the audience understood the connection. The next month, *The Citizen* reinforced the links by printing both Walker's speech and an article on Robert C. Weaver's nomination to be secretary of the new Department of Housing and Urban Affairs. Declaring that "Congress must decide if a black skin is an acceptable substitute for patriotism," it denounced the Negro nominee and devoted a page to "The Pro-Communist Record of Robert C. Weaver." The Citizens' Council believed the new department intended to destroy segregation, and it highlighted the bond between communism and integration with a one-page advertisement offering for sale recordings of the recent speeches by Putnam and Walker.[56]

The 1961 visits by Walker, Putnam, and Lowman spread the conservative gospel and alerted the public to imminent dangers, especially the burgeoning civil rights movement, and confirmed and stiffened segregationist resistance. They represented support for Mississippi's way of life by nonsouthern authorities in the church, business, and the military. The former general embodied the courage and devotion that segregationists hoped to inspire in Mississippi. Validated and inspired by the outside authorities, Mississippi's white elite could more confidently advocate segregation and expose native opponents.

In January 1962, segregationists identified one dangerous dissident, Jimmie Robertson, the *Mississippian* editor. His dissent alarmed them because he commanded a public forum at Ole Miss and he was a Mississippian. Robertson created controversy by calling for the admission of mainland China to the

United Nations, criticizing Race and Reason Day, and challenging the governor's budget predictions as "irresponsible statements which have no basis in fact."[57] When he blasted the Sovereignty Commission's investigation of Hazel Brannon Smith, the liberal editor of the *Lexington Advertiser*, he went too far. Robertson asked, "Are we, or are we not in favor of constitutional government? If we are, then included is our endorsement of the Bill of Rights."[58]

Complaining that Robertson "harps on civil rights, but not on states' rights," a *Jackson Clarion-Ledger* columnist asked, "Which side are you on, by the way?" Tom Ethridge believed that the student paper "should not give aid and comfort to those seeking to overthrow the established order." Representative Bedford Waddell from Copiah County called the editorial an "atheistic, communist brand of tomfoolery" and advocated closing Ole Miss if it did not stop publication of such ideas. Another legislator and alumnus defended the editor and freedom of the press but "disagree[d] with everything this fellow Robertson has said." Robertson's main support came from Ole Miss. The chairman of the student judicial board denied that Robertson was a communist or an atheist. Another student called Waddell a "disgrace." The *Mississippian*'s editorial staff defended Robertson as "distinctly American." From Greenville, Hodding Carter declared that Waddell had given a "clear statement of totalitarianism." The next morning an effigy identified as "Waddell" was hanged from the student union. The controversy subsided, perhaps because of the end of the semester or because the *Mississippian* ran a long article on George Monroe, a prominent conservative student and a leader of the Patriotic American Youth.[59]

Early in the spring term the newspaper again angered segregationists. Two letters supported Robertson's editorial on the Sovereignty Commission, and one suggested renaming the group the State Gestapo Commission. In response, the *Rebel Underground* accused Robertson and "his leftist minority" of having taken "complete control of" and "prostituted" the *Mississippian* behind a "veil of non-objectivism."[60]

Robertson reacted ambivalently. He ridiculed the *Rebel Underground* as a "comic strip" and disparaged the intelligence of the writers, yet he also challenged his competitors to reveal their identities and defend their positions in open debate. Though unafraid of having his editorial positions questioned, he believed fairness dictated that everyone know who his critics were and what they advocated. A few days after the appearance of the *Rebel Underground*, the student senate entertained a resolution to reprimand Robertson for misusing his editorial columns. In the meantime, the editor continued his critical commentaries. With a U.S. Senate committee investigating Edwin Walker, Robertson attacked the general's "bigoted cause" in indoctrinating soldiers and smearing public officials as communists. Robertson also persisted in his controversial attack on the state's unwritten rule prohibiting integrated athletic contests and supported the emergence of a Republican Party and two-party politics in Mississippi.[61]

A second *Rebel Underground* in the middle of February rebuked Robertson's "integration kick" and "left-wing radicalism and rabble-rousing." A letter to the *Mississippian* also chastised Robertson: "The less said about racial problems, the better off the State of Mississippi will be." In a letter from "A True Southerner," John F. Runte ranted, "When persons try to push a nigger down the White peoples throats, then in my opinion they are either communist or communist sympathizers or both." Two more editions of the *Rebel Underground* continued the attack on Robertson. Dropped from an airplane flying low over the campus, the third installment challenged the editor: "Mr. Robertson, if you are truly for segregation and the preservation of our way of life, then you will realize that there is no middle ground—either you have segregation or you do not have it." The semester's final *Rebel Underground* quoted a national conservative spokesman: "The constitutional integrity of the states is our best defense. That is why the Communists . . . have made it an important objective to destroy our states' rights."[62]

While the controversy churned, the student senate debated reprimanding Robertson. After lengthy discussion, it accepted a compromise, proposed by Senator Eastland's son-in-law Champ Terney, that stated that the senators were "not in complete agreement" with Robertson but supported the editor's "right to handle the editorial columns as he sees fit." Robertson applauded the action. After another month, the affair fizzled when the wide-ranging final report by the senate committee investigating the student newspaper made no recommendations regarding Robertson's editorials or the editorial policy in general. Robertson finished his term as editor in May 1962, and in his final editorial he stood by all of his earlier positions.[63]

Though the irritating Robertson had by the summer of 1962 departed, the United Press International reported, "Civil rights suits have been filed in flood proportions in Mississippi." Four Freedom Rider cases sought to end segregation in interstate travel facilities. One lawsuit aimed to integrate Jackson's public auditorium, parks, and libraries. The oldest lawsuit involved segregated beaches on the Gulf Coast. The federal government initiated eighteen of the lawsuits, while blacks with the help of the NAACP filed three. Most pertained to voting rights and were part of a Kennedy administration campaign to increase the number of black voters. In 1962 the possibility of more black voters took on added significance when two blacks sought election to Congress, and four of the state's congressional districts had black majorities.[64]

The state's politicians portrayed the unprecedented perils in cataclysmic terms and roused whites to the cause of segregation, states' rights, and anti-communism. In his 1962 state of the state address, Governor Barnett proclaimed that "it is imperative that we stand together in unbroken ranks to maintain the sovereignty of this great state and to keep Mississippi the true home of conservative, constitutional government." He denounced "the whims of vicious minority groups, the desire of selfish politicians, and the biased decisions of irresponsible, stacked courts." He criticized the "so-called 'Justice' Department" for filing so many lawsuits "under the now rather moth-eaten misnomer of 'civil rights.'" He concluded, "We must never give up the fight. We must never desert the field of battle. . . . We must protest every invasion. We must fight every inch of the way." In a speech to the Memphis Citizens' Council, he identified racial segregation as the fundamental value. "Integration is not inevitable. That is pure unadulterated propaganda." He argued, "The only way integration can prevail is for us to lie sublimely down and let it come." Honing his appeal, he later proclaimed "Anti-Communist Day in Mississippi" by calling on people to aid the Citizens' Council and the Sovereignty Commission in fighting "Socialism, left-wingism, and Communism."[65]

Others joined the chorus. In the spring of 1962, Ole Miss sponsored a series on the threat of communism. Assistant director of the FBI William C. Sullivan spoke to student religious groups on "Communism and Christianity"; John C. Satterfield of Yazoo City, president of the American Bar Association, talked on "They Will Bury Themselves—If We Help Them." In Jackson a scientist spoke on "Communism and Integration: Partners in Ruin!" And the president of Harding College in Arkansas spoke over a statewide radio network on "Communist Encirclement." Judge Russel Moore of Jackson, William Simmons of the Citizens' Council, and Attorney General Patterson also chimed in. Even an Episcopal rector from Texas, speaking in Jackson on "Why Integration Is Un-Christian," invoked Jesus Christ to defend segregation and racial purity and denounced integrationists who "are leveling an organized attack of the forces of hell upon God's order in nature and in human society."[66]

Additional strong support for white supremacy and racial segregation came from the state's electronic media. Thirty-seven radio stations in the Mississippi Patriotic Network frequently broadcast segregationist speeches. One influential station in the capital, WRBC, owned by the Rebel Broadcasting Company, had, according to one scholar, "a large effect on racial attitudes and behaviors in the Jackson area." It promoted the Freedom Bookstore that carried Citizens' Council publications, and it appealed for support of Barnett's segregationist positions. In the opinion of one analyst, WRBC "presented a one-sided, pro-segregationist viewpoint" and its editorials "encouraged lawlessness in the name of the preservation of states rights."[67]

One of Jackson's two television stations was part of a media powerhouse dominated by the Hederman family. With Robert and Tom Hederman as major stockholders, the Capitol Broadcasting Company owned WJTV, and the Hedermans also controlled WSLI radio, in addition to the *Clarion-Ledger* and the *Daily News*. WJTV's editorial views echoed the positions of the Hederman newspapers. Its newscasters shunned the courtesy titles of "Mr." and "Mrs." when referring to blacks, and one broadcast personality used the word "nigger" on the air. WJTV's competitor, WLBT-TV, had a complex ownership arrangement designed to skirt state law. The Lamar Life Insurance Company, owned by conservative Dallas businessmen Clint and John Murchison, started the station in 1953 but soon established a separate Lamar Life Broadcasting and sold the station to five employees, while retaining the option to repurchase it at the original price. WLBT had two sister radio stations in the state capital, WJDX and WJDX-FM. According to one student of television, WJTV and WLBT competed vigorously but were also "steadfast allies" in defending segregation and the southern way of life and together "complemented an already intimidating white power bloc."[68]

Like others in the state, the Jackson television stations carried only the segregationist point of view, and they regularly ran the Citizens' Council Forum with its slogan of "states' rights, racial integrity" and with "Dixie" as its theme music. WLBT also gave free airtime to the John Birch Society and to the Women for Constitutional Government. WLBT's station manager and part-owner, Fred L. Beard, actively supported the Citizens' Council and shaped the station's policies according to the council's ideology. During the Little Rock integration crisis in 1957, WLBT and WJDX stopped playing the national anthem at the start of each broadcast day and replaced it with an advertisement: "Don't let this happen in Mississippi, join the Citizens' Council today." To keep out all integrationist views, the television stations routinely blocked network news and entertainment shows that favorably presented blacks and racial integration. WLBT often prefaced network news with a statement to the effect that what followed was "biased, managed northern news," and the station interrupted race-related segments of *Today* and the *Huntley-Brinkley Report*, sometimes to show local news instead. In September 1955, for example, WLBT blocked an NBC interview with the NAACP's Thurgood Marshall with the explanation, "Sorry, Cable Trouble." In one two-month period in 1962, WLBT carried only one of twenty-four parts of *Today* that handled racial issues, and it broadcast only the episode of *Meet the Press* that featured Governor George C. Wallace. A WLBT newsman also used the pronunciation "nigra." Racial prejudice also affected entertainment: no blacks appeared on WLBT's locally produced *Romper Room* for children or its weekly *Teen Tempo* dance program. The unfairness and imbalance caused Medgar Evers and the NAACP starting in 1955 to protest to the Federal Communications Commission.[69] In 1962, however, the radio and television stations continued to provide another powerful bulwark against racial change.

Though the civil rights movement constituted the paramount peril, whites also understood many unrelated events to be part of a conspiracy against the South and its interests. Many whites, for example, interpreted the Supreme Court's outlawing of compulsory school prayer as part of a pattern involving race, religion, and communism. Representative Arthur Winstead saw it as another of "the numerous crackpot decisions of this Court since its infamous 1954 Black Monday ruling in the school segregation case." Referring to the Supreme Court as "Frankenstein," Charles Hills damned the "leftist" decision and complained that the Court too often used the South as a "whipping-boy." As the *Jackson Clarion-Ledger* editorialized, the prayer ruling "moved this nation in the direction of an officially godless state." To make clear the links among prayer, anticommunism, and segregation, the editor then quoted from the Communist Party's 1928 platform that declared as its goals the abolition of racial segregation, the end of Negro disfranchisement, and the elimination of laws against racial intermarriage. The *Meridian Star* reacted with similar horror to the prayer decision by exhorting, "We must take action now—before it is too late."[70]

10. "Thought Control": The Editor and the Professor

■ ■

In the summer of 1960, W. A. Lufburrow, the executive secretary of the States' Rights Council of Georgia, told William J. Simmons of the Citizens' Council about the activities of Billy Barton, an Ole Miss student intern with the *Atlanta Journal*. Lufburrow's information supposedly came from another intern, a student at Tulane University. According to the Georgia sources, Barton had participated in sit-ins and had become a protégé of Ralph McGill, the liberal editor of the *Atlanta Constitution*. In addition, Lufburrow reported Barton's alleged friendship with P. D. East, the iconoclastic publisher of the *Petal Paper* in southern Mississippi; Barton reportedly planned to visit East when he returned. Lufburrow warned that Barton was "very dangerous."[1]

Billy Clyde Barton, a farm boy from Pontotoc County just east of Oxford, enrolled at Ole Miss in the fall of 1958. A veteran of his high school newspaper, he began writing for the *Mississippian*. He became the managing editor, ran unsuccessfully for editor in his sophomore year, and prepared to run again the next year. Barton wanted to become editor in preparation for a career as a reporter and newspaperman; he had little interest in a contentious editorial page. After his sophomore year, he landed an internship with the *Atlanta Journal* and ignited a controversy.[2]

The brouhaha over Barton, and a second one over a law professor, demonstrated that Ole Miss could not remain aloof from larger controversies. The fear of subversives did not end with the dismissal of the charges brought by Edwin White and Wilburn Hooker. Segregationists demanding conformity to the racial orthodoxy monitored the university for any deviation, while anticommunists probed for disloyalty. Instead of a general attack, however, they focused on individual students such as Billy Barton and faculty like William P. Murphy.

Bill Simmons forwarded the information to the Sovereignty Commission because he "regard[ed] this information as important, and very revealing." Aware that Barton wanted to be the next *Mississippian* editor, Simmons sensed a conspiracy by integrationists "to plant sympathizers in key positions on our college campuses, where they can exert a maximum influence on student opinion." Alarmed at such subversion, Simmons believed "this is the first time we have been fortunate enough to gain knowledge of their detailed plans in advance." Within days, he spread the word; he reportedly promised one student the money necessary to defeat Barton.[3]

During the fall semester, as rumors about Barton circulated in the state and at Ole Miss, a lawyer visited Malcolm Dale, the *Mississippian* editor, to alert him that a subversive would run for editor. The attorney allegedly also conferred with Hugh Clegg. People on campus began to hear that Barton belonged to the NAACP. About the same time, a friend told Barton about the Citizens' Council's interest in him and warned him to write more conservative editorials.[4]

Barton refused to be cowed. In a series of signed editorials that fall, he challenged a proposed constitutional amendment that provided that only citizens "of good moral character" would be allowed to vote. Although he realized the amendment sought to prevent blacks from voting, Barton opposed it because it would permit an intolerable abridgement of everyone's individual rights. He warned that it not only would subject their state to justifiable ridicule, but it would invite federal legislation to eliminate literacy tests and protect voting rights. When voters in November 1960 both approved the amendment and elected unpledged, "unreconstructed" presidential electors advocated by Governor Barnett, Barton thought the state had left the Union.[5]

Pressure on Barton intensified. In the governor's office, Philip Bryant, a twenty-two-year-old legislator from Oxford, overheard Barnett's secretary mention that a member of the NAACP worked on the Ole Miss newspaper. When Bryant inquired about the individual's identity, she named Barton; when Bryant asked for proof, she referred him to Barnett. Confirming the report, Barnett declared that he did not want an NAACP member editing the newspaper. The opposition to Barton increased further in December 1960 when the director of the Citizens' Council's youth division discussed Barton's allegedly subversive activities with several Ole Miss students and organized a rival campaign for editor.[6]

Early in December 1960, editor Dale asked Barnett about reports that Barton belonged to the NAACP because the information reportedly came from the governor's office. Dale asked for evidence so that he could "correct the situation if such is the case." The governor forwarded the request to Albert Jones, the director of the Sovereignty Commission, who sent Dale a copy of Simmons's confidential report of the previous August and promised to try to find out if Barton belonged to the NAACP. Disputing the information, Dale claimed that Barton had not participated in the sit-ins but had merely covered them as a reporter, that Barton was probably not even acquainted with P. D. East, and that Barton would likely not be a candidate again.[7]

The day after Dale's reply, Barton discovered the letters in the *Mississippian* office. He was "embarrassed, chagrined, hurt, upset, and became extremely nervous and humiliated when he discovered the libelous writings." Barton decided after Christmas to appeal to the governor to "set the record straight." He told Barnett that he reported the previous summer on one sit-in at Rich's department store in Atlanta, and it was the only one he had ever seen. After the end of his *Atlanta Journal* job, he went directly to Ole Miss and did not visit P. D. East. Furthermore, he had never met East, Ralph McGill, or any member of the NAACP. Barton requested Barnett's assistance because the "untrue reports have already been very damaging to my reputation." Preoccupied with the rumors, Barton had neglected his studies. "Since these reports have resulted in an extremely bad situation," the twenty-year-old suggested, "I feel sure that you will want to correct them." He sent copies of his letter to Chancellor Williams, Hugh Clegg, and Dean L. L. Love.[8]

A week later Barnett offered an evasive reply. "To set the record straight," he emphasized that "none of the reports mentioned in your letter *originated* in my office." The governor was literally accurate, but Barton believed that the circulation within Mississippi of some allegations indeed had started in Barnett's office. Going further, Barnett alleged that the charge that Barton belonged to the NAACP began at Ole Miss because a *Mississippian* colleague mentioned it to one of Barnett's staff. While the governor claimed to hope that the rumors were false, he absolved himself of responsibility for them and seemed to deny any connection to the charges. He also did not acknowledge the involvement of the Sovereignty Commission or the Citizens' Council.[9]

Barnett's response frustrated Barton, and the rumors continued to swirl. The allegations took on additional significance when he prepared to run for editor against Jimmie Robertson, assistant editor of the *Mississippian*. Finally, on March 10, Barton responded publicly to the accusations; the state's major newspapers made it front-page news. He charged that state officials were "using Gestapo tactics" to destroy his candidacy. In addition to a "high state official," the Sovereignty Commission and the Citizens' Council had circulated "malicious lies" about him. "One outrageous charge is that I am a member of the National Association for the Advancement of Colored People and have been planted on this campus to influence student opinion. This," said the incredulous Barton, "is a preposterous and an utter lie." Referring to the confidential report on his activities, he charged, "Every report filed by this individual was completely false." Barton reiterated his intention to run for editor and announced that he was considering a slander and libel lawsuit against two representatives of the Sovereignty Commission and the Citizens' Council.[10]

When questioned about Barton's statements, Barnett denied knowing anything about "the boy" and his charges, did not remember exchanging letters with him, referred reporters to the head of the Sovereignty Commission and to the attorney general, and refused further comment. A few days later he vaguely promised that Barton would have a chance to defend himself. Albert Jones responded to questions about his letter to Dale by asking, "What letter?" Shown a copy of the letter, he dodged additional queries: "I haven't the authority to make any statement in the matter." Bill Simmons echoed, "I don't know anything about it," and he tried to disassociate the Citizens' Council from the controversy.[11]

The next day the *Jackson State Times* ran a front-page editorial entitled "Mississippi Must Not Whitewash This Obligation." Editor Oliver Emmerich questioned if the commission had "developed into a secret police organization," and he asked, "What right has the Sovereignty Commission to maintain files on any Mississippian, if no law has been violated?" He demanded that Governor Barnett immediately hold a public hearing to determine the truth of the charges. When asked about the editorial, the governor dismissed it: "You don't think I read things that Oliver Emmerich writes, do you?" Others joined Emmerich in a forceful fusillade against "the authoritarian goose-steppers." Hodding Carter contended that "we have reached the point of near insanity on any matters dealing with the race issue"; Paul Pittman of the *Tylertown Times* condemned the "McCarthylike attack on good citizens"; Hazel Brannon Smith expressed revulsion at the "lies, slander and vilification." Representative Philip Bryant, fearing a "private gestapo," called for restricting the Sovereignty Commission before it became a "state secret police."[12]

Ole Miss student leaders, including the *Mississippian* editor, cautiously supported Barton. Worried that the charges reflected on all students, they declared in a written statement that his conduct *on campus* had "been beyond reproach" and that they believed "he is innocent of each accusation." Jimmie Robertson called Barton "a personal friend of mine for nearly two years," rejected the charges against him as "totally false," and resented outsiders interfering in campus politics. The *Mississippian* also denounced the "smear campaign" and for the first time acknowledged and condemned "the vilest, most contemptible type of campaign . . . a whisper campaign" that resembled methods of the Nazi Gestapo.[13]

Four days after Barton revealed the campaign against him, the *Jackson State Times* flew him to Jackson for a lie detector test. Before the test, he signed a statement vowing to live by the results. J. D. Pittman, a Jackson private detective, administered the polygraph test. Trained by the FBI, he had worked for the Jackson Police Department and had used the device since 1947. Pittman asked the student seventeen questions. Among "Do you like to play golf?" and "Do you enjoy going fishing?" Pittman interspersed questions about Barton's supposed NAACP membership, his alleged relationships with P. D. East and Ralph McGill, and his purported participation in an Atlanta sit-in. In every case Barton repeated his earlier denials. At the end of the session, Pittman declared, "The polygraph test that I performed on Billy Barton March 14, 1961, indicates that he exercised no deception whatsoever in his answers."[14]

Under a banner headline, the afternoon *State Times* published all of the questions and answers from the interrogation. Across the top of the front page it also reproduced the polygraph chart with a caption that announced, "This polygraph chart of Barton's denials show he's telling the truth." Two days after the test, Oliver Emmerich concluded that "it is not the candidate for the editorship of the student newspaper that is dangerous but rather the tactics used against him by the State Sovereignty Commission." Comparing the tactics to a police state, he believed they could "lead to despotism and tyranny." He called for a full investigation. "Any effort to whitewash it," he said, "will be interpreted as proof of the decay of good government."[15]

When Barnett saw the *State Times* story, he refused to comment. Several members of the Sovereignty Commission also would not comment because they claimed to know nothing about Barton or the charges against him. The lieutenant governor professed that he first learned about the allegations against Barton when he read them in the newspapers, but he assumed the Sovereignty Commission would now "get all the facts." Speaker Walter Sillers did not know anything about Barton but defended the Sovereignty Commission for "warning the people of the dangers of Communism right here at home." If the commission sometimes stepped on the "toes of the innocent," Sillers believed, "that's no reason to do away with the work of patriotic citizens who are trying to save our country."[16]

A whitewash began when other Jackson papers ignored the polygraph story. Instead, the *Clarion-Ledger* covered extensively the official excuses and evasions and trumpeted that "Barnett Denies Charge of Student at Ole Miss." Barnett professed that he had routinely forwarded Mac (Malcolm) Dale's original letter to the Sovereignty Commission for a reply. "To my knowledge," claimed the governor, "I never saw the letter or heard of it until approximately a week ago. . . . That is the extent of my personal knowledge of the matter." At Barnett's direction, the Sovereignty Commission's Albert Jones released copies of the correspondence among the Georgia source, Simmons, Jones, and Dale; the *Clarion-Ledger* reprinted all of it without comment. A *Daily News* editorial conceded that the Sovereignty Commission "bungled badly by getting involved in student politics," but it dismissed the actions of the commission and the Citizens' Council as a "boo-boo" and denied that Barnett or the commission spread the rumors about Barton. The paper, nonetheless, insisted the segregationist organizations ought to defend the state against "a blood-thirsty, wild-eyed band" of integrationists.[17]

While the state's two major newspapers in Jackson tried to kill the story and end the controversy, others would not let it die. The head of the Republican Party criticized Barnett's "meddling with a basic freedom" by his involvement in the smear of Billy Barton. Calling the intrusion in the university election "another example of the governor's dictatorial actions in local affairs," the head Republican called for an apology to Barton. In the Sunday papers following Barton's lie detector test, both Hodding Carter and Oliver Emmerich repeated their stands. From Rolling Fork in the Delta, Hal DeCell claimed that Mississippi had "been brought totally under the bigotry-braided whip of the Citizen Council professionals" and that the state had unleashed upon Barton and others "the malignant influence of a purveyor of smear and suspicion." Two weeks later, DeCell's cousin, Senator Herman DeCell of Yazoo City, called for a further examination of the charges against Barton. As a member of the Sovereignty Commission, he wanted the organization to "re-examine the whole thing, and if there's been a mistake then we should do something about it." Another commissioner claimed the commission's innocence but admitted circulation of the report on Barton had been "an error, and I'm sure nothing like that will be done again."[18]

After the final spate of criticism, the controversy subsided. By denying all charges, Barnett and his associates with the Sovereignty Commission and the Citizens' Councils weathered the early spring storm. The stifling of discussion by the Jackson papers helped by reducing public awareness and discussion. The two-week tempest seemed to end.

Throughout the dispute over Barton, one voice remained deafeningly silent. No Ole Miss official made any public statement, much less defended one of its own students. The day after Barton resorted to a lie detector test, the chancellor discussed plans for the future of the medical school with the trustees; the story of his appearance contained no mention of Billy Barton.[19] Williams's silence suggested his political ineffectiveness and boded ill for his influence in any future controversy.

"In view of the slanderous attacks against my reputation by state officials and members of the Citizens' Council," Barton declared one week before the election, "I am forced to withdraw from an active campaign for the editorship of the *Mississippian*." He added, "Shortly I will file a court suit in a final effort to clear up the vicious charges made against me in the last six months. This is a last resort measure." One week later, with Barton's name still on the ballot, Robertson defeated him decisively. The controversy had an immeasurable effect. More students may have voted against Barton because of the allegations, but Robertson thought the attacks had proved an advantage for Barton. In victory Robertson expressed sadness that he had "defeated a boy whom I consider not only a close personal friend but also one of the truly outstanding young journalists I have encountered in my life." Claiming his opponent's "ability and integrity have never been questioned," Robertson hoped Barton would continue to work on the newspaper.[20]

In their zeal to defeat Billy Barton, archsegregationists failed to realize that they probably should have targeted Robertson. Distracted by the sensational reports from Georgia, Barnett, Jones, Simmons, and others neglected Robertson's writings and his background. Far more than Barton, Robertson had a keen interest in politics, and his leanings were not always conventional. In 1960, for example, he supported the Republican candidate for president instead of either the Democrat or Barnett's unpledged electors. More important, as sports editor of the *Mississippian*, he repeatedly condemned the unwritten rule banning competition against teams with black players, and he would later write many editorials critical of Barnett. While Simmons and others falsely alleged that Barton knew P. D. East, Robertson had close ties to the segregationists' despised adversary, Hodding Carter. They did not know Carter was a family friend and a client of Robertson's father and that Robertson had written sports stories for his Greenville paper while he was a high school student. Oblivious to Robertson's political preferences and personal allegiances, state officials had erroneously hounded Barton.[21]

After his defeat, Barton persistently tried to clear his name. More than a year later, in a suit field in Hinds County Circuit Court against Governor Barnett, he sought $200,000 in damages. He claimed Barnett and his agents engaged in a "plot and conspiracy" using "Gestapo tactics" to "libel and slander" him. Barton asked for $100,000 in special damages because his "reputation has been damaged to the extent that he will be economically boycotted within his native state." His alleged ties to the NAACP and the civil rights movement would make finding a job in the state "virtually impossible." The judge in Barton's case was M. M. McGowan, an ardent states' rightist and member of the Citizens' Council. Early in July, Judge McGowan threw out the case because it "does not show the times and places of such alleged slander, and doesn't charge the governor directly with making these statements." The judge also held that two people who allegedly spread the rumors against Barton were state employees and not Barnett's personal agents. Nearly six months later,

Barton filed another slander and libel suit in federal court in Oxford against Barnett, Simmons, Jones, Barnett's secretary, and the rumor's original Georgia source. The federal lawsuit failed in 1964, and the controversy finally ended.[22]

The dispute over the student editorship erupted in the middle of the longer contest over the university's dedication to the southern way of life. Orthodoxy's defenders failed to find and remove any disloyal faculty or students, but they did not relent. By the spring of 1961 they narrowed their sights to one of their earlier targets, and it was not Jim Silver. After a quarter-century of Silver's dissent, many white Mississippians may simply have grown accustomed to his protests and acknowledged their ineffectiveness. Silver was, after all, a controversialist but not an organizer, a flamboyant troublemaker but not a strategic threat. Instead they focused on law professor William Patrick Murphy. Though less well known than Silver, Murphy posed a far more serious threat to the fundamental beliefs of white Mississippians. Murphy, thoroughly southern in background, had controversial ideas about state sovereignty and states' rights that rested on his historical and legal analysis. His scholarship presented a coherent, consistent, and thoroughgoing challenge to the heart of the southern segregationist cause.[23]

Born in Memphis in 1919, William Murphy grew up there and went to Southwestern College (now Rhodes). After graduating in 1941, he joined the navy and served in combat in both the Atlantic and Pacific. After the war, Murphy married, went to law school at the University of Virginia, returned to Memphis in 1948 to clerk for a U.S. district court judge, and later practiced law there. In 1950 Murphy joined the U.S. Department of Labor. Three years later he decided to seek a postgraduate degree in law, and Yale University awarded him a fellowship beginning in the fall of 1953. Quite by chance, Murphy joined the law faculty at Ole Miss when Dean Robert J. Farley asked him to fill in for a professor who had just left. One year later, in 1954, he finally took a leave from the law faculty and went to Yale for graduate study.[24]

In his first year at the Ole Miss law school, Murphy could not avoid the race question. The new professor worked with Dean Farley, a member of the state's new Legal Educational Advisory Committee, to formulate a legal response to the 1954 *Brown* decision. Six weeks after the ruling, Murphy outlined his ideas in a letter to the *Jackson Clarion-Ledger*. First, he assumed that the decision "was validly made pursuant to its power of judicial review, this power having been part of our constitutional system since 1803." Second, Murphy maintained that neither Mississippi nor the South could "reserve to itself the right to disobey valid laws and court decisions because it is in disagreement with them" and that the ruling "will and should be effectuated." "Effectuated" obscured Murphy's meaning; he thought the decision should be enforced, and he assumed that the "adoption of legal subterfuges in an attempt to evade the decision" would be useless. Third, "It would be an unthinkable catastrophe for any of the states to abandon public school education." For Murphy, public education took precedence over the maintenance of racial segregation. In his final assertion, Murphy acknowledged that the *Brown* decision would "create for the Southern states manifold problems" in education and that judges would have to consider the varying, sometimes unique, conditions in each community. Murphy called for Congress to enact legislation that would leave implementation of the decision to each state's governor, legislature, and courts. Under his plan, Congress would be the final arbiter of the Court's decision.[25]

Murphy's letter received limited press attention, but less than a week later Bill Simmons, the future Citizens' Council leader, answered with his own letter. Sensing Farley's involvement, Simmons's reply to both professors presented many of the constitutional arguments against *Brown* that Murphy had anticipated. He protested the abuse of judicial review, stressed the "illegality and fraudulent nature of the Fourteenth Amendment," and objected to the reliance on psychology, instead of the law. His harshest criticism hit at the professor's declaration that a state cannot reserve the right to disobey decisions with which it disagrees. According to Simmons, the federal government had "been captured by the NAACP, New Dealers, Fellow Travelers and other left-wingers." He suggested that "the NAACP has captured . . . the Law School at Ole Miss." From southern Mississippi, Mary D. Cain's editorial, "Something Rotten at Ole Miss," claimed that "there is no middle ground here: One is either for segregation or for integration." Suspecting Murphy and Farley really favored integration, she suggested both should be "summarily fired." Despite the protests, the little-known professor's proposal dropped from discussion.[26]

Though Murphy's departure for Yale removed any immediate threat posed by his dissent, contemporary events spurred his interest in the history of states' rights as a concept because it lay at the heart of much southern political ideology. As a result, his dissertation examined the change from state sovereignty to national sovereignty under the Articles of Confederation and the Constitution.[27] As racial tension in the state increased, his topic's significance expanded because state sovereignty and states' rights formed an essential element in the segregationists' justification for rejecting federal interference in race relations. Increasingly supportive of civil rights, Murphy disagreed with the states' rights argument.

While working on his dissertation, Murphy continued to dissent, often in the *Mississippi Law Journal*. He wrote favorably about labor unions, and he deemed James J. Kilpatrick's view of state sovereignty "ridiculous," "untenable," and "historically untrue." More important for segregationists, he defended the Supreme Court and its authority to interpret the Constitution. Regarding its *Brown* ruling, however, he doubted the "reliability and credibility" of the findings of the social sciences, claimed the Court built its verdict on "a specious argument based on dubious sources," and suggested that to "ground a decision on such evidence may be to build on shifting sands" because the findings could change dramatically. He suggested that "it is hard to escape the conclusion that, when faced with this great challenge to judicial statesmanship, the Court did not measure up."[28] Murphy did not, however, defend segregation, white supremacy, or states' rights.

In 1959 Murphy's dissent briefly extended beyond scholarly commentary and impinged on activism. In the summer of 1955 after his year at Yale, Murphy had joined the ACLU. Aware of its controversial nature, he had first asked Hugh Clegg if he knew of any reason he should not join. After Clegg assured him that belonging to the ACLU would not cause any problem, Murphy joined (he was one of two members in Mississippi). As required by state law, he included it on his affidavit listing personal and professional memberships, but he added an objection: "This affidavit is being signed under protest. I regard it as an unwarranted invasion of my personal and private affairs." Murphy never represented the ACLU in any legal matter, and his ACLU affiliation proved uneventful until the summer of 1958 when he briefly became involved in the Clennon King case. His role in the controversy did not, however, immediately become public.[29]

A few months later, Murphy's role in the King affair, combined with his unorthodox legal opinions, evoked the first major challenge to the professor. As a target of Edwin White and Wilburn Hooker, he became embroiled in the investigation of faculty loyalty at Ole Miss. Murphy had drawn the state's archsegregationists' attention and convinced them that he was an enemy of segregation, states' rights, and the Mississippi way of life. Except for one frivolous charge, each of the accusations pertained directly to his views on racial segregation. His critics claimed, for example, that he defended the Supreme Court's position in the school segregation cases, and they accused him of belonging to the un-American ACLU and of recommending a Jackson attorney to the ACLU in the Clennon King affair. More specifically, Hooker, White, and their colleagues asserted that Murphy supported integration and that he tried to indoctrinate his law students.

When asked for information for a rebuttal, Murphy did not cower but instead expressed his indignation. Referring to his combat service during World War II, Murphy proclaimed, "I will match my patriotism and love of country with that of any man. As an American, as a lawyer, and as a teacher, I have a profound respect for the Constitution of the United States and for our system of government." Murphy conceded his authorship of various pieces but thought further comment on their contents was unnecessary: "They speak for themselves, and I stand by them." At the same time, he dismissed, defused, or ignored some serious criticisms. He mentioned, for example, the positive reactions to his letters and essays that he received from the region's politicians, other southern law professors, and the public. He did not, however, contest the charge that his comments on Kilpatrick were "a bitter attack on the doctrine of state sovereignty and interposition," and he did not dispute his critics' summary of the contents of his 1954 letter to the *Jackson Clarion-Ledger* that outlined a possible response to the *Brown* decision.[30]

To the allegations regarding the ACLU and Clennon King, Murphy stood resolute. He admitted membership and reminded his opponents that Clegg had approved his joining; his motives for belonging to the ACLU warranted no discussion. He proudly pointed out that it defended the Bill of Rights "on behalf of anybody and everybody in America," including "whites, blacks, and yellows; rich and poor; segregationists and integrationists." More important for his defense, the ACLU did not welcome anyone who held totalitarian ideas, whether communist, fascist, or Ku Klux Klan. Murphy insisted that neither the House Un-American Activities Committee nor the U.S. attorney general had ever classified it as a subversive organization. As for his involvement with Clennon King, Murphy explained exactly what he had done and pointed out that, as a result of his report, the ACLU dropped its interest in the case.[31]

Perhaps the most threatening allegation claimed that he had explicitly endorsed the *Brown* decision and integration and propagandized his students by not presenting in his classes the arguments for segregation. Murphy stressed that he had "criticized both the result of the case and the legal craftsmanship of the opinion" and had never endorsed it. He did consider it the law of the land, would not resist any law, and opposed abandoning public education to avoid integration. Regarding his teaching, Murphy declared, "I deny unequivocally that I have ever been a propagandist in any of my classes," and he emphasized his objectivity in studying the law.[32] The uproar subsided when the board accepted Ole Miss's defense of Murphy and the other professors.

In May 1962 the *Mississippi Law Journal* published Murphy's eleventh article on state sovereignty and the original intent of the nation's Founding Fathers. He charged that the "Constitution was fatal to the sovereignty of the states" because it severely limited the states' powers and firmly established national supremacy. Although politicians, statesmen, and constitutional theorists later questioned national sovereignty, Murphy "stated flatly" that no significant evidence existed among the sources from the creation of the Constitution to support a "strict construction of the Constitution, interposition or nullification, and secession." The idea of state sovereignty was "abandoned after the Civil War and may today be considered extinct, despite the recent abortive attempts to revive them in the various interposition resolutions adopted by Southern legislatures." According to Murphy, "Even the polemics of Southern Senators in the field of civil rights lack real conviction."[33]

As Murphy's articles appeared between March 1958 and May 1962, resentment against the constitutional law professor built, especially among legislators and members of the state bar who received the *Mississippi Law Journal* as the bar's official publication. In December of 1959, Judge Benjamin F. Cameron of the U.S. Court of Appeals for the Fifth Circuit confidentially protested to Chancellor Williams that he considered states' rights an "absolute" and thought an Ole Miss law professor should champion states' rights, not degrade them. Deflecting the complaint, Williams refused to intervene, but the judge's protest demonstrated the intense opposition to Murphy.[34]

In the winter of 1960, Murphy took refuge in a one-year visiting appointment at the University of Kentucky. Though he would not be on the state payroll for 1960–61, the state senate on April 19 adopted without opposition an amendment to the biennial appropriations bill for the state's colleges that barred paying anyone who belonged to "subversive" organizations such as the ACLU, the NAACP, or the Communist Party. Senator John McLaurin wanted the measure as insurance against Murphy's return. Hodding Carter, denouncing the amendment as one more example of an effort at "thought control in Mississippi," could foresee when democracy in Mississippi "will stand for the rubber-stamp assent of an unthinking electorate responding to the stimulus of perpetual demagoguery," and the result would be "totalitarianism." A few days later another senator introduced a resolution to direct the trustees "to forthwith terminate the contract of employment of Dr. William P. Murphy." Only after other senators, all Ole Miss alumni, insisted that Murphy be given an opportunity to defend himself, did the senate refer the resolution to the judiciary committee where it died along with McLaurin's proposal.[35]

The next week, after the legislative uproar over his position abated, Murphy responded for the first time to his attackers. He knew that "they are using me as a means of attempting to intimidate other teachers and professors throughout the state," but he refused to be intimidated. His prepared statement asserted, "I am not ashamed of my membership in the American Civil Liberties Union," which he described as a "respectable, patriotic and worthwhile organization" that was in no way "subversive or un-American." Regarding his teaching, Murphy announced that "it is a lie that I have ever advocated integration in my classes. It is not my job to teach either segregation or integration." When he discussed the school desegregation case, he employed a "legal and analytical" approach, not a "partisan and emotional" one. He concluded with a striking declaration: "I want to make this absolutely clear. I do not intend to give up my membership in the ACLU because of attempted political intimidation. I do not intend to tailor my teaching to satisfy any cult of crackpots, fanatics and willful ignoramuses."[36]

In the spring of 1960, a few Mississippians encouraged the embattled professor. In addition to Hodding Carter, a Eupora legislator, a Greenville lawyer, and William Winter, the state tax collector, privately expressed their support. In a petition 120 law students declared their "complete faith, trust, and absolute confidence in the teaching ability and integrity" of Murphy and requested the legislature to "abandon the attack now being made." Law school colleagues, especially Dean Farley, also supported and encouraged him. Chancellor Williams, however, offered no public defense of Murphy or academic freedom. At the time of the Kershaw controversy, Williams had in a faculty meeting assured Murphy that the "ditch to die in" would be when someone tried to fire a faculty member because of that professor's scholarly work. He apparently did not consider the Murphy imbroglio that ditch. After conceding so much ground to segregationists throughout the 1950s, the chancellor seemed unable to make a stand.[37]

Despite the pressures and stresses of the constant attacks, Murphy completed his dissertation in the spring of 1960 and later in the year received his doctorate. He also secured a summer teaching appointment at the University of Missouri. Combined with his visiting professorship at Kentucky, Murphy left all the controversies behind temporarily. During the 1960–61 academic year, he sought other employment, but Farley renewed his commitment to at least another one-year contract for Murphy and reported that the chancellor would support his recommendation. Though the dean doubted the board would approve Murphy's reappointment, he pledged to fight for it, and he declared that he was ready to resign if Murphy's contract were not renewed. Murphy prodded J. D. Williams to come to his defense, but the chancellor hoped that Ole Miss could avoid a public controversy and that Murphy would find another job.[38]

At the IHL board's regular May meeting, Chancellor Williams said that Murphy was a fine professor, that terminating a professor so late in the academic year would make obtaining another position very difficult, and that firing Murphy could lead to greater problems for the law school and the university in the form of investigations and possible censure by professional and accrediting bodies. The trustees then compromised by unanimously approving Murphy's contract for the summer session, but with one qualification —he would be paid but could not teach. The trustees delayed any action on his contract for the next term. Not waiting for a contract, Murphy requested a year's leave of absence to teach at the University of Missouri. Though he mentioned "the political opposition" to his continued teaching at Ole Miss as a reason for going to Missouri, Murphy emphasized that he was not resigning, that he expected to return to Mississippi in a year, and that his visiting appointment was contingent on his being granted a leave of absence.[39]

If J. D. Williams hoped to end the controversy and to avoid publicity, he failed. The day before Murphy asked for another leave, the *Jackson Clarion-Ledger* reported that he probably would not be rehired. The paper declared, "State College Board and University officials were doing a neat job of tossing the ticklish issue back and forth. Nobody wanted to say that Murphy has been fired, but it was plain that the decision has been made." Three days before the next board meeting, the law faculty unanimously asked the trustees to "rescind the condition attached to Professor Murphy's summer contract and restore Professor Murphy's freedom to teach." They "deplore[d]" the "political interference" that would imperil accreditation and had already hurt morale. Williams tried to reassure his faculty that the Murphy case was the ditch he had frequently mentioned.[40]

When the board met on June 29, it had several options: approve Murphy's leave of absence to teach in Missouri, with the implication that he could return in 1962; approve his contract and thereby effectively deny his leave request while keeping him on the faculty; or end his employment, either by firing him or by taking no action. Pulled on one side by many legislators, the Citizens' Council, and the governor, and on the other side by Ole Miss alumni and a few lawyers and judges, the board divided. With tensions high in a long meeting, and with the board's executive secretary and its chairman fearing a defeat for Murphy, the trustees postponed dealing with the case until they reconvened on July 7.[41]

Between June 29 and the meeting on July 7, lobbying continued. At a law school alumni luncheon in Biloxi, Farley promoted Murphy's cause with four alumni trustees. The next week in a meeting in Louisville arranged by the provost, board chairman Charles Fair assured Murphy of his support. According to Fair, the outcome remained unpredictable because of the political forces operating in the state. For example, if Murphy's contract were renewed, legislators had threatened to restructure the board of trustees, close the Ole Miss law school and create another elsewhere, and strip the board of financial control over the colleges. Though he could not offer any guarantee, Fair told Murphy that he would at least get a hearing before the board fired him.[42]

At about the same time, Dean Farley met with Governor Barnett. They had known each other since the 1920s when Barnett finished law school during

Farley's first year on the faculty. In describing the case, Farley had to explain academic tenure and accreditation before appealing to Barnett to intervene with his appointees to the board. The governor agreed to talk with the men he had named to the board before they met on July 7. The next day a *Jackson Daily News* story explained that the controversy over Murphy's contract might trigger an investigation of the law school by the American Bar Association and eventually threaten the law school's accreditation.[43]

On July 7 the trustees voted unanimously to grant Murphy a one-year leave of absence to teach in Missouri. Informally the board explained to Chancellor Williams that its action was terminal—it did not want to have deal with Murphy again. For the trustees, granting a leave of absence did not imply that Murphy could return to Ole Miss in 1962. When Provost Charles F. Haywood called Murphy the next day and explained the outcome, the professor reminded him that the chancellor had promised to support his employment as long as the dean recommended it. Haywood agreed, but he indicated that Murphy's continued employment had been removed from the chancellor's hands because everyone thought the legislature would intervene if Murphy had not resigned by the next spring.[44]

After the board's action, the controversy dissipated. Murphy drew his salary even though he did not teach, and he and his family prepared to move to Missouri. At the same time Murphy contacted officials of the AAUP, of which he was a member. The AAUP engaged in discussions with the Committee on Academic Freedom and Tenure of the Association of American Law Schools. In the summer of 1961, Murphy also communicated with the ACLU, though he thought that his ACLU membership was a primary cause of his troubles.[45] None of the organizations intervened, and in the fall of 1961, while he taught at the University of Missouri, Murphy's attention turned to the issue of his tenure at Ole Miss.

In 1950 the university had adopted a tenure policy that allowed for tenure after three years, but the university neglected to create a procedure to implement it. As a result, apparently no faculty member obtained tenure during the following decade. When Charles Haywood became provost in 1960, he moved to develop a tenure process and to maintain tenure records, and Chancellor Williams announced the tenure system in early 1961. One provision said that anyone who had taught at Ole Miss for three years and had not been approved for tenure by January 1961—the group included virtually all faculty members—could apply for tenure. At the university since 1953, Murphy believed he deserved tenure under the new procedures.[46]

Soon after Williams announced the new system, Dean Farley recommended Murphy for tenure, and the provost assured Murphy that he would discuss it with the chancellor. Murphy held some hope that tenure would end his conflict with the board. After repeated inquiries by Murphy, Chancellor Williams finally responded on December 1, 1961. He agreed that Dean Farley had recommended Murphy for tenure, but he said that the provost did not concur. Unwilling to reverse the judgment of his provost, Williams let Murphy's bid for tenure die, but he told Murphy that he would not have approved his tenure even if the provost had recommended it. Unable to withstand the attacks made by segregationists, especially on the board and in the legislature, Williams had decided Murphy's job was not the ditch he wanted to die in. The chancellor's decision did not please Murphy. He immediately requested an explanation: "I am entitled to know why I am being denied a right and status to which I appear to be unquestionably entitled." Murphy also reminded the chancellor of his earlier commitment to support Murphy for reappointment as long as Dean Farley recommended him. The tenure decision struck Murphy as "in complete variance" with the earlier pledge. The chancellor's refusal to grant him tenure "was the final straw," according to Murphy, "which persuaded me to leave."[47]

Later in December, after having been alerted to the case by the AAUP, the Committee on Academic Freedom and Tenure of the Association of American Law Schools (AALS) met with Farley and Murphy. After its hearing, the AALS committee suggested that "basic principles of academic freedom and tenure have been violated," and it dispatched two deans to meet with the IHL board and the Ole Miss administration. The next month in Jackson, Frederick Ribble of the University of Virginia and Page Keeton of the University of Texas held a cordial but frank two-hour discussion with Chancellor Williams, Dean Farley, and the board. Some trustees called for Murphy's departure, but Farley, according to Ribble, "stood out as firm as a rock speaking with courtesy but with precision and clarity" in Murphy's defense. The two visitors stressed that the trustees had to defend academic freedom and explain its importance to the public. Ribble and Keaton believed that some agreement favorable to Murphy would soon be reached, and they extracted a pledge that the board would hold a public hearing where Murphy could speak before the trustees took any action against him.[48]

While all parties considered their options, Murphy early in March 1962 accepted a permanent position at the University of Missouri law school. The controversy had suddenly ended, almost. Farley had promised Murphy a job teaching in the summer, and Murphy wanted the position because he needed the salary and because he needed to be in Oxford to arrange his family's move to Columbia, Missouri. Once again, however, two state senators introduced legislation to prohibit using state funds to pay any ACLU member. Farley assured Murphy that the trustees would approve his summer employment, but only after the legislature adjourned. On May 29, the trustees unanimously accepted Murphy's resignation from the faculty and approved his appointment for the summer, but three trustees objected even to his final summer employment.[49]

At the end of four years of personal and professional turmoil, Murphy experienced a mixture of relief, satisfaction, doubt, and disappointment. Convinced that he had not caused the controversy, he maintained that "my conscience is clear." He was, moreover, going to work at a better university for a substantially larger salary. For personal and family reasons, Murphy regretted leaving, but after so many temporary appointments, settling down in his father's home state appealed to him. After resigning, however, he wondered if he had done the right thing; he began to regret that he had helped avoid a confrontation over academic freedom when he asked for a leave of absence in the summer of 1961. To the chairman of the AALS committee that looked into his case, Murphy confessed, "I hate like hell to see the Board and the Chancellor got off without even a resolution of censure." Despite Murphy's regrets, the controversy over his employment ended, and he moved to Missouri at the end of the summer of 1962.[50]

The expulsion of Professor Murphy and the defeat of Billy Barton marked victories for the forces controlling the closed society. In each case, segregationists had quieted a potentially powerful critic. Even though Barton was a white native of Pontotoc County, was only an undergraduate, and had shown no interest in political activism, the state's leadership believed unsubstantiated allegations about him and worked to prevent his election as editor of the student newspaper. Even though Murphy had been born and educated in the South, had married into a Mississippi family, had restricted his dissent to his scholarly work, and had not engaged in any activism in support of racial equality—despite the limited nature of Murphy's dissent—the closed society could not tolerate him. To preserve and protect the southern way of life, Barton had to be blocked from the editorship and Murphy had to leave Mississippi.

The fates of Barton and Murphy warned other potential dissenters from the racial status quo, especially Ole Miss students and faculty. The university's administrators and the board of trustees yielded in each controversy to the demands of the extremists in the legislature, the Citizens' Council, and the Sovereignty Commission. In the end, J. D. Williams had once again not found the ditch he wanted to die in. Even the principles of freedom of the press and academic freedom and tenure had not protected the student or the law professor, so others at the university and across Mississippi had reason to fear if they even allegedly transgressed the racial orthodoxy. According to one observer, the university faculty took the outcome of the controversy over Murphy as "a bad omen," and they saw in it "the specter of a slow, compromising purge of faculty members in moments of crisis, an ignoble surrender by the University's trustees to the extremists, and even the possibility of the loss of University accreditation." One professor bluntly commented, "If they get away with this one, there will be more."[51] Another moment of crisis was not far away. As the experiences of Barton and Murphy had proven, Ole Miss's fate would at that time rest more in the hands of the state's segregationist politicians than with the university's leaders.

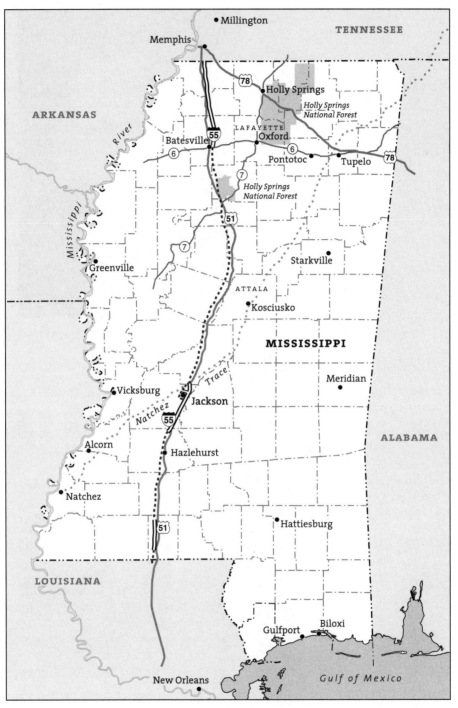

Mississippi

Chancellor J. D. Williams.
(Cofield Collection, Southern
Media Archive, Special Collections,
University of Mississippi)

"Blind Jim" Ivy.
(Archives and Special
Collections, University of
Mississippi)

Clennon King.
(Mississippi State
Sovereignty Commission,
Mississippi Department of
Archives and History)

Professor James W. Silver.
(Dain Collection, Southern
Media Archive, Special
Collections, University of
Mississippi)

Professor William P. Murphy.
(Law School, University of
Mississippi)

Legal Defense Fund lawyers Constance Baker Motley and Jack Greenberg flank their client,
James Meredith. (© Bettmann/CORBIS)

Governor Ross R. Barnett. (© Bettmann/CORBIS)

Left to right: Lieutenant Governor Paul B. Johnson reads a proclamation by Governor Barnett to Department of Justice Attorney John Doar, James Meredith, and Chief U.S. Marshal James P. McShane that Meredith will not be allowed to register. (UPI/Mississippi Department of Archives and History)

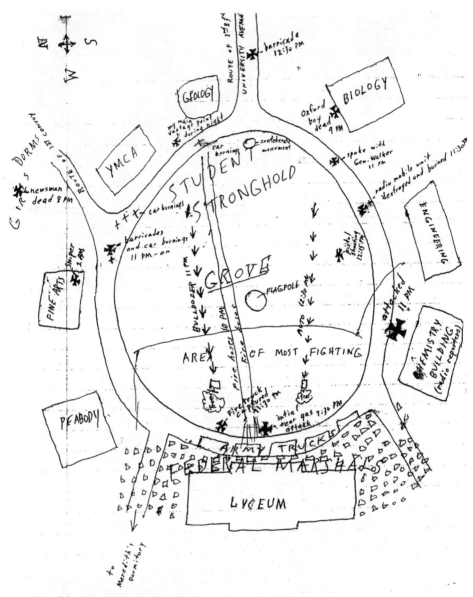

Map of the riot on September 30–October 1, 1962, over James Meredith's desegregation of Ole Miss, drawn at the time by Curtis Wilkie. (Archives and Special Collections, University of Mississippi)

The Lyceum, University of Mississippi, September 30, 1962. U.S. marshals in white helmets guard the steps of the building where Meredith was expected to attempt to register. (© Flip Schulke/CORBIS)

Highway patrolmen standing with their backs to the crowd in front of the Lyceum, September 30, 1962. (Mississippi Highway Patrol Collection, Special Collections, University of Mississippi)

Crowd in front of the Lyceum, with U.S. Army trucks in the background, September 30, 1962. (Mississippi Highway Patrol Collection, Special Collections, University of Mississippi)

Damage caused by the riot, October 1, 1962. (UPI/Mississippi Department of Archives and History)

Cartoon by Bill Mauldin, *Atlanta Constitution*, October 1, 1962. (© 1962 by Bill Mauldin; courtesy of the Mauldin Estate)

"How'd You Like Your Daughter Marryin' One Of Them?"

Cartoon by Paul Conrad, *Washington Post*, October 8, 1962. (© Tribune Media Services, Inc., all rights reserved, reprinted with permission)

"... He Took Water And Washed His Hands Before The Multitude ..."

Cartoon by Herblock, *Washington Post*, October 3, 1962. (© The Herb Block Foundation)

James Meredith formally registers for classes at Ole Miss as Robert B. Ellis, university registrar, watches, October 1, 1962. (© Bettmann/CORBIS)

James Meredith heckled by students after a class, October 8, 1962. (UPI/Mississippi Department of Archives and History)

Prayer Of Thanks, 1962

Eternal Father, thank Thee for Thy grace and Thy mercy

And thank Thee for giving us dedicated and courageous men like James Meredith

Cartoon by Thomas Stockett, *Baltimore Afro-American*, November 24, 1962. (The Afro-American Newspapers, Archives and Research Center)

James Meredith isolated in class by the refusal of white classmates to sit near him.
(Ed Meek/University of Mississippi)

James Meredith and Medgar Evers at a press conference in Jackson, January 30, 1963.
(© Bettmann/CORBIS)

Civil Rights Memorial and statue of James Meredith, University of Mississippi.
(Robert Jordan/University of Mississippi Imaging Services)

PART TWO *James Meredith*

■ ■

11. The Making of a Militant Conservative—J. H. Meredith

■ ■

On January 26, 1961, a neatly typed letter arrived at the Ole Miss registrar's office; it asked for an application for admission, a catalog, and any other useful information. As part of the daily mail in Robert B. Ellis's office, the inquiry from a man on Maple Street in Jackson seemed unexceptional. Ellis and his staff later that day sent the materials and the standard reply: "We are very pleased to know of your interest in becoming a member of our student body." And in closing, "If we can be of further help to you in making your enrollment plans, please let us know."[1]

The rapid response pleased James H. Meredith. From his apartment less than a mile north of Jackson State College, he filled out the application. On January 31, he returned it along with a letter of explanation. Acknowledging Ellis's friendly tone, Meredith trusted that "it reflects the attitude of the school, and that it will not change upon learning that I am not a White applicant." He revealed, "I am an American-Mississippi-Negro citizen." An application from a Negro would not, he assumed, surprise Ellis, though he recognized the unusual nature of his application and the controversy it would likely cause. Concerned about the university's and the public's reactions, he "hope[d] that this matter will be handled in a manner that will be complimentary to the University and to the State of Mississippi." Meredith would be the one to "suffer the greatest consequences of this event," but he told Ellis that he hoped "the complications will be as few as possible."[2]

Following the application procedures closely, Meredith contacted all the colleges he had attended to have transcripts sent to Ole Miss. He conceded, however, that he could not meet one requirement: six alumni who would act as references for him. "I am a Negro and all of the graduates of the school are White," he told Ellis. "I do not know any graduate personally." To substitute for the alumni, he sent statements from six Mississippi Negroes who confirmed his good moral character. With his application apparently complete, he asked that the university rule immediately on his admission so that he could enroll when registration for the spring semester commenced on February 6, 1961.[3] Ole Miss officials who received his application knew nothing about Meredith, his unusual background, his special motivation, or his objectives.

James Howard Meredith was a native of Attala County, in the center of the state, about seventy miles north of Jackson. The Native Americans who originally inhabited the region yielded to French control over it by the first half of the eighteenth century, until the British gained possession as a result of the French and Indian War. After the American Revolution, the territory that would comprise Attala became part of the United States, and in 1804 part of the Mississippi Territory, and after 1817 part of the state of Mississippi. The Choctaws ceded their lands to the federal government in 1820 and 1830, and after completion of surveys of the cessions, Attala became a county in 1833. The name "Attala" derived from an early nineteenth-century French novel, and its county seat from Thaddeus Kosciusko, a Polish soldier who fought with the patriots in the American Revolution.[4]

Early Spanish explorers visited the Piney Hills section, but the first white settlers came in the late eighteenth century. Many others passed through on the Natchez Trace, the Indian trail linking Natchez, Mississippi, and Nashville, Tennessee. Traversing the area from southwest to northeast, the trace served as a vital roadway in the Old South and as a major resource for Attala. Before steamboats, boatmen from Kentucky and the Old Northwest Territory floated their goods down the Mississippi River to New Orleans and then returned home cross-country via the trace. With steamboats and the decline of the Natchez Trace, and without access to a major river or any of the early railroads, Attala became much more isolated.

Though Attala farmers depended on cotton in the nineteenth century, their land was not conducive to large plantations. The county grew slowly and retained a white majority; on the eve of the Civil War it had only fourteen thousand inhabitants, about five thousand of them African American slaves. Unlike other parts of the state, in Attala few farmers had many slaves. In 1850 perhaps as few as fifteen white farmers qualified as "planters" by owning more than twenty slaves, and most owned only two or three. By 1900 the county had not even doubled its antebellum population, and it languished throughout the twentieth century. As one visitor commented, it had "no logical reason to exist" because it lacked major highways, railroads, and airports and because it had no significant natural resources. Only hardworking, resourceful people made the county survive. As Boyd Campbell, an Attala native and a president of the U.S. Chamber of Commerce in the 1950s, observed, residents of Attala "had to scratch for a living and they just kept on scratching." The folks of Attala County struggling to make a living included the forebears of James Meredith.[5]

In the 1890s, according to family lore, James Meredith's paternal grandfather moved to Attala County as a tenant farmer. Ned Meredith had been born a slave in 1850 in adjacent Neshoba County, and during the Civil War he took the name of Meredith from his former master. Ned Meredith married Ellen Franklin in January 1878 in Neshoba County, but after a few years Ellen Meredith died, probably in childbirth. Ned left an infant son with his wife's family and took his older boy, James, to Cairo, Illinois. After a few years, in the 1880s, the illiterate Ned Meredith returned to Neshoba County and married Francis Brown, a schoolteacher fifteen years his junior. Soon after the birth in 1891 of their third child, Moses Arthur, who would become the father of James Meredith, Ned and Francis Meredith moved to Attala County. Required to help in the fields, young Moses Meredith did not go to school except in inclement weather. Despite his lack of formal education, he learned to read and write because his mother taught him. In 1901, when Moses Meredith was only ten years old, his mother died giving birth to her fifteenth child.[6]

At seventeen, Moses Meredith, known as "Cap[tain]," left Attala and moved west one county to Holmes County, where he worked for black landowners; later he worked on a railroad and in a sawmill. By 1915 Cap Meredith had returned to Attala as a tenant farmer and married his childhood sweetheart, Barbara Nash, who was also literate. Over the next decade they had six children. More significant, in the fall of 1925 Cap Meredith bought eighty-four acres a few miles north of Kosciusko for $200 cash plus eight annual payments of $132.50. Through ambition and perseverance the Merediths became landowners. Though poor by most standards, they moved toward the top of the community. In 1925 fewer than four hundred of Attala's ten thousand blacks owned land, and an eighty-four-acre farm was larger than most farms in the county, white or black.[7]

On their farm, the Merediths cleared trees so they could plant cotton, grow vegetables, and raise pigs and chickens. All the while Cap Meredith walked four miles, six days a week, to work at a cottonseed oil mill. In the late 1920s, his daily wage of two dollars enabled him and his wife to meet their mortgage payments and hold onto their land; unlike many small farmers, they did not borrow to finance their cotton crop. The Merediths recognized the importance of education and insisted that their children go to school. Their children walked the couple of miles each way to attend a poorly equipped, one-room county school; the school year lasted only a few months.[8]

For farm families like the Merediths, already victims of an agricultural depression, the stock market tumble in 1929 had little effect. Tragedy did strike them late in 1929 when Barbara Meredith died in a Jackson hospital after a short illness. After her death, even with the help of their sons, thirteen and twelve years old, Cap struggled to hold onto his land and his family.[9]

In February 1931, Cap Meredith met Roxie Marie Patterson, a twenty-seven-year-old Attala native with a triracial family lineage that included whites and Indians as well as blacks. According to family stories, her maternal grandfather was Judge Harvey Davis, a prominent white man in the area known as "Mr. Big," who in 1873 had sexually abused a thirteen-year-old black girl employed to take care of his children; the resulting child, a daughter, was raised by her own maternal grandmother. Named Roxiana Lee, she took her grandmother's last name. The white father never had anything to do with his mulatto daughter and, according to some accounts, he effectively ruined the life of her young black mother. In 1891 Roxiana Lee married William S. Patterson, a son of ex-slaves who also was part Indian. The couple, whom the census described as "mulatto," eventually had fifteen children, and Roxie Patterson was their tenth child.[10]

Growing up in the Center community of southeastern Attala, Roxie Patterson finished the fourth grade, but she spent much of her youth helping on her family's farm and working long days for nearby farmers. Perhaps affected by his wife's background, a proud Will Patterson never let Roxie or his other children work for anyone who mistreated them. Once when a white farmer seemed to treat Roxie and others in the Patterson family like slaves by watching them work while he was dressed in a white shirt and tie, the Patterson children stopped picking cotton and walked back to their farm. Will Paterson's status enabled him to insist that his family be treated with respect. In 1919 he distinguished himself from most blacks in Attala when he registered to vote. By the early 1920s he owned more than two hundred acres, produced more than thirty bales of cotton each year, and had even purchased an automobile.[11]

At seventeen, Roxie Patterson became engaged, but her parents wanted her to marry someone else; the impasse meant that she did not marry. By her midtwenties she resigned herself to never marrying, in part because she considered herself the family's "ugly duckling." Instead, with her sisters married and her brothers grown and away from home, she did much of the farming after her father developed eye trouble. She also devoted herself to her church. Then she met Cap Meredith, and three months later they married, on Easter Sunday in 1931. As a new wife Roxie Meredith became stepmother to five children, and in the next fourteen years Cap and Roxie Meredith had seven children of their own, two of whom died in infancy. Their first child, born on June 25, 1933, was christened J. H. and called "J" but later became known as James Howard Meredith.[12]

During James's childhood and youth, his father farmed and worked in the cottonseed oil mill, though his wages slumped as the Depression continued. Nearly always in debt to a local bank during the 1930s, Cap Meredith nevertheless ensured that his family never went hungry and that they held onto their farm. The family did well compared to most in the community. Although lacking indoor plumbing, their eleven-room, wood frame house was never an embarrassment. It differed from many dwellings because by the mid-1930s it had electricity and a radio, so Cap Meredith listened to the news, the Grand Ole Opry, baseball, and boxing. In one of James Meredith's earliest memories, he listened with his father to Joe Louis's first championship fight in 1937.[13]

After he got big enough, James had to work in the cotton fields and tend the pigs, chickens, and cows. He spent many long, hot hours, for example, chopping and picking cotton. Like most youngsters, he did not enjoy his tasks, but he followed his father's discipline. From their parents, the children learned the importance of work and the value of money. Most of the time they worked around their farm. When the kids worked outside the family, their parents allowed them to keep their earnings, but their father monitored their spending and did not allow them to waste money—they had to report exactly how they spent it. Always thrifty, Roxie Meredith made clothes for the children, while Cap Meredith repaired their shoes and cut their hair.[14]

Ambitious for James and his siblings, Roxie and Cap Meredith stressed education. In a searing youthful experience, Cap Meredith was once called a "dumb nigger." Cap's commitment to learning increased when his lack of even a seventh-grade education later cost him a chance at a good job. Sharing his dedication to education, Roxie Meredith regretted that she had not gone further in school, and as an adult she walked to Kosciusko for adult classes at night. Her memoirs explained, "Among my great desires, education ranks among the top. . . . My desire for learning has never been abated." The parents' unwavering commitment meant that the Meredith children all went to school.[15]

James Meredith's older half brothers and sisters first attended Marble Rock School, not far from their home. The simple school had three teachers and one hundred students in eight grades. When old enough to start school, James also attended the small rural school for one year, but by 1940 he and the others walked four and a half miles to Kosciusko to attend the Attala Training School. After World War II, their father sold some timber for a thousand dollars and bought a three-year-old pickup truck that the older children drove to school. James attended Attala Training School for eleven years. The segregated school lacked indoor plumbing, playground equipment, and many amenities available at white schools. In addition, none of the black teachers had a college education. Despite the hardships, James learned a lot at the school, but much of his education still occurred at home.[16]

James learned early what he later called "the true meaning of life, . . . that death was to be preferred to indignity." Crucial were pride, order, and independence. His parents took great pride in their house, farm, and family, and they insisted that their property be kept in good order. Unlike most black residences in Attala, their house always had exterior paint, window screens, and furniture in every room. Cap Meredith maintained his fences, instead of sharing the responsibility with white neighbors, because he wanted privacy and independence. According to James Meredith, his father acted like "a king in his own domain. . . . a sovereign state and we neither recognized nor had any diplomatic relations with our neighboring states." Even Moses Meredith's nickname commanded respect, especially from whites who called him "Cap" instead of "boy" or some other disparaging term; Cap, a diminutive for captain, connoted respect if not actual equality. Deferential blacks often addressed unknown whites as "Captain." By using Cap as his nickname, he engaged in the subterfuge of scrambling typical racial categories. According to a family story, a wealthy white man once asked Cap Meredith why he did not address him as Captain "like the other niggers," and Cap responded, "Why should I call you by my own name?" The family held itself apart as special and different, both from other blacks and from whites. As Roxie Meredith remembered her own upbringing, "We were taught that we were better than no one and on the other hand, nobody was better than us."[17] The Merediths instilled in their children a similar pride and dignity, which others may have translated as a sense that they were special and even superior.

On more than one occasion, Cap Meredith demonstrated his strength and resilience in dealing with whites. One day when he walked home from the cottonseed mill, four white men accosted him, but Cap stood his ground. After he laid into one of the whites, they left him alone. Perhaps the most public demonstration of his courage came in the spring of 1919 when he registered to vote at the Kosciusko courthouse and became one of the county's few black voters. Cap raised his children to be similarly strong and assertive. When his children trekked to their school, white kids riding a bus often threw things at them as they walked along the road. Urged to stand up for themselves, they eventually threw things back at the bus; soon the incidents stopped.[18]

Cap Meredith and his wife worked to protect their family from whites. For example, although a white family lived within one hundred yards, Cap Meredith had ensured his family's privacy by leaving enough trees and underbrush to block the view of their house. Even more than privacy, safety and dignity concerned Cap and Roxie. To prevent any incident or even any ill treatment, they forbade their children to go on their white neighbors' property. As an adult, James Meredith remembered that growing up he had never been inside a white person's home, partly because his father disapproved of the indignity of using the back door, but also because he learned to avoid situations that could lead to trouble with whites. The parents' caution had a daily impact on the younger Merediths: the next-door whites had black tenants living on their land, but James and his siblings could not go to the tenants' home to play with the black children because they would have had to go on the white man's property. Instead, the neighboring black youngsters came to the Merediths' house to play.[19]

"Separation dominated my childhood completely," Meredith recalled. He had very little contact with or knowledge of whites. Even when he went to Kosciusko—to shop on Saturday, to church, or to school—race restricted his world. The heart of the town's Negro section was South Natchez Street, called Beale Street by the locals. It contained two major churches, a school, and businesses, including funeral homes, cafes, barber shops, stores, and pool halls. As a member of one of Attala's leading black families, James Meredith did not patronize the seamier spots on the lower end of Beale Street but often spent time in Bell's Café, where the black elite usually congregated. To get to the black businesses or to church or school, James did have to go through the town's white section and the town square, but he never went inside the businesses. The white grocery stores, theaters, and cafes remained unknown to him, as did, of course, the white residential areas and public schools. His segregated world was, nonetheless, a busy place.[20]

Meredith first experienced segregation's harshness outside Attala County when he was a teenager. With others in his family he visited relatives in Detroit, but he rode the train back to Mississippi by himself. On the return trip, the fifteen-year-old encountered the demands of "separate but equal" in race relations in Memphis. Before entering Mississippi, the conductor ordered James to leave the nonsegregated coach and to move to a segregated car. Despite the urgings of some whites that he remain, he went to the Jim Crow coach. The required change humiliated him and demonstrated his inferiority. As an adult, Meredith recalled, "I cried all the rest of the way home," and "I've been crying a little ever since." The experience provided his first indication of his "personal responsibility to change the status" of Negroes.[21]

Although Meredith grew up in a poor, isolated, rural county, he absorbed his family's traditional, conservative ideas and values. Like all of his grandparents, for example, his parents had a legal, stable, and durable marriage when most rural blacks established only common-law families and other "temporary associations."[22] Cap and Roxie Meredith also owned their own farm and home, and in addition Cap Meredith held a steady job during J.'s childhood. They stressed to their children frugality, hard work, education, self-esteem, and self-improvement.

Perhaps Meredith's church membership epitomized his upbringing. At his father's insistence, the family attended Kosciusko's Wesley Memorial Chapel, rather than a rural church or Roxie Meredith's Baptist church. Wesley Memorial, in the Methodist Episcopal Church, was Kosciusko's largest black church. Baptized in the church at twelve, Meredith received all his religious instruction at Wesley Memorial. Its worship services followed the structured order of urban churches more than did the rural Methodist churches or any Baptist churches. The more restrained participation had less enthusiastic shouting of "amen" and "hallelujah." In many ways mirroring qualities he learned at home, the more formal service embodied the characteristics often deemed vital by the middle class for social mobility. Meredith later appreciated that Wesley Memorial was "of great importance to the basic character" of its members.[23]

In 1950, Meredith left the familiar and secure environment of his family, farm, church, and school and moved to Florida to finish high school. His parents sent him to live with his uncle Clifford Meredith and his family in St. Petersburg. At seventeen Meredith left Attala County and never returned to live there again. In his one year at the segregated public Gibbs High School, Meredith received above-average academic marks. Although his classmates teased him because he was "always clowning, gets around, and has himself a time," he was a serious student. One highlight of his senior year came when he won an American Legion essay contest by writing on "Why I Am Proud to Be an American"; he declared his belief in the United States as a land of opportunity where an individual's ingenuity and ability, not just his race, determined his progress. J. Meredith was also a well-behaved student. A decade later an investigator for the State of Mississippi reported that Meredith had "no criminal record, or juvenile record" while in St. Petersburg. The investigator found "no evidence of his being associated with any subversive or racial groups while he resided in" the Florida city.[24]

After graduating from Gibbs High in June 1951, Meredith wanted to go to college, but he could not afford it. Instead he moved to Detroit where a stepbrother and stepsister lived. After only a few weeks in Michigan, he followed his stepbrothers into the military. His upbringing, characterized by order, discipline, pride, and personal responsibility, had prepared him well for military life. Late in July 1951, he enlisted as "James Howard Meredith" for a four-year tour of duty with the U.S. Air Force. For the small (5 foot 7 and 140 pounds) and intelligent young man, the air force at the height of the Korean War promised less physical jeopardy and more training than the army, and the air force was the least racially segregated branch of the armed services.[25]

After basic training in New York, Airman Meredith went to Western New Mexico College for training as a clerk-typist. For three months in the fall and winter of 1951–52, he studied business English, typing, and record keeping, and he made As and Bs in all his courses. The air force next assigned him as a clerk to Forbes Air Force Base just outside Topeka, where B-29 crews trained. Meredith received superior efficiency ratings and became a sergeant at the age of nineteen. In May 1954 his supervisor praised his "initiative and readiness to coordinate problems encountered," his "exemplary" devotion to duty, his cost-saving efficiencies, his "excellent attention to military courtesy and discipline," and his "loyalty and integrity beyond question." Later in 1954 the air force transferred Sergeant Meredith to Offutt Air Base near Omaha.[26]

While his commanders recognized his ability and encouraged him, Meredith in his four years in the air force displayed determination to improve himself through education. Early in 1952 he enrolled in a psychology course through the extension division of the University of Kansas. In the summer of 1953 Meredith was one of six airmen to take an exam for the U.S. Military Academy. His academic background, however, had not prepared him for West Point, and the results of a college-level GED test (similar to the later CLEP test) indicated his strengths in the natural and social sciences and his weaknesses in literature and verbal expression. By taking courses in speech, composition, and literature through the University of Kansas, he worked to overcome his deficiencies. He also took courses through the Armed Forces Institute out of Madison, Wisconsin, a political science class at Washburn University in Topeka, and several courses with the University of Omaha's adult education program.[27]

Although he sought self-improvement and advancement in the air force, Meredith did not forget his family and home in Attala County. The family's life had become more difficult by the 1950s. Suffering from severe diabetes, Cap Meredith stopped working, and his children carried on the farmwork. At the same time, Roxie Meredith began working in a school cafeteria. Although Sgt. James Meredith earned a modest salary, the disciplined and frugal financial management he had learned from his father allowed him, beginning in 1951, to send money regularly to his parents. At one point, Meredith even supplemented his military pay with a temporary, part-time job. By 1954 he claimed on his tax return that he supplied 70 percent of his parents' support. He nonetheless managed to save enough money to invest in land; on his father's advice, he purchased forty acres in Attala County in 1954 and another seventeen acres two years later. The purchases demonstrated his conservative approach to personal finances and his long-term commitment to Mississippi, as did the courses that he took in farm management, dairy farming, and real estate.[28]

In July 1955, Meredith's four-year air force hitch ended with an honorable discharge. He considered going to college under the GI Bill, had his high school transcript sent to several colleges, and obtained information from the University of Michigan. In the summer of 1955, after visiting Kosciusko and Florida, he returned to Detroit and enrolled at Wayne State University. Unhappy after just a couple of weeks in college and seventy days as a civilian, he received a bonus and his old rank when in October he reenlisted for another four years in the air force. His first assignment was to Bunker Hill Air Force Base, a dozen miles north of Kokomo, Indiana, where he served as a clerk-typist. While at Bunker Hill, he married Mary June Wiggins. Five years younger than Meredith, she was born in Oklahoma but grew up in Gary, Indiana. After high school, she lived with her parents in Gary and worked as a secretary at Bunker Hill, where she met Meredith. They married in December 1956. With their combined incomes, James and June Meredith more easily continued to support his parents.[29]

In the summer of 1957, the air force transferred Sergeant Meredith to Tachikawa AFB, twenty-five miles from Tokyo. He displayed dedication to his responsibilities, which included maintaining control of classified documents. A white airman later admitted "that Meredith was not the most popular supervisor. Not because he was colored, but because he was interested in getting the job done through hard work; an interest shared by few and viewed as an offense by many." He received the Good Conduct Medal in October 1958. In addition to his military post and her civilian job, each as a clerk for the air force, James and June Meredith took advantage of educational opportunities. She took classes for a year before she became pregnant with their first child, and he made all As and Bs in a dozen courses through the University of Maryland's Far East Division. In addition to courses in English and speech, Meredith, a patriot caught up in the cold war atmosphere of the 1950s, studied Russian for four semesters, Russian history, and the history of the Far East. He also studied economics, public relations, and grammar at the Armed Forces Institute. As a result, in 1959 he passed the college-level GED in language and literature.[30]

Repeatedly Meredith's superiors noted his devotion to education, both for himself and for his fellow airmen. As his squadron's noncommissioned education officer, he advised and counseled other airmen about their education. He also had great interest in the education of his nieces and nephews, and in 1958 he proposed to his siblings a fund to support the education of the next generation. He expressed gratitude for his parents' sacrifices so that they could all finish high school and be successful. "I personally refuse to be satisfied in stopping here," he declared. Further professional or technical education by family members would involve more expense than any one of them could afford, so he proposed that they cooperate financially. A family educational fund would help others achieve higher education.[31] Although his dream did not materialize, it exemplified his faith in education and his stress on financial management.

Meredith's entrepreneurial spirit continued in Japan. In nearly three years, he bought and sold several homes and a trailer on the base, purchased and sold a 1952 Cadillac, and continued to invest regularly in savings bonds. In 1960 he purchased his parents' farm so that they could retire to Kosciusko, and that third parcel brought his total holdings in Attala County to 141 acres. By managing their air force salaries, the Merediths continued to support his parents.[32]

Meredith credited his father with teaching him money management techniques. He learned, for example, to keep track of his money: "Literally, I could [in 1958] account for nine out of every ten dollars that I had ever made." As part of his basic philosophy, he believed that the "most efficient and effective way of doing things is usually, if not always, the simplest." Instead of buying one pack of cigarettes for 35¢, he could buy a carton of ten for $2.75 and save 75¢, and over a year the savings would accumulate. Actually, Meredith confessed, "I don't smoke so I save the whole amount." When he bought a new suit, he purchased it at a cheap store rather than buying the same suit for twice the price at an exclusive men's shop. More generally, he never bought anything while he shopped; "if it costs $100 or more, I bargain for at least two weeks; if it's $500.00 or more, I bargain at least four weeks; if it's $1000.00 or more, I stop bargaining and start negotiating which must last for at least six weeks or longer." Getting the best deal required having a good credit rating, and he diligently established good credit with a Detroit bank and with Montgomery Ward and Sears Roebuck in Indiana. For every thousand dollars spent by the average black person, Meredith estimated, he saved three hundred dollars. Thrift enabled him to buy cars, purchase land, and support his parents—to live, in effect, beyond what many considered his means. His financial acumen caused his supervisor to call him "one of the most financially responsible NCOs I have known."[33]

During his air force years, Meredith grew from an eighteen-year-old high school graduate into a mature adult. He married and became a father, but he also grew intellectually, as his experiences in a world literature class in 1959 demonstrated. In a paper on "The Value of Literature," he confessed his ignorance. "I have just recently started to read books," he wrote, "so I hope this study of literature will start me to really appreciate the real value of reading." He anticipated learning to read for "pleasure" and "guidance." In comparing the *Odyssey* and the *Aeneid*, Meredith emphasized "the political effects or influence in the books," because politics interested him, and he lacked the confidence to assess the literary styles or the portrayals of characters. Despite a preference for history and politics, he tackled the major works of literature. In a paper comparing the ideas of Chaucer, Rabelais, and Cervantes, he admitted that he had "probably made some big mistakes" but declared his interest in their ideas and what others had to say about them.[34] Though not an intellectual, Meredith benefited from his continual enrollment in a variety of academic courses, and his success boosted his confidence.

Even more than his educational experiences, living in Japan for three years had a great impact on Meredith. For the first time he experienced, just as Cap Meredith had taught him, that he did not have to be inferior because of his race. Although prejudice still existed within the air force, and he daily felt its consequences, he found that the Japanese treated him as a foreigner and as an American GI but not specifically as a Negro, especially not an inferior Negro. He later observed, "It's the only place in the world where I was near free," and the experience was a revelation to him because he realized that he "was, or certainly had been, a nigger." In the United States, and even among Americans in Japan, he had passively *accepted* inferiority. When he realized that in some places in Japan he did not experience any inferiority, he understood that racial oppression was not universal but contrived by whites to protect their social position. As he later wrote, "The greatest pain an oppressed people must bear is the knowledge of its own oppression."[35] Instead of just crying over the indignity, as he had when forced as a boy to move to a segregated railroad car, Meredith began to envision other possibilities for race relations. His Japanese experience proved that racial segregation and black inferiority did not have to continue.

Meredith's racial awakening occurred while the civil rights movement accelerated, and it may have spurred his new racial consciousness. Even at a distance, he kept informed about the movement; for instance, he knew about Clennon King's attempt to enroll at Ole Miss in 1958.[36] The changes augured by the civil rights movement reinforced his realization of the impermanence of American racial patterns. The two separate processes—one personal in Japan and the other social in the United States—prompted a complicated reaction in the air force sergeant. An imminent end to discrimination inspired him as a black Mississippian, but as an airman stationed in Japan he found his opportunities to participate in any protests severely restricted. When the sit-ins spread across the South, Meredith felt both hope and frustration. Only months away from becoming a civilian, the sergeant could not participate in any way in the social revolution at home.

While in the air force, Meredith received special inspiration from a white colonel from Mississippi. During a promotion review, the colonel noticed Meredith's Mississippi background, so he and the other board members quizzed him about their home state, asked his opinion on racial issues, and probed his attitudes. After the odd examination, the colonel explained: "We are with you, but the degree of success attained in this new move [the civil rights movement] to unify the potentials of our country will depend on you." Meredith understood that "you" referred to American blacks, and he interpreted the colonel's remark as encouragement for his later civilian attempts to combat white supremacy.[37]

Expecting to be discharged in the summer of 1960, Meredith became anxious and restless, neglected his duties, and developed, according to his superior, "a negative attitude" toward his assignments and an "antagonist attitude" toward his coworkers. In part, his performance evaluation suffered by comparison to his prior exemplary work. Even though critical, the assessment officer recommended him for a Good Conduct Medal. Meredith knew that he lost his temper too easily, was too nervous, and worried too much. Though initially well-suited for the military, he may have come to find it confining and regimented, particularly after his own development and the changes occurring back home. He complained to doctors about tension, nervousness, and an occasional nervous stomach, and in the spring of 1960 a physician referred him to an air force psychiatrist. By early 1960, Meredith, according to the psychiatrist at Tachikawa AFB, had become "extremely concerned about the 'racial problem,'" and "his symptoms intensified whenever there is a heightened tempo in the racial problems in the U.S. and Africa." He reported that Meredith felt "a strong need to fight and defy authority," though usually in "a passive, procrastinating way." Finding "no evidence of a thinking disorder," the doctor concluded that he suffered from a "Passive Aggressive Reaction, chronic, moderate" but recommended no treatment.[38]

Though in many ways liberated by his new understanding of race and by the hopes of the civil rights movement, Meredith felt constrained by his role as an airman in the air force. His awkward situation allowed him to react only passively and indirectly. He could resist authority only by neglecting his responsibilities, reducing his efficiency, and becoming less cooperative, tactful, and diplomatic at work. Meredith's last performance review before his discharge noted that he had "a quick mind" but was "not content to merely ride with the tide."[39] He would have to wait until he left the air force before he could take any kind of positive action based on his new perceptions regarding race relations and really buck the tide.

Toward the end of Meredith's duty in Japan and the air force, he and his wife decided to return to Mississippi. As a civilian, he intended to help black Americans achieve their true freedom by fighting as a different kind of soldier in a different kind of war, a war against white supremacy. For his new theater of operations he chose the place he knew best, his home state, but he did not limit his mission to Mississippi or to ending racial discrimination or unequal treatment. His new mission called for "total victory . . . over 'White Supremacy' and all its manifestations," and he believed that progress for blacks would mean the improvement of both races. "The greatest hope for a major change in the basic status of the Negro," he later argued, "is to convince the American whites that it is in their best interests."[40]

To participate in the war against white supremacy, Meredith decided that he needed to complete his education, so he enrolled in Jackson State College, in the heart of Jackson's black community. Started as a Baptist college in Natchez, Jackson College moved to the capital in 1883 and became state-supported in 1940 as Mississippi Negro Training School. After a decade as Jackson College for Negro Teachers, it became Jackson State College in 1956 and broadened its curriculum to include the liberal arts. As one of three state-supported colleges for blacks, Jackson State College offered undergraduate and graduate programs, primarily in education, but also increasingly in the liberal arts that Meredith wanted. (Neither Mississippi Vocational College nor Alcorn Agricultural and Mechanical College emphasized the liberal arts.) The Merediths also believed that their family would be more comfortable—suffer fewer indignities —in Jackson than in the small, rural Mississippi towns that were home to the state's other Negro colleges.[41]

When Meredith enrolled at Jackson State in September 1960, he had already accumulated nearly half the credits required for an undergraduate degree. Aiming toward a degree in history and political science, in 1960–61 he took classes in history, math, physical science, psychology, and education. A full-time college student for the first time, he had to confront probing questions, particularly in a provocative philosophy course.[42]

An assignment at the start of his first quarter required Meredith to explain "What I Believe." The topic's overwhelming dimensions confused him. Instead of tackling the larger philosophical questions, Meredith quickly narrowed his focus to the issue that really motivated him—"my position as a member of the minority people" and his goal of changing his place "from an unfavorable to a favorable one." Confidently declaring his faith that Negroes could "move from a position of inferiority to a position of superiority," he acknowledged the problem's complexity. Blacks were "not lazy on their own accord" but "because of the entire condition of their total situation." No single method, even education, would, therefore, suffice. And he admitted he would judge the results by the simple standard of how they affected him. As an example, he compared having Japanese women work in his home in Japan and white women in Mississippi employing black women to do their housework; he considered the former right and good and the latter wrong and bad. Back in Mississippi for the first time in more than a decade and increasingly aware of the complexities of race, Meredith conceded that he did not yet have the full answer, and he took regretful consolation from the fact that nobody else did either, because "no one has led us from our miserable position."[43]

Meredith's growing concern for "his ultimate objective in life of eventually gaining here on this earth a more equal status for all men," and his corresponding lack of concern with weighty subjects like the origin of the cosmos, came through in a rambling paper on "Why Have a Philosophy?" Perhaps parroting his professor or his textbook, he granted at the outset that ideas matter because they "are the foundation of action" and more particularly "furnish a basis for social action." A philosophy, however, should derive from one's own free thinking and not just reflect tradition or law or custom. The "paramount fallacy of our problem (the negro [sic] problem)," according to Meredith, was that "education is the answer." Although he acknowledged education's importance, Meredith maintained that the existing system of black education stifled creativity, bred acquiescence, and confused parts and wholes. It taught blacks to accept whatever they were taught, not to think for themselves, and to ignore inconsistencies in the larger society. As an example of "completely lopsided" education, he described how a professor would rebuke a student who did not address him as "Mr. Smith" but would "smile and bow with all politeness" when an eighteen-year-old white clerk in a store called him Charlie.[44]

Whites had established the state's educational goals, and not for the benefit of blacks. "No where in the history of the world," Meredith claimed, "has anyone established a goal that was more beneficial for others than for themselves." The strict disciplinary standard in black schools, for instance, not only thwarted independent thought but also tended "to make the student dependent upon directions." He observed, "This is one of the major tools of the white man to keep us in our place." The system had to be reformed for blacks to progress. He wanted his fellow Negroes to be willing to question authority, to reform the educational system, to change their ideas, and to "seek solutions to our problems ourselves directly." "If we keep waiting for someone to help us, we will always have something to look forward to," he concluded. "Because it will never happen."[45]

Blacks, in Meredith's opinion, accepted the existing world, and he worried that "some how we have lost our faith in the power to create a new order." After his change of consciousness, he could not accommodate the status quo. "If we want more equality," he declared, "we must make a condition that will lead to this end." Otherwise the white man would continue to use his power to protect his interests and "to provide conditions under which he could control every-thing around, including the black man." To contest whites' control of their lives, blacks had to unite, because none could overcome inferiority unless all did. Though whites used religion to help control blacks, he believed religious values had to play a "paramount" part in "our strive toward freedom."[46]

Meredith found especially galling that blacks feared "to speak in a society whose very existence is based on freedom of expression" and feared to meet when the Constitution guaranteed the right to assemble. "Is this life[?]" he asked. "My answer is NO." He saw only one solution to the fear and the oppression: "Unless WE do something[,] Nothing will of value be done." He realized someone would have to "weather the storm of prosecution and per-secution, suffer the consequences of facing reality and pay the price of free-dom. Who has the courage?"[47] Although Meredith did not yet have a clear program and had not figured out his role in the struggle, he thought about the growing movement and his participation in it.

Meredith's new experiences with civil rights were neither academic nor abstract. His appreciation of the need for change escalated as a result of two incidents during his first months back in Mississippi. For many years the entrepreneurial Meredith believed that "a solid economic base" was a pre-requisite "for the all-out offensive against the evils of human inequality." By saving and investing while in the air force, he tried to achieve economic strength and security for his civilian life. Interested in becoming a private entrepreneur, Meredith in the fall of 1960 met with a representative of one of Jackson's leading oil companies to talk about opening a gas station in the city's black section. The man introduced himself as "Mister" and asked Meredith his name; sensitive to disrespect by whites, he replied "Meredith." When he asked again, the white man explained that he wanted to know his first name. The second time Meredith told him his initials. Without betraying his reaction, Meredith recognized the limitations placed on his business future by the sys-tem of white supremacy that required that he address a white man as "Mister" while whites demeaned blacks by using only their first names. "I considered it unfair and unacceptable," Meredith recalled, "for a Negro to have to attempt to engage in business under these conditions." More than ever, he realized that "before I could engage in business at the level that I desired, the system [of white supremacy] would have to be broken."[48]

The second incident in the fall of 1960 involved his "first act of war against the system of 'White Supremacy' in Mississippi." An avid golfer after his years in the air force, Meredith came to Jackson just when the city had constructed a public golf course for Negroes to forestall any attempt to integrate the white courses. At the dedication of the still-unfinished course, Mayor Allen Thompson praised the fine progress of the city's blacks and applauded the capital city's peaceful race relations. After the ceremony, the mayor worked the mostly black crowd by speaking to and shaking hands with each person. When with out-stretched hand Mayor Thompson approached, Meredith refused to extend his hand. Taken aback, the mayor recovered and moved on to others. Shaking hands with Thompson, Meredith thought, would only confirm the mayor's belief that he was "a generous distributor of human justice" who had "fulfilled his obligation to the Negro community" by paternalistically building a sepa-rate, inferior golf course for them. Meredith refused to "contribute to the mayor's easy assumption that his way was the right solution."[49]

In his new role as a student, Meredith had the freedom to participate in public affairs. While in the air force in Japan, he had tried to register to vote in Mississippi, but the air force officer in charge told him that Mississippi had no provision for absentee registration, so he never registered. At Jackson State he became involved in civil rights and politics, and at the urging of the student body president and as part of a campus voter registration campaign, Meredith went to the Hinds County Courthouse to register. He told the clerk in the registrar's office that he had just been discharged from the air force, had moved back home to Attala County, and lived in Jackson to attend Jackson State. Except for the part where the applicant interpreted part of the state constitu-tion, the clerk filled out and approved Meredith's application; all Meredith had to do was just sign it and he became a registered voter.[50]

During the 1960 presidential campaign, Meredith expanded his political involvement. Thinking Democrats promised to do more for blacks than had Republicans, he supported Kennedy. The overwhelming majority of Jackson State students seemed to back the Republicans, because blacks had made prog-ress under Eisenhower and because segregationist Democrats controlled the state. For a debate on the two parties' civil rights programs, a former president of the student government agreed to speak for the Republicans, but nobody would represent the Democrats. The Republican advocate, a philosophy class-mate of Meredith, asked him if he would represent the Democrats, and Mere-dith agreed. One measure of Meredith's effectiveness came the day after the debate in a mock election: though campus political rivalries also affected the results, the Democrats won a surprising victory by thirteen votes.[51]

Meredith's role in the debate enhanced his stature on campus and led to greater involvement in various activities. In his first quarter in college, he proposed and spearheaded the formation of the Debaters Club to train stu-dents in public speaking, conducting research, and analyzing various issues. He also served as an officer of the Social Science Club. Within the organiza-tions, Meredith retained his independence. He recalled having "frustrated three power takeovers of leading student positions . . . simply by demanding that proper parliamentary procedures be used in nominating and electing officers."[52] By family background and military experience, he expected groups to follow the proper rules and procedures.

Two organizations with racial programs especially appealed to Meredith. In the winter of 1960–61, he associated with the new Mississippi Improvement Association of Students (MIAS). Although not a member of MIAS, Meredith drafted some of its statements. Formed in response to the college administration's dissolution of the student government, which it thought "an unwarranted abuse of power," MIAS defended democratic student government and opposed the "travesty" of a new constitution handed down by the college's administration. Calling the proposed new government a "puppet" group and its officers "traitors," MIAS declared, "We feel that a brow-beaten student body can never be a good student body." MIAS understood that the administration sought to keep students "docile" to please white state officials, but MIAS and Meredith sought to "break the White monopoly on elected officials" and to work to improve life and opportunity "for our people."[53] With MIAS, Meredith stood for challenging white dominance and for greater rights for blacks.

Perhaps the NAACP appealed most to Meredith. After growing up in rural Mississippi and spending nine years in the air force, he knew little about civil rights organizations; he had never heard of CORE and only knew that the NAACP had somehow been involved with the *Brown* case. He learned about the civil rights group from other students. After joining the NAACP in September, he and June began attending NAACP mass meetings, though they doubted it could develop the strength in Mississippi to challenge white supremacy. Through his initial activities he met the NAACP's state field secretary, Medgar Evers. On several occasions in the fall of 1960 Meredith discussed with Evers the idea of applying to Ole Miss. Evers, who had tried to desegregate the law school, wanted someone to challenge segregation in higher education, but Meredith told him he was not interested in making the attempt.[54]

If his conversations with the NAACP official stimulated Meredith's thinking, the impetus for his eventual decision had other sources. Dr. S. Lamar Bailey, a white physician in Attala County, had planted one of Meredith's earliest thoughts of attending Ole Miss. When as a small boy Meredith went to the doctor, he noticed a picture of the Ole Miss football team in the office, and Bailey, who had been a member of the class of 1923 and sports editor of the *Mississippian*, fascinated him with stories of the team. Captivated by the doctor's tales, Meredith, like many little boys, began to dream about attending the school with the great football team, even though he had no understanding of racial segregation in higher education. By the time he became a teenager, Meredith routinely mentioned attending Ole Miss as one of his goals.[55]

As an adult, Meredith focused not on going to Ole Miss but on ending racial inequality. "I feel there is no logical reason to justify denying a law-abiding citizen the rights of full citizenship solely on the basis of race," he explained early in 1961. When he entered Jackson State, his mission remained to challenge white supremacy. Only by breaking the "monopoly on rights and privileges held" by whites could he and other blacks achieve their potential. To challenge the control of powerful Mississippi whites, he could have selected no better initial, *tactical* target than the university in Oxford. His ultimate goal remained, however, ending white domination.[56]

A dozen Jackson State students also encouraged Meredith in his consideration of an attempt to desegregate Ole Miss. He and his colleagues frequently discussed opportunities to advance civil rights for Mississippi blacks.[57] Their moral support reinforced his inclination to seek admission to the university. His long-standing interest in attending Ole Miss, his belief in his right as a citizen to further his education at any public institution, and his commitment to achieving racial equality combined with the nurturance of the idea by his friends to push him toward applying.

In the fall and winter of 1960, Meredith sensed a "new spirit that had swept Mississippi." Among blacks, he heard increasing, though discreet, discussions of civil rights and observed more voter registration activity. Though important, the change in local attitudes and conditions proved less decisive for him than the transformation caused by the presidential election of 1960.[58]

Attacks on white colonialism in Asia and Africa and the domestic black freedom struggle pushed civil rights into the presidential campaign. The discussion energized Mississippi blacks and caused, in Meredith's opinion, a "radical change in attitude and opinion." He found John F. Kennedy "more forthright in his acknowledged commitment to work for the equality of Negro citizens" than Richard M. Nixon. Unlike any recent national candidate, however, Nixon actually brought his campaign to Jackson, and Meredith went to observe the Republican nominee. Other than insipid comments about Ole Miss football and beauty queens, Nixon said little. Meredith assumed he came only to appeal to white supremacists, not blacks. Kennedy's election finally created, according to Meredith, "the proper atmosphere" in which to act, and his inaugural address further spurred Meredith. With a Democratic president committed to civil rights, Meredith believed that the federal government would force Mississippi to yield on segregation. As a result, in late January of 1961, he began his attempt to enter the University of Mississippi.[59]

By 1961 Meredith had become unusually equipped for the enormous task of desegregating Ole Miss. In a powerful way, his ideas joined conservative elements from the two prominent and seemingly contradictory strands in black thought represented by Booker T. Washington and W. E. B. Du Bois. From his parents Meredith learned the virtues of discipline and dignity, of hard work and self-improvement. As a youth in Attala County, he found his subordination because of his race unacceptable but learned to accommodate himself to Mississippi's segregated way of life. Much like Washington, in the air force he stressed individual improvement and racial advancement through practical education and material prosperity. Though Meredith never rejected his early values, during the 1950s he also began to adopt the approach long advocated by Du Bois. He realized the importance of higher education, not merely vocational education, for blacks. He saw himself as a member of the talented and educated elite that would lead his race. As the civil rights movement gained momentum, Meredith wanted to protest injustice and to agitate for full equality; to be held as an airman on the sidelines frustrated him. A newly registered voter in 1960, Meredith recognized the need for political action to obtain equal rights and opportunities.

In 1961, therefore, Meredith was both a budding entrepreneur and an incipient activist. He was practical and idealistic. He was a curious and sometimes perplexing blend of Washington's accommodationism and Du Bois's elitism and protest. He was a militant conservative. By the time he applied to Ole Miss in 1961, he had all his life submitted to domination by whites; he had for as long as he could recall been a "conscientious objector" to his "oppressed status." For years his "long-cherished ambition ha[d] been to break the monopoly on rights and privileges held by the whites of the state of Mississippi," and now he was committed, like a soldier, to breaking white supremacy by entering the University of Mississippi. As Judge John Minor Wisdom would later describe him, Meredith had become "a man with a mission and a nervous stomach."[60]

■ ■

With the declaration that he was "not a White applicant," James Meredith's application caught Ole Miss officials only slightly by surprise. No Mississippi college or university had desegregated, but university leaders must have monitored changes across the South. If the slow desegregation of higher education frustrated many people, to white Mississippians the delays offered hope that it could be avoided. As 1961 began, the attack on segregated public universities escalated and threatened to render white resistance futile. On January 3, the first three black undergraduates enrolled at the University of Tennessee in Knoxville; at the same time the university's medical school in Memphis admitted its first black student. Also early in January, just two weeks before Meredith made his original inquiry, a federal judge ordered the University of Georgia to enroll two black undergraduates, Hamilton E. Holmes and Charlayne Hunter.[1] Only the specifics of Meredith's bid could have surprised university officials, for they must have realized that racial segregation in higher education could not remain unchallenged for long.

Following procedures, Meredith submitted a completed application, his health record, and an application for housing. In letters to his previous universities to have transcripts sent, Meredith stressed the urgency because he wanted to enroll on February 6. His request to Jackson State College asked only that the registrar forward a copy of his transcript to the university in Oxford; he avoided divulging his purpose because he feared any announcement might cause a delay by skittish bureaucrats. With his application as complete as he could make it, he asked for immediate admission so that he could enroll when registration for the spring semester began.[2]

For the first time since Clennon King tried to enroll in 1958, the university faced a breach in the racial barriers in higher education. In the intervening years, the commitment of whites to segregation had intensified, as shown in 1959 when state authorities fabricated criminal charges against Clyde Kennard to fend off his attempt to integrate Mississippi Southern College.[3]

Written on Tuesday, January 31, Meredith's application went first to registrar Robert B. Ellis. A native of Memphis and an Ole Miss graduate, thirty-nine-year-old Ellis had served as registrar for a decade. When he read Meredith's letter and reviewed his application in his second floor Lyceum office, he learned that Meredith was a Negro but also that he was unusual in other respects: he was a native-born Mississippian, an air force veteran, and a successful student at several other colleges. Ellis, who in the 1950s had handled several inquiries from blacks, knew the sensitivity of the application. He understood that he could not handle it routinely, that he had to confer with his superiors, and that they had to act fast. Ellis first notified Hugh Clegg, who had been designated to handle applications from Negroes, and he forwarded copies of Meredith's application to the attorney general and to the IHL board's executive secretary.[4]

Meredith's letter to the registrar caused university administrators to scramble because registration for the spring semester began on the following Monday. Initial discussions in the Lyceum and with officials in Jackson led to a special meeting on Saturday, February 4. According to the minutes of the meeting, it "was called for the purpose of discussing the problem of overcrowding" and the problem of more than four hundred students in academic difficulty, but the real purpose must have been to plan for the latest threat to segregation. E. R. Jobe, the board's executive secretary, considered the meeting so serious that he drove to Oxford to join Chancellor Williams, Clegg, the dean of the College of Liberal Arts (substituting for the provost), the university attorney, the comptroller, and the registrar. Jobe suggested that the university stop accepting applications on the justification that limiting the size of the student body would enhance faculty-student interaction. In support, the dean of liberal arts pointed to crowded laboratories and classrooms and to budgetary limitations on hiring additional faculty. The comptroller similarly stressed cramped dormitories and study space.[5] Although the meeting's minutes revealed no discussion of Meredith's application, it surely caused the decision to curtail enrollment for the spring.

To prevent a deluge of new students, the administrators settled on January 25 as the "best cut-off date" for new applications. Later acceptances "would result in a serious overtaxing of physical space, decreased proficiency in instruction, and general lowering of the superior academic standings to which the University must aspire." The new deadline did not apply to university employees and their families, anyone with a prior oral commitment from an Ole Miss official, and applicants to the graduate school.[6]

J. D. Williams publicly attributed the unavoidable action to inadequate state appropriations that resulted in the institution's inability to provide for the growing number of students. Hailing the university as "a prestige institution enjoying a national reputation for the quality of its teaching and research programs and for the accomplishments of its faculty, students, and alumni," he maintained, "We owe it to our students not to water down our quality program in any respect."[7]

Although Williams described the problem in grave logistical terms, he failed to mention the application by a black student that had arrived just a few days *after* the new, retroactive deadline. He also neglected to explain that the policy change would prevent the institution from being inundated by *fourteen* additional applicants. His disingenuous declaration encouraged the perception that the policy had nothing to do with race and only protected Ole Miss from overwhelming numbers. The university had, according to one historian, begun to employ a "strategy of delay, deception, and duplicity in the hope of dissuading James Meredith."[8]

After the meeting, Robert Ellis telegraphed Meredith that Ole Miss had decided to "discontinue consideration of all applications for admission or registration . . . received after January 25, 1961" and reminded him that his "was received subsequent to such date." Offering a vague and indirect "it has been found necessary" explanation, he closed by saying "we must advise you not to appear for registration." A similar message went to thirteen others, including eleven white Mississippians whose papers arrived after the new deadline.[9]

Only two days after the telegrams, registration for the spring semester began. On Monday, however, rumors suggested variously that five blacks had applied for admission, that one had mistakenly slipped through the admission process, and that no reason could be found to reject two black applicants. An "integration scare" swept the state. Fearing an attempt to integrate Ole Miss, Governor Barnett sent eight plainclothes state troopers to the campus, but when questioned, he refused comment. The attorney general's office said it did not know what was happening at Ole Miss, while patrolmen claimed to be part of a civil defense exercise or registering for graduate classes.[10]

Returning, transfer, and new students found state troopers on every road leading to campus, at the gymnasium for registration, and at the Lyceum. Though most students supported continued segregation, opinions ranged from a lack of concern to a worry that Ole Miss might close. "I just wish something would hurry up and happen once and for all," one student said. Another realized, "After seeing what happened in Georgia a few weeks ago, I don't see what else we can do." Some students who had favored closing the university to prevent integration now accepted "token integration" to keep the school open because they wanted to finish their education. The unsettled situation disappointed one segregationist student, who said, "I often wondered what would be done when this time came and now no one in charge seems to know either." Most students, however, worried more about the rainy weather and unsatisfactory class schedules.[11]

Nobody knew what to expect. The state patrol's mission and the plans of other state officials remained unknown. In Jackson, the IHL's Jobe admitted he had heard the rumor about integrating the university, but otherwise refused to comment. University leaders also remained mum, either out of ignorance or discretion. They did, however, instruct registration workers to be polite to any Negroes who appeared and to refer them to the registrar's office just as they would anyone who had not complied with registration requirements. With the chancellor out of town, a statement from Clegg conceded the university had received one inquiry from a black student, the only one since Clennon King. "No such application for admission to the University," he explained, "has been filed which was accompanied by any recommendations from alumni." If other officials feared that any statement might be used against them in court, Clegg boldly suggested that officials had turned down Meredith's application because it lacked five references.[12]

While everyone else waited, the trustees acted. On February 7 at a called meeting in Jackson, it adopted three policies to ensure continued segregation in higher education. One allowed an institution such as Ole Miss to refuse a transfer from an unaccredited college like Jackson State. According to the trustees, a school could also reject an application that contained "false, contradictory, questionable, or uncertain data" or it could submit it to the board itself for review; the university could apply the vague, elastic provision to Meredith's application. Last, the board declared that all applicants "must receive a certificate of admission before presenting themselves for registration." Because Meredith had received no such certificate, he could not properly register.[13] The new policies would, the board hoped, shore up racial barriers.

Meredith did not present himself for registration on Monday or Tuesday, February 6 and 7. He remained in Jackson. The only Negroes visible at Ole Miss were groundskeepers and custodians.[14] Meredith, however, had not given up, and the new regulations would not deter him. Not waiting passively or patiently while state leaders maneuvered to block him and university officials contrived a response to his application, he continued at Jackson State and worked further to achieve his ultimate objective.

As he prepared his application, Meredith had contacted lawyers for the NAACP and the U.S. Department of Justice and thereby had begun the process leading to a lawsuit. When he talked with Medgar Evers on January 29, the head of the state NAACP became the first person outside Jackson State friends to learn of his plan to enroll at Ole Miss. Evers, of course, supported him and suggested contacting the NAACP's Legal Defense and Educational Fund for legal assistance. Incorporated in 1939 as a tax-exempt organization independent of the NAACP, the Legal Defense Fund (LDF or, as it became known, the

Inc. Fund, or more simply, the Fund) handled litigation for the NAACP. Thurgood Marshall, the original LDF director, still held that position in 1961. A native of Baltimore and a 1933 graduate of Howard University's law school, Marshall had joined the NAACP staff in 1936. Later as head of the LDF, he had directed its successful litigation in *Brown v. Board of Education of Topeka* and in many other cases.[15]

Meredith wrote Marshall on the same day he conferred with Evers, two days before he submitted his Ole Miss application. He informed Marshall that he wanted to enter the university on February 6 and "anticipate[d] encountering some type of difficulty with the various agencies here in the state which are against my gaining entrance in the school." Without the resources to mount a legal challenge, Meredith hoped that Marshall and the Fund would provide assistance. After summarizing his life, Meredith sketched his academic background and modestly concluded that "his educational qualifications . . . are adequate." More important, Meredith tried to convince Marshall of his long commitment to breaking white supremacy in Mississippi. Aware of the potential problems, Meredith stressed, "I am fully prepared to pursue it all the way to a degree from the University of Mississippi."[16]

Soon after receiving Meredith's letter, Marshall called for more information. Before responding, Meredith consulted with Evers, and at his suggestion, they called Marshall from two telephones in the Evers home. Marshall reviewed Meredith's experiences and objectives, but his persistent questions and his request for documentary evidence annoyed Meredith, who hung up on the lawyer. Evers, however, persisted, with both men. As a result, Meredith agreed to cooperate with Marshall. He also soon learned of the NAACP's commitment to his cause. During the integration scare at registration in Oxford, Roy Wilkins, the head of the NAACP, said in a telephone interview from New York that "Ole Miss is going to be integrated" and that "the full resources of the NAACP will be at the disposal of Negro students when they want it." Though Meredith still doubted the NAACP's strength and ability to tackle discrimination in Mississippi, he had no other option. A week later, therefore, he sent Marshall copies of his academic transcripts and a copy of the Ole Miss catalog that the attorney had requested.[17]

About the time that Meredith asked for support from the LDF, he also contacted the U.S. Department of Justice. William L. Higgs, a white Jackson lawyer, facilitated his overture and in that way became Meredith's first lawyer. Meredith initially encountered Higgs on February 2 at Tougaloo College when he heard Higgs speak on Negro rights. A Greenville native, Higgs graduated in 1955 at the top of his Ole Miss class, received a Harvard University law degree in 1958, and began practicing law in Jackson at the age of twenty-two. A liberal activist, Higgs unsuccessfully ran for the state legislature in 1959 and the next year challenged Representative John Bell Williams. By February 1961 Higgs had become a hated figure in the state not only because he was the only white lawyer who accepted civil rights cases but also because his lawsuit the previous month challenged the Sovereignty Commission's subsidy of the Citizens' Council.[18]

After Higgs's lecture, the two briefly conferred. Within a few days Meredith went at Higgs's invitation to the lawyer's office, and they called Burke Marshall, the assistant attorney general of the United States. Higgs was acquainted with Marshall and thought he would be concerned about Meredith's efforts to enter Ole Miss. In their conversation, Marshall told Meredith that the Civil Rights Division would assist him in any way it could. At Higgs's urging, Meredith on February 7 wrote to the Justice Department to explain himself and his mission. Expressing grief that an American had to "suffer the embarrassments and personal humiliations" for trying to obtain his civil rights, he described his situation as "agonizing and often miserable" because he realized the unfairness of black oppression and had a conscientious compulsion to rectify it. While officials delayed acting on his application, he feared that state agencies would not protect him and indeed might intimidate or eliminate him. As evidence he pointed to Clyde Kennard who had been sent to Parchman Prison on "trumped up charges" after he tried to enroll at Mississippi Southern College. Meredith wanted the federal government to use its "power and influence . . . to insure compliance with the laws as interpreted by proper authority." His sometimes emotional and rambling appeal closed, "I simply ask that the federal agencies use the power and prestige of their positions to insure the full rights of citizenship for our people."[19]

While Meredith contacted the LDF and the Justice Department, information about his application slowly became public. On February 8 the *Jackson Daily News* reported that a Jackson State student from Kosciusko had applied to Ole Miss and that the university had soon thereafter moved the application deadline to January 25 to prevent his acceptance. Nine days later UPI reported a confidential interview with the unnamed Meredith at his Jackson apartment. He declined to answer most questions. He told the newsman, for instance, that he would not say anything about his "attempt to enter [that] the university did not reveal," and he denied that any organization had prompted his application. After disclosing that he had not spoken with any Ole Miss representative, he explained: "I feel that Ole Miss is no doubt the best institution in the state, and I think I should like to graduate from the state's best institution."[20]

More than two weeks later, and still unidentified, Meredith told UPI that he wanted to enter the university "for the good of my people, my country, my state, my family, and myself." As a father, he wanted to be able to tell his son that he had fought segregation and discrimination. He chose to take his stand in Mississippi because he was a Mississippian. "I am powerless to restrain myself from seeking to correct a condition that is certainly in need of change for the benefit of all," he declared. He believed that black persons, as full citizens, deserved full educational opportunities. Ending the hopelessness, the sense of inferiority, the fears among blacks would, he argued, benefit all Mississippians and Americans.[21]

Despite his bold ideas, Meredith moved cautiously. Always aware of Clennon King and Clyde Kennard, he kept to a "strategy to survive." He realized the value of publicity and the need to proceed quietly and secretly, and he emphasized his family's safety. Meredith did not trust the defenders of white supremacy, whose agents seemed to be everywhere. In Attala County, for example, whites sent influential blacks to his parents' home to persuade them that he should drop his plan; the visit upset Cap and Roxie Meredith, but they supported their son. In Jackson, strange cars occupied by whites cruised Meredith's apartment complex, and intimidating whites inquired about him. Protective friends and neighbors feigned ignorance but also organized watches over his home. Though helpful and reassuring, they could not really guard Meredith.[22]

Meredith recognized that, as he later recalled, "the very best possible protection against my particular enemy was the enemy himself." Police surveillance and harassment actually afforded him some protection from violent reprisals by white extremists. But the police were not alone. Within a week of his application, a Sovereignty Commission investigation uncovered the details of his Attala upbringing, his air force service, his lack of an arrest record, and his ownership of land and automobiles. A commission agent even reported his fingerprint classification.[23]

While the attention of whites troubled Meredith, it also provided reassurance. Some segregationists, he thought, actually welcomed his attempt to enroll at Ole Miss as an opportunity to mount a major defense of their way of life. They could make their stand for segregation, however, only if he were alive; if anything untoward happened to him, their cause would suffer. At the same time interest by the NAACP and the federal government encouraged him. Though he realized his increasing value to both the NAACP and Mississippi whites as a challenger of segregation, he focused on his own personal mission.[24]

In mid-February, Meredith's campaign received an enormous boost when the LDF assigned Constance Baker Motley to his case. In retrospect he believed that her joining his case was "the best possible thing that could have happened." The daughter of West Indian immigrants, Constance Baker was a native of New Haven, Connecticut. She attended Fisk University in 1942–43 before transferring to New York University. In 1945 she began working at the NAACP's LDF while a Columbia University law student, and she continued with it after graduating in 1946. (She married Joel Wilson Motley Jr. in 1946.) When in 1949 she participated in a lawsuit to equalize teacher pay, she made her first trip to Mississippi, gained her first trial experience, and met many members of Jackson's black community. In the 1950s she continued her work on teacher pay equalization lawsuits and on the cases that culminated in *Brown*. Jack Greenberg, an LDF associate, described her as "regal in appearance, deliberate in manner and speech, with somewhat of a nasal voice." Candid and tenacious, she was, according to Greenberg, "a dogged opponent of Southern segregationists, who found her tougher than Grant at Vicksburg." By 1961, Motley, who had fought to desegregate higher education in Florida, Alabama, and Louisiana, was prepared for Meredith's case. She believed that Marshall assigned her to the case because of her work with similar cases, because of her Mississippi experience, and because Mississippi might treat a black woman better than a black man.[25]

On February 16, 1961, the thirty-nine-year-old assistant LDF counsel first advised her new client. Very interested in Meredith's application, she promised to provide "whatever legal assistance appears to be necessary." Recognizing that the spring enrollment deadline had passed, she suggested that he seek admission for the fall semester but also proposed that he request the registrar make his application a "continuing application" for admission as soon as possible, either summer school in June or the next regular term. Unfamiliar with the specifics of the case, she asked for copies of his application and correspondence for confirmation that the registrar had received them too. She also advised him not to write any unnecessary letters to the university.[26]

In the next few weeks, Meredith exchanged letters with the registrar. After expressing disappointment with the abrupt decision to stop accepting applications, he requested, as Motley had recommended, consideration as a "continuing" applicant for the summer of 1961. He inquired about receipt of his transcripts and called for immediate action on his application. To minimize conflict, he thanked Ellis for the "respectable and humane manner in which you are handling this matter" and hoped that it would continue. The next day, however, when the registrar received Meredith's latest inquiry, he returned his room deposit. When Meredith received the money order, he sent it back with the reminder that he had asked to be admitted for the summer session.[27]

After two weeks the registrar had not responded, and the silence confirmed Meredith's expectation that Ole Miss would try to defeat him through delay and denial. Frustrated, on March 7 he asked Motley for advice. He told her that he could not fulfill all of her requests because he had not kept a copy of his application, did not have signed copies of his letters of references, and did not want to return to his home county to obtain his references' signatures because many people had warned him that he would be arrested in Kosciusko on unknown charges. In addition, the great fear among blacks made him unwilling to contact again his five black Attala County references unless "absolutely necessary."[28]

From New York, Motley advised him to ask the registrar for three things: status as a continuing applicant, a guarantee that his transcripts had been received in good order, and instructions about any remaining "prerequisites for admission." She also said that the Fund was "presently studying the possibilities of bringing legal action in your case." A few days later, the *Jackson Clarion-Ledger* reported that a fund-raising letter from the state NAACP announced its plan for a lawsuit to force the university to admit a black student. By the middle of March, therefore, Meredith's quest had taken a serious turn toward a major legal challenge to segregation, and any resulting lawsuit would have the backing of the NAACP's experienced litigators.[29]

The Fund's interest buoyed Meredith. He hoped it would pursue his case, but he knew the lawyers had to use their legal expertise to make their decision. Meredith again assured Motley of his commitment. "The central theme" of his ideas about "the best method of winning the fight" was, he told her, "expediency." Overcoming white supremacy by desegregating Ole Miss remained his objective, and he cared little how he achieved that result. At her urging, he renewed his requests to Ellis; he relayed a copy of his letter to Motley along with his confession that he did not expect a response from Ole Miss.[30]

After the LDF agreed to represent Meredith, Motley worked more closely with him by providing detailed advice and instructions. She wanted his application to be as unimpeachable as possible because she expected Ole Miss to use any error to justify rejecting his application. After perusing the university's admission provisions, she emphasized that he had to comply fully with every criterion. The university, for example, required five recommendations attesting to the applicant's good character but also recommending admission. His letters only testified to his character and did not explicitly endorse his admission. "This is an admission requirement," she declared, "which you should take care of immediately." She also questioned his qualifications as a Mississippi resident because he had not lived in the state for the previous twelve months, unless he had kept it as his official residence during his air force service. Resident status would entitle him to lower fees and might also strengthen his claim for admission. Practically, Motley inquired about his plans for university housing and about his veterans benefits.[31]

With lawyerly precision Motley considered the academic issues involved in Meredith's application. Referring directly to the catalog, she told him to make sure each of his transcripts included the mandatory statement that he had been honorably dismissed and was eligible for readmission. She recommended that he obtain an official registrar's assessment of which transfer credits Ole Miss would accept and that he request from the dean of liberal arts an evaluation of which credits would apply toward his degree.[32]

Though Meredith admitted that her queries caused him to "burn a little 'midnight oil,' " he got to work. At his instruction on March 26, his five original references supplied new letters of recommendation with declarations that "recommend that he be admitted to the University of Mississippi." Meredith also asked his previous schools to make sure his transcripts contained the required statement of his "good standing and eligibility for immediate readmission." The Veterans Administration confirmed his continuing eligibility for benefits. He duly reported his actions to Motley and also told her that he had applied for housing in a men's dormitory because his family would not accompany him. As for his legal residency, he had no "doubt that I am a legal resident of the state of Mississippi." Except for his air force years, he had never lived in another state for a year, and in the service he had always listed both Michigan and Mississippi; he provided a Defense Department form as evidence. He admitted that the "addresses are for military purposes only, and in no way establish or affect legal residence."[33] The care with which he and Motley approached his legal residence reflected their awareness of the scrutiny his application would receive as the university sought any reason, large or small, to justify his rejection.

On March 26, Meredith quoted to Robert Ellis the regulations on letters of recommendation and enclosed five new letters of reference. Citing the catalog, he asked Ellis to determine whether his transfer courses would count toward his degree. Meredith expected Ellis to consider his application in the customary way and to notify him as soon as possible of his acceptance or rejection. To remain cordial while forcing the issue, Meredith conceded that he was "not a usual applicant" but hoped his application would not cause a problem for the university.[34]

During the spring of 1961, Meredith enrolled in courses in psychology, education, history, and political science at Jackson State and earned four As, one B, and one C. Many of his professors supported him, either open or tacitly. He suspected that college administrators felt pressure from powerful whites to prevent his successful entry into Ole Miss; he later expressed pride that the administrators did not yield and did nothing to stop his campaign.[35]

Meredith's Jackson State friends boosted his morale, but he wanted approval from black college students across the state. To elicit endorsements, he identified himself as the black man who had applied to Ole Miss. On March 20 he distributed to Mississippi's black colleges a letter explaining that he sought not just the desegregation of Ole Miss but the greater "social, economic, and political advancement of the Negro in Mississippi." Though he knew many blacks opposed his attack on white supremacy, he called for students to give him "a vote of confidence" by signing his letter and returning it to him. Within days more than one hundred students at Jackson State alone endorsed his plan, but he needed far greater backing for such a daring move.[36]

Four days after his plea for support, Meredith circulated among blacks "Why I Plan to Go to the University of Mississippi," his fullest explanation of his motivations. He declared that a Mississippi Negro was entitled to an education at the state university. Blacks needed to become more than the teachers and preachers produced by segregated institutions. They deserved access to the ROTC program available at the white universities. More important, he sought to offer an alternative to racial segregation, discrimination, and oppression by fighting the "hopelessness," the "demoralizing" attitudes, and the "fears and inferior feelings that prevail among our people."[37]

As he had before, Meredith attributed much of his inspiration to his one-year-old son John. Repeatedly he asked how, when his son was older, he would answer his questions about segregation and discrimination. He imagined him asking, "What have you done to correct these conditions?" Knowing that "Shut up, boy" would not suffice, the father had to do something. He did not claim that only he could change the treatment, status, and condition of Mississippi blacks, only that his conscience compelled him to act.[38]

Meredith also cast his action in a larger political context. As a patriot, he believed his country was "truly the greatest among nations" but its race relations hurt it in the cold war. America's opponents used its racial practices to question the greatness of the United States, and Mississippi's racial system was the nation's worst. Whites used blacks' numerical power "to excite the hates and fears of the [white] masses in order to hamper our progress." Mississippi had to address racial inequality to ensure the nation's leadership in the world, and Meredith would do his part by desegregating the major university.[39]

While Meredith knew that whites opposed his attending Ole Miss, he maintained that white resistance would not be as uniformly intransigent as many assumed because many whites "agree that Mississippi carries segregation to unreasonable limits." He based his assessment especially on his air force experiences, where he found he could always work with white Mississippians, and back home he found whites more amenable to change than many feared. In particular, white college students realized that the progress depended on ameliorating racial problems. His basic optimism did not allay all of Meredith's concerns. Though he sought "to commit no crime, to break no law, or to infringe upon the rights of anyone," he realized the unprecedented nature of his proposal: "No Negro has gone to a school in Mississippi heretofore proclaimed for whites only." Aware of earlier defeats, he feared failure. More ominously, he recognized that something might happen to him or his family. Retribution could not dissuade him; it could not be worse than life under racial oppression.[40]

Just days after Meredith's second letter to blacks, the Mississippi civil rights movement accelerated. Soon after noon on Monday, March 27, in a direct attack on segregation, nine Tougaloo students staged a study-in protest at the main public library in downtown Jackson. Local reporters, tipped off by Medgar Evers, covered the event. When the protesters refused to leave the library, Jackson police arrested them. That evening, coordinated by the MIAS, several hundred Jackson State students, including Meredith, rallied in support of the jailed "Tougaloo Nine." After songs and prayers in front of the college library, local police and college officials broke up the gathering. The next afternoon about fifty black students attempted to march to the city jail in support of the Nine, but the police dispersed them with dogs and tear gas. The Nine were released on bond later Tuesday and appeared at an evening NAACP rally at a local church attended by four hundred supporters. On Wednesday, when they went to municipal court for trial, several hundred blacks gathered across the street, but police with clubs and dogs attacked and scattered them. Convicted by the court, each student received a one hundred-dollar fine and a thirty-day suspended sentence. As Myrlie Evers later concluded, the "change in tide in Mississippi" started in 1961 when, with the student protests in March, "Negroes took the offensive in the struggle for full citizenship." Until then, Mississippi had been a "backwater" where the greater movement caused "only minor ripples."[41]

While the larger movement developed, Meredith waited to hear from Ole Miss. In early April, Constance Motley stressed that it was "absolutely essential that you comply with all of the requirements with which it is possible for you to comply prior to bringing suit." She urged him not to worry that his new letters of reference were not from university alumni because the LDF had won a similar Georgia lawsuit. Concerned that Ole Miss had not received his transcripts, she provided a draft of a letter to send to the dean of liberal arts.[42]

By the time Meredith heard from Motley, he had grown more disheartened because he had not heard from anyone at the university, but he followed her directions and wrote to Dean A. B. Lewis. He explained that the registrar had not communicated with him since his February 4 telegram rejecting Meredith's application; Ellis had not even acknowledged any of Meredith's three subsequent inquiries. The registrar had refused to tell him if he had failed to meet any of the requirements for admission or if his application had any deficiency. In a direct challenge, Meredith "concluded that Mr. Ellis has failed to act upon my application solely because of my race and color." He asked Dean Lewis to consult with Ellis and to tell him of any problems with his application, and he specifically requested "some assurance that my race and color are not the basis for my failure to gain admission to the University."[43]

Meredith routinely shared copies of his letters with Motley. Increasingly attentive to detail, he explained to his lawyer that the University of Maryland had not assured him that his transcript contained the required statement, but he knew an earlier Maryland transcript sent to Jackson State had contained such a statement. For her files he enclosed copies of the responses he had received to his requests that his transcripts include a certification that he remained a student in good standing. He closed his brief letter with a very personal observation. While he tried to get a public education "to which I have been theoretically entitled for nearly one hundred years," twenty-seven-year-old Soviet cosmonaut Yuri Gagarin was traveling in outer space. The comparison was "amazing and perplexing" to Meredith: a Russian became the first man in space before, and apparently with less difficulty than, the first Negro could enroll in Ole Miss. He took some consolation, however, in knowing that the civil rights movement in his state had at least "got[ten] on the map" with the Jackson demonstrations a few days before the Russians conquered space.[44]

Finally, at the end of April, Meredith and Motley met. She flew to Jackson to get to know him, hear his personal history, review his struggle with the university, and discuss his case. As usual when she came to Mississippi, Motley stayed in the black community because all major hotels refused blacks. In April, Medgar Evers arranged for her to stay with one of his neighbors. When Evers introduced Meredith to Motley, she impressed him as an astute lawyer and a large, cordial woman. To Motley he seemed a small, slight man, "soft-spoken and reserved in his speech and manner," but forcefully committed. Each quickly respected the other, but they never became personal friends. In their professional relationship, they continued to address each other as "Mr. Meredith" and "Mrs. Motley."[45]

Ten days after the Jackson meeting, Meredith at last heard from the registrar. With a "Dear Sir" salutation instead of the earlier "Dear Mr. Meredith," Ellis on May 9 bureaucratically assured Meredith that his "application has been received and will receive proper attention." After acknowledging receipt of four transcripts, all in good order, he addressed the admissibility of the courses. Under the university's rules, Ellis tentatively could accept only forty-eight out of ninety semester hours, but with a crucial qualifier—"if your application for admission as a transfer student should be approved." He emphasized the guarded quality of his evaluation: "My evaluation of your credits is not in any way a determination or decision as to whether your application for admission will be approved or disapproved or of its sufficiency." In closing, Ellis asked if Meredith wanted his application to be handled as a "pending application."[46]

The registrar's response pleased Meredith, but the refusal to accept so much of his work, none from Jackson State, disappointed him. Thinking that Ellis's letter provided him justification to pursue admission for the summer term, Meredith forwarded the letter to his New York lawyer. In return mail, Motley urged him to tell Ellis immediately that he did want his application to be considered as pending for both the summer and fall terms. Exasperated by Ellis's evasiveness but concerned about the possible next step in the case, she directed Meredith to "*ask him again to advise you if there is anything further that you should do in order to complete your application.*" Meredith once again wrote to Ellis. After expressing pleasure that the university was paying "proper attention" to his application, he reiterated his wish to be considered for the summer and fall terms and asked again to be notified if he needed to do anything further to complete his application. Insisting that Ellis tell him whether his application had been accepted or rejected, Meredith, as a husband and father who had to plan for his family, told him that "it is imperative that I be informed . . . at the earliest possible date."[47]

As the pace picked up, Motley waited only a week before again asking Meredith on May 18 if he had heard from Ellis. Believing the registrar's earlier letter had "clearly indicate[d] that you are qualified for admission," she knew "no reason why you should not be admitted this summer." Motley encouraged him to ask Ellis when Ole Miss would act on summer school applications. As the June term fast approached, she grew more impatient and more determined. "If you do not hear from the registrar, I suggest that you present yourself for registration on Thursday, June 8, as indicated by the latest catalog," she advised Meredith.[48]

While waiting a week for the registrar's response, Meredith and Motley exchanged several letters. To prod Ellis one more time, Meredith took his question regarding the application as a pending one as an opportunity to say that he assumed that his application was complete and that he met all admission requirements. Worried that deficiencies remained, the meticulous Motley told Meredith to secure a statement from Wayne State University that he had honorably withdrawn in 1955 when he reenlisted in the air force. For use in a lawsuit, she also instructed him to send her the receipts he had saved from his certified mailings to the university. She insisted that he call her collect when he heard from the registrar.[49]

Before Meredith received any definitive word from the university, the racial situation took a dramatic turn on May 24 when the first Freedom Riders entered the state. Organized by CORE, the Freedom Rides began on May 4 when an integrated group of a dozen people left Washington, D.C., on two buses. They planned to travel to New Orleans to test compliance with court decisions outlawing segregation in interstate travel and the facilities serving travelers. Their trip proved largely uneventful until Alabama. After an attack on May 14 outside Anniston in which one bus was burned, the Freedom Riders endured beatings by whites later the same day in Birmingham and six days later in Montgomery. As a result, President Kennedy sent hundreds of U.S. marshals to Alabama, and the governor declared martial law in the state capital. Intense negotiations between federal officials and political leaders of Alabama and Mississippi produced guarantees of the Freedom Riders' safety when they continued from Montgomery to Jackson.[50]

On May 24, two dozen black and white activists, now including members of the Student Nonviolent Coordinating Committee (SNCC) as well as CORE, left Montgomery on two buses bound for Jackson. An agreement between Attorney General Robert F. Kennedy and Jackson's mayor, Allen Thompson, Governor Barnett, and Senator Eastland provided that state and local authorities would ensure the riders' safety, and in exchange, federal authorities would not object to their arrest in Jackson. When the two buses arrived in Jackson, no whites attacked the Freedom Riders, but police arrested them when they entered the bus terminal's "white" waiting room and restrooms. Charged with breach of the peace, they were peacefully taken to the city jail. Tried and convicted two days later, the Freedom Riders refused to pay their fines and opted to serve their sixty-day jail terms. Soon more Freedom Riders came to Jackson and went to jail; by the end of the summer more than three hundred had been arrested, tried, convicted, and jailed.[51]

Though Mississippi avoided a violent reaction to the Freedom Rides, civil rights demonstrators had brought the larger movement directly into the heart of the state. By involving CORE and SNCC as well as the NAACP, the Freedom Riders changed the movement in Mississippi. NAACP lawyers would no longer dominate the movement; CORE and SNCC each soon established a presence and intensified the challenge to white supremacy. The opposing demands for the maintenance of racial segregation became, if possible, more insistent. At the same moment, Ole Miss met Meredith's challenge.[52]

On May 25, the day after the Freedom Riders staged their initial peaceful assault on Jackson, the Ole Miss registrar responded definitively to Meredith. "I regret to inform you," Ellis's letter stated, "in answer to your recent letter, that your application for admission must be denied." In an unusual explanation, Ellis declared, "The university cannot recognize the transfer of credits from the institution which you are now attending since it is not a member of the Southern Association of Colleges and Secondary Schools. Our policy permits the transfer of credits only from member institutions of regional associations. Furthermore, students may not be accepted by the University from those institutions whose programs are not recognized." Although he believed Meredith realized his application's flaws, the registrar reminded him that "your application does not meet other requirements for admission," including inadequate letters of recommendation. Vaguely referring to other disqualifying factors, Ellis saw "no need for mentioning other deficiencies." Hoping to end the case, Ellis declared Meredith's "application file has been closed," and he returned Meredith's deposits.[53]

When Meredith called Motley with the not-unexpected news, she mentioned exploring any available appeals of the decision within the university and the board of trustees. Meredith, weary from waiting and worried about the summer school deadline, objected to any delay. As a result, lawyer and client agreed to file a federal lawsuit seeking his admission to Ole Miss. On Memorial Day, Motley flew to Jackson to consult with Meredith, finish the necessary legal papers, and present their case in federal court.[54]

The decision to file suit encountered numerous problems. Motley was not licensed in Mississippi, so Meredith needed a local counsel to file the suit. Few blacks practiced law in the state, and even fewer whites would help in such a case. A second difficulty involved securing a discreet notary public for the federal court documents. The solution to the problem of local legal representation came when R. Jess Brown, a black lawyer from Vicksburg, agreed to accept the case, and the need for a notary was satisfied when a woman in Medgar Evers's neighborhood performed the duties. A final problem involved Meredith himself: his lawyers wanted him to make the proper impression in court by shaving his full beard and by exchanging his khaki pants and shirt for more conservative clothes. Though they left the decision to him, they made their wishes clear, and when they appeared in court the next day, Meredith had done as they suggested.[55]

On May 31, Meredith, Motley, Medgar Evers, and Jess Brown drove to Meridian, ninety miles east of Jackson, where Judge Sidney C. Mize presided over the U.S. District Court for the Southern District of Mississippi. In the federal court building they did some final preparation of legal papers. Drawing on his air force clerical skills, Meredith typed some of the documents for presentation to Judge Mize. With everything in order, the four proceeded to the fourth-floor courtroom, where the judge was hearing a case. Mize interrupted the proceedings to accept the twelve-page complaint and to hear Constance Motley's argument.[56]

The next day the *Meridian Star*'s front page for the first time carried Meredith's picture, and Mississippi newspapers identified him as the black person seeking to enter Ole Miss. In Meridian he refused to tell the press where he lived or to identify his parents. Speaking briefly with reporters outside the court, Meredith said that he simply wanted to go to a better school but would "continue [his] studies at Jackson State College until such time as [he is] admitted to Ole Miss." With "no intention of antagonizing anyone," he declared that he would proceed in "an orderly and proper manner" and that he did not see "any call for violence" when he entered the university. Meredith denied any connection with the Freedom Riders and declared that he had acted on his own initiative and only later accepted legal assistance from the NAACP.[57]

The *Jackson Clarion-Ledger* ran the story of Meredith's lawsuit on the front page, but in the middle of the left side, not as the lead story on the top right. It withheld immediate editorial comment, but political columnist Charles M. Hills offered his typically intemperate commentary. Playing off a report that, at one point in his typing at the federal court in Meridian, Meredith had to ask how to spell "Biloxi," Hills observed, "The University of Mississippi is being sued to accept a student who can't even spell a three-syllable word . . . the name of probably the best known town in Mississippi . . . the nationally known resort, 'Biloxi.' " After disingenuously suggesting that the NAACP ought to find a more qualified candidate, he snidely claimed, "Of course with the help of Bobby Kennedy and Brother Jack, Sam Rayburn and Lyndon Johnson, it is probable that a Hottentot could crash the staid halls of Ole Miss. How ridiculous can this situation get, anyway?"[58]

Commenting on events in its own hometown, the *Meridian Star* showed even less restraint. A defiant editorial, "Never Say Die," foretold the reaction of the state's white leadership and urged readers not to minimize Meredith's attempt to enter Ole Miss. "Some misguided people ask what difference it makes if only a few Negroes go to a white school. The difference is that the first Negro is only the opening wedge for a flood in time to come." The result was clear: "Massive integration will mean future intermarriage. Intermarriage in the South, where we are so evenly divided white and colored, means the end of both races as such, and the emergence of a tribe of mongrels." The *Star* decried moderates as nothing but people "who want to supinely submit to the integrationists." The editorial tried desperately to rally segregationists: "If you value your racial heritage, if you have even the smallest regard for the future of this South of yours—you will be for segregation one hundred percent. We must lock shields. We must fight for our race and for the South to the last bitter ditch. We must never lose heart. We can triumph—we will triumph—we must triumph."[59]

13. *Meredith v. Fair* I: "Delay, Harassment, and Masterly Inactivity"

■ ■

On May 31, 1961, on the fourth floor of the Meridian federal courthouse, James Meredith's legal battle began before Judge Sidney Mize. LDF lawyers presented his grievances against the fifteen trustees, headed by Charles D. Fair, and three Ole Miss representatives, Chancellor Williams, Dean Lewis, and Registrar Ellis. The plaintiff wanted Judge Mize to rule on his right, and by implication the right of all blacks, to attend Ole Miss. Represented by Constance Motley, Meredith also sought a temporary restraining order to prevent the defendants from keeping him out of the university and to allow him to enroll for the summer session beginning on June 8.[1]

The case of *Meredith v. Fair* developed in two stages. In the first, fought in the U.S. District Court for Southern Mississippi, the case made its halting but predictable way through courtrooms in Meridian, Biloxi, and Jackson toward a verdict in February 1962. It started with the plaintiff's complaint and request for relief from the court. Before a hearing on the charges, the defendants obtained a detailed deposition from Meredith. After legal maneuverings, Judge Mize heard testimony on the plaintiff's claims. When Mize refused Meredith's request, the Fifth Circuit Court of Appeals directed him to conduct a full trial in the case. Spanning more than two weeks, the trial resulted again in a ruling against Meredith. When his lawyers appealed, the second stage began in New Orleans. The appellate court ruling provoked an unprecedented judicial tug-of-war between the appellate court and a district court judge that eventually the U.S. Supreme Court settled in September 1962. Along the way, the courts subjected Meredith to numerous delays and postponements. The state's wily prolonging tactics demonstrated its intransigence, and the judge's acquiescence revealed his preference for the defense.

At the outset of the first hearing, Motley explained that her client based his claim on the Fourteenth Amendment. Adopted during Reconstruction, it mandated that a state could not "deprive any person of life, liberty, or property without due process of law," nor could it "deny to any person . . . the equal protection of the laws." She asked the court to declare that Meredith and other Negro citizens of the state "have a right to attend the University of Mississippi and other state institutions of higher learning presently limited to white students upon the same terms and conditions applicable to white citizens and residents of Mississippi."[2]

In what a Jackson paper called "the first legal desegregation action involving Mississippi schools," Motley requested an injunction to prevent Ole Miss from "refusing to consider and act expeditiously" on Meredith's application and to prohibit it from rejecting him "solely because of race and color." She objected to the "policy, practice, custom and usage" that kept blacks out. Meredith had the academic prerequisites for admission. She wanted the court to prevent the defendants from doing anything that "interferes with, defeats, or thwarts" his rights.[3]

Concentrating on the admissions procedures, the twelve-page complaint recounted Meredith's correspondence with the registrar and highlighted the university's failures even to acknowledge his inquiries. Noting that the application form asked for the individual's race, the complaint stated that Meredith had readily declared that he was a Negro. The plaintiff pointed out that he received notification of the rejection of his application four months after he had applied but that he could not respond to the university's action because Ole Miss had not revealed the rationale behind its decision. Ignoring the accreditation status of Meredith's previous college, the complaint emphasized the required letters of recommendation.[4]

Unlike a non-Mississippian who needed any five people to testify to the applicant's good character and to recommend admission, a Mississippi resident had to secure recommendations from alumni in the applicant's home county. The plaintiff implied that the different requirements for in-state and out-of-state applicants violated the equal treatment clause. The major objection involved the inability of Meredith and other blacks to secure recommendations from Ole Miss's white alumni. According to the complaint, "there are not now and never have been any Negro graduates of the University of Mississippi." Meredith claimed not to know a single Ole Miss alumnus "who would recommend his admission in view of the segregation policy" that determined the university's practices. As a result, he alleged that the "alumni certificate requirement is unconstitutional" because "it places a burden on Negroes seeking admission . . . which is not shared by white residents" and because "in operation and effect it bars the admission of qualified Negroes . . . solely because they are Negroes."[5]

The white-haired, seventy-four-year-old Mize, a Mississippian and a graduate of the Ole Miss law school, reportedly looked "vaguely like Winston Churchill and Theodore Bilbo." In Gulfport, he had participated in state Democratic politics before President Franklin D. Roosevelt appointed him to the federal bench in 1937. Twenty-four years later, in June 1961, after hearing

Meredith's complaint, Mize denied the request for a restraining order that would permit Meredith to enroll at the university. The judge did, however, schedule for two weeks later in Biloxi a hearing on the larger issues presented by Meredith's complaint.[6]

The IHL board became further involved when Judge Mize directed that a deputy U.S. marshal serve on every defendant a summons to respond within twenty days to Meredith's complaint. While the university defendants accepted the summonses, most of the other defendants refused. A deputy marshal left the summonses in their presence anyway—in one case on the desk in front of the defendant, in another instance on a table in his living room, and in a third case in the window of a trustee's pickup truck with the trustee sitting inside. They tried to refuse the summonses, but they could not ignore the lawsuit. Five days after the suit was filed, the trustees called a special meeting to discuss the case. When reporters learned of the emergency gathering, board executive secretary Jobe denied any meeting was planned. After word of it leaked, the trustees postponed it until the afternoon. Though the board made no announcement and its minutes contain no references to the Meredith case, the trustees discussed the case and their response to it.[7] The more important action, however, occurred within the courts.

After Mize's initial rulings, each side sought to bolster its case by questioning individuals on the other side. When Meredith's attorneys asked to depose Ellis, Judge Mize, following procedures that allowed the defendants twenty days to respond to the original complaint, denied the request. Lawyers for two defendants sought to question Meredith, and his lawyers objected because the twenty days had not elapsed and because of the inconvenience of having him appear in Meridian instead of Jackson. Judge Mize nonetheless directed him to appear at the Meridian federal courthouse on June 8, the first day of summer school.[8]

At the deposition R. Jess Brown joined Constance Motley and Derrick Bell of the LDF. Three assistant attorneys general, Dugas Shands, Edward L. Cates, and Peter M. Stockett, represented the defendants. The lawyers agreed to meet with Mize to settle any disagreement. Less than an hour into the closed session, they recessed for lunch. When Motley asked about places to eat, a defense lawyer mentioned popular Meridian restaurants, but the plaintiff's team refused to take their lunches out the back door of white restaurants. Instead Meredith and his attorneys searched for a "colored" cafe.[9]

A long afternoon session established many issues and set the tone for the case. Meredith's chief interrogator was Dugas Shands, a fifty-five-year-old known as "the state's civil rights expert" and as the man who "stands between [the] state and integration." A native of Bolivar County in the Delta, he graduated from Vanderbilt University and the Ole Miss law school. After a private law practice and several government posts, Shands in 1954 accepted Governor J. P. Coleman's appointment as assistant attorney general. Reputedly a quick thinker even though he spoke slowly, he faced enormous challenges— Meredith's lawsuit, several federal voting rights lawsuits, the Freedom Rider cases, and a lawsuit to desegregate Gulf Coast beaches. In Meredith's deposition Shands hoped to expose the plaintiff's greater interest in integration than education, his recruitment and sponsorship by the NAACP, his incapacity for the academic work at a white university, and his moral unfitness. Shands treated him with the disrespect and disdain that many whites showed blacks. According to Meredith, he was "a master of the 'Nigger Treatment' tactic." As Meredith later explained, the "tactic is to provoke the Negro, to frighten him, and then to break him down and cross him up. The aim is to imply that the Negro is dishonest, immoral, a thief by nature, and generally unworthy of being considered fully human."[10]

Shands first asked Meredith about the preparation of his lawsuit and his contacts with the NAACP. When he queried, "Have you spent any money on this lawsuit yourself?" Motley objected, and she repeated her objection when Shands asked about his personal property. Shifting to the complaint itself, Shands asked when and where Meredith had signed it. When Motley again protested, Shands declared, "All of this goes to the veracity, the competence, intelligence and the character of the plaintiff." Changing slightly, he asked who had witnessed his signature, and, when Meredith glanced at his lawyers, Shands admonished him, "Don't look around there, you look at me." Motley repeated her objections. After the attorneys agreed to confer with Judge Mize later, Shands interrogated Meredith about his reasons for seeking admission to Ole Miss. Motley objected to any investigation of his motives as irrelevant; she also objected to queries about his personal finances, automobiles, and return to Mississippi. At one point, she charged that Shands was "harassing the witness," and later instructed her client not to answer.[11]

Undeterred, Shands probed Meredith's employment history and asked if he worked for the NAACP and if it paid his expenses. Motley insisted that the "financing of the case is not relevant." Shands began to press on the letters of recommendation but abruptly switched to Meredith's air force service. Motley objected to Shands's questions as irrelevant and immaterial. Shands argued his queries dealt with Meredith's "financial ability, . . . his good faith, . . . his veracity, . . . [and] whether or not this is his lawsuit or somebody else's lawsuit." When the judge and attorneys reviewed each question, Mize approved every one, though he acknowledged that some might not be relevant in a trial. In giving the defense wide latitude, Mize decided that the personal queries could deal with the plaintiff's "moral qualifications" for admission. When Motley protested Shands's "fishing expedition," Judge Mize conceded that each side had the right to ask him to strike any irrelevancies from the record.[12]

In examining Meredith, Shands demonstrated his white superiority. Though Meredith usually concluded his replies with "sir," Shands invariably addressed him condescendingly as "James," not "Mr. Meredith." He also refused to use a courtesy title with the LDF lawyers. When dealing with Jess Brown, Shands denied any personal or professional respect by using the demeaning "Jess." As a black woman, Constance Motley presented a different problem, but Shands resolved the difficulty by calling her neither the personal "Constance" nor the more formal "Mrs. Motley" but instead referring to her as some variation of "Plaintiff's Counsel." For her part, Motley always used "Mr. Shands."[13] The plaintiff's lawyers did not protest the disrespectful language, probably to focus on the facts of the case, but perhaps also to avoid antagonizing Judge Mize.

Freed to probe many areas of Meredith's life, Shands jumped from his connections to the NAACP and Medgar Evers, to his letters of recommendation, to his involvements at Jackson State, to his air force service, and to his personal finances. Shands peppered Meredith with questions designed to confuse, embarrass, and discredit him and to make him, not the university's rejection of him, the issue. In a tense, hostile interrogation, Shands at one point asked Meredith to spell "notary public," which the transcript showed Shands pronounced "notary republic"; Meredith pronounced it properly and spelled it correctly.[14]

Shands then bored in on the letters of reference and implied that Meredith had stolen from the air force both the typewriter and the stationery used in preparing the recommendations. Undaunted, Meredith asked, "Are you saying that I stole the paper?" Shands denied it: "I'm not saying anything, James, I am asking you facts." In response to another accusation, Meredith denied that he had taken the container in which he kept his papers from the air force, and Motley objected to the question: "You are now fishing and trying to get this man implicated in some kind of crime. . . . You are trying to entrap this man and trying to show that he stole goods." Meredith insisted, "I have never stolen anything in my life."[15]

On the form and substance of the letters, Shands pressed him. Meredith identified each of his references, explained that he had told them why he needed the letters, and had typed the original letters so his references would only have to sign them. Acknowledging that the first letters did not recommend his admission, Meredith told Shands that "we" decided to submit new letters. Seizing on the word "we," Shands claimed that it proved that Meredith had experience using the editorial "we," and he seemed to refer to radical student publications at Jackson State. Denying any such writings, Meredith mentioned his counsel had suggested the new letters. He emphasized that he had typed all of his letters except for the one to the dean of liberal arts. To prove that the NAACP had instigated the effort to integrate Ole Miss, Shands charged that the letter generated by the NAACP was "when you threw 'race or color' into it." Meredith corrected him by pointing out that his application letter had clearly stated his race, before he contacted the NAACP.[16]

Three and a half grueling hours of the "Nigger Treatment" failed to fluster Meredith. He withstood the bullying. Meredith recalled that ten minutes after the deposition began "I knew that I could out-maneuver Shands" and lead him "down many roads of no return." In fact, "there was no time while Shands asked questions that I did not feel confident that I had a definite advantage of him in the courtroom." He believed that whites did not "know their Negroes" and that he had a superior understanding of whites. "I had spent fifteen years systematically studying white folks, especially southern ones," he claimed, "and I had little doubt that I knew more about every white man than he knew himself, certainly insofar as his relationship to the Negro is concerned."[17]

The deposition preceded the important hearing that began on June 12 in federal court in Biloxi, Judge Mize's hometown. Motley surprised Mize when she named the plaintiff's witnesses; the judge apparently expected only written affidavits and oral arguments. Motley called Robert Ellis. To nearly every question Motley asked, Shands objected. For example, when she asked if Ellis had in January 1961 received a letter from Meredith, Shands objected: "Who J. H. Meredith is, this record is utterly silent about." He claimed not to know if Meredith wrote the letter. After Mize sustained the objection, Motley asked if Ellis had received a letter signed by Meredith. Again Shands: "Whether that is the same James H. Meredith in this lawsuit, the record goes entirely silent." When Mize continued to sustain Shands's objections, Motley relented, excused the registrar, and called Meredith as the next witness.[18]

Directed by Motley's methodical questioning, Meredith retraced his correspondence with the university, his acquisition of recommendations, his educational background, his air force service, and his financial affairs. Shands's repeated objections disrupted and delayed the hearing. When, for example, Motley asked if Meredith had explained the purpose of the letters to his references, Shands objected to it as hearsay. Mize agreed. Similarly, when Meredith testified that students took exams in self-taught courses in the armed forces "when you feel you have mastered the material," Shands protested that "what he feels" was unacceptable and "whether he did or did not master something is not for this witness to determine" (Mize concurred). Last, Motley asked Meredith about his registering to vote, and he declared that he registered in Jackson, where he lived.[19]

Shands pursued his voter registration. Meredith admitted that he had never voted and that a Jackson State registration drive prompted him to register in February 1961. Asked about the requirements for registering, Meredith replied, "I assume that I met them." Reporting that the voting registrar called him a "nigger," he implied that if a segregationist registrar approved his application then he must have met the requirements. Pressed by Shands, he admitted that he was not, as the law required, a Hinds County resident for the year prior to registering and that he must have, therefore, sworn to false information when he registered to vote. But Meredith explained that he simply followed the directions of the registrar who did most of the talking and did not ask many questions. Meredith testified that he told him "that I had never lived in Hinds County. I told him that I had always lived in Attala County." Because Meredith had served in the air force, the Hinds registrar, according to Meredith, gave him "this exemption that he says all military people get." Though Shands dropped his questions about Meredith's voter registration, a year later state law enforcement authorities would return to it.[20]

Shands pressed on his omission of Wayne State College from his application. Interrupting Meredith's answer, Shands tried to rattle him: "Now, when you were up at Wayne College, were you able to read and write?" Meredith admitted that as an eighteen-year-old he had had some problems with grammar. But Shands suggested he had left Wayne State off his application because of incompetence: "Could you read and write good on January 31, 1961?" Motley objected, but Shands moved on.[21]

When Meredith expressed pride in his military service, Shands asked if he would authorize the defense to review his air force records. At first Meredith expressed his reluctance. He explained that "if I'm successful in getting in the University of Mississippi, I don't want to set a bad precedent to Negroes where they have to go through a special procedure to get that; that is, by showing all these things I don't believe is required from a normal applicant." Shands fired back, "James, you don't have anything to hide in this matter do you?" When Motley objected to his tone and to his effort to trap the witness, Mize ruled that the court could only make an unfavorable inference if he refused to authorize an inspection of his records. Meredith relented. Motley, however, protested: "They denied his application on May 25 [1961] on whatever evidence they had at the time, and it did not include his Army [sic] record."[22]

When Shands tried to establish that Meredith was not a legal Mississippi resident, Meredith contended that he maintained his legal residence in Kosciusko during his military service. At the end of his last hitch, the air force paid his way either to his home or to his place of enlistment, and he went to Detroit but had his family's possessions shipped to Kosciusko, his home. He also said that when he obtained a driver's license in September 1960, he listed Attala County as his home. Confused about 1960 and 1961 but determined to trip him up, Shands suggested that he had falsely given Attala County as his home seven months after he had registered to vote in Jackson.[23]

Toward the end of the cross-examination, Shands inquired, "Now, James, do you really seriously charge that you have been kept out of the University solely because of your race and color?" Meredith replied, "Yes, sir." When the defense lawyer asked for the factual basis for his claim, Motley interrupted that the requested answer amounted to a legal opinion on the heart of the case, but Mize overruled her. Meredith then explained that the registrar's reasons—attendance at a nonaccredited college and failure to supply alumni references—"did not seem to me reasonable, logical enough, for grounds for not admitting me," so he concluded the policy must have been based on race. Shands rejected the explanation as his opinion. As for the references, Shands accused him of taking the paper when he left the air force, but Meredith countered that he had merely taken paper that had been discarded. "You mean to charge the government with throwing away perfectly good paper?" asked Shands. "Yes, sir," Meredith answered and then explained that it had been thrown away when his unit was dissolved and he had retrieved it from a trash can.[24]

Late in the afternoon, when Judge Mize realized the testimony would take several days, he suddenly halted the hearing and announced that it would resume in nearly a month. Objecting to the delay, Motley reminded Mize that her client sought to enroll for the summer session that began two days earlier and suggested that the defense expedite the case by filing a deposition along with the plaintiff's objections. Mize ruled, however, that the defense was entitled to cross-examine the plaintiff's witnesses, and he recessed the hearing until July 10.[25]

The defendants had succeeded. The long recess prevented Meredith's attendance in the first summer session and made very unlikely his enrollment for the second because any decision would come well after its July 17 start. Shands's interrogation of Meredith also opened up issues that would play significant roles in the legal battle: the plaintiff's legal residence, the legality of the information he gave when he registered to vote, and his character, if he had stolen from the military and had something to hide in his military record.

Two weeks after the hearing recessed, the state pressed the plaintiff when the Sovereignty Commission released information about Meredith and his family. It revealed Kosciusko as his hometown, told where he had attended school, and identified his parents as Cap Meredith, a retired farmer, and Roxie Meredith, a school cafeteria worker.[26] Piercing their privacy, the commission exposed him and his parents to threats and intimidation.

During much of June and July lawyers sparred over procedures. Five times in five weeks Meredith's attorneys tried to depose the registrar. They also wanted to inspect admissions documents for the spring semester of 1961, both summer terms, and the upcoming fall session. They hoped to find other applicants admitted without alumni certificates, transfers from nonaccredited institutions, and students accepted for the spring semester after the January 25 deadline. They expected the files to bolster their claim that Meredith had been rejected because of his race.[27]

The state opposed the deposition of Ellis because the hearing had already started and he had been called as a witness. Regarding admissions records, the defense said the plaintiff had not shown he could not get the information any other way or that denial of the request would work a hardship on Meredith's case; the state also argued that the law did not provide for inspection of records once the trial began. The state also sought a delay because of Shands's poor health. His work had, according to an affidavit, caused "an elevation of blood pressure and hypertension, headaches and a general intense fatigue." By the third week of June his physician hospitalized him for five days. Shands maintained that the state's other lawyers were inexperienced, that he wanted to be present for any deposition of Ellis, but that he was physically unable to carry out his duties. The defense claimed that its "motions are not made for delay but so that justice may be done."[28]

When he saw Shands, Mize concluded that "he ought to be in bed." Granting his indispensability, the judge postponed the hearing until August 10. A frustrated Motley told the court on July 10, "[A] case involving constitutional rights cannot be suspended because someone is ill," especially one "so simple that even a first-year law student could try it." On August 1, Mize finally ordered Ole Miss to make all undergraduate applications for the summer of 1961 available to the plaintiff in Jackson on August 7. He also denied a request to depose registrar Ellis.[29]

Ellis escaped a deposition, but he, alone among the defendants, had in July answered Meredith's complaint. He denied all: that Meredith's rights had been violated, that he represented a class of Negro citizens, that Ole Miss was restricted to whites, that Meredith was a legal resident when he applied, that he had been rejected because of his race, that he could not have obtained alumni recommendations from his county, that his objective was an education, that he had the "proper regard for truth and veracity," and that state law required separate institutions of higher education. Meredith's "reckless" charge that race had affected the treatment of his application was "uncalled for, unjustified, unwarranted, and constitute[d]" a "debasement of the University" and the defendants. It "shocked, surprised and disappointed" Ellis.[30]

Also in July, Meredith clarified his position. In an interview he distanced himself from the Freedom Riders and suggested more demonstrations were "senseless" and "doing more harm than good." His state's "special problems" had "to be worked out in special ways," but blacks could work "out their own problems." He declared, "The freedom riders have failed to adequately consider the needs, desires and capabilities of the local people of Mississippi."[31] By criticizing the civil rights movement, he also demonstrated that he was not a tool of the NAACP.

When, after an eight-weeks interruption, Judge Mize resumed the hearing in Jackson on August 10, he recognized Shands's poor health by permitting him to sit. Shands nonetheless grilled Meredith for eight hours on a multitude of topics; the morning session focused on his residence and income while the afternoon period examined his medical history. He worked to frustrate and confuse the witness. Finally, trying to clear up a question, Meredith declared, "I do not live in Attala County and drive here every day. I stay in Jackson and go to school here." Shands insulted him: "And you don't know what residence means?" Meredith explained that he resided in Jackson where he had his mailing address but his permanent home was Kosciusko.[32]

Switching to Meredith's civil rights activity, Shands said "Nigra." The official transcript actually reported that the word was Negro "(pronounced 'Nigra' by counsel asking question)."

Motley protested, " 'Nigra,' what is that; do you mean Negro?"

"I mean Negro [pronounced 'Nigra']," replied Shands.

"Well, I object to that, Your Honor," said Motley. "If the word is Negro I think it ought to be pronounced Negro."

"Well, pronounce it correctly, Mr. Shands, if that is what it is," directed Judge Mize. "Negro, she says, is proper pronunciation of the word, so pronounce it right."[33]

Shands shifted to Meredith's addresses when he married, got a driver's license, received a poll tax waiver, enrolled at Wayne State, and enlisted in the air force. To questioning about his registering to vote, Meredith finally said, "He [the registrar] told me I was qualified and I could register, and I took his word for it." When Shands asked exactly what he and the registrar had said, Meredith could not remember but insisted that he explained to the registrar where he lived, his military service, and his current address. "And he decided, determined," he explained, "that I was eligible to register. . . .

I assumed that he knew what the law was and if I was qualified to register he would let me register."[34]

Shands turned to Meredith's income from the GI Bill and his Attala County land, and he probed the NAACP's support. Meredith pointed out that the LDF, not the NAACP, helped with his case. When Motley objected that the lawsuit finances were irrelevant, Shands maintained that his questions involved Meredith's credibility. Mize overruled the objection. Shands asked why Meredith sought the LDF's help, and he replied, "Because I knew that they were an agency that was to help people in civil rights matters, where they were being denied their civil rights." Shands objected to Meredith's claim that his rights had been denied, but Mize permitted the answer. After lunch, Shands returned to Meredith's participation in civil rights groups at Jackson State, and Motley protested that he was engaged "in an endless effort to try to . . . trap the plaintiff into saying something that doesn't amount to a hill of beans, anyway." Judge Mize let Shands proceed. When the defense returned to Meredith's voter registration, Motley again complained. Shands moved on to ask who had helped him prepare civil rights pamphlets at Jackson State, but Meredith refused to name them. In what one observer called a "heated objection," Motley warned of retribution against black students if the court forced Meredith to name them. Mize agreed.[35]

Concentrating next on Meredith's application to Ole Miss, Shands claimed that he "sought to throw race into this lawsuit," especially when he contended in April 1961 that Ellis failed to act on his application only because of his race. "Now, how in the world did you assume all of that, James?" asked Shands. "Are you sensitive on the subject of race?" Shands's questions depended on information uncovered just the day before in Meredith's air force records in St. Louis.[36]

In reply to Shands's inquiry, Meredith replied, "Very much so."

"Oh, you are? How long have you been so sensitive on the subject of race?"

"All my recollecting life."

"All your life since childhood," Shands repeated, "isn't that right?" He continued, "You have had nervous trouble, haven't you[?]"[37]

Meredith said that "sometimes when these racial incidents would come up through the years when at the peak of them I would become a little tense in the stomach." He admitted that he was "interested in" and "very concerned" about race but denied ever losing his temper over it. Pressed, he acknowledged that his air force physical examination form showed that he had checked the box indicating "nervous trouble," yet on his Ole Miss application he had marked "no" beside "nervous trouble." He did the same for "depression or excessive worry." Shands pursued the contradictions. Meredith reported that the doctor who examined him prior to his discharge dismissed his worries and said that he had nothing that could be considered nervous trouble.[38]

Sensing a weakness, Shands alleged, "James, you have even been under psychiatric care, haven't you?" Meredith said that he had only been examined by a psychiatrist, who convinced him that he did not suffer from any nervous problem. After Meredith acknowledged that he had not seen the psychiatrist's report, Shands asked him to read it into the record: "This is a 26 year old Negro SSgt who complains of tension, nervousness, and occasional nervous stomach. Patient is extremely concerned with the 'racial problem' and his symptoms are intensified wherever there is a heightened tempo in the racial problems in the U.S. and Africa. Patient feels he has a strong need to fight and defy authority and this he does in usually a passive, procrastinating way. At times he starts a crusade to get existing rules and regulations changed. He loses his temper at times over minor incidents both at home and elsewhere. No evidence of a thinking disorder. Diagnosis: Passive Aggressive Reaction, chronic, moderate. Recommendations: No treatment recommended. Patient declined medication." When asked, Meredith could not recall the doctor's provisional diagnosis and asked Shands what the term meant. Shands again belittled him: "You don't know what a provisional diagnosis is? . . . You are ranked as a senior in college?" Still unclear, Meredith relayed that the doctor's provisional diagnosis was "obsessive compulsive neurosis." After getting the medical report into the record, Shands rehashed a hodgepodge of points before Judge Mize recessed the hearing until the next morning.[39]

The hearing reconvened in the courtroom dominated by a forty-by-twenty-foot mural on the front wall. Authorized by the Works Progress Administration in the 1930s, it depicted a plantation scene from the Old South society, built on white supremacy, black subservience, and racial segregation. Its only relevant feature was a judge—white, of course—holding a law book.[40] The painting vividly represented the society that Meredith sought to destroy, but the plaintiff did not object to it but focused on battling segregated higher education.

On the second day, the main witness was Robert Ellis.[41] To show that Meredith's application was handled differently from ones from whites, Motley had Ellis explain how his office dealt with applications. When he referred to Meredith's application as "incomplete," Motley interjected that all applications initially were "incomplete" because they awaited letters, transcripts, health records, and other documents, yet Ellis handled incomplete white applications differently. After fifteen minutes of wrangling over Shands's objection, Motley, frustrated by the defense's delaying tactics, protested the "long-winded objection in which he [Shands] repeats himself and repeats himself on the ground that it prejudices this plaintiff in this hearing because he is trying to get admitted to the next term." As the noon hour approached, Judge Mize announced a recess until the following Tuesday morning. Motley "offered strenuous objection" to yet another delay and wanted the record to show the plaintiff was "fighting and fighting and fighting to get the hearing through with." Mize, referring to "things beyond the control of this court," mentioned five voting rights suits and five Freedom Rider cases—none of which Motley could fault.[42]

Four days later, Ellis returned to answer Motley's questions. At every opportunity, Shands objected. When Meredith's counsel attempted to introduce his college transcripts, which Ellis had brought to court, Shands objected that they were hearsay and therefore lacked "certification or authentication." Mize agreed. When Motley tried to question Ellis about applicants who had been admitted and had attended classes before their transcripts had arrived, Shands objected because she did not distinguish among attendance, enrollment, and admission and had not limited the question to transfer students like the plaintiff. After Mize overruled the objection, Ellis replied, "We will permit a student to register pending the receipt of the transcripts" during the summer. When Motley extended the question to alumni recommendations, Shands protested. During the legal tussle, Ellis tried to answer, "I'm sure it is true that we do permit students to register pending the receipt . . . ," before another Shands objection cut him off. Motley then suggested, before Shands objected, that students with poor academic records had been admitted to the summer sessions.[43]

Following a brief recess, Motley asked, "Mr. Ellis, have any Negroes ever been admitted to the University of Mississippi, to your knowledge?" Shands "object[ed] to that unless this witness knows the lineage of every person who has attended" Ole Miss. Mize directed Ellis to answer the question and several succeeding similar ones. In effect, Ellis said he did not know whether a Negro had ever been admitted, that some had applied while he was registrar, and that some dark-skinned students had been on the campus, "but I can't tell you whether any of them were of the Negro race or not." Asked whether he would admit a qualified Negro who submitted a complete application and who met all the entrance requirements, Ellis claimed that he would.[44] Perhaps unwittingly, the defense had conceded the possibility that blacks had already attended Ole Miss.

After the plaintiff rested, Shands offered Meredith's air force records as evidence. Calling the file irrelevant and immaterial, Motley objected because the defense had obtained the record on August 9, ten weeks after the registrar had explained the rejection of Meredith's application in a letter dated May 25. Ignoring the chronology, Mize overruled her objection.[45]

The defense first called J. R. McLeod, the Hinds County deputy circuit clerk. He did not recognize Meredith, whom he registered as a voter six months earlier and could not remember anything Meredith said. Denying that Meredith told him he was not a resident of Hinds County, the clerk testified that if he "had told me that he was a permanent resident of Attala County he would not have registered." He declared that he had never completed a voter application form for anyone, but when Motley pressed, he admitted that one of his staff may have helped Meredith register.[46] His testimony did not clear up Meredith's voting status.

As its major witness, the defense recalled Robert Ellis. Prompted by Shands's friendly questions to "Bob," the registrar reported that neither set of Meredith's letters of recommendation met the requirement of character references from six alumni for a Mississippi resident nor did they recommend him for admission. According to Ellis, Meredith first admitted that he could not supply the required alumni letters but in an April letter claimed to "have attempted to comply with all the admission requirements." The statements were clearly "in conflict." Something else, however, disgusted the registrar: Meredith's allegation that race had caused his rejection. Ellis concluded that Meredith "was trying to get into the University because he was a Negro and not because he wanted an education" and predicted that as a student he would not follow university rules. Meredith's apparent willingness to lose both academic credits by transferring from Jackson State and his GI benefits also suggested his "very unreal approach."[47]

The next day, Shands announced, "I am exhausted to the point where I do not feel that I can properly proceed with the examination of Mr. Ellis." He would remain and participate as much as he could but Charles Clark would lead the defense effort. Motley had no objection, and Judge Mize approved the substitution.[48]

Born in Memphis in 1925, Charles Clark grew up in Cleveland in the Delta. He shared his name with an ancestor who had been wounded at Shiloh as a Confederate general, elected governor in 1863, imprisoned by Union forces in May 1865, and later appointed a university trustee. Clark's father had practiced law in Cleveland with Walter Sillers. After the death of Clark's father when the boy was only two years old, Sillers served as Clark's guardian. He attended several colleges but never received an undergraduate degree; after service in World War II, he graduated from the Ole Miss law school in 1948. Except for an interruption for the Korean War, he practiced law in Jackson throughout the 1950s. In the summer of 1961, Attorney General Patterson asked him to join his staff as a temporary special assistant to help Shands with civil rights cases. Shands, also a Cleveland native and a friend of Sillers, had known Clark's parents and the younger Clark as well, both in their hometown and in the capital. Clark's ties to Sillers may have provided the attorney general insulation from criticism by the powerful speaker of the Mississippi House of Representatives. Clark's first involvement in the case had come when he went to St. Louis to inspect Meredith's service file, fewer than ten days before he took over the defense.[49]

Clark began by having Ellis review Meredith's file. He testified that the application failed to meet the basic requirements, so Meredith received "no consideration on the merits of the application." Its major flaw was the absence of alumni recommendations. Ellis explained that his office sent each applicant a list of the alumni in the applicant's county and only asked the applicant to list six of them on the form—the admission's office would solicit the letters. His office sent Meredith the list for Hinds County, and Meredith never requested a list for Attala. Ellis admitted that he wondered if Meredith resided in Mississippi because the health form listed his wife's address as Gary, Indiana, and because his Washburn University transcript gave a Detroit home address. Ellis concluded, "I then and am now convinced that this man in terms of University regulations is a non-resident."[50]

In cross-examination, Motley established that Ellis learned that Meredith was a Negro from his application, the attached photograph, and Meredith's accompanying letter. Motley then asked Ellis why Ole Miss wanted to know an applicant's race, and he replied that "we feel we have a right to know as much about the student who wishes to enter the university as we can."

Motley queried, "Do you take race into consideration in passing upon the application?"

"No," Ellis replied.

"What is the point to it then?"

"As a matter of information."

"For what?" persisted Motley. "What purpose is this information?"

After Judge Mize overruled an objection, Ellis struggled to explain that Ole Miss wanted it "for statistical purposes, for counseling purposes, and any number of reasons."

"What statistics do you have on race?" asked Motley.

Ellis answered, "Offhand, I don't know of any."

"How does race affect your counseling service?" she continued.

"You'll have to ask the counseling service. I don't know."[51]

After asking if Ellis knew of any Ole Miss alumni who were Negro (Ellis claimed not to be in a position to know), Motley tried to establish whether "as a matter of policy, custom, and usage" segregation prevailed in the state's educational systems. To each query, Judge Mize sustained Clark's objection because they were all "foreign to the issues" in the case.[52] Despite the objections, Motley had raised such topics for the record.

Finishing her cross-examination, Motley posed two vital questions. She asked about Ellis's decision to wait until May 25 to respond to Meredith's February 20 concern about whether his application was complete. Ellis suggested the voluminous correspondence prevented his replying every time, but Motley pointed out that by February 20 he had received only a couple of communications from Meredith. Ellis then blamed "a tremendously heavy work load," "peculiar problems that I have to answer individually," and Meredith's application that "became a problem" when he announced he would not be able to supply alumni letters and would "substitute his own procedure." In the end Ellis only said that he "simply did not have the time to give attention to it that it deserved."[53]

Motley also questioned the claim that Ole Miss "cannot recognize the transfer of credits" from Jackson State because it did not belong to the Southern Association of Colleges and Schools (SACS). When she said the board adopted the policy on February 7, 1961, after Meredith's application, Ellis explained that in fact the Committee of Admissions adopted it on May 15, 1961, just days before he informed Meredith of his rejection. He insisted that the committee did not consider Meredith's application when it made the change; he asserted, "I know for a fact that there were not more than two men on this eight-person committee who had any awareness of the application of the plaintiff."[54] He did not explain their ignorance.

Ellis also testified that, of all the colleges that Meredith had attended, only Jackson State lacked accreditation. Unlike Ole Miss, it was not a member of SACS. Though SACS had for many years barred Negro institutions, in 1956 it had started a separate "approved" list of black institutions that included Jackson State. The next year SACS accepted eighteen black schools, but Jackson State was not among them. Acknowledging Jackson State's status, Motley presented a copy of "Accredited Higher Institutions, 1960," published by the U.S. Office of Education, that listed Jackson State as an accredited institution. Over repeated objections, she had Ellis read that the Mississippi College Accrediting Commission had also accredited Jackson State. Ellis admitted the accuracy of the information but could not tell the court much about the commission.[55]

After Ellis's testimony, the defense rested and the plaintiff offered no rebuttal. In her final argument, Motley contended that Meredith met the legitimate entrance requirements and had been denied admission solely because the university operated as a segregated institution for whites only. In the state's final presentation, Clark said Meredith did not meet the university's standard of "good moral character" because he was "not able to understand the meaning of what it is to be under oath and to tell the truth." Clark emphasized, "The registrar did not take his race into consideration at all with regard to his application," and he denied any "intentional or purposeful discrimination on account of his race or color."[56]

Though he held open the possibility of a ruling before the fall semester opened, Mize realized that an appeal might delay Meredith's enrollment until second semester. The court adjourned. Each side could only wait, and the wait was long. Ole Miss's September enrollment deadline passed. Thanksgiving came and went. Mize finally ruled on December 12, 1961.[57]

In his ruling, Judge Mize denied Meredith's request for a preliminary injunction. He rejected the defense argument that Meredith was not a Mississippi citizen, but in every other way he accepted the defense arguments. He declared that Ole Miss had not discriminated when it stopped admitting students after January 25 and that the admissions committee's action "was not taken in any attempt direct or indirect to discriminate against anyone solely on the ground of race or color." Mize found "conclusively that he [Ellis] gave no consideration whatsoever to the race or color of the plaintiff" and that the plaintiff "utterly failed" to prove otherwise. He scheduled the final hearing for January 16, 1962, but the plaintiff would not wait. Jess Brown immediately filed an appeal with the U.S. Fifth Circuit Court of Appeals.[58]

Chief Judge Elbert P. Tuttle granted an appeal and set January 9 for a hearing in New Orleans. Judges Richard T. Rives and John Minor Wisdom joined Tuttle. After they reviewed the record, they heard the attorneys repeat their arguments, with a few modifications. Motley emphasized that state law made conspiring to overthrow segregation a crime, and Meredith's application was an attempt to overthrow segregation. She also mentioned that Jackson State College recently gained membership in SACS. "The conclusion is inescapable," Motley argued, "that the reason that this man is not in the University of Mississippi is that he is a Negro."[59]

Clark denied that Ole Miss rejected Meredith because of his race. When Judge Tuttle asked, "Don't you think we should take judicial notice of what everyone else knows, that the alumni regulation is an effort to prevent Negroes from entering?" the defense disagreed. Shands argued that the plaintiff failed to prove any racial discrimination and had not shown that the required alumni references placed an "undue burden" on Meredith or that "white students are treated any differently." In fact, the plaintiff had failed to prove "that there has never been a Negro graduate of the University of Mississippi." Furthermore, no state law required racial segregation at the university, and the denial of admission to a black person did not prove discrimination. "Going to college," according to Shands, "is not guaranteed by the Constitution."[60]

During the arguments, the judges wondered about the propriety of reversing Mize's decision before he had a chance to hear the case on its merits in a few days, and Wisdom suggested that the appeals court simply did "not have sufficient evidence to make a decision." Motley, however, told the judges, "We have presented all the evidence we have" and more delays would give the defense "a tailor-made reason for not admitting him, and that is that he will graduate from Jackson State." Two days later, on January 12, the appellate court denied the request for an injunction and recognized that "James H. Meredith is a Mississippi Negro in search of an education." Written by Judge Wisdom, the decision complained, "This case was tried below and argued here in the eerie atmosphere of never-never land." An incredulous court observed, "Counsel for appellees [the defendants] argued that there is no state policy of maintaining segregated institutions of higher learning and that the court can take no judicial notice of this plain fact known to everyone." Clark's suggestion that the plaintiff "should have examined the genealogical records of all the students and alumni . . . to prove the University's alleged policy of restricting admissions to white students" appalled the judges who found that the state "maintains a policy of segregation in its schools and colleges." The policy, however, provided insufficient cause to rule in favor of the plaintiff because Meredith still had to prove "that the policy was applied to him to produce discrimination on the ground of race."[61]

The ruling also declared that the alumni recommendations denied blacks equal protection of the laws, and it highlighted the adoption of the requirement immediately after *Brown*. Wisdom noted that Ole Miss lacked black alumni, few "if any" white alumni would support a black applicant because of "traditional social barriers," and a cooperative white would have to worry about "the possibility of reprisals." The court said that, to the extent that Ole Miss had denied admission due to a lack of recommendations, Meredith had been "discriminated against in violation of the equal protection clause of the Fourteenth Amendment and was unlawfully denied admission to the University." Finding alumni references unconstitutional did not, however, solve the case.[62]

Relying on a "muddy" hearing record, the judges concluded that "it is impossible to determine whether there were valid, non-discriminatory grounds for the University's refusing Meredith's admission." Instead it ordered Judge Mize to proceed with the full hearing of the case and chastised him for "a welter of irrelevancies and, at the same time, a conspicuous omission of evidence that should be helpful to a proper determination of the case." The appeals court blamed the inadequate trial record on Mize's giving the defense too "much latitude" while "severely circumscrib[ing]" the plaintiff. It also found "erroneous" Mize's restricting evidence on admissions to the 1961 summer session because Meredith sought to enroll in any session and because the general "policy and practice of the University in admissions were at issue." Last, the court found unclear which transfer credits Ole Miss would accept and whether the accreditation of Jackson State would affect the case. Only a "full trial on the merits" could resolve the issues, and Meredith "should be afforded a fair, unfettered, and unharassed opportunity to prove his case." Wisdom declared, "A man should be able to find an education by taking the broad highway. . . . He should not have to take by-roads through the woods and follow winding trails through sharp thickets, in constant tension because of pitfalls and traps, and, after years of effort, perhaps attain the threshold of his goal when he is past caring about it." Mindful of the start of the semester on February 6, the court requested a prompt hearing and ruling by Mize.[63]

Judge Mize convened a hearing on January 16 in Jackson. The parties replayed the earlier proceedings, with the defense angling for delays and for restrictions on the retrieval of university documents. On the second day, the defense asked for a postponement because Shands had been hospitalized. The other defense counsel, especially Clark, claimed they were unprepared to proceed. Resisting further delay, Motley declared, "Mr. Clark was hired for the purpose of taking over and now he suggests he didn't take over. . . . It can't be both, that Mr. Shands did all the work and at the same time he was so ill that he had to hire somebody else." Mize postponed the hearing one week.[64]

Blocked by the delays and Mize's "inability" to conclude the hearing before the spring semester, Motley asked for a rehearing before the Court of Appeals and for a preliminary injunction allowing Meredith's admission, both pending the trial in Mize's court. Ed Cates, an assistant attorney general, rejected claims the state had used delays to defeat desegregation and alleged instead that Meredith's lawyers had "toyed with the Court" by seeking and then withdrawing requests for various subpoenas. A rehearing, Cates said, "would be injurious and harassing" and would cause "turmoil and confusion" between the courts. The appeals court refused a rehearing.[65]

When Mize resumed the hearing a week later, Clark again tried to derail it by claiming that the U.S. Code required that a three-judge panel hear it, but the judge rejected his claim. The plaintiff then called four Ole Miss administrators to testify about admissions. Motley asked dean of women Katherine Rea if she had ever seen a Negro student at Ole Miss, and Rea said that she had not. Clark asked her, "When does a person that you see become a Negro in your eyes?" Motley, according to one newspaper, "jumped to her feet" to object to Clark's pronunciation of "Negro."

"I think Mr. Clark ought to be able to pronounce the word 'Negro,' " Motley insisted. "It is not Negro (pronounced N-i-g-r-a); it is Negro (pronounced N-e-g-r-o), and I think you know enough to pronounce the word Negro correctly." (The *Jackson Clarion-Ledger* reported that he said the even more offensive "Niguh.")

Clark replied, "I intend no discrimination or to impugn anything at all by the pronunciation I used, and it is the pronunciation that I am used to and have heard all of my life, and I object to counsel's remark, and I will not confine my pronunciation to what she prefers unless this Court so orders me."

"Well, I understood you to say Negro," observed Judge Mize. "You might not have pronounced it as emphatically as she does, but I will let you proceed. Certainly I want you to be courteous and I know you mean no insinuation to the Negro."[66]

Motley proceeded to ask Rea, Love, Farley, and Bryant whether a Negro had ever been a student at Ole Miss. When Love said that he did not know, Motley insisted, "You don't know whether you have seen any Negroes? You know what Negroes are, don't you?" Love explained that he could not always determine race by observation and that he did not know each student's genealogy. Bryant did not know whether any blacks had attended and had "entertained the possibility some students were enrolled who were Negroes."[67] Motley did not ask why whites objected if they could not always even identify blacks. The possible absurdity of racial segregation, after all, was not at issue.

On the fourth day, Ellis, whom Judge Mize had referred to as "the main defendant," took the stand. After a procedural tussle over evidence, Motley questioned Ellis about his reasons for rejecting Meredith. He maintained that Meredith was not a Mississippi resident and that Jackson State's recent accreditation had no effect on the case. He told Motley that Meredith wanted "to make trouble for the university." Asked to elaborate, Ellis asserted that Meredith "was trying to be admitted to the University because he was a Negro." He further alleged that Meredith had "psychological problems in connection with his race" and had "a mission in life to correct all the ills of the world." The registrar had concluded that Meredith was "a trouble maker and . . . would be a very bad influence at my institution." He said that he had rejected whites for psychological causes, but could offer no examples. Ellis also testified that, when he realized Meredith's application might result in a lawsuit, he had talked about the application with Clegg and with Shands, discussed Meredith's transcript with Dean Love, but otherwise talked with nobody about it and had received no instructions about how to handle a Negro applicant.[68]

Other higher education officials told of the lack of policies and the absence of discussion about black applicants. In a deviation, trustee Dr. Verner Holmes, a Coleman appointee, responded to a question about whether

Negroes had ever enrolled by answering simply, "I do not [know]." Several trustees maintained that before Meredith's lawsuit they had never discussed racial factors in admissions, and the board secretary agreed. J. D. Williams claimed that he had never discussed the admission of blacks with the board and never received any instructions regarding Negroes. Maintaining he had never seen Meredith's application, he said he discussed it only with Love, whom he instructed to handle it in the ordinary way because they had "no authority to deny [admission] on race or color." After presenting more than twenty witnesses, the plaintiff rested.[69]

The defense then called Ellis as its only witness, but it shifted its strategy. The university, according to Ellis, still had to determine an applicant's moral character, and the attorney general supplied new documents that Ellis added to Meredith's file. Motley objected to the registrar's reopening Meredith's file, but Judge Mize overruled her complaint. The defense then introduced signed affidavits that the attorney general's office secured two weeks earlier, on January 15, from four of Meredith's five original references (the fifth, Meredith's cousin, reportedly agreed with the affidavit but refused to sign it). Repudiating the earlier letters, each one said he could not vouch for Meredith's character because he had not known Meredith since 1949, denied understanding his earlier statement's connection to a university application, and declared he had not been paid or forced to make the new statements. The affidavits implied that Meredith acted fraudulently in obtaining them in the first place and that he tried to deceive the university about his relationship with his references. Ellis concluded that "this fellow is a trouble maker" of low moral character and that Ole Miss's high moral standard caused him to reject Meredith.[70]

In a special Saturday session, Motley reiterated that Meredith had been denied admission solely because he was black. The defense claims about her client's psychological state derived solely from his air force records that the university did not even see until months *after* Meredith had been rejected. She acknowledged that merely applying to Ole Miss was "against the policy of segregation" and made one a troublemaker in the eyes of segregationists. Finally, she stressed that a decision should be reached before the spring semester started or Meredith might graduate from Jackson State. For the defense, Clark denied that Meredith had been barred because he was a Negro and charged that the plaintiff had failed to prove otherwise. Edward Cates emphasized that Meredith lacked good moral character and repeated that he was simply a troublemaker. Judge Mize closed the hearing and took the case under advisement.[71]

One week later in an eleven-page ruling, Judge Mize declared, "The only question now posed for decision is whether or not the Plaintiff was denied admission to the University of Mississippi solely because of his race or color." He decided that "the evidence shows rather conclusively that he was not denied admission because of his race." The university did not, according to Mize, have a "custom or policy" that "excluded Negroes from entering the University" and is "not a racially segregated institution." He found no evidence that anyone "has been rejected because of his race or color." Two days before the start of the spring semester, Mize, therefore, reaffirmed his earlier ruling and dismissed Meredith's complaint.[72]

14. *Meredith v. Fair* II: A "Legal Jungle"

■ ■

O
n February 5, 1962, two days after Judge Sidney Mize ruled that Ole Miss had not rejected James Meredith because of his race, and pending an appeal, Constance Motley asked the U.S. Fifth Circuit Court of Appeals to prohibit the university from blocking her client's admission. Time was crucial: the spring semester began on February 6. The appeal warned that continued denial of admission could make the case moot because if Meredith returned to Jackson State College he could graduate in June. Asst. Atty. General Edward Cates repeated the denials of discrimination and warned of an injunction's irreparable damage to Meredith and the university. Cates also argued that Meredith "cannot take both sides of the *time* factor"—both invoke Jackson State's accreditation in December 1961 to justify his transfer and also deny the state's ability to use his army records and other later evidence that "discredited" his moral character. The three-judge appellate panel agreed to hear Meredith's petition for an injunction in an unusual session the following Saturday.[1]

In the New Orleans federal courthouse, Judges Richard Rives, Elbert Tuttle, and John Minor Wisdom convened on February 10 to hear the request in *Meredith v. Fair*. The plaintiff had drawn the most receptive Fifth Circuit panel possible. President Truman had named Rives to the federal bench in 1951. An Alabamian and a former president of the state bar association, Rives spoke "with the accent but not the language of segregation" and earned a reputation as a "trailblazer" among southern judges on civil rights. He, for example, wrote the 1956 district court opinion in favor of the Montgomery bus boycott. Elbert Tuttle was born in California, grew up in Hawaii, and received his education at Cornell University, but he practiced law in Atlanta starting in the 1920s. As a Republican he campaigned for Eisenhower in 1952, but he also served as a trustee for two black colleges. Eisenhower appointed Tuttle to the bench in 1954. Before joining the court he worked in the Republican Party with John Minor Wisdom, a native of New Orleans. While practicing corporate law in New Orleans, Wisdom worked for job opportunities for blacks as a member of the Urban League and on the president's Committee on Government Contracts. Despite Wisdom's liberal leanings, Eisenhower nominated him in 1957. Wisdom gained a reputation as the court's leading legal scholar.[2]

In three hours of argument, the lawyers reprised their earlier clashes. Motley made her basic argument: "Race was the factor why he was denied admission." She dismissed all of the other explanations as irrelevant. She also contended that Meredith's references had withdrawn their endorsements of his character "out of fear" when confronted by the attorney general's men. Countering the charge that Meredith sought only to cause a controversy, she conceded, "Of course, he's a troublemaker because he is trying to change a policy which prohibits him from getting a first-class education," but he was a troublemaker "in the good sense" because "he is against the whole system" of segregation. Motley reminded the judges that "unless this relief is granted, this appeal will be moot" because Meredith would graduate from Jackson State and suffer "irreparable harm."[3]

Edward Cates, a 1952 graduate of the Ole Miss law school who had clerked for Judge Benjamin F. Cameron, repeated most of the defense argument and denied that the state had coerced Meredith's references to withdraw their recommendations. Charles Clark denied the need for immediate action and even suggested that the plaintiff should drop out of college until the court could decide his appeal on its merits. At the hearing, Attorney General Patterson participated directly for the first time when, in summing up the defense's case, he argued that Ole Miss had acted in good faith in rejecting Meredith's application and maintained that Meredith was not qualified for admission. The attorney general called on the appeals court to uphold Judge Mize's decision. When Patterson completed his summation, Judge Tuttle announced that "a decision will be made promptly," and the hearing adjourned.[4]

Within forty-eight hours, the judges voted two-to-one to reject Meredith's request. In reaching their decision, Rives and Wisdom worried that the court could cause greater harm if it issued an injunction for Meredith and later, after a full hearing on the appeal, upheld the lower court decision against the plaintiff; it would, in effect, order Meredith's admission under an injunction only to bar him later in its ultimate decision. In balancing the "hardship" to Meredith against the "possible irreparable damages" to all, Rives and Wisdom decided that the burden placed on Meredith did not outweigh the court's need to "study the full record and testimony on the hearing before the district court" before taking any action. Though the court denied the injunction, it called for an expedited appeal so it could decide the case on its merits before the start of the next fall semester. In a footnote, the majority also suggested that Meredith could avoid making his case moot by selecting "subjects of study other than those leading to his graduation."[5]

Judge Tuttle dissented. Recalling that court's own decision only three months earlier by his friend Judge Wisdom, he pointed out the court had recognized a "policy of segregation," ruled unconstitutional the alumni references, and now acknowledged Jackson State's accreditation. Predicting that the court would overturn Mize's ruling, Tuttle wanted to grant the injunction: "I do not think this Court ought to concern itself with any possible damage to the appellant by granting his motion for injunction." His dissent concluded, "He does not need for us to help him decide whether he really wants what he is here fighting so hard to get."[6]

Mississippi papers withheld comment and waited for the resolution of the pending appeal, but state leaders expressed satisfaction. "The court acted wisely," Gov. Ross Barnett told newsmen. With a big grin he said, "I am delighted over the decision of the court." Attorney General Patterson believed it was "in keeping with laws and precedent." A disappointed Meredith remained calm, but he said he did not know what he would do about continuing his lawsuit or his college education. "I'm going to rest a few weeks and then think about it," he told reporters. In New York, Motley declared that the appeal of the original decision would continue, and she expected to return to New Orleans in a few weeks to argue its merits.[7]

Meredith's equivocation reflected no flagging of his commitment but derived from his impatience with finishing his education and his wish to get on with his life. He had been making alternative plans. In addition to applying for a Woodrow Wilson Fellowship for graduate school, he had applied to the Howard University law school and for graduate study in political science at Atlanta University. The latter said he could exercise the acceptance whenever he wanted. "Without this assurance," Meredith later wrote, "I would probably have chosen to get my degree from Jackson State College [in June 1962] and go on to graduate study." Instead in late February he announced that he would return to Jackson State, register for enough credits to receive his GI benefits, but fall short of the graduation. He still hoped to enroll at Ole Miss in the summer.[8]

The Court of Appeals set April 18 to hear Meredith's appeal and, after a short delay, convened on April 20. Judge Wisdom was joined by Judge John R. Brown and Judge Dozier A. DeVane. Born in Nebraska and a graduate of its state university, Brown studied law at the University of Michigan and then joined a major firm in Houston. In 1955 Eisenhower appointed him to the appeals court, where he became known as an activist and a supporter of civil liberties. Judge DeVane balanced Brown's presence on the panel. DeVane, a Floridian, worked for several utility companies and as solicitor for the Federal Power Commission before President Roosevelt named him a federal district court judge in 1943. According to one scholar, DeVane, nearly eighty in the summer of 1962, was "a staunch believer in states' rights" and often "demonstrated his preference for segregation."[9]

With Judge Brown presiding in the New Orleans federal courthouse, Motley and Cates took two and a half hours to repeat their arguments. Motley called Mize's decision "clearly erroneous" and charged that the registrar's reasons for rejecting her client had no merit. She said that Ole Miss and state officials were "frantically searching for a legitimate nonracial reason" to reject Meredith, but they could not find one. For the state Cates claimed that Ole Miss would admit "qualified Negroes" but that Meredith was "not qualified" and "does not have good moral character" as required. Cates mentioned that Meredith had lied on his application for a poll tax exemption, misled his references about his application, and was simply not a "good faith applicant." Although officials had learned many of the details after Meredith's rejection, Cates contended that the registrar had rightly "suspected" the truth about Meredith. At the end of the hearing, the court took the case under advisement.[10]

While everyone waited for a decision, officials in Jackson intervened. Ten days after the New Orleans hearing, a bill introduced by Representative Leon Hannaford from Tate County, just northwest of Oxford, proposed that an adult had to live in the state for twelve months to qualify as a state resident; even a landowner and a qualified voter would "still be considered as being a non-resident if he has entered the state for the purpose of enrolling in an educational institution." Arguing against the bill, Joseph Wroten of Greenville declared, "If a young person interested in Mississippi cannot satisfy residency requirements by registering to vote, it has come to a sorry state." After the house approved the bill by a vote of 103–5, a motion to reconsider prevented its passage, but the legislators had made their feelings clear.[11]

Hinds County authorities also acted. The circumstances of Meredith's voter registration had first become public nearly a year earlier, and rumors circulated that the state would press charges to try to bar him from Ole Miss. On May 28, county attorney Paul G. Alexander charged that on February 2, 1960 (actually 1961), Meredith falsely registered to vote in Hinds County while a resident of Attala County. Justice of the Peace Homer Edgeworth immediately issued a bench warrant for Meredith's arrest. At dawn nine days later, a Hinds County deputy sheriff woke Meredith, gave him time to dress and call Medgar Evers, and took him to the county jail. After questioning, Meredith stayed in a large cell with many other blacks until Evers and Jack Young, a black Jackson lawyer, posted a $500 bond at about five o'clock that evening.[12]

Protesting Meredith's arrest, Evers and Aaron Henry denounced "Mississippi's method of attempting to maintain segregation by jailing those Negroes who try to enter the best institutions of higher learning." The arrest recalled the case of Clennon King in 1958 and the arrest, prosecution, and conviction of Clyde Kennard after he sought to enter Mississippi Southern College in 1959.

Evers and Henry declared, "Despite such Nazi-like harassment, Mississippi's institutions of higher learning must be opened to all persons without regard to race, creed or color."[13]

Charged under an eighty-two-year-old law against swearing falsely when registering to vote, Meredith faced a year in jail and a fine of $100. His conviction would physically prevent Meredith from enrolling, and it would justify the rejection of his application by corroborating his lack of good moral character. When Motley learned of his arrest, she promptly applied to Judge Wisdom for an order to prevent the state from continuing its case against her client. On the day before the trial in Meredith's voter registration case set for June 13, Wisdom called the charge a "punitive action" and enjoined local officials from proceeding until the federal court completed reviewing the case seeking admission to the university.[14]

Finally, on June 25, 1962, two months after the appellate court heard arguments in the case, four and half months after Judge Mize's decision, and thirteen months after Meredith filed his lawsuit, the case concluded. In what two scholars have called a "masterpiece of acid rhetoric," Judge Wisdom spoke for himself and Judge Brown in favor of Meredith. At the outset the opinion simply called Meredith "a Mississippi Negro in search of an education," but its eighteen pages thoroughly refuted the state's deficient defense and harshly rebuked Judge Mize. Meredith's willingness to lose academic credits and GI benefits by transferring demonstrated for Wisdom "his perseverance and fit in with the character of a man who is having a hard time getting a college education but is willing to pay the price exacted of a Negro for admission to the University of Mississippi." In Meredith's correspondence, Wisdom detected no "defiance," "no chip on the shoulder and no evidence of such abnormal concern" about his race characteristic of a troublemaker. His letters sometimes had what Wisdom deemed the "laconic style, barren of comment," of "a man of perseverance, but a man of patience and politeness."[15]

Meredith needed patience because, as the court bluntly declared, "from the moment the defendants discovered Meredith was a Negro they engaged in a carefully calculated campaign of delay, harassment, and masterly inactivity. It was a defense designed to discourage and to defeat by tactics which would have been a credit to Quintus Fabius Maximus" (the Roman general who successfully used cautious, evasive, delaying tactics against Hannibal's invading army). Without questioning Shands's health, the court contended "there are plenty of lawyers in Mississippi ready, able, and more than willing to represent the University," so the defense did not have to rely on him alone. The continuances "were part of the defendants' delaying action. . . . It almost worked." Wisdom blamed Mize for granting the "continuances of doubtful propriety" and unreasonable length and criticized his waiting from August 1961 until December to announce his order when "time is of the essence." Judge Wisdom also sternly criticized Mize's rulings that repeatedly restricted the black plaintiff and aided the defense. Wisdom called them "manifestly erroneous" and "a clear abuse of judicial discretion." Mize's damnable actions, the state's offensive strategy, and the lower court's mistakes were, however, insufficient to overturn Mize's decision.[16]

The claim that Mississippi had no policy of segregation in higher education struck Wisdom as preposterous, and he thought it would "startle some people in Mississippi." Earlier the appeals court had recognized that "Mississippi maintains a policy of segregation in its schools and colleges," and the court could "find nothing in this case reaching the dignity of proof to make us think we were wrong." It cited state laws on racial segregation and mentioned the widely known rule that would not allow athletic teams from the white institutions to compete against teams that had black players. Regarding alumni references, Wisdom declared that creation of the rule six months after the *Brown* decision demonstrated that it "unquestionably was part of conscious University and State policy" to "evade desegregation." After courts denied similar requirements in Louisiana and Georgia, Ole Miss's continued use provided "demonstrable evidence of a State and University policy of segregation that was applied to Meredith." In particular the court noted that the university did not give Meredith the same latitude as it did white applicants to use letters that did not mention moral character.[17]

Considering the IHL board's new policy on transfer students from unaccredited colleges, Wisdom noted that the board could prevent black transfers by operating inferior black colleges "inherently incapable of ever being approved" but pointed out that Jackson State College had made the justification irrelevant when it gained accreditation late in 1961. "The reason was never valid," the decision declared, "and again demonstrates a conscious pattern of unlawful discrimination." Wisdom further held that "the transfer policy was both discriminatorily applied and irrationally construed [by the university] in order to bar Meredith's admission."[18]

Finally, Judge Wisdom considered "the ex post facto rationalization for the turndown." The university's later explanations struck Wisdom as only fair because Meredith wanted to take advantage of subsequent changes, such as Jackson State's accreditation, but he concluded the "contention is frivolous" that Meredith swore falsely when he registered to vote and that "the facts . . . show a determined policy of discrimination by harassment." Dismissing also the charge that Meredith was a troublemaker, he sympathized, "It is certainly understandable that a sensitive Negro, especially one overseas, might have a nervous stomach over the racial problem." Instead of faulting Meredith, Wisdom declared his military records suggested that he was "just about the type of Negro who might be expected to try to crack the racial barrier at the University of Mississippi: a man with a mission and a nervous stomach." As for allegations about Meredith's moral character, Wisdom alleged the state was "scraping the bottom of the barrel" with trivial charges.[19]

After a thorough review, Wisdom found that Meredith's "application for transfer to the University of Mississippi was turned down solely because he was a Negro. We see no valid, non-discriminatory reason for the University's not accepting Meredith. Instead we see a well-defined pattern of delays and frustrations, part of a Fabian policy of worrying the enemy into defeat while time worked for the defenders." He intended that the court's decision would "pierce the veil of innocuity" surrounding the state's segregation policy, but he recognized, as he said, "There are none so blind as those that will not see." The court reversed Judge Mize's ruling and directed him to issue the injunction requested by the plaintiff. Ole Miss would have to admit its first black student.[20]

The decision came on Meredith's twenty-ninth birthday. Pleased and relieved, he said, "I always expected delays would be the state's greatest tactic, but I had hoped the delay wouldn't be so long." Being the first black at Ole Miss "really doesn't appeal to me," he said. "What I'm interested in is getting a good education and seeing that my people have an opportunity to get a good education. The question of integration or segregation hasn't been a motivating factor." Noting that other southern universities had admitted blacks "without any problem," he said, "I don't think Mississippi will be any different."[21]

White Mississippians had mixed reactions. Front-page stories in the state's major papers reminded readers it was the first federal desegregation order aimed at their state. Attorney General Patterson promised to "press every appeal possible in this case" and to "exhaust every legal means and resources at our command." Options included a reconsideration by the appeals court and an appeal to the U.S. Supreme Court. Other state officials, including Ole Miss spokesmen, had no reaction. In the days after the decision, the state's editors also withheld comment, perhaps because they knew of nothing to suggest.[22]

Unwilling to wait any longer, Meredith announced that he hoped to enter the second summer session that began on July 13. The appeals court, however, would not issue a mandate to carry out its decision until twenty-one days had passed, during which the defendants could ask for a rehearing or request a stay of the decision until they appealed to the Supreme Court. To expedite the process, Meredith's attorneys two days after the ruling asked the appellate court to issue an immediate mandate for his admission, but on July 9 the court refused. Meredith had to wait for the mandate expected on July 17. Summer school registration ended the following day, so Meredith still had a chance to enroll that summer.[23]

In the meantime, on July 10, Judge DeVane's dissent became public. Judge Brown had hoped for a unanimous decision to "arm Meredith . . . with undeniable evidence that he has the law and right on his side," but DeVane accepted Judge Mize's conclusion that Meredith was a troublemaker. Because Mize had "observed the appellant throughout the trial" while the appellate court had worked only with the "cold, printed record of the facts," DeVane deferred to the district court judge. In considering integration's effects on the university, the judge, in effect, considered Meredith a troublemaker because his actions might make trouble, might provoke a public disturbance. He wanted to avoid another Little Rock crisis, and he "fear[ed] the result of this decision may lead to another comparable situation." Despairing of judicial power, he believed, "Integration is not a question that can ever be settled by Federal Judges. It is an economic, social and religious question." He concluded that if Meredith were admitted to the university, the result would be "nothing short of a catastrophe."[24]

One week later, the state attorney general had not decided whether to ask the court of appeals for a rehearing or to go directly to the Supreme Court. As everyone waited, the situation grew more complicated when Alfanette Marie Bracey, a twenty-one-year-old Jackson State student, announced that she submitted her application to Ole Miss on July 7 but ten days later had not received a reply. Interested in physical education and health, the majorette wanted to take dance and swimming classes not offered at Jackson State. A minister's daughter, she had not included any references with her application and had not told the university that she was black.[25]

The day after Bracey's application became public, the defendants had not acted, so *Meredith v. Fair* proceeded on schedule when the Fifth Circuit sent its mandate to Judge Mize. Before he could order the university to admit Meredith, however, the defense made a surprise move: lawyers went to Meridian to ask another member of the Court of Appeals for the Fifth Circuit Court to issue a stay in the implementation of the court order.[26] Entering into the case for the first time, Judge Benjamin Franklin Cameron played an unexpected, bizarre, and unprecedented role in Meredith's lawsuit.

Cameron graduated from the University of the South and the Cumberland School of Law in Tennessee before starting his law practice in his hometown of Meridian in 1914. For forty years he developed a law practice representing Mississippi corporations. Personally puritanical, he became a Republican in 1928 and endorsed Republican Herbert Hoover when Democrat Al Smith opposed Prohibition. After his election, Hoover rewarded Cameron by appointing him U.S. attorney for the Southern District of Mississippi. Later, Hoover wanted to name Cameron to the federal bench but encountered opposition from a Mississippi senator. In 1955 Cameron, one of the state's few Republicans, came to the attention of the Eisenhower administration, and Senator James Eastland also endorsed him. John Minor Wisdom, then a lawyer in New Orleans, recommended him, the American Bar Association approved his nomination, and the NAACP endorsed him. In the spring of 1955, Cameron joined the Fifth Circuit.[27]

One study of the Court of Appeals for the Fifth Circuit has described Judge Cameron as "a well-read man, a careful researcher whose opinions were second only to Judge Wisdom's in terms of scholarly discussion." His opinions earned Cameron a reputation as a "maverick conservative," and his lengthy dissents sometimes criticized his fellow judges directly and often irritated them, particularly his more liberal colleagues. A distinctive legal perspective and a rather aloof personality removed him from judicial collegiality. In addition, declining health further isolated him. More than anything, however, his defense of a rapidly vanishing way of life set him apart.[28]

An unwavering segregationist, Cameron never accepted the *Brown* decision, but his judicial opinions lacked incendiary pronouncements and probably affected his colleagues more than they inspired segregationists. Cameron based his opinions on his views of the law and the Constitution, southern and American history, and the nature of racial differences. For him the Tenth Amendment fundamentally reserved powers to the states. He once called it "the axis upon which our entire constitutional system revolves; the heart which gives sustenance and vitality to the whole organism; the balance wheel whose steady functioning insures the smooth working of the entire mechanism." Critical of the "dangerous tendency to exalt the federal judiciary and debase the states," Cameron believed that the federal courts should whenever possible defer to the states and that district courts should take precedence in cases that warranted federal action. He trusted the wisdom and good faith of local authorities more than the courts. To do otherwise would make people resent federal action because "government from too far off is tyranny."[29]

Adopting Claude Bowers's interpretation of Reconstruction—one favorable to the unreconstructed South and hostile to the freedman—Cameron thought that the Emancipation Proclamation had freed the uneducated and "bewildered Negro" who was then exploited by "selfish politicians and conscienceless adventurers" during a time of "sadness and shame." For more than eighty years after Reconstruction, southern whites and blacks experienced "a continuing growth in mutual understanding, respect and brotherhood." The peaceful progress came under assault, Cameron believed, from judicial changes under the New Deal, from the centralization of power during the Depression and war, and from Negro bloc voting that influenced elections and national policy. As a result the federal government's attempts to change southern race relations from the outside destroyed goodwill, harmony, and peace between southern whites and blacks.[30]

Any effort to improve race relations would encounter "essential differences between the two races," and the seventy-year-old judge in 1961 identified disparities "in ambition, in tastes, in aptitudes, in standards of behavior, and in culture." The racial differences caused him to oppose integration, yet he remained pleased with the "excellent state of race relations in the South." Problems common to blacks and whites, he believed, "can best be worked out if they are left alone" to develop the "tolerance and understanding so necessary to the continued advancement of the interests of both races." Too often, he charged, "judicial fiats" provoked controversy and conflict when he preferred "statesmanship" through long-term constructive cooperation and conciliation.[31]

Judge Cameron was probably the federal judge most receptive to Mississippi's plight in the Meredith case. The day after the court of appeals' directive to Mize, the state's lawyers asked him to issue a stay that would prevent any action by Mize for thirty days so that the state could petition the Supreme Court. Cameron complied. If the Supreme Court agreed to hear an appeal after its summer recess, the stay would continue until October, after the start of the fall semester.[32]

Constance Motley wanted to move immediately to vacate or cancel Cameron's stay, but her client had misgivings about continuing. The state's strategy of delay seemed to work. In the wake of Judge Cameron's stay, Meredith wrote Motley that he had decided not to "attempt to obtain an undergraduate degree from the University of Mississippi." A proud man, Meredith concluded that he could not benefit by remaining for at least another year as an undergraduate (the prospect even frightened him) and that he should go to either graduate school or law school. Though he realized he could be an example of "fearlessness" to his people by continuing his fight, he also believed that blacks most respected success and higher education and that he was "hurting myself and my people by not developing my capabilities at a normal rate." He did not attend Jackson State's graduation because he "couldn't stomach the idea" of seeing his friends graduate while he had to wait. His family's sacrifices also worried him. As "a good soldier," he recognized that he could not fight every battle, so he decided to seek admission to the Ole Miss law school and hoped that Motley would represent him if he again encountered racial discrimination.[33]

Meredith's letter shocked Motley. At her request, he flew to New York, where she and others at the LDF worked to convince him to persist. While in

New York, in an interview with the *New York Post*'s liberal editor James A. Weschler, Meredith betrayed no lack of resolve or any change in his original objective; his "mingled serenity and solemnity" impressed the veteran New York columnist. Weschler thought the segregationists in Mississippi "are not shattering his spirit; they are fools if they believe they are."[34] His New York supporters restored Meredith's resolve.

With Meredith's renewed commitment, Motley contested Cameron's July 17 stay, but she did not have to work hard because the three-judge panel of the Fifth Circuit reacted at once. The court recalled its directive to Mize, resumed authority in the case, and asked each side to submit by July 24 arguments regarding the stay. Without oral arguments, the panel on July 27 unanimously set aside Cameron's stay. Again writing for the court, Judge Wisdom's biting decree showed impatience with further delays. At the outset it declared that "time is now of the quintessence." The court noted that the defendants had not asked for a rehearing or a stay, and Cameron had not examined the record, heard the arguments, or discussed the case with his fellow judges. Wisdom held that "it is unthinkable that a judge who was not a member of the panel should be allowed to frustrate the mandate of the Court" by issuing a stay. Wisdom saw no crisis or emergency to warrant Cameron's improper intrusion: "This is not a Chessman case. It is not a Rosenberg case. It is not a matter of life and death to the University of Mississippi." He noted that other southern universities were "not shriveling up because of the admission of Negroes."[35]

To resolve the impasse created by Cameron's stay, the three appellate judges "recalled and amended" their prior mandate that, they now recognized, contained wording "so loose as to defeat the intentions of the Court." To make "explicit the meaning that was implicit," the court issued a new mandate to the district court with a "preliminary injunction enjoining and compelling" the defendants to admit Meredith and "prohibiting and preventing" the defendants from keeping him out of the university. Judge DeVane, who had originally dissented, joined in reprimanding Judge Cameron and in attempting to enforce the court's ruling. After the decision one newsman reported, "The sweeping action apparently climaxed Meredith's long fight to enroll at Mississippi." Meredith certainly hoped so. "I'm not getting any younger," he told newsmen. "There have been so many decisions. I hope this is the last." But Judge Cameron had not finished.[36]

The next day, a Saturday, less than twenty-four hours later, Judge Cameron issued a second stay. Contradicting the appeals court, he maintained that his first "stay was and is valid and in full force and effect," and he charged the action of the three-judge panel was in "violation and contravention" of his legitimate stay. Cameron said that his fellow appellate judges had exceeded their jurisdiction in attempting to overturn his original stay, so he stayed the appeals court's latest actions and renewed and extended his July 17 stay. Lasting thirty days, his new stay again gave the defense time to appeal to the Supreme Court. Later that same day, the New Orleans appeals court panel dismissed Cameron's second stay. Three days later Cameron renewed his stay.[37]

More than a commitment to the racial status quo lay behind Cameron's unprecedented moves; he profoundly disagreed with the other judges on both substantive and procedural questions. Some issues dividing the court were well known, while others remained part of its internal workings. In dissent, Cameron had repeatedly criticized the federal judiciary, and the federal government generally, for exceeding its constitutional responsibilities, and he had on several occasions castigated other judges on his own Fifth Circuit. A 1957 dissent in a school desegregation case, for example, expressed his "fundamental disagreement with the thinking of my colleagues as to the mission and true competence, in segregation cases, of federal courts generally and of this Court in particular." He believed the majority of his brethren made a "strategic mistake of real magnitude" when they stirred up "controversy" instead of promoting "an atmosphere of repose and harmony." Insisting that the courts display a sympathy for local conditions, Cameron found that "such an understanding has been tragically lacking in many of the decisions of many of the judges of the Fifth Circuit." In dissent, Cameron lashed out at the "drastic and intemperate" rulings of the "offensive group." The court decisions were "a saddening spectacle," and he understood why southerners viewed the Fifth Circuit judges as "alien intruders."[38] By the summer of 1962, his frustration helped push him to take extraordinary measures to prevent what he saw as further judicial abuse by his own court of appeals.

Questioning the Fifth Circuit's procedures, Judge Cameron believed that the assignment of judges to appeals panels had been consistently rigged, not only to produce liberal judgments in civil rights cases but to exclude him and other conservative Mississippi judges. The "Four," his term to refer to the four liberal judges on the Fifth Circuit, controlled the court to obtain the decisions they wanted. The court simply failed to administer justice impartially or neutrally. He believed that Chief Judge Tuttle and Judge Brown always made sure that a three-judge panel had a liberal majority in civil rights cases and that Cameron himself never participated in the cases, even in ones coming from his home state. Though another year would pass before Cameron made his objections public in a dissent, he had by July 1962 voiced his concerns within the court. His dogged battle with the panel of Wisdom, Brown, and DeVane in the Meredith case may, therefore, have reflected his frustrated opposition to their tactics, in addition to his own belief in states' rights, racial segregation, and the Tenth Amendment.[39]

Judge Cameron's third stay proved no more permanent than his others. Less than a week later, on August 4, the Fifth Circuit panel of Brown, Wisdom, and DeVane responded. It declared Cameron's stays of July 28 and 31 to be "un-authorized, erroneous and improvident" and "vacated and set aside" each of them. Reaffirming its previous orders, the panel ruled that they "continue in full force and effect and require full and immediate obedience and com-pliance." The recalcitrant Cameron refused to concede. With Judge Sidney Mize failing to carry out the Fifth Circuit's order, Judge Cameron two days later for the fourth time defended his earlier stays and renewed and extended his previous stays.[40]

Motley and the LDF decided to file a motion with the U.S. Supreme Court to vacate Cameron's latest stays. On summer recess, the Court could not hear Meredith's motion until it returned on October 1. With the start of the fall semester approaching, Meredith's lawyers appealed to Justice Hugo Black, who had jurisdiction over appeals coming from the Fifth Circuit when the Supreme Court was not in session. Facing complex and conflicting requests, Black informally requested that the Department of Justice comment on the case, and as a result the Kennedy administration officially became involved in the case for the first time.[41]

In an eleven-page motion submitted to Justice Black on August 13, the NAACP's LDF asked that Black "authoritatively and beyond dispute settle the spurious question which Mississippi continues to raise as a cloud upon ap-pellant's indisputable right to attend the University of Mississippi without racial discrimination." Echoing Judge Wisdom, it claimed that "not the slight-est shadow of a doubt" existed about Meredith's right to enroll, the state's repeated request for stays was "a 'legal' tactic to frustrate" Meredith, and the case "involved no doubtful questions of law." Black should set the stays aside and reaffirm the Fifth Circuit's ruling so that Meredith could enroll for the fall semester. As Motley waited for a decision, she remained optimistic that her client would enroll and did not worry about registration deadlines because "they can't very well hold a deadline against him."[42]

Prepared by Charles Clark, the defense brief supported Judge Mize's deci-sion, criticized the Fifth's Circuit's ruling, and asked for a writ of certiorari under which the Court would rehear the case after October 1 when it returned from its summer vacation. The brief reiterated the state's allegations about Meredith's character. More important, it claimed the Fifth Circuit had only "*inferred* that the application was turned down solely because the applicant was a negro" and called the inference "unwarranted and erroneous" because it ignored the evidence and the trial court judge's decision; it amounted to the "substitution of speculation for proof." The defense further argued that the Fifth Circuit had exceeded its appellate role and engaged in "original jurisdiction contrary to the spirit and intent" of federal law. Coming several months after the facts of the case, the appellate court's injunction was "improvident, inequitable and incorrect" because it failed to consider that the facts may have changed in the interval. In a hurry, the plaintiff waived the right to respond to the broader plea by the defense.[43]

Clark claimed Ole Miss had the right to question the propriety of Meredith's " 'missionary' or non-educational" motives and did not have to admit him because he was black—"his race does not entitle him to special treatment or consideration." The defense further argued, "The Registrar's decisions should be accepted without a clear showing of abuse of discretion, which this record does not disclose." The Fifth Circuit's "obtuse" reasoning said that "because this case arose in Mississippi, and because the plaintiff is a negro, therefore, unconstitutional discrimination will be presumed and he must be entitled to special, not equal treatment." Contrary to Judge Wisdom, the defense finally argued that the "time required to permit this [full] Court's review is certainly inconsequential" because, after all, the plaintiff had waited nine years after high school before applying to the university.[44]

The Department of Justice had not paid careful attention to Meredith's lawsuit, but almost from the beginning it had followed the case, so Justice Black's request for legal advice did not catch it completely unawares. A statement prepared for Solicitor General Archibald Cox by the Civil Rights Division suggested how the Fifth Circuit's order could be carried out, and as a result the Justice Department on August 31 filed an amicus curiae brief in *Meredith v. Fair*.[45]

The Justice Department had waited to take an interest in the case because its limited resources meant it could not enter every case and because Burke Marshall, the assistant attorney general, thought Meredith's lawsuit involved no novel legal issue. Once a judgment had been reached, however, the department had an interest in the enforcement of a federal court order. Arguing that Judge Cameron "was without power" to grant the stays, the department called Cameron's actions "altogether lawless." To allow one judge the power to block the actions of his own court would, the amicus filing suggested, "be inconsistent with the orderly functioning of the judicial system. It would allow a sort of perpetual merry-go-round with the court and a single judge entertaining contrary decrees *seriatim, ad infinitum*. The situation is absurd." On the specifics, the solicitor general maintained that the defense had offered no evidence it would be "irreparably injured" by a lack of a stay and that the stay "would irreparably injure Meredith . . . because the additional time he would lose would be irretrievable." Sticking to the plaintiff's narrow request and without taking a position on the defense request for a writ of certiorari, the government asked the Court "to issue an injunction, pending disposition by the full Court, restraining the respondents from refusing to comply with the judgments and orders of the court of appeals."[46]

The Justice Department's involvement provoked many white Mississippians. It drew a harsh rebuke from Attorney General Patterson, who denounced it as "another evidence of the fact that the House of Kennedy is wholly incapable of resisting pressure from the NAACP and other radical groups." Claiming he would not respond to the allegations in the brief if it had not come from such a high official as the attorney general of the United States, Patterson dismissed the Justice Department's suggestions that Judge Cameron had acted lawlessly. Patterson compared the Justice Department's "lack of concern" over communist activities in Mississippi to its aggressive interest in integrating Ole Miss. Personalizing the state's dispute with Meredith and now the federal government, the state attorney general declared, "Robert Kennedy criticizing a judge of Judge Cameron's stature is like a jackass looking up into the sky and braying at a great American Eagle as it soars above." Other white Mississippians also defended Cameron. His hometown editor penned a paean "To Judge Cameron." Praising the judge's efforts to "secure justice for the South," an editorial in the Meridian newspaper urged, "May we never forget what he has done for us. We are proud that he is a citizen of our community."[47]

In a judgment announced on September 10, Justice Black agreed with the Fifth Circuit, and therefore the plaintiff, on every point, but he did not decide the question of certiorari. Though convinced that the Court had jurisdiction and that the Court's rules gave him as an individual judge the same authority to act alone, he explained that he had consulted with each of his colleagues and that they all individually had agreed not only with his understanding of his authority but "that under the circumstances I should exercise that power" as he did in his ruling. According to Black, Judge Cameron's stays "can only work further delay and injury to the movant [Meredith] while immediate enforcement of the judgment can do no appreciable harm to the University or other respondents." Black also saw little possibility that the entire Court would agree to hear the case and review the decision of the Court of Appeals. Until the Court finally disposed of the defense's request for a writ of certiorari, however, Black vacated Cameron's stays, declared the Fifth Circuit's decision and its mandate "should be obeyed," and prohibited the defendants "from taking any steps to prevent enforcement of the Court of Appeals' judgment and mandate."[48] He effectively ordered Meredith's immediate admission.

Reactions to Black's ruling were swift. The plaintiffs were, of course, pleased and optimistic. Calling the decision "wonderful," Constance Motley explained that she was gratified that the "legal problems have been ironed out. We have been in a kind of legal jungle since Judge Cameron started issuing stays." She declared that "as much as possible, Meredith is a student at the University of Mississippi as of now," and described him as "not a bit afraid" of entering the all-white university. Next Meredith announced that he expected to register sometime the following week, though the details had not been worked out. Expecting Meredith's matriculation during the upcoming registration period, Medgar Evers sent a telegram to Governor Barnett to ask that the governor "use the delegated as well as the Christian influence of your office to effectuate a smooth transition at the University." At the same time, Evers said the ruling encouraged his organization to go "all out to end segregation in Mississippi."[49]

When Ross Barnett first heard about Black's ruling, he said it was "just as illegal as if the Supreme Court of Kansas had issued it." He vowed to prevent Meredith from enrolling at Ole Miss, but he would not be more specific "for fear of endangering the case." Attorney General Patterson refused to comment until he had a chance to read Black's decision, and Chancellor Williams and the IHL officials also had no comment. Word quickly spread in the state capital, however, that the state would employ the 1956 legislative resolution of interposition. Urging Barnett to invoke interposition, Senator Hayden Campbell of Jackson claimed that the theory "has never failed wherever it has been used. We have a governor with the courage and the fortitude to use the interposition resolution," declared the state senator, "and every member of the legislature and the people should stand by the Governor and give him their support." At Ole Miss the night after Justice Black directed the admission of Meredith, university officials had to disperse an angry group of students, and the next night a cross was burned near the veterans apartments where many expected Meredith would live.[50] Though the Supreme Court justice had acted, the issue was clearly not settled.

In the wake of Black's ruling, the *Washington Post*'s Robert E. Baker assessed the Mississippi situation: "Ever since the Supreme Court's 1954 Desegregation decision, white Mississippi has been on an official binge of defiance and racism. . . . Clear heads and sober thoughts are needed in Mississippi now more than at any time in the past century. But instead of sobering up, white Mississippi seems to be belting down one more for the road. There could be an ugly crash. The clock is running out in Mississippi."[51]

15. Negotiations: A Game of Checkers

■ ■

The *Meridian Star* hailed the struggle over James Meredith's admission as "the battle of Armageddon between racial purity and mongrelization" and insisted, "We must prevail. We have too much to lose."[1] Though Justice Hugo Black's September 10 ruling may have seemed to resolve the legal case, the controversy only intensified. Focused on Meredith's challenge, Mississippi's leaders moved in multiple ways to shore up segregation. The governor preached defiance of the federal courts, a Jackson court convicted Meredith of a misdemeanor, and the legislature enacted laws to preserve segregation at Ole Miss. President Kennedy and his brother Robert, the attorney general, tried to compromise with Mississippi leaders to achieve Meredith's admission, and the administration also prepared to deploy troops to carry out the federal court orders.

In the weeks after Justice Black's directive, each side, facing other problems, proceeded awkwardly and tentatively. A special session of the general assembly considered legislative reapportionment, and Barnett tended to a potential disaster involving a grounded river barge loaded with chlorine gas. He also suffered the death of a sister in mid-September. The Kennedy administration, on the other hand, dealt with alarming reports of Soviet missiles based in Cuba. An even greater cause for the floundering was that neither side had a comprehensive strategy. Determined to keep Meredith out of Ole Miss, the state's leadership did not know what to do except to be obstructive. The Kennedys wanted somehow to avoid a crisis without submitting to the segregationists. Each side, hoping the other would yield, stumbled through September. A close Barnett adviser observed, "It is like a checker game and nobody can foresee the next move."[2]

As the dispute deepened, Mississippians did not know what to expect from the Kennedy administration. Though John F. Kennedy had little personal experience with blacks, only slight awareness of racial discrimination, and limited knowledge of the southern way of life, he had as a young congressman and senator consistently supported civil rights legislation. He endorsed fair employment, objected to poll taxes, and fought for home rule for District of Columbia blacks. During the Cold War, he usually connected support for civil rights to the fight against communism; racial inequality provided the Soviet Union with an embarrassing issue to use against the United States. For Kennedy, racial prejudice and discrimination posed an intellectual problem more than an emotional one. According to one student of Kennedy and race, he was in the late 1940s and early 1950s affected "more by the illogic and irrationality of racism than by its cruelty." Though he may not have appreciated the nation's racial dilemma, he supported civil rights even before 1956.[3]

In seeking the 1956 Democratic vice-presidential nomination, Kennedy appealed to southern segregationists while hoping to retain northern liberal and black support. To reconcile the conflict, he fashioned a moderate stance that supported gradual racial change achieved by voluntary reform. After he lost the nomination, Kennedy kept an eye on national politics and continued to pursue a middle position. The next year he voted for an amendment to a civil rights bill that provided for a jury trial in cases of criminal contempt; white southerners supported the amendment because it would allow a jury of whites to judge segregationists accused of violating civil rights laws. His vote disappointed blacks and pleased southern whites, but his ultimate support for the larger bill encouraged blacks and alienated segregationists.[4]

If Kennedy's inconsistent stand worried some southern whites, it had a special appeal for white Mississippians. His *Profiles in Courage*, published in 1956, subscribed to the conservative white southern interpretation of Reconstruction as a horror caused by fanatical northerners, and it praised L. Q. C. Lamar's courage in seeking reconciliation after the Civil War. The positive portrait of Lamar, the author of the Mississippi's Ordinance of Secession and a leader in whites' return to power after Reconstruction, pleased white Mississippians. At the same time, on a visit to the state during the Little Rock crisis, Kennedy told Democrats that he supported the *Brown* decision. He also questioned the scope of the federal intervention in Little Rock and challenged the state's Republicans to defend the Eisenhower administration's use of the army in the crisis.[5]

Unwilling to give up on the South, he wanted to keep white Mississippians in the party and friendly to his potential presidential candidacy. He especially courted powerful southerners in Congress. When Kennedy's flirtation with segregationists provoked harsh attacks by the NAACP, he deprecated his southern appeals and tried to repair his support among blacks. One scholar has called his attempt to straddle the civil rights issue a "profile in cowardice."[6]

In his 1960 run for the presidency, Kennedy continued playing both sides of the racial issue. He saw civil rights as a political problem to finesse. Toward the end of his campaign for the nomination, Kennedy changed his position to thwart a challenge from liberal Adlai Stevenson. After he secured the nomination, however, he again equivocated. The party platform endorsed civil rights, but his selection of Texan Lyndon B. Johnson as his running mate displeased some in the movement. Two symbolic gestures may have been crucial for Kennedy's election. First, he promised a presidential proclamation to desegregate federal housing. Second, toward the end of the campaign, the Kennedys responded to Martin Luther King's jailing in Georgia with a telephone call from Robert Kennedy to the local judge that helped secure King's release and with a call from John Kennedy to King's wife. In both instances Kennedy did nothing substantive, but his rhetoric wooed black voters without alienating too many southern whites.[7]

The winning Democrats did not carry Mississippi. To protest the party's civil rights stand, Ross Barnett had supported unpledged electors to block either candidate from an electoral college majority; the South could then bargain to protect the southern way of life. When unpledged electors won a plurality only in Mississippi, Barnett sacrificed any loyalty from the new president.

As president, John Kennedy preferred gradual, voluntary racial progress, but he moved hardly at all. Feeling constrained by his slim victory, southern congressional power, and his own lack of zeal for civil rights, the president followed a "policy of inaction": he failed to desegregate federal housing and refused to push for new civil rights legislation. Instead he largely left civil rights to his brother, the attorney general. Through a dispassionate, cautious, controlling approach, Robert Kennedy protected him by avoiding crises and controversies. To placate white southerners, the administration named segregationists to several southern federal judgeships and persuaded the Civil Rights Commission to postpone southern hearings. To manage the movement, the administration dissuaded its leaders from massive, direct-action protests in favor of voting rights. Tactically, the Kennedys preferred persuasion, negotiation, and conciliation first, then lawsuits if necessary, and a minimum use of federal power as a last resort. The administration denied that the government should provide a national police force and instead relied on local law enforcement. Only when compelled by the movement did the administration intervene directly, but reluctantly and half-heartedly. The spur usually came from federal court orders, not from any goal of racial justice.[8]

The Freedom Rides of May 1961 provided the administration's first major challenge. John Kennedy sent a contingent of U.S. marshals to Montgomery to protect the riders and to preserve law and order. Later, a compromise with Senator Eastland and Governor Barnett guaranteed the riders' safety and allowed Mississippi authorities to arrest them without a protest by the administration. The episode demonstrated that the Kennedys wanted to avoid protests that could become violent, yet they would intervene only after other means failed. Their approach disappointed both sides. Segregationists denounced the administration for coming to the support of the riders, while movement activists thought it had deceived and deserted them through its limited and irresolute response, especially its secret negotiations with southern segregationists. Many of the Kennedys' attitudes and preferences revealed in their handling of the Freedom Rides affected their involvement the next year at Ole Miss, and they also influenced the response of white Mississippians. Allowed to violate the Freedom Riders' rights by arresting them in Jackson, Barnett and others believed that the Kennedys would not overturn segregation if law and order were maintained and that the administration could be outmaneuvered in crisis negotiations.[9]

Predisposed to deemphasize civil rights, the Kennedy administration initially showed little interest in Meredith's lawsuit. In February 1961, Meredith sent the Justice Department a letter that explained his application, but the department did not respond. A few days later Burke Marshall, the assistant attorney general for civil rights, received an FBI report based on information from Hugh Clegg, and four months later Constance Motley sent him the complaint filed in Meridian. Marshall and other Justice Department lawyers followed the case. In June 1961, he warned that "the Federal Government will unquestionably have to make some preparation, including having deputy marshals available," if Meredith gained admission to the university. A year later, Marshall assured the attorney general that he was "keeping in close touch with the entire situation."[10]

Burke Marshall, a thirty-eight-year-old native of New Jersey and a Yale graduate, had joined the Justice Department in 1961 after more than a decade of legal practice in Washington as an antitrust lawyer. He directed the civil rights division even though he had no prior experience in either politics or civil rights. Described as "bland and imperturbable" and "diffident," Marshall was an adept negotiator and advocate of federalism. As he explained later in *Federalism and Civil Rights*, he preferred to defer to state and local governments to enforce the law. If they refused or failed, Marshall wanted to negotiate a remedy with them or secure court relief before considering the use of federal power, and he often found no basis for federal intervention. His approach struck some ardent supporters of civil rights as conservative and timid.[11]

On a June 1962 trip to New Orleans for an appeals court session in the Meredith case, Marshall stopped in Jackson to consult informally with the mayor and some of his assistants, including Tom Watkins. A prominent attorney and the city's chief counsel on civil rights matters, Watkins had worked with Marshall on an antitrust case, and they had talked frequently when the

Freedom Riders came to Jackson. Though they had never met, the two men had formed a professional friendship. Nothing substantive resulted from their Jackson meeting, but it did confirm a relationship that would become useful later as Watkins advised the governor.[12]

By the summer of 1962, as the Fifth Circuit Court of Appeals considered Meredith's case, Marshall informed Robert Kennedy that it would likely order Ole Miss to admit Meredith. In June, Marshall began exploring federal protection for Meredith, and he assured Robert Kennedy that he was monitoring developments. Until Meredith's lawsuit went to the Supreme Court, however, the Justice Department took no active part in the case. Its role changed when Justice Hugo Black's clerk requested the department's comment on the case, and Marshall's office prepared a statement for the solicitor general to use in filing an amicus brief.[13]

Once the department became involved, its role rapidly expanded. Even before Black issued his directive, Marshall discussed the situation with knowledgeable southerners. Early in September, he received an overture from C. Nolan Fortenberry, the chairman of the Ole Miss political science department, and they conferred briefly on September 7, when the professor attended a meeting in Washington. In a significant action, Marshall on September 5 instructed James P. McShane, the chief marshal, to prepare marshals to support Meredith's entry into Ole Miss. The assistant attorney general knew from the Freedom Rider experience that marshals would be the preferred means to carry out any court order if negotiations failed. By September 8, the army had also been notified that it might have to provide logistical support for the marshals.[14]

The day after Black acted, the other side began intense preparations to prevent the integration of Ole Miss. Barnett played the key role. Sixty-three-year-old Robert Ross Barnett was born in Standing Pine in Leake County, near the middle of the state. The son of a Civil War veteran, farmer, and sawmill operator, he cut trees, picked cotton, and plowed fields with his father. To put himself through Mississippi College and the University of Mississippi law school, young Ross Barnett worked as a barber, janitor, and high school basketball coach. In the following three decades, he gained wealth and an "almost unequaled" reputation as a plaintiff's lawyer in Jackson. The rural, folksy Barnett had amazing success with small-town juries because of his easy familiarity and his sense of humor (he told campaign audiences, "Just kick the door open and ask for Ol' Ross"). Transferring his talents to politics proved difficult, and in 1951 and 1955 he lost runs for the governorship. In 1956 Barnett gained attention when he defended whites arrested in violent protests against integration in Cleveland, Tennessee. Three years later, he campaigned for governor as a strong segregationist with the support of the Citizens' Council. Even though he had never held public office, he won the election.[15]

The new governor, who traveled the nation recruiting industry, soon lost support at home in conflicts with legislators and other political leaders. His attempts to reward political allies with jobs in state agencies, ranging from the State Textbook Commission and the Game and Fish Commission to the Sovereignty Commission, aroused protests from the agencies and from the legislature. Disputes over prisons, finances, and teacher pay also plagued his administration. A crusade against vice along the notorious Gulf Coast alienated many of his supporters, and his lavish spending on renovating the governor's mansion, especially a ten-thousand-dollar "gold-plated" bathroom, offended others. Representative Karl Wiesenburg charged the administration was "the most corrupt, the most obnoxious that has served this state since Reconstruction." With the governor's popularity plummeting, Ole Miss fans even booed him at a football game in 1960.[16]

Voters continued to support Barnett's campaign pledge to maintain segregation. He once said, "The Good Lord was the original segregationist. He made us white, and he intended that we stay that way." Barnett promised that the schools would not be integrated while he was governor. Hodding Carter defended his dedication and admitted "a small sneaking admiration for Gov. Barnett. . . . He believes in what he is doing and is quite willing to take the consequences." Other observers doubted his political skill in defending segregation because he lacked governmental experience and often seemed confused, inarticulate, and bumbling. Though audiences responded well to his speeches, often written by Citizens' Councilors, Barnett performed poorly on the stump: once he referred to a Jewish audience as "a fine Christian gathering." Reporter John Herbers, however, suggested that he was not as incompetent as he seemed and that "the appearance of confusion works to his advantage; that is, when it comes to political maneuvering." According to Herbers, Barnett may have seemed slow and distracted but was in fact aware and involved. The Kennedys would have difficulty with the enigmatic governor.[17]

After Black's September 10 ruling, Barnett conferred with state officials, his advisers, and Citizens' Council leaders to prepare the state's next move. He decided to address the state over radio and television on September 13. He remained confident that the state could prevent Meredith's enrollment. "We plan to avail ourselves of every legal weapon possible," he told reporters. "We see several possible methods of blocking his entry."[18]

The day after Black's ruling, Meredith returned to Kosciusko from visiting his wife's family in Indiana. He expected to register the following week; orientation for transfer students began on September 17 and registration two days later. Many students returned to Oxford a week early to prepare for fraternity and sorority rush, and freshmen arrived on Saturday, September 15. Among students already on campus, most assumed he would be shunned, and some expected him to fail out of school within a month. The evening after Justice Black's order, Ole Miss officials broke up a student demonstration. The next night a cross burned on campus.[19]

Despite Meredith's plans, the student protests, and Barnett's bluster, Judge Mize made the first move. On September 13, as directed by Black, he granted a permanent injunction that prohibited the IHL board and Ole Miss officials from doing anything to "frustrate or defeat" Meredith's admission or attendance. Mize ordered his own alma mater not to discriminate against Meredith "in any way whatsoever because of his race." The way finally seemed clear for Meredith.[20]

At 7:30 P.M.. on the day of Mize's injunction, Barnett spoke to the state in a live, twenty-minute radio and television broadcast. Saying the "day of expediency is past," he exhorted his listeners to realize that the "day of reckoning . . . is now upon us. This is the day and this is the hour." Twice he repeated his campaign promise that "no school in our state will be integrated while I am your Governor," and he vowed "that there is no sacrifice which I will shrink from making to preserve the racial integrity of our people and institutions." Pledging to go to jail before violating his pledge and submitting to the dictates of the federal government, he called on all other elected officials to do the same. Barnett proclaimed, "There is no case in history where the Caucasian race has survived social integration. We will not drink from the cup of genocide."[21]

Under the Tenth Amendment, Barnett asserted the state's sovereignty over its schools, colleges, and universities, and he invoked the doctrine of interposition through a gubernatorial proclamation to prevent the "unwarranted, illegal and arbitrary usurpation of [the state's] power" by federal judicial action. He warned that if Mississippi failed, "our system of government will crumble and fall, and American liberty will be lost forever in the ruins." Barnett urged his listeners to display "dignity, courage and fortitude" as they stood "together, hand in hand, mind to mind, *unyielding and unafraid*!" They had to prove that they "do not, will not surrender to the evil and illegal forces of tyranny!" The governor had, according to one reporter, "made defiance of the law a respectable, almost heroic attitude."[22]

State leaders nearly unanimously supported Barnett. In a typical evaluation, Jackson's Senator Hayden Campbell hailed his talk as "historic, masterful and courageous." The *Jackson Clarion-Ledger*'s front-page editorial judged the governor "exactly right" on states' rights. Except for one, the state's congressional delegation pledged him complete support. The lone congressional dissenter, Frank Smith, a moderate who had recently lost a reelection bid, maintained that Barnett's stand "would lead the state down another blind alley" and that it "threatens the existence of our great university." A few others also dissented. Greenville's state representative Joseph Wroten rejected the "leadership of extremism" and declared that Barnett had "called for anarchy and defiance of the United States Government." Hodding Carter derided the state's political leaders for "still echoing the hollow phrases" of interposition, a "euphemism for nullification and ultimately anarchy."[23]

On campus on the night after Barnett's speech, Meredith was hung in effigy from a lamppost in front of the student union. A sign on the figure declared: "Hail Barnett. Our Governor will not betray Mississippi. . . . We are proud that our Governor stands for constitutional sovereignty." Nearly all students considered Meredith an "intruder and troublemaker more interested in making headlines in New York papers than in seeking an education." If he attempted to enroll, they expected violence. Some preferred letting him enroll to closing the university, while others fretted more about the fate of their nationally ranked football team than about segregation or education.[24]

Chancellor Williams and his staff had already instructed students to treat Meredith as any other student. At a two-day retreat in the first week of September, student government officers, women student leaders, the newspaper editor, and others met with the chancellor, the provost, and the dean of students to plan student government's role in the growing crisis. All agreed on the need to avoid violence and keep Ole Miss open. The students recognized their responsibilities to keep their fellow students from gathering in crowds and discussing volatile racial subjects in big groups. If a disturbance did erupt, the leaders agreed to moderate it. The chancellor explained that any student who demonstrated against Meredith would be expelled, and he warned them not to discuss the situation with anyone outside the university. Later, at freshman orientation, Williams said, "This freshman class has the greatest responsibility ever placed in any freshman class in the history of the University." He urged them to avoid demonstrations and violence, to act as mature men and women, "not boys and girls," and to pray that "peace and reason will prevail." "Do nothing to make the university lose its prestige," he implored then. "Do nothing that will lead people to ask, 'Why should we keep the University open when students are acting as they are?' Be careful not to start or carry rumors. Have faith in these days of crisis."[25]

On the same day, eight Oxford ministers, without taking a stand on integration, rejected the hysteria of the white supremacists and accepted the possibility of Meredith's admission. A joint statement read during their church services recognized the "critical" federal-state conflict and urged all to "act in a manner consistent with the Christian teaching concerning the value and dignity of man." Praying for "God's guidance," the clergymen called on Christians to "exert whatever leadership and influence possible to maintain peace and order." They beseeched everyone "to resist the pressures placed upon us by emotionally excited groups," and they promoted a defense of "the honor and good name" of the university.[26]

At Oxford's First Presbyterian Church, Reverend Murphey C. Wilds called for supporting law and order, avoiding demonstrations, and speaking out for peace. At St. Peter's Episcopal Church, Reverend Duncan Gray stressed the "*heavy responsibility*" as Christians to prevent violence and to promote "Christian love and brotherhood." He took a stand: "We hope and pray that the members of St. Peter's Church and our students with us today will exercise the leadership necessary to assure the peaceful admission of James Meredith to the University, insofar as we have the power to do so." Also at St. Peter's, Reverend Wofford K. Smith warned, "When emotion is substituted for a clear head, when the mob replaces law and order, and when violence destroys the chance for peaceful arbitration, then our beloved community will have degenerated to a jungle-like state of existence." He declared that "Christ died for *him*. God, in love, made him, died to redeem him, and still loves him to the fullest."[27]

Despite all the preoccupations, preachments, and preparations in Oxford, the real players were in Jackson. The trustees' involvement deepened at their September 4 meeting when they assumed full authority over Meredith's application. On Friday, September 14, the day after Barnett's speech, the board met to respond to recent events. Attorney General Patterson and Charles Clark discussed their choices. With all legal options exhausted, the board could follow the court order and allow Meredith into Ole Miss or it could defy the court, oppose Meredith's admission, and be cited for contempt. The board divided. Seeing the futility of further resistance, six trustees preferred to admit Meredith rather than face contempt charges. Barnett's five appointees advocated defiance. Two remained undecided. The board recessed until the following Monday, September 17, when Barnett would present his strategy.[28]

Over the intervening weekend, as the governor huddled with advisers, incessant rumors agitated the state. According to one unconfirmed report, the IHL board had wavered in response to Barnett's defiant challenge to choose jail over yielding to federal integration demands. Another account alleged that the board had so disappointed the governor that he was considering naming himself registrar so he could personally reject Meredith. The trustees' temporizing prompted Lieutenant Governor Paul B. Johnson to call publicly on the board to stand with Barnett and to urge citizens to tell the trustees that "no member of the Negro race shall attend the University of Mississippi." Mississippians also debated who had the legal authority to close Ole Miss. People feared that Oxford's big welcome party for students could turn into an ugly demonstration against Meredith. Some objected to reports that Ole Miss officials might arrest protesters. Use of U.S. marshals to force Meredith's enrollment troubled segregationists, and gossips speculated on how Mississippians might react to federal force. Nobody knew if the highway patrol would try to arrest the marshals. Compared to an invasion by marshals, an "atomic bomb dropped on Mississippi would do no less damage and would be far more welcome," according to Bidwell Adam, the head of the state Democratic Party. He told Robert Kennedy that he "can kiss Mississippi and the Deep South goodbye" if he deployed federal forces in the state.[29]

Concerns that the Kennedy administration might use marshals or even the army to ensure Meredith's registration were not misplaced. Anticipating a court ruling in the Meredith case, two deputy marshals made a reconnaissance visit to Oxford in late June. Gathering demographic, topographic, and geographic data, they studied the airport, government offices, motels, access to the university, and other aspects of the town. In their July 12 report to Chief Marshal McShane, they recommended using only a small escort force of marshals because of benign public opinion in Oxford and because state law enforcement would maintain law and order. If state authorities failed, they proposed a force of at least sixty, fully equipped marshals on the campus. If the larger force were needed, they recommended flying into the Memphis airport and using facilities in Holly Springs and just south of Memphis as staging areas.[30]

In several meetings, William Geohegan, a Justice Department lawyer, discussed with the marshals, the border patrol, and others in the department the logistical problems of deploying marshals. Assuming Meredith would enroll the following Thursday or Friday, Geohegan's informal group made plans on Tuesday, September 13. They expected a dozen deputy marshals to lodge in an Oxford motel, ready to accompany Meredith to the campus, with a second group of sixty marshals and twenty-one border patrol cars in reserve in Holly Springs. Nearly two hundred marshals would prepare to mobilize on twenty-four hours' notice.[31]

On September 14, Marshall and Geohegan discussed with Secretary of the Army Cyrus Vance and military leaders the army's anticipated role. Marshall explained the likelihood that marshals would be used, and, if the situation required a large force of marshals for an extended period, the army would be expected to create an encampment for them in the Holly Springs National Forest. In addition to air transportation, the marshals would need communications links among units in Memphis, the Holly Springs tent city, and Oxford. Finally, Marshall broached the possibility that the army itself would be used in Oxford. Though Vance wanted the army to remain the last resort, he agreed to begin planning for troop deployment.[32]

After Geohegan, Marshall, and Deputy Attorney General Nicholas Katzenbach reviewed their preparations with Robert Kennedy late on September 14, Geohegan believed Kennedy wanted two hundred marshals available for Meredith's expected registration on September 20 or 21. The Marshals Service directed two groups to report to the Memphis Naval Air Station by the night of Tuesday, September 18; when Robert Kennedy learned of the deployment, he directed that only two dozen stay in Memphis and the others return home. The first to reach Memphis were, in fact, McShane and his assistant, John W. Cameron. Directed by the attorney general to check out Oxford and Ole Miss, they flew to Memphis on Saturday, September 15. After meeting Meredith for the first time, McShane, Cameron, and several other marshals on Sunday drove to Oxford, where they talked with the local marshal and toured the town and campus.[33]

While the marshals readied to assist Meredith, the army prepared to build a tent city for the marshals and, if necessary, to help maintain peace and order. It investigated the operation's possible requirements, military facilities near Oxford, available army units, and nearby reserve forces. Once the army identified the involved units, it created a command structure. As part of the planning, the army located tents, beds, showers, latrines, and lights; communications experts linked the army, the Justice Department, the Memphis Naval Air Station, and marshals in Memphis and Oxford. The operation's sensitivity required not only secrecy but that military personnel not go into Mississippi for preliminary work. As a cover, the army used an ongoing exercise called HIGH HEELS/ SPADE FORK, a test response to a natural disaster in Memphis. By September 20, the army was ready to move on twenty-four-hours' notice.[34]

The army first obtained intelligence on Mississippi from the FBI, but by September 19 the army relied on its own covert operatives in Oxford. Army intelligence maintained a small Oxford office, probably for security clearance interviews with individuals at Ole Miss, but it supplemented the local staff in September. Along with FBI agents, they reported their observations as well as relevant rumors, radio news broadcasts, and newspaper coverage. In addition, the air force flew a photo reconnaissance mission over Oxford.[35]

The administration also pursued other options. For example, Marshall asked Dean Erwin Griswold of Harvard law school to encourage John Satter-field and members of the state bar to support Meredith's enrollment as a matter of constitutional law. Marshall also had Myers McDougal of the Yale law school contact prominent Mississippians. At the same time, Marshall, with the help of the Department of Commerce, compiled a list of major businesses active in Mississippi. In a meeting at the Justice Department, several top members of the administration discussed ways to have national corporations use their Mississippi contacts to persuade the IHL board to yield on the desegregation, and they divided responsibilities for contacting more than a score of manufacturers. The Justice Department also gathered information about federal programs that assisted Ole Miss.[36]

At the same time, Barnett hid some of his actions from his constituents. Two days after his statewide address, he began secret telephone negotiations in which he betrayed little of the defiance Mississippians heard. Initiated by Robert Kennedy, the cordial discussions involved when, where, and how Meredith would register. At first Kennedy proposed that Meredith go to the university on Thursday, September 20, and Barnett pledged to cooperate. When Kennedy emphasized the need to avoid violence, the governor promised no violence would occur. Under the plan, a few marshals would accompany Meredith, Ole Miss would refuse to register him, and the federal government would seek a court order for his registration. Without objecting, Barnett observed that the litigation could last a year, but the attorney general thought that was far too long. At the end of their brief talk, Kennedy promised to call on Monday to finalize their plans.[37]

Before the negotiations resumed, the trustees reconvened to hear the governor. Thomas Tubb, the board president, invited the press into the meeting to publicize that some trustees had decided to admit Meredith, but Barnett's supporters insisted that the meeting be closed. Outside newsmen nevertheless heard "raised voices" in the acrimonious meeting where Barnett explained various possibilities: the legislature could enact new laws to give him more legal weapons; Meredith might be prosecuted for giving false information on his voter registration; the governor could close Ole Miss; and the trustees could block Meredith and go to jail for contempt. After Barnett left, the trustees argued over what contempt of court meant and whether they would be jailed for contempt. Divided, the board recessed until its regular meeting on Thursday.[38]

After the meeting, Jobe announced that the board had taken no action. Asked about closing the university, Tubb said only that the governor had the power to do so. In a statement after the meeting Dr. Verner Holmes insisted, "I will not vote to close the University of Mississippi." He would "go to jail if need be but provided that the university's integrity is maintained and that the university remains open." Holmes declared, "I am not willing to go to jail if it will accomplish nothing. This would be ridiculous and ineffective."[39]

At the same time, trustee Tally D. Riddell, a lawyer from east-central Mississippi, prepared a detailed explanation of his decision to support Meredith's admission. Though opposed to integration, he could not ignore the court orders. Riddell called further opposition "vain and futile" and sharply criticized Barnett's actions. Emphasizing that the "Governor is *not* a defendant," he suggested that Barnett had deceived the public by claiming that he would go to jail to maintain segregation when in fact the governor did not face contempt charges—the trustees did. Riddell expressed disgust that Barnett cloaked himself in the law and the constitution while using "every conceivable means of pressure to force the members of the Board to act in an unlawful manner and criminally violate the existing injunction." Closing the university would cause "irreparable injury" to students and to the state. He hoped that the public would realize that "political considerations and not the welfare of our institutions" motivated some in the present crisis.[40] Revealing deep splits on the board, his stance proved that some valued the university and the law more than segregation.

Despite board divisions, Barnett had considerable support. The *Meridian Star* agreed "100 per cent" with his go-to-jail proposal, and West Point's *Daily Times Leader* endorsed his position in "the greatest test of Constitutional authority since the Civil War." The *Jackson Clarion-Ledger* claimed Mississippians firmly backed him. Approval also came from the Mississippi Sheriffs Association, the Meadville Civitan Club, the Jackson Optimist Club, and the Mississippi Society of the Daughters of the American Revolution. Laurel's Harmony Baptist Church pledged "our absolute and unwavering support" and promised they would "NEVER surrender" any of their principles.[41]

Worried white voices also emerged and indicated a greater interest in the university's integrity than in segregation. Former lieutenant governor Sam Lumpkin of Tupelo, for example, supported racial segregation but said, "To close the university would mean a triumphant victory for the NAACP and the Kennedy boys. . . . Sensible thinking people of Mississippi do not want the university closed." Citizens worried about the financial effects of closing Ole Miss. The football team would not play, but the coaches' contracts would have to be fulfilled, the bond payments for the Jackson stadium would have to be met, and the financial guarantees to visiting teams would have to be satisfied. Furthermore, debts from building dormitories would have to be paid without student housing fees, the university medical center might close, and male students would face the military draft. The lack of educational opportunities and apparent political instability might cause the economic development to stall. Nevertheless, as one official explained, "anyone who opposed Gov. Barnett's proposal to close the university if necessary to prevent integration would be charged with favoring integration."[42]

A few accepted the risk. Hodding Carter observed, "Mississippi's course is more than reckless, it is a denial of human intelligence." He feared the state seemed headed toward a "jungle world" of "anarchy." Pascagoula's Ira Harkey asked, "How can we defy the law 'to the finish' without resorting to violence?" Predicting "the turmoil of anarchy we are approaching" would yield only hate, strife, and grief, he concluded, "In a madhouse's din, Mississippi waits. God help Mississippi."[43] Mississippi's leaders would not heed Harkey's and Carter's warnings.

Early in the evening on Monday, September 17, the governor and Robert Kennedy talked again. In a change of position, Barnett insisted that Meredith should register Thursday afternoon at the trustees' Jackson office because the board would be meeting then, the registrar would be present, and the chance of resistance would be less. Kennedy wanted to think about it and to consult with Meredith, who had to make the final decision. The next day, Kennedy told Barnett that Meredith insisted on registering in Oxford, and Kennedy supported the decision. Barnett then shifted and asked for a postponement until Friday, Saturday, or Monday, to reduce the risk of opposition. Four hours later, when Barnett called back and spoke with Burke Marshall, he insisted that he had no control over the board and reported that the trustees had the day before ordered Meredith to appear at their office in Jackson on Thursday. In response to Marshall's question, the governor said the board had not yet voted on whether to allow Meredith to register.[44] Rapidly developing events preempted all plans.

A special legislative session on reapportionment convened on Tuesday, September 18, but it immediately addressed the brewing integration crisis. First a senate resolution urged all citizens and officials to "give their full and complete support and cooperation" to Barnett's proclamation of interposition. Only an hour after the legislature opened, a joint session cheered the governor in "a hero's reception" when he came ostensibly to discuss legislative reapportionment. Lieutenant Governor Paul Johnson's introduction praised Barnett's defiance of federal power. In a three-page speech, Barnett attacked the court-ordered reapportionment because it "seriously interfere[d] with states' rights and the freedom of the people of the several sovereign states." He branded the judicial interference a "deliberate, palpable and dangerous exercise of powers not granted" to the courts by law or the Constitution. Without mentioning Meredith, Ole Miss, or segregation, the governor hoped "to stand steadfast all the way down the line" and pledged "to do everything in my power, everything that is legal and honorable, to uphold our customs and traditions."[45]

After Barnett departed, Speaker Walter Sillers introduced a resolution supporting Barnett's "fearless and courageous" defense of states' rights "against the unlawful aggression and usurpation by the federal government" and his stand against "political aggression, abuse and misrepresentation designed to disrupt and destroy Southern institutions, traditions and way of living." Without mentioning integration, the proposal endorsed Barnett's efforts to block Meredith's enrollment, and it did not call for closing the university to avoid integration. Former governor J. P. Coleman, who served as a representative, endorsed the resolution because he had "faith that Governor Barnett will do the best he can" and that the governor, the attorney general, and the trustees "will do all that they possibly can to maintain segregation" at Ole Miss. The resolution passed, with negative votes from Representatives Wroten and Wiesenburg. Later the senate also adopted it.[46]

Support for Barnett increased. Judge Tom Brady praised his "courageous stand in invoking the principle of interposition" and approved his go-to-jail policy. An equivocal former lieutenant governor, Carroll Gartin, lauded the governor's "determination to keep our schools and colleges *open* and segregated." In the *Jackson Clarion-Ledger*, Charles Hills said that the governor's speech to the legislature propelled him to unprecedented popularity, but Hills recognized its perils because Barnett had vowed that no Negro would enroll during his term as governor. Hills concluded, "Barnett must keep that promise in spite of all things, or lose face. At least he must stop Meredith at this time." Hills suggested, "If Ole Miss gets integrated this week, look out!"[47]

On the same day that Barnett addressed the legislature, the Justice Department filed a brief for the right to participate in the Meredith case "for the purpose of preserving and maintaining the due administration of justice and the integrity of the judicial processes of the United States." It claimed that interposition and nullification "obstruct and interfere with" the implementation of the court orders. Judges Griffin Bell, John Minor Wisdom, and John R. Brown granted the request and opened the possibility for civil and criminal contempt charges against the trustees if Meredith were blocked from enrolling. Mississippi's attorney general blasted the intervention as evidence that Robert Kennedy had become "general counsel for the NAACP, Martin Luther King and other radical agitators and trouble-makers."[48]

The pace of activity escalated. Wednesday morning, in a conversation with Geohegan at the Justice Department, Attorney General Patterson expressed confidence that arrangements could be worked out for Meredith to enter the campus and settle his business without being harmed, but he acknowledged that the trustees had ordered Meredith to go to Jackson and had prohibited Ole Miss officials from registering him in Oxford. Though Barnett later continued to press for Meredith's appearance in Jackson, he could not assure Robert Kennedy that the board would allow him to register. For Meredith to go to Oxford would, according to the governor, violate the trustees' directive, but the Justice Department continued to push for registration at the university. Late Wednesday afternoon, Marshall called Patterson to discuss plans for the next day. With McShane and four others listening on a speakerphone, Marshall arranged for three marshals to take Meredith to the campus at 3:00 P.M. McShane planned to call Colonel T. B. Birdsong, head of the highway patrol, so that he and other patrolmen could accompany them from Batesville to Oxford. Patterson pledged that Birdsong would insure Meredith's safety.[49]

Legal action extended beyond the legislature and the federal court. Forty-seven people, including many with children at Ole Miss, filed a complaint in state chancery court against university officers, the IHL board, and many federal officials, including Robert Kennedy and several FBI agents. They asked for an injunction barring Meredith's enrollment because they feared that some state officials were not "loyal Mississippians" and would not follow Barnett's leadership in blocking Meredith. The request went before Chancellor L. B. Porter of Union, whom Barnett had appointed to his post only six weeks earlier after the incumbent's death. On Wednesday morning the Ole Miss alumnus (class of 1936) and staunch segregationist directed the defendants not to do anything to help Meredith "enroll or register" nor to do anything to "aid or abet the integration."[50]

Shortly after lunch on Wednesday, the legal maneuvering shifted back to Hinds County Justice of the Peace Court, where Paul G. Alexander, the local prosecutor, renewed the formal charges against James Meredith for falsifying his voter application. At Motley's request, Judge Wisdom had enjoined Hinds authorities from prosecuting Meredith until after the courts had fully considered his lawsuit, and the matter seemed to have been dropped until Meredith's enrollment became imminent. When the authorities revived the charges, a trial was set for the following morning, September 20.[51]

Soon after the perjury charge was brought against Meredith, Governor Barnett expanded the purview of the special legislative session to include the segregation crisis. After a hurried conference among the governor, lieutenant governor, and legislative leaders, the legislature considered two measures. Late Wednesday afternoon, the senate took up a bill proposed by George Yarbrough, E. K. Collins, Tommy Brooks, and John McLaurin to prevent the enrollment of any individual convicted of any criminal charges or facing charges involving moral turpitude. As McLaurin explained, it was intended "simply to keep these criminals from getting into our universities and colleges." Seven minutes after the bill's introduction, the senate passed it unanimously and sent it to the house. At the same time the house considered a constitutional amendment to give the governor authority over college admissions in cases where the trustees could not decide. Over dissents by Karl Wiesenburg, Joseph Wroten, and George Rogers of Vicksburg, the house approved the amendment and forwarded it to the senate, which promptly passed it.[52]

Five minutes after okaying the constitutional amendment, the house passed the senate bill dealing with criminal charges and applicants to the university, but Wroten and Wiesenburg voiced strong objections. One newsman reported that neither Wroten nor Wiesenburg sought "the role of hero or martyr. They are two men voting their convictions." Neither man claimed to be an integrationist. Wroten believed "this kind of resistance leads to anarchy. I don't feel the people of Mississippi want to bear arms against the federal government." For Wiesenburg, "the question is simple. Can we as citizens of the United States engage in such defiance of Federal law?"[53]

Wiesenburg's motion to reconsider stopped the legislation. The house adjourned with plans to reconvene early the next day. At 12:01 A.M. the legislature reconvened. Speaker Sillers refused any discussion and the house promptly passed the bill 122–1, with Wiesenburg casting the lone negative vote and Wroten paired against it. When the senate cleared the bill and the lieutenant governor signed it, the senators cheered. The legislature had done what it could to prevent the integration of Ole Miss. Meredith was expected to try to enroll later that day, but lawmakers hoped legal charges pending against him would stymie his attempt. Some observers, however, thought that the law could not apply retroactively to Meredith's alleged perjury. Whatever its utility, the legislators sent the bill to the governor for his signature, and a gratified Barnett signed it just before 1:00 A.M.[54]

When the governor went to the capitol at about midnight, he came from the middle of a secret, five-hour meeting of the IHL board. Called at the request of one of Barnett's supporters, the meeting gave him another chance to explain his strategy for dealing with Meredith. The governor's generalities frustrated the trustees. When they pressed for an explanation, he could only reply, "The only way I know to keep him out is just don't let him in." Some trustees finally realized that he had no plan, except to drag out the controversy as long as possible and hope the federal authorities would relent. The angry, tense, and tired trustees argued with Barnett and among themselves; some nearly came to blows. Tally Riddell became so upset that he was rushed to the hospital with a suspected heart attack. In all the bickering, the board hit upon a possible solution. One of Barnett's appointees offhandedly suggested to "let you do it. We'll let you reject him." Having stripped the power from the chancellor and registrar and assumed it themselves, they decided to shift it to Barnett. He would face the contempt charges. At 2:30 A.M., the trustees chose to postpone final action until the next morning.[55]

About the time Barnett signed the legislation early Thursday morning, a twenty-seven-by-thirteen-foot cross made of oil-soaked sacks burned on the ground in front of an Ole Miss dormitory. The same evening in front of the gymnasium where transfer students were to register on Thursday, a small wooden cross bore the inscription "One Killed Here." Earlier on Wednesday, someone altered a sign at the campus's main gate to read "New *white* students report to Lyceum Building 117." The three minor events, whether the work of protesters or pranksters, evidenced serious opposition to Meredith's expected registration. Despite the incidents, the campus and the town remained quiet under an "apprehensive calm."[56]

Students registered for classes on Wednesday as usual. Students and faculty did not know what to expect from the governor, the federal government, or even their own chancellor. Few would talk about Meredith or the situation that was building on their campus. Most, especially out-of-state students, wanted the university to remain open and did not consider the principles of states' rights and segregation worth risking the closure of Ole Miss, and many seemed to expect that integration was inevitable. Among university officials only Hugh Clegg spoke to reporters: "No comment." Oxford residents were only slightly more talkative. One did say of Meredith, "He's got more guts or less brains than anybody I ever heard of." Perhaps the individual most missed was William Faulkner, the Nobel prizewinner who had died ten weeks earlier; as a Memphis reporter lamented, he would have had acute observations as the storm approached.[57]

Though Faulkner was absent, more than fifty reporters from across the country and scores of policemen converged on Oxford. The university required reporters to register and to wear name tags, but it also tried to make their visits comfortable by turning a Lyceum boardroom into a pressroom, with typewriters, telephones, free coffee, and lunches. As the radio, television, and newspaper correspondents waited, they had little to do. A bored Birmingham reporter noticed women students with hemlines one inch above the knee and happily announced that "there has been plenty to watch for besides Meredith." By Wednesday, the biggest story was the presence of scores of law enforcement officers who easily outnumbered the journalists. In addition to eight Ole Miss policemen and eight Oxford patrolmen, Sheriff Joe Ford had only two deputies. Concerned that the local forces might be inadequate, Oxford police on September 18 specially commissioned thirty-four local firemen, ten members of the American Legion, and ten members of the Veterans of Foreign Wars. Five nearby towns volunteered two policemen each for service in Oxford. County sheriffs across the state sent as many as fifty officers. By far the largest contingent came from state agencies. On Wednesday they streamed into town, some in plainclothes and unmarked cars. Arriving sometimes with three or four officers in each of more than seventy cars, they included members of the state highway patrol but also officers who investigated auto and cattle theft and who carried out routine investigations. The state officers made the National Guard armory their unofficial headquarters and installed a small radio transmitter. By late Wednesday, September 19, three hundred law enforcement officers were in Oxford and Ole Miss. The FBI also dispatched a dozen agents to Oxford.[58] All anticipated Meredith's arrival.

The week after Barnett's television address, Meredith stayed in seclusion. Concerned for her client's safety, Constance Motley insisted that he stay out of sight in Memphis. Meredith, however, wanted to remain in Mississippi and live his normal life unless a verifiable danger appeared. He believed he should wage his fight from within his state and be responsible for his own security, but he also recognized that success required his survival. A Memphis lawyer arranged for him to stay secluded in a boarding house. Meredith at first objected but was impressed by the lawyer, A. W. Willis, and complied with the plan. After one night in the boarding house, however, Meredith called a cousin in Memphis and arranged to stay with her family instead. He would remain in Memphis until he went to the university.[59]

From Memphis, Meredith watched events unfold. At his second meeting with James McShane, the chief marshal explained that his men would, for Meredith's own security, accompany him when he went to the university to register. For several reasons, the air force veteran had misgivings about the Justice Department's plan. From the beginning of his campaign, his basic concern had been for a better education for Negroes in his state; his own personal safety did not concern him. "If I went around worrying about that I'd be living a pretty miserable life," he said. "I don't worry about me." In any case, he claimed to have confidence in the state to protect him. "I don't think I'll need any federal marshals," he told an interviewer. "I believe Mississippi will protect its citizens." Many times he had defended his home state because he believed it no worse than any other state. "Mississippi does not deserve the poor reputation it has in race relations," he told an interviewer while staying in Memphis. "It is a national problem."[60]

More realistically, Meredith recognized any need for protection would extend far beyond his first days at Ole Miss. In response to McShane's plan,

Meredith argued that the marshals could not be with him at registration and then leave him by himself. Once given protection, he could not survive without it. Either Mississippians could be trusted to take care of him or they could not, reasoned Meredith; the burden could not be assumed by federal authorities and then later shifted to the state. After Meredith insisted that he either would enter, stay, and leave by himself, or he would enter, stay, and leave with federal protection, the Justice Department realized its commitment would be longer than anticipated.[61]

While he waited, Meredith was typically calm, poised, and polite, not "scared or tense." A *New York Times* reporter remarked that his "demeanor is so quiet, it almost masks his zeal to improve the lot of his race in the state of Mississippi." He appeared to be a curious blend of "almost superhuman courage and some naivete" about his mission. In interviews, he reminisced about his boyhood dreams of attending Ole Miss and explained his personal obligation to act to change society. Only with better education could the black community develop the necessary leadership among lawyers, businessmen, and politicians. The traditional black leaders, preachers and teachers, could not be expected to effect the necessary change because they were vulnerable to white authority, so people like Meredith had to act. With more and stronger leaders, blacks could work effectively to end racial discrimination. Meredith was, however, realistic about what he could accomplish. "I don't expect any spectacular things to occur when I enter Ole Miss," he admitted. "Next week a Negro will still be a Negro in Mississippi." But he was confident that Mississippi would be "the best state within 25 years," and he wanted to stay in the state and "have something to say about how Negroes will live in Mississippi."[62]

The next, crucial move in Meredith's mission would be for him to gain actual admission to the segregated university. Nearly everyone involved expected the "showdown" to come on Thursday, registration day for transfer students. Meredith's lawyers told reporters that he would enroll at the university on Thursday. According to one commentator, "The federal government can't back down, neither can Gov. Ross Barnett. . . . If Meredith is going to make his play, he must do it soon. If the Governor is to stop him, he will have to show his cards at the same time."[63]

PART THREE

A Fortress of Segregation Falls

16. Initial Skirmishing: September 20–25, 1962

On Thursday, September 20, James Meredith went to Oxford to register but was refused. In the following week he tried three more times, unsuccessfully. While he moved between Memphis, Oxford, and Jackson in his attempt to enroll, larger forces worked to assist or thwart him. The Kennedy administration tried for a peaceful solution, and the federal courts eliminated barriers to his registration. At the same time, Mississippi whites labored to prevent any breach in segregation. Governor Ross Barnett extended his secret negotiations with the Kennedys, and local courts acted to stymie Meredith. Sometimes the moves appeared orchestrated, but in other instances coordinated only by a shared objective of preventing integration. As the controversy continued, the marshals and the military escalated their preparations. Increasingly complicated by intricate strategies, multiple moves, and confusing feints, the contest resembled a chess match more than a game of checkers. In the tangled skirmishing, the university often was ignored. As one commentator noted, "Ole Miss [has become] a pawn in what promises to be a fight to the finish between segregationist Governor Barnett and the Federal Government."[1]

In the midst of the turbulence, one prophetic voice called in a different direction. In a sermon on an Oxford radio station on Thursday, September 20, Reverend Duncan Gray said that "the question now is not a matter of 'if,' but 'when.'" He identified "*three* clear and unmistakable duties." First, Christians had not just to avoid violence but to do everything possible to create a "mood and climate" that would prevent violence. Second, they had "a clear duty to obey and uphold the *Law* as it is interpreted by our court." Accepting that Meredith would enroll, Gray pointed to a third, ultimate responsibility: "we will have the *continuing* duty to see that this new student is accepted and treated *as a person*; that he is not exposed to badgering, torment, or ridicule; that he is given the opportunity to stand on his own merits as a student among students, person among persons, regardless of the color of his skin." Gray implored Christians not to shrink from the task: "We should *rejoice* in the fact that God has *chosen* us to live in this difficult period; that God is offering us the opportunity and the *privilege* to make a truly significant contribution to the history of our state and nation and to the cause of justice and peace among the sons of men."[2]

Whatever its effect in Oxford, Gray's message did not reach Jackson. At 8:30 A.M. Thursday, Justice of the Peace Homer Edgeworth heard the voting fraud case against Meredith. With neither Meredith nor his lawyer, R. Jess Brown, present, Edgeworth accepted testimony from the prosecuting attorney and from the Hinds County Circuit Court deputy clerk. After a ten-minute hearing, Edgeworth convicted Meredith, sentenced him to one year in the Hinds County jail, fined him one hundred dollars, and ordered him to pay court costs. To prevent his enrollment later that day at the university, Edgeworth ordered his immediate arrest, and officers left for Oxford.[3]

Thursday morning, lawyers for the LDF and the Department of Justice also worked to clear the legal path for Meredith's enrollment. Constance Motley filed three motions in federal district court. One asked for an injunction to stop Hinds County officers from arresting Meredith. A second sought protection against the injunction issued by chancery judge L. B. Porter that barred Meredith's enrollment. The third asked for a temporary retraining order to prevent enforcement of the new law to exclude anyone convicted of a crime involving moral turpitude. Justice Department lawyers asked the court to prevent anyone from keeping Meredith out of Ole Miss because that would "frustrate and obstruct" the court orders and mean that Meredith had been excluded "solely on account of his race and color."[4]

At about noon Judge Mize, joined by Judge Harold Cox, halted action against Meredith on his voter registration conviction under the new state law but ordered a hearing on it for the following Monday. They also deferred action on Porter's injunction until a hearing early the next week. A few minutes later during a hearing recess in Hattiesburg, a three-judge panel of the Fifth Circuit Court of Appeals responded to a Justice Department appeal by prohibiting the enforcement of Porter's injunction, in addition to confirming the district court's action against the new state law and Meredith's conviction.[5] By Thursday afternoon the federal courts had removed the legal barriers to Meredith's enrollment.

Negotiations between the Justice Department and state officials continued. Thursday morning, after Meredith's conviction, Attorney General Patterson called Burke Marshall to tell him that he could no longer guarantee their agreement of the night before; he now could not promise Meredith's safe return to Memphis because he might be arrested while in Oxford. Patterson explained that he had no control over local police and prosecutors. After learning of the changed circumstances, Marshall telephoned Tom Watkins to discuss the court order against Meredith's arrest. Watkins believed Barnett would change his mind and offered to talk to him about preventing Meredith's arrest; after he and Barnett conferred, Watkins and Patterson told Kennedy and Marshall that Barnett had ordered the police to leave Meredith alone.[6]

Still worried that someone might try to apprehend Meredith, Patterson wanted to consult directly with the governor before reactivating the plan to bring Meredith to the campus later that Thursday, but Barnett had spent the morning at his sister's funeral. Not completely confident that the plan would work, Patterson suggested that Meredith should begin his drive to Oxford. In another call just after lunch, Patterson reported to Kennedy that he had urged the district attorney in Oxford to keep the sheriff from arresting Meredith and, more important, that the governor had so informed other sheriffs. The plan proceeded. Patterson expected the highway patrol to escort Meredith and the marshals to the campus, the registrar to refuse Meredith's admission, and the patrol to get the Meredith party safely out of Oxford. Confirming the plan, Kennedy told Patterson, "I really appreciate your help. It will make a helluva difference." Subsequent calls, including one between Barnett and Kennedy, eased Washington's worries about Meredith's safety.[7]

If privately Barnett acquiesced in the plan, publicly he defied any attempt at integration. An executive order commanded the IHL board, the registrar, and "all authorities concerned" to "refuse" Meredith admission. Barnett also sued in Jackson and Oxford chancery courts to bar Meredith from Ole Miss. His complaint explained that not only were the court orders that compelled Meredith's admission illegal but his enrollment would violate state law because "James H. Meredith, the Defendant, is a colored man" and that under the state constitution and law the university was solely "for members of the white race." The governor further contended that Meredith did not meet the requirement of good character because he was a convicted criminal.[8]

Barnett insisted that Meredith could obtain an education at Jackson State but that he really wanted "to foment strife, disturbance, riot and breaches of the peace." He predicted that Meredith's entrance into the university "would be inflammatory, setting off confusion, disorder and disturbance among the students at the University, and trouble, riot and possible bloodshed threatening the safety of the Defendant and others who might be engaged in assisting him." To prevent chaos and perpetuate segregation, the governor asked for a temporary injunction against Meredith's enrollment. Chancery courts in Oxford and Jackson granted temporary injunctions blocking Meredith or anyone in his behalf from working to get him admitted.[9]

Barnett flew to Oxford on a highway patrol airplane with Paul Johnson and Dugas Shands. He expected to block Meredith's admission. The IHL board three days before had sent Meredith a telegram directing him to appear at the board office on Thursday afternoon, but everyone knew that Meredith would instead appear at the university. In a telegram to the trustees Wednesday night, Robert Kennedy announced that Meredith would go to Oxford because the Justice Department had received no assurance that he would be allowed to register in Jackson. The trustees and university administrators could, he insisted, legally do nothing to prevent his enrollment. While Kennedy expected to cooperate with Barnett "to avoid law enforcement problems," he made clear his commitment "to take all appropriate action to make the orders of the courts effective."[10]

Pressed from all sides, the trustees reconvened Thursday morning, hours after their frustrating late-night session. After a motion to admit Meredith, Jobe read Tally Riddell's explanation of why he would vote to admit Meredith. It outraged M. M. Roberts, a Hattiesburg lawyer and Barnett appointee. After intense debate, the board defeated it by a one-vote margin. During a lunch recess, the governor notified the board's secretary that he was going to Oxford and wanted authority to deal with Meredith's application. When the trustees reconvened, they discussed the possibility of flying to Oxford, but Roberts proposed that they appoint the governor the registrar and give him "the full power, authority, rights and discretion of this Board to act on all matters pertaining to or concerned with" Meredith's application. With Verner Holmes dissenting, the board approved. After Meredith failed to appear at the board office as directed, the trustees at 3:35 P.M. announced Barnett had become the Ole Miss registrar.[11]

In the morning, hundreds of students milled around in front of the Lyceum waiting for Meredith and chanting "Hotty Toddy," the school fight song, and various segregation slogans such as "Glory, glory segregation. The South shall rise again." By the middle of the afternoon the crowd had grown to more than one thousand. When Barnett arrived, he went to the Center for Continuation Study to meet Meredith. To a newsman's question about whether he intended to allow integration, the governor replied, "Hell, no." The crowd surged toward the continuation center and cheered, "Hold that line, Governor!" and "Push him back, push him back, way back!" and "Two, four, six, eight. We don't want to integrate." Barnett entered the building, closed and guarded since noon, and conferred with Clegg, Ellis, Tad Smith, and several alumni leaders who had been meeting most of the day. More than one hundred highway patrolmen, standing shoulder to shoulder, secured the front of the building and kept the crowd and scores of reporters fifty feet back. Assorted police backed up the patrolmen.[12]

On his way from Memphis, Meredith rode with St. John Barrett, a Justice Department lawyer, Chief Marshal James P. McShane, and another marshal. Barrett, a thirty-nine-year-old Californian who had worked in the Civil Rights Division since 1957, met Meredith for the first time that morning. McShane, who first met Meredith several days earlier at his lawyer's office, would play a key role in Meredith's admission. Head of the marshals for only a few months, the heavy-drinking, former welterweight Golden Gloves champion and twenty-year veteran of the New York City police "personified the Hemingwayesque image of a policeman." In the mid-1950s McShane met Robert Kennedy when Kennedy served as a counsel to the Senate's Permanent Subcommittee on Investigations (the rackets committee). Kennedy convinced McShane in 1957 to join the committee staff as an investigator. After two years, McShane went to work for the Senate Anti-Trust Committee as it began investigating professional boxing. In 1960 McShane, who had only an eighth-grade education, worked briefly on security for presidential candidate John F. Kennedy, and in May 1961 the president named him marshal for the District of Columbia. He directed the marshals in Montgomery at the time of the Freedom Rides. In May 1962 the fifty-three-year-old McShane became chief of the marshals.[13]

Reaching Batesville, twenty-five miles west of Oxford, Meredith's group stopped as planned at the highway patrol station where Colonel T. B. Birdsong, the head of the patrol, and several patrol cars joined them to provide an escort. A military helicopter waited in Memphis to retrieve Meredith and the federal officials if the situation became threatening. When the small caravan arrived at the continuation center about 4:30 P.M., hisses, boos, and cries of "Go home, nigger" and "nigger, nigger, nigger" welcomed Meredith on his first visit to Ole Miss. Accompanied by Barrett, McShane, and another marshal, Meredith, dressed in a brown suit with a white shirt and tie, entered the building without comment. All reporters remained outside.[14]

Directed to a small auditorium, Meredith's group met their adversaries, Ellis, Barnett, Paul Johnson, and Dugas Shands. Others present included one of the governor's former law partners, his cousin James Arden Barnett, university attorney Jack Doty, and several other Ole Miss friends and officials. When Barnett heard St. John Barrett's name, he asked how it was spelled. Told it was spelled without the "n," Barnett, as southerners often did, wondered if he were related to a friend named Barrett; misunderstanding the friendly comment as a put-down, Barrett momentarily bristled. Meredith observed the forced pleasantries as people shook hands and introduced themselves; as the only black person in the room, he noticed that nobody extended a hand or offered a personal greeting. Chancellor Williams and Dean Lewis were absent because Patterson had informed them that the board's action left them "without authority to take any action" regarding Meredith's admission.[15]

Barnett, Ellis, and Doty sat behind tables at the front of the room, and Meredith, Barrett, McShane, and another marshal sat on the front row of chairs, while observers sat or stood in the back. Asked by the governor to explain his presence, Barrett said that he represented the Department of Justice. When the governor asked if anyone had a statement to make, Barrett replied, "Yes, sir, we came here to have you register Meredith in accordance with the court order." Then Ellis read the trustees' resolution transferring the registrar's power to the governor. He did not refuse to register Meredith but said the board had relieved him of that authority. Barrett asked Ellis if he realized the federal courts had ordered the university to register Meredith, but Ellis had nothing more to say. He refused to respond when Barrett asked about being in contempt of court, and he refused to give Barrett a copy of his statement. He walked to the back of the room.[16]

After a pause, Governor Barnett asked Meredith, "What can I do for you?"

"I want to register," Meredith replied.

The governor then read a formal proclamation. To protect the citizens of Mississippi, Barnett declared, "You, James H. Meredith, are hereby refused admission as a student to the University of Mississippi." As registrar, Barnett repeated in more general and veiled terms the arguments that he made earlier in the day in asking for injunctions against Meredith: Ole Miss was for whites only; Meredith's admission would cause turmoil and violence; Barnett had the duty to maintain peace; and public order required continued segregation at the university. Barnett then gave Meredith a copy of the proclamation.[17]

Barrett told the governor that the federal government denied his proclamation had any legal effect because the trustees and the registrar remained under federal court order to register Meredith. To thwart the federal courts would put them in contempt. When Barrett asked Barnett if he realized that he was in contempt, Barnett bristled, "Who are you to say that I am in contempt?" Barrett conceded that he did not have the power to hold anyone in contempt. After the exchange, Meredith, Barrett, and the two marshals left the building.[18]

Outside during the twenty-minute meeting, the students sang and chanted. To some observers the crowd seemed more curious than threatening, more like a pep rally than an incipient riot. When Meredith emerged, the crowd jeered, booed, and taunted him; he responded only with the slightest smile and wave as he got in a car to return to Memphis. As it departed, some rushed to stop it but could only chase and spit on it as it left. After Meredith escaped unharmed, the police abandoned their cordon. About five minutes later when Barnett emerged, the cheering crowd rushed up to congratulate their hero. He told the throng, "The only comment I have to make is that the application of James H.

Meredith has been denied." One account reported an "ear-splitting roar of approval." The governor then flew back to the capital.[19]

On Thursday afternoon, for the first time, the two sides had come face to face outside a courtroom. Twenty months after applying, Meredith finally stepped onto the campus, and he and the governor had their first personal encounter. More important, federal officers squared off against state representatives, as their battle moved beyond the rhetorical to the physical. In their first contest, Barnett seemed the clear victor: Meredith was rejected, the federal authorities departed without a fight, and racial segregation was preserved. In his defense of the southern way of life, however, Barnett had, perhaps unwittingly, raised the ante by encouraging his constituents to believe in ultimate victory. At the same time, the Kennedy administration could not ignore the open challenge to federal authority. Even more after Thursday afternoon, neither side could yield.

The Justice Department took the next step. After conferring with his superiors, attorney Harold Flannery petitioned the federal court in Meridian for a hearing on contempt charges against the chancellor, the dean, and the registrar because they, "and other persons acting in concert with them, failed and refused to permit James Howard Meredith to register and enroll at the University of Mississippi solely on account of his race." The petition alleged that their actions "constituted disobedience and contempt of this Court's order." Early Thursday evening, as a janitor cleaned the federal office building, Flannery filed his motion with a secretary who had stayed late in the clerk's office. After she processed the papers, he took them to Mize's hotel, where he found the judge having dinner in the restaurant. Accompanied to his hotel room by Flannery, Mize signed the order for a hearing the next day. He decided that Ole Miss officials "are now failing and refusing to discontinue . . . excluding Negro students from the University of Mississippi solely because of their race and color." Late Thursday evening lawyers for the federal government asked a three-judge panel of the Court of Appeals sitting in Hattiesburg to issue a similar citation against the trustees, and the judges directed the trustees to appear in New Orleans the following Monday. The Justice Department continued to avoid a legal fight with the governor.[20]

At the hearing on contempt charges against the university leaders, three hundred observers, many of them alumni, packed the second-floor courtroom in the Meridian post office building. Powerful lawyers represented each side. From the LDF, Jack Greenberg joined Constance Motley, as did Jess Brown, Meredith's local counsel. The Department of Justice was represented by Robert Owen of the Civil Rights Division, who questioned witnesses, and Burke Marshall, who came from Washington mainly to observe. The defendants also marshaled an impressive array of legal talent—Joe Patterson, Dugas Shands, Tom Watkins, Charles Clark, and Fred B. Smith. The seventy-year-old Smith conducted most of the defense case. He had practiced law in Ripley since graduating from Ole Miss's law school in 1914. He had served several terms in the legislature and had been president of both the state bar and the state bankers association.[21]

Most of the three-hour hearing consisted of testimony by St. John Barrett. Before he took the stand, the defense asked Judge Mize to broaden the case against the three from civil contempt to include criminal contempt. The Justice Department objected, perhaps because it suspected a ploy to keep the defendants from testifying or because it realized the three could not be charged later with criminal contempt if cleared in the hearing. Judge Mize agreed to the defense request.[22]

Questioned by his colleague Robert Owen, Barrett described events of the day. According to one reporter, "Waves of unrestrained laughter twice surged over the audience" and broke the tension in Mize's courtroom—once when Barrett referred to Barnett as Governor Patterson (the governor of Alabama) and, second, when he mistakenly called Ellis the registrar of voters. Under cross-examination by Fred Smith, Barrett conceded that neither he nor Meredith asked to see the chancellor or the dean and did not ask where they were. After Barrett left the stand, the defense called Hugh Clegg and Frank Everett to testify. Clegg said that neither the chancellor nor the dean had anything to do with registration, and he pointed out that the events in question occurred more than three hundred yards from the chancellor's office. Everett, a prominent alumnus, corroborated that neither Williams nor Lewis had been present and that nobody requested to see them.[23]

Before final arguments, Judge Mize threw out the criminal contempt charges. The civil complaint remained, and Marshall then made the case against the university leaders. He rejected the claim that the defendants had only followed board orders not to admit Meredith. According to Marshall, the actions of the board and governor were "legally ineffective" in trying to take responsibility away from the university officials. Decrying defiance of the courts, Marshall claimed that the court's injunction continued to control the defendants who "still run the university." Despite the actions of others, they "should have taken stronger steps to insure the registration of Meredith." He made a simple argument: "They should be instructed whether they think they have the authority or not, to admit Meredith, to arrange his class schedule, and to take all other steps necessary to treat him as other students."[24]

Fred Smith, brought into the case by the defense at nine o'clock the night before, replied, "These men have not consciously disobeyed the court order." In fact, the chancellor and the dean had no responsibility for registration and were not in the building when Meredith was rejected. Though the registrar was present, he acted "under specific instructions of the trustees by whom he was employed" and only read a statement saying the authority over registration had been taken from him. Smith also reported Joe Patterson's call advising the three administrators to do nothing. "The matter was taken out of their hands," Smith claimed. "They had no authority. They had no power." Instead the defense lawyer blamed Barnett who "alone denied the admission."[25]

After conferring with Judge Harold Cox, who was hearing another case but occasionally came into the hearing, Judge Mize dismissed the contempt complaints. According to Mize, the trustees had withdrawn from university officials "all power . . . to act upon the application of James Meredith." In addition, Mize specifically declared that Ellis's authority had been "fully and completely withdrawn" and that he was "powerless to do anything." Mize decided, "The whole power, the entire power had been invested in the Governor of the State of Mississippi." When Mize announced his decision, the defendants smiled with relief, but their predicament had not been fully resolved. Justice Department lawyers said that, although they would not appeal, they would instead seek to have the three administrators added to the trustees' contempt hearing scheduled for Monday in New Orleans.[26]

Two other potentially significant events on Friday garnered less notice. In Miami, Henry King Stanford, the chairman of SACS's commission on colleges, said his group followed events at Ole Miss "with gravest concern." The day after Barnett rejected Meredith, Stanford pointed out that "capricious and unwarranted political interference with the operation of state colleges and universities" especially troubled SACS. It would continue to monitor developments and gather all the facts before it did anything related to accreditation. A different fiscal threat came from Representative William Ryan (D-NY) who was annoyed that the university continued to receive federal funds while the state flagrantly disobeyed federal law. Frustrated by Barnett's defiance, Ryan introduced a bill to prohibit all federal funds for institutions that deny admission on account of race.[27]

Over the weekend, as each side prepared to battle in New Orleans, tensions rose. Hodding Carter observed that the "minor skirmishing is over and the real war was scheduled to begin." Discussion of the case permeated the state; even at high school and college football games, people speculated about it. Barnett closeted Saturday with his closest counselors to consider his options in the constantly changing case. Whites seemed increasingly determined in their support of Barnett. He received endorsements from the Flora Chamber of

Commerce, the Clinton Junior Chamber of Commerce, the Mississippi Sheriff's Association, former governor Hugh L. White, and countless newspapers. The politically powerful Mississippi Association of Supervisors gave their "full, non-wavering and faithful support."[28]

Despite the apparent consensus, some whites did demur. Curtis H. Mullen, editor of the *Madison County Herald*, observed that "it seems unlikely and unrealistic that the Governor will be able to call the turn" in his showdown with the federal government. Hazel Brannon Smith blasted the governor's "emotional binge" that was "taking [the state] off down a dead-end road in an irresponsible action" reminiscent of events before the Civil War. Possibly closing the university especially troubled some. The Marshall County Bar Association, for example, resolved that the "preservation of the University of Mississippi should be a consideration paramount to all others."[29]

At the same time, in Jackson a few white business leaders worried about violence and chaos in the developing crisis. On Sunday, September 23, William H. Mounger and Calvin Wells of Lamar Life Insurance Company, Baxter Wilson of Mississippi Power and Light, and Tom Hederman of the *Jackson Clarion-Ledger* discussed for several hours in Wilson's office what to do. They did not advocate integration but wanted to avoid a disaster. They also sympathized with the unfair position of friends on the board. The next two nights Mounger arranged meetings with additional participants, but without arch-segregationists Hederman or Wells. Though the group failed to decide what to do, their meetings quietly began a movement counter to the growing hysteria. As their worries increased, they would meet again.[30]

The most determined and outspoken opposition to Barnett came from the NAACP. On Saturday, Medgar Evers announced, "We are winning. The fight is half over." He expected Meredith would finally register for the fall semester. "We feel it is now time for the federal government to step in and enforce the court decision," said the state NAACP head. "We don't want to think of federal troops coming into Mississippi, but if it takes that to enforce the court order, I think they should be brought in." A confident Constance Motley said that if Meredith got a favorable ruling in New Orleans, he would register whether he made the official deadline or not. In Detroit, Meredith's older brother Emmitt said, "It's something he has to do. I think it's the right thing." The national NAACP also came to Meredith's aid. Pointing to Barnett's willingness to "go to jail," the NAACP requested that Kennedy "call on the governor to cease and desist these defiant actions." If Barnett persisted in his defiance, the NAACP wanted the administration to use "all power of the federal government" against him.[31]

Justice Department attorneys, however, decided not to move directly against

Barnett, even if the governor sometimes seemed to be daring his federal opponents. They suspected that Barnett wanted to be jailed to help him in a 1964 senate campaign against John Stennis. The department also did not want to personalize the contest: "This is not Kennedy against Barnett in 15 rounds. The issue is the law, and it is better to keep it that way." As a result the administration left Barnett alone, at least for the moment, but he persisted. About the time of the appeals court hearing, the governor issued another executive proclamation to protect state officials convicted of contempt. Under the Tenth Amendment, he maintained, all state officials had the "legal right, obligation and duty not to acquiesce, impair, waive or surrender" the state's rights. Any federal agent who tried to arrest or fine a state official should, therefore, be "summarily arrested and jailed." When a joint legislative session heard the order, it applauded and cheered. Later Barnett told several legislators, "I'm going all the way."[32]

The Fifth Circuit Court of Appeals convened at 11:00 A.M. Monday, a mere five and a half hours before registration for the fall semester closed. All of the judges, except an ailing Ben Cameron, sat to consider the case. Outside the old post office building, a half-dozen segregationists carried Confederate flags and signs that said, "We need more people like Governor Barnett" and "God help us keep calm, cool and segregated." Of the hundreds who had gathered hours earlier, only a few got courtroom seats. In addition to the eight judges and the defendants, nearly a score of lawyers entered the courtroom. The armada of attorneys for the state included Charles Clark and former governor J. P. Coleman. The plaintiffs were represented by Burke Marshall and John Doar and by Constance Motley, Jack Greenberg, and R. Jess Brown.[33]

Judge Tuttle presided over the tense, five-hour hearing. According to one report, the "main fireworks in the courtroom action centered around barbs hurled at Mississippi attorneys from the bench. The judges cut through legal language several times to point out that the only issue so far as they were concerned was that Meredith be admitted at once." Another account referred to the "caustic remarks" from the judges. Charles Clark directed the Mississippi case, while John Doar handled most of the work for the plaintiffs. The presentation of documents for the record and arguments and summations by the lawyers took most of the time. Only Jobe and Ellis testified.[34]

As the first witness, Jobe explained that the board's directions to the university removed from its officials all authority over Meredith's application. Before Motley asked another question, Judge Brown interjected that the witness had not answered her question. Jobe then told the court, "No, it gave them no instructions when they had no authority. The board," he continued, "reserved to itself the authority in the matter of Meredith." After Jobe, Ellis took the stand and informed the court that he, the chancellor, and the dean decided, "when the decision became ours, that we would do exactly what the court told us to do, and that meant registering Meredith." Jobe's and Ellis's answers did much to relieve Ole Miss officials of responsibility and made more likely the dropping of contempt charges against them.[35] The board remained culpable.

Abstaining from calling witnesses, defense lawyers presented arguments why their clients were not in contempt of court, and the judges repeatedly showed impatience with their claims. Charles Clark, for example, maintained that the court could not act until it settled the question of whether the "power of the court is paramount to the authority of the governor." Dismissing the concern, Judge Richard Rives responded "The governor is not above the prerogatives of this court." When Malcolm M. Montgomery blamed conflicting state laws and state court injunctions, Judge Griffin Bell retorted, "They [the trustees] are constitutional officers and in my opinion the worst thing they did was abandon their authority to the governor." Agreeing with Bell, Judge Wisdom observed, "They delegated their powers to a man whose acts they could predict with absolute certainty. Is that not defiance?"[36]

Chester Curtis, a Clarksdale lawyer and Ole Miss alumnus who represented the university officials, argued that Barnett's actions had prevented the chancellor, dean, and registrar from complying with the court orders. Alumnus William Barbour of Yazoo City claimed that they had never willingly defied the court, and he urged the judges, "Put yourself in the position of a college registrar if the governor comes in to take over your office." Interrupting, Judge Joseph C. Hutcheson of Texas, first appointed to the bench by President Woodrow Wilson, corrected Barbour: "That is a misconception of the Governor's powers. In our state we impeach the Governor for interfering, and you all look like you are going to reward him." Hutcheson then asked, "Were you relying on the doctrine of interposition, which was knocked out at Appomattox?" When defense lawyers still tried to excuse the Ole Miss administrators, again Hutcheson asked, "Counsel, would you first state where in the law an injunction goes off or on according to the opinion of the enjoined person as to whether they are acting in good faith?"[37]

The judges repeatedly questioned the defense attorneys and displayed disbelief in their arguments. Just before a noon recess, Judge Tuttle observed, "I feel a prima facie case that the defendants have not complied with the court order has been made." During the afternoon, other judges indicated that they agreed. Judge Brown commented that the Hinds County justice of the peace who had convicted Meredith in the voter registration case "is in violation of the order too, isn't he?" When the defense mentioned the injunctions issued by chancery court judges, Judge Tuttle wondered if the court could enjoin all of the chancery judges from interfering in the Meredith case. Chester Curtis asked the court to dismiss the case because Judge Mize had found the defendants not guilty of contempt, but Judge Tuttle pointed out that they were charged with contempt of an order of an appeals court, not of Mize's district court. Judge Hutcheson, questioning the attorney general's legal advice to the trustees, asked, "Did you advise them that this monkey business of coming around pretending to take over the school was legal?"[38] In every way the defense was on the defensive.

In her closing, Motley proposed that "the appellant be registered right here and now in open court by the Registrar of the University of Mississippi." Burke Marshall emphasized that the "basic problem is not just the act of registration, but accepting him as a student on a continued attendance at the University." He believed the university officials would comply if the courts could "make the Board of Trustees face up to its responsibilities." In addition he wanted the court to stop Barnett's interference because, as he told the court, "Defiance of the court's order stems directly from the governor's act of rejecting Meredith." Judge Tuttle, however, pointed out, "Yet no one has suggested that the governor be cited."[39]

Charles Clark's closing argument also focused on Barnett's responsibility. He claimed the trustees' innocence because they had delegated the registrar's responsibility to Governor Barnett. Shifting the blame from his clients, Clark acknowledged Barnett wanted to frustrate the court's desegregation order: "You have the solemn declaration of the Governor of the State of Mississippi that he is going to close that institution." Judge Tuttle dismissed Barnett's threat by saying that "we have heard that of every state in the South," and Judge Wisdom refused to say the court would not move against Barnett for contempt. When a judge asked why the trustees had not sought an injunction to prevent Barnett's closing of the university, Clark only mustered, "I don't know the answer to that." Late in the afternoon, Judge Tuttle proposed that the defense legal team canvas their clients to determine if "they will immediately comply with whatever order the Court issues." The court recessed for fifteen minutes.[40]

During the recess, the trustees conferred. Ira "Shine" Morgan, who was hard of hearing, asked for an explanation:

"Did I hear that Judge say," inquired the Oxford appliance dealer and Barnett appointee who had stood with him, "that if we didn't let Meredith in Ole Miss, that he was going to fire us?"

"That's right, Shine."

"And that he would send us to jail?"

"Yes."

"And he would kick us off the Board and put people on who would let him in?"

"That's right, Shine."

"Now let me get this straight. That judge said he was going to kick us off the Board and put people on who would let Meredith in, if we didn't vote to let him go to Ole Miss, and that he was going to fine us and put us in jail!"

"That's right, Shine, and he gave you fifteen minutes to make up your mind."

"Wonder why he gave us so much time!"[41]

While the trustees agreed to comply, the judges reached a conclusion. When the hearing reconvened at 6:00 P.M., Judge Tuttle announced that the trustees had "willfully and intentionally violated the Court's order." When Tuttle asked what the board intended to do to comply with the order, the chairman promised that the trustees, individually and as a board, "will enter any order and do any act that this Court may direct them to do, as, if, and when the Court directs them to do it." Satisfied, Tuttle declared that the court would not find them in contempt but would expect the board to rescind its September 4 order stripping university officials of authority over Meredith's application and to withdraw its September 20 delegation of that power to the governor. At Motley's insistence, the court required the board to guarantee Meredith's "continued attendance." The court at first also wanted the trustees to assure his registration by noon the following day. To objections about insufficient time to return to Mississippi, Tuttle snorted, "Well, you are only 40 miles from the State of Mississippi." After discussion, the court extended the deadline until 4:00 P.M. on Tuesday, and left it up to the two sides' lawyers where the registration would occur, Oxford or Jackson. At Clark's suggestion of the closer Jackson, everyone agreed that Ellis would be at the board office the next day. After adjournment at 6:32 P.M., the judges issued the order.[42]

Monday evening at their New Orleans hotel, the trustees and their lawyers drafted an explanation of their actions. Emphasizing their unity throughout the New Orleans hearing, they declared, "It was stated from the bench that upon our disobedience the court would forthwith admit Meredith and would appoint someone to register him." The trustees admitted, "It was apparent that fine and imprisonment in amounts unknown to us would not prevent Meredith's admission." They had not defended states' rights and segregation to the very last, but they trusted that Mississippians "will understand that we have done our best in a most difficult situation."[43]

Other Mississippians wanted to take extreme measures to prevent integration. During the same evening that the trustees explained their new position,

Lafayette County sheriff Joe Ford, apparently on behalf of the Mississippi Sheriffs Association, proposed a novel plan to dig up the streets entering the campus and build barriers to Meredith's entrance. When the suggestion reached the trustees, they denied permission and declared that nobody should interfere with traffic or do anything to impede Meredith's arrival. The board directed that the court orders must be obeyed. Though rebuffed, the sheriffs remained on campus in force all week.[44]

In reaction to the appeals court's directives, James Meredith warily observed, "I've been admitted a lot of times before." He would claim success only after he enrolled. On the other side, the state attorney general said, "The constitutional rights of 5,000 students at the University of Mississippi have been ignored to gratify the pretended constitutional rights of one." The Justice Department, however, announced, "We are making arrangements for Meredith to register." He was expected to register Tuesday afternoon in Jackson, where Barnett still claimed that "we have a lot of steps left we can take."[45]

The sudden events shook the publicly resolute and confident Barnett. When Robert Kennedy told him early Monday evening that the board had agreed to register Meredith, a stunned Barnett could only ask, "Did they agree to that?" Assured that they had, Barnett replied, "All of them? That's really shocking to me." Barnett repeated his dismay: "I'm surprised at that really. They were so firm about it two days ago. . . . I thought they were going to stand steadfast." When Kennedy reminded him of the court order and tried to plan for Meredith's arrival the next day, Barnett claimed that two state court injunctions barred Meredith's admission. Unmoved, Kennedy informed him that the Court of Appeals would later restrain anyone from interfering, but Barnett balked: "They don't pay attention to the Mississippi courts. That's pretty rough, Mr. Kennedy. That's pretty low down. . . . General, that won't work." While Kennedy persisted on how to register Meredith and avoid a major violent conflict, Barnett could only manage to say, "I tell you now I won't tell you what I'm going to do. I don't know yet." When pressed, Barnett said he needed to find out more about the situation and put the attorney general off until the morning.[46]

Before Barnett and Kennedy talked again, Meredith's quest encountered a curious distraction. On September 25, newspapers reported on Harry S. Murphy, the black sailor who had passed for white in the World War II training program at Ole Miss. He revealed that he had enrolled and studied at the all-white university in 1945–46. Stories included a picture of Murphy holding his Ole Miss identification card and descriptions of his experiences as a student. Suddenly Meredith would be not the *first* black but instead the first *known* black to attend the university, but the change made little difference. Ignoring the early breach, segregationists still emphasized the necessity of keeping Meredith out despite the courts and the Kennedys.[47]

At 8:30 Tuesday morning the court of appeals issued a temporary restraining order to prevent anyone—from the governor to the local sheriffs—from obstructing Meredith's admission. Many white Mississippians, however, refused to relent. The governor issued his own order to law enforcement officers to "do all things necessary that the peace and security of the people of the State of Mississippi are fully protected," which apparently included arresting Meredith or federal officials helping him. Senators drafted a bill to impeach the trustees for deserting the state's cause. At the same time, the group that had secured an injunction from Judge Porter vowed, "If necessary we will proudly join Gov. Ross Barnett in jail." In Jackson on Tuesday morning Barnett plotted with state leaders, while scores of policemen and patrolmen guarded entrances to Ole Miss in case Meredith tried to register in Oxford.[48]

Late Tuesday morning, Robert Kennedy again called Governor Barnett to work out the arrangements for Meredith's enrollment. Asked if anyone would physically interfere with Meredith, Barnett replied, "We are going to do it peacefully. We are not going to have any violence here." At one point, after Barnett said Meredith would be told what to do, Kennedy asked who would tell him, and the governor blurted out, "I am going to tell him that." When Kennedy tried to clarify the plans, Barnett admitted he did not know what would happen but predicted a repeat of what had occurred at the university the previous week, and then another court battle. After sparring over the federal court order versus the state court injunctions, an exasperated Kennedy queried, "Do you consider yourself a part of the Union?" When Barnett defended the superiority of the state courts, Kennedy replied, "This discussion won't get us very far."[49]

Switching to what would happen later in the day, Kennedy asked if Barnett was going to obey federal law, and Barnett stressed state law in addition to federal law and his grievance that the federal courts had been "whittling it [the Constitution] away piecemeal by piecemeal." When he conceded that he ordered the police not to allow Meredith on the campus, Kennedy wondered if that meant he wanted "to fight a pitched battle." Barnett stated, "That's what it's going to boil down to—whether Mississippi can run its institutions or the federal government is going to run things." He swore to uphold state law and, unlike "weak-kneed" southerners, was willing to fight. Kennedy reminded Barnett that Mississippi was part of the United States and asked if the state were leaving. "We have been a part of the United States," Barnett responded, "but I don't know whether we are or not. . . . It looks like we are being kicked around—like we don't belong to it." And he reminded Kennedy, "General, this thing is serious."[50]

Barnett then asked if they really had to fight "over one little boy . . . backed by the NAACP which is a communist front." When Kennedy tried to ignore the question and arrange to talk with Barnett later, the governor agreed but added, "I am going to treat you with every courtesy but I won't agree to let that boy get to Ole Miss. I will never agree to that. I would rather spend the rest of my life in a penitentiary than do that." Kennedy stressed that he had a duty to enforce the law and that the "orders of the court are going to be upheld." The long conversation achieved little. Kennedy promised to call Barnett within half an hour with details about Meredith's plans, but he actually waited several hours.[51]

After huddling with advisers in the morning, at noon Barnett walked from his capitol office across the street to the IHL board office in the fifteen-story Woolfolk Building. After flying from New Orleans about nine o'clock, Dean Lewis and registrar Ellis waited in one of the trustees' offices to enroll Meredith. About the time the governor arrived, they left for lunch, and the trustees convened for a noon meeting. The board unanimously canceled its September 4 action relieving Ole Miss officials of authority over Meredith's application and withdrew its delegation of the registrar's power to Barnett. Without dissent, it also instructed the chancellor, dean, registrar, and all others at the university "to register and receive James H. Meredith for actual admission to, and continued attendance thereafter without any act of discrimination on account of race or color, at the University of Mississippi."[52]

After their meeting the trustees bided their time in their tenth-floor offices. As the hours passed, many legislators came to witness the impending events, and many went to the board's office. Newspaper and television reporters milled around the building where hundreds of spectators also gathered. By late in the day the crowd numbered close to two thousand, including a scattering of blacks. The highway patrol kept them away from the Woolfolk Building, while Jackson police cleared the parking in front of the building and maintained traffic flow.[53]

Early in the afternoon, Marshall talked with Charles Clark, who agreed that Ellis would go to the Jackson federal building to register Meredith. At 1:25 P.M. Robert Kennedy finally reached Barnett at the board office and explained that Meredith would soon land in Jackson and go to the U.S. attorney's office. Confused, Barnett asked where Meredith would try to register, and, though Kennedy seemed unsure, the plan remained the federal building. Kennedy also wanted his promise that Meredith would be protected and that nobody would interfere with him, and Barnett replied, "There will be no violence at all."

Kennedy, however, also wanted to make sure that Meredith would not encounter any interference when he tried to register, but the evasive governor only repeated his pledge about violence. Kennedy promised to call when the plans were definite.[54]

Soon after Kennedy and Barnett talked, Burke Marshall learned in a series of calls with Clark and the head of the trustees that a legislative committee's subpoena prevented Registrar Ellis from leaving the capitol, that the governor had commandeered the board's office, and that state authorities would enforce the court's 4:00 P.M. deadline. In reaction, Marshall called Judge Tuttle and arranged an extension. In a last-minute change of plans, the Justice Department had Meredith go to the Woolfolk Building.[55]

At 3:25 P.M. the border patrol plane carrying Doar, McShane, and Meredith landed in Jackson. The forty-two-year-old Doar was Marshall's assistant in the Civil Rights Division. The son of a Wisconsin lawyer, he practiced law in his home state for ten years after graduating from Princeton and the University of California's law school. A Republican, he joined the department in the Eisenhower administration's last year and stayed to serve under Kennedy. Engaged in litigation and negotiations in the South, he gained a reputation as a friend of the civil rights movement. On the flight from New Orleans, Doar and Meredith had their first real conversation. In subsequent weeks they became nearly inseparable, but never personally close.[56]

Doar, Meredith, and McShane went to the U.S. attorney's office and called Washington to make final arrangements for going to the board office. During their forty-minute stay at the federal building, Kennedy again called Barnett, and they confirmed that Meredith should enter the east entrance and use a waiting elevator to go to room 1007 where the registrar waited. To Kennedy's repeated questions, Barnett promised to control the crowds and protect Meredith. When the attorney general asked if many people were with the governor, Barnett replied, "Oh, I don't know. I can see about 15 or 18 right now. They're high class people." The brief conversation ended with Kennedy's expressing "hope this is all conducted with the dignity of the United States and the Governor of the State of Mississippi," and Barnett's reassurance, "It will be." Fifteen minutes later, Kennedy called again to say the group was on its way.[57]

When Meredith arrived at the Woolfolk Building shortly after 4:30, he found a "curious, worried" crowd of whites and a few cheering black students. With a slight smile, he went with Doar and McShane to the board office. As highway patrolmen cleared the way, they walked from the elevator down the hallway to room 1007. Acting as the doorman, a state representative knocked to announce their arrival, and Barnett, appearing to one observer "tired and pale," opened the door to confront Meredith and the federal men. Doar introduced himself, and they exchanged cordial greetings before Doar tried to hand Barnett a summons, a petition, and a temporary restraining order from the New Orleans federal court. Saying he was "not showing you any disrespect" and "grateful to you for offering it to me," the governor declared that his policy and the instructions of the state attorney general forced him to decline them. After Doar explained the restraining order issued that morning, he announced, "And we would like to get on now, governor, with the business of registering Mr. Meredith."[58]

Standing in the doorway and facing the three visitors, Barnett asked if they intended to register Meredith and if Doar were speaking for him, and Doar answered affirmatively and pointed to Meredith. "Is this James Meredith over here," asked Barnett of the man he had met five days earlier. Looking at Meredith, Barnett invoked the doctrine of interposition. In "order to prevent violence and in order to prevent a breach of peace, and in order for his own protection, and in order to preserve the peace, and in order to maintain and perpetuate the dignity and tranquility of the great and sovereign state of Mississippi," the governor did, as he had done in Oxford, "hereby now and finally deny you admission to the University of Mississippi." Listening over portable radios, the crowd outside cheered. In a gesture of southern courtesy, Barnett presented the original copy of his proclamation to Meredith.[59]

Doar then read to the governor parts of the order issued that morning by the federal appeals court and called on him to let them "see Mr. Ellis and get this young man registered." Unknown to Doar, Ellis was unavailable. Refusing to yield, Barnett responded that, under his oath as governor, he was complying with the state laws and constitution and "certainly I am complying with the constitution of the United States. I have no apology to make for it." He further declared his respect for the state legislature and emphasized his belief in the Tenth Amendment. "Gentlemen, my conscience is clear," he concluded. "Thank you." When Doar tried one final time to leave the court papers with Barnett and asked if he refused to allow them into the office, shouts of "No!" came from the room behind the governor, and he refused. "I do that politely," said Barnett, to which Doar replied, "We leave politely." As Doar, McShane, and Meredith turned to leave, Barnett offered, "Come to see us at the mansion."[60]

After the eight-minute confrontation, Doar, Meredith, and McShane left. Outside the crowd had, according to one report, become "an angry, hate-filled throng," cursing, booing, and jeering Meredith as he emerged. Cries of "Get out of here you black nigger" and "We don't want you nigger" and "Communist" greeted him. One teenager waved a Confederate flag, a couple of women danced, and a few sang "Dixie" to celebrate the victory. Protected by highway patrolmen, a serious and subdued Meredith walked to a waiting border patrol car and rode off, with one heckler kicking the car. The crowd then chanted "We want Ross, we want Ross." After watching events below from a tenth-floor window, Barnett made his way down. An overloaded elevator, stuck between floors, delayed his triumphant appearance. After fifteen minutes, the crowd believed Barnett had left by a rear door and began to disperse, but cheers and applause welcomed Barnett when he finally came out.[61]

In the first two face-to-face skirmishes, Barnett had foiled Meredith. Success emboldened the governor's supporters and caused them to believe victory would be theirs. As a result, the pressure on Barnett intensified. At the same time, the resolve of James Meredith, the Justice Department, and the federal courts never slackened; they responded to the challenges with greater determination that defiance would not prevail. In the coming days, the two sides would engage in further confrontations in the struggle over segregation at Ole Miss.

■ ■

"Everything all right down there?" Robert Kennedy asked Ross Barnett early Tuesday evening, shortly after the governor prevented Meredith's attempt to enroll at the trustees' office. The governor assured Kennedy that the crowd had only booed Meredith and cheered himself. When Barnett said that Meredith had not registered, Kennedy replied that Meredith "is going to show up at classes tomorrow." Caught off guard, Barnett asked if that meant in Oxford and how Meredith could go to classes without first registering. He confessed, "Well, I don't know what will happen now. I don't know what we will do. I didn't dream of a thing like that." When Kennedy urged him to prevent violence, the governor wavered: "There was no bloodshed today— tomorrow or any other day I can't guarantee it. I can't stay up at Ole Miss." But he promised to encourage everyone to avoid violence.[1]

In a rambling appeal, the agitated governor said, "If you knew the feeling of about 99½ percent of the people in this thing you would have this boy withdraw and go somewhere else. I'm sure though . . . you don't understand the situation down here." Once again he blamed the Communist NAACP for stirring up "hatred among the races," and he beseeched Kennedy, "I wish you would talk to them about the South. Get them to let us alone down here." After allowing Barnett to vent his feelings, Kennedy reminded him that Meredith would be in Oxford the next morning. The governor thanked him for calling.[2]

Pressured by the attorney general, the governor had to decide what to do next, but he faced other cascading, conflicting, and uncontrolled events. The Kennedy administration groped for a peaceful resolution of the controversy, and the federal courts considered contempt charges against the governor and the lieutenant governor. At the same time the state legislature whipped up segregationist fervor, and outsiders agitated for people to defend states' rights and segregation in Mississippi. Governor Barnett, who had supplanted the trustees and the Ole Miss administration, had to contend with the competing forces to negotiate his way through the controversy.

A few minutes after his first call, Kennedy telephoned again to ask if 10:00 A.M. would be a good time for Meredith to arrive; the governor agreed but appealed, "General, why don't you keep that boy away?" Referring to the rule of law, the attorney general replied, "Hell, it's my job and my responsibility." Barnett still contended, "You can never convince me that the white and Negro should go together," but Kennedy insisted that the question did not involve their personal opinions. When the governor objected that Meredith had been convicted of a crime, Kennedy reasserted that Barnett objected "because he is a Negro." Barnett then shifted to the "simple and unmistakable" claim that the *Brown* decision was "not the law of the land," but Kennedy ignored him and said, "But anyway, Governor, they will be down there at 10 o'clock." Barnett closed with an invitation to "come by to see us."[3]

Within a few hours, the legislature met in an unusual night session. One reporter compared its anger to the "pre–Civil War scenes from 'Gone with the Wind.'" John McLaurin of Brandon complained that the "President and his little brother" should instead be dealing with the communists in Cuba, while another called on the administration to focus on northern cities "where they rape young women every night." To great cheers, Laurel's E. K. Collins declared that Meredith would not enter Ole Miss "as long as there are red corpuscles in bodies of true Mississippians." The fervor of Barnett's supporters reduced his options: he could not yield to the NAACP, the Kennedys, or the courts. In New Orleans that evening, federal judges ordered the governor into court on Friday to explain why he should not be held in contempt for his directive to arrest federal agents and for his refusal to admit Meredith. After avoiding a showdown, the government now called him to account for his actions. According to the *New York Times*'s Claude Sitton, the conflict "threatened to bring the most serious Federal-state controversy since the Civil War."[4]

The next encounter came Wednesday in Oxford. The campus had settled into a routine with the start of classes and a football victory, but the atmosphere was far from normal. When J. D. Williams returned from the New Orleans hearing, he addressed students over the university radio station. "This is not the time to panic," he declared. After praising their "poise and maturity," he said he recognized that "the temptation to demonstrate is great. But the quiet determined attitude of the students to maintain a normal state of affairs is to be greatly commended." He remained confident that Ole Miss could weather the crisis and "maintain order." After he spoke, the announcer pointed out the irresponsible statements and rumors circulating and urged students to remain calm in the "coming days that may be critical." According to one report, "a tense calm prevailed." Scores of highway patrol cars rolled around campus and town, and the entire state patrol had been on alert since Monday. Countless sheriffs and deputies also deployed to the university, and officers guarded all campus entrances and questioned anyone suspicious.[5]

Faculty and student opinion on the situation varied. The editor of the student newspaper thought most students preferred closing the university to submitting to integration. One student showed little patience: "I'm so tired of this mess, I don't care if they let 50 [Negroes] in." Another said, "No matter who wins, we lose." While students felt ambivalent about segregation and their own education, one said, "We just can't let Ole Miss close. But it doesn't seem as if we'll have any say in the matter." Faculty experienced conflicts involving job security, political pressures, and segregation; one professor thought "most of them are scared." Administrators stressed keeping Ole Miss open and peaceful but realized the power to make decisions had been removed from them. Barnett still held the real power, and he was expected on the campus Wednesday.[6]

Although Barnett planned to fly to Oxford on Wednesday morning to block Meredith's attempt to enroll at 10:00, low clouds prevented his flight and forced him to rush the 165 miles north in his powder-blue Cadillac. Lieutenant Governor Paul Johnson planned to drive to Oxford, and he arrived on schedule and waited for the governor and Meredith to arrive. Flying from New Orleans, Meredith's border patrol plane landed at the Oxford airport at 9:10 A.M. After fifteen minutes of discussion with the state patrol, perhaps to delay until Barnett could arrive, Meredith, Doar, McShane, and six other marshals rode to the university in two border patrol cars as part of a caravan, including three highway patrol escorts. Approaching from the east along University Avenue, the patrol escort turned off on a side street and left the federal force alone to encounter a roadblock at the intersection with South Fifth Street, about a block east of campus.[7]

The Justice Department modified its tactics in the third attempt to enroll Meredith. In telephone negotiations the day before, Burke Marshall reminded Tom Watkins that, in the showdown Barnett seemed to want, the federal government would have more men and would surely win, so he encouraged the Jackson lawyer to advise Barnett to alter his plan. Seeking a compromise to allow the federal government to win without humiliating his state and Barnett, Watkins proposed that Meredith's escorts employ "the mildest kind of force" to "push the Governor aside physically." The use of minimal force would provide Barnett with the excuse that the federal government had "forcibly brought about desegregation." After consultations in the Department of Justice, Marshall instructed McShane and Doar to use some physical force if necessary to push beyond Barnett and to get Meredith onto the campus.[8]

Marshall and the Kennedy administration worked with Watkins because he did not display the belligerence of so many of the governor's archsegregationist advisers, led by William J. Simmons. Control of the Citizens' Councils gave Simmons great influence. Described variously by reporters as the "*eminence blanche* of the Barnett camp" and one of the state's "most radical segregationists," he denied his influence but reportedly helped write Barnett's speeches, including the televised address that invoked interposition. Though not an official member of the administration, Simmons was, according to the *New York Times*, the "chief strategist in the campaign to keep the University of Mississippi white." During the last week of September, at Barnett's request, Simmons lived in the governor's Alumni House suite and participated in the strategy sessions. The "rajah of race," according to the Sovereignty Commission's Erle Johnston, he strengthened the segregationists' cause by bolstering Barnett's resolve.[9] On Wednesday he closely watched events on University Avenue.

Earlier Wednesday morning, after sealing off the campus, a score of unarmed highway patrolmen created a human barrier across University Avenue, and one hundred feet behind them a similar line of sheriffs' deputies formed. Three parked patrol cars made a final barricade. All traffic had been cleared from the street, and most people present were either reporters or law enforcement officers. After their escort pulled onto a side street, Doar, McShane, and Meredith met the roadblock, got out of their car and, with the half-dozen marshals, walked forward. Johnson emerged from a parked car, came through the patrolmen, and stood in the middle of the street. McShane and Doar approached the lieutenant governor, while Meredith, dressed in a conservative suit and carrying a briefcase, stood silently aside. Nobody seemed to pay any attention to him. Everyone focused on the confrontation between the federal and state officials. According to one observer, the "scene was almost hushed."

After Johnson told McShane he was in charge, the marshal declared, "We want to take Mr. Meredith in under the directions of the Federal court and have him registered."

"I'm going to have to refuse Mr. Meredith," responded Johnson, who explained that in Barnett's absence he was "acting in his stead, by his direction and under his instructions." He read the same proclamation Barnett had read to Meredith in their first meeting at the university. After Johnson gave the proclamation to Meredith, the two sides sparred and scuffled. The marshals tried to elbow their way around Johnson; the patrolmen parried every thrust. Either communications or cooperation had broken down, because Johnson did not follow Watkins's plan.

Doar came forward, introduced himself as "an officer of the court," and told Johnson, "We want to register this man."

When Doar tried to give the lieutenant governor a copy of the governor's contempt citation, Johnson refused: "I do not accept [the papers]. I do this politely."

Doar then declared, "We think we are going in now."

"No, I can't let you," replied Johnson.

McShane insisted, "I think it's my duty to try to go through and get Mr. Meredith in there." Doar also explained that he was just doing his duty.

With state troopers shoulder-to-shoulder and crowding in behind him, Johnson told the federal officials, "We are going to block you," and "if there is going to be any violence, it will be on your part and the U.S. Marshals. We will meet force with force."

McShane and Johnson stood toe-to-toe with fists raised. The jostling continued. At one point, Johnson accused McShane of performing for the television cameras. Amid quiet pushing and shoving, McShane, Doar, and the marshals shifted from one side of University Avenue to the other as they looked for an opening, but Johnson and the patrolmen refused to yield. McShane asked, "Governor, are these men acting under your authority, physically preventing us from going in?"

"They are," replied Johnson.

Doar then repeated that they sought only to enforce a court order and warned Johnson that he was violating the court order. Doar directed the patrolmen to "stand aside and let this man in," but the troopers held firm. Finally, Doar relented. He asked Johnson one last time to permit them to enter the campus, and the lieutenant governor refused to respond. Thwarted again in their tense, five-minute confrontation with the state, Doar, McShane, Meredith, and the other marshals returned to the airport. Less than an hour after arriving in Oxford, Meredith commented, "Well, at least I'm getting a lot of flying time."

Back on University Avenue, the assemblage of police broke into applause for Johnson's stand, and Bill Simmons rushed to shake his hand. When Barnett arrived, just as Meredith flew from Oxford, he went straight to the Alumni House to have lunch, take a nap, and confer with Johnson, Simmons, and his other advisers. Though Barnett did not speak to the press, he seemed satisfied and gave no indication that Johnson had violated any agreement. Johnson expressed surprise that the federal agents had tried to force their way through the roadblock, but he maintained he would "do it the same way if I had it to do over again."[10]

Hours after Johnson turned Meredith away, the Fifth Circuit Court of Appeals reentered the proceedings. At the Justice Department's request, Judges Wisdom, Rives, and Brown ordered Johnson to appear at 10:00 A.M. Saturday to explain why he too should not be held in contempt.[11]

Barnett, and now Johnson, had wide support among Mississippi whites. "There has never been more harmony of purpose in Mississippi," concluded Charles Hills. A UPI survey found Mississippians solidly behind Barnett as a "governor with guts." Thousands of supporting telegrams from all over the state and the nation flooded the governor's office. One Vicksburg resident compared Barnett, "a great Southerner," to Robert E. Lee, Stonewall Jackson, and Jefferson Davis. Wednesday evening a unanimous state senate resolution praised Johnson's "outstanding service" in Oxford and recognized him as a "strong right arm to Governor Barnett." One of Barnett's close legislative advisers thought a gun battle between state and federal forces "highly possible," even "likely." The congressional delegation, except for Frank Smith, gave him their "unqualified support of your heroic efforts in defending the sovereign rights" of Mississippi. The state senators condemned "judicial tyrants," "the agents of communism," and "the power of a police state," and they worried about the "purity of their [whites'] bloodstream."[12]

A few discordant voices emerged. In a telegram released to the press, seven Oxford clergy chided Barnett over "the anarchy thrust upon us and our people through continued defiance of federal court orders." Former lieutenant governor Sam Lumpkin compared Barnett's proclamations and posturings to "braying like a jackass in a tin barn." The *Delta Democrat Times* concluded, "Mississippi stands alone. As we are sowing, so shall we reap. It will be a bitter harvest." From outside the state, Michigan's governor announced that he would ask the executive board of the National Governors' Conference to censure Barnett for his "outrageous conduct." The executive council of the Southern Association of Colleges and Schools (sacs) declared a special meeting on Friday, September 28, to decide if events had jeopardized accreditation by violating standards on political interference.[13]

In Washington, Robert Kennedy conceded that "the situation is serious" but pledged to "use whatever force is necessary to get the job done." The army continued to prepare for action, including deployment to secure access to the campus.[14]

At the same time, the Justice Department negotiated secretly with the governor and his representatives. On Wednesday afternoon, September 26, Watkins told Marshall that the Justice Department had not used enough men, and he suggested that twenty-five armed marshals should confront the state officials, who would then yield. Marshall thought it would work if the state would comply. After talking with Barnett and his advisers, Watkins confirmed the plan, with two modifications: all the marshals would draw their weapons and the state forces would leave Oxford after yielding. Late Wednesday night Marshall rejected the proposal because it left twenty-five marshals in charge of maintaining order. The next day, in conversations with Robert Kennedy, Watkins no longer called for the withdrawal of state forces and assured Kennedy that Barnett okayed the plan. Kennedy's proposal that only one marshal pull his pistol delayed an agreement.[15]

Thursday at the Alumni House, Barnett huddled with Johnson, Simmons, Billy Ferrell of the Mississippi Sheriffs Association, and others. In afternoon telephone calls with Robert Kennedy, Barnett and Johnson raised numerous objections to proceeding. At first, Barnett objected that one marshal's drawing a side-arm "could be very embarrassing"—the governor would yield to minimal force. Though Johnson stressed that all the marshals must draw their pistols, he assured Kennedy that "there won't be any shooting" because the police would be unarmed. He also pledged to "do everything to preserve law and order at all times." Just when everything seemed settled, Barnett called back to plea for a delay at least until Saturday. With Barnett's contempt hearing on Friday, Kennedy suggested that acting on Thursday would be in the governor's best interest. The governor also worried about the public finding out about his secret negotiations, but Kennedy promised no word would leak from his office. Arguing for a postponement, Johnson feared a hothead, either a sheriff or a deputy or a bystander, might start shooting. Kennedy replied that two hours remained for Meredith to register or the situation would worsen; the court would hold Barnett in contempt and order his arrest, and the government would use force to enroll Meredith and to keep Ole Miss open. After conferring with his advisers, the governor promised to try to control the two or three worst people so that Meredith could come to Ole Miss late that afternoon.[16]

Thirty minutes later, when Kennedy confessed that he was "taking a helluva chance" by relying on the governor and asked if violence were possible, Barnett guaranteed "there won't be any violence." The governor reminded him, "You understand we have had no agreement," and Kennedy agreed. At 3:35 P.M. (CST), Kennedy told Barnett that Meredith would arrive in two hours, but the attorney general worried about FBI reports that the state patrol had been told the marshals would be in charge of law and order once Meredith arrived. After equivocating, Barnett said, "I don't think I could agree to guarantee the man after he gets in." Frustrated, Kennedy retorted, "I had better call it off, Governor." When Kennedy insisted that law and order was essential and that he did not care who was in charge, Barnett vaguely guaranteed to "protect the lives and health and persons of everyone." Kennedy seemed satisfied.[17]

About 3:30 P.M., Meredith, Doar, and McShane left the Memphis Naval Air Station. More than two dozen unarmed marshals in a caravan raced down Interstate 55 toward Batesville. Veteran marshal Donald D. Forsht had instructions to draw his pistol at the appointed time and to tell Johnson the marshals backing him up would use force if needed to enroll Meredith. Though Meredith expected it would be a bluff, the group anticipated a late afternoon showdown with the governor and the state police.[18]

Waiting for them was a university experiencing "violin-string tension." Students and professors continued going to class, but in many the discussion centered on Meredith. One professor said, "We have all year to talk about geology. Today let's talk about the university." An English professor gave his class an option of several of Shakespeare's plays to read but warned, "Reading *Othello* might present a problem in Mississippi. In the play, Othello, a Moor, is a Negro, and his wife, Desdemona, is white. But it shouldn't be any serious conflict. They were just married, not trying to get into school." Many read newspapers, watched television news, and listened for radio updates, while others seemed unaware and unconcerned. According to one report, the consensus reflected a dilemma: "We don't want Meredith here—but we don't want Ole Miss to close." Hundreds of students milled around; when afternoon classes concluded, their numbers swelled.[19]

As a confrontation approached, everyone on campus waited—one hundred journalists; three hundred state patrolmen; one hundred sheriffs, deputies, and local police; and hundreds of students, all unarmed. While police protected Barnett, a score of officers manned each of the campus's five entrances, stopped all cars, and required driver identification before a vehicle could enter. Dozens of plainclothes police shed their jackets to show they carried no guns and wore identifying white arm bands. Six caged police dogs waited in police cars. At 2:00 P.M., the highway patrol reported to the National Guard Armory on the town's eastern edge for instructions that included removing their badges and name plates; the sheriffs and local police met at the county courthouse for a similar briefing. By 3:00 P.M. all returned to their posts, and the state troopers established a roadblock on University Avenue near the main entrance to campus.[20]

More than a thousand people converged near the roadblock. About 4:15 P.M., a state patrolman riding down University Avenue urged students to leave. Half an hour later, Paul Johnson used a sound truck to warn, "Someone could easily get killed" and "nothing's going to happen except we're going to turn back that nigger again. Please leave the area." Circulating student leaders also asked their cohorts to leave. Instead, the crowd grew to nearly two thousand because, as one student explained, "if too many marshals show up Ross'll need some help." At about 5:00 P.M., when Barnett drove up to the roadblock, got out of the car, and tipped his black homburg, the crowd applauded and cheered "We want Ross!" "Don't give in Ross." "We'll win, we'll win." "Ross for President!" After conferring with Johnson, Simmons, the head of the highway patrol, and Jackson attorney William Goodman, he returned to the Alumni House.[21]

At 5:35 P.M. Barnett told Kennedy, "General, I'm worried—I'm nervous, I tell you." He informed him about the many strangers in the crowd and admitted law enforcement could not control them. He warned that a "a hundred people [could be] killed there. It would ruin all of us." When Kennedy volunteered to withdraw Meredith's party, Barnett begged, "General, do that please." They agreed that Barnett would not comment but that the Justice Department would issue a statement. Kennedy directed the convoy, about thirty miles from Oxford, to return to Memphis. Marshal Forsht, who did not have to draw his pistol in a confrontation, recalled weeks later, "I was so glad." Barnett and most law enforcement officers departed, and the campus reopened to traffic.[22]

At 5:45 P.M., the Justice Department explained that the mission had been called off because the force accompanying Meredith might not have been sufficient in the face of a large crowd. Despite the embarrassing setback, Robert Kennedy reiterated the fundamental American "respect for the law and compliance with all laws—not just those with which we happen to agree." According to him, Barnett's position was "incompatible with the principles upon which this Union is based." Though Kennedy still hoped for a peaceful resolution, he repeated that the federal government would enforce the court orders, "whatever action that ultimately may require." Later he declared, "Mr. Meredith will be registered," but he did not say when.[23]

Despite Kennedy's commitment, most white Mississippians seemed determined to back Barnett. Thursday night, to protect him and Johnson, the legislature approved, unanimously in the senate and with two objections (Wiesenburg and Wroten) in the house, a bill to exempt property from seizure to pay fines for contempt. The next day legislators provided for the state to pay any fines imposed on the governor and declared "every spoken word . . . and every act done" by state officials to be "sovereign acts of the sovereign state" and not individual acts subject to punishment. A house resolution called the use of marshals "an unconstitutional and illegal attempt to subjugate free American citizens." One senator suggested sending "a petition to the United States Congress to sever relations with the State of Mississippi."[24]

Friday morning when Paul Johnson reported to the senate, he received a standing ovation. He described the issue as the danger of the "centralization of power" and lauded the police, Ole Miss students, and other state officials for their support. Later in a closed session, he suggested that violence would have resulted if Meredith had come to the campus, but he did not explain how the violence would have started if the police and students behaved so properly. Expecting more trouble and a need for reinforcements, Johnson urged Mississippians who wanted to serve to report to Judge Russel Moore in Jackson. In a radio interview, he insisted that a regiment could not have protected Meredith from the rough crowd that had formed on Thursday. If not for the state troopers, "that Negro wouldn't have lasted as long as it would take to aim a shotgun." Without a cooling-off period, Johnson predicted, "Blood is going to be on somebody's hands. I think it's going to be on the hands of the aggressors," the Kennedys.[25]

Though defiant, Barnett received serious warnings from the federal court in New Orleans, the Kennedy administration, and sacs. On Friday the court of appeals held a hearing on the Justice Department's motion to cite Ross Barnett for civil contempt. Burke Marshall, John Doar, and St. John Barrett represented the United States, and Constance Motley and Jack Greenberg appeared in court with James Meredith, who had flown in from Memphis. The defendants in *Meredith v. Fair*, including the governor, also had a team of lawyers present. Judge Elbert Tuttle opened the hearing by asking, "What says the Respondent, Ross Barnett?" John Satterfield replied that he remained in Jackson and sent no lawyer to represent him. At Satterfield's request, the court permitted him to appear as amicus curiae, but when he sought to have the charges dismissed, the court refused to let him make any motions, file any pleadings, or make any objections.[26]

The court first heard from the Department of Justice's three witnesses to prove that the court had tried diligently to serve its orders on the governor. The appellate court clerk testified that he had sent the papers to Barnett but never received proof of delivery. A marshal explained that he had tried to deliver the papers at the state capitol, in the Woolfolk Building, and at the governor's mansion. McShane told the court that the governor had refused the papers when he and Doar had tried to serve them in the Woolfolk Building.[27]

When Satterfield proposed introducing the witnesses' credentials as exhibits, the judges questioned him about his relationship with Barnett. Satterfield balked unless sworn in as a witness, but Judge Rives directed him to answer as an officer of the court. When Satterfield again objected unless he had the status of participating attorney, Rives shot back, "Yes, you may object, but I still ask for an answer." The court extracted from him that Barnett knew fully about the court's orders even if he had not accepted the papers. After a ten-minute recess, the court, because of Barnett's absence, withdrew Satterfield's amicus curiac status. After the defense attorneys conferred, Garner W. Green, a special assistant attorney general, mentioned the possibility of "bloodshed," and Judge Tuttle bristled, "We have heard about the possibility of bloodshed for the last ten years." Judge Hutcheson interrupted, "You are threatening the Court with bloodshed, are you?" Greene denied it. Tuttle ruled that the "State of Mississippi has no part in this proceeding" and denied anyone not a party to the case the right to make any motions.[28]

After more testimony from the same three witnesses and after Justice Department lawyers showed a news film of the events in the Woolfolk Building, Tuttle admitted that the court had "practically exhausted its powers" to get Meredith into the university. The "time has about come . . . when the burden now falls on the Executive Branch," and he called on the Department of Justice for guidance. Burke Marshall emphasized that state authorities had had "every opportunity . . . to meet their responsibilities." He assured the court, "There is no question that the order of the Court is going to be enforced . . . whatever force, physical force, is required" and offered three proposals. First, the court could give Barnett until Tuesday to withdraw interposition and to purge himself of contempt; Judge Hutcheson, however, impatiently denied the governor had "any right to. . . . that kind of folly. That is Alice in Wonderland stuff." Second, it could require Barnett to report by Tuesday what he had done and make clear the repercussions of noncompliance. Once again, delay disgusted Hutcheson: "Of course, if you had one good Texas Ranger, it would have been done all right." Third, according to Motley, the court could hold Barnett in contempt and use "whatever power is necessary" to enroll Meredith. Late in the afternoon, at the end of the hearing, the court found Barnett in contempt and levied a $10,000-a-day fine, but it also gave him until 11:00 A.M. Tuesday to clear the charge and avoid jail by letting Meredith into Ole Miss.[29]

While the court contended with contempt, the Kennedys confronted the resistance. On Thursday, they conferred at least five times about the Oxford situation, but the president, who had yet to receive a thorough briefing, left its management to the Justice Department. Monitoring of events, however, caused the president to reconsider plans for a family weekend at Newport and the attorney general to postpone a speaking engagement at Stanford University. The brothers instead concentrated on crafting a strategy to integrate Ole Miss without using the military, to keep from backing down without provoking violence. While willing to negotiate, they always sought to avoid force and violence. As Robert Kennedy explained, "We can't back down and we won't back down. We don't want to use troops. But if you make us use troops, we will." The administration's patience and tolerance for discussion may have appeared as a lack of commitment and may have encouraged Barnett to delay and dissemble.[30]

With no resolution of the crisis, Robert Kennedy went to the Pentagon's War Room to discuss the use of the military with General Maxwell Taylor, the chairman of the Joint Chiefs of Staff, and with Secretary of the Army Cyrus Vance. Secretary of Defense Robert McNamara flew back from Germany in case troops were needed. On Friday, Vance and the attorney general went to the White House to brief the president on the army's plans.[31]

After Thursday's aborted attempt, the marshals and soldiers quickened their activity. An engineer battalion left Fort Campbell and arrived at the Memphis Naval Air Station early Friday morning. It would erect a tent city if the marshals went to Oxford. Units at Fort Bragg and Fort Benning had also been alerted, but an army spokesman denied they had anything to do with Mississippi. At the same time, more than one hundred marshals mobilized at the naval air station, and more soon joined them. Observers expected a showdown either on Monday, to give Barnett one more chance to avoid contempt, or on Tuesday.[32]

Another harbinger emerged Friday from a meeting of the sacs executive council. After visiting Oxford for several days earlier in the week, its executive secretary reported that Ole Miss officials maintained that Barnett should have time to finish his fight with the federal government before sacs acted. Its incoming president, Dr. S. A. Brasfield of the Mississippi Department of Education, urged the council to make no statement because any declaration would be interpreted as favoring integration. Others pressured to suspend all Mississippi institutions because of the governor's actions. For seven hours, the council debated how to criticize the violations of sacs standards by the governor and the trustees without appearing to take a position on integration. In telegrams Friday evening to Barnett, to the ihl board, and to the head of each institution, the executive council, without mentioning Meredith, charged that the colleges' integrity had been "threatened by this crisis," declared the board and the governor had been "in error," and stated the council would recommend stripping the institutions' accreditation if the "unwarranted procedures" were not corrected. The council absolved the university administration of fault. Late Friday, Barnett called Henry King Stanford, the sacs president, at his home, and in a fifty-minute conversation that extended beyond midnight, he emphasized that he did not want to interfere or violate sacs standards but he worried about upholding the Tenth Amendment and the states' rights.[33] The call confirmed his awareness that sacs threatened Ole Miss's academic viability.

Ominous reports alerted the fbi of citizens mobilizing to assist Barnett. As early as September 15, the fbi investigated plans of Georgia Ku Klux Klansmen, and by the last week in September, fbi sources warned of the dispatch of four surplus P-51 fighter planes. Louisiana Klansmen allegedly had arrived on campus, and a Kansas City radio broadcast asked radical groups to prepare to join the fray. One thousand men from Memphis reportedly readied to descend on Oxford, while the National States' Rights Party on Thursday would supposedly send at least six carloads of members to Oxford. Some preparations for resistance gained considerable publicity. Two hundred armed members of the Citizens for the Preservation of Democracy planned to leave Mobile on Saturday, as did another group from Montgomery. A spokesman declared, "Every white, red-blooded Southerner should be there. This is the hour of decision." The Florida Citizens' Council offered five hundred volunteers, while Willie L. Rainach, a leader of Louisiana Citizens' Councils, met with Barnett on Friday night and pledged thousands of men. Inquiries from vigilante groups prompted Lafayette County sheriff Joe Ford, the head of the local Citizens' Council, to "implore you to stay away from Oxford . . . if you are sincere in wanting to bring about a peaceful situation."[34]

Edwin Walker instigated much of the activity. In radio interviews, he called for ten thousand patriots to meet him in Mississippi to fight for states' rights. On September 26, he alerted Shreveport listeners that "it is time to make a move" if the president used military force. He declared, "It's time to rise, to make a stand beside Governor Ross Barnett. . . . Rally to the cause of freedom." He urged people to grab "your flag, your tent and your skillet" and go to Mississippi. In interviews Friday with a New Orleans radio station and a Dallas television station, he repeated his pledge to go to Mississippi and claimed offers of help from Ohio, Minnesota, Florida, New York, California, and Washington. By Saturday he announced that thousands were already headed to Mississippi. His emergence lent the controversy over Meredith a dangerous new aspect. Not only did bringing an unorganized force to Mississippi escalate the potential for violence, but it increased the pressure on Barnett to resist to the end. According to one FBI analysis, the public support of Barnett made impossible his plan to back down in the face of federal force. A Memphis FBI agent concluded that "Governor Barnett has reversed his position and that he is no longer willing to order Mississippi state and local officers to step back and permit Meredith and U.S. Marshals to enter without resistance."[35]

When Robert Kennedy tried at midday Friday to negotiate with Barnett, the governor thanked him for letting the state officials know each time he planned to try to enroll Meredith and asked him to continue that relationship. The frustrated attorney general charged that "just notifying you stirs it up rather than helps the situation," and Barnett explained that Thursday's situation had surprised him. "I didn't dream there was so many people there," he said. "Honestly, I looked that crowd over and saw them growling and carrying on and after [that] I went back and told you that it just wouldn't do to go." To Kennedy's suggested statement in support of law and order, the governor asserted it "wouldn't amount to a hill of beans" and instead proposed a cooling-off period. Kennedy countered with the suggestion that the state patrol assume law enforcement responsibility and that its commander travel to Washington for talks, but Barnett shifted the topic to Meredith, whom he called "foolish" for insisting on going to Ole Miss. After Barnett reminded him that the state would pay for Meredith's education elsewhere, Kennedy stressed, "Governor, he's going to the University of Mississippi." When Barnett brought up Meredith's air force record, Kennedy saw "no purpose running through that again." Barnett said his lawyers would contact Kennedy for further discussions, and the conversation ended. Two hours later Kennedy reported to Barnett that he had consulted with Tom Watkins and urged the governor to talk to him too. Hemmed in, Barnett could only request that Kennedy not send any Negro marshals to the state. The press reported the Barnett-Kennedys conversations, but the specifics remained secret.[36]

Expectations focused on Monday, October 1, before Barnett's Tuesday court deadline. Although two cross burnings, one near a dormitory and one at the flagpole near the Lyceum, broke the peace very early Friday morning, by dawn nearly all of the state troopers and other out-of-town police had left, and the remaining police shed their helmets and nightsticks. On Friday they did not guard the campus entrances and no crowds formed.[37]

"Placidity has temporarily replaced paroxysm here," the *New York Times* reported Friday. Students seemed "relaxed and smiling," according to another report, and "went from class to student union, chatting and skylarking, boy-attracting and girl-watching." At the same time, an "ugly threat of violence continue[d] to lurk over the campus," and tension reduced class attendance and made studying difficult. Some students waited to buy textbooks to make sure the university stayed open. Many wanted it to remain open. Worried about what SACS might do, one student complained, "Nobody suffers from the loss of accreditation but students and they have been the most blameless in this situation." One young woman hoped that soldiers would not use barbed wire barricades—"They are bad on hose, you know." According to another student, the whole affair had to be "settled before next weekend. That's homecoming weekend here, and a lot of ripsnorters who don't like the idea of a future Negro alumnus at all will be coming back." By the end of the week, more than three thousand students had signed a resolution approving Barnett's actions and praising his "courageous defense" of states' rights.[38]

Faculty hesitated to speak publicly because, as one professor explained, the "moment is so fraught with frenzy" and faculty thought public comments were too risky. One assessment discovered the faculty's "great unhappiness" with the political leadership and widespread fear that the university would lose accreditation and be humiliated in the national academic community. Professors largely remained isolated, weak, and silent. "What really burns us," one did tell a reporter, "is that we are innocent victims in this whole darn thing." In his view the governor had wrongly involved the university in a political fight; the university got blamed when in fact "no university official has said that he would refuse to register—or to teach—Meredith." Another professor objected, "It's unnecessary to jeopardize education in Mississippi when the courts have made clear their decision. This is not 1862," he emphasized, "it is 1962." The three hundred black employees of Ole Miss were even more wary. Working "with an ill-concealed air of apprehension," according to one report, they tended to ignore questions or shrug them off.[39]

Even Oxford businessmen dedicated to segregation tired of the controversy because their businesses suffered. Gas stations and restaurants reported sharp declines as students stayed on campus. The operator of a beauty salon said her business had fallen by 50 percent because women did not want to get out in town during the uncertainty. As bad as business was, the merchants feared even more the closure of the university. Around the courthouse square a petition circulated to keep Ole Miss open, and even prominent segregationists signed it. When asked if he was a southerner, one businessmen who signed it replied, "Yes, but I'm also a businessman."[40]

Scores of journalists reported the controversy, and Friday night "The U.S. vs. Mississippi," a half-hour CBS special, provided an up-to-the-minute summary. Showing the Jackson and Oxford confrontations as examples of "Federal authority versus the sovereignty claimed by the State Government," CBS suggested that Mississippi had pushed its challenge "close to its ultimate limits" and that the situation would soon end because the opposing forces "stand face to face."[41]

At Ole Miss the air of crisis lifted on Saturday and by that night Oxford looked like a "ghost town." The electric atmosphere shifted to the state capital where most students and many Oxford residents went to watch the Rebels play Saturday night against Kentucky. In Jackson segregationists celebrated the state's rebuffs of Meredith, the Kennedys, the courts, and the NAACP. Bumper stickers proclaimed "Keep Mississippi Sovereign," "The South Shall Rise Again," and, referring to Robert Kennedy, "Beat Lil Brother." Thousands of cars sported Confederate and Mississippi flags, and radio stations repeatedly played "Dixie," "Roll with Ross," and "Go Mississippi," the new state song. Another new song, "Never, No, Never," went:

We'll never yield an inch on any field.
Fix us another toddy,
Ain't yielding to nobody,
Never, never, never, never, no never.

Ask us what we say,
It's to hell with Bobby K.
Ross's standing like Gibraltar,
He shall never falter.
Never shall our emblem go
From Colonel Rebel to Ole Black Joe.[42]

Despite the high spirits in Jackson, the controversy continued to develop. A three-judge panel in New Orleans convened a hearing on a contempt citation against the lieutenant governor. In a reprise of the day before, Johnson did not appear in court, the judges refused to let John Satterfield and Charles Clark represent the state, and each side repeated its arguments. In a new twist, the federal government's last witness, James Meredith, testified in court for the first time since January and recounted how Johnson had blocked his entrance to the university. For the federal government, John Doar asked the court to act against Johnson as it had against Barnett, but he proposed a smaller fine for Johnson. He did not call for Johnson's arrest unless he failed to purge himself of contempt after he became governor in the wake of Barnett's arrest. Constance Motley, however, made greater demands. Claiming a fine would be ineffective because others would pay it, she called for Johnson's imprisonment if he did not end his contempt, and she wanted to give him a short time in which to clear himself. After hearing counsels' recommendations, the three-judge panel shortly after 1:00 P.M. found the absent Johnson in contempt and fined him five thousand dollars per day unless he purged himself of contempt by 11:00 A.M. on Tuesday, October 2.[43]

With the court pressing for a peaceful resolution, a counterforce flew into Jackson on Saturday afternoon. Edwin Walker came to stand with Barnett for states' rights. He would not say whether Barnett had invited him but indicated he had communicated with the governor's office. James J. Kilpatrick of the *Richmond (Va.) News Leader* described Walker as "breathing Messianic fire from cold, fanatic eyes." At a news conference Walker exhorted, "Rally to the cause of freedom in righteous indignation, violent vocal protest and bitter silence under the flag of Mississippi." Calling "for a national protest against the conspiracy from within," he vowed protesters would begin arriving in Oxford on Sunday. He told reporters that after attending the Ole Miss football game, he would go to Oxford. Asked if he advocated violence, Walker responded, "Any violence or bloodshed in Mississippi . . . would only be initiated by the federal government."[44]

While Walker rallied opposition in Jackson, the Kennedys searched for a solution to the Mississippi situation. To keep an eye on developments, the president delayed going to Newport and Robert Kennedy canceled his California trip. The attorney general's planned speech, which he released to the press, explained the Kennedys' frustration. The "absence of any expression of support from the many distinguished lawyers in that state" especially disappointed him. Defending compliance with the law and with the court orders "would be unpopular and require great courage," but the members of the state bar "still have their obligations as lawyers and they are remaining silent." "Courage is the most important attribute of a lawyer," and the attorney general found little of it among Mississippi lawyers.[45]

To break the stalemate and fashion a settlement, the president entered the negotiations on Saturday, September 29. His main interests, he explained to the governor, were the execution of the court order and Barnett's help in an "amicable" solution where nobody would be "hurt or killed." Speaking from his office guarded by state highway patrolmen, Barnett mentioned his oath to follow Mississippi law, including the new law barring anyone convicted of a crime from enrolling in the university. "I'm on the spot here, you know," he admitted, but Kennedy replied, "I've got my responsibility just like you have yours." When Barnett seemed to assume that Tom Watkins had reached an understanding with the attorney general, the president denied any agreement and suggested that Watkins confer with the attorney general. By promising that Watkins would fly to Washington on Sunday, Barnett avoided any settlement and could continue discussions until Tuesday, beyond Meredith's expected arrival. As the conversation concluded, the governor added, "Appreciate your interest in our poultry program and all those things." In response to the non sequitur, Kennedy could only say, "Okay, Governor, thank you."[46]

In discussions with the Justice Department, Watkins made little progress. Saturday afternoon he apparently suggested registering Meredith in Jackson, possibly at the IHL board office or the university medical school, while Barnett made a show of resistance in Oxford. After Meredith registered, Barnett could claim that the federal government had tricked him. The idea offered something for everyone: enforced court orders, Meredith's enrollment, peace at Ole Miss, and an alibi for Barnett so that he could say he had fought to the bitter end. The principals involved, however, had not approved the plan.[47]

Less than an hour after his first call, the president, with the attorney general present, called Barnett. Though the governor had not talked with Watkins, Robert Kennedy had, and he reported that Watkins offered no new solution. The attorney general agreed to meet with Watkins in Washington but believed it would be a waste of time unless Watkins had specific new ideas about maintaining law and order. Robert Kennedy asked Barnett to avoid a mob scene by prohibiting people from congregating in Oxford, but Barnett ignored the proposal and fell back on Watkins's latest idea. Reentering the conversation, the president returned to the question of what Barnett and the highway patrol would "do to maintain law and order to prevent the gathering of a mob and action taken by a mob. Can they stop that?" he asked. Barnett said, "I'll do everything in my power to maintain order. . . . We don't want any shooting," but when President Kennedy pressed, he wavered: "That's what I'm worried about. I don't know whether I can or not." After President Kennedy offered to help find a way that "causes the least chances of damage to the people in Mississippi," Barnett wanted a delay "to let people cool off on the whole thing." The president asked, "How long?" When the governor proposed two or three weeks and refused to guarantee even then that he would support registering Meredith, Kennedy laughingly deflected the idea.[48]

Toward the end of their conversation, Barnett vowed to cooperate and then added an enigmatic statement: "I might not know when you're going to register him, you know." The president responded with a "Well, now governor" and suggested that Barnett consult with Watkins and report back to the attorney general. Barnett may have referred to Watkins's last proposal, and the president's reply may have cinched the deal. In the afternoon's third conversation, the governor more directly reviewed with the president their "plan" to have Meredith secretly enrolled in Jackson on Monday. Saturday evening, however, the plan came apart when Barnett called Robert Kennedy at home and backed out of the deal.[49] The inability to achieve any concrete agreement frustrated the Kennedys and forced them to proceed with their own plans.

Saturday evening, while the Kennedys prepared their next moves, Ross Barnett attended the Rebels' football game. One reporter described the crowd as courteous and gracious, full of "love for their state and their university," but also permeated with "a strain of bitter violence." When Barnett entered the stadium just before the kickoff, the crowd cheered and waved Confederate flags in support of their embattled governor and his stand for states' rights and racial segregation. Barnett and his family joined forty-two thousand fans. At halftime, the crowd chanted "We want Ross," and he descended to a microphone on the playing field to help dedicate the new official state song, "Go Mississippi," a variant of his 1959 campaign song. To a "wild ovation" from the all-white crowd, the governor, with "clenched fist raised high," simply declared, "My fellow Mississippians, I love Mississippi. I love her people, our customs. I love and respect our heritage." Everyone in the stadium understood what he meant. In eighteen words he reaffirmed his full devotion to their way of life and did nothing to ease tensions or reduce the resistance. Instead, though he had been secretly negotiating with the Kennedys, Barnett ritualistically repeated his vow to defend state sovereignty and white supremacy in the face of all threats. The crowd went wild. One report said, "Bedlam broke out when the Governor finished. Confederate flags waved, rebel yells echoed through the stadium and the [university] band alternated between 'Go Mississippi' and 'Dixie.'" Erle Johnston later maintained that Barnett "was cheered as had no man in history."[50]

Some Ole Miss partisans tempered their support for the governor with loyalty to the university. Though they voiced support for Barnett's stand, alumni groups insisted that the university remain open no matter what happened. The Hinds County alumni chapter, for example, resolved that closing the university "would have a catastrophic effect . . . upon all the people of this great state," but it also called on the state's elected leaders "to use every moral and legal means to prevent integration." They believed that Barnett could both keep the institution open and maintain racial segregation. The potentially contradictory position in effect valued education and the university more than racial segregation, white supremacy, and the much-vaunted Mississippi way of life. It represented a moderate position in Mississippi. Tom Gregory, a Meridian reporter and Ole Miss alumnus, argued that the "battle at Oxford" had "developed into a personal battle between the White House and the Governor's mansion" and that Meredith had become "a pawn," but he believed that "Ole Miss shouldn't be" one too. It should not be jeopardized.[51]

A statewide chorus nevertheless praised Barnett. The Patriotic American Youth commended his defense of the Tenth Amendment, and the Greenville Chamber of Commerce lauded his "courageous" stand. Twenty-eight employees of a Jackson company protested the "dictatorial tyranny on the part of the central government," and the Airport Baptist Church near Greenville praised Barnett's role in the "battle for freedom" against "a crooked and perverse den of socialism that calls itself the Federal Government of the United States." At the Clay County Fair, two major state politicians, Charles Sullivan and Rubel Phillips, castigated the national Democrats and supported Barnett. The head of the Mississippi Republicans also praised Barnett's dedication to states' rights and individual freedom.[52]

With tensions increasing by the hour, on Sunday, September 30, three commentators defended their state and explained its position. The *Meridian Star* declared that the "Meredith-NAACP vs. Mississippi battle has developed into a do-or-die fight" over the centralized power of a socialistic government. The editor exhorted, "Let us stand together—for freedom." Proclaiming that Barnett's stand "has electrified the South," Judge M. M. McGowan insisted in the *Jackson Clarion-Ledger* that Mississippians "rally behind Governor Barnett in his gallant effort" against socialism, communism, "power drunk bureaucrats," the United Nations, "judicial tyranny," "vicious assaults" of various kinds, conspiracies, a "godless government," and "an endless train of other abuses cruelly designed to stamp out the last vestiges of our constitutional rights." Clarifying the issues, Charles Hills expressed the worries of whites about losing control of their state's large black population. "If Meredith gains entry to Ole Miss," Hills feared, "it may well mean breaking down of all controls" and the creation of the "unleashed furies of the Congo." Mississippians did not seek to deprive blacks of their civil rights, but Meredith sought something else. "We do not regard the privilege of association as a civil right," Hills explained. "The white people of Mississippi simply do not care to 'take a Negro to lunch.'" Hills regretfully concluded, "Whatever comes of all this, the Negro in Mississippi may well find in the long run that he has not profited himself, for the hand of friendship reaches far deeper than the hand of force."[53]

Saturday night the Kennedy administration prepared to wield its forceful hand. For more than a week, the Pentagon and the Justice Department had planned for using marshals, supported by the army. More than two thousand soldiers in three task forces—two military police units from Fort Bragg and Fort Dix plus an infantry one from Fort Benning—waited on alert for orders to move to Memphis or to Columbus Air Force Base in Mississippi, and on Saturday the army formed a fourth task force of twelve hundred infantrymen at Fort Benning. With the new code name of Operation Rapid Road, the operation included possible deployment to Jackson if the army needed to support the arrest of Barnett for contempt of court. Although everything depended on what Barnett decided to do, Monday seemed the most likely day for military operations. As a precaution, however, the army prepared for action as early as Sunday.[54]

While the Kennedys talked with Barnett and Watkins on Saturday, they and their assistants also prepared in case the negotiations failed. Saturday morning Robert Kennedy conferred with Burke Marshall, Nicholas Katzenbach, and Edwin Guthman in the Justice Department. After a disappointing noon call from Watkins, Kennedy concluded that a compromise looked unlikely and that military action would probably be necessary. Following a quick call to the president, the attorney general and Marshall went to the White House to help draft a speech for television Sunday evening. President Kennedy also conferred by telephone with Robert McNamara and in person with General Maxwell Taylor and Cyrus Vance. He also finally canceled vacation plans. Lawyers meanwhile drafted the relevant presidential documents for the administration to use the army. The administration interrupted the drafting of documents and canceled plans for the president's Sunday televised address when a deal seemed to have been made to sneak Meredith into Jackson Monday for registration. Marshall and Robert Kennedy left the White House, where the president went to the residential quarters for dinner. In the early evening Ross Barnett called the attorney general at his home to renege on the plan, but the two men did agree that Meredith would register at Ole Miss on Monday morning.[55]

With the deal changed, work resumed late Saturday night on a presidential proclamation addressing the obstruction of justice in Mississippi, on an executive order federalizing the Mississippi National Guard, and on a speech for Sunday night. A few minutes before midnight, Major General Chester V. Clinton, a military aide to the president, and Norbert Schlei, an assistant attorney general, brought the proclamation and the order to the White House. Right after midnight, the president signed the documents at a desk that U. S. Grant had used, but Kennedy, fearing a revival of memories of the Civil War and Reconstruction, directed that nobody mention the desk. Proclamation No. 3497, "Obstruction of Justice in the State of Mississippi," declared that Barnett and other officials had prevented the enforcement of court orders, and it called on them to cease their obstruction. In an unusual move, President Kennedy gave no time for them to stop but instead simultaneously issued Executive Order No. 11053, "Assistance for Removal of Unlawful Obstructions of Justice in the State of Mississippi." Because the presidential proclamation had not been obeyed, he directed the secretary of defense "to take all necessary steps to enforce" the court orders and "to remove all obstructions of justice" in Mississippi. To carry out the order, McNamara could use the armed forces and could federalize the National Guard in Mississippi.[56]

General Clinton promptly notified McNamara, who issued orders to have the presidential decrees carried out. Two minutes after midnight on September 30, he activated the Mississippi National Guard and brought it under federal control. Soon the Pentagon's War Room became the command post for military operations in Mississippi. A fifth task force made up of military police formed at Fort Hood in Texas very early Sunday morning, and it and the other alerted military units prepared to move to Memphis.[57]

On Saturday, a Memphis journalist had observed that "barring a sudden attack of sanity at Jackson, the ugly threat of violence continues to lurk over the campus." By the wee hours of September 30, a major battle between federal and state power was imminent.[58]

18. "A Maelstrom of Savagery and Hatred": The Riot

∎ ∎

In a modern version of David versus Goliath, Governor Ross Barnett, the rural Mississippian who had put himself through college working as a barber and door-to-door salesman, battled President John F. Kennedy, the Harvard-educated scion of a wealthy Boston family. Kennedy federalized the state's National Guard and mobilized the army and the U.S. marshals to enforce the order of the Fifth Circuit Court of Appeals despite whatever opposition might develop. By late Sunday, September 30, the contest had devolved into an unforgettable night of chaotic violence as a "deserted peaceful campus" transformed in a few hours into "one of almost unbelievable horror . . . [with] mob violence and martial law."[1] Neither side had thoroughly prepared for the confrontation; instead, each stumbled through a confused night of uncoordinated actions and reactions.

Earlier Sunday the presidential order worked its way down the chain of command from the secretary of defense to the members of Mississippi's Army and Air National Guards. Guardsmen who obeyed federal orders included Barnett's son and his son-in-law, Senator John C. Stennis's son, eleven state legislators, several college students, and Charles Sullivan, a 1959 gubernatorial candidate. By noon more than 80 percent of the eleven thousand guardsmen had reported to armories or air bases, and the Mississippi adjutant general created an Oxford task force of three thousand soldiers from three Guard units. Because Washington officials had decided only in the last few days to call up the National Guard, they had had minimal discussion with Guard leaders and knew little about the units. Sunday afternoon, in a two-hour meeting at the Memphis Naval Air Station, the army field commander, General Charles Billingslea, learned from the three Guard commanders about the units. He directed them to be prepared to move to Oxford no later than Monday morning.[2]

An engineer battalion from Fort Campbell proceeded early Sunday to the Holly Springs National Forest in northeastern Lafayette County to construct a tent city for as many as three hundred marshals. Before dawn, additional regular army task forces, including five hundred military police from Fort Hood, continued to converge on the Memphis Naval Air Station; by midday, more than four thousand soldiers massed at the base. They expected action on Monday.[3]

Using army units to desegregate a southern university introduced a problem: the use of black soldiers. Six years earlier, during the Little Rock crisis, the army removed more than one hundred blacks from the 101st Airborne Division, but in the 1961 deployment to Montgomery, black GIs remained in their assigned units. For the Kennedy administration in 1962 to segregate blacks would have been hypocritical. Instructions from a Pentagon planning session on September 17 called for leaving them with their units, but the policy remained unclear to many. According to General Creighton Abrams, for example, a more complex plan discussed with the attorney general allowed integrated units in the general area but required the withholding of black soldiers when the units came in contact with civilians. Abrams believed that blacks could not, therefore, drive trucks or ride in jeeps as radio operators. Some units withheld black soldiers, but most maintained integrated ranks.[4] The confusion exemplified the poor military planning.

The army and National Guard were to serve as support and possible reinforcement for the marshals. By Sunday, more than 600 marshals had assembled at the naval base. The chief marshal, James McShane, could only request the participation of other marshals or their deputies, and only 125 full-time deputy marshals agreed to serve, so he depended upon 316 border patrolmen and nearly 100 Bureau of Prisons guards serving as special deputy marshals.[5]

The six hundred marshals averaged thirty-six years of age, and nearly 90 percent had served in the military. Although 90 percent had graduated from high school, only 40 percent had gone on to college and only 10 percent had graduated. All were white, and more than two-thirds were from the South. Many were segregationists who did their job anyway. Most had several years of professional experience. Each border patrolman had received fourteen weeks of instruction in firearms, arrests, prisoner protocol, and legal procedures, and nearly every prison guard had riot-control training. The permanent deputy marshals usually had several years of law enforcement experience; all had been trained in riot and mob control, tear gas usage, and prisoners management; and one-third had protected the Freedom Riders in Montgomery in 1961. Three had led dozens of riot control training sessions for other marshals.[6]

The missions of the marshals, the army, and the National Guard developed from the decisions of Barnett and the Kennedys. The national administration had committed to enforcing the court orders, but Barnett had not figured out how to foil that objective. His advisers, all segregationists, pulled him in different directions. One cautious group, which included Tom Watkins,

William F. Goodman, and perhaps Joe Patterson, urged him to fight for states' rights on legal and constitutional grounds, but they also wanted to maintain law and order. A second, larger group, including Bill Simmons and Russel Moore, pressed him to do anything necessary to prevent integration, even go to jail. The latter group surrounded him and made access difficult, even for the state attorney general. Barnett wavered but usually sided with the archsegregationists.[7]

Shortly before 11:00 A.M. Sunday, Barnett resumed discussions with Robert Kennedy. Still hoping to avoid the shame of an end to segregation during his governorship, Barnett told him that "you should postpone" forcing the integration of Ole Miss. When Kennedy dismissed further delay, Barnett described another scenario. Hundreds of unarmed highway patrolmen, sheriffs, and other "soldiers" would back him up as he denied Meredith's entrance at a blocked street and called for "no violence, no bloodshed." "When you draw the guns," he told Kennedy, " . . . we will step aside and you can walk in." Kennedy rejected it as "silly," "dangerous," and politically inspired.[8]

Claiming that the whole matter had "gone beyond politics," Kennedy charged that Barnett placed his own political needs ahead of the best interests of his state and nation. Barnett admitted his desperate political predicament: "I have said so many times—we couldn't have integration and I have got to do something. I can't just walk back." Kennedy suggested that Barnett announce that the National Guard had been taken over by the federal government and that the governor did not want any Mississippian to be "responsible for placing Mr. Meredith in the institution." Then Barnett could "step aside." The governor agreed but insisted, "I have to be confronted with your troops." Ignoring that idea, Kennedy countered with a proposal that three hundred marshals secure the campus later that day before a crowd could resist or Barnett react; Meredith would arrive also and enroll the next morning. A Sunday surprise, the attorney general thought, would avoid any "gunfighting" and give Barnett an alibi because he could announce that the marshals had surprised him. The governor could then urge "everyone to behave themselves."[9]

At first the governor liked the plan, especially as it occurred on Monday, but when Kennedy explained that waiting would risk violence, Barnett balked. The attorney general then warned that the president would say on television that evening that Barnett had agreed on Saturday to have "Meredith go to Jackson to register" but that on Sunday Barnett "broke [his] word to him." Barnett begged, "You don't mean the President is going to say that tonight?" When assured that he would explain their deal, Barnett pleaded, "Don't say that. Please don't mention it." Pinned between his pledges to the people and his promises to the president, he offered a desperate new tactic: "Why don't you fly him in this afternoon; please let us treat what we say as confidential." Kennedy refused to discuss it further and told Barnett to settle on a plan and call him back that afternoon. When Watkins apologized for any misunderstanding, Kennedy said he was "sick and tired" of Barnett's trying to make himself "a great political hero."[10]

As the discussion continued, Watkins acknowledged that the governor accepted Meredith's arrival on the campus that afternoon, but Marshall insisted that Barnett "would have to say the State has given up before the physical force of the Government" and that "the State police will have to help keep order." Watkins agreed and pledged that the governor would order the highway patrol to maintain law and order and not to resist the marshals. When Robert Kennedy rejoined the conversation, he and Watkins agreed to get Meredith on campus before the president's televised address at 5:30 P.M. (CST) and before dark fell in Oxford; if their plan failed, the president would reveal the governor's broken promise. According to Watkins, Barnett would dispatch Colonel T. B. Birdsong, and once he arrived the marshals could be deployed, with Meredith soon to follow.[11]

Toward the end of the conversation, the Mississippians tried again to limit their political vulnerability. Watkins claimed that their discussions had been "in perfect confidence," but Marshall insisted that "it is absurd to think you can reach an agreement with the President of the United States and then call it off." Watkins beseeched Kennedy to offer his apology to the president and to "ask him please not to say anything about these talks." Barnett was "sorry about the misunderstanding last night." When Kennedy reassured them that the president would not mention their talks if everything were "straightened out" before he spoke, Barnett appealed, "Please let's don't have a fuss about what we talked about," and Kennedy agreed. Finally, when the governor explained that he might publicly "raise cain" about what they had agreed to, Kennedy said, "I don't mind that; just say law and order will be maintained," and he did not object to Barnett's continuing his fight in the federal courts.[12]

For confirmation, the president in a telegram asked if Barnett would follow and enforce the court's orders. If he would not so pledge, Kennedy wanted to know whether he would continue to interfere. More crucial, he inquired if "state law enforcement officials [would] cooperate in maintaining law and order and preventing violence in connection with Federal enforcement of the court orders." Suggesting that mobs should not gather or students demonstrate, he finally asked if Barnett would "take responsibility for maintaining law and order in that state when the court orders are put into effect."[13] Kennedy never received a reply.

On Sunday the president did hear from the state's congressional delegation.

Except for Frank Smith, they urged him not to use the military and demanded cancellation of the orders federalizing and mobilizing the National Guard. Not only did they oppose all efforts at integration, they also feared that using the armed forces in a civilian controversy could result in a disaster.[14]

After making a deal, each side sent a delegation to Oxford. Late Sunday morning Barnett directed Colonel Birdsong to establish roadblocks at the campus entrances and to clear the campus of nonuniversity people. Birdsong then ordered almost the entire highway patrol to Oxford, with one officer left in each district to handle automobile accidents. Shortly after noon, Birdsong and Dave T. Gayden, his assistant and the chief of the patrol, flew to Oxford. With a dozen patrolmen already on the scene, at about 1:45 P.M. they began carrying out their orders.[15]

Barnett's agreement with Robert Kennedy did not call for him to go to Oxford, but he dispatched four personal representatives. To head the delegation he tapped George Yarbrough, president pro tempore of the senate. He was joined by Senator John C. McLaurin, a staunch opponent of Meredith and the integration of Ole Miss, and Representative C. B. "Buddie" Newman, a protégé of Walter Sillers. The fourth, intransigent segregationist Judge Russel B. Moore, had the previous week coordinated for Barnett the highway patrol and the sheriffs on campus. Before leaving Jackson, Moore directed sheriffs and local police to report to Oxford as soon as possible. While Yarbrough flew home and then rode in a highway patrol car to the university, the other three flew in a state airplane to Oxford. They planned to meet at the Alumni House at 6:00 P.M.[16]

In the meantime, Robert Kennedy dispatched five young Justice Department officials to direct the work of the marshals and to assist in the enforcement of the court order. Nicholas deB. Katzenbach, forty-year-old deputy attorney general, led the group. Norbert A. Schlei, the thirty-three-year-old head of the department's Office of Legal Counsel, also joined the mission. To help with public relations, Kennedy sent Edwin O. Guthman, the department's press secretary and a Pulitzer prizewinning reporter. Harold F. Reis, another lawyer with the Office of Legal Counsel, and Dean Markham, a lawyer and an old friend of the attorney general, rounded out the delegation. They flew on a government jet at 3:30 P.M. Sunday.[17]

As forces converged on Oxford, tensions and anxieties escalated, and a climax seemed imminent, a few Mississippi voices urged peace and brotherhood. At St. Andrew's Episcopal Church in Jackson, Wofford K. Smith repeated the sermon he had delivered in Oxford two weeks earlier. In Oxford, Murphy C. Wilds told Presbyterians that the "world around us is being shaken . . . by rumors, by uncertainty, by words and action, by helmets and gas masks and night sticks and dogs, by fear." In a rebuke of the state's leaders, he mocked "state sovereignty" by proclaiming, "No state is sovereign. No nation is sovereign. There is only one sovereign: God!"[18]

At St. Peter's Episcopal Church, Reverend Duncan M. Gray Jr., the grandson of a St. Peter's rector in the 1930s and the son of the Episcopal bishop of Mississippi, addressed the controversy. According to Gray, "we do *not* have the right to defy and disobey the law," and to do so would lead to anarchy. He posed the basic question: "Are we *morally* justified in refusing to admit to the University of Mississippi any student who meets all the necessary requirements *except* for the color of his skin? Remember, the question here is not 'What would I *like*?' or 'What do I *want*?' The question is simply, 'What is *just* and *right*?'" Gray maintained the state's cause was not "righteous and just." Leading to a different understanding, Gray said that "*no university in the world would defend this [the state's] position rationally, and no Christian Church in the world would defend it morally*. And I do not believe any one us here today would stand in the presence of Jesus of Nazareth, look him squarely in the eye, and say, 'We will not admit a Negro to the University of Mississippi.' For it was our Lord who said, 'Inasmuch as ye have done it unto one of the least of these my brethren, ye have done it unto *me*.'" Reverend Gray decided "there can be only one resolution to this crisis: the admission of James Meredith."[19]

The clergy had no effect on plotting in Jackson and Washington. At the Memphis Naval Air Station, Meredith knew he would go to Oxford, but not when. After flying from New Orleans that morning, he watched football on television, snacked, and awaited directions. In Oxford, Chancellor Williams made no special preparations because he had received no official word from anyone; he expected Meredith and his federal escorts on Monday. Nobody had told him of the Barnett-Kennedy agreement, but he and Clegg had wondered if Meredith might be brought to campus Sunday. Even the army by midday Sunday had not been notified of plans to bring Meredith to campus Sunday; military leaders would learn of the decision late Sunday afternoon.[20]

A popular army of protest reportedly continued to mobilize. The FBI heard countless alerts about individuals and groups going to Oxford to help Barnett. Similar reports appeared in newspapers. A Shreveport paper, for example, announced that a sheriff would on Sunday lead a caravan of 150 cars to defend Ole Miss. Even on Sunday, offers of assistance inundated the governor's office. Members and officials of the Ku Klux Klan, the National States' Rights Party, and various Citizens' Councils volunteered, as well as sheriffs and individual citizens.[21]

After fomenting protests for a week, Edwin Walker drove to Oxford after the football game and checked into a motel shortly after midnight. Sunday morning he offered his services to Sheriff Ford, who turned him down but permitted him to stay as an observer. About 5:00 P.M. Walker spoke to the press. His rambling responses, aversion to photographs from the side, and insistence that everyone stand in front of him made him seem mentally unbalanced. Alleging that the Fourteenth Amendment did not call for integration, he proposed a peaceful protest and repeated his support for Barnett, whose "lawful stand for state sovereignty is supported by thousands of people beyond the state borders now on their way to join you at Oxford."[22]

In agitating resistance and defiance, Walker was not alone. During the weekend, radio and television stations incited support for Barnett's indomitable stand against integration and the federal government. Sunday in Jackson WRBC appealed for (white) citizens to go to the governor's mansion to protect him from any federal threat. In addition, radio stations all day Sunday broadcast news updates on the situation in Oxford. Journalists returning to Oxford from the football game kept abreast of developments by listening to their car radios, and Ole Miss students monitored the situation through reports from their own university station, WCBH. Radio reports spurred many with no connection to Ole Miss to go to the campus. In Columbus on Sunday, WCBI editorials labeled Meredith's enrollment an "unlawful invasion of the rights of our state" and asserted that citizens ought to "make a pilgrimage to Oxford."[23]

As uncounted individuals, scores of highway patrolmen, and several official delegations moved toward Oxford, the marshals marked time near Memphis. About noon Mississippi time, Burke Marshall told Tom Watkins that the marshals would have to leave Memphis soon to complete their deployment in Oxford that afternoon, and he called John Doar in Memphis to direct the marshals to move out. Later Watkins suggested that Marshall should call Robert Ellis to alert him that Meredith was on his way to enroll. Marshall agreed but insisted, "We are not going to put Meredith in until the situation is physically stabilized." Meredith's security required marshals on the campus. By 2:30 that afternoon, the first group of marshals had taken off for Oxford.[24]

The university's airport became the first focus of afternoon activity. Built in 1955 a mile north of campus, it had one 4,200-foot east-west runway capable of handling small-to-medium-sized planes. One of the first to land carried Birdsong and Gayden of the highway patrol. Met by one of the dozen state patrolmen already in Oxford, they went to the university gymnasium to establish the patrol headquarters (the Guard unit preempted their first choice, the National Guard armory). Responding to a radio message, Colonel Birdsong next went to the Alumni House to meet with Joseph A. Dolan, an assistant to Katzenbach. Earlier, after word reached Memphis Naval Air Station that the marshals would go to the university that day, Dolan accompanied a reconnaissance force to the tent city in the Holly Springs National Forest and then proceeded into Oxford. At his request, Birdsong showed him the campus and then took him to the airport.[25]

During Birdsong and Dolan's drive, several Ole Miss officials, assuming Meredith would appear Monday morning, met at the chancellor's home at 2:00 P.M. to prepare appeals to the students to avoid trouble, remain peaceful and orderly, and not interfere with authorities. Williams, Love, and Clegg planned for their statements to appear in a special edition of the *Mississippian* available at every dorm room before Meredith's expected arrival on Monday, and to be broadcast over the local radio stations and over the student union loudspeaker. Clegg tried unsuccessfully to secure similar statements from the governor and lieutenant governor. The university also prepared to mobilize its own security force, the Oxford Police, Lafayette County law enforcement personnel, and police from nearby communities.[26]

At the chancellor's home, university leaders received a call from Marshall, who informed them that Meredith would arrive that afternoon. The news surprised them because they had not been involved in any of the negotiations. Though caught off guard, Clegg warned Marshall several times of campus conditions that included an inability to implement plans to ensure order because many student leaders had not yet returned to campus. He told Marshall that only the trustees could authorize Meredith's admission and that the registrar was unavailable anyway. In addition to objecting to a Sabbath registration, Ole Miss officials cautioned about the combination of returning students exuberant after the football victory and fast-approaching dusk. Marshall only repeated that Meredith would soon be on the campus. When Marshall rejected housing Meredith off campus, Clegg said he could use a dorm apartment that also contained cots for marshals.[27]

Clegg's conversations with Marshall made the chancellor realize that he had lost control of the university. With little warning of the change in plans, he went to the campus radio station to tape a message for broadcast. Appealing to pride and loyalty, he began, "Ole Miss is great. You are helping make it greater." He urged everyone living on campus to "stay on campus" and to "attend classes and proceed with normal assignments." Williams suggested everyone "avoid congregating in large groups," "not participate in demonstrations of any kind," "report agitators to Campus Police," and "keep away from points of danger." After WCBH went on the air at 6:00 P.M., it broadcast his appeal a dozen times before signing off at midnight Sunday.[28]

Even before Birdsong and Dolan arrived at the airport, the first 170 marshals landed about 2:30 P.M. in five border patrol C-130 transports. A crowd of curious, though generally orderly and peaceful, students, townspeople, and reporters watched; some shouted and jeered at the marshals waiting on the grass near the runway. About 4:00 P.M., the five-member Justice Department delegation arrived. In a call from an airport pay telephone to Robert Kennedy, Katzenbach learned of Dolan's meeting with Birdsong and received instructions to proceed to campus. The army had dispatched seven trucks from the Holly Springs camp to bring the marshals back for the evening, but under the new plan rode instead to campus. The army had not expected such a public role, so four of the trucks had black drivers. With the Justice men in border patrol cars, a caravan set out. As it approached the airport gate, it encountered Colonel Birdsong and Dolan. After conferring, Birdsong agreed to lead them to campus, keep open the road between the airport and campus, and cooperate with the federal forces. As the motorcade passed more crowds of onlookers, traffic increased with some civilian cars breaking into the convoy. Highway patrolmen directed traffic and tried to keep the road open, while other units cleared the street in front of the Lyceum. The marshals reached the campus about 4:15 P.M.[29]

Right after the marshals stopped in front of the Lyceum, Clegg and university police chief Burnes Tatum arrived. When they made no objection, Katzenbach directed McShane to deploy the marshals in a line on the Lyceum's east side. Clegg unlocked the Lyceum and the group went to his office on the west side of the building. For thirty minutes, Katzenbach, Dolan, Guthman, Schlei, Clegg, and Birdsong held an impromptu meeting, with other university officials joining as they arrived. When the Justice Department representatives mentioned registering Meredith, Clegg surprised them by announcing that he would register the next morning.[30]

The original plan that had called for Meredith's matriculation on Sunday sent the marshals to the Lyceum where the registrar had his office, but the postponement left the force without a purpose. As nightfall approached, with few options and having received no helpful advice from Washington, Katzenbach had to decide what to do with hundreds of marshals. To remove them and Meredith would yield to the segregationists and thwart the court orders. Meredith had to remain and the marshals had to protect him. Katzenbach could not send the marshals to the distant tent city, the National Guard armory was unavailable, and the state highway patrol had occupied the gymnasium. To redeploy the marshals to Meredith's location would highlight it and increase his danger. Katzenbach instructed Dolan to find a place on campus for the marshals to stay overnight, and in the meantime he directed McShane to have them maintain their formation in front of the Lyceum. Before Dolan could locate an appropriate site, events made leaving the Lyceum impossible. The marshals therefore remained at their posts guarding, or appearing to occupy, the antebellum building at the physical and symbolic heart of Ole Miss.[31]

Dressed mostly in coats and ties, the marshals wore white helmet liners with "U.S. Marshal" stenciled on the front and orange arm bands bearing "U.S. Marshal." Each carried a riot club, a loaded .38 revolver, and, with a few exceptions, a gas mask. Many carried tear gas guns and wore orange vests filled with tear gas canisters. At the edge of the street in front of the Lyceum, the first marshals lined up shoulder-to-shoulder facing toward the Circle, a park-like area four hundred feet in diameter just east of the Lyceum. In the Circle's center rose the university flagpole, and at its eastern edge, opposite the Lyceum, stood a twenty-nine-foot-tall marble Confederate soldier.[32]

With the marshals outside, Katzenbach, Clegg, and the others continued their discussions. University officials informed Katzenbach of arrangements for Meredith to stay in Baxter Hall, a men's dormitory honoring the 1943 student body president, killed as an infantryman in Germany. On the second floor of the forty-seven-room men's dorm built in 1947, the accommodations consisted of a bedroom, living room, kitchenette, and separate bathroom. The apartment also had room for several marshals and immediate outside access through a private door that opened onto a landing with stairs to the ground. The remote location at the west end of the westernmost dorm made access and security simple.[33]

At the Lyceum the Justice Department representatives established communication links with Washington. Dolan used a hallway pay phone to call the White House collect, and he kept the line open the rest of the night. A few minutes later, Harold Reis asked Love if he could use a telephone, and Love directed him to other public phones in the hall. Persisting, Reis inquired if he could use a phone in the dean's first-floor offices on the south side of the Lyceum, and Love reluctantly agreed. Reis then called the Justice Department and asked an official to call him back, and the line also remained open. Virtually taking over Love's offices, they brought in other communications gear, including a radio to communicate with the border patrol cars.[34]

The links from the Lyceum supplemented connections established from Oxford to Washington. On September 17, technicians had installed a direct line from the U.S. attorney's office on the town square to the Justice Department. Nine days later the border patrol installed a radio in the Alcohol and Tobacco Tax office in the post office basement on the opposite side of the square, and another line joined the two offices. On Saturday, September 29, the lines were consolidated in the civil service examination room in the post office basement, which became the Oxford base for the federal operation.[35] Despite several lines between Oxford and Washington and between units in the town and campus, communications proved difficult throughout the crisis and no connection joined the chancellor to any of the federal posts.

A link to a border patrol car became important when the meeting in Clegg's office broke up and the participants dispersed. About five o'clock, Katzenbach informed the attorney general that Meredith should be brought to campus, and Marshall told Doar to have Meredith at the Oxford airport within the hour. Before Katzenbach and Guthman left to meet Meredith's plane, Katzenbach told McShane to secure the Baxter Hall area, and two dozen men went to the dormitory. Chief Tatum knew the way and had the keys to Meredith's rooms, but because he lacked a car the highway patrol drove him the one-third mile to Baxter Hall. At the same time Birdsong drove toward the airport to check traffic conditions but was interrupted by instructions to report to the Alumni House to confer with Barnett's four representatives. Guthman and Katzenbach, meanwhile, left the Lyceum in a border patrol car to go to the airport to meet Meredith. Schlei and McShane remained in charge of the marshals at the Lyceum.[36]

When 120 more marshals arrived at the Lyceum at 4:40 P.M., several dozen people milled around—students on dates, families with young children, and strangers who had come to witness the unfolding events. Perhaps twenty highway patrolmen assigned to the front of the Lyceum kept the crowd orderly. To the patrolmen and marshals, the gathering seemed more like the start of a college pep rally than the makings of a mob. A few Confederate flags appeared, and one student in a Confederate uniform ran around. Patrolmen mingled and chatted with people, and a few marshals, in violation of protocols, even talked with students. As they returned to campus, more and more curious students walked to the Lyceum. Crowds and police had become almost commonplace on campus, but as word spread that the marshals had taken up their positions at the Lyceum, more people gathered in the Circle across the street from the building's front door. The numbers grew to more than two hundred by 5:30 P.M., when thirty more marshals arrived in a fifteen-car convoy. The mood became a bit more assertive and testy. Highway patrol roadblocks at the campus entrances barred individuals unaffiliated with the university; even journalists accredited by the university could not get onto campus, though some did sneak in.[37]

About the same time that the third contingent of marshals arrived, the noisy crowds on campus began to alarm the chancellor. The announcement of Meredith's pending arrival surprised Williams, but the convoy of army trucks rolling past his residence shocked him. Though he realized that he had no control over events, the fate of his students in such volatile and dangerous conditions concerned him. While the radio station broadcast his appeal, he drove toward the Lyceum. Parking on the Circle, he mingled with the crowd, which he believed was still largely comprised of students. When he saw that the patrol and the marshals were not in conflict, he pointed their cooperation out to the students and urged them to return to their dormitories. For nearly an hour, Williams worked to protect the students.[38]

As the crowd grew it became noisier, but the marshals maintained their positions. They had been trained to act in coordination, be impersonal but courteous, ignore insults, take no side in a dispute but maintain law and order, exercise calm judgment and common sense, and prevent an unruly crowd from becoming a violent mob. Their training stressed the importance of an initial display of significant force under the direction of a vigorous leader because a show of strength often caused crowds to break up. If the crowd failed to disband and became a mob, the marshals would use tear gas to prevent harm. If tear gas failed, they could use firearms, but only in self-defense or to protect lives.[39]

By sunset, more than 150 additional marshals reinforced the first groups. At the same time, the crowd in front of the Lyceum increased to several hundred, mostly students, with many wearing their freshman beanies. Joking, they chanted "Hotty Toddy" and other college cheers, and they also hollered "two, one, four, three, we hate Kennedy." Though an occasional "nigger lover" pierced the air, they good-naturedly called a few marshals by nicknames, like "Smiley" and "Mr. Clean." Some tossed cigarette butts, loose gravel, pennies, and rolls of toilet paper toward the marshals. They booed and hissed the marshals but cheered when army trucks drove off, one with a Confederate flag attached and another with a sign that said "Yankees Go Home." Though the heckling became more abusive, it still seemed to one reporter "more like jest than maliciousness." The marshals remained alert, impassive, and unperturbed. They ignored the remarks and the missiles. By 6:00 P.M., with the crowd approaching one thousand, the marshals stood steadfast. The highway patrolmen directed traffic but otherwise stood in small groups and watched, with an occasional laugh at the antics of the crowd.[40]

Observers later contended that the disorder could have been squashed if a state or Ole Miss official had stepped forward to control the gathering. Kenneth L. Dixon, the *Meridian Star*'s managing editor, lamented that not "one respected school official" had "made an effort to control the crowd." He said his World War II friend Bill Mauldin asked, "Who in the world ever let this thing get this much out of control?" Another reporter despaired that "the complete silence of voices of reason" from Ole Miss leaders "left the way open for the voices of emotion to hold sway." Walking among the students, Chancellor Williams and individual faculty members quietly appealed to individual students, but none tried to assert authority. Over the previous decade, and especially the last year, the chancellor and the administration had ceded control of racial matters to the trustees and to the politicians. Their acquiescence had undermined and disabled their own authority. Even the Kennedy administration had ignored Williams. At twilight on Sunday, therefore, Ole Miss leaders stood helpless to prevent a tragedy.[41]

On their way to the airport, Katzenbach and Guthman, after stopping downtown for gas, got lost. After radioing for directions, they finally found the airport. Though a large hostile crowd had formed, Katzenbach deemed the area secure and judged the route to campus safely under the highway patrol's control, so he directed that the border patrol airplane carrying Meredith proceed to land. A few minutes after 6:00 P.M., fifteen minutes after sunset, Meredith landed. After Katzenbach and Guthman greeted him and John Doar, the four loaded into a border patrol car and joined a procession to campus. The highway patrol's Gayden led two army trucks with about a dozen marshals each and three border patrol cars. They arrived at Baxter Hall about 6:30 P.M.[42]

Going through the campus's western entrance, Meredith saw little. A few students congregating near the dorm occasionally threw rocks and bottles at a contingent of marshals patrolling the immediate area, and the marshals replied with tear gas. By early morning, however, nearby dormitory residents brought hot coffee and hamburgers to the marshals. The intense action at the Lyceum remained out of Meredith's sight and hearing. He made his bed with linens supplied by the university, read a newspaper or magazine, and went to bed about 10:00 P.M. Except for some commotion that woke him a few times, he knew little of the tumultuous events of his first night at Ole Miss. When Robert Kennedy knew that Meredith had arrived, he notified Barnett.[43]

Satisfied with his safety, Katzenbach, Guthman, and Doar returned to the Lyceum shortly before seven o'clock to discover more marshals and a larger, noisier crowd. The worsening situation still did not seem dangerous, but the mood would deteriorate within half an hour. As dusk faded into darkness. the night's greater secrecy and anonymity emboldened the crowd, and the marshals' white helmets stood out in front of the lighted Lyceum. About 6:30 P.M. campus roadblocks eased, and more reporters came onto campus, where their flashbulbs highlighted the positions of the unwanted outsiders. At the same time, the increasing numbers of marshals posed a greater threat. Black army truck drivers outraged the crowd, as did news of Meredith's arrival. Word spread that someone had betrayed their cause. The crowd became a mob.[44]

During the transformation, hostile challenges to the marshals increased.

The distance between the marshals and the burgeoning mob shrank as people pushed closer to the Lyceum. Stationed in the street between the two groups, highway patrolmen refused to prevent violence toward the marshals or the few soldiers accompanying them. When Marshal Bennie E. Brake from Charleston, South Carolina, spoke to highway patrol major Bob Fyke, whom he had known since 1958 when they met at the FBI National Academy, Fyke refused to shake the marshal's hand and did nothing to control the crown. Instead some troopers laughed and joked with the crowd. When individuals moved from the Circle into the street to cut the brake lines of the army trucks parked in front of the Lyceum, the patrolmen watched, turned their backs, or walked away. The state policemen also did nothing when someone burst toward an army truck, grabbed a fire extinguisher, and discharged it into the face of a black truck driver. The crowd roared approval. One patrolman even suggested that a protester not deflate an army truck's tires by slicing them but instead that he cut off the tires' valve stems close to the wheel rims to make them difficult to repair. One student reportedly said that a patrolman had given him his slap jack, a type of billy club or night stick with weights in the end to make it more harmful. As darkness fell, many patrolmen shined flashlights into the marshals' faces to make them more visible but also to blind them to the oncoming missiles.[45]

The size of objects hurled at the line of marshals grew from pennies and pebbles to rocks, bottles, and brickbats. When more marshals came, jeering people assaulted their vehicles and shattered windshields and windows. When one student attacked a border patrol car, state patrolmen volunteered to take care of him, which they did by rescuing him from the marshals and sending him back into the crowd. Another student distributed eggs to throw at the marshals. Lighted cigarettes set ablaze the army trucks' canvas tops, and a black driver waiting behind the steering wheel scrambled to put out the flames. When an observer told a state patrolman about the attempts to set a truck on fire, he replied, "Let 'em do it."[46]

Verbal abuse escalated to harassment. Annoying became threatening. The throng hollered, "We want Meredith," "Get the nigger out," and "Get a rope" and "Burn the Kennedys and the niggers." The language descended from sophomoric to profane. Cries included "Oh, you nigger-lover, oh you mother——." The marshals were accused of having "nigger children" and being "nigger fuckers." Some taunted them with "Marshal, where's your wife tonight? Home with a nigger?" Individuals rushed up and spat on the marshals and soldiers. In spite of it all, the marshals did not break ranks to retaliate, but many were frightened.[47]

Assaults on newsmen demonstrated the crowd's changing nature. More than 359 journalists had registered with the university, though not all of them were on campus Sunday evening. Shortly before 7:30 P.M., Gordon Yoder, a white news cameraman from Dallas, accompanied by his wife, parked his station wagon on the Circle near the Lyceum. He tried to film the scene, but elements of the mob attacked him. While state patrolmen and, a little further away, marshals watched, the mob beat Yoder to the ground and destroyed his three-thousand-dollar equipment. When he tried to retreat to his automobile where his wife waited, they attacked the car. State police ignored his pleas. In response to one man's request to assist Yoder, a trooper replied, "Let them kill the nigger!" After breaking out all the windows and battering the car, the mob rocked the car to overturn it. Only when the Yoders seemed critically imperiled did patrolmen intervene to hustle them to safety. Other reporters realized their danger when they heard shouts of "Let's kill all the reporters" and when strangers threatened them, grabbed and destroyed their cameras, or slugged them. Journalists warned arriving colleagues not to carry cameras and equipment that identified them as reporters. After being roughed up because he had a camera, one reporter hid it in some bushes to recover it later. Their professional appearance and lack of participation in the protests made reporters stand out, and the sudden arrival of many more in the area of the Circle when the highway patrol let them in before 7:00 P.M. made them more conspicuous.[48]

The crowd viewed journalists as obnoxious outsiders who gave Ole Miss and the state a bad name. Though Mississippi and Memphis media had reporters present, the majority represented more distant news organizations. As outsiders, they were assumed to be unfriendly to local customs and traditions and to represent the forces of integration almost as much as did the marshals. Their presence angered the crowd and incited it to further violence. Some protesters may also have attacked cameramen out of concern that pictures would end their anonymity.[49]

The attack on Yoder demonstrated that by 7:30 P.M. the crowd had become a mob, and the conflict had changed from pep rally to violent clash. The mob had no intention of beginning a revolt against federal authority, had no plan to overthrow the federal government. It engaged instead in a wild, violent protest against the national administration's use of force to achieve integration. One news account announced, "The war had begun." The experience reminded one marshal of Korea when the Chinese army had overrun his unit, except in Korea "we could shoot back." Even though the conflict was a riot and not a war or insurrection, United Press International declared Gordon Yoder the "first casualty."[50]

Just as the riot began, three of the governor's representatives went to the

Lyceum to meet with their Justice Department counterparts. About the time Meredith had arrived, Judge Russel Moore, Representative Newman, and Senator McLaurin had also landed and gone to the Alumni House to meet Senator Yarbrough. At Yarbrough's direction, Birdsong had come to the Alumni House to update them on the situation. The governor's delegates, instead of meeting to prepare a strategy for the next day, had consulted with Barnett and decided that the sheriffs and their deputies would not be needed. A few minutes after 7:00 P.M., Moore had ordered over the highway patrol radio all sheriffs and deputies to return to their homes. He then went to meet with the sheriffs and deputies, while Yarbrough, McLaurin, and Newman went to the Lyceum with Birdsong to investigate conditions and to confer with Katzenbach and his team.[51]

In Clegg's office, Yarbrough expressed displeasure that the federal forces had occupied the campus and charged that federal authorities would be responsible for what happened. He then announced his intention to withdraw the state patrol to avoid conflict between state and federal forces. If the patrol withdrew, he said, federal forces would have responsibility for maintaining the peace. Taken aback, Katzenbach argued that state authorities had not been relieved of responsibility for preserving law and order. Calling it a mistake, he suggested that withdrawing the state patrol would increase the likelihood of violence by leaving no buffer between the crowd and the marshals. When Yarbrough disagreed and indicated he would order the patrol to leave, Katzenbach suggested that the senator call Barnett.[52]

At the very moment of Yarbrough and Katzenbach's disagreement, Robert Kennedy called Katzenbach. Told of Yarbrough's plan, the attorney general told him to inform the senator that if he did not withdraw that order immediately, President Kennedy would announce in his nationwide address at 8:00 P.M. that the patrol had been withdrawn in direct violation of the administration's agreement with the governor. Robert Kennedy then called Barnett, who in turn called Yarbrough. After talking with the governor, Yarbrough agreed that the patrol would remain. The change made little difference, however. During the negotiations in the Lyceum, the FBI learned that a 7:25 P.M. radio message had ordered the highway patrol to leave the campus; Yarbrough apparently had issued the order before he entered the Lyceum and could not rescind it in time. Dozens of patrol cars and officers began pulling out; others left their blockades at the campus entrances. Though some patrolmen returned a few minutes later to the Lyceum vicinity, the departure of most patrolmen opened the campus to outsiders, ceded control to the marshals, and signaled to the mob that the state would not halt them.[53] The action inspired the mob.

At 7:30 P.M., in the midst of the descent into violence, Barnett over statewide radio and television tried desperately to reconcile his public and private positions. After explaining that Robert Kennedy had just told him that Meredith was on the Ole Miss campus, the governor, as the Kennedy administration had hoped, said, "I urge all Mississippians and instruct every state officer under my command to do everything in their power to preserve peace and to avoid violence in any form." But his next equivocal sentence declared that even though surrounded and "overpowered" by "the armed forces and oppressive power of the United States of America, my courage and my convictions do not waver" and "our principles remain true." He repeated his emotional words from the football game the night before: "I love Mississippi. I love her people." Far from accepting the court orders and the integration of Ole Miss, his "heart still says never, but my calm judgment abhors the violence that will follow." He did not say that violence "might" follow but instead predicted that it would, despite his earlier appeal to preserve peace and avoid violence.[54]

To convince white Mississippians that, despite appearing to yield, he remained true to the their way of life, Barnett once more declared: "To the officials of the Federal Government, I say: Gentlemen, you are tramping on the sovereignty of this great state and depriving it of every vestige of honor and respect as a member of the union of States. You are destroying the Constitution of this great nation. May God have mercy on your souls. Mississippi will continue to fight the Meredith case and all similar cases through the courts to restore the sovereignty of the state and constitutional government."[55] Barnett could say that he had called for law and order, but his attack on the national government and his defense of states' rights provoked resistance. His statement, therefore, satisfied no party; his most adamant advisers saw it as a sellout, while the Kennedys resented his defiance. In any case, he spoke too late to dissuade anyone from rioting.

By nightfall most of the state patrol had departed, and the violent assault, particularly on the east side of the Lyceum, intensified. The horde edged closer and their shouts became more vulgar, angry, and threatening. More cigarette butts, bottles, boards, and bricks rained down on the marshals encircling the building. Molotov cocktails exploded. The few remaining state troopers took little action, and the marshals tried to dodge the missiles while holding their passive positions. A few minutes after the attack on Gordon Yoder, a broken Coke bottle seriously cut the eye of a Texas marshal, and he was taken to the university infirmary for treatment. Flying debris battered and bruised other marshals. Fearing for their safety, they asked permission to use tear gas to repel the mob, but McShane refused. His assistant, John Cameron, finally ordered the marshals to don their gas masks preliminary to firing tear gas. Some observers interpreted the action correctly and fled the scene, but many in the mob retreated only across the street with state troopers again standing between the marshals and the protesters. The gas masks, however, failed to intimidate the crowd, and some took them as a challenge. After only a few minutes the protesters again pushed into the street and crowded in on the marshals.[56]

By the time the meeting in Clegg's office concluded, the situation had worsened so much that Yarbrough and Dean Love volunteered to calm the crowd. About 7:40 P.M., they emerged onto the Lyceum's east steps to face the crowd in the Circle. Shocked by the marshals' gas masks, Yarbrough insisted that they not fire gas, so McShane ordered the marshals to remove their masks. Identifying himself as the governor's representative and a neighbor from Red Banks, Yarbrough urged students to stop the violence and return to their dorms. Without a loudspeaker, his appeals had little effect. People yelled for Barnett, and Yarbrough agreed to try to get the governor to come to Oxford if the crowd would back up into the Circle. He directed the few state patrolmen to push people out of the street and into the Circle; the troopers tried but lacked the manpower.[57]

When Guthman reported to Robert Kennedy, the attorney general expressed reluctance to use tear gas and asked to speak with Colonel Birdsong. In front of the Lyceum, meanwhile, a flying piece of pipe felled a marshal, and another suffered burns, perhaps from acid thrown from the mob. McShane consulted with his assistants and decided to act. Before Kennedy could talk with Birdsong, McShane commanded the marshals to put on their masks. A couple of minutes before 8:00 P.M., he ordered the release of the first tear gas volley. Canisters spewed into the Circle, and the mob retreated, briefly. Westerly winds carried the gas back toward the marshals, and as the air cleared, the mob surged toward the Lyceum. A pattern of attack, gas, and retreat continued for hours. After the marshals fired the first tear gas, Katzenbach apologetically told Robert Kennedy what the marshals had had to do. The attorney general regretted the escalation and rushed to tell his brother before he addressed the nation, but he was too late.[58]

Minutes after the order to fire, President Kennedy spoke on national radio and television about the Mississippi crisis. By delaying his talk from 5:30 until 8:00 P.M. (CST), he allowed events to overrun his message; he was unaware of the latest events in Oxford. First the president announced that, pursuant to the federal court orders, "Mr. James Meredith is now in residence on the campus of the University of Mississippi." Emphasizing that no troops had been used, he "hoped" that the marshals and local law enforcement agencies would be sufficient to allow everyone to "return to their normal activities." For him, the key principle was "the integrity of American law." Pointing out that the law included court decisions as well as legislation, he argued that "law is the eternal safeguard of liberty—and defiance of the law is the surest road to tyranny." He stressed, "Americans are free, in short, to disagree with the law—but not to disobey it."[59]

After noting that Meredith filed his own lawsuit, Kennedy reminded white Mississippians that eight southern judges on the Court of Appeals rendered the final decision. Once it ruled, the federal government had to carry out its order; his responsibility was "inescapable." He wanted to employ "as little force" and create the least possible disruption of the community. He regretted that the executive branch had to get involved and had "tried and exhausted" all other options. Mississippi authorities had "deliberately and unlawfully blocked" the court orders so "a peaceable and sensible solution . . . without any federal intervention" became impossible.[60]

To avoid offending white southerners, the president did not directly mention blacks, civil rights, integration, segregation, or states' rights, and he used the term "race relations" only once. Kennedy blunted his criticism even more by praising nine other southern states that had admitted all races to their universities. He also acknowledged that the "present period of transition and adjustment in our nation's Southland is a hard one for many people" and that the responsibility for any failures "must be shared by all of us, by every state, by every citizen," not just the South.[61]

Four concluding paragraphs of his nine-minute presentation flattered white Mississippians. Kennedy praised L. Q. C. Lamar and other native sons, including five Medal of Honor winners in the Korean conflict, for placing "national good ahead of sectional interest." Seeking support from Ole Miss students, he lauded their football team's "tradition of honor and courage," and he called on the students to display their "patriotism and integrity" and "courage" by obeying the law, even if they disagreed with it. According to Kennedy, "the honor of your University and the state are in the balance."[62] His first national broadcast on civil rights had no effect on the Ole Miss campus. Many rioters and observers listened to Kennedy on portable or car radios, but his appeals failed. The riot had already begun and oratory would not stop it.

Before the marshals released tear gas, one marshal alerted the patrolmen and suggested that they move out of the area. Thinking the gas unnecessary, the patrolmen cursed and ignored the warning. One patrolman threatened: "If y'all hurt one of those students I am going to take this magnum I have and kill every god damn one of you." At the first use of gas, the troopers on the edge of the crowd moved back because they had no gas masks, but parts of gas cartridges hit several patrolmen standing directly in front of the marshals. The patrolmen retreated to get their gas masks from their patrol cars, and Dave Gayden instructed them to leave their weapons locked in their car trunks.

When they returned to the vicinity of the Lyceum, they discovered their World War I vintage masks were ineffective and returned again to their headquarters in the gymnasium. After an hour and a half, with the gas continuing to spread, Birdsong and Gayden discussed the use of the patrol with Katzenbach and Doar. As a result, Birdsong ordered all the patrolmen to leave campus, regroup west of Oxford, and then establish roadblocks on entrances to Oxford. The state patrol, therefore, finally left the university completely in the hands of the federal marshals. The gates to the university opened to all.[63]

In the riot's first hours, outsiders streamed in and swelled the mob to more than two thousand. During the evening more people came from various Mississippi communities but also from neighboring states. Marshals also continued to arrive. Fourteen cars with nearly one hundred marshals arrived about twenty minutes into the rioting, and an hour later forty more. For almost three hours, they defended their position around the Lyceum in the face of repeated mob attacks. Confederate flags flew among the rioters, and often a rebel yell announced a charge. In all the shouting, few referred to James Meredith; the mob directed its wrath instead at the federal marshals. The marshals repeatedly charged into the Circle to use tear gas to force the mob to disperse; many retreated toward the Confederate monument until the gas cleared enough for another assault. Rioters scavenged bricks and boards from the science building construction site, and they stole chemicals from the chemistry labs. As nonstudents joined the mob, gunfire also erupted. With the street lights on the Circle shot out, the Lyceum's porch lights made the marshals standing beneath them easy targets. Bullets from unknown sources hit dozens of marshals, and the Lyceum became a first aid center with wounded marshals lining the halls.[64]

The marshals found themselves unprepared for the violence they faced. They needed better communications, both among themselves and with officials in Washington, equipment to light the area and to address the mob, and medical personnel and provisions. They had no stretchers to carry the wounded, and a lack of planning left the Lyceum's rear (west) door locked so the wounded had to pass through the more dangerous east entrance facing the Circle. The marshals also lacked ambulances to transport critical cases to the hospital. When a tear gas canister struck patrolman Welby Brunt in the head early in the conflict, Justice Department representatives realized they could offer no medical assistance and had no way to transport him to the airport; two hours elapsed before an ambulance could take the critically injured trooper from the university infirmary to the Oxford airport for a lifesaving flight to the university medical center in Jackson.[65]

By 8:15 P.M., some marshals needed more tear gas. Repeated radio requests failed to get it. When tear gas finally did arrive from the airport, it was not enough to supply all of them. Hours after the riot began, the marshals still called for more tear gas. Several squads of marshals also needed helmets and gas masks because their own gas often blew back at them. Truck drivers lacked basic directions for getting from the airport to the university and for driving around the town and campus. Their uncertainty delayed their work and made them easy targets.[66]

The night's easiest target may have been thirty-year-old Paul Leslie Guihard, a British reporter for a French news agency and a stringer for the *London Daily Sketch*. The British son of a Frenchman and a British woman, he was a British army veteran and had reported for a decade, more than two years in the New York bureau of Agence France Presse. Enthusiastic and aggressive, "Flash" flew into Jackson on Sunday and in the afternoon witnessed the scene at the governor's mansion, ventured across the street to the Citizens' Council's headquarters, and telephoned a report to New York. Late in the afternoon he and his photographer drove to Oxford and arrived soon after the riot commenced. Within an hour, he lay dead. Students found his body a dozen feet from Ward Hall and about five hundred feet from the Lyceum; they gave him heart massage because they assumed that he had suffered a heart attack. After they failed to secure an ambulance, a student drove him to the hospital, but he was already dead. From a distance of less than one foot, an unknown assailant had shot Guihard in the middle of the back; the .38 caliber bullet pierced his heart. Dressed in a white shirt and brown suit coat and sporting a red beard, he was a conspicuous outsider even if his killer never heard him speak.[67]

A more famous and dangerous visitor was Edwin Walker. After his news conference, Walker tried to enter the campus about 6:00 P.M., but the highway patrol prevented him. He then went to the courthouse, where he talked informally with sheriffs and deputies. About 7:30 P.M., he ate supper at the Mansion Restaurant and listened to the president's address. A disgusted Walker then proceeded toward campus. Parking east of the university, he walked toward the action. Dressed in a dark suit, white shirt, and tie, Walker stopped across from the Confederate monument and talked with students on the fringe of the crowd. Moving toward the flagpole in the center of the Circle, he discussed the situation for fifteen minutes. When people saw the Texan wearing a Stetson hat, they called out, "We have a leader," and "General, will you lead us to the steps?" After huddling with protesters, he announced, "Well, we are ready." They then moved toward the Lyceum, but a blast of tear gas forced them to retreat. Walker heard cries of "Will you get us organized, will you lead us?" and "Would you lead us in a charge?" He later claimed that he never led anyone that night, but others thought they saw him nod his head.[68]

About 9:00 P.M., while Walker stood between the monument and the flag-pole, Reverend Gray recognized him from television and newspapers. Gray had first come to campus before 6:00 P.M. at the request of a parent to retrieve her daughter from her dormitory. After eating supper at his church and watch-ing Kennedy on television at Jim Silver's home, the rector returned to campus. Alarmed at the rioting, Gray appealed unsuccessfully to a deputy sheriff to restore order and then ventured out into the Circle to try to stop the rioting. Occasionally taking refuge in the Y Building, Gray worked in the growing darkness to persuade students to return to their dorms and anyone else present to drop their weapons. When he saw Walker, he realized that many considered Walker their leader, so he approached to ask the general for help in stopping the riot.[69]

To Gray's requests, Walker responded that he had no interest in stopping students who had a right to protest and that he was only an observer. "Who are you anyway," Walker challenged, "and what are *you* doing here?" Explaining that he was the Episcopal rector, Gray said he wanted to avoid injuries and pre-vent any further damage to the state or university. Walker commented, "You are the kind of minister that makes me ashamed to be an Episcopalian." The rector said that he had a right to be concerned about his hometown and suggested that Walker should have stayed at his home in Texas. Gray tried to convince people nearby to leave. In the meantime, Walker turned and walked toward the monument. When men accompanying Walker prevented Gray from following, he returned to the Y Building to watch the continuing action.[70]

As Walker walked westward through the Circle, hundreds moved with him to the flagpole and then toward the Lyceum. When they surged at the Lyceum, many hurled objects at the marshals. Watching the crowd approach, the mar-shals responded again with a volley of tear gas. To escape the noxious fumes, the throng retreated toward the statue, where Walker again spoke to them. "If you can't win, go home," he shouted. "But, let's not quit. We can win."[71]

After a few minutes in the Y Building, Gray went back outside where he noticed part of the crowd clustered around Walker perched on the side of the Confederate monument. Gray walked over to hear him congratulate the stu-dents for their stand. Walker assured them of their right to protest and the justness of their cause. He claimed that troops should have been in Cuba, not Mississippi, and he explained the presence of federal forces by telling the throng that they had been "sold out." To shouts asking who had sold them out, Walker replied that "Birdsong let you down." Despite the alleged treachery, Walker beseeched them, "Don't let your governor down" and "Stay with Ross Barnett." He told them reinforcements would soon arrive from all over the na-tion and any bloodshed would be "on the hands of the Federal Government."[72]

Reverend Gray climbed onto the base of the statue but could not make his way to the side where Walker addressed the crowd. When Gray walked up to him, the general announced that the group contained an Episcopal minister whose position embarrassed him as an Episcopalian. Four men pulled Gray aside, roughed him up, and sent him away. Friendly people helped Gray escape to the Y Building. In the meantime, Walker had encouraged the crowd to "go get 'em boys" and instructed them to "charge." When Gray returned a few minutes later, Walker and others were going toward the Lyceum. Gray persisted in his efforts to persuade individuals to refrain from violence, looked for his colleague Reverend Wofford Smith, and finally, about 10:00 P.M., left campus when he helped a friend by driving a car away from the university.[73]

Chaplain Smith, meanwhile, circulating among the mob, also appealed for an end to the disorder and violence. He periodically returned to the Y Building for respite from the gas and chaos. On one stop at the Y shortly after 9:00 P.M., Smith heard that several students had been shot, apparently by the marshals. Horrified, he decided to confront the marshals. Waving a white flag, he rushed toward the Lyceum and marshals ushered him inside. Discussions persuaded Smith that they had not fired on the students, but, after seeing wounded marshals lying on the hall floors waiting for first aid, he realized that he had to do whatever possible to stop the bloodshed. When a marshal suggested that he appeal to the crowd for calm, Smith agreed to try.[74]

With objects and debris pummeling marshals outside the Lyceum, Smith, accompanied by a marshal, went out the east door, walked into the street, and shouted for attention. When some rioters saw his clerical collar, the onslaught abated. In response to his appeal and the marshals' request for someone to speak for the mob, a young man stepped out of the crowd. Smith offered to discuss the situation, but the freshman—undoubtedly, with a beanie and a shaved head—said that he did not feel qualified to speak. When the marshals called for a senior, George M. "Buck" Randall stepped forward. Smith recognized him as a football player because he had seen him in Jackson on Saturday. Randall, a fullback, explained that the crowd wanted to storm the Lyceum to get Meredith. A cheer at the pep rally the day before had declared, "Hotty, toddy, we want a body." Smith explained that Meredith was not inside, and Randall relayed the information and tried to get the crowd to disperse, but the rioters refused to listen and recommenced hurling curses and missiles at the marshals, who responded with more of their dwindling supply of tear gas. The dispirited Smith retreated into the Lyceum, and Randall soon returned to his dormitory. The melee resumed.[75]

About 9:30 P.M., when the remnant of the highway patrol withdrew, several hundred marshals tried to defend the Lyceum, while six hundred yards away a smaller contingent protected Baxter Hall and Meredith. According to a marshal directing traffic, one of the patrol cars, in a final protest, tried to run him down as the troopers left. Under the new circumstances around the Lyceum, the marshals could hardly maintain order. Pandemonium prevailed. The mob controlled most of the Circle, while smaller bands roamed the heart of the campus. In a symbolic protest, someone raised the Confederate flag. Tear gas permeated the center of the campus, and an occasional breeze blew it farther around the campus. Rumors also abounded. One claimed that a coed had been killed, another that Birdsong had been shot.[76]

As the siege of the Lyceum continued, the rioters used vehicles to attack the marshals' position. At about the time the highway patrol exited, someone stole a fire truck from the university power plant and drove it toward the Lyceum. University employees pursued the truck until tear gas around the Circle halted them. The driver stopped it near the Y Building, where others hooked its hose to a fire hydrant and tried to spray the marshals. In reaction several marshals launched tear gas canisters toward the fire hose, forced the would-be firemen to abandon the truck and its hose, and cut the truck's ignition wires. After resuming their posts at the Lyceum, the marshals heard that the crowd wanted to block the street around the Circle by turning over the fire truck. Desperate for tear gas and reinforcements, the marshals went back to the truck to keep the street clear. While holding the crowd at bay until more tear gas arrived, the marshals shot several bullets into the hose to cripple it. They returned to the vicinity of the Lyceum when army trucks brought additional tear gas.[77]

No sooner had the marshals disposed of the fire truck than they faced a bulldozer. Rioters commandeered it from a construction site and drove it through the Circle toward the Lyceum. Volleys of tear gas, some fired directly into the cab, forced the driver to flee, and then marshals jumped on board and stopped the bulldozer. About twenty minutes later, the rioters restarted the bulldozer and aimed it again at the Lyceum, with a crowd following behind hurling all kinds of projectiles. The marshals stopped it thirty feet from the Lyceum's front door. Ten minutes later rioters sent toward the Lyceum an unoccupied 1954 Chevrolet with doors locked and windows closed. At first the marshals could not see it through the haze but heard it approach from the flagpole area. When the car emerged into the open, at least one marshal fired his pistol at it as it passed by him, but the bullets had little effect. Another marshal turned the bulldozer toward the approaching car and let it crash into the bulldozer's blade. The marshals left the bulldozer in a defensive position facing the mob.[78]

Thwarted in using the bulldozer and the automobile, rioters restarted the fire truck about 11:20 P.M. and drove it in front of the Lyceum. The driver aimed the truck at the marshals, who avoided being hit by jumping out of its path. As the truck circled several times, a few protesters held on while others ran safely behind it; all of them threw things at the marshals. On its last pass, several marshals shot at the truck's tires and engine while others sent tear gas into the truck's cab. Affected by the gas, the driver swerved and drove into a tree in the Circle. After the marshals apprehended the driver, a sailor from Memphis Naval Air Station, a marshal parked the fire truck beside the Lyceum and cut the wires to the distributor.[79]

Throughout the frenzy that began with the first tear gas, people poured onto the campus. According to eyewitnesses, within a couple of hours the crowd shifted from primarily Ole Miss students to mostly older strangers. With the outsiders, the level and volume of violence mounted. Gunfire especially increased. Countless unknown assailants, some in the Circle's trees, peppered the marshals' position with pistol, rifle, and shotgun fire. With their views hindered by darkness and obstructed by the tear gas in the air, the snipers and other assailants often fired randomly in the direction of the Lyceum or other targets. Their fusillade nonetheless wounded dozens of marshals. When the mob heard that a marshal had been shot, it let out a cheer.[80]

Among the marshals, thirty-nine-year-old Graham E. Same from Indianapolis received the most grievous injury when one buckshot pellet struck him in his carotid artery. Fearing that he was dying, marshals carried him into the Lyceum, where a border patrolman temporarily stopped the bleeding. No doctor was available. A university physician had been at the Lyceum for an hour after the riot started but then went to the infirmary to treat the wounded. After more than two hours of rioting, Clegg called to ask Dr. L. G. Hopkins, a local general practitioner, to come to the Lyceum. With the help of the state highway patrol, Hopkins arrived about midnight and began treating the wounded. Marshal Same's condition was critical, so when conditions outside permitted, he was evacuated to the airport and flown to Memphis for treatment. Rumors spread that he had died, but, in fact, no marshal perished.[81]

A local civilian was not as fortunate. After dove hunting Sunday afternoon, Walter Ray Gunter and Charlie Berryhill went to Ole Miss to see what was going on. Gunter, a twenty-three-year-old, lived in Abbeville, just north of Oxford, while his friend lived outside Oxford and worked at the university as a painter. A high school dropout, Gunter repaired jukeboxes, enjoyed drag racing, hunted and fished, and, with his eighteen-year-old wife, expected their first child within a few days. The two men came to campus before dark but left to eat supper. About 9:30 they returned, milled around the Confederate statue, and then walked to a construction site two hundred yards southeast of the Lyceum where for a good view the two friends stood on a stack of eighteen-inch concrete drainage pipes. Watching over the heads of others standing nearby, the two men observed the assaults on news cameramen and the episode with the bulldozer. When the rioting moved in their direction or when gunfire seemed threatening, they retreated between buildings but returned when the action shifted. Shortly after 10:30 P.M., when protesters rushed toward Gunter's position with marshals in pursuit, his friend jumped down and suggested they leave. Gunter never followed. With only a "dull thud," a .38 caliber bullet struck him in the middle of his forehead and he slumped onto the pipes. When Berryhill turned to hurry Gunter along and saw him sitting with blood running from his head, he and several strangers picked him up and rushed him to the hospital, but Gunter died on the way. Authorities never charged anyone in his death; the Lafayette County sheriff believed that he had been killed by a stray shot. Nine days after his death, Gunter's wife delivered their baby daughter.[82]

As the disturbance descended into a deadly riot, the Kennedy administration kept in contact with officials on the scene via telephone. After his televised address, the president, the attorney general, and several aides worked for three hours out of the Cabinet Room in the White House. Within the first hour, the White House group suggested that the Justice Department delegation in the Lyceum ask coach John Vaught to appeal to the mob for peace, but they could not locate him. After hearing of the severity of the attacks and the death of Guihard, the Kennedys worried about Meredith's safety. The withdrawal of the state highway patrol especially concerned them.[83]

At 9:30 Sunday evening, Secretary of the Army Vance directed General Billingslea to send troops to Oxford. The order dramatically accelerated the deployment scheduled for Monday. A few minutes later Katzenbach asked for troops and received authority from Washington to direct the local National Guard unit to the Lyceum to reinforce the marshals. A few minutes after 10:00 P.M., Katzenbach called Colonel Murry Falkner at the Oxford armory and instructed him to bring Troop E of the 108th Armored Cavalry Regiment to the Lyceum.[84]

About the time Falkner and his unit of four officers and seventy enlisted men left the armory, President Kennedy called Barnett to protest the patrol's removal and to demand that state authorities end the riot. He volunteered that continued rioting made it unsafe to remove Meredith. To the governor, mentioning a withdrawal of Meredith demonstrated an encouraging lack of federal resolve. After reporting that he had ordered Birdsong to commit as many patrolmen as possible to restoring order, Barnett proposed to go to Oxford to tell the mob that Kennedy had agreed to remove Meredith from Ole Miss. Kennedy, wondering how long such a trip would take, speculated that even an hour might be too long to wait. Concern only increased when Barnett announced (incorrectly) that a state patrolman had just died. To Barnett's plea to remove Meredith, Kennedy repeated that he could not be removed during rioting. Barnett pledged to try to restore order. The president then agreed to talk again, after order had been restored, "about what's the best thing to do with Meredith." His implied concession suggested to Barnett that the fight was not over.[85]

The governor needed little encouragement. Pressured by segregationist advisers, he worried that his earlier statement in response to the marshals' invasion had, despite its defiance, seemed like a change of position. To correct any impression that he had backed down, Barnett late Sunday evening made another public statement. "Some reports interpreting my statement tonight as altering my stand in any way," he declared, "are wholly untrue and completely unfounded." To shore up his reputation as a strict segregationist, he said, "I repeat to the people of Mississippi I will never yield a single inch in my determination to win the fight we are all engaged in. I call on all Mississippians to keep up this faith and courage." And he swore, "I will never surrender."[86]

While Kennedy and Barnett spoke, the lieutenant governor arrived in Oxford. Earlier in the evening, after reports of the marshals' arrival on campus, Paul Johnson had rushed to the governor's mansion, where they decided that he would go to Ole Miss. He arrived after 10:00 P.M. He and Birdsong rendezvoused just west of the university in a bowling alley parking lot where highway patrolmen had retreated. They drove to the Lyceum to confront Katzenbach and Doar with their demand that the marshals stop using tear gas if they wanted the patrol to return to help restore order. But Katzenbach objected. Instead they agreed that the state patrol would establish new roadblocks around Oxford to keep more outsiders from flooding onto the campus. Nearly one hundred patrolmen deployed on the major roads leading into town.[87]

The situation at the university worsened, despite the highway patrol's success in blocking many people from the campus. Dozens went around the roadblocks, across the countryside, and into the melee. The growing crowds attacked journalists' vehicles and army trucks, and on the Circle they set several private automobiles on fire. At least a half-dozen vehicles owned by university faculty and staff suffered major damage.[88]

More serious than property damage, the number of injured soared; they mainly suffered the effects of tear gas, bricks, bottles, and gunshots. Before the night ended, nearly 40 percent of the more than five hundred marshals were injured. They had broken bones, cuts and scrapes, burns caused by chemicals from nearby labs, and respiratory problems brought on by their own tear gas.

Bullets, buckshot, or birdshot struck twenty-nine marshals. Many received assistance in the Lyceum's makeshift first-aid station, but some, along with students and others, went to the student health service, where doctors and nurses treated them throughout the long night.[89]

In Washington, the group in the Cabinet Room received distressing reports of the deteriorating conditions. Thinking about his talk with the governor, the president asked his advisers, "What about removing him if Barnett says that he can restore law and order?" When nobody responded, the discussion continued to focus on the safety of the marshals and of Meredith. The marshals wanted to protect themselves by firing back at the protesters, but when Katzenbach asked about the marshals' returning fire, Robert Kennedy told him only, "Oh, I think they can fire to save *him*." While urging Katzenbach to "hold out" for another hour and to protect Meredith, the attorney general and the others expressed frustration that the National Guard and the army were taking so long to get to the university.[90]

When Troop E of the National Guard finally reached campus in its four jeeps and two trucks, it proceeded straight through the heart of the riot. The mob screamed epithets at the men, threw missiles at the convoy, and shot at the vehicles as they maneuvered around the Circle through barricades erected by the protesters. The soldiers had on their gas masks and rode under the trucks' tarpaulins, but they could not escape the violence. A brick thrown through his jeep windshield broke Falkner's arm. When they finally arrived shortly before 11:00 P.M., Falkner deployed his men with the marshals along the Lyceum's north side, but half a dozen had already suffered injuries and went inside for first aid. Though white and undoubtedly sympathetic to segregation, the Guardsmen fought the rioters, many also Mississippians. As one Guardsman said, "When they start bouncing bricks off your helmet, you don't care what state they're from." A nephew of William Faulkner, Colonel Falkner used a bullhorn to appeal unsuccessfully to the crowd. Learning of the marshals' low supply of tear gas, Falkner dispatched trucks to the airport. Shortly after 11:30 P.M., before the Guard trucks could reach the airport, an army truck arrived from the airport with four marshals, twenty-two prison guards, and twenty-two cases of gas grenades. Within two hours other elements of the Guard's 108th Armored Cavalry Regiment arrived at the Lyceum. In the meantime violence continued and the need increased for regular army troops and others to reinforce the beleaguered forces at the Lyceum.[91]

The first National Guard units did not alleviate all the problems facing the Justice Department representatives in Oxford. Though the meeting in the Cabinet Room broke up at 1:00 A.M. (11:00 P.M. CST), the Kennedy brothers monitored the situation from the White House for another three and a half hours. Worried about reports of snipers and dissatisfied with the highway patrol's inaction, at fifteen minutes before midnight President Kennedy called Barnett and insisted that "we've got to get this situation under control." The governor volunteered to "issue any statement, any time about peace and violence," and he explained that public pressure had forced him to say that he refused to give up. He told Kennedy, "You understand. That's just to Mississippi people." Claiming to understand, Kennedy accepted that nobody "in Mississippi or anyplace else wants a lot of people killed." The call ended when Barnett agreed to send highway patrolmen to the campus to restore order.[92]

When they talked five minutes later, Barnett reported that Colonel Birdsong had about one hundred and fifty men in Oxford. Kennedy asked about patrolmen sitting in their cars several blocks from the campus. Barnett reported, "I told 'em, just like you asked me, to get *moving*." He also assured the president that Birdsong had called for fifty more patrolmen to report to Oxford and that he would do all he could to stop the shooting. When Kennedy also requested that Birdsong "get those students to go to bed," he showed his misapprehension of the magnitude of the crisis.[93]

The president grew increasingly disgusted with the army's slow deployment, but poor communications between Washington, Memphis, and Oxford, especially at the airport, meant that nobody had an explanation. By late Sunday night, the army had not fulfilled the promise of its Operation *Rapid* Road. General Billingslea flew from Memphis and arrived at the Oxford airport about midnight. A company of more than one hundred MPs followed in helicopters, but confusion and difficulties at Memphis Naval Air Station delayed them. By 11:45 P.M., their tardy departure had frustrated President Kennedy. At the university, federal agents expected the MPs to land on the campus about 12:15 A.M. at an improvised site next to the football stadium. Katzenbach, worried about the marshals' safety, repeatedly asked where Billingslea and his forces were. After the MPs finally began landing at the Oxford airport at 1:00 A.M., Katzenbach prodded them to get to campus. From the White House, an exasperated President Kennedy at 1:30 A.M. CST demanded that Billingslea move his troops immediately.[94]

While the MPs made their way from Memphis, trouble continued all around campus. Ominous reports included outsiders preparing for more assaults. Federal officials had particular concern about Walker's activities. After mingling with protesters near the Confederate monument until a few minutes after 1:00 A.M. Monday, Walker drove with a companion to a gas station on Highway 6 near the university's western entrance. He shook hands and talked with about twenty men and crossed the highway to chat with highway patrolmen. About 2:15 A.M., when a station wagon drove up to the gas station and four men got out and went into a building next door, Walker followed. The men got a case of empty soft drink bottles, filled a five-gallon can with gasoline, and drove off toward campus. Walker walked to the campus entrance where he talked with a few patrolmen. He may have briefly returned to campus, but about 3:30 A.M. he apparently ended his intrigues and returned to his motel room for the remainder of the night.[95]

While Walker agitated west of campus, the army proceeded to Ole Miss. Shortly before 2:00 A.M., the convoy departed from the Oxford airport. The plan called for them to approach the Lyceum from the west, but ten minutes later the caravan erroneously approached the campus entrance at the north end of Sorority Row. When state patrolmen stopped the buses, the troops armed with rifles, bayonets, helmets, and gas masks unloaded and marched to the Lyceum. Weathering abuse and attacks, the one hundred MPs passed the chancellor's residence and continued through tear gas, burning vehicles, smoke, and debris on the Circle as they came to the Lyceum from the northeast. From inside the building one Washington journalist reported, "At 2:15 A.M. came a spontaneous shout that I will never forget: 'They're here. They're here.' "[96]

Four hours after first summoned to the campus, Company A of the 503rd Military Police Battalion from Fort Bragg joined the marshals and Guardsmen in encircling the Lyceum. They did not immediately vanquish the rioters; suppression of the riot depended on the arrival of additional troops. An hour later two squadrons of the 108th Armored Cavalry of the National Guard arrived at the Lyceum. Lacking maps of the university, the National Guard units had to rely on sketchy information supplied by the Guardsmen themselves to plan their deployment. Six hundred marshals and soldiers finally began to gain control of the campus by sweeping the mob back from the Lyceum and eventually from the campus. More military forces, including the 716th Military Police Battalion, continued to converge on the campus throughout early Monday morning. One company of soldiers marched to Baxter Hall where James Meredith slept and secured it by dawn. At 6:15 A.M. Monday, General Billingslea announced, "I now declare this area [the campus] secure."[97]

Early Monday morning, four trustees also issued their own reassuring statement. Shortly after the rioting started the previous evening, Chancellor Williams called Charles Fair in Louisville to report on events and to request that some trustees come to campus. Fair agreed and persuaded Thomas Tubb of West Point to join him; Tubb then did the same with S. R. Evans in Greenwood and Verner Holmes in McComb. Though Holmes arrived on the train shortly before dawn, the other trustees drove, arrived by midnight, and stayed with Williams and Clegg throughout the night. After Holmes joined them, they announced that "peace and quiet were established." The four trustees concluded that most rioters were not students, many not even Mississippians. With the army in control, the trustees were "satisfied that there will be no repetition of the horrible experiences of Sunday night on the campus." Calling the campus "completely normal," they promised parents that "students will be fully protected as long as they obey the rules and regulations of the University." The trustees and the chancellor hoped to keep Ole Miss open.[98]

In securing the campus, the army pushed the rioters into Oxford. Violence and chaos had not been completely eliminated but merely transferred from gown to town. By 7:30 A.M., Mayor Richard W. Elliott observed rioting on the Oxford square. With only seven policemen and thirty special deputies, the city could not handle the intruders. After appealing over an Oxford radio station for citizens to stay home, Elliott tried to get the highway patrol to stop the rioting, but the remaining troopers in town refused because their orders did not allow it. Unwilling to see his town destroyed, Mayor Elliott contacted the local FBI agent and requested federal assistance. Within twenty minutes the army appeared downtown to suppress the rioting and restore order.[99]

As the army secured the campus and restored order around the courthouse square, one phase of the struggle to desegregate the University of Mississippi ended, and James Meredith prepared to start the next phase as the first known black student to enroll at Ole Miss.

19. "Prisoner of War in a Strange Struggle": Meredith at Ole Miss

■ ■

Monday morning after the riot, James Meredith skipped breakfast and went to the Lyceum. Escorted by John Doar, James McShane, and several marshals, he rode from Baxter Hall in a riot-damaged border patrol car. Dressed in a suit and tie, he entered the Lyceum for the first time at 8:15 A.M. and proceeded to the registrar's office. In what the Associated Press called "a strange and eerie sight," with tear gas lingering in the air, marshals and troops encircling the building, and a group of students protesting across the street, he matriculated at Ole Miss. After completing the necessary forms, including ones for late registration and for the Veterans Administration, he paid his tuition and fees with $230 in cash. Registrar Robert Ellis then gave him the class schedule prepared two weeks earlier by the dean of liberal arts. After fifty-five minutes, Meredith left for his first class. Ellis refused to comment. When a reporter asked Meredith if he was happy to be registered, he only said, "This is not a happy day." Soon a proclamation appeared on the Lyceum's pressroom door: "Pursuant to the mandate of the Federal Courts, the orders for the registration of James Meredith have been followed."[1]

Outside the Confederate flag flew at half-staff and students cried, "Nigger go home" and "How's it feel to have blood on your hands?" With the slightest smile, Meredith ignored the taunts. Edwin Guthman, Justice Department press officer, announced, "Marshals will escort Meredith about the campus as long as necessary. They won't leave him as long as he is in danger." Occasionally rubbing his eyes and holding a handkerchief to his face because of tear gas, Meredith walked to his first class.[2]

He arrived at the nine o'clock class in colonial American history fourteen minutes late. Only nine of twelve students were present in the Graduate Building classroom. Professor Clare Marquette, who had known for more than a week that Meredith would be in his class, interrupted his lecture on "The Beginnings of English Colonization" to answer the door. After meeting Doar and McShane, he welcomed his new student and showed him to a seat; the escorts remained outside the room. The professor provided his unprepared pupil with paper and explained how far he had gone in the lecture. At first the others seemed to ignore Meredith, but several soon left. At the end of the hour he left with his escorts and returned to his dorm. Marquette later observed that Meredith's attendance amounted to "a revolution in the prevailing customs in the state."[3]

After forgoing lunch, Meredith rode with McShane and other marshals to his Spanish class. The other students stayed away because they heard he would be in the class, so the instructor called off class. Lingering tear gas forced the cancellation of his math class. Monday evening in his dorm room, Meredith ate dinner prepared by the army. He had achieved his goal "to breach the system of 'White Supremacy.' "[4]

Meredith's surroundings resembled an "eerie military camp." Riot debris littered the heart of the campus. Soldiers manned all entrances and patrolled the town and campus. MPs guarded Baxter Hall, while marshals rested in and around the Lyceum. A field hospital occupied an athletic field, and the army converted an intramural field into a motor pool. While the student union grill remained closed, the campus cafeteria served meals with paper plates and plastic utensils, but without its black employees, who all stayed away.[5]

Hundreds of students had fled, and some parents had driven to Oxford to retrieve their children. Seventy-five percent of the females may have left. At least fifty students sought to transfer to three private colleges in Jackson, while others tried to switch to Tennessee schools. As a result, attendance Monday dropped 70 percent.[6]

Monday's extra edition of the *Mississippian* published pleas from student and university leaders. Editor Sidna Brower urged students not to bring "dishonor and shame" by engaging in violence. Acknowledging that Ole Miss was "caught in the middle," she observed that federal authority would prevail as it had in the Civil War when the nation divided over nearly identical issues. The student government president warned that rioters and demonstrators could face expulsion. Messages from Chancellor Williams and Dean Love, prepared before Sunday night, pled for calm and cooperation.[7]

Students nevertheless protested Meredith's presence. They yelled, "You won't live long, nigger," and "Dirty bugger, go home." Homecoming decorations at the Delta Kappa Epsilon house included imitation guns behind barricades made of hay bales along with a sign proclaiming, "You may take the campus, but you will play hell with the DEKES." Late Tuesday night, after hearing grenades and weapons fire, soldiers rushed to Fraternity Row but discovered only a record player blaring from the DEKE house. A black effigy hanged from a window across from Baxter Hall, students set off firecrackers and threw rocks at the building, and a sign declared, "We're gonna miss you when you're gone." A second effigy accompanied by a Confederate flag ordered, "Go back to Africa where you belong." Authorities made no arrests. On Wednesday an unemployed white man from northeastern Mississippi who said, "I'll kill him, so help me God, if I can get my hands on him," tried to enter Baxter Hall, but soldiers apprehended him.[8]

Returning students pushed attendance to 50 percent by Wednesday and 75 percent the next day. Though Meredith spent several hours Tuesday taking tests required for transfer students, he continued attending classes. Justice Department representatives drove him to his classes and waited outside the classrooms, while MPs sat in nearby jeeps. The army continued to provide his meals in Baxter Hall. On Thursday he walked unescorted to one of his classes, ate his first meal in the cafeteria, and visited the campus post office, with his escorts always close by. He often drew a taunting, jeering crowd who threw rocks and exploded firecrackers. He usually ignored the insults or replied with a wave or a smile. On a Thursday afternoon walk he got only about halfway from his last class to the library before a female student asked, "Why doesn't somebody kill him?" Marshals loaded him in their car for the ride to the library.[9]

In the library one student came out of a room to say to a marshal, "Tell him he can study in here if he wants to smoke." When Meredith went to his math class one afternoon, a student sitting outside a building said hello, and a smiling Meredith returned the greeting. Though most diners hushed when he entered the cafeteria, and a few left, one young man shook hands with him, sat down, and talked for a few minutes. Most students gradually adopted an "ignore the whole thing" attitude. As one freshman who had thought he would leave the university said, "Now that he's in I think I can live with it." Another decided, "We should all be thankful that the Army is here, otherwise there might be no university standing today." A raucous two or three hundred out of nearly five thousand agitated the campus and worried authorities.[10]

The first major threat to the developing peace came with the homecoming football game scheduled for Meredith's first Saturday in Oxford. The undefeated Rebels' game against the Houston Cougars would attract more than thirty thousand, and the influx worried federal officials. On Tuesday, when federal and university officials conferred, the army and the chancellor thought playing the game in Oxford would demonstrate the restoration of peace and order, and Williams announced homecoming would take place as planned. A Justice Department spokesman suggested, however, that the game might not be played in Oxford because crowds could cause violence and disruptions. Some local merchants as well as university students also feared violence. One student feared "the rednecks in for a football game." The head of the Mississippi Sheriffs Association warned of a potential "holocaust." The University of Houston compounded the problem when it announced it did not want to play in Oxford.[11]

Military intelligence reported that an Oxford game could produce another explosion. A bomb threat against Baxter Hall and shots fired at an MP patrol also concerned the military, but army leaders supported the home game. On Wednesday, Katzenbach and Guthman flew to Washington to confer with the attorney general and Pentagon officials. After the consultations, the Defense Department announced early Thursday morning that the game would not be played in Oxford because it might lead to "disorder and injury." Federal authorities would allow the game to be played in either Houston or Jackson. Ole Miss immediately canceled all homecoming activities and moved the game to Jackson's 45,000-seat Memorial Stadium.[12]

Governor Ross Barnett "personally guaranteed" all students a ride to the game, and he personally borrowed nearly five thousand dollars to charter a train to Jackson. Saturday morning one thousand students boarded a twenty-two-car "Freedom Train" for the four-hour ride. Sporting Confederate flags and chanting "Six, five, four, three, go to hell Kennedy," they joined seventeen thousand fans at Memorial Stadium. Students handed out decals picturing a black Colonel Rebel saying, "Go Rebels! That's a court order!" The crowd greeted Barnett with "an ear-splitting," "frantic explosion of applause," the loudest outburst of the afternoon. In his invocation, Episcopal bishop John Maury Allen prayed, "Save us from violence, discord and confusion," but Rebel fans expressed their contrary feelings when they cheered "Dixie" and the announcement that Michigan had defeated Army. The Rebels' 40–7 victory seemed almost an anticlimax.[13]

Ignoring football, Meredith, as he would during the upcoming months, left on Friday to spend the weekend in Memphis with his wife, one of his lawyers, and friends. Though his first week had been difficult, Meredith told reporters that he had "lived under adverse circumstances all my life." Despite starting a week late, he denied any academic difficulty and reported that the faculty had impressed him as "a more professional group" than he had seen at other institutions. When asked if he would persist at Ole Miss, he laughingly assured newsmen that he would not have tried to enroll if he had not been fully prepared to stay. He could not judge whether the campus situation had improved but wanted it "back to normal as soon as possible so students can continue their studies normally." Despite his hopes, Meredith faced continual harassment and remained isolated. He had become, one reporter observed, a "prisoner of war in a strange struggle."[14]

The Justice Department, realizing it could not force students to like Meredith or to approve integration, worked for a better college atmosphere. By widening his campus activities, a Justice Department lawyer explained, "We want him to become as common a sight here as one of the trees." To improve conditions, Katzenbach met with two student groups. At the law school on Monday of the second week, he defended the government, criticized state leaders, and reminded the students that court orders had to be obeyed. Future events were "very much more in the hands of the students than anyone else," so he urged them to "accept the fact that Meredith will be on the campus and get on with the job of studying." He encouraged a smaller group of student leaders to assume some responsibility for their university, but he refused to tell them how to do it.[15]

At the law school, Katzenbach brought up the question of black soldiers. Their presence had drawn complaints, while Meredith objected to their segregation. To fashion a solution President Kennedy directed that the army assign black soldiers to all jobs except sentinel duty at Baxter Hall. Two days later Katzenbach reignited a controversy when he told the law students that using blacks soldiers as truck drivers the night of the riot had appalled him. Aware that it could incite the crowd, he admitted, "I could have dropped dead."[16]

After Katzenbach's comments, unaware that weekend patrols had included black MPs, Meredith renewed his demand for an end to the segregation. On his way to class, he handed a reporter a handwritten, three-page statement attacking the army's use of black soldiers. Though the first integrated army units deployed on the campus "looked like American units," a later purge "re-segregated" them. After his complaint he noticed that blacks on a "garbage detail truck [were] unarmed" while whites carried weapons. He called it "intolerable" and "a dishonor and a disgrace" to other black servicemen. According to Secretary Vance, the army had initially acted "to avoid unnecessary incidents," but "after the situation became more stabilized" restored blacks to "all normal functions." He insisted that the army had removed them for their own protection. To prevent conflict, army leaders in Mississippi kept black troops from situations where they would directly interact with white students. The issue had been resolved.[17]

Katzenbach's law school comments provoked other protests. Henry Hederman, an owner of the *Jackson Clarion-Ledger*, charged that Katzenbach tried to "indoctrinate" students, while Fred Beard saw the "brainwashing" as an example of university cooperation with the federal government. To rebut Katzenbach, Attorney General Joe Patterson demanded equal time. In the mid-1950s he had followed a more moderate course on segregation than most Mississippi leaders by supporting the construction of an integrated Veterans Administration hospital in Jackson and by remaining loyal to the national Democratic ticket in 1960. In the weeks before Meredith's arrival, Barnett did not include Patterson among his close advisers. According to one observer, he had by October 1962 become "a political target for some of Gov. Barnett's close friends," so perhaps he responded to Katzenbach to protect himself politically before an election year.[18]

While Patterson waited, students continued to harass Meredith. On the evening of Sunday, October 7, more than one hundred harassed him when he left the cafeteria. During dinner the next night in the most serious demonstration since the riot, a rock shattered a cafeteria window, and glass hit Meredith's table. Meredith and the marshals finished their meal, while outside several hundred shouted "get that nigger" and "Kennedy is a coon keeper" and threw rocks, bottles, lighted cigarettes, and firecrackers at the MPs. Someone also let the air out of two tires on a car driven by marshals. MP reinforcements quickly arrived, and marshals removed Meredith through a rear door and returned to Baxter Hall.[19]

In reaction to protests, demands on Ole Miss's leaders increased. Faculty, especially the AAUP chapter, pressed for action. At its urging, the chancellor met with faculty Monday afternoon after the riot to assure them that the university was safe, would not close, and would retain accreditation. The next day the AAUP declared, "Riots, weapons, and agitators have no place at a university." A reluctance to enforce discipline frustrated some faculty. On October 9, seven law professors petitioned the chancellor to expel rioters and to prevent further disorder. At the same time the faculty senate debated resolutions for stronger discipline.[20]

Pressure also came from an unexpected source. On October 9, Hal Holbrook brought to the campus his "Mark Twain Tonight" performance. In one segment called "The Silent Lie," Mark Twain skewered the human propensity to conform, remain silent in the face of injustice, and ignore the truth. He declared that "there is no art to this silent lie. It is timid and shabby." Mark Twain also belittled people who believed that they had found the truth: "They spend the rest of their lives putting shingles around their truth to protect it from the weather." Holbrook's demand for facing the truth in the name of justice elicited an ovation.[21]

Responding to the pressures, Chancellor Williams on Thursday evening, October 11, spoke several times over the campus radio station. "Do not panic, riot, or in any way incite a riot," he pleaded. "No student, who loves Ole Miss," he maintained, "will do anything to bring dishonor to her or to the State and the nation." The next day Dean Love formally "deplore[d]" violence, insisted that it "cease immediately," and warned of "immediate and drastic disciplinary action." The faculty senate, faculty in Phi Beta Kappa, and the *Mississippian* endorsed the policy. The student government on October 16 condemned violent student demonstrations, though it also protested "the forced admission of an unqualified student," and ODK-Mortar Board endorsed "non-violent opposition" and urged an end to actions that could damage Ole Miss.[22]

Believing the university had temporized with unruly students, several professors threatened to lower the grade of any student who protested against Meredith. To rumors of possible academic retribution, one student leader denied that discipline was a faculty prerogative and denounced the "shocking abandonment of academic integrity and a frontal assault on academic freedom." The university's academic council criticized as improper any use of grades as a means of discipline, and Provost Haywood declared academic reprisals a violation of academic freedom.[23]

From the moment Meredith arrived, student behavior concerned both university and federal officials. The several hundred people detained by the marshals and the army on September 30–October 1 included more than one hundred students, most from thirteen other colleges. For the fewer than thirty Ole Miss students detained, the disposition of their cases proved difficult. To avoid making them martyrs, federal authorities turned over to the university the names of thirteen students. Dean Love followed procedures to prevent any appearance of yielding to political pressure, which would jeopardize accreditation. Aggressive prosecution, however, might appear as kowtowing to the Kennedys and spark retaliation against Ole Miss by Mississippi whites. Katzenbach questioned the delay and insisted on action against the rioters.[24]

Though Love routinely forwarded the list of students to the Student Judicial Council, the chancellor asked the student group to defer action while he sent the names to Attorney General Patterson, who refused to act. The governor, however, had his own plans. First, he proposed that the IHL board expel Meredith as mentally incompetent, but the chairman said that it had no such authority and warned that it could be in contempt of court and imperil accreditation. Second, Barnett appointed nine lawyers to provide free legal defense for students facing charges.[25]

Segregationist intransigence became clear when, eight days after Katzenbach, Patterson spoke to the law school. He defended the protesters and attacked the Kennedys. Denying any political motivation, he lambasted their "political skullduggery" and "ruthless politics" in using troops, and he suggested they should have dispatched troops "to put that bearded beatnik of Cuba, Castro, in his place." Referring to Meredith as "this humble one" who claimed only to seek an education, he refused to "consider Ole Miss now integrated" because the courts had forced one black man in and force of arms kept him there. He suggested that students had a constitutional right "to ignore and ostracize any undesirable student." Patterson resented Robert Kennedy's criticism of the lack of disciplinary action and denied Kennedy had any authority over Ole Miss students. He vowed that Kennedy "is not going to browbeat and intimidate the officials of this university, its students, nor the attorney general of Mississippi."[26]

Many other friends of Ole Miss urged the chancellor not to punish students for opposing Meredith, and they protested his pledge to comply with court orders. Charging that he and liberal, nonsouthern professors favored integration, one suggested that the NAACP targeted Ole Miss because of the faculty's pro-integration views. Williams also heard that segregation and states' rights took precedence over accreditation. Of course, the chancellor had supporters. His most significant endorsement came on October 18 when the trustees expressed their "fullest confidence and deepest gratitude for a job of highest competence which has been extraordinarily well done."[27]

Following procedures, the administration allowed the Student Judicial Council to handle the discipline. Established in 1951, it had five members; all had to be at least seniors and two had to be law students. The student body elected the chairman, but the student government appointed the others. In the fall of 1962 John F. Lynch, a Memphis engineering student, chaired it. During regular closed meetings on Thursday afternoons, it heard evidence and called witnesses, and it recommended punishment to the dean and the chancellor, who set the penalties. In more than twelve hundred cases in eleven years, the administration had overruled it in only one minor case.[28]

The Justice Department on October 10 sent the names of eleven students taken into custody during the riot to Dean Love, and he placed each on temporary probation and gave the names to the Judicial Council. In the next few days he repeated the procedure when he received additional names. One individual was not a student, another had withdrawn, and a third was found to have been uninvolved in any disturbances. Though the Justice Department withdrew allegations against five students, the council proceeded with cases against them for violating university regulations. On October 18 the council began closed hearings on the eight students and concluded its work within a week by recommending one semester of disciplinary probation for six students and suspension for one semester and probation for the remainder of their careers at Ole Miss for two others. At Love's recommendation the sentences were reduced to permanent disciplinary probation. The results were announced on October 27. The eight students were the only individuals ever punished for participating in the riot.[29]

The absence for several weeks of other major protests encouraged Love to seek an agreement with the Justice Department to reward good behavior and encourage orderly conduct. By October 29, they agreed to reduce restrictions on students in Baxter Hall and nearby dorms, and Love planned to meet with Baxter residents at 10:00 P.M. on Monday to announce the policy.[30]

Despite Love's hopes, three factors indicated more trouble for the last week of October. First, Tuesday night was Halloween, a time for mischief. Second, for Thursday night students planned a pep rally before the Rebels' football game Saturday against the LSU Tigers. Third, on October 25, the *Rebel Underground* promoted organized resistance and proclaimed it would "never accept integration." It interpreted Meredith's presence as "the beginning of organized aggression to bring about Negro political domination and racial amalgamation throughout the South." With troops and marshals on the campus and with "carpetbaggers and scalawags on the faculty," it recognized "resistance is necessarily underground." Officials heard reports that Citizens' Councils had provided money for fireworks and that someone had brought more than four thousand cherry bombs to campus on Sunday, October 28.[31]

Amid such provocations, disorder continued. On Meredith's first visit to the student union grill, the other students, except for one woman, walked out; after a mob gathered outside, marshals hustled Meredith away. In the most serious harassment, Taylor Robertson, a Baxter Hall resident, repeatedly printed the words "WHITES ONLY" above the water fountain, and several times students prevented Meredith from using it. Once Meredith scuffled with a student before MPs hauled the offender away to the marshals, who soon released him.[32]

Monday evening, October 29, while Meredith and two federal lawyers ate in the cafeteria, outside cherry bombs exploded and a crowd formed. He walked back to his room unharmed, but eggs and bottles hit his army escort. Fireworks continued through the early evening. While Dean Love talked with Baxter Hall residents, more than one hundred students gathered and hundreds of explosions occurred, with some cherry bombs aimed with slingshots at army sentinels. From windows students threw objects, including Molotov cocktails. A letter tossed from Baxter Hall declared, "James Meredith is a dead nigger living on federal time"; a sticker on the back said, "Citizens' Council, states rights, racial integrity." After Love's tough talk, he and the police took seven students into custody and the crowd dispersed.[33]

Throughout the night, cherry bombs and other firecrackers rained down on MPs posted in the vicinity of Baxter Hall. After early evening duty, Pfc. Dominick A. Niglia resumed his watch at 5:00 A.M. A few minutes later, thrown from a Mayes Hall third-floor window, a Coke bottle filled with explosives exploded at Niglia's feet. A short time later, when he thought he saw at the same window someone lighting a fuse, he fired his M-1 rifle at the window. A single bullet passed through the window and wound up in a hallway door frame. He had fired, he told his superiors, in self-defense. After his unauthorized use of his rifle, the army dispatched him to his home base of Fort Dix while it investigated.[34]

Niglia's shot gave critics ammunition. Claiming "indiscriminate" gunfire would "inflame students," Representative John Bell Williams called it "perhaps the most reprehensible action" at the university and demanded that the army take all the "unnecessary" weapons from the soldiers. Senator John Stennis called for an investigation to hold Pfc. Niglia "accountable for his unauthorized and dangerous action." After a student who admitted throwing firecrackers told the Lafayette County Citizens' Council that the bullet had missed his head by only six inches, the council voted to condemn the "brutalities by Negro MPS." Niglia was white.[35]

After Monday night, Chancellor Williams suggested that the "first emotional crisis is over" and pledged to guarantee that students could pursue their education. Tuesday morning, classics professor William H. Willis discussed the violence with the provost and with the chairman of the faculty senate. At the provost's urging, three senators, three AAUP members, and three professors at large formed a Committee of Nine to work with Dean Love on student discipline. Tuesday afternoon, the new group declared, "If order cannot be promptly restored and maintained, the University is not only sure to lose its accreditation, but deserves to lose it." Concerned that a "self-styled vigilante committee is aggressively intimidating students," it said "the restoration of order is the first duty of the University administration" and called for expulsion of disorderly students. The AAUP instituted evening faculty patrols of the dormitory areas.[36]

University leaders continued to meet with federal representatives on campus. Katzenbach asserted that the university had shirked responsibility to punish students, and he intimated that the federal government might take legal action if the university failed to act. Haywood responded that some offending students had decided to assist the university, the situation had improved until the last couple of days, and the recent outbreak sought not to oust Meredith but to close Ole Miss. Love pointed also to state political pressures.[37]

To maintain order the army, marshals, and campus police intensified their efforts. A search of a dorm room discovered firecrackers, marbles, and a slingshot; cases against two students were referred to the Judicial Council. The Justice Department announced that demonstrating students would face contempt of court charges. Washington worries also prompted Katzenbach's return to Oxford late Tuesday, where he, too, emphasized that anyone arrested would face federal charges.[38]

As the resistance continued, the *Mississippian* editor condemned "civil savagery" and "barbarism." Sidna Brower called for forceful action and questioned why Ole Miss expelled students for panty raids but not for assaults on soldiers. Protests made "the University and the state appear to be a rural, isolated land of uneducated and savage people." Agreeing, more than sixty students called for "drastic action" against agitators and urged their expulsion.[39]

Student declarations failed to quell the disorder. Outside Baxter Hall on Tuesday afternoon hundreds of handbills addressed to "Soldiers of America" appealed to the MPs not to "be tricked into fighting your fellow Americans." They described their common foe, "Red Jack Kennedy," as "a sick, sick Communist" and "the most dangerous enemy America has ever had." Students also threw cherry bombs, eggs, and bottles at Baxter Hall and the guards. Inside harassment included slamming doors, moving furniture, and shouting. On Meredith's ride back to Baxter Hall after supper, a bottle crashed through the car's rear window and the flying glass cut a marshal.[40]

While Meredith ate dinner Tuesday, after reports of an imminent attack on his dorm and after a student said that a third-floor room in Baxter Hall contained seventeen sticks of dynamite, the police chief led marshals and army officers in a search of the dorm. Guards with fixed bayonets prevented anyone from entering or leaving. In sophomore Taylor Robertson's suitcase in his third-floor room, they discovered cherry bombs and other fireworks, university ID cards, and a two-gallon gas can. They retrieved "a live plastic baseball CN grenade" (tear gas) from a trash can outside his room, and in another room they found cherry bombs and a box of shotgun shells.[41]

During the search of Baxter, someone in Lester Hall threw a firecracker that injured an MP. University officials allowed soldiers to cordon off Lester Hall. While a crowd of three hundred gathered outside, the room-to-room hunt for contraband shifted from Baxter to Lester. The nearly two-hour search yielded an empty five-gallon gasoline can, a rifle and ammunition, a hand grenade filled with nails, knives and a machete, and an ice pick. Dean Love forwarded evidence of misconduct to the Judicial Council. Urging students to return to their dormitories, he warned that soldiers "will shoot. For the sake of your mothers, you had better leave." They dispersed. Faculty patrols reappeared, and, at the request of the sheriff and university police, a half-dozen highway patrol cars also returned to patrol the campus on Halloween night.[42]

On Wednesday, October 31, the chancellor spoke to all male students and vowed "swift and drastic disciplinary action" if disruptions continued. A university required "free and open discussion," he declared, and "intimidation of persons holding opposite views has no place in a university." He condemned violence: "If there are any who cannot support the establishment of peaceful and orderly conditions, I am prepared to see us part company."[43]

Despite Williams's stern warning, the *Rebel Underground* on Tuesday announced its "primary objective" to get Meredith to transfer and predicted that many northern colleges would happily make him their " 'Tar Baby.' " It "URGE[D] THE ORGANIZATION OF 'UNDERGROUND' TEAMS AND UNITS" in all the dorms, sororities, and fraternities. It identified Professor Russell Barrett as one who had eaten a meal with Meredith and labeled him and other faculty seen as sympathetic as "Honorary Niggers"; it further proposed that Barrett, Farley, Silver, and other "racial perverts" should teach at Tougaloo College or Tuskegee Institute.[44]

In a virtual reply Wednesday afternoon, the Committee of Nine urged the administration to "acknowledge openly and publicly" Meredith's rights as a student and the university's obligation to protect his rights. It also insisted that the university not yield to political pressures in prosecuting disruptive students, and it rejected protection for dissenting professors. The faculty group called for employing a public relations specialist to rebut the Citizens' Council's "concerted and massive propaganda barrage." To convince SACS of the university's integrity, it urged an end to the screening of campus speakers and to required faculty affidavits, and it contended that the administrators should assume responsibility for disciplining students.[45]

Despite the committee's recommendation, the Judicial Council considered evidence against students involved in the disturbances or who possessed banned articles. Supported by the chancellor's statement, it showed less leniency in the new cases. It placed one student on disciplinary probation and voted to expel four others. On November 3, the chancellor approved its recommendations, and Dean Love notified the students.[46] One case, however, was far from over.

Leroy Taylor Robertson, the Baxter Hall student pinpointed in the room search, was charged with possession of cherry bombs and forged ID cards and with harassment of soldiers and Meredith. Robertson had explained to the FBI that he took the rejected ID cards at registration and used them to get friends into football games and that he never used the fireworks against soldiers. After testimony from a soldier, FBI agents, and a marshal, he admitted using fireworks, painting a racist sign over the Baxter water fountain, and possessing false ID cards. The council "recommend[ed] nothing less than expulsion." It denied him a rehearing, and the IHL board deferred to the university. Before the university could hear an appeal, Robertson's minister, chancery judge Stokes Robertson, circuit judge Leon F. Hendrick, John C. Satterfield, and the president of Belhaven College attested to his character but pointed out tragedies in his life. At an appeal hearing on November 21, Robertson conceded the charges against him, expressed remorse, and requested an opportunity to demonstrate that he could behave. Finding the offenses "serious and sustained," not "casual and impulsive," the administration denied the appeal.[47]

Robertson then filed a lawsuit charging that Ole Miss officials expelled him to "placate" the Justice Department and SACS. At the end of November, a Hinds County chancery judge temporarily ordered his reinstatement, and he returned under disciplinary probation to Baxter Hall. The order disgusted many at the university. Administrators worried that it would invite constant challenges to disciplinary decisions and would strip them of control, and rumors suggested that J. D. Williams and others might resign if Robertson prevailed. Faculty implored the trustees to secure a "prompt" reversal. Robertson did not return for the spring semester, and the judge at the plaintiff's request in late March dismissed the case without prejudice. The delays convinced some at the university that the IHL board had temporized and may have lacked commitment to its own independence and integrity. In part as a result, Provost Haywood resigned in late December.[48]

As Robertson's case dragged on, the campus calmed down after the Halloween uproar. For the remainder of 1962, the army noted a marked reduction of incidents, and the Judicial Council acted on only a half-dozen cases. Excitement about the football team's five consecutive victories helped divert the campus. Fifteen hundred students boosted school spirit at a pep rally Thursday evening after Halloween. "It was the healthiest sign since the September 30 nightmare," according to Coach Vaught. After the Rebels defeated LSU, 15–7, the *Mississippian* crowed, "We're Number One," and the editor announced that the paper would no longer discuss the "issues that have interrupted the regular routine of college life" unless somebody "renews the agitation." Vaught claimed, "The minds of the students were off campus troubles and on football."[49]

With Ole Miss returning to normal, critics concluded that two dozen dissidents, aided by another two hundred, had fomented the trouble. The Citizens' Councils, at least in spirit, supported them. In the face of more stringent discipline on campus, however, the troublemakers employed more subtle methods of what one reporter called "a guerilla campaign of psychological warfare."[50]

A week after Halloween a second flyer appeared, the *Rebel Resistance*, reprinted with permission from the *Gulf Coast Gazette*. Two Ole Miss students paid an Oxford print shop thirty dollars for four thousand copies that they distributed on campus. Members of the local Citizens' Council contributed the money to pay the bill. The flyer identified three stages in racial integration and offered a "Strategy for Students at Oxford." First came "physical proximity," which Meredith and black university workers had achieved. To limit relations to physical proximity and thus defeat integration, students needed to resist "social acceptance" or "social miscegenation": they should keep "the colored boy in a state of constant isolation" by not speaking to "the NAACP leper," and they should "banish" and "ostracize" anyone who did. To prevent the "ultimate goal" of biological amalgamation required the students' constant vigilance.[51]

Students watched Meredith settle into his quarters, develop his routine, and expand his campus activities. MPs always guarded his apartment's private entrance and stairway as well as the dormitory's front door. To enter, other residents had to show identification cards. As many as fifty students may have moved out of the dorm in protest, and the remaining residents did not all appreciate his presence; their ruckus made studying and sleeping difficult for him. Several windows displayed Confederate flags and stickers declaring, "I protest Meredith's presence at Ole Miss" and "Brotherhood by bayonet."[52]

In the larger corner room of Meredith's suite, the ever-present marshals and Justice Department men stored equipment and kept cots. With a bare floor, unadorned walls, and blinds on the four windows closed for security, the room appeared gray and austere. Between the marshals' quarters and Meredith's room were a bathroom, an unfurnished small kitchen, and a dining nook. Meredith's room also suffered from a lack of natural light because its two windows were covered. To personalize his room, he displayed mementos from Japan on his dresser and a calendar from a black barbershop on one wall. Under his neatly made bed he arranged his shoes, while books, school papers, and stacks of mail covered a spare bed.[53]

Even before he enrolled, Meredith received hundreds of letters and packages. In late September, for example, Rosa Parks, Wyatt T. Walker, Septima Clark, and others at the annual SCLC meeting individually sent words of support. Others came from all over the nation and from other countries. In addition to dozens of telegrams, Meredith received money, books, and other gifts. Hate mail also flooded his mailbox. One letter from California was addressed to "'Mr.' James Meredith (DECEASED),'" while a Pennsylvanian called him a "stinking black bastard" and a "black savage." For safety, postal inspectors opened all packages. Throughout his first semester, letters poured in, sometimes several hundred in one day. He often took bundles of mail with him when he left on the weekends.[54]

Marshals and soldiers accompanied him everywhere on campus. From a peak of 12,000 army and National Guard soldiers within sixteen miles of

Oxford on October 2, the force declined by October 15 to 5,000, with only the local National Guard unit still in Oxford. The maximum troop level on the campus was 4,550 on October 2. By the end of the month it had decreased to a few hundred in Oxford and only about 70 on campus. In addition to spotlights on Baxter Hall, the army provided nearly a dozen guards inside and outside Meredith's dorm. When he left Baxter, a jeep patrol known as the "Peanut Patrol" followed, another one remained in his vicinity, and several others stayed inconspicuously nearby. A reinforcement platoon camped close to Baxter Hall, while a second stayed in reserve in town. An army car patrolled Oxford day and night, helicopters occasionally flew over, and intelligence agents worked the area.[55]

The number of marshals similarly declined. A week after Meredith's enrollment, the army closed the camp in the Holly Springs National Forest, and about a dozen marshals remained. A three-man shift of marshals accompanied Meredith wherever he went on campus, a similar group waited on call, and a third relaxed off-duty. At first they drove him to his classes, but after a couple of weeks he often walked. Preceding him, one marshal checked the building. A second walked near Meredith, while a third followed in a car. One marshal stood outside the classroom, another down the hall or on the stairwell, and a third at the front door. Each could see the next and the man at the building entrance was in sight of the Peanut Patrol; if needed they could move swiftly. When Meredith was in his room, three marshals were always on duty in the adjoining room, and at night one always remained awake.[56]

After a couple of weeks, one remaining Justice Department lawyer coordinated protection and maintained contact with Washington through a direct telephone line from the Baxter Hall to the attorney general's office. To make protection easier, he sought Meredith's cooperation. First John Doar and then Arvid Sather went everywhere and ate many meals with Meredith. For the first few weeks, one of the lawyers even slept in Meredith's room. The Justice Department agents established a first-name basis with Meredith but engaged in no personal conversations with him and never became personally close to their charge.[57]

Though appreciative of the protection, Meredith chafed under its restrictions. He could go nowhere without his guardians. Even in his quarters they were always present and often noisy. He may have been lonely, but never alone. As tensions subsided, he grew restless and rebellious. His unpredictable ways could confound them. For example, if he decided on the spur of the moment to leave Baxter Hall, the marshals had to scramble to protect him.[58]

Late in the afternoon of October 18, Angela Sullivan, a white Justice Department secretary, went to Meredith's apartment, a violation of the prohibition against women in men's dormitories that could have led to his expulsion. He invited her to dinner with him and two marshals, and for the first time a white woman ate with a black person on the Ole Miss campus. By flouting racial taboos, he made the marshals cope with a potentially explosive situation. According to one account, the dinner "attracted considerable attention" and caused "some grumbling and stares," but "there was no incident."[59]

Though he tested his protectors' patience, Meredith never made their job impossible, and they encouraged him to walk around as independently as his safety would allow. He walked to classes, the laundry, the post office, the library, and the cafeteria. The marshals and MPs always remained close by because his survival depended on them. Five weeks after he enrolled, Meredith participated in his first extracurricular activity when he attended a symphony performance in Fulton Chapel. Accompanied by a Justice Department lawyer and seven marshals, he entered through a side door and sat within thirty feet of the chancellor and his wife. Few seemed to notice him, but six jeeps of soldiers and a handful of university police waited outside just in case. After the two-hour concert, he returned to Baxter Hall without incident.[60]

As Meredith moved around campus, he tried to be friendly and polite, and he described most students as courteous. Occasionally he exchanged greetings with students, and some engaged him in brief conversation. In class the few friendly students usually did little more than say hello. In the cafeteria a student chatted with him even though others jeered outside. Once, at the post office, one female and two male students talked with him for a few minutes. Beneath the pleasantries, hostility prevailed, and students continued to heckle and annoy him. He tried to maintain a sense of detachment and even humor. "I think it's tragic that they have to have this kind of fun with me," he said, "but many of them are the children of the men who lead Mississippi today, and I would not expect them to act any other way. They have to act the way they do."[61] His interactions with students became so routine that newspapers increasingly ignored them.

An event on November 15, however, did generate considerable publicity: as planned by two Mississippians, seven students had dinner with Meredith. Other students had warned them to leave Meredith alone. James Defibaugh, a freshman from Gulfport, later explained, "He is human and I refuse to admit that anyone or any group has the right to tell me what to do." One met Meredith at the cafeteria door and invited him to join them at a quiet corner table. Hostile students soon moved around and made insulting and threatening comments while the six white men and one white woman had a tense dinner with Meredith. Outside an angry crowd gathered. After their meal, the students returned to their rooms. At Howry Hall, freshmen Craig Knobles from Meridian and William Temple from Washington, D.C., discovered that their unlocked room had been vandalized. Someone had scrawled "nigger lover" on the door and on a wall, heaped Knobles's clothes and records on the floor, and poured water on the pile and on his bed.[62]

Knobles succumbed to the harassment and the next weekend left Ole Miss. His former roommate endured constant irritation. Someone rolled three cherry bombs into a bathroom stall occupied by Temple. Lighter fluid poured under his door was set afire, and bottles were thrown through the transom. For her participation, Jennifer Harmon from New Orleans endured threatening telephone calls and other harassment. The university investigated but never developed a case to send to the Judicial Council. At the end of the semester several of the seven quit, and at the end of the academic year the others left.[63] The segregationists' plan to isolate Meredith and hound his supporters seemed to work.

A week later, the segregationists' ire shifted to the editor of the *Mississippian*, Sidna Brower, the daughter of a Memphis businessman and a member of Kappa Kappa Gamma sorority. Five days after Temple and Knobles's room had been vandalized, she pointed out the hypocrisy of a minority's wanting the right to protest Meredith while denying another minority the opportunity to befriend him. She declared that "all students should have the right to associate with whom they please and be able to say what they please without the fear of being chastised." Her stand culminated a number of editorials offensive to segregationists. Ten days before the riot, her front-page editorial had criticized the *Jackson Daily News* for its "screaming headlines and sensationalized stories" on Meredith's attempts to register. After the riot, she joined others in calling for an end to the disturbances and violence. Later she denounced the Halloween upheavals and urged Ole Miss to get tough with the demonstrators.[64]

Brower's editorials brought national attention. The Scripps-Howard newspapers awarded her an internship even though she had not applied, and she flew to New York to appear on a national news show. At the invitation of the liberal *Nation*, she contributed to an essay on events at Ole Miss. Mississippians, she wrote, regarded Governor Barnett as a "demigod" and expected him to protect southern traditions even if they did not know what the traditions were. Brower disparaged white supremacists because "many of those who most fear for the 'degeneration' of the white race are the products of the degeneration of their own fine old families."[65]

Brower's commentary and the resulting acclaim earned her many critics. The conservative Patriotic American Youth and the Citizens' Councils reportedly engineered a campaign against her. The *Rebel Underground* sarcastically urged students not to "upset Sidna. She may win a Pulitzer Prize."

Shortly before Thanksgiving, George Monroe of Newton introduced a resolution into the student senate to censure her because she "has editorially opposed student opinion and has failed in a time of crisis to support the rights of her fellow students." The senate also considered a reprimand, although it endorsed editorial freedom and commended her for opposing violence. Brower defended her editorials and said that if she had made any error it had been to neglect the federal government's side in the dispute. Anti-Brower petitions circulated, and letters on both sides appeared in the newspaper. Early in December, the senate voted 63–27 to reprimand her. The faculty senate, however, commended her because she had "significantly contributed to the preservation of the University's integrity."[66]

The attacks on Knobles, Temple, and Brower fit the plan to ostracize friendly whites and to isolate Meredith. In November fewer students spoke to him. Most seemed resigned to his presence, even if they did not accept him as an Ole Miss student. Catcalls and taunts diminished, but an occasional student still jeered. One reporter concluded, "Mr. Meredith is not so much ignored as simply, by act of will, not seen." He may indeed have been, as editor Jimmy Ward claimed in the *Jackson Daily News*, "the most segregated Negro in Mississippi."[67]

Amidst all the controversies, Meredith the person had been overlooked. Late in October, Russell Barrett of the political science department demonstrated his acceptance of Meredith by having coffee with him in the cafeteria, but others did not follow his example. Barrett later acknowledged that "almost everyone—including his friends—forgot about Meredith. We were busy and intent on saving the University, so that James Meredith sometimes seemed to be incidental." Even the Committee of Nine failed to focus on him or on his academic progress.[68] When professors finally reached out to him, he needed the attention because he was under enormous pressure.

To get away and to see his family and friends, Meredith left campus every weekend. On Thursday, November 8, upset and frustrated with tests, he took a long weekend and missed two more tests on Friday. At a news conference, he admitted that he had "started getting bags under my eyes and feeling pressure I have never felt before." He objected to all the attention focused on him: "The greatest problem I have is that everybody thinks everything I do or think is of public importance." Repeated requests for interviews and photographs prevented a normal existence. While he understood his importance as a "symbol," he wanted to be an individual. He protested the continued presence of soldiers and marshals. "I don't see a cause [for them to be there]," he announced. Suggesting the real problem was the persistence of troublemakers, he claimed the federal agents would not be needed if the university eliminated threats to peace and order.[69]

Reports circulated that Meredith feared he was failing and wanted to quit. He did concede that the atmosphere made studying nearly impossible. When queried about his grades and the tests he had skipped, he replied, "That is a relationship between a student and his teacher." He asserted, "That's not the important thing. What we are involved with is the right to get an education. The right to fail is just as important as the right to succeed." Though he seemed to equivocate when he said he would "try to stay at the school," he declared, "I have never given any consideration to withdrawing." Privately, he had concerns about his academic progress. In mid-November he reminded Dean Lewis that he had started two weeks late and had "not been able to both catch-up and keep-up." He asked for extra time at the end of the semester. The following week Lewis sent a form letter announcing his "unsatisfactory record." At the end of the semester after Meredith again appealed unsuccessfully for an extension in his algebra course, he soldiered on.[70]

Nearly two months after he enrolled, Meredith retained his "granite attitude" about his mission and understood his presence had importance because he was black. Dismissing grades, he worried that if he excelled people would attribute his success to exceptional abilities and continue to deny other blacks a similar chance. He wanted to prove that all blacks deserved equal opportunities, especially in education. But integrating Ole Miss was only preliminary to the larger issues of political and economic equality. "Not one problem has been solved," he insisted; "Negroes are still Negroes in Mississippi."[71]

Despite the ostracism, Meredith remained "optimistic about everything." Refusing to acknowledge loneliness, he knew that "most of the people in the whole world are behind me—I stand for them." He also recognized his good fortune. "I am a lot better off than most members of my race," he told the *Chicago Defender*. "I've got a lot of freedoms that haven't come to the others yet." Professors and marshals, for example, addressed him as Mr. Meredith. One day, in the presence of a Negro janitor, he kidded around with a marshal in Baxter Hall. When Meredith told the marshal "to go to hell," he saw that the custodian "nearly turned white. . . . He was proud of me. You see," he explained, "if he told a white man to go to hell, he'd be whipped." At the same time, Meredith admitted that he got angry and dejected when he saw black maids sweeping floors. But he kept his mind on his mission and reminded himself, "You got to stay operational."[72]

Meredith's comments sometimes startled his university supporters, who found themselves caught among contending forces. Segregationists denounced them as a "small group of left wing professors," and they distributed thousands of postcards addressed to the IHL board and to the chancellor that called for the immediate firing of Silver, Barrett, Farley, and "other integrationists." At the same time, northern liberals criticized their timidity. The besieged faculty felt a new, odd freedom because of "a sort of 'don't give a damn' attitude toward the state. Now we feel we've got to speak out to save the university." Preventing control by the Citizens' Council and preserving the university's integrity required Meredith's enrollment.[73]

The week after Meredith's news conference, a worried Russell Barrett again sought him out. Meredith assured him that he would stay unless he flunked out or became physically unable to continue. The two also discussed his growing isolation. Until Barrett explained, Meredith was unaware of the campaign to ostracize him. To Barrett's claim of support on campus, Meredith countered that only open support mattered. As a result of their hour-long talk, Barrett recognized Meredith's need for ordinary conversation and understood the benefit of attending public events without the burden of guards. The two also conferred about his academic progress. The noisy, omnipresent guards made even reading in Baxter Hall difficult, and security made studying in the library problematic, though he had read in the library and wanted to do it more often. Concerned that he may have fallen behind, Barrett suggested tutoring. Despite his aversion to special help, Meredith had a math tutor but, especially in his major, refused to accept other assistance. Barrett also reminded him that his professors would help him outside of class as part of their routine duties.[74]

Barrett subsequently proposed to the Committee of Nine that faculty and students have coffee and meals with Meredith, his professors offer academic assistance, newsmen allow more privacy, and faculty replace his guards at public functions. He also recommended a reduction in the number of guards and advocated Meredith's right "to attend the University *on the same basis* as other students." When the last point irritated some of the committee as too radical, he retracted his report, and the committee did nothing formally to alleviate Meredith's difficulties.[75]

While the Committee of Nine and the administration avoided helping Meredith, other faculty did. Although on leave, Jim Silver met with him several times in the fall. On perhaps the first occasion in late October, he noticed Meredith eating breakfast in the cafeteria and told him he had received several books for him. Meredith stood, they shook hands, and Silver sat down with him while he continued eating. Soon the wives of two professors joined them. In later meetings, Meredith and Silver discussed writing a book together, but their plans quickly diverged. As they got to know each other over coffee in the cafeteria, Silver became convinced that Meredith could succeed at the university: "There's no question about his capacity; no question about his emotional stability." Impressed by Meredith's determination, Silver thought the harassment would not affect him. Others sat with him in the cafeteria or entertained him in their homes. In December, *Ebony* carried a picture of Meredith in the cafeteria chatting with Silver and two other professors.[76]

Despite a few friendly professors, the pressures bore down. Anonymous telephone calls, disturbing dorm noises, fireworks outside, and students with rifles riding by Baxter Hall exacerbated the other snubs and discourtesies. Irritants included a cigarette lighter that played "Dixie" when a student flipped it open in class. Death threats also brought concern. When Meredith attended a talk and sat with a white friend of the speaker, an angry female student sitting behind them declared, "Ah'm gonna get mahself a gun—Ah truly am!" Nothing happened, but he did once find a dead raccoon on his car. William Higgs feared that someone would kill him and predicted he would not graduate. Russell Barrett, however, saw only "the remote possibility that some nut might try to harm him." Toward the end of 1962, his refusal to discuss grades intensified speculation that he would not pass. After weeks of suggestions, Meredith accepted tutoring in French, and at Constance Motley's urging, he agreed to spend ten days over the holidays studying with tutors for his exams.[77]

In mid-December a serious incident occurred during a visit to Kosciusko with his wife to celebrate their seventh anniversary. When he left a barber shop after getting a shoe shine Saturday evening, police stopped him for failing to yield the right-of-way at an intersection. After being taken to the police station, Meredith posted his own ten-dollar bond. He later claimed the police had treated him "like a dog," called him "nigger," and cursed him. "It was typical of the way Negroes are treated in Mississippi," he said. On his way back to Oxford on Sunday, he reported three carloads of harassing whites. The Kosciusko newspaper editor called Meredith's arrest "unfair and unjust" and worried that the town would become involved in more "useless and tragic violence." On Wednesday, fearing another, possibly violent, incident, Meredith did not return for a court appearance and forfeited his bond.[78]

Instead of appearing in traffic court, Meredith after his last class before Christmas flew to the Northeast for tutoring. In New Haven, Constance Motley arranged for Yale faculty to help him, but after one unsuccessful day "alone and unhappy," he decided to join his wife visiting comedian Dick Gregory in Chicago. When he arrived on Sunday, December 23, he heard radio reports that shortly after midnight several shotgun blasts had broken windows in his parents' home and nearly hit one of his younger sisters. Returning immediately to Mississippi, he knew that "you just can't convict white people for doing these things."[79]

Accompanied by Negro marshals, Meredith spent the remainder of his holidays with family and friends in Jackson. The holidays, he later said, constituted "a turning point in my struggle against the evils of 'White Supremacy.'" At his favorite haunts around the city, he witnessed the pride blacks took in the marshals and in his own accomplishments. "This was," he reminisced, "what I was fighting for: The pride of my people." He delighted in seeing them dancing and having a good time. At one place he realized, "The average income among this group was certainly less than fifteen dollars a week. It was these people that I felt obligated to raise from this blind pit of helplessness. It was for them that I would give my life." But he wanted to battle in his own way. Not wanting any advantage that would be unavailable later to other blacks, he refused "any kind of outside help," even math tutoring from a Jackson State professor.[80]

After the holidays, the atmosphere at Ole Miss changed. Following nearly two months free of a major incident, segregationists renewed a campaign of protests. On his drive back, Meredith got an indication of what lay ahead. Though marshals provided an escort, students harassed them by passing and then slowing down, shining their bright lights, and making repeated gestures to Meredith. On Sunday evening, the *Rebel Underground* called for the "separation of the coon from the curriculum" and announced riot veterans had formed the "Brick and Bottle Minutemen" to seek the "impeachment, removal and execution" of President Kennedy and people who conspired with him. Another *Rebel Underground* competed in stirring opposition to Meredith and integration.[81]

At 8:00 A.M. on the first day of classes in 1963, Meredith escalated the conflict with a typed, two-page statement. "I have decided not to register for classes during the second semester at the University of Mississippi," began his startling declaration, but the sentence continued, "unless very definite and positive changes are made to make my situation more conducive to learning." He emphasized that, although he had "not made a decision" to quit, he had decided not to attend "under the present circumstances." Aware of the "bitter war for the 'equality of opportunity,'" he recognized that "there is too much doubt and uncertainty regarding the procedure to be followed in settling our problems. No major issues have been decided legally or officially, illegally or unofficially." The veteran wanted the rules of engagement clarified before he would continue. Refusing to answer questions, he had nothing else to say until the end of the semester.[82]

Meredith surprised everyone; reactions came swiftly. Perceiving a challenge, students resumed their harassment. When he emerged from class, several hundred jeered. Monday evening students hissed as he entered the cafeteria, and one hundred walked out. The next few evenings students in the cafeteria banged trays and silverware on the tables, crowded around his table, and walked out. At Thursday dinner, four hundred staged the largest demonstration since November, with some shouting "Go home, you nigger." When Meredith and his escort left, students followed them and dispersed only when the campus police chief tried to apprehend them.[83]

Robert Kennedy charged that the university had failed to create conditions conducive to Meredith's education. Kennedy expected Ole Miss to rectify the situation and hoped that Meredith would remember the many persons who had worked for his admission and for his right to remain. Meredith's withdrawal would, Kennedy contended, reflect badly on the university, the state, and the nation. In response the chancellor defended his institution's compliance with court orders and pointed out that the previous week federal representatives had made "no complaint, suggestion or criticism." Williams expressed pride in keeping the university open, maintaining accreditation, and providing "a favorable climate for learning."[84]

Observers interpreted Meredith's statement as a publicity grab, an empty threat, a rationale for bad grades, an effort by Robert Kennedy to "squeeze a little more political mileage" out of the controversy,"and "an attempt to mobilize outside public opinion against Mississippi and the university." A Memphis newspaper columnist called it a "wild tirade" of "reckless and unfounded charges of harassment and persecution." The chancellor appreciated the writer's comments, but Jim Silver believed they suffered from a "colossal misunderstanding" of Meredith. He described Meredith as "a very complicated human being . . . [and] an individualist" who "makes his own plans, usually without script," and he challenged assumptions about Meredith's academic failure.[85]

Four days after Meredith's statement, the sparring continued. An aide to Robert Kennedy blamed "weak administrators" for much of the lack of discipline. In response, Dean Love warned students that the administration would not tolerate further disorder. The chancellor suggested Meredith's statement had disrupted the peaceful and quiet campus but downplayed the resulting incidents because they did not involve violence or interrupt classes and occurred mainly at the dinner hour. Unusually warm weather and a full moon may also have helped spawn the recent protests, and the chancellor allowed, "I doubt that Mr. Kennedy's statement helped us."[86]

Pressure on Williams increased. The local AAUP criticized failures to discipline "unruly and dissident students" and deplored Williams's attempts to minimize disturbances. More important, the professors claimed, "unsympathetic" members of the administrative staff "sabotaged" his authority and discipline by suggesting that Meredith was unqualified and by alleging that he was failing his courses. Some administrators also refused to arrest violent students and did not act or speak against the "scurrilous and humiliating" *Rebel Underground*. According to the professors, after a student threw a bottle, a university policeman told another student, "Don't tell me his name; we have enough trouble already." The AAUP implored Williams to take "moral responsibility" for enforcing court orders "without equivocation or delay." In the meantime it requested that three hundred soldiers remain on campus.[87]

Russell Barrett took the administration to task for failing to punish students who trashed Knobles and Temple's room. He criticized it for not voicing disapproval of the *Rebel Underground* and not supporting students and faculty friendly to Meredith. As a result, the campus had become inhospitable to academic life. If nothing changed, Barrett predicted, Ole Miss would suffer a loss of both faculty and students and an eroding of relations between faculty and administration. He also warned Williams that Meredith would withdraw, an action he described as "disastrous for the university." Ultimately he feared the university would lose accreditation.[88]

In a special evening meeting on January 11, the Judicial Council considered a case against a student for demonstrating the previous night. It recommended suspension until the fall semester, and the administration concurred. The action seemed to reflect growing intolerance for disorder, but the *Rebel Underground* alleged that the "crime" involved "yelling 'nigger' at a coon," which it considered unremarkable because blacks "have been called (and are) niggers in this area for centuries." Labeling Williams "our Quisling Chancellor" and "a LIAR," the *Rebel Underground* claimed the council had unanimously voted to dismiss charges but that the administration, in "an example of Soviet type government at its worst," had suspended the student and blamed the decision on the Judicial Council. Its chairman denied the allegation.[89]

To placate critics and recover authority, Williams declared the disruptions "unworthy of an American institution of higher education," though he seemed to dismiss them as "ill conduct and rowdyism." To obtain student cooperation, he invoked their love of Ole Miss and reminded them that disorder hurt the institution's reputation and diminished the value of their own degrees. Last, he defended "the right of every student to pursue his educational program in a normal academic atmosphere" and warned that violators "invited the sternest disciplinary action." He did not mention Meredith, threaten retaliation, or refer to any specific problems. He did not see that Ole Miss had become, as one editorial described it, "a jungle of fear and hatred," and he accepted none of the responsibility for its "degeneration" or for the discord across the campus.[90]

During the uproar over Meredith's announcement and campus discipline,

Sidna Brower was nominated for a Pulitzer prize for editorial writing. The recognition provoked attacks. In the *Jackson Clarion-Ledger*, Tom Ethridge suggested that the Pulitzer had "become a gimmick for promoting integration and rewarding Southern turncoats" and any Mississippi editor could qualify for it by "singing the surrender song so dear to Columbia University's mix-minded board of judges." The *Rebel Underground* blasted the prizes as tools of the "Communist Conspiracy." Judging her work "mediocre and dishonest," it attributed her nomination to her betrayal of the southern way of life.[91]

While Brower waited to find out if she would receive the prize, Ole Miss waited to see what Meredith would do. In the meantime, he endured exams. For the first time he spent a weekend on campus before his last two exams on Monday. After his English test, he stopped by Silver's office and conferred with him, Barrett, and Willis. Even though he did not even take his algebra exam, he did not worry about his academic standing. The professors, however, fretted and impressed on him the importance of his returning. They worried withdrawal would be interpreted as a victory for Barnett and the segregationists. Silver feared his departure might "wipe out all the gains that have been made" and allow the Citizens' Council to take over education. Although Meredith appreciated their interest, he could not tell them whether he would return or not.[92]

Meredith received abundant support for returning. His mathematics teacher wrote, "I do hope you will *come back*. Don't give up." One political scientist, who was an Ole Miss alumnus and a Mississippian, wanted him to return and told him, "The courage which you have displayed is most commendable, in fact incredible." Registrar Ellis said, "I hope that Meredith comes back, for the university's sake, for his sake also. I don't think we could survive another crisis." A marshal also wanted him to return because "we'd hate to do it all over again next September." President Kennedy appreciated Meredith's difficulties but said he would be "sorry" if Meredith quit and "I hope he continues." Constance Motley believed he would return in September 1963, if not in the spring, and by the fall semester he would not be the only black at Ole Miss. If Meredith did quit, said the NAACP's Roy Wilkins, it would be a "blessing in reverse" because it would demonstrate to all Americans the "bitter, fanatical opposition of many Mississippi whites to Constitutional rights for all." One pessimistic reporter thought, "If he does not return to Ole Miss it will reinforce the it-just-never-happened psychology. It will be offered as evidence that integration can't be made to work here, . . . and that the violence of last fall served its dark purpose."[93]

Uncertain about his future, Meredith packed his ten-year-old Cadillac and prepared to visit his wife and son in Jackson during the semester break. That he left many of his belongings in his room suggested that he had not decided to quit. When he tried to leave, however, he experienced what one observer called a "final indignity"—his car would not start. A newsman concluded that "the dispirited automobile seemed to do what all the moral preachments in the world had been unable to do:. . . . [it made Meredith] just a guy with a broken-down automobile. . . . just not that much different from the rest of us."[94]

Few students shared the hopeful interpretation. After reporters, campus police, and bystanders helped get his car running by pushing it into the street and down a hill, perhaps a score of cars full of harassing students followed him out of town. They gradually ended their pursuit of the small caravan of Meredith, marshals, and newsmen. Meredith first drove to Memphis to get his car repaired and then during the middle of the night drove to Jackson. When he arrived about 4:00 A.M., his future at Ole Miss remained unresolved.[95]

20. J. H. Meredith, Class of '63

"I have concluded that the 'Negro' should not return to the University of Mississippi. The prospects for him are too unpromising," announced James Meredith at a Jackson news conference on January 30, 1963. His statement stunned the fifty newsmen and one hundred African Americans in the Negro Masonic Temple's auditorium, though one white newsman did applaud. Several reporters ran to phone in the story. "However," he continued, "I have decided that I, J. H. Meredith, will register for the second semester at the University of Mississippi." Applause and cheers greeted his declaration, but several local reporters looked dejected. "I see signs," he said, "that I will be able to go to school in the future under adequate, if not ideal, circumstances." Refusing to blame Ole Miss students for his troubles, he explained that they "are just like students elsewhere, they are basically good people." With Medgar Evers at his side for the fifteen-minute news conference, Meredith said that he was in good academic standing. When asked about his safety, he downplayed his special risk: "I think Negroes are in constant danger in Mississippi." He also reported that the chancellor had assured him that the situation would improve. Though he echoed his earlier plea that he be treated as an individual and not as a symbol, Meredith expressed gratitude for support from all over the nation.[1]

In the previous week, Meredith had discussed his future with his friends and family and with a steady parade of visitors. James Baldwin returned for a second visit within a month. A. W. Willis, Meredith's Memphis lawyer, and Jack Greenberg came to confer with him. Medgar Evers also discussed the future with Meredith. He kept his plans to himself, not even revealing them at the state NAACP meeting, where he received a standing ovation. Moving his family into a new Jackson apartment only complicated speculation, and postponing his news conference to the last day before spring registration heightened anticipation.[2]

Meredith's perception of his role seemed confused. In warning that he might not return, he recognized his symbolic role and asked for less attention to himself personally and to his daily actions, yet in his announcement he stressed that he would enroll as an individual and not as a symbol. Critics, charging duplicity, gleefully pointed out the impossibility of separating the two. Tom Ethridge said, "The truth is the Negro is returning with him" and suggested that he decided to return only because of the pressure on the symbol from the Kennedys and the NAACP. Charging that Meredith had "spent all too much time complaining and calling attention to himself through public statements and press conferences, to be considered a serious student seeking nothing more than an education," Ethridge intimated that faculty friends "have gotten him passing grades he didn't earn." Charles Hills argued Meredith's goal had always been to desegregate Ole Miss and that his statements indicated that he "has forgotten his main purpose in being there." He also proposed that Meredith may have simply misjudged the situation he would encounter.[3]

Under stress, Meredith may have been unable to keep his priorities clear. He wanted to represent his race and to be an individual, to break down segregation and to get an education, but doing both posed a conflict. To deal with the pressure, Meredith emphasized whichever role served his survival. His reactions may have made him appear uncertain, but they also revealed a real person, not a superhuman hero. As Jim Silver understood, "James Meredith is a human being, a very complex human being, and not an institution."[4]

In response to Meredith's decision, the chancellor did not yield to Barnett and pledged to ensure that he was treated just like other students, as the courts required. To avoid a repetition of the fall's events, Williams vowed to protect the institution and its students from the "irresponsible behavior" of interfering outsiders. He welcomed only students with a "serious intent" to get an education and believed that the large majority were "mature, law-abiding Americans" and serious students. Others who engaged in "demonstrations, harassment of persons, distribution of unauthorized publications, or other actions disruptive of orderly academic life" would receive "swift and severe disciplinary action." He insisted that students' activities had to be legal and orderly.[5]

An hour later, the university banned unauthorized media representatives and prohibited even registered newsmen and photographers from a large part of the campus during registration. The idea may have come from Clemson University, where such a ban had been part of its peaceful desegregation. The Ole Miss restrictions covered most of the places Meredith might go, including Baxter Hall, the cafeteria and student union, and most academic buildings. The next day, Williams declared unacceptable "public statements and press, radio, and television interviews which appear likely to create disorder or impair the effectiveness of the educational program." Though trying to avoid abridging First Amendment rights, he promised to punish violators.[6]

The journalism faculty defended the First Amendment and protested that the restrictions violated the "American heritage of freedom" and the Constitution. They reminded the chancellor that "truth, on which freedom is built, is always distasteful to someone when it is significant enough to be news," and that limiting the press did not solve any problem. The new rules "cannot be enforced" and confirmed the negative view many had of the "limited status of freedom at Ole Miss." Pointing to events of the fall, the professors contended, "The press did not create the situation at Ole Miss. Free expression did not stifle reason. Indeed, if more people had spoken more freely, more openly, more quickly, the crisis might have been tempered." The faculty senate considered the journalism professors' protest but tabled a motion to endorse the chancellor because it might appear to criticize their colleagues and the press.[7]

The Committee of Nine worried that the policy might restrict academic freedom and subject professors to discipline for speaking unwisely. It interpreted the policy to mean that Williams thought someone had acted improperly; the nine pressed for examples, but Williams could not provide one. Fearing that the chancellor had set a standard that Meredith could not meet and that "might be used under outside pressure to precipitate his expulsion," they also warned that the regulation might also open Williams to political pressures if outsiders thought the policy had been violated. The chancellor claimed he had only restated an existing policy to remind everyone not to make statements damaging to the institution.[8]

After the criticisms, Chancellor Williams tempered his position. Once the semester began successfully, he congratulated the community for its "restraint, dignity, and good judgment" and reminded it of the "twin ideals of freedom and responsibility." Although promising to protect "freedom of thought and expression," he stressed that "irresponsible behavior can do the University incalculable harm." His tone had changed but the restrictions remained and the promised retribution stayed in effect.[9]

Williams's stand affected news coverage. The army's commander in Oxford said that the Jackson press had "been geared up to keep the issue alive," but beginning in February, the number of news stories, editorials, and columns declined dramatically, probably because of media restrictions. The lack of publicity may have reduced protests and demonstrations. By mid-February one marshal concluded that "as long as the press stays away things go pretty well."[10]

When Meredith reentered the campus on January 31, he sparked no controversy. Jeeps of MPs and unmarked cars of marshals patrolled, and an army helicopter circled above. The university had brought in more than a dozen extra policeman. After his drive from his parents' home, Meredith stopped by Baxter Hall before going to the Lyceum to confer with an assistant dean and then to talk privately with Chancellor Williams. According to Meredith, they had a pleasant chat except that he balked at Williams's request for a public statement that his only reason for attending Ole Miss was to receive an education. He said any black person who did what he had done only to get an education would be "crazy," and he reminded the chancellor of his goal to "break the system of 'White Supremacy.' "[11]

After eating lunch with John Doar, consulting with two political science professors, and picking up his mail, Meredith stood in the registration line. He signed up for six classes, including algebra, a repeat from first semester. One official observed that the process was "smooth" and that Meredith went "completely unnoticed." The other students did not, however, welcome him back. Their mood, according to one newsman, was one of "glum resignation rather than acceptance." One student said, "I'm sorry he came back. I'm tired of hearing about the whole thing." Another claimed that Meredith returned only because of the pressure from the Kennedys and the NAACP.[12]

Meredith's registration shared the spotlight with another black man's attempt to enroll at Ole Miss. Twenty-one-year-old Dewey Roosevelt Greene Jr. was a native of Greenwood, where his father was a house painter. According to the Sovereignty Commission, his parents, especially his father, had a reputation as troublemakers because they "always upheld the children for what devilment they got into at school." In January 1954 the parents had registered to vote, but they had not voted because they never paid their poll taxes. Dewey Greene Sr. served as president of the NAACP local in the 1950s, and the Greenes were early activists with SNCC.[13]

After graduating from high school, Greene served three years in the navy. During the Clennon King controversy, his navy friends challenged him to bring about change in his home state. When he left the navy in 1961 and returned to Mississippi, Greene worked at a Greenwood motel and enrolled at Mississippi Vocational College. He found the college too conservative because its students "had an unrealistic attitude on the racial problem itself" and considered the Constitution "as something for white men!" After Greene worked with SNCC, the college's president described him as a "racial trouble-maker" and planned to deny him reenrollment in the fall of 1962. In the summer of 1962 Greene worked as a reporter and photographer for the *Mississippi Free Press*, a weekly newspaper in Jackson, and was a plaintiff in an August 1962 lawsuit to desegregate the Jackson airport restaurant.[14]

Within weeks of Meredith's enrollment, Greene applied, and officials rejected his transfer from an unaccredited college. The registrar judged his "limited level of [academic] achievement" unacceptable, but Greene decided to try to enroll anyway. Learning of his plan, Ellis in a telegram on Wednesday, January 30, asked him not to appear for registration because he would not be accepted. Greene apparently did not receive the telegram before he left for

Oxford. Thursday morning, while Meredith visited Baxter Hall, Greene arrived at the Lyceum. An assistant dean of students helped him find the registrar's office, where Ellis read him the telegram and explained his rejection. When Greene asked about further steps he could take, Ellis explained the appeal process. With nothing else to say, Ellis asked him to leave peaceably. After less than half an hour, Greene left and ignored the few reporters outside.[15]

Greene's attorneys immediately announced they would pursue his admission through the federal courts, and the next day, February 1, William L. Higgs filed a lawsuit in federal district court in Jackson. Claiming that *Meredith v. Fair* had been a class action on behalf of all blacks, the legal challenge argued that the registrar had acted in contempt of the federal court by rejecting Greene's transfer from an unaccredited college. Judge Sidney Mize announced he would hold a hearing on the following Monday, February 4. Greene would be represented by Higgs, who had earlier advised Meredith and was increasingly involved in civil rights. As a result of his work, Higgs suffered constant intimidation and harassment, but he also developed close ties with the growing civil rights movement, with whites like Jim Silver and Hodding Carter, and with national figures including Burke Marshall and William Kuntsler. In September 1962, *Life* magazine recognized Higgs as one of the nation's "red-hot hundred" young leaders.[16]

Three hours after Higgs filed Greene's suit, Jackson police arrested Higgs and charged him with "indulging in acts of unnatural and perverted sex" with a sixteen-year-old Pennsylvania male. Hinds County judge Russel Moore postponed Higgs's trial so he could receive an ACLU award in New York. When he failed to appear for his rescheduled trial, Moore granted another postponement, but Higgs, fearing that he would be charged with a felony and face imprisonment, did not return. Judge Moore appointed lawyers to defend Higgs, and a jury of twelve white men convicted him *in absentia*. Later, Judge Stokes Robertson ordered Higgs's disbarment.[17]

Other lawyers represented Greene in his attempt to enter Ole Miss. In Hattiesburg on February 4, Judge Mize told Greene that he would not act until Greene exhausted the university's appeals process. Two weeks later a three-judge appeals court panel upheld Mize's action. Greene then filed an appeal with the university's admissions committee, but he never achieved acceptance.[18] Mississippi's treatment of Greene and Higgs demonstrated, even after Meredith's enrollment, the extent of segregationists' defense of the southern way of life.

During the controversies over Higgs and Greene, several other questions preoccupied many at the university and in the state. Though just a few hundred soldiers remained in and around Oxford, the army continued to use the

National Guard armory but needed other facilities to quarter troops. When in early 1963 federal authorities started to build a temporary camp near the airport at a cost of nearly one hundred thousand dollars, Barnett protested it as "both criminal and civil trespass of the worst type," and he called on all state and local authorities to fight the action. The state attorney general, joined by two district attorneys and the Lafayette County Board of Supervisors, sued in state court to block the construction, and in mid-January a chancery judge granted a temporary injunction to stop it. The army canceled the construction and moved its troops to facilities purchased by the U.S. Forest Service south of Oxford.[19]

At the same time the National Guard objected to the federal occupation of most of its armory. After failed negotiations and several formal protests, Captain Murry Falkner sued to force the army out of the armory. He claimed the army's occupancy was "arbitrary, capricious, unreasonable, and unlawful," prevented the Guard from training, and violated the Guard's lease with the city. Before the case could be heard, the army moved to its new camp south of Oxford. Later in the spring the state filed a lawsuit to remove all troops from the campus because they had been sent there illegally, but the troops withdrew before the case could be pursued.[20]

More relevant for the university, reports of departing faculty circulated. As early as mid-October newspapers reported that disgruntled faculty had begun to look for other jobs. The first and most prominent to depart was Provost Charles Haywood. Many had expected the thirty-five-year-old to become chancellor when Williams retired, but instead he returned to the banking industry. In early 1963 the *New York Times* estimated that faculty turnover could be three times higher than normal with as many as thirty leaving. One professor predicted 20 percent would quit. University spokesmen dismissed suggestions of an exodus. According to Jim Silver, however, "It's not the number of men leaving, it's who is leaving," and he believed that they included top quality faculty who would be difficult to replace. As he said, "The dopes will remain." Worries about the institution's integrity, academic freedom, accreditation, student discipline, and Citizens' Council influence prompted many to look for other jobs. Because Ole Miss salaries trailed considerably the regional and national averages, better positions with higher salaries could be found at other schools. Faculty also feared Ole Miss would attract inferior students from out of state and would be unable to hire quality professors. To Silver the university seemed "doomed," while the Associated Press reported faculty sentiment that "the death knell may have already sounded," and one professor pointed to "the hopelessness of the whole state."[21]

"Prophets of gloom and doom," according to Tom Ethridge, "are predicting decay and dissolution," but he expected growth and prosperity "without raising the white flag or remaking our social order according to the whims of Kennedyism and its NAACP masters." The *Jackson Daily News* bid "good riddance" to the "egotistical" liberals without "guts and dedication." To reports that faculty would quit *en masse* to embarrass the university, the paper blasted the "warped mentality or twisted ego [that] would stoop to such a Hollywood-ish stunt." If indeed they quit, it "would be an event for high jubilation."[22]

By the end of the academic year, more than thirty professors had accepted positions at the state universities of Colorado, Florida, Illinois, Michigan, and North Carolina, as well as smaller colleges. In reporting to the IHL board, the chancellor repeated their complaints to emphasize the ramifications of recent events. A physicist declared his "unwillingness to swear allegiance to a state whose constitution . . . is in basic disagreement with the United States Constitution," while a philosopher sought "a political atmosphere more congenial to an American." A political scientist objected to "strong and sinister influence in the government of the university of reactionary political forces in the state," and another physicist wanted "the cherished right to a life for myself and my family devoid of outright fear." A sociologist believed the administration "will continue to be prostituted for political expediency." Departures hit the chemistry, physics, philosophy, and classics departments hard. Acknowledging that reports had been accurate, Williams conceded, "Others would like to leave, but they can't find a job. I expect they'll be going too."[23]

Not all faculty wanted to leave. Some professors had loyalty to Ole Miss or roots in the community. Conservatives had less inclination to move.[24] Some had familial reasons to remain. Others stayed because they could not compete for other positions. The overwhelming majority of faculty, therefore, returned.

Despite minor controversies, James Meredith had a much more normal existence during his second semester. Harassment and threats became sporadic. Many more days passed uneventfully, and early in the semester the army reported that Meredith was "receiving no attention what so ever. He is being treated with complete disdain [by other students]." The marshals and the army repeatedly observed that he had "conducted his campus activities without incident" and, for the entire month of April, that he had "moved about campus with a great amount of freedom, and with few incidents."[25] None of the events, however irritating and embarrassing, precipitated a crisis.

On Thursday afternoon during the second week of classes, Meredith drove downtown to buy a rocking chair. He went into several businesses without any trouble and purchased a chair at a store owned by Ira L. "Shine" Morgan, a member of the IHL board. Though stores served black customers, Meredith's visit irritated many merchants and townspeople. After shopping, he returned to his car, where a merchant accosted him, cursed him, and spat on his automobile. Marshals suspected further trouble if he returned downtown often; Sheriff Ford told a military representative that Meredith would be arrested if he did. The threat convinced federal officials of the danger, but they also feared that Meredith might take the warning as a dare.[26]

Most untoward incidents happened on campus, and a few could have proven disastrous. A week and a half after shopping in Oxford, as Meredith walked back to Baxter Hall late in the afternoon, someone on the third floor of Vardaman Hall dropped a two-foot rope tied into a noose. Though Meredith saw it and continued walking, he could not have missed its message. The day before, Meredith had told a marshal that if the troops and marshals left, he would soon be killed. He had overheard students say that they would kill him if they could be assured of a trial by a Mississippi jury. The marshals at Baxter also occasionally received threatening calls. The most serious threat came in February when a caller warned that Meredith would be killed before he left the cafeteria that evening, but nothing happened.[27]

In March the only serious harassment came one morning as Meredith walked to class. Someone dropped two plastic bags of water from a second floor hall window of Howry men's dormitory; landing near Meredith, they splashed water on his shoes and pants. Meredith and the marshal with him charged into the dorm, knocked on several doors, and asked if anyone knew who had thrown the water bombs; unable to find the perpetrator, Meredith went on to class. The marshals also continued to receive a few threatening messages, but the calls to Meredith decreased to one or two per week in March. Twice in April, callers warned marshals of bombs in the library, and campus police had to evacuate the building. In April soldiers discovered unexploded Molotov cocktails, one in an army truck and another where the alert platoon waited. Neither device exploded, but they alerted everyone to the reality of the threats.[28]

Students also targeted Meredith's car. While he played golf in late March, someone let the air out of two tires. In mid-May he drove his new 1963 Thunderbird to campus for the first time, and students reacted by clustering around the car and making unsavory comments. That night someone pelted it with eggs.[29]

During the spring provocative publications continued to appear. Two versions of an *Ole Miss Coloring Book* skewered nearly everyone. The first, a seventeen-page mimeographed pamphlet of simple sketches, made fun of local authorities. Distributed in late January, it showed, for example, a wooden board and suggested, "This is the Board of Trustees. Color the Knot-holes." Under a running rooster, it directed, "This is the Chancellor. Color him red, white, blue or yellow." Seven headless caps and gowns depicted the faculty—"Color it silent." A remarkable likeness of Meredith, "a new student," did not need to be colored because "He is already colored." A second *Ole Miss Coloring Book*, professionally illustrated and published in Florida, appeared in April and was dedicated to the leading segregationists, including George Monroe, Taylor Robertson, Bill Simmons, and Judge Russel Moore. Denouncing federal authorities and praising Barnett and Walker, it wanted the campus colored "bloody" and the soldiers in front of the Lyceum "red (inspired)." For a marshal, "Color him green. Color his trigger happy." As for the Kennedys, the attorney general was to be colored "yellow" and the president "pink."[30] The books suggested that the controversy had devolved into humor.

Two weeks after Meredith's shopping venture, during the night of February 21, small cards saying "ignore the nigger with vigor" appeared on the marshals' cars around Baxter Hall. Each carried the stamp "Rebel Underground." Also in February, the *Rebel Underground* began to arrive through the mail. Authorities attempted without success to trace its origin. In March, Hugh Clegg had decided the Citizens' Council in Greenwood had published early issues, but the army's commanding officer in Oxford reported that Chancellor Williams and others believed that Joe Ford published the *Rebel Underground* from the Lafayette County sheriff's office.[31]

Six issues appeared during the spring semester.[32] Calling Meredith "a cunning and deliberate troublemaker" and "a partially domesticated, semi-literate member of a cannibalistic race," it questioned his academic eligibility. It blamed Meredith's presence on the "head Coon Keepers in Washington" and called for the "ARRAIGNMENT, INDICTMENT, TRIAL, CONVICTION, CONFIRMATION and the EXECUTION of John Fitzgerald Kennedy" and his agents. The renegade publication named faculty who seemed friendly toward Meredith—Russell Barrett, Frank Howard, Jim "Thirty Pieces" Silver, Anna L. Gareau, Clare Marquette, Mildred Topp, Robert L. Rands, and Charles Fortenberry—and in several cases encouraged harassment by publishing their home telephone numbers. It criticized Fortenberry, chairman of the political science department, for sponsoring a social for political science majors, including Meredith; the event, it said, was "FORCING us to Mix and Mingle with the coon on pain of being busted out" of the program.[33]

In what one observer called "unbelievable depths of depravity," the *Rebel Underground* suggested "licentious and adulterous relationships between some of these coon coddling, libbie faculty members." It condemned Sidna Brower as "our Pink Pulitzer Princess," labeled her the "Foul Harlot of Journalism" and suggested that she and Meredith "sure do sit close together in class." It also went after Judith Gardner, a Jackson sophomore who sat next to Meredith in one of Barrett's classes and who had criticized the *Rebel Underground* in a letter to the *Mississippian*. Calling her a "wench," it claimed she "doth socialize and chit-chat with the coon." As a result of the attack on Gardner, which included publishing her parents' Jackson address, she left Ole Miss and her family moved from Mississippi.[34]

In perhaps its most outrageous charge, the *Rebel Underground* claimed not only that Jim Silver, an "ol' Lewd Lecher," had a grand collection of pornography but that Mildred Topp, a novelist and creative writing teacher, had posed for some of the pictures. After signing the AAUP statement the previous fall, Topp had taken down the names of her students during a major protest in January and had chatted with Meredith at the end of the first semester. To the pornography charge the sixty-five-year-old grandmother laughed and responded through a letter to the *Mississippian* that the accusation was "the only funny thing I have been able to find in the *Underground*." A frail ninety-five pounds, she allowed that a picture of her "would mean the end of the pornographic industry." Though in ill health and near death, she predicted that "the forces of evil, the powers of darkness that are now trying to destroy this University will not prevail." After she died later in 1963, Russell Barrett maintained that "her life was definitely shortened" by the year of turmoil and by the *Rebel Underground*.[35]

If the *Rebel Underground* fomented protests in the fall, the lack of disorders in the spring indicated its increasing ineffectiveness. In February soldiers judged that student interest had declined. A few weeks later army officials observed "little significant reaction" to it. The commander reported that "students are reading it just to keep up with the latest campus gossip." It had deteriorated into a diversion.[36]

With no crises during the spring, Meredith expanded his activities. He golfed on the university's nine-hole course, located just across the street from the gymnasium, between the football stadium and the Confederate cemetery. His golfing partners included Silver, Barrett, and William Strickland, a professor of French; local ministers and an army officer also played occasionally. In golf he pursued an interest developed as a caddy in Kosciusko and while in Japan, and it allowed him to escape his responsibilities and to interact normally with people.[37]

On Valentine's Day, Meredith played his first round with Silver and Cliff McKay, the Presbyterian chaplain. Meredith signaled his plans by purchasing a ticket for ten rounds. The army, marshals, and local police provided protection; an army helicopter hovered overhead. Silver later reported Meredith was anxious and nervous the whole time but "we joked and had an all-round good time." On the windy, cold, but crowded course, everyone was friendly, though the noise from walkie-talkies and laughing spectators distracted the golfers. Two weeks later Meredith played eighteen holes, and during the rest of the spring he frequently worked in a round. With the danger level declining, security decreased to a few marshals.[38]

Meredith's faculty contacts developed beyond golf. Increasingly professors had coffee or ate a meal with him in the cafeteria, and they also hosted Meredith in their homes. In the fall he had eaten in the campus apartment of art professor Ray Kerciu and in the Oxford homes of chemist Russell Maatman and of economist Frank Howard. During the spring more professors invited him into their homes for a meal. In addition to Kerciu and Howard, Richard Joslin of the art department and anthropologist Paul Hahn entertained him in their residences. For each visit, guards went too, and as a result, Meredith said, "There was no one in Oxford and few people in Mississippi who did not know that I was dining out with 'white folks.' "[39]

Inviting Meredith into their home caused the Howards to suffer retaliation. According to Meredith, pressure forced their older son to quit Boy Scouts, and in her elementary school class their youngest child received for Christmas a black doll labeled "nigger lover." The Howards nevertheless continued to have Meredith as a guest. Partly as a result of the harassment, Howard resigned and tried to sell his house. The Howards could not find a buyer until gossip predicted Meredith would buy it and live in it, and then the house sold.[40]

Two of Meredith's strongest faculty supporters never invited him to their homes. Russell Barrett refused unless he could come on his own without the security forces because the visit could not be relaxed. Jim Silver also never had him into his home on campus, and an incident in March 1963 revealed why. When a friend suggested that several professors invite Meredith over to Silver's home for steaks, Silver could not refuse. When his wife heard about the invitation, she, according to Silver, "blew her top" and refused to have Meredith in her home. Silver arranged to have the dinner at Howard's home, and in deference to his wife's wishes Meredith never visited the professor's home. Mrs. Silver, an Alabamian, could not accept blacks as equals, particularly in a social setting. As Silver later explained, "It's her department. I don't believe people should be forced to associate with Negroes in their homes against their will."[41]

Meredith's extracurricular life also included attendance at campus functions. When the San Francisco Ballet came in February, he met several dancers and walked with a few in the troupe to Fulton Chapel where he watched their performance. Afterward he visited in the home of Wofford Smith without any untoward events. Two weeks later he dined in the cafeteria with Professor Kerciu and members of the New York classical music ensemble Pro Musica before their performance. Though he went to the concert with two other students, one male and one female, and later in the evening stopped by the Kerciu apartment, no incidents occurred.[42]

In the spring Meredith enjoyed wider contacts among local blacks, particularly Roger Thompson, a sixty-three-year-old farmer and retired university carpenter. In October 1962, Thompson told a reporter, "I'm so glad there's a black face over there. I'm proud of it and I hope there will be more." An activist in the NAACP and the Regional Council of Negro Leadership, he declared, "I'm not afraid. And you can use my name." In early December he became the first black to visit Meredith at Baxter Hall; he wanted to make sure that he was not lonely. He returned several times, and occasionally Meredith drove to Thompson's home just west of Oxford. One Sunday in early January, Thompson took his friend to a funeral and afterwards around the county to visit several black families. Meredith recalled, "I met almost every Negro family within ten miles of Oxford." When they stopped at the home of a Jackson State classmate who taught at the high school, the response shocked Meredith: he and his wife refused to let Meredith into their home. The teacher later told Meredith that his principal had said that he would fire anyone who associated with Meredith. His acquaintance, Meredith realized, had lost the "minimum of self-respect and self-direction that a human must maintain in order to be an individual." The experience steeled Meredith to continue.[43]

Other blacks also visited Meredith. Aaron Henry stopped by one Sunday in March, and Meredith gave him a tour of Ole Miss. A friend from Jackson, James Allen Jr. came to campus in March to take Meredith's car to Jackson and later returned to give him a ride to Memphis for a weekend. During one week in May, Meredith drove to Holly Springs to see black students at Rust College and the Mississippi Industrial College, conferred with Medgar Evers in Oxford, talked in Baxter Hall with local black activist William Redmond, and ate lunch with his cousin James C. Meredith in the cafeteria. As a courtesy to his cousin, an air force captain, the army provided him a place to sleep. One Saturday in June, two of Meredith's sisters and his father came for a visit; they had lunch in the cafeteria and toured the campus and town before driving home. None of the visits provoked any disturbance. Meredith also visited the homes of other Oxford blacks, patronized their businesses, and attended services at their churches.[44]

Meredith still encountered hecklers, firecrackers, hostility, and disturbances, particularly in Baxter Hall. As his activity increased, his protectors worried that he might create a dangerous situation or trigger a violent outburst. With warm weather, for example, they discussed his possible use of the Ole Miss outdoor swimming pool; they believed they "could expect trouble" if he did. A greater possibility involved his attendance at a Rebels baseball game. "If this should happen," concluded the army commander, "indications are that he would be directed to the segregated section." Federal officials decided to act only if "there is disorder and/or Mr. Meredith is in danger," but he never tried to swim in the pool or attend a baseball game.[45]

The decline in campus disruptions had many causes. In addition to the reduced press attention, students seemed tired of the integration issue. Under surveillance by the army and marshals and pressure from the administration, they resigned themselves to Meredith's presence. They also learned that protests and demonstrations failed. In the wider state, other controversies took precedence. Ross Barnett and Paul Johnson fought their federal contempt charges, and election year politicking, which involved the desegregation of Ole Miss, also took the spotlight away. Even more, events at Mississippi State University captured headlines in March. After winning the SEC basketball tournament, the issue of whether the Bulldogs should compete in the NCAA tournament against integrated teams provoked a debate. With the university president's support and despite objections by segregationists, the State team overcame the "unwritten rule" and went to the tournament.[46] The change may have signaled a slight alteration in the attitudes of some whites as the push for racial equality in the state escalated.

Many other events also made Meredith recede in the public mind. In early January, twenty-eight white Methodist ministers issued a "Born of Conviction" declaration of moral opposition to racial discrimination and support for public education. The Justice Department sued to end school segregation in Biloxi and Gulfport, and in March blacks filed suits to desegregate public schools in the City of Jackson and in Leake County. Rumors about a black applicant swirled around the University of Southern Mississippi. A federal court heard arguments in a Justice Department challenge to voter registration laws, while demonstrations in support of black registration spawned violence in Greenwood. In Alabama, the SCLC's Birmingham campaign began in April, and two months later George Wallace made his infamous stand at the University of Alabama.[47]

Attention returned to Ole Miss as a result of a controversial art exhibit. In September 1962, landscape artist G. Ray Kerciu joined the faculty for a one-year position. The twenty-nine-year-old Michigan native had served at Keesler Air Force Base on the Gulf Coast before earning degrees from Michigan State and the Cranbrook Academy of Art. Toward the end of his year at Ole Miss, Kerciu staged a one-man show of fifty-six paintings and prints, including five on the racial crisis at the university. Using the techniques of what one critic called the New Realism or pop art, Kerciu reproduced on canvases the images and words that he had observed at the time of the riot and later. The *New Yorker* explained that his works were "in the tradition of political art that holds the mirror up to the environment without offering directives for changing it." One work portrayed a Confederate flag on which he had written slogans such as "Impeach JFK," "Would you want your sister to marry one?" and "[deleted] the NAACP." Other paintings contained "We will never surrender," "Go home nigger," "Kennedy's Koon Keepers," "Brotherhood by bayonet," "States Rights," "Never," and "White supremacy." Opening on March 31, the exhibition hung in the art gallery for several days without any public comment.[48]

Richard Calloway, owner of an Oxford music store and a member of the Citizens' Council, went to the show with a deputy sheriff, took pictures of the works, and, along with a few students, complained of obscenity. The following day a representative of the United Daughters of the Confederacy protested the defamation of the Confederate flag. With the chancellor out of town, Provost Charles Noyes summoned Kerciu and his department chairman to a meeting where a law professor explained that some paintings violated state laws against obscenity and against defacing the Confederate flag or any representation of it. At the provost's insistence Kerciu removed the offending paintings. In a news release, the university acknowledged that the administration had learned that the "representations of the Confederate flag have been taken by many viewers as indicating a slighting attitude toward the flag itself and all that it may mean to Southerners." The statement did not identify the "many," failed to mention the applicable state law, and ignored the opinions of blacks. After declaring that Kerciu had not intended to demean the Confederate flag, it defended "his right to hold and express through his art any political and social convictions he may have," but because his works "have given distress and offense to many through the use made of the Confederate flag," the university "asked" him to take the paintings down.[49]

In Saturday's *Jackson Clarion-Ledger*, Tom Ethridge reported Calloway's charges, summarized the state laws, and suggested that the Sons of Confederate Veterans and the United Daughters of the Confederacy might investigate the case. "I thought this only happened in Nazi Germany and Communist Russia," complained one professor. Two anonymous, fearful faculty members charged that the administration had "bowed to a small pressure group," and they claimed that academic freedom "is melting away like an ice cream cone." On Monday, Ethridge reproduced one of Kerciu's paintings and called the paintings unlawful and obscene. Later that morning, eight students picketed outside the art gallery to protest with signs that read "censorship" and "freedom?"[50]

Late Monday a law student's complaint prompted a justice of the peace to issue a warrant for Kerciu's arrest for violating state laws against obscenity and desecrating the Confederate flag. Charles G. Blackwell, a twenty-four-year-old father of two from Ellisville, was a well-known segregationist, past state president of the Patriotic American Youth, and a member of the Citizens' Councils in Jackson, Laurel, and Oxford. A National Guard veteran, Blackwell had been in the first unit that arrived on the campus during the riot on September 30. In the spring of 1963, he had declared his candidacy for the state legislature from Jones County. Claiming "nothing personal against Mr. Kerciu," the politician believed that laws had to be enforced. Early Tuesday afternoon a sheriff's deputy arrested Kerciu in his office, but he gained his release by posting a five-hundred-dollar bond.[51]

Hours after Kerciu's arrest, the AAUP chapter called on the administration to defend his "right and duty" to express himself. An alumnus in Arkansas warned, "If we deny freedom of expression to one of the faculty, we are destroying academic freedom." He worried that Ole Miss might enforce "the petty orthodoxies of the White Citizen's Council and the so-called Patriotic American Youth." The *Mississippian* asked, "Is Ole Miss truly a University?" On the other side, a Jackson man said that academic freedom "grows more hateful everyday" because it supports positions at odds with Mississippi's "mores and social customs." Two members of the Sons of Confederate Veterans objected to "a profanation of an ensign sacred to Mississippians." The *Rebel Underground* praised Blackwell and had fun with Provost Noyes's equivocation in ordering or requesting the removal of the artworks: "Wasn't that a Cool Caper that Provost NO-YES pulled in the 'Art' mess? That Slippery Reptile certainly lived up to his contradictory name." It called the university leaders "Dishonest and Rascally Scoundrels."[52]

Pressed from all sides, Chancellor Williams decided accreditation required that the university provide Kerciu with legal counsel, but he also continued to support the decision to have the paintings removed because of concern that they violated state law. The chancellor was not the only person under pressure. Claiming he had been harassed, Charles Blackwell said, "This suit has proven that the integrationists will use every tactic and method against me that Meredith claims has been used against him." As a result, on April 17, two and a half weeks after Kerciu's art show opened, Blackwell dropped his charges. He soon finished law school, Kerciu left for a California teaching position, and the university retained accreditation. Ole Miss and its chancellor, however, incurred wounds for appearing irresolute in defending academic freedom. Williams's conduct greatly disappointed Silver, who had considered him "an honest if vacillating and weak man." In April 1963 he concluded that Williams was "about as conniving (though more pious)" as other state leaders. The university's troubling response provided others with additional reasons to leave.[53]

Unaffected by the art brouhaha, Meredith went to class, played golf, and traveled regularly to Jackson and Memphis. The campaign to ostracize him continued, but the stress eased a bit as overt harassment declined. In April the army noted an increase in disturbances, but most aimed more at soldiers than Meredith. With equanimity, the army commander considered the rise "not unusual. . . . The students are restless and looking forward to graduation or the summer vacation." A less forgiving Student Judicial Council convicted a student of repeatedly using obscene language and gestures at MPs and of trying to run a jeep of MPs off the road, and it put him on disciplinary probation for the rest of his time at Ole Miss.[54]

In the spring, Meredith became more visible. He spoke out more frequently, confidently, and comfortably about his experiences and beliefs. Early in April his second article in a major news magazine appeared in *Look*, and the following month a letter and an interview appeared in the *Mississippian*. Toward the end of his year at Ole Miss, he traveled to Washington, Chicago, and Los Angeles. John Corlew, the *Mississippian*'s new editor, interviewed Meredith in his dorm room and found him "sometimes serious, sometimes nonchalant— but always quietly confident." In Washington, under the pressure of television lights and journalists' questions on *Meet the Press*, he acquitted himself "damned well," according to Jim Silver. In each interview and in his writings, Meredith stressed issues larger than himself. Greater opportunity for Mississippi blacks and "uplift for the Negro in general" drove him more than his own college degree. Though he expected the change to be "rough," he increasingly thought that most blacks had decided that they "are prepared for whatever is to come."[55]

Meredith considered his effort part of both American history and the cold war. Referring to the Civil War, he said "we're still wrestling with the same problem," the "civil rights and basic freedoms" of the American Negro. The international fight against communism and the emergence of new African nations also demanded the elimination of racial discrimination because the leader of the *free* world had "to bring itself nearer to this ideal of human equality," and he saw his campaign as part of that larger effort. He supported "strong legislation" by Congress, but he emphasized that he sought to end white supremacy, not to achieve racial integration or to force people "to enter into association with anyone else unless they so desire." He told Ole Miss students, "I do not want to join your fraternities." He repeatedly maintained that he wanted basic rights and opportunities for himself and for other blacks and wanted society to come "to the point where an individual is not judged by his race." For him both integration and segregation emphasized race, not individuality.[56]

In explaining what had happened at the university, he admitted that he had expected opposition to last only two weeks. Refusing to blame students or rednecks, he decided that the "real problem is the power structure. . . . the system of law and the legal structure" and political leadership. As a result, the campus protesters "had no choice but to act as they did." His ostracism, like segregation, "results in a reduction in everybody's rights" because it affected any white student who wanted to associate with him. "The students are still not free to associate with me," he said on *Meet the Press*. Although optimistic about graduating in August, he regretted that so little had changed. The marshals and soldiers frustrated him; he was almost never alone, and their continued presence meant that nobody had addressed the underlying causes of the riot and the campus disturbances. The enrollment of other blacks would, he believed, require marshals and soldiers for security. Despite his experiences at Ole Miss, Meredith predicted that positive changes in race relations would come fast in his home state, perhaps because it had the highest percentage of blacks and the problems were "most pressing" there.[57]

Meredith himself kept pushing for change. In April he applied for an apartment in married student housing for the summer. His wife graduated from Jackson State, and he hoped that she and their son could join him for the summer. Before his admission in the fall of 1962, Meredith had sent a twenty-five-dollar deposit for an apartment "in which I plan to live beginning with the first summer term of 1963." When he later inquired about an apartment, the registrar replied that his deposit had been returned to him as part of an agreement approved by the court. Robert Ellis then said Meredith would have to file an application, but the university considered applications in the order in which deposits were received. By the time the bursar received his check on April 18, no apartment was available for the summer.[58]

When students heard about Meredith's application, a protest resulted. At a student senate meeting, George Monroe charged "there are two sets of rules on this campus. There is one set for James Meredith and his friends and another for the 4,500 white students." He alleged that the chancellor showed a "pattern of inconsistency" and a bias toward "certain minority groups of students." After enthusiastic applause, the senators considered a resolution requesting the denial of Meredith's application because the presence of marshals and troops proved that Meredith was in danger on the campus. If he lived in the apartments, the other spouses and children would also be in danger. To protect them, Meredith should not be assigned an apartment. One senator suggested that the soldiers and marshals themselves "would be a real menace to the wives and children living there." The resolution passed unanimously.[59]

On May 16, the chancellor reported the application to the IHL board and Judge Mize. Although Williams asked for their guidance, he concluded that giving Meredith an apartment would "create problems" that would interfere with the provision of "education opportunities." He argued that having Meredith's family in married student housing would probably "jeopardize accreditation" because it would lead to "a repetition of acts of disorder and violence" and "aggravation of existing tensions." Seeming to agree that the male federal agents would endanger wives and children, he said that "unattached and detached marshals and guards" in the area "would cause serious concern in the minds of the students for the welfare of their families." Finally, he doubted that the injunction governing Meredith's enrollment applied to housing, much less family housing. He concluded that Baxter Hall provided the "best available housing for Meredith."[60]

Meredith's attorneys filed in U.S. district court an appeal of the university's decision. Seeking his access to family housing, they recounted his attempts to make a deposit for an apartment and Ellis's refusal to accept them. According to the plaintiff, the chancellor's worries about disturbances did not "provide a valid basis for denial of his application." Instead, "the denial of the housing application is based solely on the fact of his race" and violated the court orders that he be treated as any other student. On May 28 Judge Mize heard motions in Biloxi on Meredith's request. At the same time he dealt with another case involving Ole Miss.[61]

At the May meeting of the IHL board, Williams reported an application for law school beginning June 5 from Cleve McDowell, a Jackson State graduate. The board unanimously instructed the registrar to "defer and withhold action" on the application; it directed its lawyer to seek from the U.S. district court an explanation of the board's responsibilities under the injunction of September 13, 1963, in *Meredith v. Fair*.[62] Lawyers for the NAACP, however, asked Mize for a temporary restraining order against the university and the IHL board to allow McDowell's admission to the law school.

The sixth of ten children of a tenant farmer in Drew, McDowell had just graduated with honors from Jackson State, where he had known Meredith. In the fall of 1962 the twenty-one-year-old had considered applying to enter the university in January to finish his undergraduate education. After conferring with Meredith, he decided to apply instead to law school and sought the legal help of Constance Motley. He applied in November 1962 and again the following February after the law school revised its application form. In April 1963, the chancellor directed the law school to send the files of black applicants to the IHL board and to notify him when the school accepted one. Dean Farley forwarded copies of McDowell's documents to the board but told its executive secretary that he was "somewhat disturbed" about having to do more than just notify the board of the application; concerned about accreditation and complying with the court order, Farley feared that the abnormal procedure "may be interpreted as being beyond compliance with the injunction [in *Meredith v. Fair*] and imply a discrimination in dealing with applications of law students." Judge Mize granted the restraining order and set hearings for the following Monday in both the McDowell and Meredith cases.[63]

When Mize heard arguments in Biloxi on June 3, the state's lawyers maintained that all married student apartments were filled. The university, furthermore, had no record of Meredith's deposit, so he was not on the list for family housing. In correcting the board's lawyers, Motley pointed out that court records from *Meredith v. Fair* showed that the university had received his deposit in the summer of 1962 and returned it to him. The next day Mize refused to order the university to provide an apartment for Meredith because he decided the university had rejected Meredith because of a lack of space, not because of racial discrimination.[64]

In McDowell's case, the state argued that *Meredith v. Fair* had not been a class action; even if it had been a class action, it might not apply to McDowell because he only "*claims* to be a member of the Negro race." For the board, Charles Clark also argued that admitting McDowell would be a "catastrophe" and would lead to bloodshed. The case was a "question of integration and not education," and Meredith's behavior demonstrated his lack of interest in a real education. "Meredith has continuously made an issue of his race," charged the defense, and it suggested that his "publicity campaign and press conferences" caused his allegedly marginal academic performance. Just as Meredith's presence had "been destructive of educational opportunities," the defendants suggested McDowell's would be also. Mize reportedly took only ten minutes to reject Clark's arguments and to order McDowell's admission the very next day.[65]

Across the state, rumors, plots, and plans proliferated. Governor Barnett heard pleas for resistance from John McLaurin, Russel Moore, Bill Simmons, and other segregationists. Gossip claimed that the governor and lieutenant governor would again go to Oxford to prevent integration. Bill Minor of the *New Orleans Times-Picayune* later reported that Barnett and Representative John Bell Williams even considered having the state's congressional delegation join the governor in Oxford for a defiant stand, but the scheme collapsed when Senator Stennis and others refused to participate. In another plan, one of the governor's advisers drew up an executive order to close the law school. When the board's executive secretary said it would effectively close the entire higher education system because all schools would lose accreditation, calmer voices, including Tom Watkins's and Erle Johnston's, prevailed.[66]

Chancellor Williams pledged to carry out any court order. He repeated his opposition to outside interference, intolerance for demonstrations and harassment, support for law enforcement, and intention to discipline troublemakers. The calm chancellor said, "I personally don't feel there will be any trouble." An Ole Miss spokesman predicted, "They will stand in line just like everyone else," and an unconcerned student observed, "What's one more Negro, more or less?" Police in Oxford and nearby towns nevertheless stood ready to assist. Federal officials also brought in four additional marshals, while John Doar and others from the Department of Justice were in Oxford for another trial.[67]

About noon on June 5, the governor addressed Mississippi on television. "The State of Mississippi cannot cope with the United States Army and the Federal armed forces," conceded Barnett. "It would be unwise and futile to enter into a physical or a shooting combat with the United States Army." He nevertheless made a "positive and determined protest" of McDowell's unconstitutional forced entry and argued that Ole Miss still had not been integrated. Unwavering in his support of segregation, Barnett advocated the "purity and integrity of the white and Negro races." He reiterated his opposition to "dictatorial powers and polices" to overturn segregation and explained that "integration is the primary facet of the conspiracy to socialize and communize America." Far from yielding, Barnett encouraged perseverance because "we can all surge forward to a complete and honorable victory."[68]

Late Wednesday afternoon McDowell registered anyway. With army planes overhead, soldiers and marshals remained vigilant, and a few trustees observed, but nothing unusual happened. A pool of newsmen had little to report. Wednesday evening, McDowell dined with John Doar in the cafeteria before spending the night in the empty Baxter Hall, where he and Meredith would share a room for the summer. The next day Meredith enrolled. At the end of June, the army commander reported that they had "attended classes without incident."[69]

On June 10, the army turned Baxter Hall security over to the marshals. Four soldiers remained off campus ready for immediate deployment, and a squad was on fifteen-minute alert. The next night Meredith suffered a major shock when Byron De La Beckwith assassinated Medgar Evers in Jackson. Meredith's wife called to tell him that Evers had been shot, and he learned later that his friend was dead. He described the effect of Evers's death as "profound." Evers had been one of his "best and most beloved friends," but Meredith felt his death even more acutely because he believed that he himself, not Evers, "had been considered the most likely victim."[70]

As Meredith struggled the next day to continue, newsmen asked for a statement. He released a statement to the Associated Press and then conferred with professors Silver and Willis. Silver considered some of Meredith's words "really inflammatory, as well as . . . libelous," and he arranged for the AP to hold the story. After Meredith went to class and Silver consulted with Russell Barrett, the historian retrieved Meredith from class and persuaded him to omit two sentences: "If I were charged with the responsibility of finding Medgar Evers' killer, I would look first and last among the ranks of law officers of this state. The chances are at least 100 to 1 that there is where the killer is to be found." The wire services deleted the worrisome words.[71]

"A Negro's life is not worth the air it requires to keep it alive in Mississippi," Meredith declared. He blamed Evers's death on "defiant and provocative actions" of Governors Barnett and Wallace, federal inaction that encouraged white supremacists, and "blind courts and prejudiced juries" that refused to punish a white man for a crime against a black man. As evidence that "a white man can do anything he wishes to a Negro and go unhampered," he pointed to "what had happened to the guilty parties in the University of Mississippi riots. Nothing!" Invoking Patrick Henry's "Give me liberty, or give me death," he called on blacks to continue Evers's campaign for equality and justice by instituting "a general boycott of 'everything possible' by 'all' Negroes" in the state and by uniting "to protect our persons and our property, and our loved ones." Meredith felt the need for protection because the army's departure had left him more vulnerable than ever.[72]

The press release had no effect on Meredith's security. Marshals continued to protect him, and the army did not return. With 130 soldiers leaving Oxford on June 17, troop levels continued to fall until by July 25 the entire army force had pulled out of the area and turned the task over to the marshals and local police; the army's total expenditure in the Meredith operation had approached four and a half million dollars. After Evers's death, Meredith and McDowell had, according to the army commander in Oxford, been "frightened and unsettled," and the army's departure did not increase their feelings of security. For McDowell, the federal responsibility remained unclear, and the uncertainty caused worry and anxiety for both men. No significant disturbances occurred in June or July, so the remaining forces proved adequate.[73]

Meredith's statement had unintended repercussions. When asked about the applicability of the January 31 restrictions on statements to the press, Williams defended the policy and vowed to apply it to all students. The administration discussed Meredith's statements and delegated Dean Love to warn him to abide by the earlier rules. On the Monday morning after Evers's Sunday funeral in Jackson, a hand-delivered note from Love ordered Meredith to a meeting at 1:00 P.M.. In a thirty-minute meeting, Love expressed his concerns, and Meredith described his friendship with Evers and his problems with reporters on campus. Though Meredith did not expect to make additional statements, he agreed to clear any with the university news bureau.[74]

Four days later, the Sovereignty Commission asked the IHL board to investigate Meredith's two formal statements. If they violated the rules, the commission recommended "punitive action be taken immediately." As the AAUP had worried, Meredith's opponents wanted to use the rules against him. A few weeks later the trustees appointed a committee to investigate. The board chairman said, "Meredith's actions since he became a student have proven our theories he was more interested in a springboard for vocal utterances than an education." At the same time he acknowledged that lawyers advising the chancellor had concluded that getting the federal courts' permission to expel Meredith would be impossible; they also worried that his expulsion would jeopardize accreditation.[75]

Meredith's remarks after Evers's assassination were not his last public comments as an Ole Miss student. He traveled and spoke extensively in 1963. In March, for example, he flew to Tampa, Florida, to be honored at the Southeast Regional Conference of the NAACP. On Easter weekend in April, Meredith went to Los Angeles to receive the Booker T. Washington Award from the Tuskegee Alumni Association for bringing "outstanding progress in the field of human rights."[76] The appearances caused no controversy, unlike two of his later speeches.

At NAACP meetings in the early summer, Meredith gave two formal talks that caused consternation. On June 2, two days before Judge Mize ordered McDowell's admission and ten days before Evers's murder, Meredith told the state convention that he believed in "rewarding my friends and punishing my enemies," and he urged them to trade with the black businesses that advertised in their program. As for blacks who did not support the NAACP, Meredith declared, "We will treat them like we treat the whites who do not support us." With black support, black businesses could succeed, just as Barnett had boasted, but he questioned the governor's contention that whites treated blacks well in Mississippi. With statistics on income, life expectancy, health care, and education, he challenged Barnett's claims. He called on blacks to "eliminate the gap between us and human dignity" in the next twenty years by ending white supremacy. He targeted biological white supremacy but also "de facto" and "developmental white supremacy." The destruction of all forms of white supremacy would come, according to Meredith, "because the nigger will no longer play the nigger's role." Though he also called for additional federal legislation, Meredith stressed the need for individual action.[77]

The tough comments caused no stir in part because the local media, including the *Jackson Advocate*, paid no attention. A month later at the NAACP's national convention in Chicago he had a different experience. Invited by the National Youth Work Committee to speak on "Emancipation's Unfinished Business," he spoke to 650 people attending its banquet. He declared, "My purpose here tonight is to provoke." He challenged the audience with the topic assigned him: "Of all the things that have occurred affecting the Negro in the United States, I consider the issuance of the Emancipation Proclamation as being the most detrimental." It provided an excuse not to free slaves when the Union took control of the South. At the end of the Civil War, the nation made no provision for the freedmen, so "they were left attachless, with nothing, no land, and nowhere to go except back to the slave masters." As a result, "a human social system was created worse than any form of slavery" because under slavery "everyone had a place. The freed Negro had no place."[78]

"My greatest dissatisfaction today," Meredith said, "is the existence of the very low quality of leadership present among our young Negroes and the childish nature of their activities." Youth in the sit-ins, Freedom Rides, and voter registration drives failed to impress him. He blamed the sorry leadership on adult interference, but he also criticized the youth for a lack of "discipline and knowledge." Among young blacks he found a "yeah maybe, but not me" attitude, to which he responded, "Bull! Anyone of you burr heads out there could be the owner or manager of a large department store, president of a corporation, or even maybe mayor of the city of Chicago." Encouraging them to believe in themselves and in the possibilities for change, he proposed that in "twenty years Mississippi is going to be the Negro showplace of the world and the United States of America is going to be truly the land of the free and the home of the brave."[79]

On the planned March on Washington, Meredith declared that it "would not be in the best interest of our cause." Though he supported any oppressed people's efforts to "secure redress of its grievances," he wanted the movement's next objective to be effective national civil rights laws, and he questioned the march's effectiveness in producing helpful legislation. He did not oppose the march but urged people to seek the advice of black politicians and governmental leaders.[80]

In closing, Meredith indulged in a conjecture about "pride and recognition." Saying that many, including the mayor of New York City, had compared his entrance into Ole Miss to the astronauts' explorations, he wondered if he would receive a ticker tape parade in New York City and an invitation to address Congress. "Or will it be the same old story," he speculated: " 'But you are a Negro.' " Though he seemed to understand that, as a Negro, he still did not fully have a place, Meredith craved the recognition granted astronauts and other brave adventurers. His self-serving comments, however, did not attract the criticism heaped on other parts of his talk. The NAACP had made his speech available before he spoke, and rumors circulated that the audience would boo him, but instead they "listened politely but coolly."[81]

John Davis, a twenty-two-year-old Rutgers University student who served on the national NAACP board, followed Meredith to the podium and rejected his criticisms. He objected to the dismissal of the student leaders. Davis also denied that Meredith was a black leader or an expert on the civil rights movement. The audience, according to the United Press International, responded to Davis with "standing, shouting applause." As Davis rebuked Meredith, Roy Wilkins commented about Meredith, "He's not really representative of young Negroes."[82]

The next day reactions intensified. Meredith admitted that the "intolerance and bigotry" of the NAACP gathering caused him to cry for the first time since he was a young boy. He told reporters that the "discourtesy" and "dishonor" shown him by his fellow blacks had "overwhelmed" him and kept him from sleeping. Wilkins, however, had no sympathy. "Did he say he was responsible for the treatment he received?" he asked. "Did he say that he was criticized because he called the audience 'burr head' or did he otherwise tell why he was treated as he was?" Wilkins refused to apologize and argued that Meredith should apologize. Meredith declined but said that "everything I have been fighting for, the basic principles of tolerance, dignity, and respect, I was denied there in Chicago." Later he complained to Arthur B. Spingarn of the NAACP that he had been a victim of a "well planned plot to discredit" him, but Spingarn and other NAACP leaders denied any plot and regretted the unproductive controversy.[83]

Meredith's Chicago performance again revealed his unpredictability. He would not conform to others' expectations or subscribe to conventional ideas, but instead he was independent, iconoclastic—a militant conservative. In the tradition of Booker T. Washington, Meredith lectured the NAACP youth on the traditional conservative principles of careful personal financial management— spending wisely through comparative shopping, saving for future needs, and establishing a good credit rating. Like W. E. B. Du Bois, he also demanded "full citizenship" for blacks and called for the "racial pride" necessary to achieve their goals. Unlike some radical African Americans, however, he remained optimistic: "I do believe that this world can be made into a better place in which to live." To bring progress, however, he wanted the movement to stress the importance of legislation and other traditional solutions, not mass demonstrations. After his speech Meredith explained, "I am not any more against anti-segregation mobs than pro-segregation mobs. I just don't believe in mobs." In the developing split within the movement caused by the emergence of youth-oriented groups such as SNCC and their direct action tactics, Meredith preferred the established organizations' more formal methods of litigation, lobbying, and legislation. But his Chicago speech revealed his discomfort even with the NAACP.[84]

Back in Mississippi, the *Jackson Clarion-Ledger* relished Meredith's embarrassment and played it as the lead front-page story for two days. Four-column headlines almost gloated, "NAACP Youth Leaders Blast James Meredith" and "Wilkins, NAACP Blasts Cause Meredith to Cry." Though the headlines suggested that he had been discredited, segregationists did not waste much time on the story because they had other complaints to pursue against Meredith. His opponents sensed that his emotional statement after Evers's death presented their best opportunity to block his graduation on August 18. The responsibility for determining if his words had violated the chancellor's directives rested with a special committee set up by trustees.[85]

The four-member committee held a hearing in Biloxi on July 18 as part of the board's monthly meeting. Four lawyers constituted the committee: M. M. Roberts, appointed by Barnett; Tally Riddell, appointed by J. P. Coleman; and Thomas J. Tubb and Charles Fair, appointed by Hugh White. As a consequence, the committee did not include the four other Barnett appointees who were, with Roberts, the strongest segregationists. First, E. R. Jobe read to the committee the chancellor's January 31 directive and Meredith's statements after Evers's death. Provost Noyes next explained the circumstances surrounding the chancellor's policy and how the administration dealt with Meredith's statements. Dean Love then recounted his interview with Meredith, and Vice Chancellor Alton Bryant explained that administrators had to be concerned about how rules were implemented and the effects of carrying them out as much as their literal meaning. As an example, Bryant mentioned the wise decision not to act against Professor Kerciu, and he said the chancellor had acted similarly with Meredith.[86]

While the committee waited to report to the entire board, Meredith finished his ten and a half months at Ole Miss in relative peace. On his last day of exams, he donned a "Never" button that segregationists had worn, except that he victoriously wore his upside down. As the university prepared for summer graduation, a special committee worked to insure "an orderly and dignified academic occasion." The university barred newsmen from the campus except for the Grove, the scene of graduation, and reporters could not conduct any campus interviews. Campus police, backed up by local officers, prepared to barricade the campus to allow only authorized individuals to enter, and the chief of buildings and grounds planned to search and secure the building closest to the graduation area. In case of rain, the blockade would be dropped and commencement would move indoors. One professor was assigned "to man the microphone in case of panic."[87]

The committee prepared for a number of African Americans on campus. If possible, Meredith and his guests would stay in Baxter Hall until just before the ceremony, and the committee hoped they would approach the graduation area from the rear, apparently to offer as little disruption as possible. If blacks entered the cafeteria, police should be present, and if any blacks asked to use a restroom, an usher should take them to the Lyceum. After the ceremony, Meredith could leave his cap and gown in Baxter Hall before departing the campus. The committee tried to anticipate every possible problem, even disruptions by outsiders. It expected extra marshals to supplement the regular contingent.[88]

Clegg used his contacts to learn of possible plans for trouble. Only two concerns came to the attention of the FBI and the Justice Department. A report from Memphis suggested that a large number of blacks planned to attend the graduation ceremony and would be armed in case anyone tried to prevent them from being seated. After investigating, the FBI found no evidence to confirm it. Rumors also circulated that, immediately after Meredith received his diploma, authorities would arrest him, probably on the outstanding voter registration charge or for a traffic violation. At John Doar's insistence, the FBI checked with law enforcement authorities and found that nobody planned to arrest Meredith.[89]

Other pressures on the university and on the trustees also increased. The AAUP asked for clarification of reports that the board was considering expelling Meredith. From another perspective came letters and telegrams urging Williams to deny Meredith his degree. A Pontotoc lawyer called for "punitive action" that included not awarding his diploma until authorities completed a full investigation. Ole Miss supporters from the Delta told the chancellor, "If you allow Meredith to obtain an Ole Miss degree then a degree from Ole Miss is not worth the paper it is written upon." Calling a diploma "a certificate of HONOR," another declared Meredith "has not, does not, and never will, deserve and merit it."[90]

In the week before commencement, Barnett renewed the Sovereignty Commission's call to deny Meredith his degree pending further investigation. To buttress his request, Barnett repeated Meredith's statements about boycotts and ending white supremacy. Frustrated by the university's inaction, the State Building Commission decided on August 14 to act. Including Chairman Barnett and Speaker Sillers, all eight commissioners called Meredith's statements "derogatory and harmful" and concluded that he had tried to "harm and injure" Ole Miss and the state and to disparage the integrity of state officials. Unless the trustees could prove that Meredith did not make the statements, the commission requested he not be awarded a degree.[91]

The night before the full board's August meeting, the board committee met to decide what to recommend. The chancellor told the committee that Meredith's June 12 statement had not mentioned the university and had not elicited any reaction on campus, and he reiterated the university's position that Meredith's actions did "not justify expulsion" and constituted "no basis for properly and legally denying him" a diploma. Williams further argued that withholding his degree would jeopardize accreditation. The chancellor also pointed out the tolerance of Ray Kerciu's dissent earlier in the spring. At its closed meeting the committee voted 3–1, with M. M. Roberts dissenting, that Meredith's statements were insufficient to warrant withholding his degree. The next morning the board received the recommendation that it take no action against Meredith, and in a public meeting the trustees voted 6–5 to accept the recommendation. The five dissenters were all Barnett appointees. After the vote, Chairman Tubb and four colleagues criticized Barnett's "political interference" with the board. Three days before commencement, Meredith had by a one-vote margin been approved for graduation. On Saturday the university faculty formally approved his application for a degree in political science.[92]

Meredith spent the few days between his last exam and the Sunday graduation at his Jackson home. On the day of commencement, the Merediths drove in a caravan with friends and marshals to Kosciusko for dinner with his parents and in the afternoon to Oxford. Meredith and the nearly four hundred other graduates gathered near the library and then marched to the Grove. They passed the scenes of rioting nearly eleven months earlier: they went through the Lyceum, across the Circle, past the Confederate monument, and into the Grove. Perhaps forty blacks joined twenty-five hundred whites in the audience. The seating was not segregated, though most African Americans sat together in the back, and they included Meredith's parents, his wife and their child, Myrlie Evers, Aaron Henry, R. Jess Brown, and other friends.[93]

Speakers during the commencement exercises made only a few oblique references to the unique graduate and the year he had endured. In his invocation, Reverend William Arthur Pennington, a Methodist from Oxford, acknowledged "that we live in a difficult time when . . . men do not love one another," and he asked for God's help to "bring unity out of discord, trust out of suspicion." The main commencement speaker, President John Anderson Hunter of Louisiana State University, declared that, despite his institution's athletic rivalry with Ole Miss, the people of LSU "have been intensely sympathetic toward you in your time of crisis." He also complimented the university:

"It is to the credit of this institution, its officials, its faculty and student body, that the academic traditions of Ole Miss have been sustained."[94]

At 5:12 P.M. on August 19, 1963, thirty-one months after first applying to the university, James Meredith walked to the platform and received his Ole Miss diploma, a handshake, and "congratulations and good luck" from Chancellor Williams. After the exercises, he returned to Baxter Hall one last time, where he greeted friends and family and gave them a tour of his old home. Sunday evening, escorted by marshals, Meredith and his family drove to Memphis, where he stayed with a cousin before flying the next day to Gary, Indiana, for a speaking engagement.[95]

After his mission ended, Meredith remained uncertain about what he had accomplished. He believed that he had made some progress in insuring that every American had an equal chance for an education, but he denied any ultimate triumph against his primary target, the system of white supremacy. As a radical, Meredith would not be satisfied with partial victories; he disparaged the idea of making incremental gains. "You can't make gains," he explained to a reporter. "There's no in-between; either a citizen has equal protection or he doesn't."[96] He modestly knew that the freedom struggle had not ended, that many fights remained. Despite his unwillingness to claim success, Meredith had indeed proven that even Mississippi could not save segregation. Ross Barnett, the Citizens' Councils, and other forces of white supremacy had been forced to yield to Meredith's determination, backed by the NAACP, the federal courts, the Kennedy administration, and the army. Meredith had not broken white supremacy, but he had made a crucial advance toward equality by defeating segregationists in the most recalcitrant southern state and in an all-out battle over a hallowed symbol of their southern way of life, Ole Miss.

21. "The Fight for Men's Minds"

■ ■

Ten days after the riot in the fall of 1962, a Scripps-Howard reporter concluded that in "the one battlefield that counts most: The fight for men's minds," desegregationists had won a major battle at Ole Miss. They had demonstrated dedication, intelligence, and a "willingness, if not an inclination, to martyrdom." On the other side, the leaderless, "hodge-podge 'troops'" of the segregationists seemed "as much anti-authority as anti-negro" and "manage[d] to terrorize even other Southerners." Refusing to be provoked, James Meredith "did not gloat" and did not make "a single public relations mistake," while his opponents reacted with "obscene shouts" and "choked-up fury." In the "psychological warfare," Meredith, the NAACP, and the Kennedys seemed to have prevailed. In early October, however, the struggle over public opinion had not ended. The immediate public relations contest involving disputes over the causes and meaning of the Oxford disaster and efforts to allot responsibility for it continued for months. At the same time, a larger, more important struggle occurred in the minds of whites grappling with desegregation. As Gunnar Myrdal had observed in 1944, the American race problem was essentially a problem in the white mind. In the face of federal forces, Ole Miss and Mississippi whites had acquiesced in Meredith's enrollment, but the ultimate fight over their accommodation to, or acceptance of, racial equality would last much longer and produce more ambiguous results.[1]

In the fall of 1962, arguments developed over blame for the riot. Though Barnett's critics did not agree on everything, they generally deplored violence, called for obedience to the law and the Constitution, criticized his leadership, and defended the Kennedys' actions. The opposing position, which dominated the discussion in Mississippi, praised Barnett's defense of states' rights and the southern way of life, excoriated the Kennedys for what they saw as violation of the Constitution, and blamed the marshals for precipitating the riot. Though many Barnett defenders rejected violence, they remained defiant in their opposition to integration. Conducted largely through the media, the first rounds of the debate by commentators, civilian organizations, and citizens, as well as participants in the events, produced polarized exchanges.[2]

One of the first to speak out was William H. Mounger, the president of Lamar Life Insurance Company. At 7:40 A.M. on Monday, October 1, he interrupted the regular broadcast of his company's Jackson television station to speak extemporaneously for eight minutes. He deplored the violence and declared, "We are a part of the United States of America, and we must obey the laws of the United States of America." In addition to calling for the arrest of all rioters, he wanted the state's leaders to reveal any agreements made with the federal government and to explain "the basic law upon which they are proceeding."[3]

The next day Mounger's moderation received support from 127 bankers, lumbermen, attorneys, farmers, industrialists, and politicians meeting in Jackson. Convened by Mounger and other Jackson civic leaders, they expressed grief over events at Ole Miss, advocated law and order, wanted an investigation of the riot, and defended the university. The pillars of corporate life also called for unity so the state could "continue to march forward" and sustain its "tremendous—almost unbelievable—progress." They reasserted that the *Brown* decision "was morally and legally wrong."[4] Their temperate stance did not prevail.

Soon after the riot, state and national leaders began trading charges about the melee. On Monday the state's congressional delegation, except for Frank Smith, blamed it on the federal courts, the Kennedy administration, and the marshals. In reply the Justice Department defended the marshals and pointed to Barnett's failure to maintain law and order, especially when the state patrol left the campus Sunday night. Monday evening during an interview on national television, the governor justified his actions, and early Tuesday morning Assistant Attorney General Burke Marshall responded on *The Today Show*. At a news conference in Jackson later that day, Paul Johnson and other state officials rebutted Marshall, and on Wednesday a resolute Barnett on statewide television called for calm and patience but also proclaimed, "We will oppose this illegal invasion by every legal means. . . . [and] we shall, in the end attain victory."[5]

The Kennedy administration continued to back the marshals and soldiers, and it took some satisfaction that its actions in Mississippi had not harmed the president politically. Among northern liberals and blacks, support for Kennedy increased, without serious decline in the South.[6] At the same time, American prestige abroad did not suffer seriously as it had after the Little Rock crisis in 1957. The Kennedy administration had little time to appreciate the results in Mississippi because on October 15, two weeks after the riot at Ole Miss, intelligence photographs revealed Soviet missiles in Cuba, and the nation entered the most fearful crisis of the Cold War. Mississippi, integration, and states' rights yielded to communism, nuclear war, and national survival.

Among Mississippians, however, the riot debate persisted. In Oxford Reverend Duncan Gray called Barnett "a living symbol of lawlessness," and the university chapter of the AAUP charged that blaming the marshals was "not only unfair and reprehensible, but . . . almost completely false." In response Charles Hills blasted "scaly-backed professors and Judas-enrolled psalmists around the University of Mississippi" who had demonstrated their disloyalty by agreeing with Washington critics and the national media. According to Hills, federal forces "punished" his state "because it objected to being mongrelized. . . . because it did not care to be negroid in totality." He specifically blamed the marshals and soldiers as the "perpetrators" of violence.[7]

Barnett's support among white Mississippians remained strong, and the Citizens' Councils remained defiant. Two days after the riot, the senate commended the governor. Automobile bumper stickers boasted "Ross Is Right," and some women walking by the governor's mansion carried small Rebel flags. The Jackson Legal Secretaries Association, the Lexington Rotary Club, the Mt. Olivet Veterans of Foreign Wars and American Legion, and the Newton Chamber of Commerce proclaimed their support for Barnett and their criticism of the Kennedys. Late in October the newly formed Women for Constitutional Government echoed complaints about an "unlawful invasion" of Mississippi, federal tyranny, and biased national press coverage.[8]

Many small-town papers also backed the governor, but Hodding Carter, Hazel Brannon Smith, and other editors spoke out in opposition. Pascagoula's Ira Harkey, whose editorials would win a 1963 Pulitzer prize, called state leaders "false prophets who deluded the people for eight years into believing we could maintain school segregation" and blamed them for the "appalling climax of murder, mayhem, and destruction." His paper also published Representative Karl Wiesenburg's five-part analysis, *The Oxford Disaster . . . Price of Defiance*, in which he argued that Barnett "led his state down a path that inevitably led to riot, destruction and death."[9]

Though some southern newspapers sided with the state's segregationists, outside the region most of the nation's press deplored lawlessness, criticized Mississippi officials, and defended the Kennedy administration. Two nationally syndicated conservative columnists, Arthur Krock and David Lawrence, criticized federal authorities for moving too swiftly, but even they did not defend Barnett. And William F. Buckley, a supporter of states' rights, could not defend Mississippi's racial policies. *Look* magazine for December 31 pieced together the intricate stories of the secret negotiations, the deployment of marshals and troops, Edwin Walker's incitement of armed resistance, and the riot itself. The article, the most widely read account of the riot, exposed Barnett's duplicitous dealings. A Justice Department spokesman said the article was accurate, and Chancellor Williams judged it "thoroughly researched and most carefully written." Barnett dismissed it as "completely ridiculous," while Paul Johnson denounced its "grotesque exaggerations." A few weeks later in the *Economist*, Jim Silver contended that "all the world except Mississippi" recognized the fraudulent attempt by the state's leaders to shift the blame for the riot to the marshals and the Kennedys.[10]

As the lines of debate hardened, nearly everyone called for some kind of investigation or evaluation. One of the first was Senator Eastland, but a Senate inquiry apparently soon died. The Justice Department and the army engaged in self-examinations of their operations. The FBI, along with state and local authorities, investigated the deaths of Paul Guihard and Ray Gunter, but none uncovered conclusive evidence. Within a month of the riot, a Citizens' Council brochure entitled "Operation Ole Miss" and the Junior Chamber of Commerce's "Oxford: A Warning for Americans" reported what had happened and justified Barnett's actions.[11]

For many whites, the General Legislative Investigating Committee made the most significant inquiry. Starting on October 4 and continuing for seven months, it heard testimony from more than one hundred witnesses in nineteen sessions. After it hired John Satterfield as counsel early in February, it sought to prove that the marshals started the riot. In April its fifty-five-page report condoned the actions of Mississippi officials and condemned the behavior of the federal government. Though many state leaders hailed the report, it failed to persuade everyone. Ira Harkey, for example, called it "useless" and "cynical." The Justice Department branded it an "untruth document" full of "bias, factual errors, and misstatement."[12]

On the same day that the legislative committee released its report, an Oxford theater showed *Oxford U.S.A.* Produced under a contract with the Sovereignty Commission to "point out the true facts," the forty-three-minute documentary substantiated the official state version of the riot. Advertisements announced, "Verifies Legislative Investigation" and "Federal Atrocities Revealed." The Sovereignty Commission used it to spread the segregationist interpretation of the riot. Within eighteen months groups from Massachusetts to California viewed the state's most visible entry in the public relations war.[13]

While the two sides battled through the media, they also fought legal contests that implicitly aimed to establish responsibility. Within hours of the riot, federal officers charged Edwin Walker with seditious conspiracy.[14] Before a federal grand jury could meet to consider charges, a Lafayette County grand jury convened in mid-November. The judge's charge to the jury blasted the "diabolical political Supreme Court" and the Kennedy administration as "hungry, mad, ruthless, ungodly power mad men" and demanded that "criminal acts against . . . necessary segregation laws [not] go unpunished." After hearing nineteen witnesses and studying state and federal reports, the grand jury criticized the actions of the federal marshals. Their "arbitrary and unnecessary action" in surrounding the Lyceum had "the sole purpose of agitating and provoking violence," and their unwarranted use of tear gas "set off the tragic violence that followed." The report condemned the "many cruel and inhuman acts of violence inflicted by the marshals" on prisoners. At the same time the jury also commended the highway patrol for having control of the situation until the marshals used tear gas, and it praised the work of the Lafayette sheriff. In addition to its general assessment of the riot, the jury indicted Pfc. Dominic Niglia for firing a rifle shot into a dormitory and James McShane for "unlawfully and feloniously" firing tear gas that "did incite a riot." Niglia's case was soon dropped, and after a continuance, the court on September 15, 1964, dropped the McShane case. McShane and other Justice Department employees faced civil lawsuits brought by an Ole Miss student who claimed they had started the riot and by three men detained during the riot who alleged their civil rights had been violated, but courts eventually dismissed them.[15]

Other cases also developed out of the riot. A federal grand jury in Oxford early in 1963 indicted four men for interfering with and obstructing marshals; subsequent trials convicted none. Meanwhile, the government dropped charges against Edwin Walker and six others. Perhaps the most important legal action involved contempt charges against the governor and lieutenant governor. For more than two and a half years, the cases divided the Fifth Circuit Court of Appeals over civil versus criminal contempt, the right to a jury trial, and the appropriate court to handle the cases. Finally in May 1965, after Barnett had yielded the governorship to Paul Johnson in the election of 1963, the court decided 4–3 that a trial would not serve the public interest.[16]

While the courts contemplated contempt charges and others battled over blame, Ole Miss struggled to understand its responsibility for the crisis. In their first public comments in the weeks after the riot, university leaders portrayed the school as a victim of larger forces. In mid-November the university's forty-two-page report concluded that it had "maintained its academic integrity" and that the courts "had completely cleared" its leaders of contempt. Though the analysis viewed the controversy as a political conflict between state and federal power, it denied that the university had experienced "political interference"; any pressures "were never intended to interfere with the internal operation of the University." Recognizing that political interference constituted "grounds for disaccreditation," the report tried to protect the university's accreditation and reputation by emphasizing its own limited role in the entire affair.[17]

The Southern Association of Colleges and Schools, concerned about political interference, monitored the Meredith case. At its annual meeting before Thanksgiving, SACS put all the state's public colleges in an "extraordinary status" that neither revoked accreditation nor exonerated the schools but instead "placed [them] under continued and careful observation" until its next meeting. The American Council on Education unanimously criticized the "shocking invasion of political power," and the Association of State Universities and Land Grant Colleges adopted a similar resolution. The national office of the American Association of University Professors maintained contact with people at the university because it wanted assurances that academic freedom had not been abridged. The Association of American Law Schools found the law school had done "almost everything" it could to protect its integrity and took no disciplinary action.[18]

After all the investigations, lawsuits, hearings, and trials, no one was fined or served a jail sentence, nor did anyone establish responsibility for the disorder or the deaths. Neither side convinced the other of its culpability. In the longer term, however, nearly all historians have agreed that responsibility rested with Governor Barnett and other state officials. One remarkable exception came in a former Ole Miss professor's analysis of the "confrontation at Ole Miss." William T. Doherty, born and educated in Missouri, served as history department chairman until 1963 when he moved to West Virginia University. In 1973 he excoriated the moral failure of participants in 1962 and, in passing, also damned "bland journalists and historians" who excused them by viewing events in terms of politics and not morality. Though he even chided James Meredith for "undue individualism" and ignorance of the larger civil rights movement, Doherty acknowledged that he "did nothing immoral" and had given a "heroic solo performance." The historian reserved his harshest judgments for state and national leaders. He blamed the naive Kennedys for failing to understand the state, its leaders, and the political pressures on the university. Doherty damned the "daffy" state legislature, the "fascistic" Citizens' Council, and the duplicitous, political Barnett who chose "brinksmanship" instead of "statesmanship." At the same time, he criticized the "academic Pilates" and "educational eunuchs" who demonstrated "moral obtuseness" and cowardice by not defending academic freedom, the rule of law, and Meredith's right to admission. Doherty concluded that "all participants . . . were morally fried in the Ole Miss holocaust of 1962." Everyone paid a price for the state's defiance.[19]

Despite the prolonged and sometimes bitter public debate over the causes of the violence at Ole Miss, the disaster did have positive ramifications. In South Carolina, for example, four months after Meredith's enrollment, leaders who knew about the Ole Miss debacle engineered Harvey Gantt's desegregation of Clemson College without incident. Later in the spring of 1963, Governor George Wallace made his futile stand in the schoolhouse door to prevent the admission of blacks to the University of Alabama, but the governor, university leaders, and the federal officials understood that they had to avoid a violent confrontation. As a result, Wallace yielded, and Vivian Malone and James Hood registered at the state university. Though not complete, the desegregation of southern higher education had been achieved.[20]

Within the larger black freedom struggle, events in Oxford established that the Kennedy administration would use federal power to enforce the law. Though Meredith's achievement remained largely an isolated event, it spurred popular support and added momentum to a movement that in the following year included the Birmingham campaign—with its fire hoses, police dogs, and children's crusade—and Martin Luther King's "I Have a Dream" speech at the March on Washington. In Mississippi, Meredith's breach of segregation inspired the movement to work for further advances against white supremacy. Weeks after he enrolled, black students began a boycott of Jackson's discriminatory white businesses. The crisis at Ole Miss also marked the high point of massive resistance in the state. In 1963 Paul Johnson won the governorship partly based on his stand against Meredith, but in his inaugural address in January 1964, only five months after Meredith's graduation, he promised to fight "not a rearguard defense of yesterday . . . but for our share of tomorrow." In a major break with the policies of Ross Barnett, he employed the rhetoric of reconciliation when he told his fellow Mississippians, "We are Americans as well as Mississippians. Hate or prejudice will not lead Mississippi while I sit in the governor's chair."[21] While racial segregation and prejudice remained, the state had passed a critical point in its race relations.

Ole Miss did not escape the effects of its ordeal over integration or the legacies of the riot. In October 1962 one observer predicted "that the university has been damaged brutally, that its reputation is so besmirched it will take years to banish the stain of bloodshed on the campus." In the national culture, Ole Miss soon symbolized white supremacy, segregation, and states' rights. Popular music propagated its reputation for retrograde racial and political attitudes and for racial violence. In 1963 the Chad Mitchell Trio's "Alma Mater" helped solidify the negative image. Sung partly to the tune of "America the Beautiful," the satirical reminiscences of Ole Miss alums included "the rich wonderful experiences," the "shining moments of our youth" that included the "teargas raids, the Army tanks, those riots after class." The song skewered the school proud of its Miss Americas by recalling, "My girl was only seventeen, when she was chosen riot queen." Nostalgic for "hand grenades" and the "effigies we burned," it closed with a touching "God bless thee, Ross Barnett." That same year Bob Dylan's "Oxford Town" mourned the dark place where "the sun don't shine above the ground" and where a man could not enter a door "because of the color of his skin." Dylan sang, "Guns and clubs followed him down / All because his face was brown." Remembering that two men died, Dylan in sorrow warned, "Better get away from Oxford Town." In the wake of 1962, Oxford and Ole Miss became national pariahs.[22]

As the reputations of the town and university suffered, each entered long periods of lassitude, a lingering effect of defiance. Even the Rebels football team endured diminished success. In 1963 it won the SEC championship, but the next year the team that had won 85 percent of its games and played in eight major bowl games in nine seasons slipped to a 5–5–1 record. The glory days had ended. For forty-five years the Rebels did not win another SEC football title. Known also for its Miss Americas, Ole Miss failed to produce another until 1986. Instead of the "babes" and "brutes" of the 1950s, the university's notoriety after 1962 rested on riots and racism.[23]

J. D. Williams played out his last years at Ole Miss, until his retirement in 1968, without ever finding the ditch he would die in. To succeed him, the trustees selected Porter L. Fortune Jr. A World War II veteran with a doctorate in history, he had worked at the University of Southern Mississippi for a dozen years before becoming executive secretary of the National Exchange Club. M. M. Roberts of Hattiesburg and other Barnett appointees considered Fortune a safe and reliable candidate. For the next sixteen years Fortune presided over a stagnant institution. Enrollment grew in the 1960s and 1970s, but Ole Miss missed much of the exciting, explosive expansion of comparable institutions, including the University of Southern Mississippi and Mississippi State University. Only in 1984 with the appointment as chancellor of R. Gerald Turner, a young and energetic Texan, did the university experience a revitalization and resurgence.[24]

During the same years, Oxford shared Ole Miss's inertia. In the fall of 1962 the town stood poised for dramatic development. A county hospital and jail and a municipal high school were under construction. The state was building limited-access north-south and east-west highways on the edges of town, and the interstate highway from Batesville to Memphis opened. In August 1962

Oxford switched from operator-assisted to direct-dial telephone service. With an improving infrastructure, the town appeared ready for growth. Instead it languished: the 1960 population of 5,528 took more than thirty years to reach 10,000.[25]

While the events of 1962 had long-term deleterious effects on Oxford and Ole Miss, the decade-long controversy over race had immediate consequences for many individual participants. In 1956 Will Campbell lost his job as chaplain and went on to work for the National Council of Churches before developing a career as an author and public speaker. After Billy Barton's unsuccessful campaign to become editor of the *Mississippian*, he tried to pursue a journalism career in Mississippi but had to accept working for the Associated Press outside the state. After suffering a serious wound as an AP reporter in Vietnam, he returned to Pontotoc to recuperate and died in an automobile accident in 1972. Law professor William Murphy found better fortune at the University of Missouri and later at the University of North Carolina.[26]

When Robert Farley approached mandatory retirement at the end of 1963, he expected to relinquish his law deanship but continue teaching temporarily beyond sixty-five as the university often permitted. His reappointment promised controversy because he had consistently opposed segregation, so to avoid causing conflicts with the trustees and within the state bar, Farley resigned in the spring of 1963 and moved to the University of Florida. A more egregious fate awaited Jim Silver. In 1963 the history professor's presidential address to the Southern Historical Association was titled "Mississippi: The Closed Society"; a book-length version followed in the summer of 1964. His critical, even caustic, comments caused consternation among conservatives. A movement formed to oust him from Ole Miss, but he left in the summer of 1964 for a one-year appointment at Notre Dame University before the trustees could act. The hostility induced him to stay at Notre Dame, and in 1969 he moved to the University of South Florida.[27]

The 1962 disaster affected many others, and a few were especially unfortunate. After loyally testifying for the state, registrar Robert Ellis continued to work at the university but was soon shunted off to the School of Education. In 1965 Russell Barrett, the political science professor who had befriended Meredith, wrote his account of *Integration at Ole Miss*. Relentlessly attacked by segregationists in subsequent years, he slipped into severe mental illness and died in 1980. Dean L. L. Love moved to Colorado, where he committed suicide in 1968. In addition to losing his lawsuit against the Associated Press, Edwin Walker in 1963 survived an assassination attempt by Lee Harvey Oswald and lost a bid for governor of Texas. A decade later, Dallas police twice arrested Walker for public lewdness after making sexual advances on plainclothes policemen in a restroom in a public park. Walker pled no contest to the misdemeanors. He died in 1993.[28]

The battle over Ole Miss also had political ramifications. In Paul Johnson's gubernatorial victory in 1963, he had defeated J. P. Coleman in a runoff by tying the former governor to the hated Kennedys. In the same election, John McLaurin, one of the four men Barnett sent to Ole Miss on the night of the riot, challenged Attorney General Joe Patterson by pledging to be a "*strong*" attorney general, but the criticism failed to stick. Four years later Ross Barnett lost when he again ran for governor.[29]

Two years after Coleman's loss in the gubernatorial election, President Lyndon B. Johnson nominated him for the U.S. Fifth Circuit Court of Appeals; Coleman served until 1991, his final decade as chief judge. In 1965 Johnson named Constance Baker Motley, the former NAACP lawyer, to the federal bench in New York. Four years later President Richard M. Nixon appointed her opposing counsel, Charles Clark, to the Fifth Circuit Court of Appeals, where he served with Coleman and succeeded him as chief judge. Though Clark and Motley often attended the same federal judicial conferences, they never spoke about their battles in the Meredith case.[30]

The crisis at the university had its greatest effect on James Meredith, who would always be known as the man who integrated Ole Miss. After graduating in August 1963, he studied for a year at Ibadan University in Nigeria before entering law school at Columbia University. In June 1966, when Meredith was on a solitary March against Fear through the Delta from Memphis to Jackson, a sniper shot and wounded him. While a law student, Meredith invested in Bronx real estate and made a brief run against Representative Adam Clayton Powell. After receiving his law degree in 1968, he returned to Mississippi, where he engaged in a variety of businesses and ran several times for public office. In 1984 he moved to Cincinnati, where he taught African American studies for a year at the University of Cincinnati, ran unsuccessfully for the school board, and continued to lecture around the country. In 1989 Meredith moved to Washington to join the staff of Republican Jesse Helms, an archconservative senator from North Carolina, and two years later Meredith endorsed Ku Klux Klan leader David Duke for governor of Louisiana.[31]

Meredith's post-1963 career has baffled many observers because he violated the expectations for a civil rights hero. While Meredith the maverick pursued an unpredictable path, he remained guided by a belief in his own divine responsibility, a commitment to black pride and progress, and a conservative stress on individual responsibility and achievement. His lonely but public experience at Ole Miss reinforced his individualism and encouraged a desire for public attention. In subsequent efforts for black advancement, Meredith acted alone and rejected the established civil rights organizations and their conventional remedies. At the same time, he often took audacious, controversial stands that garnered public attention for himself and his causes, in part because he had grown accustomed to the limelight. More than most commentators have realized, Meredith followed a steady course after his year at Ole Miss. The same individualism and self-confidence that enabled him to survive the challenges of the early 1960s also fueled his later endeavors.

As Meredith recognized, however, enrolling at Ole Miss involved more than just one black man: he represented his race. His symbolic accomplishment did not end with his graduation; other black students made his achievement permanent and made their own contributions. The number of African American students at Ole Miss increased to 16 by 1966, nearly 200 in 1970, and more than 700 by 1982. Cleve McDowell, who entered law school the summer before Meredith's graduation, tried after Meredith's departure to endure without any federal protection. Arming himself for protection, McDowell on September 23, 1963, dropped his gun as he ran into the law school. Police arrested him and Ole Miss expelled him. The following June, under a court order, Cleveland Donald, a sophomore from Jackson, transferred from Tougaloo College. In the fall of 1964 Reuben V. Anderson became the second black student to enter the law school, and Irvin Walker the first to enroll as a freshman. Among the many firsts achieved by black students, Anderson earned the first law degree in 1967, and the next year Robert Walker received the first graduate degree, a master's in history. By 1968 the university had enough black students to form a Black Student Union. Basketball player Coolidge Ball became the first black athlete in 1970, and in 1972 Ben Williams became the first black football player; three years later students elected him the first black Colonel Rebel, and his teammates selected him team captain.[32]

While the black presence and accomplishments on campus grew, racial tensions and conflicts continued. Even if vanquished in the fall of 1962, defenders of the southern way of life persisted, and the battle for men's minds continued. One indication of change came when Senator Robert Kennedy spoke at Ole Miss in March 1966. Invited by law students, he sought to move beyond 1962 toward reconciliation. The friendly reception, including a standing ovation, by five thousand at the coliseum suggested that the defiance of the early 1960s had dissipated, if not disappeared.[33]

In February 1970, a peaceful protest by black students disrupted a concert, and police arrested about ninety black students and sent some temporarily to the state penitentiary at Parchman. Eight students were suspended and forty-five put on probation. Later in the year, however, the university hired its first black professor and initiated a black studies program. In 1982 a perennially irritating rebel flag provoked a controversy after the first black cheerleader vowed not to wave it. At the same time, James Meredith marked the twentieth anniversary of his admission by speaking at a convocation, and a few weeks later the Ku Klux Klan rallied on the Oxford square. Though white students defended the banner, the university in the spring of 1983 severed all connections to the Confederate battle flag. In the wake of the fights over the flag, black enrollment fell from 715 in 1982 to only 536 in 1984. Partly in response, the following year new chancellor Gerald Turner stressed the need for more black students when he repeatedly declared that progress depended on "more Ole Miss rings on black fingers." By 1995 the number of black students at Ole Miss had nearly doubled to 1,043, more than 10 percent of the total enrollment. Damon Moore, class of '86, became the university's first black Rhodes Scholar. In 1990 students chose Kimzey O'Neal to be Miss Ole Miss and Lee Eric Smith editor of the *Daily Mississippian*.[34]

As racial problems periodically roiled the campus, two embarrassing incidents involved the segregated fraternities. In 1988, when Phi Beta Sigma, a black fraternity, prepared to move into a former white fraternity house on Fraternity Row, the house mysteriously burned. With financial assistance from friends and other fraternities, Phi Beta Sigma did later move into another house on Fraternity Row. A year after the fire, several members of the all-white Beta Theta Pi fraternity stripped two members, painted racial slurs on their bodies, and left them at Rust College, a black school thirty minutes away in Holly Springs. In addition to apologizing to the college, Ole Miss disciplined the students and banned Beta Theta Pi for three years.[35]

Despite such ugly events, the university had, according to one historian, "made remarkable progress" in accommodating racial change. One indicator came in the fall of 1995 when students began an ad hoc effort to create a civil rights memorial at Ole Miss. In a discussion of campus symbols, whites in a southern folklore class recognized the absence of anything to balance the antebellum Lyceum, the Confederate soldier monument, and the Confederate flag and "Dixie." Led by John T. Edge, a thirty-two-year-old Georgian, southern studies students in November 1995 discussed the idea with the Black Graduate and Professional Student Association. Within weeks a biracial group organized to "construct a sculptural commemoration of the Civil Rights Struggle on the Ole Miss campus." In February 1996 Chancellor Robert C. Khayat supported the project but declared that the university "would like to assure its quality and aesthetic control by inviting competitive bids that reflect a variety of architectural ideas." He assigned a vice chancellor and the university architect to work with the group, which had grown to include faculty and staff.[36]

The new Civil Rights Commemoration Initiative (CRCI), which soon brought in members of the Oxford community, launched a grassroots fundraising effort. Though the university could not provide funds, the chancellor decided that the memorial should go on the ellipse between the Lyceum and the library instead of opposite the Confederate memorial on the Circle. After agreeing to fund an art consultant, he made a commitment to raising private money. While the volunteer group worked in the late 1990s to acquire the $150,000 needed to erect a memorial, several other events also boded well for changing attitudes.[37]

In February 1997, Myrlie Evers-Williams spoke as part of Black History Month, and the next month in an act of reconciliation, James Meredith presented his collection of personal papers to the university archives. One year later, representatives of the advisory board for President Bill Clinton's Initiative on Race held a town meeting on the campus. Former governor William Winter, a member of the board, had encouraged the forum to discuss racial problems and their solutions. After months of interracial meetings in the community, the event's success highlighted the changing racial atmosphere in the state and at the university. To continue the interracial dialogue, the university, at the suggestion of both Winter and Judge Charles W. Pickering, the following year organized what became known as the William Winter Institute for Racial Reconciliation. Susan Glisson, the institute's director, worked with Edge to create a civil rights memorial.[38]

Early in 2000, the Mississippi Department of Archives and History awarded the CRCI $75,000 under its African-American Heritage program. Combined with an $8,000 grant from the National Endowment for the Arts, large gifts from Dr. Watt Bishop of Oxford and P. D. Fyke of New York, and many smaller donations, the CRCI came close to its goal. In 2001 the university issued a call for a "work of art to Commemorate Mississippi's Role in Civil Rights."[39] The solicitation directed that the artwork should recognize both the "conflicts and achievements" related to "equal access to educational opportunity," particularly the "tragedy of exclusion, the drive for equal access . . . , and the enormous progress made since 1962." It should "honor those who fought for and won equal educational opportunity" in Mississippi. In addition to concern about the viewing public's safety, the university expected the memorial to be "aesthetically and conceptually" fitting for the campus ellipse. Plans called for five experts in contemporary visual and public art to select five finalists in a public meeting. The finalists would present their models in a second open meeting. With advice from representatives of the Ole Miss and Oxford communities, the panel would "recommend the artwork to be executed for the project to the gifts and facilities committees." The plan called for installation of the artwork in time for the fortieth anniversary of Meredith's enrollment.[40]

While planning and fund-raising continued, the university scored several public relations victories on race. On February 24, 2000, students elected the first black president of the student body, and the first African American woman was selected to edit the *Daily Mississippian*. Early in 2001 the Gospel Choir received a Grammy nomination for the Best Gospel Choir or Chorus Album of the Year. At commencement the following year the School of Business Administration honored doctoral recipient Joseph Meredith, son of James Meredith, as its best graduate student.[41]

The biggest public relations coup came in the spring of 2001 when the Rebels won the SEC basketball championship and advanced to the NCAA Midwest regional in Kansas City against Iona College. Publicity about the two teams' only previous meeting at a tournament in Kentucky embarrassed Ole Miss officials: in 1957 the Rebels had refused to play because Iona had a black player. Forty-four years later, when eleven of fourteen Rebels were African Americans, Chancellor Robert Khayat invited Stanley Hill, the black former Iona player, to sit with him at the game in Kansas City. After the men, their wives, and the Mississippi governor watched the Rebels win, news accounts across the country praised the gesture of reconciliation.[42]

Despite the public relations successes, the memorial project fell behind schedule. In early 2002, after receiving more than four hundred inquiries, the jurors chose five finalists to present formal proposals and models. Though the university administration wanted to select the ultimate design from a ranked list of three finalists, Edge, Glisson, and the CRCI insisted that the final decision emerge from the established open-selection process. In May the jury accepted a design submitted by Terry Adkins, a New York-born African American artist at the University of Pennsylvania. The referees hailed the design's dignity, universality, simplicity, elegance, and eloquence. It featured two nineteen-foot-tall arches inset with eleven-foot-high glass doors bearing the phrases "Teach in Fear No More," "United in Fear No More," "Learn in Fear No More," and "Insist in Fear No More." Above the doors appeared "Freedom Henceforth" and "Justice Forevermore." Two months later the IHL board approved the project.[43]

Adkins's work suddenly stirred controversy. A local architect criticized it for employing the "same architectural language as the Lyceum, which stood for years as a fortress of segregation." Referring to the words emblazoned over the doors, he asked, "Freedom for whom? Given by whom?" Adkins's use of two doors struck the architect and others as "ominously reminiscent of the 'separate but equal' policies of our recent past," and he imagined "substituting

'White' and 'Colored'" over the doors. Chancellor Khayat also had multiple concerns. He found Adkins's work lacked any mention of the university's role in desegregating higher education, he objected to placing the doors on the sidewalk between the Lyceum and the library, and he found the high arches incompatible with the surrounding buildings. Last, preferring "strong and positive" words, Khayat "balked" at the repeated use of the word "fear." Others objected that the Adkins design did not mention James Meredith or his admission to the university.[44]

Discussion of Adkins's work also derived from larger unacknowledged differences over the artistic nature of the memorial: whether it should directly represent its subject or present a more abstract interpretation. The project's purpose divided the community between people seeking to honor the larger civil rights movement and others wanting to focus on Meredith and 1962. The controversy also pitted people for whom the civil rights movement was in the past against activists who wanted to use the memorial as part of a continuing struggle. The greatest implicit conflict, however, occurred over which interpretation of the past it should portray; disagreement over the word "fear" captured the essence of the conflict. *Fear* described the feelings of black people during an ugly time of discrimination and oppression; to include *fear* would acknowledge the suffering endured by African Americans and recognize the deplorable actions of Mississippi whites that caused their *fear*, both in the past and in the present. To omit *fear* to create a more optimistic, hopeful perspective would allow people, particularly whites, to celebrate progress without facing the realities both of black life and of the past actions of whites. The struggle, therefore, signified a battle over the state's history, who would determine its content, and how to honor it.

Disagreements delayed the memorial and prevented its planned completion by the fall of 2002. Without a memorial, Ole Miss nevertheless staged an extravaganza to mark the fortieth anniversary of James Meredith's enrollment. A yearlong "Open Doors" program recognized the desegregation of the university and celebrated the subsequent changes in race relations. Participants in the opening ceremony included Myrlie Evers-Williams, Bishop Duncan Gray, and former governor William Winter. Later events featured Constance Baker Motley and soldiers and veterans of the U.S. Marshals Service who served in the 1962 crisis. The events at Ole Miss received widespread positive media attention.[45]

Continuing work for a civil rights memorial, however, encountered a new, formidable impediment: money. When the university received bids for construction of the doors in late 2004, the cost had soared to $225,000. More money had to be raised. As the student newspaper noted, "Progress stalled."

Supporters of CRCI had to turn their attention again to raising more money, but during the delay discussions over the memorial continued.[46]

Khayat, Edge, Glisson, and Adkins attempted to resolve their differences, but negotiations failed. Finally, in October 2005, citing concerns about cost, safety, location, and architecture, Khayat rejected Adkins's model and announced that a new monument would be designed by James H. Eley and Associates, a Jackson architectural firm, and erected within eight months. By canceling Adkins's contract, the chancellor revealed that ultimately he would control the memorial and its meaning. His decision sparked outrage among supporters of the nine-year effort.[47]

The *Daily Mississippian* immediately charged that the administration had all along engaged in "nothing more than window dressing" in its support for a civil rights memorial. It had "failed to honor the legacy of the civil rights movement" and sought instead "to hide the awful past" and to "whitewash" history. The editorial concluded, "We have not overcome." The next day, in an open letter to Khayat, Susan Glisson contended that "race lies at the heart of this debate." Suggesting that the chancellor's "amnesia of our history is dangerous," she defended the use of *fear* because a "banal memorial that doesn't acknowledge the fear ... communicates that all is well, that justice and equality have been achieved for everyone, that the struggle is over." She also protested his insistence "that he is the ultimate arbiter of all that transpires" at the university because the chancellor's intervention had violated the project's essential democratic process.[48]

Despite additional criticisms from Adkins and members of the university community, the administration prevailed and days later revealed the new plans. To be located in the southern half of the Lyceum-library ellipse, the memorial featured a covered seventeen-foot-tall walkway formed by two pairs of limestone columns. Over the passageway appeared the word *Freedom*, and on the two walls connecting the pairs of columns plaques explained the university's role in integration. Calling the new design "cold and unwelcoming," the *Daily Mississippian* conceded Khayat would get what he wanted, "for better or worse," because he operated "above the democratic process." The editor charged that the chancellor's "authoritarian attitudes toward others' input is almost comedic." Within two weeks, however, the administration yielded to complaints by adding a statue of James Meredith. Though it provoked a few protests, the statue remained in the revised plan.[49]

Construction delays did not interrupt the university's plan to dedicate the memorial exactly forty-four years after Meredith enrolled. A twenty-member interracial committee of administrators, faculty, and students selected quotations for the memorial and planned a gala outdoor ceremony for Sunday,

October 1. It featured three university singing groups, several speeches, and an audience of hundreds. Worried officials allowed Dr. Joe Meredith, James Meredith's son, to speak but did not provide an opportunity for the unpredictable Meredith. After a powerful keynote address by movement veteran Representative John Lewis, the chancellor unveiled Meredith's statue.[50]

At the base of the slightly larger-than-life statue of Meredith, an eight-inch-square plaque provided the only identification:

> James L. [*sic*] Meredith, a Mississippi native of Kosciusko, stepped into the pages of history on October 1, 1962[,] when he opened the doors to higher education at the University of Mississippi and in the South. As a major figure in the American civil rights movement, he helped lead the way to justice and equality for all citizens.

In small letters difficult for an adult to read from a standing position, the marker failed to explain that Meredith was the African American who had desegregated Ole Miss. (Months after the dedication, the university corrected the mistake in Meredith's name.)

Fifteen feet from the statue, each of the memorial's four sides bore a single word: *Opportunity*, *Courage*, *Perseverance*, and *Knowledge*. Missing was *Fear*, but also *Freedom*, *Equality*, *Justice*, and other words often associated with the civil rights movement. Inside the narrow walkway four plaques reproduced statements by William Winter, Myrlie Evers-Williams, Robert Khayat, and James Meredith. The first two came from the fortieth anniversary observance of the desegregation of the university. In 2002 the former governor had declared, "Today, we place a marker on that road. It is a marker that tells us not only where we have been, but where we need to be going," and Evers-Williams had observed, "Yes, Mississippi was. But Mississippi is, and we are proud of what we have become." The quotation from Chancellor Khayat came from the memorial's dedication when he said, "Our university offers hope and a bright future for all who come here to learn. We are committed to respect for the dignity of every person, and this monument stands as tangible evidence of that commitment." The longest quotation came from Meredith's memoir, *Three Years in Mississippi*. Selected by the dedication committee, it read:

> Always, without fail, regardless of the number of times I enter Mississippi, it creates within me feelings that are felt at no other time . . . joy . . . hope . . . love. I have always felt that Mississippi belonged to me and one must love what is his.

For all its successes, the 2006 celebration betrayed the limitations of the racial change that had occurred at the university and in the state. The Meredith quotation selected to appear on the civil rights monument revealed the difficulty many whites still had in grappling with the often unpleasant and disturbing complexities of race. In his memoir, Meredith's entire original statement referred to his reaction to seeing along the highway a "Welcome to Mississippi" sign. The far richer unexpurgated passage, as reproduced here, includes the few "selected words" in italics:

> This sign arouses mixed emotions in the thousands of Negroes who pass it. For many it is a joke; for others it recalls the days gone by, their work in the cotton fields in Mississippi, their migration to the North, their jobs in the war plants during the forties and in the factories of today.
>
> For me, it is indeed a sign of frustration. *Always, without fail, regardless of the number of times I enter Mississippi, it creates within me feelings that are felt at no other time.* There is the feeling of *joy*. Joy because I have once again lived to enter the land of my fathers, the land of my birth, the only land in which I feel at home. It also inspires a feeling of *hope* because where there is life there is also hope, a chance. At the same time, there is a feeling of sadness. Sadness because I am immediately aware of the special subhuman role that I must play, because I am a Negro, or die. Sadness because it is the home of the greatest number of Negroes outside Africa, yet my people suffer from want of everything in a rich land of plenty, and, most of all, they must endure the inconvenience of indignity.
>
> Then, there is the feeling of *love*. Love of the land. To me, Mississippi is the most beautiful country in the world, during all seasons. In the spring, all is green and fresh, the air is clean and sweet, and everything is healthy. As a boy I knew that any running stream of water was fit to drink. *I feel love because I have always felt that Mississippi belonged to me and one must love what is his.*

A few lines later Meredith also praised the beauty of summer in Mississippi but added, "Summer is also the most suitable season for lynching."[51]

The quotation on the civil rights memorial suppressed all of Meredith's references to the "joke" of welcoming blacks to the state and to the black migration out of Mississippi. It conveniently disregarded his feelings of "frustration" and "sadness" over the Negro's "special subhuman role" and over blacks' suffering from poverty and "indignity." The quotation, of course, also ignored his fear of death and his description of summer as a time for lynchings. More generally, the bowdlerized quotation suggested that he loved the state of Mississippi, but actually Meredith the farm boy loved the Mississippi land, not the political entity. Ole Miss had simply whitewashed what he wrote to make it more palatable to white Mississippians.

More than forty years after the riot, the expurgated version of James Meredith's poetic words exposed the continuing inability or unwillingness of some whites to engage the complexity and tragic history of race in Mississippi. Ole Miss stifled the power and passion of Meredith's words because it did not appreciate the depths of frustration, sadness, and indignity in the lives of African Americans. It had not reconciled its segregated past and the vaunted southern way of life with the inequality, discrimination, and prejudice in the history of the state's blacks. Though it had admitted and adjusted to black students, it had not accepted them as equal, integral parts of the institution. In fundamental ways, Ole Miss still existed apart from and in conflict with blacks.

By 2006 the fight for white men's and women's minds had, therefore, not yet resulted in a victory for equality at Ole Miss, just as it had not in the rest of the nation. The University of Mississippi was not unique because, as Gunnar Myrdal had explained a half-century earlier, the race problem in the white mind was not a problem specific to Ole Miss, Mississippi, or the South: it was *an American dilemma*. Conflicts between ideals and practices characterized race relations throughout the nation, not just in Mississippi or at Ole Miss. When a racial incident occurred at Ole Miss, the university often felt victimized by special scrutiny, but the events of 1962 and the university's responses prompted the special attention.

The dedication of the civil rights monument provided a positive celebration of progress and generated extensive regional and national attention for a university often plagued by negative publicity. The university, which in 1962 had suffered a deadly riot to prevent integration, built in 2006 a monument to the civil rights movement and erected a statue of the man who broke down segregation at Ole Miss. The festivities emphasized progress, achievement, and the future, and the words on the monument conveyed love for and pride in Mississippi. But what was left unsaid spoke more eloquently of what had not changed and what remained to be done.

It is, of course, James Meredith who emerges as the heroic figure, though so quietly and in so low a key that the drama of his courage lies forever beyond the language of headlines. There is no dramatic sprint and slam-bang in Meredith's sort of heroism. He is more nearly the marathoner, a man plodding step by step, . . . to conserve his energies by keeping the most austere and sustained watch on himself and his every gesture.

God knows what it must cost a man inside himself to plod that course, to keep himself forever under his own surveillance, to realize that he must present himself in public not as a man but as an image and that the least impetuous gesture from inside the man might destroy what that image must accomplish.

How does a man manage to keep himself so rigidly on guard and still listen to his lectures, read his lessons, prepare his papers, eat, sleep, breathe, be lonely for his wife, and carry all the irrational powers and persuasions any psyche moves to? How does he keep from punching a wall, or throwing a book through the window, or just standing up in his room alone and howling?

Only a terrifying dedication can sustain that man. But before we admire, we will do well to remember that we are all guilty of the crime of forcing that dedication upon him, of taking the spontaneity and the irrationality and the jokes and the romps out of this man's life and of replacing all those easy natural impulses with this austerity of self-watchfulness.

JOHN CIARDI, *Saturday Review*, June 29, 1963

Notes

Abbreviations

BN	*Birmingham (Ala.) News*
CD	*Chicago Defender*
DDT	*Greenville (Miss.) Delta Democrat Times*
DM	*Daily Mississippian*
JA	*Jackson (Miss.) Advocate*
JCL	*Jackson (Miss.) Clarion-Ledger*
JDN	*Jackson (Miss.) Daily News*
JST	*Jackson (Miss.) State Times*
KNS	*Knoxville (Tenn.) News-Sentinel*
MCA	*Memphis (Tenn.) Commercial Appeal*
MEJ	*McComb (Miss.) Enterprise-Journal*
Miss.	*Mississippian*
MLJ	*Mississippi Law Journal*
MPS	*Memphis (Tenn.) Press-Scimitar*
MS	*Meridian (Miss.) Star*
NOTP	*New Orleans Times-Picayune*
NT	*Nashville Tennessean*
NYT	*New York Times*
OE	*Oxford (Miss.) Eagle*
RRLR	*Race Relations Law Reporter*
RU	*Rebel Underground*
SSN	*Southern School News*
WP	*Washington Post*

ARCHIVES AND MANUSCRIPT COLLECTIONS

AALSP	Association of American Law Schools Papers, University of Illinois, Urbana, Ill.
AAUPP	American Association of University Professors Papers, Washington, D.C.
AKP	Alvin Kershaw Papers, private collection, Louisville, Ky.
ASCUM	Archives and Special Collections, J. D. Williams Library, University of Mississippi, University, Miss.

BMP	Burke Marshall Papers, John F. Kennedy Presidential Library, Boston, Mass.
BSP	James William (Bill) Silver Papers, private collection, San Francisco, Calif.
CLMP	Clare L. Marquette Papers, Archives and Special Collections, J. D. Williams Library, University of Mississippi, University, Miss.
FBI Files	Federal Bureau of Investigation Files, Washington, D.C.
GLICP	General Legislative Investigating Committee Papers, Mississippi State Records Center, Jackson, Miss.
GMSP	George M. Street Papers, Archives and Special Collections, J. D. Williams Library, University of Mississippi, University, Miss.
HCP	Hodding Carter Papers, Special Collections, Mitchell Memorial Library, Mississippi State University, Starkville, Miss.
HCP-RA	Hodding Carter Papers, Robertshaw Addition, Special Collections, Mitchell Memorial Library, Mississippi State University, Starkville, Miss.
IHLP	Mississippi Institutions of Higher Learning Papers, Mississippi Department of Archives and History, Jackson, Miss.
JDWP	John Davis Williams Papers, Archives and Special Collections, J. D. Williams Library, University of Mississippi, University, Miss.
JHMP	James H. Meredith Papers, Archives and Special Collections, J. D. Williams Library, University of Mississippi, University, Miss.
JMWP	John Minor Wisdom Papers, Law School, Tulane University, New Orleans, La.
JWSP	James Wesley Silver Papers, Archives and Special Collections, J. D. Williams Library, University of Mississippi, University, Miss.
LAF	College of Liberal Arts Files, College of Liberal Arts, University of Mississippi, University, Miss.
MAGP	Mississippi Attorneys General Papers, Mississippi Department of Archives and History, Jackson, Miss.
MBMP	M. B. Mayfield Papers, private collection, Ecru, Miss.
MDAH	Mississippi Department of Archives and History, Jackson, Miss.
Meredith v. Fair	Case file of *James H. Meredith v. Charles Dickson Fair, President of the Board of Trustees of State Institutions of Higher Learning of the State of Mississippi, et al.*, U.S. District Court for the Southern District of Mississippi, 1962, RG 21, National Archives and Records Administration–Southeast Region, Atlanta, Ga.
MLUSM	McCain Library, University of Southern Mississippi, Hattiesburg, Miss.
MSSCP	Mississippi State Sovereignty Commission Papers, Mississippi Department of Archives and History, Jackson, Miss.
MSSCP-USM	Mississippi State Sovereignty Commission Papers, McCain Library, University of Southern Mississippi, Hattiesburg, Miss.
RBP	Russell Barrett Papers, Archives and Special Collections, J. D. Williams Library, University of Mississippi, University, Miss.

RG 21   Records of the District Courts of the United States, National Archives and
            Records Administration–Southeast Region, Atlanta, Ga.
RG 267   Records of the U.S. Supreme Court, National Archives and Records
            Administration, Washington, D.C.
RG 319   Records of the [U.S. Army] Oxford, Mississippi, Operation, 1961–63, National
            Archives and Records Administration, College Park, Md.
RG 527   Records of the U.S. Marshals Service, Northern District of Mississippi, Oxford
            Division, Investigation into the University of Mississippi Desegregation Riots,
            1962–63, National Archives and Records Administration–Southeast Region,
            Atlanta, Ga.
SCMSU   Special Collections, Mitchell Memorial Library, Mississippi State
            University, Starkville, Miss.
UF   University Files, Archives and Special Collections, J. D. Williams Library,
            University of Mississippi, University, Miss.
USMP   U.S. Marshals Papers, Arlington, Va.
WPMP   William P. Murphy Papers, private collection, Chapel Hill, N.C.
WSP   Walter Sillers Papers, Charles W. Capps Jr. Archives and Museum, Delta
            State University, Cleveland, Miss.

Introduction

1. Myrlie B. Evers, with William Peters, *For Us, the Living* (Garden City, N.Y.: Doubleday, 1967), 202 and 235. For a discussion of the early years of the movement in Mississippi, see John Dittmer, *Local People: The Struggle for Civil Rights in Mississippi* (Urbana: University of Illinois Press, 1994), 1–89.

2. *SSN*, February and May 1961. See also Reed Sarratt, *The Ordeal of Desegregation* (New York: Harper and Row, 1966); and Peter Wallenstein, "Black Southerners and Non-Black Universities: Desegregating Higher Education, 1936–1967," *History of Higher Education Annual* 19 (1999): 12–48.

3. *SSN*, February 1961.

4. James W. Silver, *Mississippi: The Closed Society* (New York: Harcourt, Brace and World, 1964); Walter Lord, *The Past That Would Not Die* (New York: Harper and Row, 1965); Russell H. Barrett, *Integration at Ole Miss* (Chicago: Quadrangle, 1965); James Meredith, *Three Years in Mississippi* (Bloomington: Indiana University Press, 1966). A decade later another Ole Miss professor of history, William T. Doherty, provided a shorter account in "Confrontation at Ole Miss: A Southern Political Barbecue, 1962," *North Dakota Quarterly* 41 (Winter 1973): 5–36.

5. Nadine Cohodas, *The Band Played Dixie: Race and Liberal Conscience at Ole Miss* (New York: Free Press, 1997); William Doyle, *An American Insurrection: The Battle of Oxford, Mississippi, 1962* (New York: Doubleday, 2001); Paul Hendrickson, *Sons of Mississippi: A Story of Race and Its Legacy* (New York: Knopf, 2003).

6. For two examples, see Taylor Branch, *Parting the Waters: America in the King Years,*

1954–1963 (New York: Simon and Schuster, 1988), chapter 17, "The Fall of Ole Miss," 633–72; and Nick Bryant, *The Bystander: John F. Kennedy and the Struggle for Black Equality* (New York: Basic Books, 2006), chapter 20, " 'Go Mississippi,' " 329–56.

Chapter One

1. *Miss.*, September 13, 1959. The phrase varied: in 1962 it was quoted as "Welcome to Ole Miss. Everyone speaks." See *Miss.*, September 18, 1962. The student newspaper was a weekly until becoming a daily on September 22, 1961, but did not change its name to *Daily Mississippian* until February 1, 1968.

2. Joe David Brown, "Babes, Brutes, and Ole Miss," *Sports Illustrated*, September 19, 1960. The photograph is on 116, and the quotation is in the picture's caption.

3. *JCL*, September 7 and 8, 1958; *Miss.*, September 12, 1958.

4. *JCL*, September 13, 14, and 15, 1959; *Miss.*, September 13 and 24, 1959.

5. *JCL*, August 13 and September 7, 1961, and March 24 and August 4, 1962; David G. Sansing, *The University of Mississippi: A Sesquicentennial History* (Jackson: University Press of Mississippi, 1999), 160.

6. Sansing, *The University*, 160; *Miss.*, October 8, 1959. See various editions of the student yearbook, *The Ole Miss*, 1897–1963.

7. C. Vanderburgh, "Draftee's Diary from the Mississippi Front," *Harper's*, February 1964, 38; *NOTP*, September 30, 1962; *KNS*, September 28, 1962.

8. The students were Warner Alford and Kay Swayze; her father was Tom Swayze, for whom the baseball field was named in 1989. The Academic All-American football player and all-SEC baseball player who dated both Miss Americas was Robert Khayat, later chancellor.

9. William W. Sorrels and Charles Cavagnaro, *Ole Miss Rebels: Mississippi Football* (Huntsville, Ala.: Strode Publishers, 1976), 203. On Rebel football see also John Vaught, *Rebel Coach: My Football Family* (Memphis: Memphis State University Press, 1971), 203; "Coach Johnny Reb," *Time*, November 28, 1960, 34–35; Brown, "Babes, Brutes, and Ole Miss," 116ff.; and *1999 Rebel Football Media Guide*, ed. Langston Rogers (University: University of Mississippi, Sports Information Department, 1999). At the time, many groups or individuals ranked college football teams and every year designated a national champion. In 1959 and 1960 one or another so ranked the Rebels.

10. Curtis Wilkie, *Dixie: A Personal Odyssey through Events That Shaped the Modern South* (New York: Scribner, 2001), 83–86; "Coach Johnny Reb," 34.

11. The successes of the baseball teams can, of course, be followed in the *Mississippian* in 1959 and 1960 and in the state's daily newspapers. See also *Annual Report of the Chancellor of the University of Mississippi to the Board of Trustees of the Institutions of Higher Learning*, 1958–59 and 1959–60.

12. *NYT*, October 21, 1962; C. Robert Pace, "The Influence of Academic and Student Subcultures in College and University Environments," Cooperative Research Project no. 1083, Office of Education, U.S. Department of Health, Education, and Welfare (1964), ERIC Document no. 003037. Pace, a professor of higher education at UCLA, specialized in quan-

titative measurement of the college environment's effects on students' experiences and opinions. His major comparative study focused on nine American colleges and universities: in addition to the University of Mississippi, they included two church-related colleges (St. Olaf and Pace's alma mater, De Pauw), two private nonsectarian colleges (Antioch and Swarthmore), and three other public institutions (Eastern Washington State College, the University of Florida, and San Jose State College). Pace and his research team in 1961 administered hundreds of survey "questions" to more than thirteen hundred students, including more than three hundred upperclassmen on the Oxford campus. Much of the information in the next several paragraphs relies on Pace's findings.

13. *Miss.*, September 13, 1959, and September 18, 1962; *The Ole Miss M Book, 1962–63*, ed. Ruby Kathryn Clegg and Dicki Lee (University: University of Mississippi, Department of Religious Life and the Ole Miss Christian Associations, 1962), 12; *NOTP*, September 30, 1962; Pace, "The Influence," 137–58; *NYT*, October 21, 1962. Unless otherwise noted, all University of Mississippi publications can be found in ASCUM.

14. Pace, "The Influence."

15. *NYT*, October 21, 1962; Pace, "The Influence"; George M. Street to S. F., November 29, 1962, in GMSP.

16. Information on the Rhodes scholars was found in various university publications. The university has long prided itself on the production of Rhodes scholars. After the 1962 riot, an Ole Miss public relations official defended the school's academic quality by citing the number of them; see letter to the editor, *NYT*, November 27, 1962. In response the editor of the *American Oxonian* claimed the use of the numbers had been "a bit beguiling," pointed out that the figures had been "used out of context," and suggested that "population factors, the district selection system, the sizes of the student bodies at the various institutions, among other items, must be taken into account in judging the significance of the figures." See "Addendum: Scholarship at Ole Miss," *American Oxonian*, January 1963, 61–62, in CLMP.

17. Report of the Liberal Arts Development Committee, in *Annual Report of the Chancellor*, 1952–53, 216; Jane Krieger Rosen, "At Home and Abroad: A Visit to Ole Miss," *Reporter*, December 20, 1962, 19. The quotations from the professor also appeared in *CD*, December 15–21, 1962.

18. Pace, "The Influence."

19. *NYT*, October 8 and 21, 1962; *Time*, November 16, 1962, 43.

20. *The Ole Miss M Book, 1962–63*, 10–13; *WP*, October 21, 1962; Pace, "The Influence."

21. *NYT*, October 21, 1962; Wilkie, *Dixie*, 82; *Time*, November 16, 1962, 43; *Miss.*, May 11, 1956; Pace, "The Influence."

22. *Miss.*, October 8, 1959; Pace, "The Influence"; COUSAFOX [Commanding Officer U.S. Army Forces Oxford] to [Defense Department] War Room, May 2, 1963, in RG 319. For a description of the Dixie National Baton Twirling Institute held at Ole Miss, see Terry Southern, "Twirling at Ole Miss," *Esquire*, February 1963.

23. Foreword to *Annual Reports to the Chancellor by the Dean of the University of Mississippi* (University of Mississippi, 1946–47); *Time*, November 16, 1962, 43; *Annual Report of the Chancellor*, 1954–55, 3; and 1955–56, 2.

24. *Annual Reports to the Chancellor*, 1949–50, 12; *Annual Report of the Chancellor*, 1956–57, 12; Pace, "The Influence."

25. *NYT*, October 21, 1962; Pace, "The Influence."

26. *Miss.*, October 24, 1947; *Ole Miss Alumni Review*, January 1948, and January 1949; *OE*, March 25, 1954; *Annual Report of the Chancellor*, 1952–53, 219–20; and 1953–54, 181.

27. Sansing, *The University*, 13 and 27. For the history of the university, in addition to Sansing's work, see Allen Cabaniss, *A History of the University of Mississippi* (University: University of Mississippi, 1949).

28. Sansing, *The University*, 28, 64, 81, and 102.

29. Ibid., 106–16, passim.

30. Michael Alan Upton, " 'Keeping the Faith with the University Greys': Ole Miss as *Lieux de Memoire*" (M.A. thesis, University of Mississippi, 2002), 35; Sansing, *The University*, 122–23.

31. Upton, "Keeping the Faith"; Sansing, *The University*.

32. Upton, "Keeping the Faith," 54–55, 62, and 78.

33. *Miss.*, May 18, 1939; L. A. Smith, "Origins of 'Ole Miss,' " *Ole Miss Alumni News*, November 1932, 11.

34. Upton, "Keeping the Faith," 44–46.

35. Sansing, *The University*, 139; Cabaniss, *A History*.

36. Sansing, *The University*, 156–62, 179–80, and 183.

37. Ibid., 222, 233, 225, and 227.

38. Cabaniss, *A History*, 158–69; David G. Sansing, *Making Haste Slowly: The Troubled History of Higher Education in Mississippi* (Jackson: University Press of Mississippi, 1990), 91–110; Hardy Poindexter Graham, "Bilbo and the University of Mississippi, 1928–1932" (M.A. thesis, University of Mississippi, 1965).

39. For discussions of the university's symbols see Upton, "Keeping the Faith"; Kevin Pierce Thornton, "Symbolism at Ole Miss and the Crisis of Southern Identity," *South Atlantic Quarterly* 86, no. 3 (Summer 1987): 254–68; and John M. Coski, *The Confederate Battle Flag: America's Most Embattled Emblem* (Cambridge: Harvard University Press, 2005). The student paper reported the flag's dimensions as 40 by 70 feet; see *Miss.*, October 15, 1948. Whatever the actual dimensions, it was very large. The cover photograph of the September 24, 1962, *Sports Illustrated* showed the Ole Miss Rebelettes, a dance team, waving Confederate flags at a football game.

40. *Miss.*, September 23, 1943, and March 21 and October 1, 1947; "Army Administration School," *Ole Miss Alumni News*, October 1942, 7; "The ASTP at Ole Miss," *Ole Miss Alumni News*, June 1943, 3; Alfred Hume, "On Ole Miss' War Program," The Chancellor's Page, *Ole Miss Alumni News*, March 1942, 5.

41. *Atlanta Daily World*, May 16, 1991; *MCA*, *NYT*, and *New York World-Telegram*, September 25, 1962; "First Black to Enroll at University of Mississippi Found Dead in Atlanta," *Jet*, May 27, 1991, 18; *Ole Miss Student Directory, 1945–1946* (University: University of Mississippi, Associated Student Body Executive Committee, 1945).

42. *MCA*, *NYT*, *New York World-Telegram*, *MS*, and *JCL*, September 25, 1962.

43. See the references in note 42, above.

44. Vanderburgh, "Draftee's Diary from the Mississippi Front," 38; *NYT*, October 8, 1962; *Rolling Fork Deer Creek Pilot*, October 5, 1962; *Miss.*, November 21, 1947, and October 21, 1949; George M. Street to J. D. Williams, no date [1950], in GMSP; Williams to Arthur A. Madden, June 22, 1954, in UF. Even Williams could not shake the Confederacy's influence; in a 1953 speech to the state convention of the United Daughters of the Confederacy, he called Ole Miss "A Daughter of the Confederacy." See Upton, "Keeping the Faith," 98.

45. *MS*, July 22, 1962. A 1959 graduate, Dearman had edited the *Mississippian* and in 1962 worked for the *Meridian Star*.

46. See discussions of the state's colleges in Sansing, *The University*, especially 264–65; and Sansing, *Making Haste*, 154.

47. *WP*, October 21, 1962; *Rolling Fork Deer Creek Pilot*, October 5, 1962; Sansing, *The University*, 86 and 263–64; *Time*, October 5, 1962, 16; *NYT*, October 8 and 21, 1962. The quotation from the *Deer Creek Pilot* appeared fewer than ten days after the *Oxford Eagle* used the same phrase in a guest editorial by Harry Marsh, a former Mississippian and member of the *New York Herald Tribune* editorial board. See *OE*, September 27, 1962.

48. *NYT*, October 21, 1962; Wilkie, *Dixie*, 82; John Egerton, "Shake-up at Ole Miss," *Chance* (Winter 1972–73): 24–29 (quoting *Time* on 26). Though Egerton wrote more than a decade later than events discussed here, his assessment seems applicable.

49. *JCL*, March 1, 9, 12, 18, 21, and 30, 1962. Based on extensive reading of the state's newspapers, the coverage in March 1962 seemed rather typical.

50. *The Ole Miss, 1961* (yearbook), 2, quoted in Upton, "Keeping the Faith," 102; *Pittsburgh Courier*, October 20, 1962. The *Courier*'s source was a column by Max Lerner.

51. *OE*, September 27, 1962. For Meredith's views, see his *Three Years in Mississippi* (Bloomington: Indiana University Press, 1966).

Chapter Two

1. J. D. Williams to H. L. Donovan, February 15, 1947, in JDWP; *MCA*, June 15, 1956; *NYT*, October 8, 1962; David G. Sansing, *Making Haste Slowly: The Troubled History of Higher Education in Mississippi* (Jackson: University Press of Mississippi, 1990), 130–31; James C. Read, "The Williams Chancellorship at the University of Mississippi, 1946–1968" (Ph.D. diss., University of Mississippi, 1978), 26–27.

2. *Miss.*, September 15–18, 1957; *Ole Miss Alumni Review*, October 1957, 17; *JCL*, September 23, 1962; *NYT*, October 8, 1962; Read, "The Williams Chancellorship," 9–21; J. D. Williams, "The Standardization and Classification of One-Teacher Rural Schools and a Proposal Plan for Standardization for Kentucky" (M.A. thesis, University of Kentucky, 1930).

3. Charles Hill Moffat, *Marshall University: An Institution Comes of Age, 1837–1980* (Huntington, W.Va.: Marshall University Alumni Association, 1981), 116–22.

4. Williams to Edwin White, February 20, 1956; and Williams to Gaines S. Dobbins, January 9, 1951, in UF; "University of Mississippi Response to Hooker-White Charges," [1959], in IHLP.

5. Williams to Sue Ankrom, November 21, 1962; and Williams to Claude S. Shotts, March 27, 1956, in UF.

6. Moffat, *Marshall University*, 122; Herbert L. Seamans, "Education and Intergroup Relations," *Educational Record* 27 (January 1946): 87–95; [George F. Zook], "The President's Annual Report," *Educational Record* 27 (July 1946): 323–28; Lloyd Allen Cook, "The College Study in Intergroup Relations: A Progress Report, 1945–46," *Educational Record* 27 (October 1946): 452–65; J. D. Williams, "A Program for the Education of Returning Veterans," *Quarterly Review of Higher Education among Negroes* 13 (April 1945): 77–83.

7. Moffat, *Marshall University*, 122.

8. J. D. Williams, "Regional Pacts as an Answer to Educational Inequalities," *College and University Business* 7 (October 1949): opposite page 1; Williams to J. P. Coleman, August 23, 1954; Williams to Gaines S. Dobbins, January 9, 1951; and Williams to Guy H. Wells, June 5, 1958, in UF; "University of Mississippi Response to Hooker-White Charges," [1959], in IHLP. Williams referred to research compiled and annotated by J. W. Bunkley and Ford W. Hall in *General Laws Pertaining to the State Institutions of Higher Learning of the State of Mississippi* (Jackson: University of Mississippi, Board of Trustees, 1949).

9. Williams to Claude S. Shotts, March 27, 1956; and Williams to J. Oliver Emmerich, August 4, 1954, in UF.

10. Ben F. Hilbun to William B. Dickson, March 17, 1959; and Hilbun to William McGraw, April 20, 1959, in Ben F. Hilbun Papers, SCMSU; "Address by W. D. McCain, President of Mississippi Southern College, Hattiesburg, Mississippi, before the Pro-American Forum at Chicago, Illinois, September 9, 1960," in Paul B. Johnson Jr. Papers, MLUSM; Stephen Beach III to Sir (form letter), November 27, 1962, in UF; W. D. McCain to John K. Bettersworth, October 23, 1955, in John K. Bettersworth Papers, SCMSU.

11. The assessment of Williams derives largely from impressions gained during research.

12. Williams to J. H. White, July 14, 1959; and Williams to Dr. and Mrs. Harold Stoke, January 9, 1956, in UF; Williams to B. A. Jones, March 6, 1950; and Williams to W. M. Drake, April 11, 1961, in JDWP.

13. *Miss.*, July 26, 1946; Williams to H. L. Donovan, February 15, 1947, in JDWP; Tina Blackshare and Otis R. Tims, "Building a University," *Ole Miss Alumni Review*, Spring 1980, 11–14; Read, "Williams Chancellorship," 35–55. See the following in *Annual Report of the Chancellor of the University of Mississippi to the Board of Trustees for the Institutions of Higher Learning*, 1946–47: Pete Kyle McCarter, "Office of the Dean of the University," 1; Carroll W. North, "Division of the Comptroller," 1; Marvin M. Black, "Department of Public Relations," 24; and William S. Griffin, "University of Mississippi Alumni Association," 22. Williams's publications dealt with higher education and administration. See, for example, "A Program for the Education of Veterans" and "Regional Pacts as an Answer to Educational Inequalities" (cited in notes 6 and 8, above); "Higher Education in the South: An Account of the New Regional Program," *NEA Journal* 39 (February 1950): 108–9; "A Report on PR Cooperation," *College Public Relations Quarterly* 1 (July 1954): 14–17; "Financing Liberal Education (State-Supported Institutions)," *Association of American Colleges Bulletin* 40 (March 1954): 80–84; "Record of Progress," *Public Administration Survey* 7 (September 1960): 2–6; and "The Right to Know," *Public Administration Survey* 21 (November 1973): 1–5.

14. J. D. Williams, "The Chancellor's Page," *Ole Miss Alumni Review*, July 1947, 5; J. D. Williams, foreword to *Annual Report of the Chancellor* (University of Mississippi, 1946–47 and 1948–49); McCarter, "Office of the Dean of the University," in *Annual Report of the Chancellor*, 1946–47, 1–4; and 1948–49, 3; University Planning Committee, "Statistical Data for the Board of Directors of the Alumni Association," October 9, 1948, in UF; *MPS*, July 17, 1947; *MCA*, July 29, 1947; Read, "Williams Chancellorship," 64; "Division of the Comptroller," in *Annual Report of the Chancellor*, 1946–47, 8–9; *Miss.*, July 31, 1947; "Department of Buildings and Ground," in *Annual Report of the Chancellor*, 1947–48, 102 and 105; *OE*, August 9, 1956; Marvin M. Black, "Ole Miss in the Post-War Years," *Ole Miss Alumni Review*, July 1960, 12.

15. J. D. Williams, "The Chancellor's Page," *Ole Miss Alumni Review*, January 1951, 2; April 1951, 2; October 1948, 6; and April 1959, 7; Williams, foreword to *Annual Report of the Chancellor*, 1946–47; 1948–49; 1949–50; and 1951–52; "Office of the Dean of the University," in *Annual Report of the Chancellor*, 1946–47, 2–3; 1947–48, 2; 1949–50, 2; and 1950–51, 1; "The Graduate School," in *Annual Report of the Chancellor*, 1946–47, 7–8 and 12; 1947–48, 78; 1948–49, 77; and 1956–57, 86; "College of Liberal Arts," in *Annual Report of the Chancellor*, 1946–47, 15; Read, "Williams Chancellorship," 65–67; Williams to Alexander Capurso, November 13, 1952, in JDWP; "The University of Mississippi Ten-Year Report [1946–56]," no date; and University Planning Committee, "Statistical Data for the Board of Directors of the Alumni Association," October 9, 1948, in UF.

16. Williams, "Regional Pacts as an Answer to Educational Inequalities," and "Higher Education in the South"; *Miss.*, April 11, 1952; *OE*, April 17, 1952; George Brown Tindall, *Emergence of the New South, 1913–1945* (Baton Rouge: Louisiana State University Press, 1967), 259; Edouard D. Eller to J. D. Williams, April 6, 1951, and April 3, 1952; Williams to Edouard D. Eller, April 23, 1952; Williams to Friends, April 29, 1952; and Alton W. Bryant to J. W. Cohen, June 7, 1958, in UF; J. D. Williams, "The Chancellor's Page," *Ole Miss Alumni Review*, June 1952, 3; Williams to the Board of Trustees, in *Annual Report of the Chancellor*, 1955–56. See also J. D. Williams, "Keeping Abreast in Education," *Phi Delta Kappan*, May 1949, 389; and Williams, "Financing Liberal Education (State-Supported Institutions)."

17. For background see chapter 1; and David G. Sansing, *The University of Mississippi: A Sesquicentennial History* (Jackson: University Press of Mississippi, 1999); Neil R. McMillen, *Dark Journey: Black Mississippians in the Age of Jim Crow* (Urbana: University of Illinois Press, 1989); John Dittmer, *Local People: The Struggle for Civil Rights in Mississippi* (Urbana: University of Illinois Press, 1994); Charles C. Bolton, *The Hardest Deal of All: The Battle over School Integration in Mississippi, 1870–1980* (Jackson: University Press of Mississippi, 2005).

18. *Miss.*, October 4, 1946, and March 7 and 21, 1947.

19. *Miss.*, January 10 and March 21, 1947.

20. *Miss.*, April 25, 1947.

21. Ibid. For background on NSA, see Philip G. Atlbach, "The National Student Association in the Fifties: Flawed Conscience of the Silent Generation," *Youth and Society* 5(December 1973): 184–211.

22. *Miss.*, January 9 and 16, 1948.

23. *Miss.*, July 22 and 29, and August 5, 1948; Robert A. Garson, *The Democratic Party and the Politics of Sectionalism, 1941–1948* (Baton Rouge: Louisiana State University, 1974).

24. *Miss.*, April 30, August 12, and October 1 and 22, 1948.

25. Garson, *The Democratic Party*, 311.

26. *Miss.*, March 21, 1952.

27. *Miss.*, April 11 and 25, 1952.

28. *Miss.*, May 2, 1952.

29. Statement of Williams, May 8, 1952; and Morton B. King to Williams, May 9, 1952, in JDWP; *Miss.*, May 9, 1952.

30. W. Alton Bryant to David Cottrell Jr., February 6, 1954, in UF; "Department of Sociology," in *Annual Report of the Chancellor*, 1948–49, 31–32; "Department of Sociology and Anthropology," in *Annual Report of the Chancellor*, 1949–50, 33; 1950–51, 29; and 1951–52, 32–33; J. D. Williams, "The Chancellor's Page," *Ole Miss Alumni Review*, October 1948, 6; Alfred C. Schnur, "Correctional Research: A Review and Critique," *American Journal of Corrections* 42 (January–February 1962): 25; "Recommended Criminology Program," curriculum vita of Alfred C. Schnur, and Williams to Judge Luther Manship, November 15, 1951, in LAF; *Miss.*, March 16, 1951; William Banks Taylor, *Brokered Justice: Race, Politics, and Mississippi Prisons, 1798–1992* (Columbus: Ohio State University Press, 1993), 145.

31. Author's interview with Jacqueline Schnur, April 17, 1998; Williams to J. F. Hicks, April 25, 1951, in LAF; Taylor, *Brokered Justice*, especially 105–64; David M. Oshinsky, *"Worse than Slavery": Parchman Farm and the Ordeal of Jim Crow Justice* (New York: Free Press, 1996), 149–51.

32. Oshinsky, *"Worse than Slavery,"* 149–51; Taylor, *Brokered Justice*, 138–40.

33. *JDN*, February 21, 1952; "Excerpt from Doctor Alfred C. Schnur's Speech 'Crime in Mississippi,'" no date, in UF. The excerpt notes that the speech was given many times thereafter.

34. *JDN*, February 24, 1952.

35. *Miss.*, February 29, 1952.

36. Taylor, *Brokered Justice*, 142–45; *Time*, March 22, 1954.

37. Penitentiary Committee, Mississippi House of Representatives, to Williams, March 2, 1954, in UF; Taylor, *Brokered Justice*, 124.

38. Penitentiary Committee to Williams, March 2, 1954.

39. *DDT*, March 5, 1954; *MCA* and *JCL*, March 6, 1954; *Time*, March 22, 1954; Williams to Robert Hinchman Jr., March 23, 1954; Williams to Harold Stoke, March 31, 1954; and Williams to P. K. McCarter, March 31, 1954, in JDWP.

40. *JDN*, March 5, 1954; *JCL*, March 6, 1954; Hugh L. White to Williams, March 6, 1954, in UF.

41. Williams to Hugh L. White, March 9, 1954; Williams to Charlie Beauchamp (chairman of House Penitentiary Committee), March 9, 1954; Williams to Inman Moore Jr., March 22, 1954; and Williams to Ellis Bodron, March 24, 1954, in UF; Williams to Robert Hinchman Jr., March 23, 1954; Williams to Harold Stoke, March 31, 1954; and Williams to P. K. McCarter, March 31, 1954, in JDWP.

42. *DDT*, March 7, 8, 9, and 12, 1954; *JDN*, March 7, 1954.

43. *DDT* and *MCA*, March 7, 1954; *MEJ*, March 8, 1954; Williams to Frank Ahlgren, March 8, 1954, in UF. See also Millsaps College, *Purple and Gold*, March 19, 1954.

44. *JDN*, March 7, 1954.

45. Taylor, *Brokered Justice*, 146–47; Schnur, "Correctional Research," 25.

46. Allen Cabaniss, *A History of the University of Mississippi* (University: University of Mississippi, 1949), 162; *MCA*, March 7, 1954; Williams to Power Hearn, March 8, 1954, in UF.

Chapter Three

1. Neil R. McMillen, *Dark Journey: Black Mississippians in the Age of Jim Crow* (Urbana: University of Illinois Press, 1989), 8–10.

2. Gunnar Myrdal, *An American Dilemma: The Negro Problem and Modern Democracy* (New York: Harper and Row, 1944), 605–39 and 1362n8. See also Bertram Doyle, *The Etiquette of Race Relations: A Study in Social Control* (Chicago: University of Chicago Press, 1937).

3. *St. Petersburg (Fla.) Times*, December 16, 1962; *MPS*, September 29, 1962; *Miss.*, May 2 and October 30, 1962; *Christian Science Monitor*, October 1, 1962.

4. Author's interviews with Ollie Lee McEwen, December 6, 1998, and Murray Patton, December 31, 1998.

5. *Miss.* October 9, 1942, September 13, 1953, and September 23, 1955; "Blind Jim Feels Squeeze of Wartime Restrictions," *Ole Miss Alumni News*, October 1942, 4; *OE*, March 10, 1949; Anthony James, "Paternalism's Demise: Blind Jim Ivy and Ole Miss, 1896–1955," *Mississippi Folklife*, Spring 1995, 17–24. Accounts of Ivy's life contain inconsistencies. One (*Miss.*, September 23, 1955) suggested that he lost his sight in 1892 while working on a courthouse. Another (*JCL*, October 24, 1955) said that he had first come to students' attention when cheering for the football team against the University of Texas, but Ole Miss first played Texas in football in 1912 (in Austin). James mistakes Ivy's birth date for 1870 instead of 1872.

6. *Miss.*, October 9, 1942, and September 13, 1955; *Ole Miss Alumni Review*, September 1953, 12; *JST*, October 31, 1955.

7. *OE*, September 17, 1953, and August 19, 1954; *Miss.*, October 1, 1948, and September 23 and October 21, 1955; *JDN*, October 22, 1955.

8. *Miss.*, October 9, 1942, and October 21, 1955; *JCL* and *JDN*, October 22, 1955. The phrase modified or corrupted an Alabama cheer. See Warren St. John, *Rammer Jammer Yellow Hammer: A Journey into the Heart of Fan Mania* (New York: Crown, 2004).

9. *Ole Miss Alumni Review*, September 1953, 12; *Miss.*, September 13, 1953; *OE*, September 17, 1953; Frances A. Koestler, *The Unseen Minority: A Social History of Blindness in America* (New York: David McKay, 1976), 194–99.

10. "On the Campus," *Ole Miss Alumni News*, December 1936–January 1937, 6; "Blind Jim Feels the Squeeze of Wartime Restrictions," *Ole Miss Alumni News*, October 1942, 4; *JDN*, November 11, 1936; *Miss.*, September 26, October 17 and 24, and November 14 and 21, 1936.

11. *Miss.*, October 9, 1942.

12. *OE*, August 19, 1954, and October 17 and 20, 1955; *Miss.*, April 28, 1950, December 7, 1951, and September 23 and October 21, 1955; *JCL*, October 21 and 22, 1955; *JDN* and *JST*, October 22, 1955. According to one account, James E. Ivy Jr. of Chicago was Blind Jim's nephew. See *JST*, October 31, 1955.

13. Resolution, Alumni Association of the University of Mississippi, October 22, 1955, Alumni Association Files. The resolutions committee included Congressman Jamie Whitten.

14. *JDN*, October 22 and 28, 1955.

15. *JDN* and *JST*, October 31, 1955; *OE*, November 3, 1955; *Tupelo Daily Journal*, October 29, 1955; "Remarks by George M. Street, Director of Placement, University of Mississippi, at the Memorial Service for James Ivy (Blind Jim) Held at the Second Baptist Church, Oxford, Mississippi, October 30, 1955," in GMSP.

16. *JCL*, October 24, 1955.

17. *Miss.*, September 26, October 21 and 24, 1936, and October 28, 1950; *JDN*, November 17, 1936.

18. *Miss.*, October 24, 1936, and September 23, 1955.

19. *OE*, March 10, 1949; W. M. Reed, "As Blind Jim Sees It," *Ole Miss Alumni News*, March 1934, 6; James, "Paternalism's Demise," 21.

20. Hector Chevigny and Sydell Braverman, *The Adjustment of the Blind* (New Haven: Yale University Press, 1950), 145–72 (quotations on 146, 147, and 152); Thomas J. Carroll, *Blindness: What It Is, What It Does, and How to Live with It* (Boston: Little, Brown, 1961).

21. Chevigny and Braverman, *The Adjustment of the Blind*, 191.

22. Ibid., 167–72; *Miss.*, October 28, 1949; Reed, "As Blind Jim Sees It," 6; Stephen J. Whitfield, *A Death in the Delta: The Story of Emmett Till* (New York: Free Press, 1988); Howard Smead, *Blood Justice: The Lynching of Mack Charles Parker* (New York: Oxford University Press, 1986).

23. *Miss.*, April 2, 1955; receipts and expenditures from James E. Ivy Sr. Fund [February 1956?], in GMSP; Minutes, IHL Board, April 19, 1956, in Records of the IHL Board, Jackson, Miss.

24. All information about M. B. Mayfield in this and succeeding paragraphs comes from his undated, handwritten autobiography, "The Baby Who Crawled Backwards," in MBMP; and *Miss.*, April 28, 1950. Information about Stuart R. Purser comes from his memoir, *Applehead (Part One and Part Two)* (Gainesville, Fla.: Purser Publications, 1979). See also *OE*, March 24, 1949; and *Tupelo Daily Journal*, August 7, 1953. For efforts to start an art department, see LAF.

25. "A One-Man Retrospective Exhibition of Works by Stuart R. Purser," University Gallery, University of Florida, November 7–December 19, 1976 (furnished by George Allsup, who taught with Purser at the Universities of Mississippi and Florida).

26. Mayfield, "The Baby Who Crawled Backwards," and "An Autobiography," January 1979, in MBMP; Father Paul Fredette, "The Look of an Original: M. B. Mayfield," *The Glenmary Challenge*, Spring 1995, 10–13; *Pontotoc Progress*, December 26, 1985; *Tupelo Daily Journal*, January 31–February 1, 1987; *MPS*, January 25, 1979; *JCL*, June 5, 1988; *New Albany Gazette*, February 22, 1989; author's interview with M. B. Mayfield, November 20, 1998.

27. Mayfield, "The Baby Who Walked Backwards"; *New Albany Gazette*, February 22,

1989; author's interview with Mayfield. University personnel records indicate Mayfield's date of employment as October 1, 1949.

28. Mayfield, "The Baby Who Walked Backwards."

29. Ibid.; *Miss.*, April 28, 1950.

30. *Miss.*, April 28, 1950; Mayfield, "The Wishbook: A True Story" (March 1975), and "The Baby Who Walked Backwards," in MBMP; author's interview with Mayfield.

31. Mayfield, "The Baby Who Walked Backwards"; author's interview with Mayfield; "Veterans' Testing Service, Tests of General Educational Development: High School Level," July 1951, in MBMP. Mayfield's papers also include a form reporting the results of his GED test. Alice R. Butler of Jackson College signed it and commented, "Satisfactory for Jackson College." Mayfield apparently scored in the forty-ninth percentile overall and in the ninety-fifth percentile on "Correctness and Effectiveness of Expression," but only in the tenth percentile on "Interpretation of Reading Materials in the Natural Sciences."

32. Mayfield to Mrs. Ella Rucker, May 18, 1951, and Mayfield, "The Baby Who Walked Backwards," in MBMP; *JCL*, July 27, 1986; *Oxford Town* (supplement to *OE*), May 14, 1997; author's interview with Mayfield.

33. Mayfield, "The Baby Who Walked Backwards"; author's interview with Mayfield.

34. For a discussion of white attitudes toward black artists, musicians, and performers, see Myrdal, *An American Dilemma*, 329–30, 654–55, and 986–90, passim.

35. Author's interview with Ollie Lee McEwen, December 6, 1998; "University of Mississippi Response to Hooker-White Charges," in IHLP. Ollie Lee McEwen is Ernest McEwen's younger brother. The charges by Wilburn Hooker and Edwin White will be discussed in chapter 9.

36. *Miss.*, October 21, 1949, October 30, 1953, and November 8, 1957; "University of Mississippi Response to Hooker-White Charges," in IHLP; author's interview with Ollie Lee McEwen.

37. See the references in note 36, above. A controversy at Alcorn involving McEwen is examined in chapter 5.

38. Evidence of blacks entertaining at fraternity parties is limited to yearbook photographs. See Anthony W. James, "The Defenders of Tradition: College Social Fraternities, Race, and Gender, 1945–1980" (Ph.D. diss., University of Mississippi, 1998), 253.

39. *Miss.*, February 15 and 29, 1952; *OE*, February 28, 1952.

40. *Miss.*, February 29 and March 7 and 21, 1952.

41. *Miss.*, April 2, 1954; *MS*, December 31, 1962; Lionel Hampton with James Haskins, *Hamp: An Autobiography* (New York: Warner Books, 1989), 103. In his memoir, Hampton confuses his first and second appearances at the university.

42. *Miss.*, February 25 and March 4, 1955.

43. *Miss.*, May 4, 1956; John Edward Hasse, *Beyond Category: The Life and Genius of Duke Ellington* (New York: Simon and Schuster, 1993), 316–22.

44. James Lincoln Collier, *Louis Armstrong: An American Genius* (New York: Oxford University Press, 1983), 319.

45. Robert B. Patterson to Ed White, March 3, 1955, in WSP. Patterson copied the letter to Sillers and others.

46. *Miss.*, April 29, 1955, and February 3, 1956.

47. *Miss.*, November 10, 1950, October 9, 1953, November 5, 1954, and April 26 and May 2 and 4, 1962. The co-chairman of the 1962 Dixie Week, which included a slave auction, was Trent Lott. See *Miss.*, April 18, 1962. See also Michael Upton, " 'Keeping the Faith with the University Greys': Ole Miss as *Lieux de Memoire*" (M.A. thesis, University of Mississippi, 2002), 85–90, passim; James, "The Defenders of Tradition," 213; and Kevin Pierce Thornton, "Symbolism at Ole Miss and the Crisis of Southern Identity," *South Atlantic Quarterly* 86, no. 3 (Summer 1987): 254–68.

48. *Miss.*, December 6, 1946, April 2 and 9, 1948, April 11, 1952, and May 15, 1953.

49. *Miss.*, April 2 and 9, 1948, April 25, 1952, May 1, 1953, May 6, 1955, and April 13, 1956.

50. *OE*, March 1, 1951, and May 15, 1952.

Chapter Four

1. *Miss.*, October 27, 1950; *JDN*, October 28 and November 5, 1950; *DDT*, November 5, 1950.

2. *Miss.*, October 27, 1950.

3. Ibid.

4. Author's interview with Albin Krebs, November 7, 1998.

5. *Miss.*, October 6, 1950.

6. Author's interview with Albin Krebs.

7. *Miss.*, May 12, 1950.

8. *Miss.*, December 2, 1949, and September 29, 1950. The 1949 editorial was signed by Krebs.

9. *Miss.*, October 13, 1950.

10. Ibid.; Ira B. Harkey Jr., *The Smell of Burning Crosses: An Autobiography of a Mississippi Newspaperman* (Jacksonville, Ill.: Harris-Wolfe and Co., 1967).

11. *Miss.*, April 15 and 29, June 9 and 30, October 28, and November 4, 11, and 18, 1949; *Key West (Fla.) News*, June 4, 2002. Krebs retired to Key West, Florida, in the 1990s and died there on May 31, 2002. The article published a few days after his death described him as a gay man. In an interview with the author, he refused to acknowledge that he was gay.

12. *Miss.*, November 5, 1948; L. L. Love to Williams, January 4 and March 24, 1950, in UF.

13. Loren Miller, *The Petitioners: The Story of the Supreme Court of the United States and the Negro* (New York: Pantheon, 1966), 334–40.

14. *Miss.*, February 6, 1948.

15. *OE*, June 15, 1950; *JA*, October 14, 1950; *JDN*, October 17, 1950; *Miss.*, October 20, 1950.

16. *JCL*, October 28 and 29, 1950; *JDN* and *MCA*, October 28, 1950; Minutes, General Faculty Meeting, November 2, 1950, in UF.

17. *JCL*, November 1 and 5, 1950; *DDT*, November 5, 1950; Wiley H. Critz to L. L. Love, October 31, 1950; L. L. Love to Williams, November 9, 1950; and Thomas E. Bailey Jr., undated statement, in UF; author's interview with Albin Krebs.

18. See the references in note 17, above. See also *Miss.*, November 3, 1950; Williams to L. B. Porter, November 7, 1950; and Williams to Brant Coopersmith, November 10, 1950, in UF.

19. Author's interview with Albin Krebs; *Miss.*, November 3, 1950; *JCL*, November 8, 1950.

20. *Miss.*, November 3 and 4, 1950; *MCA*, November 8 and 12, 1950; *JCL*, November 4, 1950; *DDT*, November 5, 1950. For Carter's column, see also *JDN*, November 6, 1950. Krebs also received discreet endorsements from some at the university. John Falkner, who taught him creative writing, urged him not to let his critics bother him, and his brother William Faulkner also supported Krebs. See Joseph Blotner, *Faulkner: A Biography* (New York: Random House, 1974), 2:1370; and *MCA*, December 10, 1950; author's interview with Albin Krebs.

21. *Miss.*, November 3, 1950; William D. Garrett to Williams, October 31, 1950; and R. Taylor Keys to Williams, November 2, 1950, in UF; Mississippi Southern College, *The Student Printz*, November 12, 1950.

22. Harkey, *The Smell of Burning Crosses*, 71–72; *Tupelo Daily Journal*, October 31, 1950; *DDT*, November 5, 1950; author's interview with Albin Krebs; *Miss.*, November 3, 1950; *JCL*, October 31, 1950; Presley J. Snow to Williams, November 4, 1950; Harry R. Sullivan to Williams, October 30, 1950; and R. D. Maum to Williams, October 30, 1950, in UF.

23. R. Taylor Keys to Williams, November 1, 1950; L. B. Porter to Williams, November 2, 1950; William D. Garrett to Williams, October 31, 1950; and R. D. Maum to Williams, October 30, 1950, in UF; *JCL*, November 3, 1950.

24. Minutes, General Faculty Meeting, November 2, 1950, in UF; Williams to E. K. Lumpkin, October 31, 1950; Williams to Taylor Keyes, November 2, 1950; Williams to L. B. Porter, November 7, 1950; and Williams to Brant Coopersmith, November 10, 1950, in UF.

25. *JDN* and *DDT*, November 5, 1950; *Miss.*, November 3, 1950.

26. *Miss.*, November 3, 1950.

27. *JCL* and *JDN*, November 9, 1950; *Miss.*, November 10, 1950.

28. *DDT*, November 1, 1950; *JDN*, November 7 and 10, 1950.

29. Author's interview with Albin Krebs. When Murphy in 1962 revealed his experience of having passed as white at Ole Miss, he lived in New York City, where Krebs also lived and worked for *Newsweek*. When Krebs saw the news articles about Murphy, he contacted him and they got together again in the city.

30. A. B. Butts to H. C. Byrd, February 13, 1939; A. B. Butts to Fred C. Smith, July 11, 1939; and W. C. Wells to A. B. Butts, July 12, 1939, in UF.

31. Alfred Hume to Syrreb Debaters of Berry College, December 10, 1942, in UF.

32. Williams to A. J. Lawrence, July 24, 1948; A. J. Lawrence to E. R. Jobe, July 24, 1948; and A. J. Lawrence to Charles H. Gray, July 24, 1948, in UF.

33. Pauline Y. Weathersby to the Registrar, June 19, 1950; Williams to R. B. Ellis, June 23, 1950; Ellis to E. R. Jobe, July 7, 1950; and Minutes, Admissions Committee, July 20, 1950, in UF; Minutes, IHL Board, August 15, 1950, in Records of the IHL Board, Jackson, Miss.

34. Williams to Gaines S. Dobbins, January 9, 1951; and Williams to Richard L. Jeffreys, June 26, 1953, in UF.

35. Charles C. Bolton, *The Hardest Deal of All: The Battle over School Integration in Mississippi, 1870–1980* (Jackson: University Press of Mississippi, 2005), 33–60; John Dittmer, *Local People: The Struggle for Civil Rights in Mississippi* (Urbana: University of Illinois Press, 1994), 35–37.

36. *JA*, October 14, 21, and 28, 1950, November 11, 1950, and January 6, 1951.

37. Robert J. Farley to Dean Page Keeton, September 24, 1962, AALSP. Neil Robinson provided photocopies of relevant documents from the AALSP.

38. *JA*, October 24, 1953. The biographical information on Charles Dubra comes from author's interviews with Dubra'a niece Sadie O. Jones and nephew Charles Evans Dubra, June 25, 1998, and from materials they provided.

39. *OE*, November 5, 1953.

40. *JA*, October 24 and 31, 1953.

41. "A Ditch to Die In," anonymous, undated manuscript on the history of civil rights at the University of Mississippi, in UF; David G. Sansing, *Making Haste Slowly: The Troubled History of Higher Education in Mississippi* (Jackson: University Press of Mississippi, 1990), 142; Robert J. Farley to Dean Page Keeton, September 24, 1954, in AALSP.

42. *Miss.*, January 8, 1954; Resse Cleghorn, "A Dean Departs Ole Miss," *Reporter*, October 24, 1963, 42; *JDN*, January 25, 1962; "A Ditch to Die In"; Sansing, *Making Haste*, 142.

43. Charles Dubra died of a heart attack on August 29, 1955. *JA*, September 3, 1955.

44. E. J. Stringer to Mississippi State Conference of the NAACP, December 15, 1953 (reel 10), and January 25, 1954 (reel 15); and Officers of the Mississippi State Conference of NAACP Branches, January 1, 1954 (reel 15), in Papers of the NAACP, National Archives and Records Administration, Washington, D.C.; Myrlie B. Evers, with William Peters, *For Us, the Living* (Garden City, N.Y.: Doubleday, 1967), 98–102.

45. For biographical details on Medgar Evers, see Evers and Peters, *For Us, the Living*; George Alexander Sewall and Margaret L. Dwight, "Medgar Evers, Civil Rights Advocate," in *Mississippi Black History Makers*, rev. ed. (Jackson: University Press of Mississippi, 1984), 117–22; and Jack Mendelsohn, *The Martyrs: Sixteen Who Gave Their Lives for Racial Justice* (New York: Harper and Row, 1966), 64–87.

46. *JDN*, January 23 and 24, 1954; *OE*, January 28, 1954.

47. *JDN*, January 22 and 23, 1954.

48. *JDN*, January 24, 1954; Evers and Peters, *For Us, the Living*, 114; *Miss.*, February 5, 1954.

49. *JA*, January 16 and February 6 and 13, 1954.

50. Evers and Peters, *For Us, the Living*, 98–106.

51. *JCL*, May 18, 1954; *OE*, June 3, 1954.

52. *JDN*, August 12, 1954.

53. Neil R. McMillen, *The Citizens' Council: Organized Resistance to the Second Reconstruction, 1954–64* (Urbana: University of Illinois Press, 1971), 15–18, passim; Numan V. Bartley, *The Rise of Massive Resistance: Race and Politics in the South during the 1950s* (Baton Rouge: Louisiana State University Press, 1969), 82–86; *SSN*, September 3, 1954, 8.

54. Robert J. Farley to Medgar W. Evers, June 14, 1954, in UF; E. R. Jobe to Medgar W. Evers, August 23 and 26, 1954, Alexander Pierre Tureaud Papers, Amistad Research Center, Tulane University; Evers and Peters, *For Us, the Living*, 114–15.

55. A. P. Tureaud to Robert L. Carter, September 1, 1954, Tureaud Papers; Howard Smead, *Blood Justice: The Lynching of Mack Charles Parker* (New York: Oxford University Press, 1986), 68; Evers and Peters, *For Us, the Living*, 114–15.

56. Tureaud to Carter, September 1, 1954; Evers and Peters, *For Us, the Living*, 115.

57. Tureaud to Carter, September 1, 1954; Evers and Peters, *For Us, the Living*, 115. No contemporary record remains of Evers's replies to Coleman's queries, but the answers can be roughly surmised. The quote is from the book by Evers's widow.

58. Tureaud to Carter, September 1, 1954; Evers and Peters, *For Us, the Living*, 115.

59. The best source on the history of the IHL board is Sansing, *Making Haste*.

60. Minutes, IHL Board, September 16, 1954; *DDT*, September 17, 1954.

61. Minutes, IHL Board, September 16, 1954; *DDT*, September 17, 1954.

62. Minutes, IHL Board, September 16, 1954.

63. *DDT*, September 19, 1954; *JDN*, September 18, 1954.

64. Evers and Peters, *For Us, the Living*, 119.

65. Ibid.; Minutes, IHL Board, December 16, 1954.

Chapter Five

1. Clennon King, *Black-ology* (Miami: privately printed, 1997), 59–61; *Atlanta Journal-Constitution*, March 26, 2000; author's interviews with Clennon King's brother Paul D. King, April 4, 1999, and a nephew, Clennon King, September 14, 1994. The children in the King family were seven sons—Clennon, Slater, Marvin, C. B., Paul, Allen, and Preston. The newspaper article on the King family (in the "Dixie Living" section) was prompted by Preston's return to the United States for his brother Clennon's funeral. Preston King, who had a doctorate from the London School of Economics, had been in exile in England for thirty-nine years after he refused induction into the army until the local draft board addressed him with the courtesy title of "Mr." When sentenced to prison, he fled to England.

2. See the references in note 1, above.

3. See the references in note 1, above. See also Clennon King, "I Speak as a Southern Negro," *American Mercury*, January 1958, 26; and *Dallas Morning News*, May 8, 1958.

4. Clennon King, *Black-ology*, 59–61; author's interview with Paul D. King; S. V. Sanford to Clennon King, April 15, 1940; King to Walter White, April 18, 1940; and Thurgood Marshall to King, April 24, 1940, in Papers of the NAACP, Series B: 1940–1950, Legal File: University of Georgia, 1940–1946, National Archives and Records Administration, Washington, D.C.

5. Clennon King, *Black-ology*, 59–61; Clennon King to Roy Wilkins, January 23, 1956; and flyer for the International African Progress Brotherhood (IAPB), both in Papers of the NAACP, Series A: 1956–1965, Special Subjects: General, 1956–1959; author's interview with Paul D. King.

6. Josephine McCann Posey, *Against Great Odds: The History of Alcorn State University* (Jackson: University Press of Mississippi, 1994), ix and 5–9; *DDT*, March 10, 1957; *JST*,

March 24, 1957; David G. Sansing, *Making Haste Slowly: The Troubled History of Higher Education in Mississippi* (Jackson: University Press of Mississippi, 1990), 130; John E. Brewton, director, *Higher Education in Mississippi: A Survey Report* (Jackson: Board of Trustees, 1954), 142, 156, 233, and 268–70; Joseph E. Gibson, director, *Mississippi Study of Higher Education, 1945* (Jackson: Board of Trustees, 1945), 317–21. See also Melerson Guy Dunham, *Centennial History of Alcorn A&M College* (Jackson: University Press of Mississippi, 1971).

7. *JST*, November 5 and December 10, 1956.

8. *NOTP*, March 10, 1957; Clennon King to Ney M. Gore Jr., January 25, 1957; and Ney M. Gore Jr. to King, January 28, 1957, in MSSCP.

9. *JCL*, March 9, 1957; *DDT*, March 7, 1957; *JST*, March 3 and 4, 1957. The series appeared in the *Jackson State Times* daily March 3–4 and 6–11, 1957; later the newspaper reprinted the articles in pamphlet form with an introduction by the managing editor as *The Clennon King Story*.

10. *DDT*, March 7, 1957; *JCL*, March 9, 1957. At the same time the board also had to deal with apparently unrelated student demands at Mississippi Vocational College for a student government and with student protests at Jackson State College over the forced withdrawal of the college's basketball team from a national tournament because of the rule against integrated athletic contests. Hal DeCell, a Sovereignty Commission employee, suspected the Alcorn protests did have a direct link to the actions at the other Negro schools. Apparently, the commission could uncover no connection, so its involvement in the matter ended. Hal DeCell to Ney M. Gore Jr., March 5 and 14, 1957, in MSSCP.

11. *JDN* and *NT*, March 8, 1957; *JCL*, March 9, 1957; Minutes, IHL Board, March 9, 1957, in Records of the IHL Board, Jackson, Miss.; *JA*, March 9 and 16, 1957.

12. *JST*, March 7 and 8, 1957.

13. *JDN* and *NT*, March 8, 1957; *DDT*, March 7, 1957.

14. *DDT*, March 8, 1957; *JCL* and *NYT*, March 9, 1957; *JDN*, March 10, 1957.

15. *NT*, *JCL*, and *NYT*, March 10, 1957. In a telegram to the student council, the Jackson NAACP did applaud the opposition to King's views but deplored any denial of his right to free speech. See *JA*, March 30, 1957. The Sovereignty Commission also contended that the demonstrations did not originate with the students and after an investigation concluded that Otis himself had been "a primary instigator." See Hal C. DeCell to Ney M. Gore Jr., March 14, 1957, in MSSCP; and *JA*, March 16 and 30, 1957.

16. Clennon King to *Time* magazine, March 15, 1957, in MSSCP. King sent a copy of his letter to Ney Gore at the Sovereignty Commission, but the letter never appeared in *Time*.

17. Minutes, IHL Board, February 21 and March 9, 1957; *NOTP*, *MCA*, and *JDN*, March 10, 1957; *JA*, March 16, 1957.

18. *Pittsburgh Courier*, March 16, 1957, copy in MSSCP.

19. *JCL*, March 10 and 11, 1957; *NT*, March 10, 1957; *JDN*, March 11, 1957; *DDT*, March 12, 1957.

20. *JST*, March 10 and 11, 1957.

21. *JCL*, March 9, 1957; *JDN*, March 10, 1957; *DDT*, March 10 and 12, 1957; *NOTP*, March 10 and 15, 1957; *MCA*, March 15, 1957; *JA*, March 23 and April 13, 1957.

22. "The Witling of Alcorn," *The Crisis*, May 1957, 290–91; Clennon King to Roy Wilkins, May 24 and August 2, 1957; King to Arthur B. Spingarn, June 3, 1957; Roy Wilkins to King, June 7 and 17 and August 15, 1957; and Roy Wilkins to Mr. [?] Ivy, June 13, 1957, in Papers of the NAACP, Series A: 1956–1965, Special Subjects: General, 1956–1959. The NAACP Papers also contain correspondence about King's futile attempt in the fall of 1957 to gain a nomination to its board.

23. *NT*, March 10, 1957; *JST*, March 17, 1957; *JCL*, March 13, 1957; *JA*, April 6, 1957; receipt from The Office Supply Company of Jackson to the Sovereignty Commission, August 14, 1957, in MSSCP. See also Ruby Hurley to Roy Wilkins, December 31, 1957, in Papers of the NAACP, Series B: 1956–1965, Special Subjects: Clennon King, 1956–1960.

24. *DDT*, March 12, 1957, and June 5, 1958; *JST*, April 8 and 9, 1957; *JA*, April 13, 1957; *Montgomery Advertiser*, June 16, 1957.

25. *JDN, JCL,* and *JST,* July 6 and 7, 1957; *DDT,* July 4 and 7, 1957.

26. *JCL, JST,* and *JDN,* July 19, 1957.

27. Clennon King, "I Speak as a Southern Negro," *American Mercury*, January 1958, 23–33. For reactions, see Roy Wilkins to William La Varre, telegram, December 24, 1957; and NAACP's Reply to Prof. King's Attack, February 21, 1957 [1958], both in Papers of the NAACP, Series A: 1956–1965, Special Subjects: General, 1956–1959. See also the *Dallas Morning News*, May 7, 8, and 9, 1958. In early 1958, King exchanged letters with W. E. B. Du Bois about Washington and Garvey. See Herbert Aptheker, ed., *The Correspondence of W. E. B. Du Bois*, vol. 3, *Selections, 1944–1963* (Amherst: University of Massachusetts Press, 1978), 421–22.

28. *JDN*, May 4, 1958; *SSN*, June 1958; *Columbia (S.C.) State*, May 3, 1958.

29. *NOTP, DDT,* and *Charleston (S.C.) News and Courier*, May 12, 1958.

30. See the references in note 29, above.

31. Clennon King to Registrar's Office, May 11, 1958; and R. B. Ellis to King, May 13, 1958, in UF; *JDN*, May 13, 1958; *OE*, May 15, 1958; *Miss.*, May 16, 1958. The minutes of the board specifically called for "at least five (5) letters," but the standard form sent to King called for six. See Minutes, IHL Board, September 16, 1954.

32. Clennon King to Registrar's Office, May 11, 1958; and R. B. Ellis to King, May 13, 1958, in UF; *JDN*, May 13, 1958; *OE*, May 15, 1958; *Miss.*, May 16, 1958; King to "All Former Students of the University of Mississippi [in] Harrison County," May 18, 1958, in UF and in *Gulfport Daily Herald*, May 19, 1958.

33. Clennon King to J. D. Williams, no date [June 11, 1958], in UF.

34. Clennon King to R. B. Ellis, May 26, 1958; and Ellis to King, May 28, 1958, in UF; *JST*, May 29, 1958.

35. Hugh Clegg, memoranda to file, May 27 and 28, 1958, in UF.

36. Clennon King to R. B. Ellis, May 26 and 31, 1958; and King to J. D. Williams, no date [June 11, 1958], in UF.

37. Clayborne Carson et al., eds., *The Papers of Martin Luther King Jr.*, vol. 4, *Symbol of the Movement, January 1957–December 1958* (Berkeley: University of California Press, 2000), 415–16 and 419; Clennon King to Roy Wilkins, May 22, 1958; John A. Morsell to C. R.

Darden, May 29, 1958; John A. Morsell to King, May 29, 1958; and James R. Robinson to King, June 4, 1958, in Papers of the NAACP, Series A: 1956–1965, Special Subjects: General, 1956–1959.

38. Clennon King to R. B. Ellis, May 31, 1958, in UF; *DDT* and *JST*, June 3, 1958.

39. Hugh Clegg, memoranda to file, June 4, 1958; Burnes Tatum to FBI, telegram, June 4, 1958; and Burnes Tatum to Chief of Police, Albany, Georgia, telegram, June 4, 1958, in UF; *JDN*, June 4, 1958.

40. Account of the morning of June 5 is drawn from the following: *JST*, June 5 and 7, 1958; *JDN*, June 5, 1958; *NYT*, *Arkansas Gazette*, and *JCL*, June 6, 1958; *SSN*, July 1958; joint statement of Gov. J. P. Coleman and Atty. Gen. Joe T. Patterson, no date, in MSSCP; report of Hugh Clegg concerning joint interview with Clennon King, June 5, 1958; report of Tom S. Hines concerning joint interview with Clennon King, June 7, 1958; and report of Robert B. Ellis, re: Clennon King, no date, in UF; David Sansing, interview with J. P. Coleman, in ASCUM.

41. Clennon King's application for admission to the Graduate School, June 5, 1958; T. G. James to the University of Mississippi, May 28, 1958; William L. Power to Registrar, no date; and "Facts relating to the Application of Rev. Clennon King for Admission to the University of Mississippi," June 6, 1958, in UF.

42. *NYT* and *Arkansas Gazette*, June 6, 1958; *JST*, June 19, 1958.

43. *JDN* and *DDT*, June 6, 1958.

44. Joint statement of Gov. Coleman and Atty. Gen. Patterson, no date, in MSSCP. Internal evidence suggests the statement was issued just before the lunacy hearing.

45. *JDN*, *DDT*, and *Arkansas Gazette*, June 6, 1958; author's interviews with Dr. Mary Alice Lee, May 18, 1995, and William L. Power, May 15, 1997.

46. *JST*, June 6, 1958; *JDN*, June 7, 1958; *JA*, June 14, 1958; physician's report of patient, by Mary Lee and Beverly E. Smith, June 6, 1958; and order by Chancellor Stokes V. Robertson Jr., June 6, 1958, in Hinds County Chancery Court records; author's interviews with Charles Dunagin, May 26, 1995, Stokes V. Robertson Jr., May 18, 1995, and Dr. Mary Alice Lee.

47. *JCL*, November 13, 1955; clippings in W. L. Jaquith Papers, in MDAH; *JST* and *JDN*, June 7, 1958.

48. "Petition for Writ of Habeas Corpus by Mrs. Anne King, Next of Kin, in Behalf of Clennon W. King, Circuit Court of Hinds County, Mississippi," June 10, 1958; amendment to petition, June 12, 1958; "Answer to Petition for Writ of Habeas Corpus, Circuit Court of Hinds County," no date; order, Circuit Court of Hinds County, June 16, 1958, all in Papers of Mississippi Attorney General, State Records Center, MDAH; *JST*, June 11, 16, and 18, 1958; *JA*, June 14, 1958; *NYT*, June 15, 1958; *SSN*, July 1958.

49. *JDN*, June 7, 1958; *Washington Evening Star*, June 11, 1958; *JST*, June 8 and 11, 1958; *DDT*, June 8, 1958; Roy Wilkins to J. P. Coleman, June 6, 1958, in Papers of the NAACP, Series A: 1956–1965, Special Subjects: General, 1956–1959; Martin Luther King Jr. to J. P. Coleman, June 7, 1958, in Carson et al., *The Papers of Martin Luther King Jr.*, 4:419–20.

50. W. P. Murphy to Scott Tennyson, June 9, 1958; Tennyson to Murphy, June 16, 1958; Murphy to Tennyson, June 20, 1958; and Tennyson to Murphy, June 21, 1958, in WPMP; author's interview with William P. Murphy, June 21, 1991.

51. See the references in note 50, above.

52. *DDT* and *JCL*, June 8, 1958.

53. *JDN* and *JST*, June 19, 1958; W. L. Jaquith, M.D., and director of the Mississippi State Hospital, to Chancellor Stokes V. Robertson Jr., June 18, 1958, in Hinds County Chancery Court records.

54. *JST* and *JDN*, June 20 and July 3, 1958; *MCA*, June 20, 1958; *NT*, October 8, 1958; *Nashville Banner*, September 8, 1958; Clennon King to J. D. Williams, no date [June 11, 1958], in UF.

55. *JST*, September 1, 2, and 3 and October 5, 1958, and February 25, 1959; *JCL*, February 25, 1959, and July 2, 1970; *MCA*, October 27, 1959, and April 27 and May 12, 1960; *JA*, January 2, 1960; *JDN*, January 20, 1960; *Miami New Times*, February 24, 1993; *Time*, November 22, 1976, 21. The Sovereignty Commission continued to keep clippings on King long after he left the state.

Chapter Six

1. John Dittmer, *Local People: The Struggle for Civil Rights in Mississippi* (Urbana: University of Illinois Press, 1994), 41.

2. On Brady, see Daniel Miles Hoehler, "Thomas P. Brady" (M.A. thesis, University of Mississippi, 1998); James Graham Cook, *The Segregationists* (New York: Appleton-Century-Crofts, 1962), 14–30; and Neil R. McMillen, *The Citizens' Council: Organized Resistance to the Second Reconstruction, 1954–64* (Urbana: University of Illinois Press, 1971), 17–18.

3. McMillen, *Citizens' Council*, 15–40, especially 16–20.

4. Cook, *Segregationists*, 66; McMillen, *Citizens' Council*, 25–27; H. E. F., "Tornado Weather in Dixie," *Christian Century*, February 29, 1956, 264.

5. H. E. F., "Tornado Weather in Dixie," 264; Hodding Carter, *The South Strikes Back* (Garden City, N.Y.: Doubleday, 1959), 177.

6. *SSN*, April 1956, 10. The legislature passed other laws buttressing segregation. See *RRLR*, April 1956, 430–32 and 439.

7. Yasuhiro Katagiri, *The Mississippi State Sovereignty Commission: Civil Rights and States' Rights* (Jackson: University Press of Mississippi, 2001), 6.

8. Ibid., 3–18.

9. Ibid., 18–21.

10. Both Katagiri, *Sovereignty Commission*, and McMillen, *Citizens' Council*, discuss the rivalries between the commission and the council.

11. *DDT*, September 15, 17, and 19, 1954. See also Carter, *The South Strikes Back*, 145–46.

12. *DDT*, September 19 and 22, 1954. In two editorials, Hodding Carter criticized the segregationist opposition to the integrated game. See *DDT*, September 21 and 22, 1954.

13. *DDT*, September 21, 1954.

14. John Vaught, *Rebel Coach: My Football Family* (Memphis: Memphis State University Press, 1971), 6; William W. Sorrels and Charles Cavagnaro, *Ole Miss Rebels: Mississippi Football* (Huntsville, Alabama: Strode, 1976).

15. *JST*, February 5, 1959; Kathy Bartelt to author, December 14, 1999; Thomas D. Clark, *My Century in History: Memoirs* (Lexington: University Press of Kentucky, 2006), 244. The Evansville team had one Negro player. The *Jackson State Times* provides the most information on controversies over integrated sports because of the reporting of Jimmie McDowell, the sports editor. Later McDowell said that Sun Bowl officials in 1953 tried to claim that the Negro player for the College of the Pacific team was Hawaiian, but he saw the player in the locker room after the game and recognized that he was an American black. Author's interview with Jimmie McDowell, November 22, 1998.

16. On segregation in southern athletics, see, for example, Charles H. Martin, "Racial Change and 'Big-Time' College Football in Georgia: The Age of Segregation, 1892–1957," *Georgia Historical Quarterly* 80, no. 3 (1996): 532–62; Robert W. Dubay, "Pigmentation and Pigskin: A Jones County Junior College Dilemma," *Journal of Mississippi History* 46 (February 1984): 43–50, and "Politics, Pigmentation, and Pigskin: The Georgia Tech Sugar Bowl Controversy of 1955," *Atlanta History* 39 (Spring 1995): 21–35; Russell J. Henderson, "The 1963 Mississippi State University Basketball Controversy and the Repeal of the Unwritten Law: 'Something More than the Game Will Be Lost,'" *Journal of Southern History* 63 (November 1997): 827–54; Michael Oriard, *King Football: Sport and Spectacle in the Golden Age of Radio and Newsreels, Movies and Magazines, and the Weekly and Daily Press* (Chapel Hill: University of North Carolina Press, 2001), 283–327; and Frank Fitzpatrick, *And the Walls Came Tumbling Down: Kentucky, Texas Western, and the Game That Changed American Sports* (New York: Simon and Schuster, 1999).

17. Fitzpatrick, *And the Walls*, 46; Charles H. Martin, "Jim Crow in the Gymnasium: The Integration of College Basketball in the American South," *International Journal of the History of Sport* 10, no. 1 (1993): 71.

18. *JST*, November 14, 16, 22, and 26, 1955; J. D. Williams to Pete Kyle McCarter, December 1, 1955, in UF. See Henderson, "The 1963 Basketball Controversy"; Dubay, "Pigmentation and Pigskin," and "Politics, Pigmentation, and Pigskin." Williams told McCarter that Pittsburgh had three black players.

19. *JST*, November 27 and 28, 1959; Williams to McCarter, December 1, 1955.

20. *JST*, December 2, 3, 4, and 5, 1955; Dubay, "Politics, Pigmentation, and Pigskin," 21–35; *RRLR* 1 (1956): 953–54; and 3 (1958): 132–35.

21. *JST*, October 27, November 15, 21, 29, and 30, and December 4, 1955.

22. *JST*, November 29 and December 4, 5, and 7, 1955; *JCL*, December 10, 1955.

23. *JST*, December 11, 1955; *JCL*, December 21, 1955.

24. *JCL*, February 22, 1959; *SSN*, December 1956.

25. *JDN*, December 29, 30, and 31, 1956; *SSN*, February 1957.

26. *JDN* and *JST*, December 31, 1956; *DDT*, January 1, 1957; *SSN*, February 1957; J. D. Williams to W. C. Trotter, January 2, 1957, in UF.

27. *JDN*, December 31, 1956; *DDT*, January 2, 1957; C. B. "Buddie" Newman to Hilbun, December 31, 1955, in Ben F. Hilbun Papers, SCMSU.

28. A. S. Coody to Hilbun, January 1, 1956 [1957]; and Jean Scruggs to Hilbun, January 8, 1957, in Hilbun Papers; *JST*, January 2, 4, 6, and 8, 1957; *DDT*, January 3, 1957; *Miss.*, January 11, 1957.

29. *JCL*, March 6, 1957; *DDT*, March 6 and 7, 1957; *JA*, March 9, 1957; *SSN*, April 1957.

30. *The Citizens' Council*, April 1958. An examination of other newspapers from the spring of 1958 failed to uncover any other coverage of the event.

31. *JST*, November 1, 2, 4, 16, and 30, 1958, and February 10 and May 19, 1959; *Miss.*, November 14 and December 5, 1958.

32. Author's interview with Jimmie McDowell. Years later, McDowell remembered little discussion of racial matters among sports reporters, no knowledge of the racial attitudes of coaches or athletic directors, and no criticism of his stand against the unwritten law.

33. *JST*, February 10, 11, and 18, 1959.

34. *JST*, February 10, 11, 13, and 25, 1959; *SSN*, March 1959.

35. *JST*, February 10, 11, 13, 18, 24, and 25, 1959.

36. *Miss.*, February 13 and 20, 1959.

37. *JST*, February 22 and 25, 1959; *JCL*, February 12 and 19, and March 3, 1959.

38. *JCL*, February 19, 1959; *JST*, February 19, 20, and 22, 1959.

39. *JST*, February 17, 20, 24, 25, and 28, 1959; *JCL*, February 20, 1959; Jerry Clower to Ben F. Hilbun, February 26, 1959; Rev. S. M. Butts to Hilbun, February 25, 1959; and Dick Sanders to Hilbun, February 26, 1959, in Hilbun Papers, SCMSU. The Bible verse Clower referred Hilbun to reads: "If any of you lacks wisdom, let him ask of God, who gives it all liberally and without reproach, and it will be given to him" (James 5:1).

40. *JCL*, March 1, 1959; *JST*, March 2, 1959; *SSN*, April 1959; Hilbun to Dean Boggs, March 17, 1959; Hilbun to William B. Dickson, March 17, 1959; Hilbun to William McGraw, April 20, 1959; and Hilbun to James W. Lambert, March 6, 1959, in Hilbun Papers.

41. *Miss.*, March 6, 1959.

42. *Miss.*, May 15, 1959; *JST*, May 16, 1959.

43. *JST*, May 18, 19, and 24. On the Mack Charles Parker case, see Howard Smead, *Blood Justice: The Lynching of Mack Charles Parker* (New York: Oxford University Press, 1986).

44. *JST*, May 2, 8, 18, 20, 21, and 22, 1960; *JCL*, May 21, 1960. Copies of the *Mississippian* after March 10 are not available for the remainder of the spring semester.

45. Vaught, *Rebel Coach*, 108; *JST*, November 27 and 29, 1960, and November 8 and 14, 1961.

46. *Miss.*, December 1 and 15, 1960.

47. *JCL*, March 1, 1961; *JST*, March 2 and 6, and November 9 and 20, 1961; *DDT*, March 2, 1961.

48. *JST*, November 5, 7, 21, 26, and 30, and December 3 and 12, 1961.

49. Author's interview with James L. Robertson, October 4, 1998.

50. Ibid.

51. *DM*, February 21, 1962.

52. *DM*, March 2, 1962; *JDN*, March 4, 1962; *JCL*, March 3, 1962.

53. *JCL*, February 14 and 16, and March 5, 1962; Dean W. Colvard, *Mixed Emotions, as Racial Barriers Fell: A University President Remembers* (Danville, Ill.: Interstate Printers, 1985), 19.

54. *DM*, March 6 and 7, 1962. The editor of Mississippi State's *Daily Reflector* is quoted in the *Daily Mississippian* for March 7. The walls of segregation in athletics finally were

surmounted by the Mississippi State basketball team in the early spring of 1963; see Henderson, "The 1963 Basketball Controversy."

55. *DM*, March 1, 13, and 14, 1962.

56. *RU* [February 27 and March 1, 1962]. The dates for the two issues cited have been determined by internal evidence. The *Rebel Underground*, a mimeographed paper of two to four pages, appeared irregularly during 1962 and 1963; the earliest may have been February 2, 1962. Each issue omitted any indication of editors or publishers. The issues did not look alike and may have come from different sources. No complete set of the *Rebel Underground* exists, but the archives at the University of Mississippi contain the largest collection.

Chapter Seven

1. House Bill 58, Extraordinary Session of 1954 and 1955, September 7–30, 1954, Sec. 1, Para. 7, "An Act to Amend Section 2056, Mississippi Code of 1942, So as to Further Define Conspiracy," *Laws of the State of Mississippi* (Jackson: Office of the Secretary of State, 1955), 24. See also William F. Winter, "Mississippi's Legislative Approach to the School Segregation Problem," *MLJ* 26 (March 1955): 165–73. For a longer version of the chapter, see Charles W. Eagles, "The Closing of Mississippi Society: Will Campbell, 'The $64,000 Question,' and Religious Emphasis Week at the University of Mississippi," *Journal of Southern History* 67 (May 2001): 331–72.

2. *JCL*, January 29, 1955; *Hattiesburg American*, March 11 and 14, 1955. The controversy at Mississippi Southern College can be followed in the *Hattiesburg American*, February 11, 14, 15, 16, 17, 21, 23, and 25 and March 12, 1955; and in the Mississippi Southern College newspaper *Student Printz*, February 4 and 25, April 29, and May 6, 20, and 27, 1955.

3. Minutes, IHL Board, February 17, 1955, in Records of the IHL Board, Jackson, Miss.; *JDN*, February 23, 1955; *Miss.*, March 8, April 22, and May 6, 1955; *Student Printz*, February 25 and April 29, 1955; *DDT*, April 22, 1955.

4. Neil R. McMillen, *The Citizens' Council: Organized Resistance to the Second Reconstruction, 1954–64* (Urbana: University of Illinois Press, 1971); NAACP, *M Is for Mississippi and Murder* (New York: NAACP, 1955).

5. Thomas L. Connelly, *Will Campbell and the Soul of the South* (New York: Continuum, 1982), 41, 42, 52–53, 62, and 79–81; Will D. Campbell, *Brother to a Dragonfly* (New York: Seabury Press, 1977), 97. For biographical information on Campbell, see his other books (particularly *Forty Acres and a Goat*), and his oral history with Orley B. Caudill, in MDAH.

6. *Religious Life at the University of Mississippi, 1955–1956* (University: University of Mississippi, 1955), 5–14.

7. Ibid., 5–6; W. Alton Bryant, "Report to the Board of Trustees of Institutions of Higher Learning on the Invitation to Participate in the Religious Emphasis Week Program Extended to Rev. Alvin Kershaw of Oxford, Ohio, by the Committee of One Hundred at the University of Mississippi," no date; and Campbell to Williams, December 9, 1955, in UF; Morton B. King to Ralph F. Fuchs, March 28, 1956, in Morton B. King Papers, ASCUM.

More generally, see Leland Miles, "What Do You Mean, 'Religious Emphasis Week'?" *Bulletin of the American Association of University Professors* 42 (Winter 1956): 679–84.

8. Author's interviews with Will D. Campbell, November 12, 1994, and September 12, 1997; Will Campbell, "Brer Fox and Brer Tarrypin and the Crisis at Ole Miss," *Christianity and Crisis*, October 17, 1977, 233; Campbell to Williams, December 9, 1955, in UF. One of the original speakers was Ralph McGill, the liberal editor of the *Atlanta Constitution*, but he withdrew after controversy erupted over REW. McGill thought he would be too controversial because of his recent comments on the Emmett Till case and integrated athletics. Ralph McGill to Campbell, December 16, 1955, in UF. McGill was apparently replaced by Rabbi Milton Grafman of Birmingham. *St. Louis Post-Dispatch*, February 11, 1956.

9. Will Campbell, *Providence* (Atlanta: Longstreet, 1992), 3–7; Campbell to "Friend" (form letter), October 10, 1955, in UF.

10. G. McLeod Bryan, "Facing the Cultural Crisis," speech delivered October 12, 1955, in Religious Emphasis Week series, University of Mississippi, in UF.

11. Ibid.

12. Williams to Campbell, October 12, 1955, in UF.

13. Campbell, *Providence*, 3–24; Kieran W. Taylor, "'I Done Made Up My Mind': The Legacy of the Providence Cooperative Farm" (M.A. thesis, University of Mississippi, 1998), 9–17.

14. Campbell, *Providence*, 3–24. Campbell recalled that it was a state "senator," but it undoubtedly was Rep. Wilburn Hooker. See Hooker testimony on October 29, 1959, in GLICP.

15. Author's interview with Alvin Kershaw, November 11, 1994; clippings from *Newsweek*, November 14, 1955, and *Baltimore Afro-American*, November 12, 1955, in AKP.

16. *MCA*, November 2, 1955; *JST*, November 2, 1955; author's interview with Kershaw.

17. *JDN*, November 12, 1955; Williams to Pete Kyle McCarter, December 1, 1955; Hugh V. Wall to Williams, November 3, 1955; R. Pearce Phillips to Williams, November 7, 1955; V. B. Montgomery to Williams, November 8, 1955; and Robert B. Haltom to Williams, November 13, 1955, in UF; Campbell, *Brother to a Dragonfly*, 114.

18. A. E. Smith to Vice Chancellor[?], November 14, 1955; Mrs. Walter Sillers Sr. to Williams, November 14, 1955; Florence Sillers Ogden to Williams, November 14, 1955; Dave Womack to Williams, November 11, 1955; J. A. Phillips to Williams, November 12, 1955; Lamar Moss to Williams, November 10, 1955; Richard P. Birchett to Williams, November 11, 1955; and Albert S. Gardner to Williams, November 11, 1955, in UF.

19. James A. Morrow Jr., to Williams, November 4, 1955, in UF; *JCL*, November 9, 1955. The *Jackson Clarion-Ledger* of November 20, 1955, summarized opinions on the Kershaw affair.

20. *OE*, November 17, 1955; *JST*, November 24, 1955; W. Alton Bryant to Hugh V. Wall, November 9, 1955; and Williams to Hugh V. Wall, November 22, 1995, in UF.

21. *JCL*, November 13, 1955; *DDT*, November 15, 1955; and Williams to Pete Kyle McCarter, December 1, 1955, in UF.

22. Maurice Dantin to Williams, November 18, 1955; Thomas B. Bourdeaux to Williams,

November 14, 1955; Archie L. Meadows to Williams, December 13, 1955; Duncan M. Hobart to Williams, November 18, 1955; A. Emile Joffrion to Williams, December 12, 1955; Duncan M. Gray Sr. to Williams, December 8, 1955; and Duncan M. Gray Jr. to Williams, November 15, 1955, in UF.

23. *Miss.*, November 11 and 18, 1955; *JST*, November 15, 1955; *MCA*, November 17, 1955; Resolution no. 2, "A Resolution to Request the Chancellor of the University of Mississippi Not to Cancel the Invitation Extended to Rev. Alvin Kershaw to Be One of the Speakers for the Annual Religious Emphasis Week in 1956," no date, in UF.

24. *Miss.*, October 23, 1953; *JCL*, November 20, 1955; Bryant, "Report to the Board of Trustees"; and Williams to Pete Kyle McCarter, December 1, 1955, in UF; Lucie Robertson Bridgforth, " 'Bomb the Ban': A Study of the Legal Controversy Surrounding Off-Campus Speakers at Mississippi Institutions of Higher Learning" (M.A. thesis, University of Mississippi, 1979).

25. *MCA*, November 11, 1955.

26. *JCL*, November 19, 1955 (emphasis added). See also *MCA*, November 20, 1955.

27. *Itawamba County Times*, quoted in *JCL*, November 21, 1955; *Kosciusko Star*, quoted in *JCL*, December 4, 1955; *JCL*, December 4, 1955; *Miss.*, November 18, 1955.

28. *Miss.*, December 2 and 9, 1955; *JST*, November 23, 1955.

29. Author's interviews with Campbell; Campbell to Kershaw, November 9, 1955, in AKP.

30. Author's interviews with Campbell; *OE*, January 21, 1954, and June 13, 1957; *NYT*, February 12, 1956; Emile Joffrion to Kershaw, November 5, 1955; Campbell to Al and Doris Kershaw, March 9, 1956; Emile Joffrion to Duncan M. Gray, Duncan Hobart, and Duncan M. Gray Jr., November 5, 1955; and Campbell to Kershaw, November 9, 1955, in AKP.

31. R. K. Daniel to Kershaw, November 4, 1955; Adele du Bois to Kershaw, no date [November 3, 1955]; Margaret (Mrs. Joe D.) Lyons to Kershaw, no date [November 20, 1955]; and Frank W. Ellis to Kershaw, November 22, 1955, in AKP.

32. Campbell, *Brother to a Dragonfly*, 115–18.

33. *JDN*, December 15, 1955.

34. *JCL*, December 16 and 17, 1955; *JST*, December 15, 1955; "A Petition to the Chancellor of the University of Mississippi Requesting that the Invitation to the Reverend Alvin Kershaw to Be One of the Speakers for the Annual Religious Emphasis Week in 1956 Be Canceled," no date, in UF. In addition to the sons of Thomas Brady and Wilburn Hooker, signers of the anti-Kershaw petition included a future lieutenant governor (Brad Dye Jr.), a future Miss America (Mary Anne Mobley), and a future federal judge (Grady Jolly Jr.).

35. See for example, *JCL*, December 18 and 21, 1955.

36. *JDN*, January 19, 1956; *JCL*, January 20 and February 4, 1956; Minutes, IHL Board, February 17, 1955, and January 19, 1956; Williams to James P. Walker Jr. and Bradford Dye Jr., January 20, 1956, in UF. Kershaw's "Notes on Telephone Call from Oliver Emmerich, January 19, 1956" (in AKP) was a copy of Emmerich's statement about his call to Kershaw.

37. Minutes, IHL Board, January 19, 1956; Williams to Kershaw, January 20, 1956, in AKP.

38. See the references in note 37, above.

39. Statement released by James A. Morrow Jr., January 20, 1956, copy in Ben F. Hilbun Papers, SCMSU.

40. Williams to James A. Morrow Jr., January 21, 1956; Williams to Tom J. Tubb, January 21, 1956; Williams to Charles D. Fair, January 23, 1956; and Williams to J. Oliver Emmerich, January 23, 1956, in UF; Williams to Kershaw, January 20, 1956, in AKP.

41. Campbell to Kershaw, no date [received January 28, 1959], in AKP.

42. Wallace Sherwood to Kershaw, January 23, 1956; and Kershaw to Williams, January 28, 1956, in AKP; *Miss.*, February 3, 1956.

43. Kershaw to Williams, January 28, 1956, in AKP; *Miss.*, February 3, 1956.

44. Campbell, *Brother to a Dragonfly*, 119–20; Williams to Kershaw, February 2, 1956; and Williams to Joe Earl Elmore, February 20, 1956, in UF.

45. *JCL*, February 5, 1956; *JDN*, February 23, 1956.

46. Morton B. King to David Halberstam, May 23, 1956, in King Papers, ASCUM; *DDT*, February 9, 1956; *Miss.*, February 10, 1956; E. Culpepper Clark, *The Schoolhouse Door: Segregation's Last Stand at the University of Alabama* (New York: Oxford University Press, 1993), 71–90.

47. Morton B. King to Alton Bryant, December 9, 1955, in AAUPP; Morton B. King Jr. to Williams, February 3, 1956, in King Papers; *NT*, February 8, 1956; Williams to Morton B. King Jr., February 4, 1956, in UF.

48. Harris G. Warren to Ralph F. Fuchs, March 10, 1956; and Morton B. King to Ralph F. Fuchs, March 29, 1956, in AAUPP; Morton B. King to Williams, May 26, 1956, in UF.

49. University of Mississippi press release regarding King's resignation, February 7, 1956, in King Papers; *Miss.*, February 10, 1956.

50. *JDN*, February 8, 1956; *MCA*, February 9, 1956; *JCL*, February 9, 1956.

51. William Buchanan to Ben F. Hilbun, February 8, 1956; and Ben F. Hilbun to William Buchanan, February 9, 1956, in Hilbun Papers; *JCL*, February 10, 1956.

52. *JCL*, February 11, 1956; House Concurrent Resolution no. 21, Mississippi Legislature, Regular Session 1956, in *RRLR* 1 (1956): 423.

53. *JDN*, February 10, 1956; *JCL*, February 11 and 15, 1956; *MCA*, February 22, 1956; *Miss.*, February 10, 1956; Frank E. Everett Jr. to Williams, February 4, 1956; Stokes V. Robertson Jr. to Williams, February 16, 1956; and Tom P. Brady to Williams, February 25, 1956, in UF. The *Mississippian*, February 24, 1956, contained a letter to the editor from "Byron de la Bukuth" of Greenwood that congratulated the university for denying Kershaw's invitation. He was probably Byron de la Beckwith, who later assassinated Medgar Evers.

54. Edwin White to Williams, February 9, 1956, in UF; H. H. Hailey, George M. Yarbrough, Russell H. Fox, Buddy Newman, Preacher Weems, and Z. B. Whisnant to Ben F. Hilbun, February 10, 1956; Wilburn Hooker, Jim Morrow, and sixteen other members of the legislature to Hilbun, February 10, 1956; Charles L. Garrett to Hilbun, February 10, 1956; L. T. Newman to Hilbun, February 10, 1956; Joe Lee Smith to Hilbun, February 10, 1956; and Charles Wilkinson Jr. to Hilbun, February 11, 1956, in Hilbun Papers.

55. Campbell to Al and Doris Kershaw, March 9, 1956; and Francis Pickens Miller

to Campbell [no date], in AKP; Joseph H. Fichter to Campbell, February 5, 1956; and George A. Chauncey to Bess Moore and Willis Connell, February 8, 1956, in UF.

56. "Mississippi Abandons Its Religious Emphasis Week," *The Christian Century*, February 29, 1956, 260.

57. Joe Earl Elmore to the Committee of One Hundred in care of Campbell, no date, in AKP; Joe Earl Elmore to Williams, February 14, 1956, in UF.

58. Bess Moore and Willis Connell to Kershaw, February 23, 1956; and Campbell to Al and Doris Kershaw, March 9, 1956, in AKP; *JCL*, February 14, 1956; *DDT*, February 14, 1956.

59. Campbell to Al and Doris Kershaw, March 9, 1956, in AKP; *Miss.*, February 17, 1956; and Bess Moore and Willis Connell to Committee of One Hundred, February 15, 1956, in UF; *OE*, February 16, 1856.

60. *JCL*, February 15, 1956; Bess Moore and Willis Connell to Committee of One Hundred, February 15, 1956, in UF; *Miss.*, February 17, 1956.

61. Campbell to Kershaw, November 9 and 15, 1955; and Campbell to "Friends," Thanksgiving 1955, in AKP.

62. Campbell to "Friends," February 11, 1956; and Campbell to Al and Doris Kershaw, March 9, 1956, in AKP; Campbell, *Brother to a Dragonfly*, 257. Campbell had written a song, "Mississippi Magic," about a young Mississippian who escaped the state by riding the rails to Chicago; in the song the young man yearns for the return of "Mississippi magic"—" 'fore we was born we was all kin. / When we dead we'll be kinfolks again."

63. L. L. Love to Campbell, May 19, 1956; Williams to Campbell, May 22, 1956; and Campbell to Williams, January 21, 1957, in UF; "University of Mississippi Response to Charges," no date [1959], in IHLP.

64. Campbell, *Brother to a Dragonfly*, 127; Connelly, *Will Campbell*, 86.

65. Campbell, *Brother to a Dragonfly*, 126–27; interviews with Will Campbell, and with John E. Cameron, January 31, 1999.

66. Campbell, *Brother to a Dragonfly*, 125–26; W. M. Ellis to Board of Trustees of Institutions of Higher Learning, October 14, 1958, in George Neal McIlhenny Papers, SCMSU; "University of Mississippi Response to Charges," no date [1959], in IHLP; interviews with John E. Cameron, and with William M. Ellis, March 2, 1999. The chronology of events at the end of Campbell's tenure at the university remains a bit unclear. The Ping-Pong game and the punch bowl incident apparently happened close together, but the order is confusing. Campbell remembers the events in late May and June that contributed to his decision to resign, but documents indicate that he resigned in mid-April and the events most likely both occurred in June.

67. Williams to Harold Stoke, April 5, 1956, in UF

68. Edwin White to Williams, February 9, 1956, in UF.

69. Morton B. King to Alton Bryant, December 9, 1955; King to Ralph F. Fuchs, July 7, 1956; and King to Harris G. Warren, August 1, 1956, King Papers, in ASCUM; Harris G. Warren to Ralph F. Fuchs, March 10, 1956, in AAUPP; *DDT*, July 14, 15, and 16, 1957; *BN*, July 18, 1957. The 1957 exodus included Harris Warren, who left the university to take a job at Miami University, which had, he said, "an atmosphere more congenial to higher education. I'm tired of the attitude in this state toward higher education." *DDT*, July 14, 1957.

Chapter Eight

1. See James W. Silver, "Mississippi: The Closed Society," *Journal of Southern History* 30 (February 1964): 3–34, and his book of the same name. The reference to Silver as "the most hated man in Mississippi" was found in an undated clipping of Patrick J. Owens, "There Comes a Time: Dr. Silver of Ole Miss," in JWSP.

2. For background on Jim Silver's family, see James W. Silver, ed., "Diary of a One-Horse Entrepreneur: Fifty Years Ago in Up-State New York," *New York History* 33 (April 1952): 164–91, and "Making a Living in Rochester: The Diary of Henry D. Silver, 1906–1914," *Rochester History* 15 (October 1953): 1–28; James W. Silver, *Running Scared: Silver in Mississippi* (Jackson: University Press of Mississippi, 1984), especially 1–8; and various autobiographical writings by Silver in JWSP. For a description of Southern Pines, see Federal Writers' Project of the Federal Works Agency, Works Progress Administration, *North Carolina: A Guide to the Old North State* (Chapel Hill: University of North Carolina Press, 1939), 349–50.

3. Silver, *Running Scared*, 7–12.

4. Ibid., 12–15.

5. Bennett H. Wall to Silver, February 15, 1956; and [Elwood R. Maunder] to Silver, April 2, 1958, in JWSP. Silver recounts many stories about his and his family's activities in *Running Scared*.

6. Silver, *Running Scared*, 18–32, 56; *Miss.*, November 12 and 19, 1938, November 11 and 18, 1939, March 17, 1944, September 19, 1936, and September 24, 1938; *The Ole Miss* (student yearbook), 1942, 230; and *The Ole Miss*, 1943, 224; Bell I. Wiley to V. A. Coulter, May 20, 1940, and July 2, 1946, in LAF.

7. See James W. Silver, "Edmund Pendleton Gaines and Frontier Problems," *Journal of Southern History* 1 (August 1935): 320–44, "General Edmund Pendleton Gaines and the Protection of Southwestern Frontiers," *Louisiana Historical Quarterly* 20 (January 1937): 3–11, "A Counter-Proposal to the Indian Removal Policy of Andrew Jackson," *Journal of Mississippi History* 4 (October 1942): 207–15, and "C. P. J. Mooney of the Memphis *Commercial Appeal*, Crusader for Diversification," *Agricultural History* 17 (April 1943): 81–89.

8. On the relationship between biographer and subject, see Leon Edel, "Transference: The Biographer's Dilemma," *Biography* 7 (Fall 1984): 283–91; Leon Edel, *Writing Lives: Principia Biographica* (New York: Norton, 1994); and Eva Schepeler, "The Biographer's Transference: A Chapter in Psychobiographical Epistemology," *Biography* 13 (Spring 1990): 111–29.

9. James W. Silver, *Edmund Pendleton Gaines: Frontier General* (Baton Rouge: Louisiana State University Press, 1949), vii–xv.

10. *Miss.*, November 18, 1939, and February 24 and April 13, 1940; Silver to the editor, *JST*, May 12, 1955; Silver to Williams, January 26, 1954; Williams to Silver, January 10, 1949; and Silver to Sidna Brower, March 15, 1963, in JWSP; Silver, *Running Scared*, 34–35. The *Mississippian* regularly carried lists of speakers and articles on their appearances; see, for example, October 4, 1946, October 24, 1947, and January 13, 1949, issues.

11. In *Confederate Morale and Church Propaganda* (Tuscaloosa: Confederate Publishing, 1957), Silver admitted that the "author has no interest in religion as such" (8). As an adult,

Silver never attended church. Author's interviews with William Silver and Elizabeth Silver Little, June 1, 2000.

12. Silver, *Running Scared*, 20; James W. Silver, "A Personalized History [1978]," in JWSP. Silver's account could not be entirely accurate. He claimed that the chairman of the trustees came to his defense because he knew of Mrs. Silver's work tutoring a star football player named John Whittington. The events recounted by Silver most likely occurred in 1939, the year after the Wages and Hours Act was passed, and Whittington was a football running back from 1937 to 1939. The *Clarksdale Register and Daily News* for 1939 is unavailable to offer corroboration because of a fire in 1940. Martin V. B. Miller of Meridian served on the board of trustees only from May 1944 to May 1956 and more likely came to Silver's defense in 1948 when the professor was under attack by state legislators. Silver, therefore, garbled the story or conflated different stories, but the general outlines (his defense of the minimum wage and a critical local response) seem credible. See the 1938 and 1939 editions of the student annual, *The Ole Miss*, pages 129 and 145 respectively; and *Bulletin of the University of Mississippi*, April 1, 1944, 7 and 24–25.

13. Mrs. J. W. McKellar to Silver, March 27 and April 10, 1941, in JWSP; *Clarksdale Register and Daily News*, April 23, 24, and 25, 1941. An earlier appearance did not prompt any protest. See *Greenwood Commonwealth*, March 26, 27, 29, and 31, and April 1, 1941.

14. J. W. Silver, notes for talk on World War II, no date; and Luther A. Smith to A. B. Butts, November 4, 1941, in JWSP. When Chancellor A. B. Butts told him about Smith's objections, Silver admitted that he may have failed to present a balanced discussion of interventionist and isolationist views, but he denied any sympathy for Hitler. In fact, Silver supported the British. The chancellor forwarded Silver's response to Smith and added his personal assurance that Silver was "a safe and sound member of the History Department." Silver was not one of Butts's favorite professors, but the chancellor took no retribution because of Smith's complaint. Silver to Butts, November 11, 1941; and Butts to Luther A. Smith, November 13, 1941, in JWSP. For disagreements between Silver and Butts, see Silver, *Running Scared*, 33–34.

15. *MCA*, January 6 (Silver to the editor), 12 (Boyce Henderson to the editor), 14, 20 (J. L. McKinstry to the editor), and 21 (Silver to the editor), 1943; J. D. Roberts to Silver, January 17, 1943; and Tom L. Gibson to Silver, January 23, 1943, in JWSP.

16. [Unsigned] to Silver, February 12, 1944, in JWSP; *Miss.*, February 11 and 12, 1944.

17. William C. Berman, *The Politics of Civil Rights in the Truman Administration* (Columbus: Ohio State University Press, 1970), 79–134; Numan V. Bartley, *The New South, 1945–1980* (Baton Rouge: Louisiana State University Press, 1995), 74–104.

18. *JCL*, February 4 and 16, 1948.

19. *JCL*, February 7, 1948; James W. Silver, "A Professor Speakes [*sic*] Back" [April 20, 1948], in JWSP. On the legislative activity, see Senate Concurrent Resolution no. 18, Authorizing Joint Committee to Visit Institutions of Higher Learning, *Journal of the Senate of the State of Mississippi*, Extraordinary Session, January 6–April 14, 1948, 235, 250, and 255–56; House Concurrent Resolution no. 49, Appoint Recess Committee to Study Institutions of Higher Learning, *Journal of the Senate of the State of Mississippi*, Extraordinary Session, January 6–April 14, 1948, 507.

20. Silver, "A Professor Speakes [*sic*] Back." Edward A. Khayat, who had known Silver when Khayat served as an instructor with the Army Specialized Training Program at the university during the war, invited the professor to speak. See *Miss.*, September 24, 1943.

21. Silver, "A Professor Speakes [*sic*] Back."

22. Ibid. See Martha H. Swain, *Pat Harrison: The New Deal Years* (Jackson: University Press of Mississippi, 1978), 210–18.

23. Silver to the editor, *Biloxi Daily Herald*, April 22, 1948; Williams to W. Ed Wiggins, April 23, 1948; and Williams to L. A. Watts, April 26, 1948, in JWSP.

24. *DDT*, April 25, 1948; Toni [?] to Silver, June 26, 1948; Ben [?] to Silver, July 12, 1948; May Spencer Ringold to Silver, September 12, 1948; and Silver to Martin V. B. Miller, April 9, 1948, in JWSP. Carter told Silver that he was Professor X. See Carter to Silver, April 20, 1948, in JWSP. Carter must have received an advance copy of Silver's typed speech.

25. Martin V. B. Miller to Williams, April 28, 1948, in UF; Martin V. B. Miller to Silver, August 4, 1948; Mrs. Martin Miller to Silver, August 13, 1948; and Silver to Mr. and Mrs. Martin V. B. Miller, November 22, 1948, in JWSP; Silver, *Running Scared*, 20. See note 12 above.

26. Walter Sillers to Silver, January 15 and 26, 1949; Silver to Sillers, January 28, 1949; and Silver to Sillers, January 28, 1949, in JWSP. Sillers's letter of January 26 quotes Silver's letter of January 17, which is not found in the Silver Papers.

27. See the references in note 26, above.

28. Chapter 281, Laws of 1946 (House Bill no. 372), State of Mississippi; Chapter 456, Laws of 1950 (Senate Bill no. 53), State of Mississippi.

29. Hugh H. Clegg, "Someone Jumped the Gun," unpublished manuscript, no date, copy in ASCUM.

30. *DDT*, February 5, 1950. For a discussion of the controversy of 1950, see chapter 9.

31. Gene [?] to Dr. Stalin, February 13, 1950, in JWSP. Correspondence in the James Wesley Silver papers discussed Silver's essays from Britain and their circulation through forty American newspapers. The "Report from Britain," February 12, 1950, is reprinted in *Running Scared*, 144–46.

32. Silver, "Report from Britain."

33. *OE*, March 9, 1950.

34. Silver, "The Next Depression," speech at Young Men's Business Club, Moss Point, Mississippi, June 13, 1949; Silver to Walter Sillers, January 28, 1949; Silver to Ellis T. Woolfolk, December 8, 1950; Silver to Harold G. Brown, July 19 and 25, 1950; Silver to David Potter, July 16, 1951; Silver to Dean of the Graduate School of Arts and Sciences, Harvard University, July 16, 1951; Silver to Dean of Special Students, Harvard University, July 23, 1951; Silver to V. A. Coulter, August 11, 1951; and Silver to Dorothy Soderlund, January 7, 1952, all in JWSP.

35. Silver, *Running Scared*, 22, 25, 48–64, passim.

36. Ibid., 21–22; Silver, "A Personalized History [1978]"; and [unsigned] to Silver, February 12, 1944, in JWSP; *Miss.*, February 12, 1944, and June 23 and 30, 1949. On the brief controversy over the 1937 YMCA program, see *Miss.*, October 30, and November 6, 12, and 25, 1937.

37. Silver to Walter Sillers, January 28, 1949, in JWSP; *Miss.*, June 23, 1949.

38. Silver to Edward A. Weeks Jr., April 21, 1952; Silver to Nancy Balfour, September 4, 1952; and untitled speech on William Faulkner, [1972?], in JWSP; A Correspondent Recently in Mississippi [Silver], "Legacies of the Civil War," *The Economist*, December 8, 1951, 1401–2. Silver's essays in *The Economist* were unsigned except for something like "A Correspondent Recently in Mississippi"; his papers contain a list of the articles.

39. Silver to the editor of *The Boston Post Magazine*, April 29, 1952; and Silver to James A. Dombrowski, August 10, 1949, in JWSP; [Silver], "Legacies of the Civil War," 1401.

40. Silver, untitled speech on William Faulkner, [1972?], in JWSP; Silver, *Running Scared*, 36–44, 59–61. Faulkner's ideas on race were, in Noel Polk's phrase, "a hellishly complex topic," but Polk agrees that Faulkner was in many ways a southern moderate. See Noel Polk, "Man in the Middle: Faulkner and the Southern White Moderate," in *Faulkner and Race*, ed. Doreen Fowler and Ann J. Abadie (Jackson: University Press of Mississippi, 1987), 130–51. The next year, after a series of meetings in Faulkner's home with a few like-minded Mississippians, they satirized the Citizens' Council in the only issue of the anonymously published *Southern Reposure*.

41. Silver, *Running Scared*, 48–50.

42. Ibid.

43. Silver, notes for commencement speech, Oxford Training School, May 28, 1954; and Silver, ed., "Mississippi versus the United States: Documents in the Meredith Case," in JWSP; Silver, *Running Scared*, 58.

44. John Dittmer, *Local People: The Struggle for Civil Rights in Mississippi* (Urbana: University of Illinois Press, 1994), 38–40; Silver, "A Personalized History"; Charles C. Bolton, *The Hardest Deal of All: The Battle over School Integration in Mississippi, 1870–1980* (Jackson: University Press of Mississippi, 2005), 61–66.

45. Neil R. McMillen, *The Citizens' Council: Organized Resistance to the Second Reconstruction, 1954–64* (Urbana: University of Illinois Press, 1971), 18–20; Silver, "A Personalized History."

46. Silver, *Confederate Morale and Church Propaganda*, 8. See also Silver to John E. Pomfret, September 11, 1952; and Silver to Elbridge Sibley, October 8, 1953, in JWSP.

47. Silver to Williams, May 7, 1955, in UF; Silver to Committee on Faculty Research, December 9, 1946, in JWSP; *Tupelo Daily Journal*, December 12, 1954; William P. Murphy to the editor, *JCL*, June 30, 1954. Jack Reed suggested Silver as a speaker for the Kiwanis Club. See W. J. Cunningham to Silver, October 22, 1954, in JWSP.

48. *DDT*, April 22, 1955; *JST*, Silver to the editor, May 12, 1955, and editorial May 14, 1955; *Miss.*, March 18, 1955; *DDT*, April 22, 1955; Silver to Joe L. Gillespie, March 13, 1955; and Norman Bradley to Silver, May 13, 1955, in JWSP; Lucie Robertson Bridgforth, "'Bomb the Ban': A Study of the Legal Controversy Surrounding Off-Campus Speakers at Mississippi Institutions of Higher Learning" (M.A. thesis, University of Mississippi, 1979), 27–30. LeRoy P. Percy also supported the position Silver took before Percy's Greenville Rotary Club. See Percy to Silver, April 21, 1955, in JWSP.

49. [J. W. Silver], "Little White School-House?" *The Economist*, January 1, 1955, 30–31.

50. [J. W. Silver], "South of the Twentieth Century," *The Economist*, March 24, 1956, 647–48.

51. Silver to E. R. Jobe, October 29, 1956, in UF. In Jackson, Silver spoke only from notes. In his letter to Jobe, Silver set down in narrative form the points that he had retained only in outline form. The quotations from the speech, therefore, come actually from the version relayed to Jobe in the later letter.

52. Edgar S. Anderson to Coleman, October 16, 1956, in Governor J. P. Coleman Papers, in MDAH; *JCL*, October 26, 1956; *JDN*, November 1 and 3, 1956.

53. E. R. Jobe to Silver, October 27, 1956, in JWSP; Silver to E. R. Jobe, October 29, 1956, in UF.

54. William F. Winter to Silver, November 7, 1956; J. P. Coleman to Silver, November 5, 1956; Coleman to E. R. Jobe, November 5, 1956; Silver to Coleman, October 24, 1952; and Coleman to Silver, January 19, 1955, and December 10, 1956, in JWSP. See also Silver, *Running Scared*, 63–64, for Silver on Governor Coleman. Silver had provided historical advice on interposition and on Mississippi's Constitution of 1890. For other support of Silver, see Gwen Glade Hopper to Silver, October 30, 1956; Arch Dalrymple III to Silver, November 2, 1956; and Howard M—[illegible] to Silver [fall 1956?], in JWSP.

55. J. O. Emmerich to Silver, November 10, 1956; and Arch Dalrymple to Silver, March 31 [1957?], in JWSP.

56. Silver to James Hand Jr., December 2, 1956, in JWSP.

57. *MCA*, January 31, 1959; L. L. Martin to J. P. Coleman, February 21, 1959; and Williams to Coleman, February 28, 1959, in UF; Silver to A. B. Lewis, April 22, 1959, in JWSP. Silver specifically pointed to James W. Garner's 1901 study of Mississippi during Reconstruction and John K. Bettersworth's work in the 1940s on the Confederacy in the state.

58. William T. Doherty to Williams, February 12, 1960, in LAF; Joseph J. Mathews to Silver, August 9, 1958, and May 6, 1959, in JWSP. Doherty's letter provides a detailed chronology.

59. Marcia M. Mathews, "The Difference between Black and White," *Saturday Evening Post*, January 16, 1960, 13–15 and 56–57; Joseph J. Mathews to Silver, May 6, 1959, in JWSP.

60. William T. Doherty to Williams, February 12, 1960, in LAF; Alton Bryant to Mrs. Harry Ogden, February 26, 1960, in JWSP; Joseph J. Mathews to David M. Potter, January 30, 1960, quoted in Michael Kammen, *In the Past Lane: Historical Perspectives on American Culture* (New York: Oxford University Press, 1997), 37.

61. William T. Doherty to Williams, February 12, 1960, in LAF; Minutes, Department of History Meetings, January 13 and 14, 1960; and Silver to Jimmie Robertson, December 11, 1968, in JWSP.

62. Affidavit of James W. Silver, *Donald R. Stacy, et al. v. John D. Williams*, May 1969; Elwood R. Maunder to Silver, April 9, 1959; Silver to Betty [?], May 8, 1959; and Silver to Paul Pittman, January 1, 1961, in JWSP. Silver did not include the episode in *Running Scared*.

Chapter Nine

1. *JCL*, January 28, 1950. On the red scare's relationship to the civil rights movement and southern white racial attitudes, see George Lewis, *The White South and the Red Menace: Segregationists, Anticommunism, and Massive Resistance, 1945–1965* (Gainesville: University

Press of Florida, 2004); and Jeff Woods, *Black Struggle, Red Scare: Segregation and Anti-Communism in the South, 1948–1968* (Baton Rouge: Louisiana State University Press, 2004).

2. John Egerton, *Speak Now against the Day: The Generation before the Civil Rights Movement in the South* (New York: Knopf, 1994), 561; Wilson Record, *The Negro in the Communist Party* (Chapel Hill: University of North Carolina Press, 1951).

3. *Miss.*, February 10 and March 17, 1950; *DDT*, February 5, 19, and 20, and March 19, 1950; *JCL*, February 7, 1950; *JDN*, February 5 and 7, 1950. McKenzie also named Dean Forrest Murphy of the School of Education and English professor A. Wigfall Green. William Winter, a member of the legislature in 1950, furnished a copy of the early edition of the *Jackson Daily News* for February 2, 1950, that contained the names of three professors. The "final home" edition on microfilm did not contain the names. No other newspaper in the state apparently carried the list.

4. *Miss.*, February 10, 1950; *JDN*, February 5 and 7, 1950; *DDT*, February 19 and 20, 1950.

5. *OE*, February 9, 1950; *JDN*, February 8 and 9, 1950; *DDT*, February 10 and March 21 and 31, 1950; *JCL*, February 7 and 23, 1950; *Miss.*, July 6, 1950.

6. *JCL*, June 10, 11, and 12, 1956.

7. Robert B. Patterson to Hugh H. Clegg, June 29, 1955, in UF. Clegg sent copies of the exchange with Patterson to Walter Sillers. See WSPS.

8. On the hiring of Clegg, see Irene C. Smith to A. J. Lawrence, May 7, 1952, in JDWP; Clegg to Williams, January 22, 1954, in UF; *OE*, January 21, 1954; *Miss.*, February 5, 1954. On Clegg's background, see Clegg to Gene Holcomb, March 25, 1940, in Subject File, MDAH; Clegg, University of Mississippi Personal Data Sheet, January 12, 1954, in GMSP; *Ole Miss Alumni Review*, April 1954, 8. On Clegg's earlier ties to the university, see *MCA*, June 26, 1946; and *Miss.*, June 21, 1946, and April 20, 1951. On the variety of Clegg's activities, see Clegg to Williams, January 7, 1955; Clegg to Rep. John Bell Williams, December 10, 1955; Clegg to Walter Sillers, June 24, 1959; Clegg to Louis B. Nichols, July 18, 1956; and Patriotic American Youth letterhead, November 27, 1962, in UF; Minutes, University of Mississippi AAUP Chapter, November 29, 1960, in RBP; interview with Alton Bryant, January 16, 1964, in AAUPP; *DDT*, February 9, 1956.

9. Clegg to Patterson, July 26, 1955, in UF.

10. M. Mabry to Patterson, September 2, 1956, in UF.

11. *Miss.*, February 17, 1950; Will M. Whittington to W. C. Trotter, October 10, 1946; and Trotter to George McLean, November 26, 1946, in JDWP; *Ole Miss Alumni Review*, July 1947, 21; January 1950, 4; and June 1956, 6; *OE*, February 9, 1950, and March 8 and August 30, 1956; W. C. Wells to J. D. Williams, December 31, 1946; Williams to C. M. Smith, October 22, 1955; Williams to Trotter, September 10, 1956; Trotter to Williams, October 18 and 21, 1956; Williams to Trotter, October 31, 1956; Williams to Pete Kyle McCarter, November 15, 1956; McCarter to Williams, August 11, 1959; and Williams to McCarter, August 15, 1959, in UF; brochure for "Statewide Scholarship Essay Contest for Mississippi High School Students" [1958], in John Bell Williams Papers, MDAH; Robert J. Farley to Morton B. King, August 8, 1957, in Morton B. King Papers, ASCUM.

12. Testimony of W. C. Trotter, February 12, 1957, in GLICP.

13. Testimony of Joseph Jeffreys, February 12, 1957, in GLICP.

14. Testimony of George Milton Case, February 12, 1957; untitled document, August 23, 1956; and Charter of Incorporation of Conservative Club, University of Mississippi, February 23, 1956, in GLICP; *Miss.*, April 27, and May 4 and 11, 1956. The untitled document undoubtedly was the list of books prepared by Case. The books included Otto Klineberg's *Negro Intelligence and Selective Migration*, Ashley Montagu's *Man's Most Dangerous Myth: The Fallacy of Race*, *The Negro in American Life and Thought* by Rayford W. Logan, and Claude Levi-Strauss's *Race and History*. The five incorporators included two sons of Judge Tom Brady, a son of state representative E. Wilburn Hooker of Holmes County, and Bradford Dye Jr. (a future Democratic lieutenant governor).

15. Testimony of R. L. Thorn and Malcolm Mabry, February, 19, 1957, in GLICP.

16. Hooker to Sillers, May 28, 1959, in WSP; Minutes, Joint Meeting of the Board of Directors of the Alumni Association and the University Development Committee, October 9, 1953, in Alumni Association Files; author's interview with Edwin Wilburn Hooker Jr., May 14, 1998. Wilburn Hooker Sr. served as chairman of the committee planning a new airport for the university.

17. See the references in note 16, above.

18. Testimonies of Hillery Edwin White and Edwin Hooker Sr., October 20, 1959, in GLICP.

19. Testimony of Hooker, October 20, 1959, and White to Board of Trustees, October 30, 1958, in GLICP; Minutes, IHL Board, September 18, 1958, in Records of the IHL Board, Jackson, Miss.; Hooker to R. D. Morrow, November 18, 1958, in JWSP.

20. Author's interview with William M. Ellis, March 2, 1999.

21. William M. Ellis to Board of Trustees, October 24, 1958, in GLICP; author's interview with William M. Ellis.

22. Minutes of the Faculty, University of Mississippi, July 30, 1959, in UF; *Miss.*, October 23, 1953; *OE*, January 17, 1958; J. D. Williams to Ellis Finger, July 21, 1959, in UF. Hugh H. Clegg, "Someone Jumped the Gun" (unpublished manuscript in author's possession) is the most convenient summary of the allegations, but similar materials exist in the University Files and in the IHL Papers. The investigation did not affect the sciences, the schools of pharmacy and engineering, the fine arts, or athletics.

23. Hugh Clegg to Walter Sillers, June 24, 1959, in UF. Wilburn Hooker had also appealed to Sillers for support to save the university from "foreign" ideas. See Hooker to Sillers, May 28, 1959, in WSP; and Clegg, "Someone Jumped the Gun."

24. For examples of correspondence, see James W. Silver to A. B. Lewis, March 9 and April 22, 1959, in JWSP; L. L. Love to W. Alton Bryant, April 23, 1959; and Harley F. Garrett to W. Alton Bryant, April 23, 1959, in UF; and many undated memoranda in the IHLP.

25. "Reply to Allegations concerning Certain Members of the Faculty and Staff of the University of Mississippi, 1ˢᵗ Writing," March 17, 1959, in UF.

26. For similar points see [James W. Silver], "Little White School-House?" *The Economist*, January 1, 1955, 30–31; and Alton Bryant's presentation to the faculty, in Minutes of the Faculty, July 30, 1959.

27. "Reply to Allegations concerning Certain Members of the Faculty and Staff of the University of Mississippi," no date, in UF. Hereinafter referred to as "Reply to Allegations."

28. "Reply to Allegations"; *OE*, May 29, 1958, and July 30, 1959; Quinter M. Lyon, *The Great Religions* (New York: Odyssey Press, 1957). Attacks on Weigle also included that he had been involved with the creation of the Revised Standard Version of the Bible.

29. "Reply to Allegations."

30. Ibid.; Thomas S. Hines to James W. Silver, July 16, 1959, in JWSP. Hines, the son of an Ole Miss administrator, earned undergraduate and master's degrees in history at the university.

31. "Reply to Allegations." Hooker and White also criticized William P. Murphy of the law school, and his case will be discussed in chapter 10.

32. Minutes, IHL Board, June 11, 1959; W. E. Howard Jr. to Williams, June 9, 1959, in UF; Hooker to Mayes McGehee, June 5, 1959; and E. R. Jobe to White, July 3, 1959, in GLICP; *MEJ*, July 9, 1959; *JDN*, July 10, 1959; *JCL*, July 10, 1959; *JST*, July 12, 1959; Minutes of the Faculty, July 30, 1959. The accusations against Ole Miss did not affect the runoff in the Democratic primary for governor that August. See *JST*, August 16, 1959; *JCL*, August 11, 1959; and Earl Black, *Southern Governors and Civil Rights: Racial Segregation as a Campaign Issue in the Second Reconstruction* (Cambridge: Harvard University Press, 1976), 167, 170–71.

33. *JCL*, July 14, 1959; interviews with E. Wilburn Hooker Jr. and with William Spell, May 15, 1998. In working with the press, Hooker and White received advice and assistance from Spell, a Jackson lawyer, former journalist, and lobbyist.

34. Minutes of the Faculty, July 30, 1959; M. A. Pigford Jr. to E. R. Jobe, August 19, 1959, in IHLP; *JST*, July 15 and August 2 and 17, 1959; *MCA*, July 24 and August 17, 1959; *DDT*, July 20, 1959; *NOTP*, August 2, 1959; R. D. Wilcox to Chester H. Curtis, July 24, 1959; Thomas J. Tubb to Chester H. Curtis, July 27, 1959; Edward A. DeMiller Jr. to Chester H. Curtis, July 28, 1959; Jack Reed to J. D. Williams, July 11, 1959; Ellis Finger to J. D. Williams, July 13, 1959; and W. T. McKinney to Chester H. Curtis, July 23, 1959, all in UF; Alton Bryant to James W. Silver, July 25, 1959, in JWSP; *Tupelo Daily Journal*, July 17, 1959; *DDT*, July 14, 1959; *Madison County Herald*, August 1, 1959; *Lexington Advertiser*, July 23, 1959; *JCL*, July 15, 20, and 28 and August 10, 1959.

35. Minutes, IHL Board, August 27, 1959; *JST* and *MCA*, August 28, 1959.

36. *JDN*, October 27, 1959; Williams to Pete Kyle McCarter, August 15, 1959, in UF; Hooker to H. B. Mayes McGehee, June 5, 1959; McGehee to Hooker, July 3, 1959; White and Hooker to E. R. Jobe, September 1, 1959; H. B. Mayes McGehee to Hooker, September 25, 1959; and testimonies of White and Hooker, October 20, 1959, in GLICP; *JST*, December 4, 1959.

37. E. R. Jobe to White and Hooker, November 23, 1959, in GLICP; Williams to the Board of Trustees, November 5, 1959, in *Annual Report of the Chancellor*, 1958–59.

38. *MCA*, April 1, 1960; *DDT*, April 3, 1960. The offending piece must have appeared later in March, but extant issues of the paper for the 1959–60 school year stop at March 10, 1960.

39. See Richard Kirkendall, "Tom C. Clark," in *The Justices of the United States Supreme Court, 1789–1969: Their Lives and Major Opinions*, vol. 4, ed. Leon Friedman and Fred L. Israel, 2665–77 (New York: R. R. Bowker, 1969); Richard Kluger, *Simple Justice* (New York: Knopf, 1975); and Michael R. Gardner, *Harry Truman and Civil Rights: Moral Courage and Political Risks* (Carbondale: Southern Illinois University Press, 2002).

40. *DDT*, February 10 and 13, 1961; *OE*, February 16, 1961; *JST* and *MCA*, February 13, 1961; Walter Sillers to Eugene Sykes, February 17, 1961; and Sillers to Sam H. Long, February 15, 1961, in WSP.

41. *MCA*, February 15, 1961; *JCL*, February 14 and 15, 1961; *JST*, February 15 and 19, 1961.

42. Department of Christian Social Relations, Protestant Episcopal Church, "Sowing Dissension in the Churches," copy in Joseph W. Wroten Papers, private collection, Aberdeen, Miss.; *JCL*, January 17, 1961; Yasuhiro Katagiri, *The Mississippi State Sovereignty Commission: Civil Rights and States' Rights* (Jackson: University Press of Mississippi, 2001), 89; *JST*, February 17, 1961.

43. *JCL* and *JST*, January 17, 1961; Katagiri, *Sovereignty Commission*, 87–94; press releases and "Report of Mrs. Harry Scrivner," no date [March 1961], in MSSCP.

44. Barnett to J. D. Williams, January 24, 1961; Williams to Barnett, January 27, 1961, in UF; "Report of Mrs. Harry Scrivner"; *MCA*, February 13, 1961; James W. Silver to Sidna Brower, March 15, 1962, in JWSP; *JST*, March 4, 1961.

45. *JST*, March 4, 1961; Lowman to the editor, *JST*, March 10, 1961. See also Silver's recollection a year later in Silver to Sidna Brower, March 15, 1962, in JWSP.

46. Mrs. Orley Hood to the editor, *JST*, March 9, 1961; Lowman to the editor, *JST*, March 10, 1961; Silver to the editor, *JST*, March 15, 16, and 20, 1960. Naomi Scrivner, a Sovereignty Commission employee, filed a report on Lowman's visit that included a scathing commentary on Silver. See "Report of Mrs. Harry Scrivner" [March 1961].

47. On Putnam, see his *Race and Reason: A Yankee View* (Washington: Public Affairs Press, 1961), especially 1–5. See also *Life*, September 22, 1958; *NYT*, March 16, 1998; Carleton Putnam to editor, *MCA*, September 28, 1958. On his visit to Mississippi, see I. A. Newby, *Challenge to the Court: Social Scientists and the Defense of Segregation, 1954–1966* (Baton Rouge: Louisiana State University Press, rev. ed. 1969), 148–66; Neil R. McMillen, *The Citizens' Council: Organized Resistance to the Second Reconstruction, 1954–64* (Urbana: University of Illinois Press, 1971), 165–68; Corey T. Lesseig, "Roast Beef and Racial Integrity: Mississippi's 'Race and Reason Day,' October 26, 1961," *Journal of Mississippi History* 56 (February 1994): 1–16.

48. Putnam, *Race and Reason*, 82, 73, 114, 17, 15, and 7. The letter to Eisenhower was reprinted on pages 5–9, the letter to the attorney general on pages 21–29. References to *Race and Reason* include only quotations because Putnam repeats himself many times in the book.

49. *JCL*, April 20, May 14, August 9 and 10, September 28, and October 22, 1961; *The Citizens' Council*, April–May, 1961, 1.

50. *JCL*, October 22 and 26, 1961; *DDT* and *MS*, October 27, 1961; *JDN*, October 26, 1961. Leaders of the effort included former governor Hugh L. White, lawyers Thomas H. Watkins and Robert C. Cannada, Judge M. M. McGowan, William J. Simmons, editor Elmore D. Greaves, Dr. M. Ney Williams, Rep. John C. McLaurin, and business leaders George W. Goodwin Sr., Boyd Campbell, Richard D. Morphew, Stuart Irby Jr., Richard D. and Sam P. McRae, Aleck Primos, R. Baxter Wilson, and Henry and Thomas Hederman of the *JCL*. See *JCL*, October 22, 1961; and *The Citizen*, November 1961, 42–45.

51. Louis W. Hollis, "Here's How We Did It!" *The Citizen*, November 1961, 39–41; Dr. W. D. McCain, "Who Is Carleton Putnam?" *The Citizen*, November 1961, 9–11.

52. *JCL*, October 28 and 29, 1961; "The Turning Point," *The Citizen*, November 1961, 2.

53. *JCL*, December 13, 17, and 24, 1961; *NYT*, June 13, October 14, and November 3, 1961. See also, for example, "Misfit in Mufti," *Time*, December 25, 1961, 11–12; "Texas: General Walker Speaks," *Newsweek*, December 25, 1961, 19–20; John J. Lindsay, "The Case of Gen. Walker," *Nation*, October 14, 1961, 245–48; "The Walker Affair," *New Republic*, November 20, 1961, 3–4; "Citizen Edwin A. Walker: An Interview with Medford Evans," *National Review*, December 16, 1961, 411–12; "General Walker Tells Why He Is Resigning," *U.S. News and World Report*, November 13, 1961, 99–100. The group had some of the same members as the Putnam committee, but it also drew from across the state.

54. *JCL*, June 16, October 20, and December 13, 17, 20, 23, 24, 29, and 30, 1961, and December 19 and 20, 1962; *MS*, December 28, 1961; *JDN*, December 29, 1961. Also at the airport were four students from Jackson's Murrah High School who protested Walker's visit.

55. For Walker's speech, see Edwin A. Walker, "There Is No Substitute for Victory!" *The Citizen*, January 1962, 8–25. See also *JCL*, December 30, 1961.

56. Richard D. Morphew, "It's Testing Time for 'Conservatives,'" and "The Pro-Communist Record of Robert C. Weaver," *The Citizen*, January 1962, 5–6 and 7.

57. *Miss.*, November 1, 1961, and January 9, 1962. It became a daily in the fall of 1961.

58. *Miss.*, January 10 and 18, 1962. For more on Hazel Brannon Smith, see Mark Newman, "Hazel Brannon Smith and Holmes County, Mississippi, 1936–1964: The Making of a Pulitzer Prize Winner," *Journal of Mississippi History* 54 (1992): 59–87, and Matthew J. Bosissio, "Hazel Brannon Smith: Pursuing Truth at Her Peril," *American Journalism* 18 (2001): 69–83. Katagiri fails to mention the controversy involving Smith in *Sovereignty Commission*.

59. *JCL*, January 23, 24, and 25, 1962; *MS* and *MCA*, January 25, 1962; *Miss.*, January 24 and 25, and February 9, 1962; *DDT*, January 24, 1962. Albin Krebs also wrote in support of Robertson. See *Miss.*, February 9 and March 6, 1962.

60. *Miss.*, February 9 and 13, 1962; *RU*, no date [February 12, 1962].

61. *Miss.*, February 13, 14, 15, 21, 27, and 28, March 2 and 6, and May 9, 1962.

62. *RU*, no date [February 16 and 27 and March 1, 1962]; Tom Brightman to the editor, *Miss.*, February 16 and 23; John F. Runte to the editor, *Miss.*, February 27 and May 30, 1962; *JCL*, February 17, 1962; *MS*, February 28, 1962.

63. *Miss.*, February 15, 16, and 21, 1962.

64. For the UPI article, see *JCL* and *MS*, August 3, 1962. See also Louis E. Lomax, "The Kennedys Move In on Dixie," *Harper's*, May 1962, 27–33.

65. *JCL*, January 4, March 17, and May 20, 1962. The newspaper quotes Barnett as saying "sublimely." Barnett was well known for his malaprops, so he may have meant to say "supinely."

66. *Miss.*, March 7, 1962; *JCL*, March 19 and 20, May 13 and 18, and July 25, 1962; *JDN*, July 31, 1962; *MS*, August 22, 1962.

67. *JCL*, January 19 and March 21, 1962; Julian Williams, "Improper Conduct: WLBT Programming and Operations, 1955–1965" (M.A. thesis, University of Florida, 1987), 78–81.

68. Steven D. Classen, *Watching Jim Crow: The Struggles over Mississippi TV, 1955–1969* (Durham, N.C.: Duke University Press, 2004), 1–2 and 34–36; Charles Clift III, "The WLBT-

TV Case, 1964–1969: An Historical Analysis," (Ph.D. diss., Indiana University, 1976), 70–75; Julian Williams, "Improper Conduct," 85–87. See also Kay Mills, *Changing Channels: The Civil Rights Case That Transformed Television* (Jackson: University Press of Mississippi, 2004); Edwin Ernest Meek, "WLBT's Interim Operation: A Historical and Analytical Study" (Ph.D. diss., University of Southern Mississippi, 1974); Elaine Elizabeth Jones, "WLBT-TV, 1964–1979: A Case History of Progress" (M.A. thesis, Iowa State University, 1984).

69. Classen, *Watching Jim Crow*, 36–43; Clift, "The WLBT-TV Case," 44, 128; Julian Williams, "Improper Conduct," 90. See also *Federal Communications Commission Reports*, 1144. Beard later admitted using the "Sorry, Cable Trouble" announcement. See Mills, *Changing Channels*, 127.

70. *MS*, June 28, 1962; *JCL*, June 28 and July 1, 1962.

Chapter Ten

1. W. J. Simmons to Albert Jones, August 17, 1960, in MSSCP.

2. Complaint, *Billy Clyde Barton v. Ross R. Barnett et al.*, in A. E. Cox Papers, SCMSU; *Miss.*, April 21, 22, and 24, 1998; author's interview with James L.(Jimmie) Robertson, October 4, 1998.

3. See the references in note 2, above.

4. Complaint in *Barton v. Barnett*.

5. *Miss.*, October 20 and 27 and November 3 and 10, 1960.

6. Complaint in *Barton v. Barnett*; Sara McCorkle, monthly report, Women's Division and Youth Activities, Citizens' Council, December 1960 (exhibit B in *Barton v. Barnett* file, in Cox Papers, SCMSU); *JST*, March 12, 1961.

7. Malcolm Dale to Ross Barnett, December 6, 1960; Albert Jones to Dale, December 9, 1960; and Dale to Jones, December 10, 1960, in MSSCP.

8. Billy Barton to Ross Barnett, January 9, 1960, in complaint in *Barton v. Barnett*.

9. Barnett to Barton, January 18, 1961, in complaint in *Barton v. Barnett*.

10. *MCA*, *JCL*, and *JST*, March 11, 1961; *DDT*, March 12, 1961.

11. *JCL*, March 11 and 15, 1961; *MCA*, March 11, 1961.

12. *JST*, March 12, 14, 15, and 17, 1961; *DDT*, March 13, 1961; *Jackson Northside Reporter*, March 16, 1961; *DDT*, March 14, 1962; *JCL*, March 12, 1961.

13. *JCL*, *DDT*, and *Miss.*, March 16, 1961; *JST*, June 16, 1961.

14. *JST* and *DDT*, March 15, 1961.

15. *JST*, March 15 and 16, 1961.

16. *JST*, March 16, 1961.

17. *JCL*, March 16, 1961; *JDN*, March 17, 1961.

18. *DDT*, March 19 and 20, 1961; *JST*, March 19 and April 4, 1961.

19. *JCL*, March 17, 1961.

20. *DDT*, April 13 and 19, 1961; *MCA*, April 19, 1961; *Miss.*, April 27, 1961.

21. *DDT*, April 19, 1961; author's interview with Jimmie Robertson.

22. *JCL*, May 14, June 30, and July 3, 1962; *DDT*, May 24 and July 3, 1962; *NOTP*, July 3,

1962; *MS*, *MCA*, and *Chattanooga Times*, December 16, 1962; *Barton v. Barnett et al.*, 226 F. Supp. 375 (1964). On Judge McGowan, see *JCL*, February 2, 1956; *Miss.*, October 19, 1956; *SSN*, January 1959; and M. M. McGowan to William Colmer, April 24, 1956, in William Colmer Papers, MLUSM.

23. On Murphy, see Reese Cleghorn, "Tiger at Ole Miss," *Progressive*, June 1962, 21–24; and Charles W. Eagles, " 'Thought Control' in Mississippi: The Case of William P. Murphy," *Journal of Mississippi History* 66 (Summer 2004): 151–98.

24. William Patrick Murphy, Personal Data Sheet, University of Mississippi, August 19, 1953, in IHLP; author's interview with William P. Murphy, June 21, 1991; undated clipping from *Neshoba Democrat* of Philadelphia, Miss., in WPMP.

25. Murphy to the editor, *JCL*, June 30, 1954.

26. Simmons to the editor, *JCL*, July 5, 1954; *Summit Sun*, July 15, 1954. Some of Murphy's students came to his defense. See Hunter D. Gholson to Mary D. Cain, July 19, 1954; and Ralph White to Mary D. Cain, July 21, 1954, in WPMP. Murphy's critics included Tom L. Gibson, who had also attacked Jim Silver. See Gibson to Murphy, July 20, 1954, in WPMP.

27. Author's interview with William P. Murphy.

28. See review of *Constitutional Law, Cases and Materials*, by Paul G. Kauper, *MLJ* 26 (March 1955): 204–5; review of *American Constitutional Law*, by Bernard Schwartz, *MLJ* 27 (May 1956): 264–66; review of *The Sovereign States*, by James Jackson Kilpatrick, *MLJ* 29 (December 1957): 110–12; review of *Desegregation and the Law: The Meaning and Effect of the School Segregation Cases*, by Albert P. Blaustein and Clarence Clyde Ferguson, *MLJ* 29 (May 1958): 361–69; William P. Murphy to the editor, *MCA*, August 4, 1957.

29. William Patrick Murphy, "Affidavit required under conditions of House Bill No. 17, passed by the regular legislative session of Mississippi, 1956," July 29, 1957; "Reply of William P. Murphy," in WPMP; author's interview with William P. Murphy.

30. "Reply of William P. Murphy"; Hugh H. Clegg, "Someone Jumped the Gun" (unpublished manuscript), 92.

31. "Reply of William P. Murphy"; Clegg, "Someone Jumped the Gun," 91–94.

32. "Reply of William P. Murphy"; Allen Gardner to W. P. Murphy, April 22, 1960; and Les Prichard to Murphy, July 10, 1959, in WPMP; Clegg, "Someone Jumped the Gun," 91–94. Students wrote to encourage their former professor. See Mrs. Bobby R. Payne to Murphy, July 10, 1959; Thomas R. Jones to Murphy, July 15, 1959; Les Prichard to Murphy, July 10, 1959; and Lawrence J. Franck to Williams, July 22, 1959, in WPMP.

33. W. P. Murphy, "State Sovereignty and the Constitution: A Summary View," *MLJ* 33 (May 1962): 353–59.

34. Benjamin F. Cameron to J. D. Williams, December 29, 1959; and Williams to Cameron, January 8, 1960, in UF.

35. Minutes, IHL Board, March 17, 1960, in Records of the IHL Board, Jackson, Miss.; *JDN*, April 20, 1960; Senate Concurrent Resolution no. 135, Mississippi Legislature, Regular Session, 1960, copy in WPMP; *DDT*, April 20, 1960; *JDN*, April 22, 1960; *MCA*, April 20, 22, and 27, 1960; *JST*, April 25, 1960. Hodding Carter retorted that the senator who proposed firing Murphy "apparently believes that our way of life is so doubtful that it can only be protected by using techniques of suppression perfected by Adolf Hitler." Murphy, "like any

intelligent man, is not going to remain long in a state where jackasses roam the legislative halls, braying at their betters." See *DDT*, April 22, 1960.

36. *MCA*, April 22 and 27, 1960; *JST*, April 21 and 25, 1960; Murphy to Beverly S. Burbage, May 3, 1960, in WPMP. All quotations from Murphy's statement can be found in its reprinted form in *MCA*, April 28, 1960; *DDT*, May 3, 1960; and *JST*, May 14, 1960.

37. *DDT*, April 20, 1960; Allen Gardner to Murphy, April 22, 1960; Fred C. De Long Jr. to Murphy, April 23, 1960; William Winter to Murphy, May 19, 1960; Resolution of the Student Body of the University of Mississippi Law School, May 28, 1960, in WPMP; author's interview with William P. Murphy; W. P. Murphy, *The Triumph of Nationalism: State Sovereignty, the Founding Fathers, and the Making of the Constitution* (Chicago: Quadrangle, 1967), vi. The "ditch to die in" quotation attributed to Williams appeared in many sources, not just the interview with Murphy. See, for example, the unsigned "A Ditch to Die In," in UF.

38. Murphy to Alan Reitman, May 10, 1960; Murphy to Roy M. Mersky, May 12, 1960; Murphy to Robert J. Farley, February 27 and March 4, 1961; Murphy to Williams, March 2, 1961; Williams to Murphy, March 13, 1961; and Murphy, memorandum to file, April 12, 1961, in WPMP; author's interview with William P. Murphy.

39. Murphy, memoranda to file, May 19 and June 12, 1961; and Charles F. Haywood to Murphy, May 20, 1961, in WPMP; author's interview with William P. Murphy.

40. *JCL*, June 11, 1961; "Statement of the Faculty of the Law School," June 26, 1961, in WPMP; Russell H. Barrett to Charles F. Haywood, June 21, 1961; and Russell H. Barrett to Barton Milligan, June 23, 1961, in RBP. Barrett sent the provost a copy of the AAUP's "1940 Statement of Principles on Academic Freedom and Tenure."

41. Murphy, memorandum to file, July 3, 1961, in WPMP; Russell H. Barrett to William P. Fidler, June 22, 1961, in RBP; Minutes, IHL Board, June 29, 1961. Barrett, a professor of political science, established contacts with Fidler, the head of the AAUP in Washington, D.C.

42. Murphy, memorandum to file, July 3 (completed July 8), 1961, in WPMP.

43. Ibid.; *JDN*, July 6, 1961.

44. Murphy, memoranda to file, July 3 (completed July 8) and 10, 1961, in WPMP; Minutes, IHL Board, July 7, 1961. Asst. Atty. Gen. Dugas Shands requested to appear before the board because he feared the board's action might affect the state's case against James Meredith, but it considered Murphy's leave before it heard from Shands.

45. Russell H. Barrett to William P. Fidler, June 22 and July 3, 1961; and Barrett to Herman I. Orentlicher, June 23, 1961, in RBP; Orentlicher to Murphy, July 11, 1961; Murphy to Fidler, August 2, 1961; George Neff Stevens to Orentlicher, September 25, 1961; and Orentlicher to George Neff Stevens, October 2, 1961, in AAUPP; Murphy to Rowland Watts, August 22, 1961, in WPMP.

46. For the history of tenure at the university, see Williams to Faculty, January 17, 1961, in RBP; and Williams to Walter Gellhorn, January 31, 1963, in AALSP. Other provisions provided that any faculty member who had been hired before 1950 and had taught since then automatically had tenure. Everyone who had been hired since 1950 and had worked for three continuous years would be reviewed for tenure.

47. Murphy to Haywood, October 4 and November 16, 1961; Williams to Murphy,

December 1, 1961; and Murphy to Reese Cleghorn, May 10, 1962, in WPMP; Murphy to Williams, December 8, 1961, and Russell H. Barrett to Orentlicher, April 4, 1962, in RBP.

48. David H. Vernon to Robert Farley, January 2, 1962; and "Report of the Committee on Academic Freedom and Tenure," in *Program and Reports of Committees*, 1962 Annual Meeting of AALS, in AALSP; F. D. G. Ribble to Murphy, March 13, 1962, in WPMP; Orentlicher to Barrett, March 12, 1962, in RBP; F. D. G. Ribble to David H. Vernon, March 6, 1962; and Page Keeton to David H. Vernon, March 16, 1962, in AAUPP. Ribble served as the chair of the ABA section of legal education, while Keeton had just served a term as president of the AALS.

49. Murphy to Farley, March 5, 1962; Murphy to Myers McDougall, March 7, 1962; and Murphy to David H. Vernon, March 12, 1962, in WPMP; Senate Bill 1612, Mississippi Legislature, Regular Session, 1962; Minutes, IHL Board, May 29, 1962 (reconvened from meeting of May 17, 1962).

50. Murphy to W. N. Ethridge Jr., March 18, 1962; Murphy to Reese Cleghorn, May 10, 1962; and Murphy to David H. Vernon, May 29 and June 8, 1962, in WPMP; *NOTP*, August 5, 1962; *MCA*, August 6, 1962.

51. *Providence (R.I.) Evening Bulletin*, September 20, 1962; Cleghorn, "Tiger at Ole Miss," 22 and 24. Cleghorn also wrote the article that appeared in the Providence newspaper.

Chapter Eleven

1. Meredith to Registrar, no date [received January 26, 1961]; and Robert B. Ellis to Meredith, January 26, 1961, in UF; author's interview with James Meredith, May 13–16, 1996.

2. Meredith to Ellis, January 31, 1961, in UF.

3. Ibid.

4. See Kosciusko-Attala Historical Society, *Kosciusko-Attala History* (n.p., 1976); and François René de Chateaubriand, *Attala, ou les amours de deus sauvages dans le desert* (1818).

5. *Kosciusko-Attala History*, 191.

6. Hazel [Meredith] Coleman, "A Path, a Road, a Highway, Tomorrow (A Family History)," in JHMP; Neshoba County, Mississippi, Marriage Records prior to 1926, 1:46; *Twelfth Census of the United States* (1900), Schedule 1: Population, Miss., Attala County.

7. "Man behind the Headlines," *Ebony*, December 1962, 30; Coleman, "A Path"; *Fourteenth Census of the United States* (1920), Schedule 1: Population, Miss., Attala County; Mrs. Eunice P. Comfort to Cap Meredith, October 8, 1925, Deed Book 58, p. 396, Chancery Court, Attala County, Miss.; *Fifteenth Census of the United States* (1930), *Agriculture*, vol. 2, pt. 2, 1056 and 1062; vol. 3, pt. 2, 717 and 753.

8. Coleman, "A Path"; *Fourteenth Census* (1920), Population, Attala County; Deed Books no. 58, p. 396; no. 184, p. 71; no. 63, p. 208; no. 82, p. 230, Chancery Court, Attala County, Miss.

9. Coleman, "A Path."

10. Roxie Patterson Meredith told her story in one untitled piece, in "My Life Story," and

in "The Roxie Meredith Story," in JHMP (hereinafter collectively cited as Roxie Meredith Writings). See also, Coleman, "A Path"; and *Twelfth Census* (1900), Population, Attala County. They had probably met years earlier because Roxie's sister Caroline was married to Emmitt Nash, Cap's brother-in-law from his first marriage.

11. Roxie Meredith Writings; Coleman, "A Path"; Voter Registration Book, Attala County, Miss., March 6, 1919, in Attala County Courthouse; Deed Books PP, p. 242; RR, p. 326; and VV, p. 13, Chancery Court, Attala County, Miss.

12. Roxie Meredith Writings; Coleman, "A Path"; "Man behind the Headlines," 30; James Meredith, *Three Years in Mississippi* (Bloomington: Indiana University Press, 1966), 51. He took the name James Howard when he enlisted in the air force.

13. Roxie Meredith Writings; Coleman, "A Path"; "Man behind the Headlines," 30; Meredith, *Three Years*, 19–20; *Sixteenth Census of the United States* (1940), *Agriculture*, vol. 1, pt. 4, 454; and *Housing*, vol. 2, 794 and 881.

14. Coleman, "A Path"; Roxie Meredith Writings.

15. See the references in note 14, above.

16. See the references in note 14, above. See also Meredith, *Three Years*, 14–15.

17. Meredith, *Three Years*, 19–20; Roxie Meredith Writings.

18. Coleman, "A Path"; Roxie Meredith Writings; Voter Registration Book, Attala County, Miss., April 24, 1920.

19. Meredith, *Three Years*, 19–20; Coleman, "A Path."

20. Meredith, *Three Years*, 8–15.

21. *Providence (R.I.) Evening Bulletin*, September 20, 1962; "Man behind the Headlines," 32; Meredith, *Three Years*, 21.

22. Hortense Powdermaker, *After Freedom: A Cultural Study in the Deep South* (New York: Viking, 1939), 149.

23. Meredith, *Three Years*, 14.

24. "Man behind the Headlines," 32; Sam R. Ivy to Joe Patterson, June 15, 1961, in MAGP; Meredith, *Three Years*, 61.

25. "Man behind the Headlines," 32.

26. Lt. Leonard F. Petroni to Meredith, May 18, 1954, in JHMP; testimony of James Meredith, June 12, 1961, Hearing on Motion for a Temporary Restraining Order and Preliminary Injunction, in *Meredith v. Fair*.

27. Meredith testimony, June 12, 1961; Meredith transcript, Jackson State College, 1962, in UF. The Meredith Papers contain documents related to the courses he took in the air force.

28. Meredith to District Director, Internal Revenue Service, no date [1960 or 1961], in JHMP; Alberta Estes to Meredith, April 22, 1954, Deed Book no. 162, pp. 372–73; and Robert and Mary Carr to Meredith, March 27, 1956, Deed Book no. 172, 51, Chancery Court, Attala County, Miss.; Meredith transcript, Jackson State College.

29. J. K. Neal to Meredith, no date [April 26, 1954]; and Mary June Wiggins, standard Certificate of Birth, Oklahoma State Health Department, in JHMP; *Baltimore Afro-American*, September 15, 1962; deposition of James Meredith, June 8, 1961, in *Meredith v. Fair*; Meredith testimony, June 12, 1961.

30. *Baltimore Afro-American*, September 15, 1962, and February 24, 1963; Meredith testimony, June 12, 1961; Meredith transcript, Jackson State College; report, United States Armed Forces Institute, Japan [1960]; and Military Test Report, March 20, 1959, in JHMP.

31. Meredith's Airman Performance Reports, May 22 and November 6, 1959, in GLICP; Meredith to Sisters and Brothers, July 4, 1958; and Meredith to Delma Meredith, no date [follow-up to July 4 letter], in JHMP.

32. Records for purchases of homes and trailer, automobile, and savings bonds, in JHMP. For purchase of his parents' farm, see Cap and Roxie Meredith to James Meredith, April 6, 1960, Deed Book no. 198, p. 131, Chancery Court, Attala County, Miss. For Meredith's support of his parents, see correspondence with the IRS in JHMP.

33. Address by Meredith, NAACP 54th Annual Convention, Chicago, Ill., July 5, 1963, in JHMP; Meredith's Airman Performance Report, May 22, 1959, in GLICP. On his credit references, see Meredith, statement of personal history, August 5, 1958, in JHMP.

34. Meredith, "The Value of Literature" (January 27, 1959), "A Comparison of the Odyssey and the Aeneid" (February 17, 1959), and "A Comparison of the Views of Life of Chaucer, Rabelais, and Cervantes" (March 17, 1959), in JHMP; interview with James Meredith, October 12, 1967, Civil Rights Documentation Project, Howard University, Washington, D.C. (hereinafter referred to as Meredith CRDP Interview).

35. *JCL*, August 18, 1963; Meredith CRDP Interview; Meredith, *Three Years*, 25; *Providence (R.I.) Evening Bulletin*, September 20, 1962.

36. *Providence Evening Bulletin*, September 20, 1962.

37. Meredith, *Three Years*, 89–90.

38. Meredith's Airman Performance Reports, November 6, 1959, and July 18, 1960; Report of Medical History, June 7, 1960; and Chronological Report of Medical Care, Clinical Record, Consultation Sheet, April 29, 1960, in GLICP.

39. Meredith's Airman Performance Report, July 18, 1960, in GLICP.

40. Meredith, *Three Years*, 20–22; Meredith CRDP Interview; Meredith to Registrar, Jackson State College, February 15, 1960, in JHMP.

41. Meredith, *Three Years*, 23; Lelia Gaston Rhodes, *Jackson State University: The First Hundred Years, 1877–1977* (Jackson: University Press of Mississippi, 1979).

42. Meredith testimony, June 12, 1961; Meredith, *Three Years*, 2–22; Meredith transcript, Jackson State College.

43. Meredith, "What I Believe," September 23, 1960, in JHMP; Meredith, *Three Years*, 47–48.

44. Meredith, "Why Have a Philosophy?," no date [fall 1960], in JHMP.

45. Ibid.

46. Ibid.

47. Ibid.

48. Meredith, *Three Years*, 52–53.

49. Ibid., 26–29.

50. Meredith testimony, August 10, 1961, in *Meredith v. Fair*.

51. Meredith, *Three Years*, 42–45.

52. Meredith, "Proposal to Establish a Debating Organization on the Jackson State

College Campus," no date [fall 1960?]; and Meredith, announcement of Social Science Club meeting, October 1960, in JHMP; Meredith, *Three Years*, 44–45 and 49.

53. Mississippi Improvement Association of Students, Action Order no. 1 [January 1961?]; and Policy Letter no. 3, April 20, 1961, in JHMP; Meredith testimony, August 10, 1961.

54. Meredith, *Three Years*, 47 and 56; Meredith testimony, August 10, 1961; and deposition of Meredith, June 8, 1961, in *Meredith v. Fair*.

55. *Providence Evening Bulletin*, September 20, 1962; "Man Behind the Headlines," 30 and 32; Meredith, *Three Years*, 50. Barbara Shelton of the state medical association helped identify Bailey. See *Kosciusko Star-Herald*, October 16, 1986.

56. Meredith to Thurgood Marshall, January 29 and February 7, 1961, quoted in Meredith, *Three Years*, 59 and 56, respectively; Meredith CRDP Interview.

57. Meredith, *Three Years*, 50–51.

58. Ibid., 50–52.

59. Ibid., 42–47 and 50–52.

60. Meredith to Thurgood Marshall, January 29, 1961, quoted in Meredith, *Three Years*, 56; Judge Wisdom's comment appeared in the decision by the Fifth Circuit Court of Appeals in *Meredith v. Fair*, June 25, 1962. The term "militant conservative" plays off August Meier's use of "conservative militant" in "On the Role of Martin Luther King," *New Politics* 4 (Winter 1965): 52–59.

Chapter Twelve

1. *SSN*, February 1961.

2. J. H. Meredith to Robert B. Ellis, January 31, 1961 (with enclosures), in UF; James Meredith, *Three Years in Mississippi* (Bloomington: Indiana University Press, 1966), 54. For the requirement of five letters from alumni, see Minutes, IHL Board, September 16, 1954, in Records of the IHL Board, Jackson, Miss.

3. John Dittmer, *Local People: The Struggle for Civil Rights in Mississippi* (Urbana: University of Illinois Press, 1994), 79–83.

4. Ibid.; *Miss.*, October 25, 1957; David G. Sansing, *Making Haste Slowly: The Troubled History of Higher Education in Mississippi* (Jackson: University Press of Mississippi, 1990), 159.

5. Tentative draft of minutes, Division Heads Meeting, University of Mississippi, February 4, 1961, in UF.

6. Ibid.

7. J. D. Williams, official announcement, February 4, 1961, in UF.

8. Sansing, *Making Haste*, 159. Fourteen students received the telegram sent by Ellis on February 4, 1961: two in Arkansas, one in North Carolina, and eleven in Mississippi.

9. Ellis to Meredith, telegram, February 4, 1961, in UF. Much of the correspondence to and from Meredith is reprinted in his *Three Years*.

10. *SSN*, March 1961; *DDT*, February 7, 1961; *JDN*, February 8, 1961.

11. *JCL*, February 7 and 8, 1961; *JDN*, February 8, 1961.

12. See the references in note 11, above. See also Meredith to Ellis, January 31, 1961, in UF.

13. Minutes, IHL Board, February 7, 1961.

14. *JDN*, February 8, 1961.

15. Meredith, *Three Years*, 55. See Mark V. Tushnet, *Making Civil Rights Law: Thurgood Marshall and the Supreme Court, 1936–1961* (New York: Oxford University Press, 1994).

16. Meredith to Thurgood Marshall, January 26, 1961, in Meredith, *Three Years*, 55–56.

17. *JCL*, February 8, 1961; Meredith, *Three Years*, 56–57; Thurgood Marshall to Meredith, February 7, 1961; and Meredith to Marshall, February 10, 1961, in Meredith, *Three Years*, 61–62.

18. On Higgs, see Barbara Carter, "A Lawyer Leaves Mississippi," *Reporter*, May 9, 1963, 33–35; John Howard, *Men Like That: A Southern Queer History* (Chicago: University of Chicago Press, 1999), 150–58. The Mississippi State Sovereignty Commission Papers and Higgs's FBI file (in author's possession) contain numerous documents about Higgs.

19. Meredith to U.S. Justice Department, February 7, 1961, in BMP.

20. *JDN* and *JST*, February 17, 1961. See Meredith, *Three Years*, 85–86.

21. *DDT*, March 6, 1961.

22. Meredith, *Three Years*, 78–85.

23. Ibid., 80; A. L. Hopkins, investigative report on J. H. Meredith, February 24, 1961, in MSSCP. An earlier report of February 9, 1961, was not in the Sovereignty Commission's papers.

24. Meredith, *Three Years*, 84.

25. Ibid., 62; Jack Greenberg, *Crusaders in the Courts: How a Dedicated Band of Lawyers Fought for the Civil Rights Revolution* (New York: Basic Books, 1994), 33–34. See also Constance Baker Motley, *Equal Justice under Law: An Autobiography* (New York: Farrar, Straus and Giroux, 1998); and Marie Brenner, "Judge Motley's Verdict," *New Yorker*, May 16, 1994. On the 1948 Mississippi case, see Charles C. Bolton, *The Hardest Deal of All: The Battle over School Integration in Mississippi, 1870–1980* (Jackson: University Press of Mississippi, 2005), 46–48.

26. Constance Motley to Meredith, February 16, 1961, in Meredith, *Three Years*, 62–63.

27. Meredith to Ellis, February 20, 1961; Ellis to Meredith, February 21, 1961; and Meredith to Ellis, February 23, 1961, in UF.

28. Meredith to Motley, March 7, 1961, in Meredith, *Three Years*, 64–65.

29. Motley to Meredith, March 14, 1961, in Meredith, *Three Years*, 65; *JCL*, March 19, 1961.

30. Meredith to Motley, March 20, 1961, in Meredith, *Three Years*, 66; Meredith to Ellis, March 18, 1961, in UF.

31. Motley to Meredith, March [24], 1961, in Meredith, *Three Years*, 66–67. Meredith states that he received the letter *on* March 24, but in his reply to Motley he refers to her letter *of* March 24. Compare pages 66 and 67.

32. Motley to Meredith, March [24], 1961, in Meredith, *Three Years*, 66–67.

33. Meredith to Motley, March 26, 1961; Henry Newell to Registrar, March 26, 1961; Meredith letters to Washburn University, University of Kansas, University of Maryland, and Jackson State College, March 26, 1961, in Meredith, *Three Years*, 67–69.

34. Meredith to Ellis, March 26, 1961, in UF.

35. Meredith transcript, Jackson State College, in UF; Meredith, *Three Years*, 86–87.

36. Meredith to "Fellow Students," March 20, 1961, in Meredith, *Three Years*, 87.

37. Meredith, "Why I Plan to Go to the University of Mississippi," in Meredith, *Three Years*, 87–90.

38. Ibid.

39. Ibid.

40. Ibid.

41. *JCL*, March 28, 29, 30, and 31, 1961; Dittmer, *Local People*, 87–89; Meredith, *Three Years*, 92–98; Myrlie B. Evers, with William Peters, *For Us, the Living* (Garden City, N.Y.: Doubleday, 1967), 235 and 202.

42. Motley to Meredith, April 11, 1961, in Meredith, *Three Years*, 70–71.

43. Meredith to Arthur Beverly Lewis, April 12, 1961, in UF.

44. Meredith to Motley, April 15, 1961, in Meredith, *Three Years*, 72.

45. The timing of the meeting is not entirely certain. In their correspondence, they mention April 29, but in her memoirs Motley only mentions meeting Meredith one month later. Meredith also mentions the later meeting but says that he had met Motley one previous time. See Meredith, *Three Years*, 105; and Motley, *Equal Justice*, 164–66.

46. Ellis to Meredith, May 9, 1961, in UF.

47. Meredith to Motley, May 10, 1961; Motley to Meredith, May 11, 1961; and Meredith to Ellis, May 15, 1961, in Meredith, *Three Years*, 73–75. Meredith enclosed a letter applying for an apartment but also acknowledged that a dormitory room just for himself would be acceptable if an apartment were not available when he was admitted. See Meredith to Director of Men's Housing, May 15, 1961, in Meredith, *Three Years*, 75.

48. Motley to Meredith, May 18, 1961, in Meredith, *Three Years*, 75.

49. Meredith to Motley, May 21, 1961; Meredith to Ellis, May 21, 1961; Motley to Meredith, May 23, 1961; and Meredith to Motley, May 26, 1961, in Meredith, *Three Years*, 76–77.

50. Raymond Arsenault, *Freedom Riders: 1961 and the Struggle for Racial Justice* (New York: Oxford University Press, 2006); Dittmer, *Local People*, 90–99.

51. See the references in note 50, above.

52. See the references in note 50, above.

53. Ellis to Meredith, May 25, 1961, in UF.

54. Meredith, *Three Years*, 105.

55. Ibid., 105–6; Motley, *Equal Justice*, 166; Brenner, "Judge Motley's Verdict," 70.

56. Meredith, *Three Years*, 106–7.

57. *JCL*, June 1, 1961; *JDN*, June 1, 1961; Meredith, *Three Years*, 107.

58. *JCL*, June 1 and 2, 1961.

59. *MS*, June 1, 1961.

Chapter Thirteen

1. Plaintiff's Complaint, May 31, 1961, in *Meredith v. Fair*. Newspaper coverage of the filing can be followed in the *Jackson Clarion-Ledger* and the *Meridian Star*. The chapter's subtitle comes from a later appeals court decision.

2. Plaintiff's Complaint.

3. *JCL*, June 1, 1961; Plaintiff's Complaint.

4. Plaintiff's Complaint.

5. Ibid.

6. *MS*, May 31, 1961, September 22, 1962; Plaintiff's Complaint; *JCL* and *JDN*, June 1, 1961. See Martha H. Swain, *Pat Harrison: The New Deal Years* (Jackson: University Press of Mississippi, 1978), 133; and Howard Smead, *Blood Justice: The Lynching of Mack Charles Parker* (New York: Oxford University Press, 1986), 179.

7. Summonses and Deputy Marshals' Returns of Service of Writ, in *Meredith v. Fair*. See also *JCL*, June 4, 1961; and *JDN*, June 5, 6, and 13, 1961.

8. The motions, objections, and orders are all on record in *Meredith v. Fair*. See also *MS*, June 6, 1961; and *JCL*, June 7, 1961.

9. Meredith deposition, June 8, 1961, in *Meredith v. Fair*; Meredith, *Three Years*, 118. See also *MS*, June 9, 1961; and *JDN*, June 9, 1961.

10. *JDN*, August 1 and 13, 1962; *JCL*, August 13, 1961; Meredith, *Three Years*, 109.

11. Meredith deposition.

12. Ibid.

13. Ibid. The deposition itself, prepared by the deputy clerk of court Esther Carr, displayed sensibilities similar to Shands's by not capitalizing the word "Negro." A similar disrespect appeared in many newspaper accounts of the proceedings in the case. The *Jackson Clarion-Ledger* referred to Constance Baker Motley as the "Motley woman." See, for example, *JCL*, June 13, 1961.

14. Meredith deposition.

15. Ibid.

16. Ibid.

17. Meredith, *Three Years*, 109.

18. Ibid., 119; Hearing on Motion for a Temporary Restraining Order and Preliminary Injunction, June 12, 1961, in *Meredith v. Fair* (hereinafter cited as Hearing, *Meredith v. Fair*. See also *MS*, June 12 and 13, 1961; *JCL*, *JDN*, and *DDT*, June 13, 1961. In his memoir, Meredith confuses the hearing held in Biloxi with the hearing in Jackson later in August.

19. Hearing, *Meredith v. Fair*.

20. Ibid.

21. Ibid.

22. Ibid.

23. Ibid.

24. Ibid.

25. Ibid.

26. *JCL*, June 16, 1961. See, for example, A. L. Hopkins, Report: "J. H. Meredith, colored, male, student at the Jackson College . . . ," February 24, 1961, in MSSCP.

27. Motion for Order Requiring the Defendant Registrar to Appear for the Taking of His Deposition and Motion for Production; Motion for Production; and Notice of Taking Deposition on Oral Examination, in *Meredith v. Fair*. For the legal wrangling in the sum-

mer, see, for example, *MS*, June 6 and July 28, 1961; *DDT*, June 13, 1961; and *JCL*, June 28 and July 11 and 28, 1961.

28. Motion of Defendant, Robert B. Ellis, Registrar of the University of Mississippi, to Vacate Plaintiff's Notice of Taking His Deposition; Affidavit of Dugas Shands; and Motion of Defendants for Extension of Time within Which to Plead, in *Meredith v. Fair*.

29. On Motions for Additional Time; Order [in re production of documents]; Order Sustaining Defendants' Motions . . . the Taking of Defendant Ellis' Deposition; and on Dates for Filing of Answer and Arguments of Motions, in *Meredith v. Fair*; *JCL*, June 13 and 18, and July 11, 1961; *MS*, August 1, 1961; *JDN*, August 1, 1961.

30. Separate Answer of Defendant, Robert B. Ellis, Registrar of the University of Mississippi, in *Meredith v. Fair*.

31. *JCL*, July 1, 1961.

32. Hearing, *Meredith v. Fair*.

33. Ibid.; *MS*, August 11, 1961; *JDN*, August 11, 1961. According to one reporter covering the hearing, Shands had pronounced the word "Nig-row," which was the way "the majority of Southerners do." See *JCL*, August 11, 1961.

34. Hearing, *Meredith v. Fair*.

35. Ibid.; *JCL*, August 11, 1961.

36. Hearing, *Meredith v. Fair*. Clark had reviewed the part of Meredith's air force file available in St. Louis (about one-half inch of documents) and photocopied about twenty-five relevant pages.

37. Ibid.

38. Ibid.

39. Ibid.

40. On the mural, see *JCL*, December 7, 1961; Jack Bass, *Unlikely Heroes* (New York: Simon and Schuster, 1981), 13; and Meredith, *Three Years*, 131. In 1972, after objections to the mural, the court installed a curtain to cover it; the curtain was opened only on February 25, 1988, during a ceremony to hang a portrait of Judge Harold Cox. See *JCL*, May 2, 1989.

41. Meredith answered a few questions before Clark was called to testify about Meredith's air force records that he had examined in St. Louis.

42. Hearing, *Meredith v. Fair*; *JCL*, August 12, 1961.

43. Hearing, *Meredith v. Fair*. See also A. L. Hopkins, Report, "Attending trial in Federal Court in Jackson . . . ," August 18, 1961, in MSSCP.

44. Hearing, *Meredith v. Fair*.

45. Ibid.

46. Ibid.

47. Ibid.

48. Ibid.

49. Author's interview with Charles Clark, January 3, 1992; *JCL*, October 18, 1961. See note 36 above.

50. Hearing, *Meredith v. Fair*.

51. Ibid.

52. Ibid.

53. Ibid.

54. Ibid.

55. Ibid. On SACS and black institutions, see George Jackson Allen Jr., "A History of the Commission on Colleges of the Southern Association of Colleges and Schools, 1949–1975" (Ph.D. diss., Georgia State University, 1978). See also *JCL*, December 12, 1961.

56. *MS*, August 17, 1961; *JCL*, August 17, 1961. The transcript of the hearing typically did not include the closing arguments.

57. Hearing, *Meredith v. Fair*; *MS*, August 17 and December 13, 1961; *DDT*, December 14, 1961; *JCL*, August 17 and December 14, 1961.

58. Opinion of the Court, *Meredith v. Fair*, 199 F.Supp. 754 (1961); Notice of Appeal, in *Meredith v. Fair*; *MS*, December 13, 1961; *JCL* and *DDT*, December 14, 1961.

59. *JCL*, December 14 and 22, 1961, and January 10, 1962; *MS* and *NOTP*, January 10, 1962. For an account of Jackson State's recent accreditation, see *JCL*, December 12, 1961.

60. *NOTP*, *MS*, and *JCL*, January 10, 1962.

61. *JCL*, *MS*, and *NOTP*, January 10, 1962; Order by U.S. Fifth Circuit Court of Appeals, *Meredith v. Fair*, 298 F.2d 696 (1962).

62. Order by U.S. Fifth Circuit Court of Appeals, in *Meredith v. Fair*.

63. Ibid.

64. Second Hearing, January 16, 1962, in *Meredith v. Fair*; *JCL*, January 17 and 18, 1962.

65. Petition for Rehearing; and Points in Response to Appellant's Petition, in *Meredith v. Fair*. In a letter to his colleagues, Judge Rives expressed "our strong sense of social injustice" but insisted on "discipline" in strictly observing the "legal rules." He suspected they "are apt to cause much more harm than good" by creating a conflict with the lower court in the Meredith case. See Richard T. Rives to Elbert P. Tuttle and John Minor Wisdom, January 19, 1962, in JMWP.

66. Second Hearing; *JCL* and *JDN*, January 25, 1962.

67. Second Hearing; *DDT*, *JCL*, and *JDN*, January 25, 1962.

68. Second Hearing; *JCL*, January 26, 1962; *DDT* and *MS*, January 25, 1962.

69. Second Hearing; *MS*, *JDN*, and *DDT*, January 25, 1962; *JCL*, January 26, 1962. In an exchange with Motley, trustee Tally Riddell said, "The Board has never had the question of any distinction between whites and nigras at any time at any institution since been [*sic*] on the Board." Motley shot back, "Did you say 'niggers'?" Trustee J. N. Lipscomb, when asked if the board had ever talked with university officials about Meredith's application, politely replied to Constance Motley, "No, ma'am."

70. Second Hearing; *JCL*, *MS*, and *NOTP*, January 27, 1962.

71. *JCL*, *JDN*, and *MS*, January 28, 1962.

72. Opinion of the Court, *Meredith v. Fair*, 202 F.Supp. 224 (1962); *JCL*, *JDN*, *DDT*, and *MS*, February 4, 1962.

Chapter Fourteen

1. Brief for Appellant in Support of Motion for Injunction Pending Appeal, and Appellees' Points in Opposition to Appellant's Motion for Injunction Pending Appeal, *Meredith v.*

Fair, in JMWP; *DDT* and *JDN*, February 5, 1962; *MS*, February 5 and 7, 1962; *JCL*, February 5 and 6, 1962.

2. On Rives, Tuttle, and Wisdom, see Jack Bass, *Unlikely Heroes* (New York: Simon and Schuster, 1981); J. W. Peltason, *Fifty-eight Lonely Men: Southern Federal Judges and School Desegregation* (New York: Harcourt, Brace and World, 1961), especially 26; Frank T. Read and Lucy S. McGough, *Let Them Be Judged: The Judicial Integration of the Deep South* (Metuchen, N.J.: Scarecrow, 1978); Anne S. Emanuel, "Forming the Historic Fifth Circuit: The Eisenhower Years," *Texas Forum on Civil Liberties and Civil Rights* 6 (Winter 2002): 233–59; and *Time*, December 5, 1960, 14–15. Rives, Tuttle, and Wisdom, along with John R. Brown, became known as the four liberals on the Fifth Circuit Court of Appeals.

3. *MS, JCL, DDT*, and *NOTP*, February 11, 1962. Newspaper accounts have been used because no transcript of the hearing could be located; apparently federal appellate courts did not routinely use court reporters.

4. *DDT, MS, JCL*, and *NOTP*, February 11, 1962.

5. *Meredith v. Fair*, 305 F.2d 341 (1962) (Tuttle dissenting). See also *JCL, JDN, MS, DDT*, and *NOTP*, February 13, 1962.

6. *Meredith v. Fair*, 305 F.2d 341 (1962).

7. *JCL, JDN, MS, DDT*, and *NYT*, February 13, 1962.

8. Meredith, *Three Years*, 139–42; *JCL* and *JDN*, February 19, 1962.

9. *JCL* and *NOTP*, February 22, 1962; Read and McGough, *Let Them Be Judged*, 52–53; Peltason, *Fifty-eight*, 147.

10. *JCL* and *NOTP*, April 21, 1962; *DDT*, April 22, 1962. The court gave the attorneys fifteen days to submit additional briefs, but neither the docket sheet nor the case file contains any entries for briefs filed with the court, either before the April 20 hearing or after.

11. *JDN*, May 1, 1962.

12. Paul G. Alexander, General Affidavit, May 28, 1962, and Homer Edgeworth, J.P., Bench Warrant, May 28, 1962, Hinds County, Miss., Criminal Case no. 15-242, in *Meredith v. Fair*; Russell H. Barrett, *Integration at Ole Miss* (Chicago: Quadrangle, 1965), 77; *DDT, JDN*, and *MS*, June 6, 1962; *JCL*, June 7, 1962; Meredith, *Three Years*, 168–69.

13. *MEJ*, June 8, 1962. On the case of Clyde Kennard, see David G. Sansing, *Making Haste Slowly: The Troubled History of Higher Education in Mississippi* (Jackson: University Press of Mississippi, 1990), 148–54; and John Dittmer, *Local People: The Struggle for Civil Rights in Mississippi* (Urbana: University of Illinois Press, 1994), 79–83.

14. *JCL*, June 13, 1962. For an inaccurate account, see Constance Baker Motley, *Equal Justice under Law: An Autobiography* (New York: Farrar, Straus and Giroux, 1998), 174.

15. Read and McGough, *Let Them Be Judged*, 218; Appellate Court ruling, *Meredith v. Fair*, 305 F.2d 343 (1962).

16. Appellate Court ruling.

17. Ibid.

18. Ibid.

19. Ibid.

20. Ibid. Judge Brown praised the unprecedented "power and correctness" of Wisdom's

opinion. Brown to Wisdom, June 20, 1962, in JMWP. Elbert P. Tuttle expressed his "greatest admiration" for the opinion. Tuttle to Wisdom, June 27, 1962, in JMWP.

21. *JCL*, June 27, 1962; *DDT* and *JDN*, June 26, 1962.

22. *JCL*, June 27 and 28, 1962; *MS*, June 27, 1962.

23. *DDT*, July 10, 1962; *JCL*, July 17, 1962.

24. John R. Brown to John Minor Wisdom, June 20, 1962, in JMWP; DeVane's dissent in Appellate Court ruling, *Meredith v. Fair*, 305 F.2d 361 (1962); *JCL*, *DDT*, and *MS*, July 11, 1962. In a revealing letter to Wisdom, DeVane expressed his pride that most blacks, just like most whites, "violently opposed" integration, and he declared his lack of sympathy for self-righteous blacks who "go about making trouble." Dozier A. DeVane to Wisdom, June 21, 1962, in JMWP.

25. *JCL*, *MS*, and *JDN*, July 17, 1962. In the first week of October 1962, the registrar announced the rejection of Bracey's application because it was incomplete—it lacked a full transcript of her academic work. See *NOTP*, October 6, 1962.

26. *JCL*, July 18 and 20, 1962; *JDN* and *DDT*, July 20, 1962; *NOTP*, July 18, 1962; *MS*, July 19 and 20, 1962.

27. On Cameron, see Bass, *Unlikely Heroes*, 84–88; Read and McGough, *Let Them Be Judged*, 44–48; and Emanuel, "Forming the Historic Fifth Circuit."

28. Read and McGough, *Let Them Be Judged*, 45–47; Bass, *Unlikely Heroes*, 84–96; Emanuel, "Forming the Historic Fifth Circuit," 242–43.

29. *Denton v. City of Carrollton*, 235 F.2d 481, 487 (5th Cir. 1956) (Cameron dissenting); *U.S. v. Wood*, 295 F.2d 772, 785 (5th Cir. 1961) (Cameron dissenting); *Boman v. Birmingham Transit Company*, 292 F.2d 4 (5th Cir. 1961) (Cameron dissenting); *Sharp v. Lucky*, 252 F.2d 910, 913 (5th Cir. 1958) (Cameron dissenting). See also *Darby v. Daniel*, 168 F.Supp. 170 (U.S. Dist. 1958); *Avery v. Wichita Falls Independent School District*, 241 F.2d 230, 235 (5th Cir. 1957) (Cameron dissenting); *Dixon v. Alabama State Board of Education*, 294 F.2d 150, 159 (5th Cir. 1961) (Cameron dissenting); *Boson v. Rippy*, 275 F.2d 850, 853 (5th Cir. 1960). The Tenth Amendment says, "The powers not delegated to the United States by the Constitution, nor prohibited by it to the States, are reserved to the States respectively, or to the people."

30. *Boman v. Birmingham Transit Company*. Cameron's dissent has been called both an "incredible tour de force" and "a tendentious history of race relations in the South." See J. Robert Brown Jr. and Alison Herren Lee, "Neutral Assignment of Judges at the Court of Appeals," *Texas Law Review* 78 (April 2000): 1037–115.

31. *Boman v. Birmingham Transit Company*; *Avery v. Wichita Falls Independent School District*; *U.S. v. Wood*. See also *Darby v. Daniel*.

32. *MS*, July 19, 1962; *JCL*, *JDN*, and *DDT*, July 20, 1962. Cameron's stay can be found in *RRLR* 7 (1962): 741–42.

33. Motley reproduced Meredith's letter in her *Equal Justice*, 175–78.

34. Motley, *Equal Justice*, 178; *New York Post*, July 24, 1962. Meredith mentions the interview with Weschler in his *Three Years* (169) but explains it as having occurred shortly after his jailing on the voter registration charge, not after Judge Cameron's stay.

35. *JCL*, *MS*, and *JDN*, July 28, 1962; *DDT*, July 29, 1962; Court of Appeals Order,

Meredith v. Fair, 306 F.2d 374 (1962). The article in the *Jackson Clarion-Ledger* was a UPI dispatch from New Orleans.

36. Court Order; *JCL*, *MS*, and *JDN*, July 28, 1962; *DDT*, July 29, 1962.

37. *MS* and *DDT*, July 30, 1962. Cameron's stays can be found in *RRLR* 7 (1962): 742–43.

38. *Avery v. Wichita Falls Independent School District*; *Boman v. Birmingham Transit Company*. Cameron deplored a *Time* magazine article that praised Judges Wisdom and Rives as "trail-blazers" who were leading a "civil rights offensive." See *Time*, December 5, 1960, 14. See also *Hecht v. Bowles*, 321 U.S. 321; 64 S. Ct. 587; 88 L. Ed. 754 (1944).

39. For Cameron's open break with the Fifth Circuit, see his dissent in *Armstrong v. Board of Education of the City of Birmingham*, 323 F.2d 333 (1963); he uses the term "The Four" in note 1 on page 353. For discussions of Cameron's charges of partiality in the assignment of judges, see Bass, *Unlikely Heroes*, 233–47; Read and McGough, *Let Them Be Judged*, 266–76; Barrow and Walker, *A Court Divided*, 55–60; Brown and Lee, "Neutral Assignment of Judges at the Court of Appeals"; and Jonathan L. Entin, "Constitutional Law and Civil Rights Symposium, Part I: The Sign of 'The Four': Judicial Assignment and the Rule of Law," *MLJ* 68 (Fall 1998): 369–89. Defenders of the Four, at the time and since, tended to dismiss Cameron's criticisms as the complaints of an unreconstructed conservative crank. The most recent and thorough scholarly examinations of the assignment of judges within the Fifth Circuit, however, have found considerable merit in Cameron's charges. In general, among students of the Fifth Circuit, Bass discounts Cameron's allegations, Barrow and Walker found more merit in them, as did Entin, and Brown and Lee thought they had considerable validity.

40. Court of Appeals Order Reconfirmed, August 4, 1962, *RRLR* 7 (1962): 743–44; Judge Cameron's Stay Order, August 6, 1962, *RRLR* 7 (1962): 744–45; *JCL* and *MS*, August 5 and 6, 1962; *JDN*, August 7, 1962.

41. *JCL*, *JDN*, and *MS*, August 7, 1962; Memorandum for the Attorney General—Monday Report, from Burke Marshall, August 27, 1962, in BMP.

42. Motion for Vacation of "Stay Order" or for Such Other, Further and Appropriate Relief as May Be Deemed Just, August 13, 1962, in *Meredith v. Fair*, Appellate Jurisdiction Case Files, 1792–1999, 347, October Term 1962, Entry 21, RG 267; *MS*, August 13, 1962; *JCL*, August 14, 1962; *MCA*, September 4, 1962.

43. *MS*, August 16, 1962; Defense brief in *Meredith v. Fair*.

44. Defense brief in *Meredith v. Fair*.

45. Meredith to the Justice Department, February 7, 1961; Burke Marshall to Byron White, Deputy Attorney General, June 30, 1961; Memorandum for the Attorney General—Monday Report, from Burke Marshall, June 16, 1962, and August 27, 1962, in BMP.

46. Memorandum for the United States as Amicus Curiae on Motion for Vacation of Stay Orders, August 31, 1962, *Meredith v. Fair*, RG 267; *JCL*, *MS*, and *NYT*, September 1, 1962; Burke Marshall to Grenville Clark, October 9, 1962, in BMP.

47. *JDN* and *JCL*, September 2, 1962; *MS*, August 7 and September 2, 1962.

48. *Meredith v. Fair*, 83 S.Ct. 10. For examples of newspaper coverage see *MS* and *DDT*, September 10, 1962; and *JCL*, September 11, 1962.

49. *MCA*, September 11, 1962; *JCL*, September 11 and 12, 1962.

50. *DDT*, September 10, 1962; *JCL* and *MS*, September 11 and 12, 1962; *MCA*, September 11, 1962.

51. *WP*, September 11, 1962. Robert E. Lee Baker had extensive experience covering the civil rights movement, including Mississippi. See Gene Roberts and Hank Klibanoff, *The Race Beat: The Press, the Civil Rights Struggle, and the Awakening of a Nation* (New York: Knopf, 2006), 91–92 and 196–99.

Chapter Fifteen

1. *MS*, August 5, 1962.

2. *JCL*, September 28, 1962.

3. Nick Bryant, *The Bystander: John F. Kennedy and the Struggle for Black Equality* (New York: Basic Books, 2006), 30. See also Carl M. Brauer, *John F. Kennedy and the Second Reconstruction* (New York: Columbia University Press, 1977); David Niven, *The Politics of Injustice: The Kennedys, the Freedom Rides, and the Electoral Consequences of a Moral Compromise* (Knoxville: University of Tennessee Press, 2003); Mark Stern, *Calculating Visions: Kennedy, Johnson, and Civil Rights* (New Brunswick: Rutgers University Press, 1992). For a review of the literature, see Donald W. Jackson and James W. Riddlesperger Jr., "John F. Kennedy and the Politics of Civil Rights," in *Presidential Leadership and Civil Rights Policy*, ed. Riddlesperger and Jackson (Westport, Conn.: Greenwood, 1995), 109–16. For nonscholarly works, see Victor Navasky, *Kennedy Justice* (New York: Atheneum, 1971); and Edwin Guthman, *We Band of Brothers* (New York: Harper and Row, 1971).

4. Nick Bryant, *Bystander*, 54–58; Brauer, *Kennedy*, 16–22.

5. Brauer, *Kennedy*, 16–17, 20–23; Nick Bryant, *Bystander*, 54–58.

6. Brauer, *Kennedy*, 23–29; Nick Bryant, *Bystander*, 67–87, passim. The quotation from Brauer refers to James McGregor Burns's *John Kennedy: A Political Profile* (New York: Harcourt, Brace, 1959).

7. Nick Bryant, *Bystander*, 139–90; Brauer, *Kennedy*, 30–60; Jeffrey D. Meyer, *Running on Race: Racial Politics in Presidential Campaigns, 1960–2000* (New York: Random House, 2002), 18–39.

8. Nick Bryant, *Bystander*, 11 and 209–42, passim; Stern, *Calculating Visions*, 40–58; Brauer, *Kennedy*, 51–88. The Kennedy administration relied on Burke Marshall's emerging ideas on federalism. See his *Federalism and Civil Rights* (New York: Columbia University Press, 1964).

9. Nick Bryant, *Bystander*, 261–82; Niven, *Politics of Injustice*, 101–24; Brauer, *Kennedy*, 98–112.

10. Meredith to the Justice Department, February 7, 1961; J. Edgar Hoover, FBI Director, to Assistant Attorney General, Civil Rights Division, February 13, 1961; Burke Marshall to Motley, June 3, 1961; Marshall to Byron White, Deputy Attorney General, June 30, 1961; and Memorandum for the Attorney General—Monday Report, from Marshall, June 16, 1962, in BMP. A May 8 document on Potomac Institute stationery suggests that the Justice Depart-

ment was involved in a meeting of sympathetic Mississippians at the Potomac Institute on May 11, 1961, to discuss race relations in their home state. The invitees apparently included James Silver, Paul Pittman, Hodding Carter III, William Higgs, Hazel Brannon Smith, Easton King, A. E. Cox, Will Campbell, and several other ministers. See BMP.

11. Nick Bryant, *Bystander*, 246–47; Navasky, *Kennedy Justice*, 182–83, 190–91, 209; Brauer, *Kennedy*, 93–94, 110–11; Marshall, *Federalism and Civil Rights*.

12. *JDN*, June 26, 1962. See also correspondence between Marshall and Watkins, in BMP.

13. Memorandum for the Attorney General—Monday Report [Marshall to Kennedy], June 11, 1962, and August 27, 1962, in BMP.

14. Chronology of the Meredith Case, May 31, 1961, through September 24, 1962, no date (hereinafter referred to as Marshall's Chronology). Burke Marshall probably prepared the chronology. C. N. Fortenberry to Marshall, August 30, 1962, in BMP; *Miss.*, March 16, 1961; *OE*, July 13, 1961; Edwin O. Guthman, *We Band of Brothers* (New York: Harper and Row, 1972), 183–84; "Summary of Participation of Deputy Assistant Attorney General William A. Geohegan in Matters relating to the Admission of James Meredith to the University of Mississippi," no date, in USMP. Hereinafter referred to as Geohegan's Summary.

15. *MPS*, September 20 and 21, 1962; *NYT*, September 20, 1962; *JDN*, September 21, 1962; *JCL*, November 7, 1987. See also two books by Erle Johnston, *I Rolled with Ross* (Baton Rouge: Moran, 1980) and *Politics: Mississippi Style* (Forest, Miss.: Lake Harbor, 1993).

16. The best coverage of the Barnett administration's foibles and failures appeared in the work of Bill Minor; for example, see *NOTP*, June 19 and July 10, 1960, September 24, 1961, September 30, 1962, and February 2, 1964. See also *JCL*, September 17, 1961; Wayne Dowdy, "Words from Wayne," Millsaps College *Purple and Gold*, October 2, 1962; *DDT*, April 29 and June 10, 1962; *Wall Street Journal*, October 1, 1962; *Time*, October 5, 1962, 17.

17. *NYT* and *MPS*, September 20, 1962; *DDT*, June 10 and September 20, 1962.

18. *DDT*, September 12, 1962; *JCL*, *JDN*, *MCA*, and *MS*, September 12 and 13, 1962.

19. *JDN*, *MPS*, *MCA*, and *JCL*, September 12, 1962; *OE*, September 13, 1962; SAC [Special Agent in Charge] Memphis to Director FBI, September 13, 1962 (#14), in FBI Files. According to the FBI, the president of the Lafayette County Citizens' Council, Sheriff Joe W. Ford, denied the Citizens' Council was responsible for the cross burning. The FBI Files were obtained under the Freedom of Information Act. Each document will be cited by the last series of numbers in its document number (e.g., #157-401-14 is cited above as #14).

20. Judge Mize's injunction can be found in *RRLR* 7 (1962): 746–48. See also *OE*, September 13, 1962; *MS*, September 14, 1962; and *JDN* and *NOTP*, September 15, 1962.

21. Gov. Ross Barnett's TV-radio address, September 13, 1962, in *Meredith v. Fair*. The Citizens' Council's *The Citizen* for September 1962 also reprinted the entire speech as Barnett, "Mississippi Still Says Never!" See also *JCL*, September 14, 1962; and *DDT*, *MS*, and *MCA*, September 12, 1962. Earlier in May, Judge Russel Moore had proposed that public officials should be willing to go jail for defying federal orders ending segregation, and the state should continue to pay them while in jail. The only major public opposition came from Jackson mayor Allen Thompson and from McComb editor Oliver Emmerich. See *JCL*, May 2 and July 26, 1962; *JDN*, July 27 and 30, 1962; and *MEJ*, July 27, 1962.

22. Gov. Ross Barnett's TV-radio address; *KNS*, October 4, 1962.

23. *MCA* and *JCL*, September 14, 1962; *MS*, September 15 and 16, 1962; *DDT*, September 12, 14, and 16.

24. *DDT*, September 14, 1962; *JCL*, *MS*, *MCA*, and *NOTP*, September 16, 1962; *National Observer*, September 17, 1962. The dummy wore a University of Georgia jacket because that school had recently desegregated.

25. Testimonies of L. L. Love, October 18, 1962, and Sidna Brower, March 8, 1963, in GLICP; Richard B. Wilson Jr., Associated Student Body, in *Annual Report of the Chancellor to the Board of Trustees of Institutions of Higher Learning*, 1962–1963, 223–24; statement submitted by Hugh H. Clegg, no date, in IHLP; *MCA*, November 1, 1962; *MPS* and *DDT*, September 17, 1962. The retreat was held at Enid Shores Lodge, a private lodge at the southern edge of Panola County just north of the dam on Enid Lake.

26. Statement signed by Don H. Anderson, Duncan Gray, Walter Maloney, Wayne Coleman, Clifford A. McKay, Wofford K. Smith, Murphey Wilds, and Bill Pennington, no date [delivered September 16, 1962], in RBP and UF.

27. Rev. Murphey C. Wilds's sermon, September 16, 1962; Rev. Duncan Gray, "A Pastoral Word," Bulletin for St. Peter's Episcopal Church, September 16, 1962; and Rev. Wofford K. Smith's sermon, September 16, 1962, in RBP. Smith preached at St. Peter's because Gray was away preaching in Como, Mississippi; he preached the same sermon at St. Andrew's Episcopal Church in Jackson two weeks later.

28. Minutes, IHL Board, September 14, 1962, in Records of the IHL Board, Jackson, Miss.; David G. Sansing, *Making Haste Slowly: The Troubled History of Higher Education in Mississippi* (Jackson: University Press of Mississippi, 1990), 167–69; *NOTP*, *JCL*, and *JDN*, September 15, 1962; *MCA* and *MS*, September 16, 1962. The minutes of the meeting of the IHL Board are unrevealing of most of the substance of the discussions. Based on many interviews, Sansing's book provides the most thorough and revealing account of the trustees' deliberations.

29. *JCL*, *JDN*, and *MCA*, September 16 and 17, 1962; *NOTP*, September 16, 1962; *MS* and *DDT*, September 17, 1962.

30. Geohegan's Summary; and Paskal D. Bowser and John D. Rogers to J. P. McShane, July 12, 1962, in USMP.

31. Geohegan's Summary.

32. Maj. Gen. Creighton W. Abrams, memorandum for the record, September 14, 1962, in RG 319; Geohegan's Summary. The official military history of the army's involvement suggests that the meeting may have taken place *before* Barnett's address or later that night after the speech, but neither timing seems likely. Geohegan's account dates the meeting on September 14. See Paul J. Scheips, "The Role of the Army in the Oxford, Mississippi, Incident, 1962–1963," Histories Division, Office of the Chief of Military History, Department of the Army, June 24, 1965. One army after-action report also suggests the meeting occurred on September 13, but the same report misdates other events of September 13–16, 1962. See [OASCI], "After-Action Report pertaining to Oxford, Mississippi Operation," in RG 319. Marshall's Chronology failed to mention the meeting. William Doyle's *An American Insurrection: The Battle of Oxford, Mississippi, 1962* (New York: Doubleday, 2001) used

Scheips's history but not Record Group 319 in the National Archives. Doyle also apparently did not look at the U.S. Marshals Papers.

33. Geohegan's Summary; statement of James McShane, no date, in USMP. McShane's statement accompanies a copy of his testimony before the U.S. Court of Appeals for the Fifth Circuit on September 28, 1962.

34. CG USCONARC/CINCARSTRIKE TO CG USARMYTHREE FTMCPHERSON GA HIGH HEELS II/SPADE FORK, September 17 and 18, 1962; DCSOPS Department of the Army to CONARC, September 19, 1962; Col. Walter S. Schlotzhauer Jr., ODCSOPS, memorandum for the record, September 19, 1962, all in RG 319; Scheips, "Role of the Army," 14–20.

35. [OASCI], "After-Action Report"; Scheips, "Role of the Army," 20 and 35n.10.

36. Marshall's Chronology; *MCA*, September 17, 1962. For example, McDougall called John C. Satterfield to urge him to speak out about observing the law. See secretary's notes on telephone message left by McDougall in Satterfield's absence, September 18, 1962, in John Satterfield Papers, ASCUM.

37. Transcript of Conversation between Atty. Gen. Robert Kennedy and Gov. Ross Barnett, 2:15 P.M., September 15, 1962, in BMP. Although referred to as transcripts, the documents are not always exact and complete but include also summaries and paraphrased notes of conversations. Unlike the taped presidential conversations, the origin of the Justice Department documents remains unclear. Because the transcripts were made by the Justice Department, the times were all Washington time, which was two hours ahead of Mississippi; Mississippi was not on daylight saving time and Washington was. The transcripts of many of the telephone conversations are reproduced in Victor S. Navasky, *Kennedy Justice* (New York: Atheneum, 1971).

38. Sansing, *Making Haste*, 170–71; *DDT*, *JCL*, *MCA*, *NOTP*, *NYT*, and *BN*, September 18, 1962; Minutes, IHL Board, September 17, 1962.

39. Sansing, *Making Haste*, 171; *JDN*, September 18, 1962.

40. "Explanation of Position of Tally D. Riddell, Member of the Board of Trustees of Institutions of Higher Learning," Supplement to Minutes, IHL Board, September 19, 1962.

41. *West Point Daily Times Leader* quoted in *JDN*, September 18 and 19, 1962; *JCL*, September 17 and 19, 1962; *MS*, *DDT*, and *NYT*, September 18, 1962; *NOTP*, September 19, 1962. At Ole Miss, an anonymous, two-page mimeographed *Liberty Bulletin* damned the "entire unlawful business" involving the integration of the university, claimed it was "being conducted solely to buy the votes to perpetrate the Kennedy dynasty and promote the Communist conspiracy," and encouraged students to "[p]lace yourself under the direction of Gov. Barnett" and not the "leftist school administrators and officials." See *Liberty Bulletin*, Fall 1962, in UF.

42. *MCA*, September 18, 1962.

43. *DDT* and *Pascagoula Chronicle*, September 19, 1962.

44. Transcripts of conversations between Robert Kennedy and Ross Barnett, 7:00 P.M., September 17, and 12:30 P.M., September 18, 1962; and between Burke Marshall and Ross Barnett, 6:05 P.M., September 18, 1962, in BMP.

45. *NYT, NOTP, JDN,* and *JCL,* September 19, 1962.

46. *JCL, NOTP,* and *MCA,* September 19, 1962; *NYT,* September 16, 1962.

47. *JDN* and *JCL,* September 19, 1962. Emphasis added.

48. Application for Amicus, in *Meredith v. Fair; JDN* and *NOTP,* September 19, 1962; *JCL,* September 30, 1962.

49. William A. Geohegan, memorandum of telephone call with Attorney General Patterson, no date [September 19, 1962]; transcripts of conversations between Robert Kennedy and Ross Barnett, 1:30 P.M. (approx.), and between Joe Patterson and Burke Marshall, 4:00 P.M. (approx.), September 19, 1962, in BMP.

50. *Gulfport Daily Herald, Hattiesburg American,* and *MS,* September 19, 1962; *NOTP,* September 20, 1962; Meredith, *Three Years,* 182. Meredith reprints the injunction in his book. The description of Porter derives from his protests to Chancellor Williams over Albin Krebs's editorial in 1950 and his attempt to prevent the Mississippi State basketball team from participating in the integrated NCAA tournament. See L. B. Porter to J. D. Williams, November 7, 1950, and September 24, 1951, in UF; *JDN,* March 14, 1963; Russell J. Henderson, "The 1963 Mississippi State University Basketball Controversy and the Repeal of the Unwritten Law: 'Something More than the Game Will Be Lost,' " *Journal of Southern History* 63 (November 1997): 827–54.

51. *JDN* and *MCA,* September 20, 1962.

52. *NOTP, JCL,* and *MCA,* September 20, 1962.

53. *MCA,* September 20 and 21, 1962; *JCL,* September 20, 1962; *JDN,* September 21, 1962. On Wiesenburg, see *MCEJ,* February 16, 1983; and on Wroten, see his oral history memoir of July 7, 1976, with Hank T. Holmes and John Marshall Alexander, in MDAH.

54. *JCL, MCA, JDN,* and *NOTP,* September 20, 1962.

55. Sansing, *Making Haste,* 173–75; *JCL, JDN, MS, DDT, MCA, MPS,* and *NOTP,* September 20, 1962.

56. *DDT,* September 19, 1962; *JDN, JCL, MPS,* and *MS,* September 20, 1962.

57. *MCA,* September 18, 1962; *MPS,* September 18, 19, and 20, 1962; *JCL, NOTP, BN,* and *OE,* September 20, 1962.

58. *BN,* September 19 and 20, 1962; *MPS,* September 18, 19, and 20, 1962; *JDN,* September 18 and 19, 1962; *DDT,* September 19, 1962; *JCL* and *MCA,* September 20, 1962; SAC Memphis to Director FBI, September 18, 1962 (#25), and A. Rosen to Belmont, September 20, 1962 (#74), in FBI files.

59. *DDT,* September 16, 1962; Meredith, *Three Years,* 174–77, 181.

60. *MS, DDT,* and *MPS,* September 19, 1962. See also *DDT* and *NOTP,* September 16, 1962; *NYT* and *Atlanta Journal,* September 21, 1962; *MCA,* September 16 and 19, 1962; *MPS,* September 18, 1962; *Baltimore Afro-American,* September 15, 1962; *JCL,* September 19, 1962; *MS,* September 19 and 20, 1962; and *Providence (R.I.) Evening Bulletin,* September 20, 1962.

61. Meredith, *Three Years,* 178–80.

62. *DDT,* September 16, 1962; *NYT,* September 21, 1962; *MCA,* September 16 and 19, 1962; *MPS,* September 18 and 19, 1962.

63. *JCL,* September 20, 1962.

Chapter Sixteen

1. *Louisville (Ky.) Courier-Journal*, September 23, 1962.

2. Sermon by Rev. Duncan M. Gray, September 20, 1962, in RBP. A note (and internal evidence) indicates he had delivered a variation of the sermon at St. Peter's Episcopal Church in Oxford on February 11, 1962, which was Race Relations Sunday.

3. *JDN*, September 20 and 21, 1962; *MS* and *MPS*, September 20, 1962; *JCL* and *MCA*, September 21, 1962; SAC New Orleans to FBI Director, September 20, 1962 (#48), FBI files; Motion for Injunction, U.S. District Court, Southern District of Mississippi, September 20, 1962, in *Meredith v. Fair*.

4. *MS*, *MCA*, *JDN*, *JCL*, and *NOTP*, September 21, 1962; Department of Justice, Application for a Temporary Restraining Order, September 20, 1962, U.S. District Court, in *Meredith v. Fair*. The motions filed in and the orders issued by the U.S. District Court in Meridian are in the case file, *Meredith v. Fair*.

5. *JDN*, September 20 and 21, 1962; *MS* and *MPS*, September 20, 1962; *JCL* and *MCA*, September 21, 1962; SAC New Orleans to FBI Director, September 20, 1962 (#48), FBI Files.

6. Transcripts of conversations between Joe Patterson and Burke Marshall, 9:50 A.M.; and between Joe Patterson (with Tom Watkins present) and Robert Kennedy and Burke Marshall, 12:30 P.M.; and Burke Marshall, summary of telephone calls to Tom Watkins, all on September 20, 1962, in BMP.

7. Transcripts of conversations between Joe Patterson and Robert Kennedy, 1:50 P.M., 3:15 P.M., 4:40 P.M., and 5:10 P.M.; and between Ross Barnett and Robert Kennedy, 4:53 P.M., all on September 20, 1962, in BMP.

8. Order of Gov. Ross R. Barnett, September 20, 1962; Bill of Complaint, *State of Mississippi ex rel. Ross R. Barnett, Governor v. James H. Meredith*, Chancery Court, First Judicial District of Hinds County, Mississippi, in *Meredith v. Fair*; *JCL* and *MCA*, September 21, 1962. *Meredith v. Fair* also contains a copy of the same complaint filed in chancery court in Oxford.

9. Bill of Complaint; and Order Granting Temporary Injunction, *State of Mississippi ex rel. Ross R. Barnett, Governor v. James H. Meredith*, Chancery Court, First Judicial District of Hinds County, Mississippi, in *Meredith v. Fair*; *MCA*, September 21, 1962. The press immediately reported the complaint filed in Oxford but, did not learn about the Hinds complaint until the following Monday, September 24, when the first stories appeared. See *DDT* and *JDN*, September 24, 1962; and *NOTP* and *JCL*, September 25, 1962.

10. *NYT*, *MPS*, *NOTP*, *JDN*, and *MS*, September 21, 1962; E. R. Jobe to James H. Meredith, September 17, 1962, copy in certificate signed by Jobe in *Meredith v. Fair*; Robert F. Kennedy to Euclid Ray Jobe, no date [September 20, 1962], in BMP. Newspapers reported the same telegram went to Chancellor Williams, Dean Lewis, and Registrar Ellis.

11. *NOTP*, *MCA*, and *JCL*, September 21, 1962; Minutes, IHL Board, September 21, 1962, in Records of the IHL Board, Jackson, Miss.; David G. Sansing, *Making Haste Slowly: The Troubled History of Higher Education in Mississippi* (Jackson: University Press of Mississippi, 1990), 175–76.

12. *MCA*, *JDN*, and *JCL*, September 21, 1962; *DDT*, September 20, 1962; *MPS*, September 20 and 21, 1962. An unidentified interviewee (name blocked out under FOIPA) told the FBI that Barnett also conferred with Dugas Shands and Jack Doty, university attorney (#1755), in FBI Files.

13. Deposition of James Joseph P. McShane, *Cyril T. Faneca v. United States of America*, U.S. District Court for the Southern District of Mississippi, December 11, 1962, in USMP; Frederick S. Calhoun, *The Lawmen: United States Marshals and Their Deputies, 1789–1989* (Washington: Smithsonian, 1989), 258–59; *JCL*, May 11, 1962; *MCA*, September 22, 1962; *MS*, September 28, 1962.

14. *JDN*, *JCL*, and *MCA*, September 21, 1962; *DDT* and *MPS*, September 20, 1962; James Meredith, *Three Years in Mississippi* (Bloomington: Indiana University Press, 1966), 184–86; A. Rosen to Belmont, September 20, 1962 (#74), in FBI Files.

15. Joe T. Patterson to Williams, Ellis, and Lewis, September 20, 1962, in *Meredith v. Fair*; *MCA*, September 22, 1962; *JDN*, September 24, 1962. The best source for the Meredith-Barnett meeting is testimony at a hearing the following day in U.S. District Court in Meridian. See testimony of St. John Barrett, Hearing, September 21, 1961, U.S. District Court, Meridian, Miss. For a transcript of the hearing, see *Meredith v. Fair* case file. Ellis's interview with the FBI on December 10, 1962, also provided details (#1755). For another eyewitness account, see the statement by U.S. Marshal Ellis G. Duley, undated, in RG 527. For newspaper coverage of the incident described in succeeding paragraphs, see *JCL*, *JDN*, *MCA*, *MPS*, *NOTP*, *MS*, *DDT*, and *NYT*, September 21, 1962. According to some accounts, at one point early in the meeting the governor asked, "Which one of you is Meredith?" Clark Porteous reported, however, that Barnett told the story in regard to a later meeting in Jackson; see *MPS*, September 27, 1962.

16. *JDN*, September 21, 1962; testimony of Barrett.

17. Testimony of Barrett; Gov. Ross Barnett, Proclamation, September 21, 1962, in *Meredith v. Fair*.

18. Barnett quoted in testimony of Barrett.

19. *MCA*, September 21, 1962.

20. Petition of the United States, U.S. District Court, September 20, 1962, and Order to Show Cause, September 20, 1962, in *Meredith v. Fair*; *MS*, *MCA*, *NOTP*, *DDT*, and *JDN*, September 21, 1962.

21. *MS*, *JCL*, *JDN*, and *NYT*, September 22, 1962; *MCA*, October 3, 1962; Fred B. Smith Subject File, in MDAH.

22. *MS* and *JDN*, September 22, 1962.

23. *MS*, September 22, 1962; testimony of Frank Everett, Hearing, September 21, 1962, U.S. District Court, Meridian, Miss., in *Meredith v. Fair*.

24. *NYT*, *JCL*, *MS*, and *JDN*, September 22, 1962. The transcript of the hearing did not contain the final arguments to the court.

25. See the references in note 24, above.

26. See the references in note 24, above. See also Judge Mize's ruling, Hearing, September 21, 1962, U.S. District Court, Meridian, Miss., in *Meredith v. Fair*.

27. *JCL*, September 22, 1962; U.S. Congress, Senate, 87th Cong., 2nd sess., *Congressional Record* 108, no. 15 (September 21, 1962): 20274.

28. *DDT* and *MEJ*, September 24, 1962; Sansing, *Making Haste*, 178–79; *JCL* and *JDN*, September 20 and 24, 1962; *MS*, September 23, 1962; *NOTP*, September 21, 1962; Jack Hollingsworth Jr. to John Minor Wisdom, September 24, 1962, in JMWP. Many examples of editorial opinion appeared in a survey in Tom Ethridge's "Mississippi Notebook" column; see *JCL*, September 24, 1962.

29. *Madison County Herald*, *Lexington Advertiser*, and *JCL*, September 20, 1962; *MS*, September 23, 1962.

30. David Sansing interview with William H. Mounger, in Verner Holmes Papers, ASCUM.

31. *JCL*, September 23 and 24, 1962; *MS*, *NYT*, and *JDN*, September 24, 1962.

32. "A Public Proclamation of the Governor of the State of Mississippi," September 24, 1962, in *Meredith v. Fair*; *JDN* and *DDT*, September 24, 1962; *NYT*, September 24 and 25, 1962; *NOTP*, September 25, 1962.

33. *MCA* and *JCL*, September 23 and 25, 1962; *JDN*, September 23, 1962; *NOTP*, September 25, 1962; A. Rosen to Belmont, September 24, 1962 (#68), FBI files. Trustee Tally Riddell remained hospitalized. Other lawyers included Charles Sullivan, Malcolm Montgomery, Frank Everett, Will Hickman, Jack Doty, Chester Curtis, O. H. Smith, William H. Barbour, Atty. Gen. Joe Patterson, and Will Wells.

34. *MCA*, September 25, 1962; transcript, Hearing on Order to Show Cause Why the Board of Governors and Certain University Officials Should Not Be Cited for Civil Contempt, *Meredith v. Fair*, in JMWP (hereinafter cited as Contempt Hearing).

35. Contempt Hearing; *JCL*, September 25, 1962; Russell H. Barrett, *Integration at Ole Miss* (Chicago: Quadrangle, 1965), 111.

36. Contempt Hearing; *NOTP*, September 25, 1962.

37. Contempt Hearing; *NOTP*, September 25, 1962; Barrett, *Integration*, 111.

38. Contempt Hearing; *MCA* and *JCL*, September 25, 1962; Barrett, *Integration*, 111.

39. Contempt Hearing; Barrett, *Integration*, 111–12; *JCL*, September 25, 1962.

40. Contempt Hearing; Barrett, *Integration*, 112; *JCL*, September 25, 1962. Some accounts indicated the recess was for twenty minutes.

41. Sansing, *Making Haste*, 179–80. Sansing based his account on interviews with board members and with Morgan's son.

42. Contempt Hearing; Barrett, *Integration*, 112; *JDN*, September 25, 1962. The Fifth Circuit Court of Appeals order can be found at *RRLR* 7 (1962): 755–56.

43. The statement was reprinted in *DDT* and *NOTP*, September 25, 1962.

44. George M. Street, memo to file, no date [September 23, 1962], in GMSP. In "Someone Jumped the Gun" (142–43), Hugh Clegg erroneously places the events on September 22 and 23.

45. *JCL* and *NOTP*, September 25, 1962.

46. Transcript of conversation between Robert Kennedy and Ross Barnett, 9:50 P.M., September 24, 1962, in BMP.

47. *JCL*, *MCA*, *MS*, and *NYT*, September 25, 1962. An unidentified clipping shows Murphy holding his Ole Miss ID card. See also a story on a dozen "dark skinned Hindu students from Bombay, India," in *MPS*, September 29, 1962.

48. Order of Gov. Ross R. Barnett, September 25, 1962, in *Meredith v. Fair*; *JCL*, *MS*, *DDT*, *NOTP*, and *JDN*, September 25, 1962; C. A. Evans to Belmont, September 25, 1962 (#62), and A. Rosen to Belmont, September 25, 1962 (#85), in FBI Files. The Fifth Circuit Court of Appeals' Temporary Restraining Order can be found in *RRLR* 7 (1962): 756–57. For dissenting views, see *DDT*, September 25, 1962; and *MEJ*, September 26, 1962.

49. Transcript of conversation between Robert Kennedy and Ross Barnett, 12:20 P.M., September 25, 1962, in BMP.

50. Ibid.

51. Ibid.

52. Minutes, IHL Board, September 25, 1962; A. Rosen to Belmont, September 25, 1962 (#83, #84), in FBI Files; statement by J. D. Doty, university attorney, September 26, 1962; and report of respondents Williams, Lewis, and Ellis, in *Meredith v. Fair*, both in JMWP. By the time the board met, Williams had flown back to Oxford. Description of the events of September 25, 1962, largely derives from coverage in *JCL*, *JDN*, *NOTP*, *MS*, *NYT*, and *DDT*, September 26, 1962. In the paragraphs that follow, only additional sources and the sources of quotations will be specifically cited.

53. A. Rosen to Belmont, September 25, 1962 (#83), in FBI Files.

54. Summary of additional telephone conversations by Burke Marshall, September 25, 1962; transcript of conversation between Robert Kennedy and Ross Barnett, 3:25 P.M., September 25, 1962, in BMP.

55. Summary of additional telephone conversations by Burke Marshall, September 25, 1962.

56. A. Rosen to Belmont, September 25, 1962 (#95), FBI Files. The description of Doar derives from innumerable works that mention him and discuss his work.

57. Transcript of conversations between Robert Kennedy and Ross Barnett, 6:10 P.M. and 6:25 P.M., September 25, 1962, in BMP; A. Rosen to Belmont, September 25, 1962 (#95), in FBI Files.

58. *MS*, September 26, 1962. Quotations from a news film found at the National Archives and Records Administration–Southeast Region, Atlanta, Ga. (hereinafter referred to as Recording, September 25, 1962). Some newspaper accounts and later books are inaccurate. See, for example, William Doyle, *An American Insurrection: The Battle of Oxford, Mississippi, 1962* (New York: Doubleday, 2001), 82–83, that quotes Barnett as asking, "Which one of you is Meredith?" Even Meredith reported that Barnett asked, "Which one is Meredith?" (*Three Years*, 196). The recording indicates that Barnett actually asked John Doar, "Is this James Meredith over here?" For a misinterpretation, see Joseph Crespino, *In Search of Another South: Mississippi and the Conservative Counterrevolution* (Princeton: Princeton University Press, 2007), 15–16.

59. Recording, September 25, 1962. A copy of Barnett's proclamation can be found in *RRLR* 7 (1962): 759.

60. Recording, September 25, 1962; *NOTP*, September 26, 1962.

61. *MS*, *DDT*, and *NYT*, September 26, 1962; statement by J. D. Doty, university attorney, September 26, 1962; and report of respondents Williams, Lewis, and Ellis, in JMWP. Ellis said that he had been kept from Meredith by a subpoena from a legislative committee, which met in the board's office. Report of interview, December 10, 1962 (#1755), in FBI Files.

Chapter Seventeen

1. Transcript of conversation between Robert Kennedy and Ross Barnett, 7:25 P.M., September 25, 1962, in BMP.

2. Ibid.

3. Transcript of conversation between Robert Kennedy and Ross Barnett, 7:35 P.M., September 25, 1962, in BMP.

4. *JCL*, *DDT*, and *NOTP*, September 26, 1962; *MS*, September 25 and 26, 1962; Order, U.S. Circuit Court of Appeals for the Fifth Circuit, September 25, 1962, in *Meredith v. Fair*; *NYT*, September 25, 1962.

5. *MS*, September 25, 1962; *JCL*, September 25, 26, 27, and 30, 1962; *MCA*, 25 and 26, 1962. The sheriffs' vigorous support for Barnett may in part have been in hopes of gaining the governor's support for a bill that would allow sheriffs to succeed themselves; in June voters had approved a constitutional amendment allowing sheriff succession.

6. *MS* and *NYT*, September 25, 1962; *MCA*, September 25 and 26, 1962; *DDT*, September 27, 1962; *JCL*, September 18, 25, 26, and 30, 1962.

7. The following description of events on September 26, 1962, derives primarily from accounts in *JCL*, *JDN*, *MS*, *MCA*, *MPS*, *NOTP*, *WP*, and *NYT*; testimony of U.S. Marshal Cecil Harry Miller, in Hearing to Show Cause Why Lieutenant Governor Paul B. Johnson Should Not Be Cited for Civil Contempt; and testimony of James P. McShane, in Hearing to Show Cause Why Governor Ross R. Barnett Should Not Be Cited for Civil Contempt, both in *Meredith v. Fair*.

8. [Burke Marshall], memorandum [to Atty. Gen. Robert Kennedy], summary of the day's telephone calls to Tom Watkins, September 27, 1962, in BMP.

9. *NYT*, September 28, 1962; *U.S. News and World Report*, October 8, 1962, 37; *JDN*, December 11, 1962; *SSN*, July 1962, 2; *NOTP*, September 30, 1962, and January 13, 1963; *MCA*, September 28 and December 16, 1962, and January 13, 1963.

10. *JCL*, September 27, 1962; *MPS* and *MS*, September 26, 1962; SAC Memphis to Director of FBI, September 28, 1962 (#634), in FBI Files.

11. *New Orleans States-Item*, September 27, 1962.

12. *DDT*, *JDN*, *NOTP*, and *JCL*, September 27, 1962; *MPS*, September 26, 1962; U.S. Congress, Senate, 87th Cong., 2nd sess., *Congressional Record* 108, no. 15 (September 26, 1962): 20804, 20805, 20816, 20817, and 20883. The *Jackson Clarion-Ledger* pointed out that the senators spoke to a nearly empty chamber.

13. *JDN*, *NYT*, and *NOTP*, September 27, 1962; *DDT*, September 26 and 27, 1962; *JCL*,

September 26, 1962. On SACS, see George Jackson Allen Jr., "A History of the Commission on Colleges of the Southern Association of Colleges and Schools," (Ph.D. diss., Georgia State University, 1978), 189–90.

14. *MCA*, September 27, 1962; CG USCONARC/CINCARSTRIKE to CG USARMY THREE FT MCPHERSON GA, September 17, 1962; memorandum for the record by Col. Walter S. Schlotzhauer Jr., September 19, 1962; Maj. Gen. Creighton Abrams to Commanding General USCONARC, September 20 and 22, 1962; and Maj. Gen. Creighton Abrams to CONARC and Third Army, September 27, 1962, all in RG 319.

15. [Burke Marshall], memorandum [to Atty. Gen. Kennedy], summary of day's telephone calls to Tom Watkins, September 27, 1962; and [summary of] telephone conversation between Tom Watkins and Robert Kennedy, September 27, 1962, in BMP.

16. Transcripts of conversations between Robert Kennedy and Ross Barnett, 2:50 P.M. and 3:50 P.M., September 27, 1962, in BMP.

17. Transcripts of conversations between Robert Kennedy and Ross Barnett, 4:20 P.M. and 5:35 P.M., September 27, 1962, in BMP.

18. James Meredith, *Three Years in Mississippi* (Bloomington: Indiana University Press, 1966), 204–6; statement of Donald D. Forsht, November 27–29, 1962, in RG 527.

19. *MPS*, September 26, 1962; *MCA*, *MS*, and *Christian Science Monitor*, September 27, 1962.

20. *MS*, *MPS*, *JDN*, *DDT*, and *BN*, September 27 and 28, 1962; *JCL*, *MCA*, and *NOTP*, September 28, 1962; SAC Memphis to Director of FBI, September 28, 1962 (#634), in FBI Files.

21. *JCL*, *DDT*, *NOTP*, *MS*, and *MPS*, September 28, 1962; SAC Memphis to Director of FBI, September 28, 1962 (#634), in FBI Files.

22. Transcripts of conversation between Robert Kennedy and Ross Barnett, 6:35 P.M., September 27, 1962, in BMP; *JDN* and *MCA*, September 28, 1962; Meredith, *Three Years*, 205–6; SAC Memphis to Director of FBI, September 28, 1962 (#634), FBI Files; statement of Donald D. Forsht.

23. Statement of the Attorney General, Robert F. Kennedy, September 27, 1962, in BMP; *BN*, September 28, 1962.

24. *DDT*, *NYT*, and *JCL*, September 28, 1962.

25. *MS*, *JDN*, and *JCL*, September 28, 1962; *JDN* and *NOTP*, September 29, 1962.

26. Hearing on Order to Show Cause, September 28, 1962, in *Meredith v. Fair*. Major newspaper coverage of events can be found in *JCL*, *MCA*, *NOTP*, and *WP*, September 29, 1962. See also Rosen to Belmont, September 28, 1962 (#195), and SAC New Orleans to Director of FBI, October 5, 1962 (#495), FBI Files.

27. Hearing on Order to Show Cause, September 28, 1962, in *Meredith v. Fair*.

28. Ibid.

29. Ibid.; *Meredith v. Fair*, 313 F.2d 532 (1962). Ruling is reprinted in *RRLR* 7 (1962): 761–62. See also SAC New Orleans to Director of FBI, October 5, 1962 (#495), FBI Files.

30. *NYT*, *Miami Herald*, and *WP*, September 29, 1962; *JCL*, September 28 and 29, 1962; *MS* and *DDT*, September 28, 1962.

31. See the references in note 30, above. See also Nick Bryant, *The Bystander: John F. Kennedy and the Struggle for Black Equality* (New York: Basic Books, 2006), 338 and 340.

32. *MPS*, September 28 and 29, 1962; *DDT* and *BN*, September 28, 1962; *JCL* and *JDN*, September 29, 1962; Paul J. Scheips, "The Role of the Army in the Oxford, Mississippi, Incident, 1962–1963," Histories Division, Office of the Chief of Military History, Department of the Army, June 24, 1965, 26–27. Many of documents collected and used by Scheips can be found in RG 319.

33. All quotations from the telegram reproduced in the Minutes of the Commission on Colleges, *Proceedings of SACS*, November 26–29, 1962, in the papers of the Southern Association of Colleges and Schools, Atlanta, Ga. See also Allen, "A History of the Commission on Colleges," 190–91; and *JCL*, *MCA*, and *Atlanta Constitution*, September 29, 1962. One member of the executive council was H. E. Finger, president of Millsaps College.

34. SAC Birmingham to FBI Director, SACs Memphis and Mobile, September 19, 1962 (#19 and #27); FBI Director to SACs Chicago, Memphis, and New Orleans, September 29, 1962 (#112); FBI Director to SACs Kansas City et al., September 28, 1962 (#113); SAC Memphis to FBI Director, September 29, 1962 (#121); SAC Atlanta to FBI Director and SAC Memphis, September 28, 1962 (#246); SAC New Orleans to FBI Director, September 29, 1962 (#122); SAC New Orleans to FBI Director and SACs New Orleans, Memphis, and Birmingham, September 28, 1962 (#126); SAC Mobile to Director FBI and SACs Memphis, Birmingham, and New Orleans, September 29, 1962 (#119), in FBI Files; *MS*, *MPS*, and *DDT*, September 29, 1962.

35. Transcript of Walker's radio interview with KWKH in SAC New Orleans to Director of FBI and SACs in Memphis and Dallas, October 9, 1962 (#62), and SAC Dallas to FBI Director, September 29, 1962 (#202); SAC Memphis to FBI Director, September 29, 1962 (#121); Rosen to Belmont, September 29, 1962 (#190), in FBI Files; *JCL* and *NOTP*, September 28, 1962; transcript of Walker's interview with WNOE, September 28, 1962, in HCP-RA. The Hodding Carter Papers contain an addition provided by James Robertshaw, Carter's attorney in a lawsuit brought later by Edwin Walker.

36. Transcript of conversations between Robert Kennedy and Ross Barnett, 1:35 P.M. and 4:00 P.M., September 28, 1962, in BMP; *JCL*, *MS*, and *Christian Science Monitor*, September 29, 1962.

37. *JCL*, *MS*, and *Christian Science Monitor*, September 29, 1962; SAC Memphis to FBI Director, September 28, 1962 (#151), in FBI Files; *NOTP* and *NYT*, September 30, 1962. The unguarded entrances allowed James L. Hicks of the *Amsterdam News* to enter and to try to obtain press credentials like the two hundred visiting white reporters. For three days police had prevented the editor of the nation's largest black weekly newspaper from entering. He went to the Lyceum's improvised pressroom where he met Pat Smith, the director of the university's news service. Smith denied Hicks press credentials and explained, "We have a very small [campus] police force here. As you realize the situation is tense. It is for your own protection. We feel you should not be on the campus." For the first time, officials had hindered Hicks's reporting. At the direction of Smith, Hicks left the campus. *MPS*, September 29, 1962.

38. *NYT*, *NOTP*, and *JCL*, September 30, 1962; *MPS*, *Christian Science Monitor*, *Baltimore Sun*, and *JDN*, September 29, 1962; *MCA*, September 29 and 30, 1962.

39. *NOTP*, September 29 and 30, 1962; *Chicago Sun-Times*, September 30, 1962; *Christian Science Monitor*, September 29, 1962.

40. *Christian Science Monitor* and *MPS*, September 29, 1962; *MCA*, September 28, 1962.

41. Transcript of "Eyewitness: The U.S. vs. Mississippi," CBS Television Network, Friday, September 28, 1962, 10:30–11:00 P.M., EDT (#2346), in FBI Files.

42. *MS*, September 30, 1962; *JDN*, September 29 and 30, 1962; *NYT*, September 30, 1962 (song's lyrics).

43. Hearing on Order to Show Cause, September 29, 1962, *Meredith v. Fair*, 313 F.2d 534 (1962); SAC New Orleans to Director of FBI, October 5, 1962 (#495), in FBI Papers. Court's ruling is reprinted in *RRLR* 7 (1962): 762–63. Marshal Henry E. Rowe testified that he had tried to serve the order and other papers on Johnson. When he discovered the lieutenant governor was not at his office, Rowe went to his Hattiesburg home where Mrs. Johnson refused the documents, so Rowe placed them in the screen door. Later Thursday afternoon, Rowe tried again to leave the papers at Johnson's capitol office, but seven policemen threatened to arrest him for littering if he left them on the floor.

44. *Richmond News Leader*, October 1, 1962; *JCL*, *NOTP*, and *MS*, September 30, 1962.

45. *JCL* and *NYT*, September 30, 1962. Copy of Robert Kennedy's speech in Robert F. Kennedy Papers, John F. Kennedy Presidential Library, Boston, Mass.

46. Transcript of conversation between John F. Kennedy and Ross Barnett, 2:30 P.M., September 29, 1962, in BMP; *MS*, September 29, 1962. Jonathan Rosenberg and Zachary Karabell put the time of the call at 2:00 P.M., EDT, in their *Kennedy, Johnson, and the Quest for Justice: The Civil Rights Tapes* (New York: W. W. Norton, 2003), 36–40, but the handwritten time on the transcript in the Marshall Papers is clearly "2:30 P.M."

47. Transcript of conversation between John F. Kennedy, Robert Kennedy, and Ross Barnett, 3:15 P.M., September 29, 1962, BMP. Again, Rosenberg and Karabell put the time of the call at 2:50 P.M., EDT, in *Quest for Justice*, 40–46.

48. Transcript of conversation between John F. Kennedy, Robert Kennedy, and Ross Barnett, 3:15 P.M., September 29, 1962.

49. Ibid. The third and fourth conversations on Saturday between Barnett and the president and the attorney general were not recorded. For accounts of the calls, see George B. Leonard, T. George Harris, and Christopher S. Wren, "How a Secret Deal Prevented a Massacre at Ole Miss," *Look*, December 31, 1962, 22; Walter Lord, *The Past That Would Not Die* (New York: Harper and Row, 1965), 188–90; and Rosenberg and Karabell, *Quest for Justice*, 46. Nick Bryant said Barnett called the plan off after he had been "energized by the frenzied reaction" of the crowd at the Ole Miss-Kentucky football game; he "left the stadium and immediately called Robert Kennedy." Given the two-hour differential between Central Standard Time and Eastern Daylight Saving Time, Barnett hardly had time after the evening game to call Washington early enough for the administration to have the president sign the requisite documents by midnight. He must have called before the game; a Justice Department memo suggests that Barnett did call Robert Kennedy at 7:12 P.M. (EDT) on Saturday.

See Nick Bryant, *Bystander*, 353; and Angela M. Novello to Burke Marshall, February 19, 1963, in BMP.

50. *Richmond News Leader*, October 1, 1962; *NOTP*, September 30, 1962; *MCA* and *JCL*, September 30, 1962; "Fighting Back, 1957–1962," Part 2 of *Eyes on the Prize*, documentary film by Blackside, Inc., Harry Hampton, president and executive producer (Boston, 1987); Erle Johnston, *I Rolled with Ross* (Baton Rouge: Moran, 1980), 104; *NYT* and *Nashville Banner*, September 30, 1962. Barnett's statement at halftime of the football game was misquoted in many newspapers at the time and has since been erroneously reported many places. James J. Kilpatrick pointed out that the water boy for the Rebels, "and obviously part of the team, . . . trotted briskly on the field at every time out, unmistakably accepted, unmistakably Negro." See *Richmond News Leader*, October 1, 1962.

51. *JCL*, *MS*, and *DDT*, September 30, 1962.

52. *JCL*, September 28 and 29, 1962; *DDT*, September 28, 1962; Rev. James E. Pugh to the editor, *DDT*, September 30, 1962; *MS*, September 28, 29, and 30, 1962.

53. *MS* and *JCL*, September 30, 1962.

54. On the military preparations, see Scheips, "The Role of the Army," especially 26–33, 41–45, and 61–64.

55. *NYT*, September 30, 1962; *WP*, October 1, 1962; Leonard, Harris, and Wren, "How a Secret Deal," 21–22; Lord, *The Past That Would Not Die*, 188–90.

56. Scheips, "The Role of the Army," 64–65; *NYT*, September 30, 1962; *WP*, October 1, 1962; Leonard, Harris, and Wren, "How a Secret Deal," 22; Lord, *The Past That Would Not Die*, 190.

57. *WP*, October 1, 1962; Scheips, "The Role of the Army," 65–66.

58. *MPS*, September 30, 1962.

Chapter Eighteen

1. *MS*, October 1, 1962; *Wall Street Journal*, October 1, 1962; *Washington Evening Star*, October 1, 1962. Sources for this chapter are so varied and extensive that the citations cannot be comprehensive. Not all of the relevant documents in the extensive files of the FBI and the U.S. Marshals Service will be cited. Only a few examples from the abundant newspaper accounts are mentioned. Few of the plentiful secondary sources are included.

2. "OXFORD! Mississippi National Guard Stands Fast!" *The National Guardsman*, November 1962, 4–5; Paul J. Scheips, "The Role of the Army in the Oxford, Mississippi, Incident, 1962–1963," Histories Division, Office of the Chief of Military History, Department of the Army, June 24, 1965, 65–72; Claude F. Clayton to Gen. Creighton W. Abrams, October 1, 1962, in RG 319; FBI Agent Lynn P. Smith, report on interview with William John Hays, October 31, 1962, and FBI Agent Sam H. Allen Jr., report on interview with William Herman Camp, October 16, 1962, in RG 527; *MS*, *MCA*, and *MPS*, October 1, 1962. Claude F. Clayton, the senior commander of the National Guard, remained a civilian, however, because of his role as a federal district judge in northern Mississippi.

3. Scheips, "Role of the Army," 24, 63, 78.

4. Ibid., 57–59.

5. Frederick S. Calhoun, *The Lawmen: United States Marshals and Their Deputies, 1798–1989* (Washington, D.C.: Smithsonian, 1990), 265. See also statistical data on marshals from untitled and undated document; and "Background Statement for Riot Control Manual," *Deputy United States Marshals Training Manual: Riot Control* (1962), 7, both in USMP. The total number of marshals, special and permanent, involved in Oxford varies among the sources.

6. Statistical data, no date, USMP; interview with Ellis G. Duley, USM, undated (#1722), in FBI Files; *MPS*, October 3, 1962; *Raleigh News and Observer*, October 7, 1962. The "southern" states include the District of Columbia and seventeen states from Maryland and Delaware to Missouri, Oklahoma, and Texas.

7. *MCA*, October 18 and December 7 and 16, 1962; Tom Watkins to Erle Johnston, October 6, 1962, MSSCP. Hardliners also included the men he sent to Ole Miss on Sunday.

8. Transcript of conversation between Robert Kennedy and Ross Barnett, 12:45 P.M. (EDT), September 30, 1962, in BMP. Later Tom Watkins and Burke Marshall joined the conversation. Note the two-hour difference between Washington and Mississippi because the state did not follow Daylight Saving Time.

9. Ibid.

10. Ibid.

11. Ibid.

12. Ibid.

13. *NYT*, October 1, 1962. The paper reproduced the telegram in full.

14. Ibid.

15. Mississippi Highway Patrol, official report, no date, MSSCP-USM; testimonies of Col. T. B. Birdsong, October 30, 1962, and Chief Dave Gayden, October 31, 1962, in GLICP.

16. Testimonies of George Yarbrough and John C. McLaurin, October 4, 1972, Russel B. Moore, November 1, 1962, and C. B. Newman, March 4, 1963, in GLICP.

17. Interview with Nicholas deB. Katzenbach, no date (#1873), statement of Harold F. Reis, November 30, 1962 (#1873), and statement of Edwin O. Guthman, October 17, 1962 (#1722), all in FBI Files; statement of Norbert A. Schlei, in USMP; *NYT*, October 1, 1962. As in the first two citations, two or more FBI documents can have the same number if they are parts of a larger set of documents. For Katzenbach's error-filled reminiscences, see Nicholas deB. Katzenbach, *Some of It Was Fun: Working with RFK and LBJ* (New York: Norton, 2008), especially 73–84.

18. Sermons by Rev. Wofford K. Smith, September 16 and 30, 1962, and by Rev. Murphey C. Wilds, September 30, 1962, in RBP.

19. Sermon by Rev. Duncan M. Gray, September 30, 1962 (emphasis in original), in RBP; *OE*, September 5, 1957.

20. James Meredith, *Three Years in Mississippi* (Bloomington: Indiana University Press, 1966), 210–11; interview with Cecil Miller by Andrew Solt Productions, no date; Scheips, "Role of the Army," 91; Hugh Clegg, "Someone Jumped the Gun" (unpublished manuscript), 188. Andrew Solt Productions interviewed Miller and other U.S. marshals for a

television documentary, and producer Ken Wiederhorn made the transcripts of the interviews available to the author.

21. *DDT*, September 29, 1962; *MS*, September 29 and 30, 1962; *DDT*, *MPS*, *Shreveport Journal*, and *JCL*, September 29, 1962; *NOTP*, October 1, 1962.

22. Walker's deposition, July 6, 1964, in *Walker v. The Pulitzer Publishing Company*, in HCP-RA; SAC WFO to Director FBI, October 12, 1962 (#709), and report of SA, October 12, 1962 (#866), both in FBI Files; FBI Agent Robin O. Cotten, report on October 9, 1962, interview with Joe W. Ford, in RG 527.

23. *JCL*, September 30, 1962; *NYT*, December 15, 1962; testimony of George Yarbrough, October 4, 1962, in GLICP; report of SA on interview with Washington journalists, November 9, 1962 (#1432), and report of SA, including 218 interviews, October 6, 1962 (#791), both in FBI Files; *MCA*, September 27, 1962; FCC, *Federal Communications Commission Reports* (Washington, D.C.: GPO, 1965), 40:556–70 and 641–46.

24. Notes on two conversations between Tom Watkins and Burke Marshall, September 30, 1962; John Doar to Nicholas deB. Katzenbach, "Chronology of Events, 1:00 P.M.–8:00 P.M., Sunday, September 30, 1962" (hereinafter referred to as Doar Chronology), in USMP. Marshall made the first call and Watkins the second.

25. *OE*, October 27, 1955; Paskal D. Bowser and John D. Rogers to James J. P. McShane, July 12, 1962, in USMP; testimonies of Col. T. B. Birdsong, October 30, 1962, of Dave Gayden, October 31, 1962, and of D. B. Crockett, November 2, 1962, in GLICP; Mississippi Highway Patrol, official report, no date, MSSCP-USM; statement of Edwin O. Guthman, no date (#1722), in FBI Files. In September 1962, Southern Airways served the airport with two flights each day from both Memphis and Jackson. The largest plane regularly using the airport was a DC-3.

26. Testimonies of Hugh H. Clegg, October 17, 1962, of L. L. Love, October 18, 1962, and of J. D. Williams, November 8, 1962, in GLICP; affidavit of J. D. Williams, September 5, 1963, in UF; Clegg, "Someone Jumped the Gun," 188–89.

27. Testimonies of Clegg, Love, and Williams; affidavit of Williams; affidavit of Burke Marshall, U.S. Court of Appeals for the Fifth Circuit, October 24, 1962, in USMP; Clegg, "Someone Jumped the Gun," 190–91.

28. Statement of radio broadcast, September 30, 1962, in GMSP; affidavit of Williams; *The Ole Miss M Book, 1962–1963*, 19. The radio transcript was signed by Duncan Whiteside, the station director.

29. Testimony of Col. Birdsong; Doar Chronology; statement of Norbert A. Schlei, no date, in USMP; interview with Nicholas deB. Katzenbach, no date (#1873); statements of Harold F. Reis, November 30, 1962 (#1873), Edwin O. Guthman, October 17, 1962 (#1722), and two unidentified officials, no date (#1873), in FBI Files; Mississippi Highway Patrol, official report; Scheips, "Role of the Army," 89. The two officials who provided the statement to the FBI were radio coordinators assigned to the Oxford Base Operations in the basement of the post office; in the interview they referred to their log of all radio traffic (hereinafter referred to as Statement Based on Radio Log). For the eleven-page log for September 30–October 1, 1962, titled "Traffic at Base Radio" (hereinafter referred to as Base Camp Radio Log), see USMP. It was prepared by border patrol inspectors Bob Christesson

and C. V. Williams. A typed note at the end concedes "some mistakes in spelling due to fact that much of this was typed by flashlight at the fish camp, but times and facts correct." For a "statement" by or an interview with "Bobby Christensen" and "Donald R. Copoch [or Copech]" about the creation of the log, see the Ramsey Clark Papers, Lyndon Baines Johnson Library, Austin, Tex., and #1873 in FBI Files.

30. Statement of Norbert A. Schlei, no date; fragmentary statement by Burke Marshall, no date; and deposition of James Joseph P. McShane, in *Cyril T. Faneca v. United States of America* (U.S.S.D. Miss.), December 11, 1962, in USMP; interview with Nicholas deB. Katzenbach, no date (#1873); and statement of Edwin O. Guthman, October 17, 1962 (#1722), both in FBI Files; testimonies of Burnes Tatum, January 29, 1963, and Hugh H. Clegg, October 17, 1962, in GLICP. In testimony, Clegg omitted any discussion of the meeting in the Lyceum, and Tatum emphasized that he did not unlock the Lyceum.

31. Scheips incorrectly explained the presence of the marshals around the Lyceum in a different way: "This deployment, it should be explained, was a decoy operation to draw attention from Baxter Hall, the men's residence where Meredith would live" ("Role of the Army," 89–90). William Doyle also speculates regarding the placement of the marshals. See *An American Insurrection: The Battle of Oxford, Mississippi, 1962* (New York: Doubleday, 2001), 132.

32. Descriptions of the marshals comes from newspaper accounts and from the many interviews with marshals found in the FBI Files.

33. Interview with Katzenbach; statement of Schlei; testimony of Tatum; *OE*, July 31, 1947; Mississippi State Building Commission, *Physical Facilities, Institutions of Higher Learning, State of Mississippi: Public and Private Institutions, 1967–68* (University: University of Mississippi, 1969), 419–26. The family of George M. Street had lived in the Baxter apartment but had moved in the summer of 1962, as Robin Street, the daughter of George Street, confirmed.

34. Statement of Harold F. Reis, November 30, 1962, in USMP; statement of Schlei; testimony of L. L. Love, October 18, 1962, in GLICP; testimony of Tatum. See also "Summary of Participation of Assistant Deputy Attorney General William A. Geohegan in Matters relating to the Admission of James Meredith to the University of Mississippi," no date, in USMP.

35. Complete statement of U.S. Attorney Hosea M. Ray, no date (#1873), in FBI files.

36. Doar Chronology, and statement of Schlei; interview with Katzenbach; testimony of Col. T. B. Birdsong, October 30, 1962, in GLICP; testimony of Tatum; statement of Edwin O. Guthman, October 17, 1962 (#1722), in FBI Files; Mississippi Highway Patrol, official report, no date, in MSSCP-USM.

37. Statement Based on Radio Log, no date (#1873), in FBI Files. Descriptions based on hundreds of pages of interviews conducted in the weeks after October 1, 1962, in FBI Files.

38. Testimony of Chancellor J. D. Williams, November 8, 1962, in GLICP; affidavit of J. D. Williams, September 5, 1963, in UF; interviews with unidentified student, October·17, 1962 (#1043), and with Chancellor J. D. Williams, October 29, 1962 (#1433), in report of SA, November 6, 1962, in FBI Files.

39. *Deputy United States Marshals Training Manual: Riot Control*, 30–32. For example,

see statement of U.S. Border Patrolman, Oceanside, Calif., November 2, 1962 (#866), in FBI Files.

40. Statement Based on Radio Log, no date (#1873), in FBI Files; Russell H. Barrett, *Integration at Ole Miss* (Chicago: Quadrangle, 1965), 139; George B. Leonard, T. George Harris, and Christopher S. Wren, "How a Secret Deal Prevented a Massacre at Ole Miss," *Look*, December 31, 1962, 24; interviews with U.S. marshal, October 12, 1962 (#866), and with student, October 17, 1962 (#1043), in FBI Files; *NOTP*, October 1, 1962.

41. *MS* and *Christian Science Monitor*, October 1, 1962.

42. Interview with Katzenbach (#1873); statement of Edwin O. Guthman, October 17, 1962 (#1722); and Statement Based on Radio Log, no date (#1873), in FBI Files; statement of Lloyd A. Short, October 4, 1962, in RG 527; *MPS*, October 1, 1962. The sources disagree about the number of marshals and vehicles involved.

43. Meredith, *Three Years*, 211–12; Doar Chronology; statement of Guthman; interview with Cecil Miller by Andrew Solt Productions, no date; notes on additional conversation with Governor Barnett on September 30, 1962; and affidavit of Burke Marshall, U.S. Court of Appeals for the Fifth Circuit, October 24, 1962, in USMP; statement of Lloyd A. Short. Miller remembered placing mattresses over the windows for protection and hiding Meredith under a mattress in a closet during the night when the marshals ran low on tear gas and feared a mob attack, but Meredith's memoir reported no such events. In his call to Barnett, the attorney general explained that the federal agents had taken Meredith to Oxford by plane and to campus by car, not by helicopter as they had assumed in previous conversations. Earlier Barnett had prepared a formal statement to be released when Meredith arrived on campus, and it mentioned the use of a helicopter. Attorney General Kennedy had reviewed a copy that had been dictated to his office, and in their conversation Kennedy pointed out the factual error involving the helicopter. Barnett could only say that the statement would be issued with the mistake because he had no typist.

44. Statement of Guthman; report of SA, November 6, 1962 (#1433); report of SA, November 14, 1962 (#1494); and Statement Based on Radio Log, no date (#1873), in FBI Files. Between 6:30 and 7:00 P.M., about the time the crowd became a mob, army mess hall workers left the Holly Springs camp with food for three hundred. By the time the five soldiers arrived in a truck at the Lyceum, the marshals had fired tear gas, and the mob had attacked the truck. Apparently hours passed before anyone ate any food. See statement of Spec. 4 Guy R. Spencer, no date, in RG 527. For one journalist's analysis of the mob psychology, see Richard Starnes in the *Knoxville Tennessean*, October 4, 1962. Numerous interviews with the marshals described the evolution of the mob. See interviews in FBI Files. For a more melodramatic account of violence and derring-do during the riot in the style of old-fashioned military history, see Doyle, *An American Insurrection*. Doyle relied heavily on interviews decades later; he did not look at the more contemporaneous accounts available in the U.S. Marshals Papers, the files created by the GLIC investigation, or the Sovereignty Commission papers. He did not use, for example, Christesson and Williams's log of radio traffic. On one point, however, Doyle is indisputably correct: establishing the exact times for specific events is nearly impossible.

45. Interviews with Spec. 5 John Richard Miller, no date (#1722), with border patrol

inspector Edwin C. Dennis, no date (#1722), and with Texas border patrolman, in report of SA, October 12, 1962 (#866), in FBI Files; Frank F. Schweib [?] to John Doar, November 26, 1962, Department of Justice, Civil Rights Division Files; Bennie E. Marshall, office memorandum, October 19, 1962, in RG 527; *Washington Evening Star*, October 1, 1962. The materials from the Civil Rights Division were obtained under a FOIPA request. The memo to Doar was an analysis of the "Conduct of State Troopers during Oxford Crisis" that Doar had requested; it apparently was based largely on reports by the marshals.

46. Interviews with Lee Vandenberg, border patrol inspector, no date (#1722), with three journalists [Louisville, Ky.?], November 2, 1962 (#1316), with an unnamed person, November 6, 1962 (#1433), with Spec. 5 John Richard Miller, no date (#1722), and with border patrol inspector Edwin C. Dennis, no date (#1722), in FBI Files; Frank F. Schweib [?] to John Doar, November 26, 1962, Department of Justice, Civil Rights Division Files.

47. *Christian Science Monitor*, *MCA*, and *Washington Evening Star*, October 1, 1962; *WP*, October 14, 1962; interview with Tampa, Florida, journalist, October 31, 1962, in report of SA, November 5, 1962 (#1364); interviews with Spec. 5 Miller, and border patrol inspector Dennis; interview with Texas border patrolman, no date, in report of SA, October 12, 1962 (#866), in FBI Files; statement of Harold F. Reis, November 30, 1962, in USMP.

48. Statements of Gordon Yoder and Mrs. Gordon Yoder, no date, in RG 527; SAC Memphis to Director FBI, October 22, 1962 (#957), in FBI Files; *MPS*, October 1, 1962; *NYT* October 2, 1962; *Newsweek*, October 15, 1962, 99; *U.S. News and World Report*, October 15, 1962, 44; *Newsweek*, October 15, 1962, 99; interviews with Houston photographer [Dan McCoy?], October 11, 1962 (#786), and Chicago journalist, November 1, 1962, in report of SA, November 8, 1962 (#1426); interview with Texas Border Patrol inspector, no date; and interview with Miami Immigration and Naturalization Service inspector, no date, both in report of SA, October 12, 1962 (#866), in FBI Files; Schweib [?] to Doar, November 26, 1962, Department of Justice, Civil Rights Division Files. Robert Massie designated the arrival of news photographers as the "spark that brought violence." He also identified Yoder's wife as "from Jackson, Mississippi." Robert Massie, "What Next in Mississippi?" *Saturday Evening Post*, November 10, 1962, 18.

49. For an account of an attack on a *Newsweek* photographer, see FBI Agents Graham W. Kitchel and Edwin Dalrymple, report on October 18, 1962, interview with Daniel Joseph McCoy, in RG 527. Apparently no literature exists on journalists as targets or victims of domestic disorders. One editor commented that "a mobster sees in the press a menace. A free press will tell the whole world what dirty business he wants to sweep under the rug, and how he goes about trying to do it." See *MPS*, October 3, 1962. In the words of Gene Roberts and Hank Klibanoff, John Lewis during the Freedom Rides realized that segregationists "hoped to destroy the movement by destroying its witnesses, the reporters" (*The Race Beat: The Press, the Civil Rights Struggle, and the Awakening of a Nation* [New York: Knopf, 2006], 253). Alumnus Albin Krebs's " 'Kill the Reporters!' " in the October 15, 1962, *Newsweek* (100–101) discussed the attacks on journalists. Journalists also faced technical obstacles in filing reports because the number of long distance calls tripled during the riot and its immediate aftermath; attempts to call out often got a busy signal. See *OE*, October 4, 1962; *NT*, October 7, 1962; and *JDN*, October 10, 1962. For journalists' accounts, see Dan Rather with Mickey

Herskowitz, *The Camera Never Blinks: Adventures of a TV Journalist* (New York: William Morrow, 1977), 65–82; George Leonard, *Walking on the Edge of the World* (Boston: Houghton Mifflin, 1988), 92–104; Bob Schieffer, *This Just In: What I Couldn't Tell You on TV* (New York: G. P. Putnam's Sons, 2003), 23–34; Karl Fleming, *Son of the Rough South: An Uncivil Memoir* (New York: Public Affairs, 2005), 264–89.

50. *MS*, October 9, 1962; Thomas H. Waddill to James McShane, October 21, 1962, in RG 527. William Doyle offers no explanation for his use of the term "insurrection" (see *An American Insurrection*). On civil disorders and riots, see Ronald Gottesman and Richard Maxwell Brown, eds., *Violence in America: An Encyclopedia* (New York: Scribner's, 1999).

51. Testimonies of George Yarbrough and John C. McLaurin, October 4, 1972, Russel B. Moore, November 1, 1962, and C. B. Newman, March 4, 1963, in GLICP; Statement Based on Radio Log, no date (#1873), in FBI Files.

52. Interview with Katzenbach; statement of Guthman; testimony of Yarbrough; statement of Schlei; Doar Chronology.

53. See the references in note 52, above.

54. *JDN*, October 1, 1962.

55. Ibid.

56. Testimony of James P. McShane; statement of Schlei; and Base Camp Radio Log, in USMP. The context of McShane's testimony remains unclear. See also the many interviews with individual marshals in the FBI Files (especially at #866 and #1722) and many newspaper accounts. The most extensive journalistic account from the time was Leonard, Harris, and Wren, "How a Secret Deal," 18–20, 22–24, 29–30, 32, 34, and 36.

57. Testimony of Yarbrough; interview with Katzenbach; statement of Guthman; testimony of McShane; statement of Schlei; Leonard, Harris, and Wren, "How a Secret Deal," 29.

58. Statement of Guthman; testimony of McShane; Leonard, Harris, and Wren, "How a Secret Deal," 30.

59. *Public Papers of the Presidents of the United States, John F. Kennedy; Containing the Public Messages, Speeches, and Statements of the President, January 1 to December 31, 1962* (Washington, D.C.: GPO, 1963), 726–27. Based on Burke Marshall's oral history, Nick Bryant suggests that Marshall, Ted Sorenson, and Robert Kennedy "had completely rewritten" the speech in response to Barnett's 7:30 P.M. statement, but less than thirty minutes seems insufficient time for such a large task. See Nick Bryant, *Bystander: John F. Kennedy and the Struggle for Black Equality* (New York: Basic Books, 2006), 346.

60. *Public Papers of John F. Kennedy, 1962*, 727.

61. Ibid., 727–28.

62. Ibid., 728.

63. Frank F. Schweib [?] to John Doar, November 26, 1962, Department of Justice, Civil Rights Division Files; Gwin Cole to Dave Gayden, October 9, 1962, MSSCP-USM; deposition of James Joseph P. McShane, in *Cyril T. Faneca v. United States of America* (U.S.S.D. Miss.), December 11, 1962, in USMP; Mississippi Highway Patrol, official report, no date, in MSSCP-USM; Statement Based on Radio Log, no date (#1873), in FBI Files; *MPS*, October 3, 1962.

64. *New Orleans States-Item*, October 1, 1962; *MS*, October 1, 1962. In addition to nu-

merous newspaper accounts and many interviews with marshals and others in the FBI Files and the U.S. Marshals Papers, descriptions of the riot can be found in Leonard, Harris, and Wren, "How a Secret Deal," 30, 32, 34, and 36; and in Doyle, *An American Insurrection*.

65. Base Camp Radio Log; Mississippi Highway Patrol, official report; *JDN*, October 3, 1962; testimony of Welby J. Brunt, February 5, 1965, in GLICP. Interviews with marshals in the FBI Files confirmed the deficiencies described in the log of radio traffic.

66. Base Camp Radio Log.

67. *NOTP* and *MPS*, October 1, 1962; *MCA*, October 2, 1962; report to SAC Memphis, October 10, 1962 (#582); report on interview with Dr. Jerry T. Francisco, October 1, 1962 (#791); report of SA, October 12, 1962 (#866); SAC Memphis to Director FBI, October 8, 1962 (#949), and October 18, 1962 (#974); and FBI laboratory report, November 6, 1962 (#1433), in FBI Files; FBI Agent Robin O. Cotten, reports on interviews with Mrs. H. H. McLarty, October 4, 1962, and with Hugh Calvin Murray, October 11, 1962; and Department of Justice Attorney Victor C. Woerheide, interview with Thomas A. Brown, October 8, 1962, all in RG 527. William Doyle suggests the possibility that a U.S. marshal, a Mississippi highway patrolman, or a sheriff's deputy could have killed Guihard. Absent any evidence, however, the likelihood seems so remote that Doyle's speculation does a disservice to the marshals, patrolmen, and deputies on the campus that night. See *An American Insurrection*, 165–66. Ward Hall was on the site of the current student union building.

68. Walker's deposition, July 6, 1964, in *Walker v. The Pulitzer Publishing Company*; statement of Henry Van Savell, no date; and notes respecting General Edwin A. Walker, September 28–October 1, 1962, no date, in HCP-RA.

69. Duncan M. Gray Jr. to Paul J. Scheips, April 25, 1963, in HCP-RA; statement of Rev. Duncan M. Gray Jr., October 2, 1962, in RG 527. Scheips was author of the history of the army's involvement in Oxford.

70. Duncan M. Gray Jr. to Paul J. Scheips, April 25, 1963; statement of Van Henry Savell, no date; and deposition of Edwin A. Walker, July 6, 1964, in *Walker v. The Pulitzer Publishing Company*, in HCP-RA; statement of Rev. Gray. In Gray's account, he places Walker's comments about being ashamed to be an Episcopalian at both his first and his second encounter with the minister.

71. *New Orleans States-Item*, October 1, 1962.

72. Duncan M. Gray Jr. to Paul J. Scheips, April 25, 1963; statement of Van Henry Savell, no date; Walker deposition; and John E. (Jack) King to Lynn P. Smith, December 10, 1962, in HCP-RA; interview with University Police officer in report of SA, October 12, 1962 (#866), in FBI Files; statement of Rev. Gray; *MCA*, October 1, 1962. John E. King was a reporter from West Point, Miss., with radio stations WROB and WANY, and Lynn P. Smith was an FBI agent in Columbus, Miss.

73. Duncan M. Gray Jr. to Paul J. Scheips, April 25, 1963, in HCP-RA; interview with University Police officer in report of SA, October 9, 1962 (#866); and interview with University Police officer in report of SA, October 12, 1962 (#866), in FBI Files; statement of Rev. Gray. The two University Policemen reported hearing Walker give orders to the crowd. Curtis Wilkie, a January 1963 graduate of the university who worked as a reporter for the *Clarksdale Press Register*, later told lawyers for Hodding Carter that he never heard Walker

give any orders the night of the riot. See notes on interview with Wilkie, in HCP-RA. Walker later filed libel lawsuits against the Associated Press, the Times-Picayune Publishing Corp., the Pulitzer Publishing Co., the Courier-Journal and Louisville Times Co., WHA Inc., Van Henry Savell, and others whom he claimed had libeled him by saying he had led the riot. In 1967 in a very complicated split decision, the U.S. Supreme Court essentially decided that Wally Butts, the University of Georgia football coach who had sued the *Saturday Evening Post*, and Edwin Walker were public figures who could sue for libel only under the same restricted conditions that applied to public officials; in effect, it dismissed the libel suits brought by Walker and Butts. See *Curtis Publishing Co. v. Butts*, 338 U.S. 130 (1967).

74. Statement of Wofford K. Smith, no date, in HCP-RA; Leonard, Harris, and Wren, "How a Secret Deal," 32 and 34.

75. Statement of W. K. Smith in HCP-RA; Leonard, Harris, and Wren, "How a Secret Deal," 32 and 34; statement of Wofford K. Smith, no date [October 2 or 3, 1962], in RG 527. See also slightly different versions of the encounter in FBI Agents Earl L. Hassell and Richard A. Smallwood, report on interview with Joseph Bryan Cummings Jr., October 11, 1962; FBI Agent James P. Hosty Jr., report on interview with Don Williams, November 7, 1962; and FBI Agent James J. Conway, report on interview with George Marvin Randall, December 18, 1962, in RG 527. William Doyle omits any mention of Smith and, based largely on an interview with Randall thirty-eight years later, portrays Randall's participation in more benign, even heroic terms. See *An American Insurrection*, 181–83. Doyle apparently did not see Smith's statement.

76. *MS* and *MCA*, October 1, 1962; *JDN*, October 4, 1962.

77. FBI Agents Donald P. McDermott and Robert E. Beams, report on November 6, 1962, interview with E. M. Tubbs; FBI Agents William S. Ovitt and Robert S. Baker, report on November 7, 1962, interview with Albert S. Taylor; and statement of Donald D. Forsht, November 27–29, 1962, in RG 527. For the episodes involving the fire truck, bulldozer, and automobile, see the FBI files and Denis E. Dillon to John Doar, "The Fire Truck and Bulldozer Incidents," March 22, 1963, in Department of Justice, Civil Rights Division Files. See, for example, interview with New Orleans journalist, October 16, 1962 (#1280); interview with Memphis newsman, November 6, 1962 (#1433); interview with border patrolman, November 21, 1962 (#1428); statement of deputy U.S. marshal, October 25, 1962 (#1305); statements of border patrolmen, November 2 and 5, 1962 (#1317); statement of border patrolman, November 2, 1962 (#1277); and statement of border patrolman, November 5, 1962 (#1275). Tubbs, supervisor of the power plant, reported 50 holes in the 250-foot hose, with only one 10-foot section without holes.

78. FBI Agents Donald P. McDermott and Timothy M. Casey Jr., report on interview with Betty Cleveland, October 4, 1962; FBI Agents Gene H. Studebaker and Harland D. Shaw, report on October 8, 1962, interview with Marvin C. Morrisette; FBI Agent James J. Conway, report on interview with Edward T. Barthelomew, January 1, 1963; Carl A. Ryan to James McShane, no date, in RG 527. Based on a marshal's belief that the driver of the bulldozer sustained a head injury and on records for the university and Oxford hospitals, the FBI identified a man from Memphis as one likely driver.

79. In addition to the sources cited in notes 77 and 78, above, see also FBI Agents Jo-

seph A. Canale and Joseph H. Kearney Jr., report on interview with George Howard Jetton Jr., October 18, 1962; FBI Agents Robert P. Hennelly and Robert Murphy, report on interview with Seibert W. Locknman, November 1, 1962; FBI Agents Holloway Cromer Jr. and Timothy M. Casey Jr., report on interview with Harvey Hall Ferguson, November 13, 1962, in RG 527. The time of the last incident involving the fire truck comes from Base Camp Radio Log, in USMP, and statement of Hosea M. Ray, no date (#1873), in FBI Files. Jetton told the FBI that he was hitchhiking back to the Millington, Tenn., naval base, from a visit with his parents (his eighteenth birthday was September 29) when two young men, reportedly students at the University of Alabama, gave him a ride. With them he rode to Oxford and became involved in the riot. After being on the campus just a few minutes, he followed them onto the fire truck; only he was apprehended by the marshals.

80. Discussion of the violence can be found in innumerable interviews in the FBI Files and newspaper accounts. The Base Camp Radio Log also contains references to many violent incidents.

81. *MCA*, October 1, 2, and 5, 1962; *MPS*, October 1 and 5, 1962; *Miami Herald*, October 2, 1962; statements of Dr. L. G. Hopkins and Dr. Ray Windham, October 29, 1962, before the GLIC, in GLICP; Base Camp Radio Log.

82. *MPS*, October 12, 1962; *JDN*, November 8 and 19, 1962; *MS*, November 8, 1962; *NYT*, November 17, 1962; Herbert J. Miller Jr. to Jesse L. Yancey, November 15, 1962, in GLICP; autopsy of Walter Ray Gunter, October 1, 1962, in GLICP (copy also in FBI Files at #1306); reports of SAs, October 12, 1962 (#866); SAC Memphis to Director FBI, November 2, 1962 (#1178), and November 13, 1962 (#1312); interview with unknown, November 8, 1962 (#1306); FBI Agent Robin O. Cotten, report on interview with Charlie Berryhill, October 4, 1962; FBI Agents Joseph G. Peggs and Stephen M. Callender, report on interview with Charlie Berryhill, October 8, 1962; FBI Agents Donald P. McDermott and James J. Conway, report on interview with Charlie Berryhill, November 19, 1962; FBI Agents Robert E. Beams and Donald P. McDermott, report on interview with George W. Buffaloe, November 8, 1962; FBI Agent Robin O. Cotten, report on interview with Mrs. G. H. McLarty, November 4, 1962, all in RG 527. Doyle also suggests that a marshal's pistol could have fired the bullet that killed Gunter, even though later FBI tests failed to establish any link between a weapon used by a federal agent and Gunter's death. At least he did concede, "If the bullet that killed Ray Gunter came from a marshal's gun, it was without question an accident" (*An American Insurrection*, 216).

83. Jonathan Rosenberg and Zachary Karabell, *Kennedy, Johnson, and the Quest for Justice: The Civil Rights Tapes* (New York: W. W. Norton, 2003), 49–68. Rosenberg and Karabell provide a transcription of the tape-recorded discussion in the Cabinet Room, though it is sometimes incomplete and incomprehensible because of the multiple voices and conversations taking place at the same time.

84. Scheips, "Role of the Army," 94–98; "OXFORD! Mississippi National Guard Stands Fast!" *The National Guardsman*, November 1962, 5.

85. Transcript of conversation between John F. Kennedy and Ross Barnett, 10:14 P.M., September 30, 1962, in USMP, and in Rosenberg and Karabell, *Quest for Racial Justice*, 68–70.

86. *NOTP*, October 1, 1962. For a slightly different version, see USMP.

87. Testimony of Paul B. Johnson, February 29–30, 1963, in GLICP; Mississippi Highway Patrol, official report. The latter document places the negotiations with the Justice Department men earlier in the evening (about 9:30 or 10:00 P.M.) and does not mention Johnson's participation.

88. Tom S. Hines to J. C. White, November 7, 1962; and E. E. Davidson to Rufus Jones, December 10, 1962, in IHLP; interview with William Crowder, in report of SA, October 12, 1962 (#866), in FBI Files. Hines's Chevrolet may also have been the unoccupied car aimed at the marshals earlier that evening.

89. Testimonies of Dr. L. G. Hopkins, Dr. Ray Windham, Betty Dugger, Mrs. Russell Thompson, Betty Harper Cleveland, and Tommy Wayne Scott, October 29, 1962; and Mississippi Bureau of Identification case report, by Charles Snodgrass, March 11, 1963, in GLICP; "Army, Marshal, Border Patrol, and National Guard Personnel Treated at Student Health Service, University, Mississippi" [September 30–October 2, 1962], October 5, 1962, in USMP; MPS, October 1, 1962. See also "Department of Justice Personnel Who Served at the University of Mississippi—September 30 to October 1, 1962," no date, in USMP.

90. Rosenberg and Karabell, Quest for Racial Justice, 70–78.

91. MPS, October 1, 1962; Scheips, "Role of the Army," 98–100; "OXFORD! Mississippi National Guard Stands Fast!" The National Guardsman, November 1962, 5.

92. Transcript of conversation between John F. Kennedy and Ross Barnett [11:45 P.M.], September 30, 1962, in BMP; Rosenberg and Karabell, Quest for Racial Justice, 79–80. The transcriptions in Burke Marshall's papers and in Rosenberg and Karabell vary slightly in wording, but the Marshall version has combined the two parts of the conversation in an incorrect order and seems to have put them at an incorrect time.

93. Rosenberg and Karabell, Quest for Racial Justice, 80–81; transcript of conversation between John F. Kennedy and Ross Barnett [11:50 P.M.], September 30, 1962, in BMP.

94. Base Camp Radio Log, USMP; Scheips, "Role of the Army," 105–10.

95. SAC Memphis to Director FBI, October 1, 1962 (#441); and SA [name deleted] report, October 1, 1962 (#502), in FBI Files; Base Camp Radio Log; notes respecting General Edwin A. Walker, September 28–October 1, 1962, no date, in HCP-RA.

96. Scheips, "Role of the Army," 110–12; Base Camp Radio Log; Washington Evening Star, October 1, 1962.

97. Scheips, "Role of the Army," 102–5 and 121–22; New Orleans States-Item, October 1, 1962.

98. JDN, October 2, 1962; David G. Sansing, Making Haste Slowly: The Troubled History of Higher Education in Mississippi (Jackson: University Press of Mississippi, 1990), 193–94.

99. MS and JDN, October 4, 1962; MCA and MPS, October 5, 1962; testimony of Richard W. Elliott, January 30, 1963, in GLICP; statement of Richard W. Elliott, no date, in RG 527.

Chapter Nineteen

1. New Orleans States-Item, MPS, and BN, October 1, 1962; JDN and MCA, October 2, 1962; James Meredith, Three Years in Mississippi (Bloomington: Indiana University Press,

1966), 212–13; Clare L. Marquette, "The 'Meredith Incident' at the University of Mississippi," *Milton Today* [Milton College alumni magazine], May 1963, 9–13. Newspaper reports varied, sometimes widely. The *Times* of London, for example, described Meredith's suit on Monday as gray and his tie as red. See *Times*, October 2, 1962.

2. *MS*, October 1 and 2, 1962; *Washington Evening Star* and *New Orleans States-Item*, October 1, 1962; *BN* and *JDN*, October 2, 1962; Meredith, *Three Years*, 213–14.

3. Marquette, "The 'Meredith Incident' "; Marquette to Frank Warren Crow, October 17, 1962, in CLMP; *MCA* and *MS*, October 2, 1962. The *Memphis Commercial Appeal* reported that one crying young woman dashed from the class, but Marquette later denied it in the letter to Frank Crow. The graduate building later was named Bondurant Hall.

4. *JDN*, *MPS*, and *St. Louis Post-Dispatch*, October 2, 1962; Meredith, *Three Years*, 214.

5. *MCA*, October 2, 1962; *JDN*, October 2 and 3, 1962; *JCL*, October 3, 1962.

6. *JDN* and *BN*, October 2, 1962; *NT*, October 3 and 4, 1962; *NYT*, October 3, 1962.

7. *Miss.*, October 1, 1962.

8. *KNS*, October 7, 1962; ASCI Report, October 3, 1962 (?) (#360), and McGowan to Rosen, October 3, 1962 (#319), in FBI Files; *NT*, October 3 and 4, 1962; *MS* and *MPS*, October 3, 1962; *MCA* and *NOTP*, October 4, 1962; *NYT*, October 4, 1962.

9. *MPS*, October 3, 1962; *MCA*, October 5, 1962; *NYT* and *Shreveport Times*, October 4, 1962; *MS*, October 9, 1962; *KNS*, October 7, 1962; *JCL*, *JDN*, *NOTP*, and *MCA*, October 5, 1962.

10. *Providence (R.I.) Evening Bulletin*, October 2, 1962; *Miami Herald*, October 3, 1962; *MCA* and *Shreveport Times*, October 4, 1962; *JDN*, October 5, 1962; *KNS*, October 7, 1962; *Baltimore Sun*, October 12, 1962.

11. *MCA* and *MS*, October 3 and 4, 1962; *JCL*, October 3 and 5, 1962; *BN*, October 3, 1962; *NYT* and *Shreveport Times*, October 4, 1962; William T. Ferrell to J. D. Williams, October 3, 1962, in UF; Maj. Gen. Edwin H. J. Carns, memorandum for the record, October 4, 1962, RG 319; Paul J. Scheips, "The Role of the Army in the Oxford, Mississippi, Incident, 1962–1963," Histories Division, Office of the Chief of Military History, Department of the Army, June 24, 1965, 155–56.

12. Scheips, "Role of the Army," 156–57; *NYT* and *JCL*, October 5, 1962; *MPS*, *JDN*, *NOTP*, *Shreveport Times*, and *BN*, October 4, 1962. The army had 2,000 paratroopers at the Columbus Air Force Base ready to move to Jackson if trouble developed. See Scheips, "Role of the Army," 159–60.

13. *BN*, October 4, 1962; *MPS*, October 5, 1962; *JDN*, October 5 and 6, 1962; *WP*, October 6, 1962; *MCA*, *NOTP*, *NT*, and *NYT*, October 7, 1962; *MS*, October 6 and 7, 1962; *JCL*, October 5, 7, and 25, 1962. Millsaps College also had a home football game scheduled for Saturday but agreed to play later Saturday.

14. *JCL*, October 5 and 9, 1962; *MCA*, October 3 and 7, 1962; *KNS*, October 7, 1962.

15. *JDN*, October 7 and 8, 1962; *JCL*, October 9 and 14, 1962; J. D. Williams to Lowell D. Hamilton, October 13, 1962, in UF.

16. Scheips, "Role of the Army," 164–66; *JCL*, October 9, 1962.

17. Scheips, "Role of the Army," 164–68; *JCL*, October 9 and 10, 1962; *MPS*, October 9, 1962; *MS*, October 9 and 10, 1962; *JDN*, October 10, 1962; *WP*, October 10, 1962; Meredith,

Three Years, 215–16. Meredith also responded to Aaron Henry's suggestion that the NAACP had chosen him; later Henry, state president of the NAACP, claimed his comments had been misquoted and misinterpreted. See *JDN* and *MPS*, October 10, 1962. Scheips notes that CBS news film recorded blacks troops on patrol on October 6 and 7.

18. Henry Hederman to J. D. Williams, October 9, 1962, in UF; statement by Leone Davis King, October 9, 1962; and George M. Street to Hugh Clegg, October 9, 1962, in GMSP; Erle Johnston, *Mississippi's Defiant Years, 1953–1973* (Forest, Miss.: Lake Harbor, 1990), 56 and 124; *MCA*, October 18, 1962.

19. *JCL*, October 8 and 9, 1962; *JDN* and *MPS*, October 9, 1962; C. L. McGowan to Rosen, October 9, 1962, (#460), in FBI Files.

20. Russell H. Barrett, *Integration at Ole Miss* (Chicago: Quadrangle, 1965), 180–81, AAUP statement reprinted on 181; *Miss.*, October 2 and 9, 1962; Seven Law School Faculty to J. D. Williams, in UF; *JCL*, October 11 and 12, 1962.

21. *MS*, November 10 and 11, 1962; *NYT*, February 13, 2003. In 2003, Holbrook said that in forty-nine years, "The Silent Lie" routine had elicited applause only three times: in 1961 in Hamburg, Germany; in 1962 in Oxford; and in 1985 in Prague, Czechoslovakia.

22. Transcript of J. D. Williams's appeal, October 11, 1962, in Charles Haywood Papers, in his personal possession, Lexington, Ky.; official notice by L. L. Love, [October 12, 1962]; resolution of the University of Mississippi Faculty Senate, October 13, 1962, in UF; statement of Phi Beta Kappa Associates, October 17, 1962, in Verner Holmes Papers, ASCUM; *JCL*, October 9, 1962; *JDN*, October 16, 1962; *MCA*, October 17 and 18, 1962; *New Orleans States-Item*, October 18, 1962; *Miss.*, October 16 and 19, 1962.

23. George M. Street, memo to file, October 9, 1962, in GMSP; Charles F. Haywood to William P. Fidler, October 17, 1962; and Russell H. Barrett to Fidler, October 17, 1962, in AAUPP; Haywood to J. D. Williams, January 8, 1963, in UF; Brad Lawrence, letter to the editor, *Miss.*, October 16, 1962; Barrett, *Integration*, 187–88; *JCL*, October 18, 1962; statement adopted by the Academic Council of the University of Mississippi, October 16, 1062, in IHLP. For statements by professors, see testimony of Charles Haywood, October 18 and 26, 1962, in GLICP.

24. Nicholas deB. Katzenbach to Russell L. Fox, March 15, 1963, in GLICP; Katzenbach to J. D. Williams, October 10 and 11, 1962; and Norbert A. Schlei to Williams, October 15, 1962, in UF; *NYT*, October 6, 1962; *JCL*, October 10 and 11, 1962; *JDN* and *MPS*, October 10, 1962; *MCA*, *MS*, *Baltimore Sun*, and *Miss.*, October 11, 1962; testimony of Dean L. L. Love, October 18, 1962, in GLICP. Exact figures on the number of people detained, taken into custody, or arrested cannot be determined; similarly, the number of students involved cannot be fixed with certainty.

25. J. D. Williams to Joe T. Patterson, October 11, 1962, in GMSP; *JCL*, October 11, 12, 13, and 14; *JDN*, *NOTP*, and *MS*, October 12, 1962; *NYT*, October 13, 1962; *MCA*, October 12 and 14, 1962. For examples of pressure on the chancellor, see letters to Williams from Charles C. Jacobs Jr., October 11, 1962; William B. Alexander, October 12, 1962; Leonard B. Melvin Sr., October 11, 1962; Mrs. W. D. Womack Jr., October 13, 1962; and James B. Sigler, October 15, 1962, in UF. The lawyers were Glenn Fant, Will Hickman, Murray Williams, Jack Doty, Byrd Mauldin, Paul Moore, O. R. Smith Sr., and Russel Moore. Students are not

named here unless a case became prominent in the press or the individual later achieved some fame or notoriety.

26. Joe T. Patterson's speech to the University of Mississippi Law School, October 16, 1962, in GLICP; *MS*, October 16, 1962; *JCL*, *JDN*, and *MCA*, October 17, 1962.

27. For criticism of Williams, see the letters to him from Malcolm H. Mabry Jr., October 6, 1962; R. N. Beck, October 17, 1962; Mary Odin Hess, October 9, 1962; Sylvia Collins Garber, October 15, 1962; E. C. Cobb, October 13, 1962; and Kenneth O. Williams, October 16, 1962, in UF. For examples of support for Williams, see the letters to him from Forrest G. Cooper, October 5, 1962; John C. Halbrook Jr., October 15, 1962; Jack Reed, R. W. Reed Jr., and W. R. Reed, October 17, 1962; W. M. McGough, October 22, 1962; J. G. Babb, October 18, 1962; and William Winter, October 3, 1962, in UF. See also Minutes, IHL Board, October 18, 1962, in Records of the IHL Board, Jackson, Miss.

28. *MCA* and *MPS*, October 10, 1962; *JCL*, October 12, 1962; testimony of Dean L. L. Love, October 18, 1962, in GLICP.

29. Nicholas deB. Katzenbach to J. D. Williams, October 10 and 11, 1962; and Norbert Schlei to Leston L. Love, October 16, 1962, in GMSP; Report to the Committee on Racial Discrimination, American Association of Law Schools, no date [after November 1963], in UF (hereinafter referred to as Report to AALS); testimony of Dean Love; Barrett, *Integration*, 186; *The University of Mississippi and the Meredith Case* (mimeographed, November 15, 1962), 26. In some sources, the number of students referred to university authorities and the number of cases considered by the Student Judicial Council do not add up. Sources seem to agree on the conviction of eight. For the clearest accounting see *JCL*, October 31, 1962. The Report to AALS compiled by Dean Love offers the best summary of discipline cases from October 1, 1962, to November 25, 1962.

30. *University and the Meredith Case*, 28.

31. *JDN*, October 30 and 31, November 1, 1962; *RU*, 1, no. 1 (October 25, 1962); Barrett, *Integration*, 190; SAC Memphis to Director FBI, October 30, 1962 (#1104 and #1106); and A. Rosen to Belmont, October 30, 1962 (#1129), in FBI Files; *MS* and *DDT*, October 26, 1962; *JCL*, October 27, 1962.

32. SAC Memphis to Director FBI, October 25, 1962 (#1018), in FBI Files; undated clipping [ca. March 7, 1978]; and L. L. Love to Jack Lynch, November 1, 1962, in UF; Burke Marshall to Marion Wright, October 4, 1963, in AALSP; intelligence summary on Mississippi situation, 251600 to 260300, October 1962, in RG 319; FBI Agent James W. Brady, report on Robertson Case, November 19, 1962, in RG 527.

33. *JCL*, *MS*, *MCA*, and *NYT*, October 30, 1962; statement of Lt. Col. Whitney D. Stuart, *PMS*, October 30, 1962; and Lt. Col. L. E. Orr, memorandum to file, October 31, 1962, in RG 319; SAC Memphis to Director FBI, October 30, 1962 (#1104), in FBI Files; *University and the Meredith Case*, 28.

34. Office of the Provost Marshal, report of military investigation, November 11, 1962, in RG 319. The report includes statements by Niglia, a lab report, and a report of a neuropsychiatric examination of Niglia. Related materials appear in RG 319, GLICP, and the FBI Files.

35. *JDN*, November 1 and 2, 1962; *MS*, November 2, 1962; *MCA*, November 4, 1962; Scheips, "Role of the Army," 202–3.

36. *JCL*, October 31, 1962; Randolph G. Kinnabrew (chairman of the Faculty Senate), "Origin of Temporary Faculty Committee," November 20, 1962; Committee of Nine to Provost Charles Haywood, October 30, 1962, in UF; Barrett, *Integration*, 193. The Committee of Nine consisted of Ronald Carrier, John Moore, Julien Tatum, Frank Anderson, Duncan Whiteside, John Wolfe, Hector Currie, Nolen Fortenberry, and William Willis, who chaired the committee. The committee's existence was not secret; see *NOTP*, November 2, 1962.

37. Lt. Col. L. E. Orr, memorandum for record, October 31, 1962, and [unsigned], memo for record, November 1, 1962, in RG 319.

38. Burnes Tatum, call report, Department of Public Safety, November 1, 1962; and L. L. Love to Jack Lynch, November 1, 1962, in GMSP; *JCL*, October 30 and 31, 1962; *JDN*, *MS*, and *NOTP*, October 31, 1962.

39. *Miss.*, October 31 and November 2, 1962; *BN* and *JCL*, November 1, 1962.

40. "Soldiers of America," in SAC Memphis to Director FBI, November 2, 1962 (#1294), in FBI Files; *JDN*, *JCL*, and *MS*, October 31, 1962; *NOTP*, October 31 and November 1, 1962; *MCA*, October 30, 1962; *NYT*, November 1, 1962. The FBI identified one student who tossed hundreds of copies of the leaflet out of his dorm window. See FBI Agents Gerald B. Brown and Bruce C. Hodge, report on November 8, 1962, interview with David Melvin Geer, in RG 527. See also their reports on November 13, 1962, interviews with Jonathan Nash and Jim Brown, in RG 527.

41. Maj. Thomas J. Griffin to L. L. Love, November 1, 1962; Commanding Officer, U.S. Army, Oxford, to Gen. [Earle D.] Wheeler, Chief of Staff, U.S. Army, November 1, 1962; and Lt. Col. G. C. Jung, memorandum for record, no date, in RG 319; Burnes Tatum, call report, Department of Public Safety, October 31, 1962, in GMSP; *JCL*, *NYT*, and *NOTP*, November 1, 1962.

42. *JDN* and *MS*, November 1, 1962; Major Griffin to Love, November 1, 1962; Commanding Officer to General Wheeler, November 1, 1962; and Lt. Col. Jung memorandum, in RG 319; *JCL*, *MCA*, and *NOTP*, November 1, 1962.

43. *Miss.*, November 2, 1962.

44. *RU* 1, no. 2 (October 1962); *NYT* and *JDN*, November 2, 1962.

45. Committee of Nine, memorandum to the provost, October 31 and November 2, 1962, in UF.

46. Report to AALS; Committee of Nine, memorandum to the provost, November 5, 1962, in UF; Barrett, *Integration*, 195; *JDN*, December 1, 1962. The Street Papers contain reports of testimony in some cases that grew out of the October 30 and 31 disturbances. Two of the expelled students came from Mississippi, and the other two were from Louisiana and New Jersey. Record Group 527 also contains detailed FBI reports on the Judicial Council's actions in early November against several students.

47. Dean L. L. Love to Jack Lynch, November 1, 1962; Lynch to Leroy Taylor Robertson, November 1, 1962; testimony before Student Judicial Council concerning the case of Leroy Taylor Robertson, November 2, 1962; Lynch to Love, November 3, 1962; Love to Leroy Taylor

Robertson, November 3, 1962; Melvin B. Bishop to E. R. Jobe, November 14, 1962; Henry M. Hope Jr. to J. D. Williams, November 21, 1962; Stokes V. Robertson to Williams, November 12, 1962; Leon F. Hendrick to Whom It May Concern, November 13, 1962; John C. Satterfield to Thomas J. Tubb, November 16, 1962; Howard J. Cleland to Members of the Judicial Council, University of Mississippi, November 21, 1962; Minutes, Meeting of the Division Heads, November 21, 1962; Williams to Melvin B. Bishop, November 23, 1962, in UF; Bill of Complaint, *Taylor Robertson, Minor, and Jack W. Robertson Jr. v. Board of Trustees, Institutions of Higher Learning of the State of Mississippi*, Chancery Court of First Judicial District, Hinds County, Miss., November 29, 1962 (No. 62,366); FBI Agents Bruce C. Hodge and Orville V. Johnson, report on October 30, 1962, interview with Leroy Taylor Robertson, November 8, 1962; and FBI Agent James W. Brady, report on Robertson case, November 19, 1962, in RG 527. Jack W. Robertson Jr., an older brother with whom Taylor Robertson lived, filed the suit in his behalf because he was a minor. Stokes V. Robertson was not related to Taylor Robertson. Bishop was Robertson's lawyer.

48. Bill of Complaint, in *Robertson v. Board of Trustees*; Faculty Resolution, "Commendation of Disciplinary Action," December 6, 1962, in UF; Tom S. Hines to Leroy Taylor Robertson, November 30, 1962, in UF; COUSAFOX to War Room, December 2, 1962, in RG 319; Russell H. Barrett to Louis Joughlin, December 19, 1962, in AAUPP; *MS*, December 1, 7, and 22, 1962; *NYT*, December 5, 1962; Minutes, IHL Board, December 20, 1962, and January 17, 1963; *MCA*, December 3 and 22, 1962; Reese Cleghorn, "Revolt of the Professors," *New Republic*, February 2, 1963, 5–6; Agreed Order of Dismissal, *Robertson v. Board of Trustees*, March 26, 1963. The two sides apparently engaged in extensive negotiations regarding his withdrawal; see Nan [?] to Dr. E. R. Jobe, January 8, 1962, in IHLP.

49. *University and the Meredith Case*, 29; *NYT* and *MCA*, November 4, 1962; *Nashville Banner*, December 19, 1962; report to AALS; Joseph A. Califano Jr. to J. Harold Flannery, June 6, 1963, in RG 319. John Vaught, *Rebel Coach: My Football Family* (Memphis: Memphis State University Press, 1971), 120–21; *Miss.*, November 6, 1962; *NOTP*, November 2, 1962. In his memoir, Vaught presumptuously entitled the chapter on the 1962 season "Football Saves a School."

50. *MS*, November 5, 1962; *NYT*, November 4, 1962; *Baltimore Sun*, October 12, 1962; Barrett, *Integration*, 196–97.

51. *Rebel Resistance*, no date [November 7, 1962?], in UF; CO US Army Forces Oxford to Department of the Army, War Room, Washington, D.C., November 8, 1962, in RG 319; FBI Agents Gerald B. Brown and Bruce C. Hodge, report on November 14, 1962, interview with James Modell Norris, and reports on November 16, 1962, with Wilson Jerome Foster Jr. and Henry Louis Restarick Jr., in RG 527. The strategy originally appeared in the *Gulf Coast Gazette* on October 10, 1962.

52. *CD*, December 15–21, 1962; *NT*, October 3, 1962.

53. *MPS*, October 2, 1962; *NT* and *NYT*, October 3, 1962; *Baltimore Sun*, October 10, 1962; *NOTP*, December 7, 1962; *CD*, December 15–21, 1962. A floor plan of Baxter Hall established his apartment's exact location. See Mississippi State Building Commission et al., *Physical Facilities, Institutions of Higher Learning, State of Mississippi: Public and Private Institutions, 1967–68* (University of Mississippi, 1969?).

54. Postcards from Rosa Parks to Meredith, September 27, 1962; Wyatt T. Walker to Meredith, September 28, 1962; Septima Clark to Meredith, August [September] 27, 1962; [anonymous] to Meredith, October 1, 1962 (it also contained a coupon for Purina Dog Chow); and "A Nigger Hater" to Meredith, October 2, 1962, in JHMP; SAC Memphis to Director FBI, January 11, 1963 (#2023), in FBI Files; JCL, October 11, 1962.

55. Joseph A. Califano Jr. to J. Harold Flannery, June 6, 1963, in RG 319; Scheips, "Role of the Army," 161–64. At the maximum, army forces in Oxford totaled 6,100 on October 1, 1962, with an additional 1,975 National Guardsmen. Larger figures included soldiers at nearby bases. In December 1962, an FBI report estimated the bureau's involvement in the case had cost $80,366, with a maximum of 214 special agents working on it for 4,420 hours of unpaid overtime; and FBI cars logged 69,535 miles. See N. P. Callahan to [?] Mohr, December 6, 1962 (#1587), in FBI Files.

56. Scheips, "Role of the Army," 162; "Revised Security Plan," November 21, 1962, in USMP.

57. SAC Memphis to Director FBI, October 18, 1962 (#878), in FBI Files; author's interview with Arvid A. "Bud" Sather, April 18, 2005 (hereinafter referred to as Sather interview).

58. Meredith, *Three Years*, 230–31; Sather interview.

59. *MS* and *MCA*, October 19, 1962; L. L. Love to George M. Street, December 18, 1962, in GMSP; Sather interview.

60. *NOTP*, November 7, 8, and 12, 1962; SAC Memphis to Director FBI, November 7, 1962 (#1240), in FBI Files.

61. *JDN*, November 16, 1962; Meredith, *Three Years*, 227; *NYT*, October 3, 1962; *NOTP* and *WP*, October 12, 1962; *MEJ*, October 19, 1962; *CD*, December 15–21, 1962; *Nashville Banner*, December 19, 1962. The Meredith quotation first appeared in his article in the *Saturday Evening Post*, November 10, 1962, 14–17.

62. *MS*, November 16 and 19, 1962; *NOTP*, November 16, 1962; *NYT*, January 17, 1963; *WP*, January 27, 1963; Burnes Tatum and Binford Nash to L. L. Love, December 7, 1962, in GMSP. Tatum, the chief of university police, and Nash, the head of student housing, investigated.

63. *NYT*, January 17, 1963; *MS*, November 16 and 19, 1962; *JDN*, November 16, 1962; *JCL*, November 20, 1962; *MCA*, January 25, 1963; *WP*, January 27, 1963; Jane Krieger Rosen, "At Home and Abroad: A Visit to Ole Miss," *Reporter*, December 20, 1962, 18–20; George M. Street to Mrs. Louis McDonald, February 14, 1963, in GMSP; SAC Memphis to Director FBI, November 16, 1962 (#1421), in FBI Files.

64. *Miss.*, September 20, October 1 and 31, and November 20, 1962; *MPS*, October 5, 1962.

65. *MPS*, October 5, 1962; *MS*, October 16, 1962; *Charleston (W.Va.) Gazette*, December 8, 1962; Sidna Brower, "Mississippi Mud," *The Nation*, October 27, 1962, 266.

66. *NYT*, December 3, 1962; *RU*, October 1962; *MCA*, November 21, 1962; *JDN*, December 4, 1962; *MS*, November 21 and 30, and December 4, 5, and 7, 1962; *Miss.*, November 27, 28, 29, and 30, and December 4 and 6, 1962. For local commentary on Brower, see *MS*, December 7 and 9, 1962; and *MEJ*, December 7, 1962.

67. *NYT*, December 4, 1962; *JDN*, November 16, 1962; *MS*, November 5, 1962; Barrett, *Integration*, 198.

68. Barrett, *Integration*, 191 and 198–200.

69. *MS*, *MCA*, and *JCL*, November 11, 1962; SAC Memphis to Director FBI, November 8, 1962 (#1293), in FBI Files.

70. *MCA*, *MS*, and *JCL*, November 11, 1962; James Meredith to A. B. Lewis, November 15, 1962, and January 14, 1963; and A. B. Lewis to James Meredith, November 20, 1962, and January 15, 1963, in JHMP.

71. Larry Still, "Man behind the Headlines," *Ebony*, December 1962, 28; *NYT*, December 4, 1962; *NOTP*, December 7, 1962; *CD*, December 15–21, 1962.

72. *NOTP*, December 7, 1962; *CD*, December 15–21, 1962; Still, "Man behind the Headlines," 28; *NYT*, December 4, 1962.

73. *DDT* and *MCA*, November 28, 1962; *St. Petersburg (Fla.) Times*, December 16, 1962; *NYT*, November 1, 1962; *JDN*, November 1 and 29, 1962; *KNS*, November 29, 1962; *MS*, December 10, 1962; *Nashville Banner*, December 19, 1962.

74. [Russell H. Barrett] to William Willis, November 15, 1962, in RBP. Barrett also comments on his visit and the resulting report to the Committee of Nine (see *Integration*, 200).

75. [Barrett] to Willis, November 15, 1962; Barrett, *Integration*, 200. The minutes of the Committee of Nine do not include any discussion of Barrett's proposals.

76. J. D. Williams to Ross Barnett, November 26, 1962, in UF; *NOTP*, December 7, 1962; James W. Silver to A. W. Willis, November 21, 1962; Silver to Sanford Higginbotham, Bell Wiley, William Doherty, Harris Warren, and George Carbone [all former history department colleagues], January 16, 1963, in JWSP; Silver to Bill and Betty Silver, November 21, 1962, in BSP; James Meredith, "I'll Know Victory or Defeat," *Saturday Evening Post*, November 10, 1962, 14–17; photograph of Meredith, *Ebony*, January 1963, 84; Burnes Tatum to Russell Fox, February 5, 1963, in GLICP. At the governor's request, the chancellor reported on Silver's first meeting with Meredith. The two wives were Anna L. Gareau, whose husband taught political science (and she was a part-time instructor in modern languages), and Sara Lynn Kerciu, who was married to a visiting art professor. Southern historians Dewey W. Grantham, George B. Tindall, C. Vann Woodward, and Bell I. Wiley had sent Silver copies of their own books for Meredith. See correspondence in JWSP. The photograph of Silver and Meredith was reprinted in Silver's *Running Scared: Silver in Mississippi* (Jackson: University Press of Mississippi, 1984), 79. Professor Lucy Turnbull commented on her association with Meredith in the *Lancaster (Ohio) Eagle-Gazette*, undated clipping [but before January 15, 1963], in UF; and in a letter to the editor of the *Bryn Mawr Alumni Bulletin*, Winter 1963. Weekly reports filed by the U.S. marshals catalogue, among many events, the meals Meredith had in faculty homes; see, for example, the report of dinner at Professor Russell Maatman's home in F. E. Vandergrift, weekly report, December 2–8, 1962, in USMP.

77. "Man behind the Headlines," *Ebony*, December 1962, 30; *JDN*, November 14, 1962; *NYT*, December 4, 1962; *NOTP*, December 7, 1962; *CD*, December 15–21, 1962; *Atlanta Daily World* and *Nashville Banner*, December 19, 1962; Russell Barrett to George P. Backus, December 19, 1962; Barrett to Max Ascoli, December 14, 1962; and Barrett to J. D. Williams, December 4, 1962, in RBP; Committee of Nine, memorandum to the provost, December 7, 1962, in UF; Rosen, "At Home Abroad," 20; *Miss.*, November 28, 1962; James W. Silver to

Arthur M. Schlesinger Jr., January 1, 16, and 23, 1963, in BMP; Constance Baker Motley, *Equal Justice under Law: An Autobiography* (New York: Farrar, Straus and Giroux, 1998), 183. If Barrett sounded confident of Meredith's safety in December, six weeks earlier he had been more worried when he wrote Hugh Downs of *The Today Show* that as many as 300 students could engage in violent behavior and "probably 20 or 25 among this group would be willing to commit major acts of personal violence against Mr. Meredith if he were not closely guarded." See Barrett to Downs, October 31, 1962, in RBP.

78. *MS*, December 16 and 21, 1962; *DDT*, December 17 and 18, 1962; *MCA*, December 17, 1962; *JDN*, December 20, 1962.

79. Meredith, *Three Years*, 232–37; *Nashville Banner*, December 25, 1962; *Atlanta Constitution* and *KNS*, December 24, 1962.

80. Meredith, *Three Years*, 237 and 240–42. In his memoir, Meredith also mentions that James Baldwin visited him in Jackson on New Year's Day.

81. U.S. Marshals, weekly report, January 2–12, 1963, in USMP; *RU*, no date [January 6, 1962]; *DDT*, January 7, 1962; *NOTP*, January 8, 1962.

82. Meredith's statement appears in his *Three Years*, 206–7. See also U.S. Marshals, weekly report, January 2–12, 1963.

83. *MPS* and *JCL*, January 11, 1963; *DDT*, January 8 and 10, 1963; *NT* and *Miss.*, January 8, 1963; *JDN*, January 9, 1963; *National Observer*, January 14, 1963.

84. *MCA*, January 9, 1963; *NOTP*, *JCL*, and *DDT*, January 8, 1963; *MPS*, January 11, 1963.

85. *NOTP* and *JDN*, January 9, 1963; *MCA*, January 9, 13, and 15, 1963; *Miss.* and *Macon (Ga.) Telegraph*, January 8, 1963; *JCL*, January 8 and 9, 1963; James W. Silver to Paul Flowers, January 18, 1963, as reprinted in Meredith, *Three Years*, 255–57; J. D. Williams to Paul Flowers, January 15, 1963, in UF.

86. *JCL*, *JDN*, and *Arkansas Gazette*, January 12, 1963.

87. Barton Milligan and Russell H. Barrett to J. D. Williams, January 12, 1963, in UF.

88. Barrett, *Integration*, 209–10; Barrett to J. D. Williams, January 11, 1963, in RBP.

89. *MCA*, January 12 and 17, 1963; *JCL*, January 12, 1963; *RU*, no date [January 12, 1963?]; *Miss.*, January 15 and 16, 1963.

90. *Miss.*, January 15, 1962; *Louisville Courier-Journal*, January 17, 1962.

91. *Miss.*, January 11, 1963; *JCL*, January 16, 1963; *RU*, no date [January 12, 1963?]. In the next two years, Ira B. Harkey Jr. and Hazel Brannon Smith won Pulitzer prizes for editorial writing.

92. *Washington Evening Star*, January 20, 1963; Meredith, *Three Years*, 258–59; Barrett, *Integration*, 210; *NOTP*, January 19, 1963; *DDT*, January 21, 1963; *Washington Daily News*, January 24, 1963; James W. Silver to Arthur M. Schlesinger Jr., January 23, 1963, in BMP.

93. B. J. Harrison to James Meredith, January 24, 1963; and L. E. Noble Jr. to James Meredith, January 24, 1963, in JHMP; *JCL*, January 27, 1963; *Denver Post*, January 23, 1963; *Baltimore Sun*, January 25, 1963; *Baltimore Afro-American*, January 19, 1963; *Washington Daily News*, January 24, 1963. Meredith said that when he read Ellis's comment he was "so shocked that I put down the paper." See *NOTP*, January 28, 1963.

94. *KNS* and *JDN*, January 23, 1963; Meredith, *Three Years*, 259–60. Meredith's car had been vandalized the previous weekend when he had left it on campus during his visit to

Memphis. See U.S. Marshals, weekly report, January 13–19, 1963, in USMP. In his memoirs, Meredith reported that in a second incident when his car would not start, vandals had poured sugar into the gas tank or engine. See *Three Years*, 260.

95. *JDN*, *MCA*, and *Winston-Salem Sentinel*, January 23, 1963; *NOTP*, January 24, 1963; Meredith, *Three Years*, 260–61.

Chapter Twenty

1. *KNS*, January 30, 1963; *JCL*, *NOTP*, *JDN*, and *NT*, January 31, 1963; James Meredith, *Three Years in Mississippi* (Bloomington: Indiana University Press, 1966), 269–70. The FBI Files contain a slightly different version of Meredith's statement. See document #2200, January 30, 1962. The state NAACP office was in the Masonic Temple building.

2. *JCL*, January 13 and 24, 1963; *JDN*, January 13, 1963; *NOTP*, January 24 and 28, 1963; *MCA*, January 12 and 29, 1963; *NT*, January 30, 1963; Meredith, *Three Years*, 265–67.

3. *JCL*, January 24 and February 1, 1963. Ethridge quoted an editorial from the *Tulsa Tribune*, and Hills referred to one from the *Cincinnati Enquirer*.

4. *JCL*, January 26, 1963.

5. J. D. Williams to faculty, staff, and students of the University of Mississippi, January 30, 1963, in UF; SAC Memphis to Director FBI and SAC New Orleans, January 29, 1963 (#2164), in FBI Files. See also *JCL*, January 31, 1963.

6. Williams to faculty, staff, and students of the University of Mississippi, January 31, 1963, in UF. See also *JCL*, January 31 and February 2, 1963; and Russell H. Barrett, *Integration at Ole Miss* (Chicago: Quadrangle, 1965), 212–13.

7. Faculty of Journalism Department to Faculty Senate and for information to the Chancellor and Hugh Clegg, February 6, 1963, in UF; *JCL*, February 14, 1963; Tom J. Truss Jr. to Louis Joughlin, March 10, 1963, in AAUPP. See also Joughlin to Noyes, March 7, 1963, in AAUPP.

8. Committee of Nine to Chairman of the Faculty Senate, Chairman of the Committee on Committees, and President of University of Mississippi Chapter of AAUP, February 13, 1963, in UF. At its February 6 meeting, the Committee of Nine voted unanimously to disband.

9. Williams to faculty, staff, and students, February 25, 1963, in UF.

10. Command report for December 1–31, 1962, in RG 319; [name deleted] to Robert L. Haislip, weekly report, February 11, 1963, in USMP.

11. Meredith, *Three Years*, 272–73; *NT*, January 31, 1963; *NOTP*, *MCA*, *KNS*, and *JCL*, February 1, 1963.

12. *NT*, January 31, 1963; *KNS*, *NOTP*, and *JCL*, February 1, 1963.

13. Tom Scarbrough, investigative report on "Dewey Greene Jr.," November 6, 1962, in MSSCP; *JCL*, February 1, 1963; *Montgomery Advertiser*, February 2, 1963; John Dittmer, *Local People: The Struggle for Civil Rights in Mississippi* (Urbana: University of Illinois Press, 1994), 135. On Greene's application, see *NYT*, October 6, 1962; and *JDN*, October 8 and 9, 1962.

14. *Montgomery Advertiser*, February 2, 1963; Tom Scarbrough, investigative reports on

"Lafayette County (University of Mississippi)," January 29, 1963, and "Dewey Greene Jr.," in MSSCP; *JDN*, August 6, 1962; Dittmer, *Local People*, 132.

15. Tom S. Hines to L. L. Love, January 31, 1963, in UF; *Atlanta Daily World*, February 5, 1963; *NT*, January 31, 1963; *JCL* and *MCA*, February 1, 1963. Ellis asked Hines, as assistant dean, to sit in on the meeting with Greene.

16. *JCL*, February 2, 3, and 4, 1963; *MCA*, February 2, 1963; *MEJ*, February 4, 1963; Barbara Carter, "A Lawyer Leaves Mississippi," *Reporter*, May 9, 1963, 33–35; *JCL*, April 2 and May 1, 1960; *SSN*, February 1961, 4; *JDN*, July 3 and August 2, 1962, and January 3, 1963; *NYT*, August 12, 1962; *William L. Higgs et al. v. Evelyn Gandy et al.* (U.S.S.D. Miss.), in WSP; John Howard, *Men Like That: A Southern Queer History* (Chicago: University of Chicago Press, 1999), 150–58; "A Red-Hot Hundred: Gallery of Young Leaders on the Big Break-through," *Life*, September 4, 1962, 4. On January 2, 1963, Higgs and William Kuntsler filed a lawsuit in the U.S. District Court in Washington, D.C., against the Department of Justice and the FBI; it alleged that federal officials had not protected the voting rights of blacks in Mississippi. See *JDN*, January 3, 1963, and Carter, "A Lawyer Leaves Mississippi," 35. In Greene's case Higgs was assisted by Jerry Brown, a Yale law student and son of the governor of California.

17. *JCL*, February 2, 15, and 16, 1963; *JDN*, February 2, 7, 14, 15, and 16, and June 10, 1963; *DDT*, February 3, 1963; *MCA*, July 4, 1963; Carter, "A Lawyer Leaves Mississippi." See also Al Hopkins, "Trial of Attorney William Higgs," February 18, 1963, in MSSCP. William Winter told Jim Silver that most people thought "Higgs probably was guilty" but also that Higgs had "become a marked man because of his activities." See Winter to Silver, July 15, 1963, in JWSP.

18. *JCL*, February 4, 5, 16, and 19, 1963; *NYT*, March 17, 1963.

19. *JCL*, January 5, 12, 15, and 16, 1963; *MCA*, January 25 and February 2 and 20, 1963; Paul J. Scheips, "The Role of the Army in the Oxford, Mississippi, Incident, 1962–1963," Histories Division, Office of the Chief of Military History, Department of the Army, June 24, 1965, 214–19.

20. Petition for Injunction, *State of Mississippi ex rel. Murry C. Falkner v. Warren D. Hodges et al.*, February 22, 1963, Chancery Court of Lafayette County, Miss.; Scheips, "Role of the Army," 214–19; "Narrative of Events concerning the Occupancy and Use of Oxford National Guard Armory by the Active Army Units on Duty in the Oxford Area," no date [but after February 15, 1963], in Record Group 48, MAGP; *JCL*, January 17 and 20, 1963. Falkner withdrew his petition on March 16, 1963; see Dismissal without Prejudice, in case file. On the state's suit, see *JDN*, May 23, 1963; and *JCL* and *NOTP*, May 24, 1963.

21. *MCA*, January 19 and 25, 1963; *JDN*, January 27, 1963; James W. Silver to Bill Silver, January 6, 1963, in BSP; *NYT*, January 11, 1963; *Baltimore Sun*, October 12, 1963; *Washington Daily News*, January 24, 1963; *Washington Evening Star*, January 20, 1963; *JCL*, January 27, 1963.

22. *JCL*, January 28, 1963; *JDN*, January 18 and 22, 1963.

23. On the resignations, see "Report of the Chancellor to the Board of Trustees of Institutions of Higher Learning," May 6, 1963, 4; July 8, 1963, 6; August 5, 1963, 10; and September 9, 1963, 9; and *NYT*, June 9, 1963.

24. *JCL*, January 27, 1963.

25. COUSAFOX to War Room, February 5, 1963, and command report for April 1–30, 1963, in RG 319; Chester A. Smith, weekly report, February 26–March 5, 1963, in USMP.

26. Weekly report, February 3–9, 1963, and [deleted] to Robert L. Haislip, February 11, 1963, in USMP; COUSAFOX to War Room, February 8 and 10, 1963, in RG 319; *Miss.*, March 30, 1963; SAC Memphis to Director FBI, February 8, 1963 (#2265), in FBI Files.

27. Command report for February 1–28, 1963; and COUSAFOX to War Room, February 16 and 26, 1963, in RG 319; weekly report, February 17–24, 1963, in USMP.

28. Weekly report, March 12–16, 1963, in USMP; command reports for March 1–31 and April 1–30, 1963; COUSAFOX to War Room, March 20 and 26, 1963, in RG 319. In late March someone also stole Meredith's glasses from a table in the library while he left the room for a moment, and marshals reported the theft to campus police. See weekly report, March 24–29, 1963, in USMP; and Meredith, *Three Years*, 275–76.

29. Command reports for March 1–31 and May 1–31, 1963, in RG 319; weekly report, March 24–30, in USMP.

30. *The Ole Miss Coloring Book* (mimeographed, no date); *The Ole Miss Coloring Book* (Tallahassee: D. Ross Thompson, 1963). The illustrator was Burk Sauls. Copies can be found in the U.S. Marshals Papers (USMP) and in the University Archives (UF). For dating their arrival, see COUSAFOX to War Room, March 21, 1963, and command report for April 1–30, 1963, in RG 319; Tom J. Truss Jr. to Louis Joughlin, March 10, 1963, and Charles F. Haywood to William P. Fidler, February 26, 1963, in AAUPP; and James W. Silver to Bill Silver, January 31, 1963, in BSP.

31. Weekly report, February 17–23, 1963, in USMP; command report for March 1–31, 1963, and COUSAFOX to War Room, April 23, 1963, in RG 319; report of Memphis SA, March 11, 1963 (#2478), in FBI Files; *National Observer*, January 12, 1963.

32. Counting and dating the issues of the *Rebel Underground* presents many problems. Few carried any date of publication, though some had volume numbers. With differing formats, the publications appeared to come from more than one source. Barrett declared that it came out during the first five weeks of the second semester and that the "final issue" appeared in early March. Two subsequent issues have, however, been found, one for Easter 1963 and one in May 1963. See Barrett, *Integration*, 215.

33. *RU* 3, no. 1 (February 1963); *RU* 3, no. 2 (February 1963); *RU* 3, no. 4 (March 1963). The first February 1963 issue may have been distributed by hand, not through the mail. See SAC Memphis to Director FBI, February 11 (#2287) and 29 (#2334), 1963, in FBI Files.

34. *Miss.*, February 26, and March 5, 1963; *RU* 3, no. 2 (February 1963); *RU* 3, no. 4 (March 1963); *RU* 3, no. 5 (Easter 1963); Barrett, *Integration*, 215.

35. *RU* 3, no. 4 (March 1963); *Miss.*, March 30, 1963; Russell H. Barrett to Ivan Dee, November 22, 1964, in RBP; Barrett, *Integration*, 215–16; *OE*, October 22, 1953; *MPS*, January 11, 1963; *Denver Post*, January 23, 1963. Topp was one of the individuals to whom Barrett dedicated his book.

36. COUSAFOX to War Room, February 20, 1963, and command report for February 1–28, 1963, in RG 319.

37. Meredith, *Three Years*, 282–86; Barrett, *Integration*, 215.

38. James W. Silver to Bill Silver and Betty Silver, February 15, 1963, in JWSP; COUSAFOX to War Room, February 15, March 1, 20, and 29, April 12 and 24, and May 21, 1963, in RG 319; Meredith, *Three Years*, 283–85.

39. Burnes Tatum to Russell Fox, February 5, 1963, in GLICP; COUSAFOX to War Room, February 5, March 11 and 13, and May 8, 1963, in RG 319; weekly report, December 2–8, 1963, in USMP; Meredith, *Three Years*, 279–80.

40. Meredith, *Three Years*, 279–80; daily staff journal or duty officers log, May 28, 1963, in RG 319. Howard's motivation for leaving remains unclear; one news account said it was for reasons other than the crisis over Meredith. See *JCL*, January 27, 1963.

41. James W. Silver to George [Carbone?], March 14, 1963, and undated clipping, Patrick J. Owens, "There Comes a Time: Dr. Silver at Ole Miss," in JWSP; Silver to Bill Silver, January 6, 1963, in BSP.

42. Weekly reports for February 17–23 and February 26–March 5, 1963, in USMP; command report for February 1–28, 1963, in RG 319. The FBI reported that Meredith planned to dine in the cafeteria with a white female dancer, but he never did. See SAC Memphis to Director FBI, February 18 (#2331) and 19 (#2333), 1963, in FBI Files.

43. *WP*, October 14, 1962; Meredith, *Three Years*, 279; "Tag Numbers [automobile license plates] of People Attending the Regional Council of Negro Leadership Held in Clarksdale, Mississippi—Sunday, December 8, 1957," in MSSCP; Tom Scarbrough, "Further Investigation of NAACP Activities in Lafayette County," June 14, 1960, and "Report on Lafayette County," January 29, 1963, in MSSCP; weekly reports, December 2–8, 1962, and March 6–11 and 24–30, 1963, in USMP; James H. Meredith, "I Can't Fight Alone," *Look*, April 9, 1963, 71–72.

44. Weekly reports, March 6–11 and 17–23, 1963, in USMP; command reports for March 1–31, May 1–31, and June 1–31, 1963, in RG 319.

45. COUSAFOX to War Room, April 18 and 24, 1963, in RG 319.

46. For example, see *JCL*, February 1, 2, and 14, 1963. See also Russell J. Henderson, "The 1963 Mississippi State University Basketball Controversy and the Repeal of the Unwritten Law: 'Something More than the Game Will Be Lost,'" *Journal of Southern History* 63 (November 1997): 827–54.

47. For example, see the front-page coverage in the *JCL*, January 24, February 13, March 5, 8, 13, and 15, and April 8, 1963. RG 319 contains materials concerning the possible use of USAFOX units in connection with the Greenwood disorder.

48. "Report of the Chancellor to the Board of Trustees of Institutions of Higher Learning," September 10, 1962; *MCA*, April 11, 1963; *New Yorker*, May 29, 1963, 69–70; Barrett, *Integration*, 217; *Time*, April 19, 1963. See also *SSN*, May 1963; Tom J. Truss Jr. to Louis Joughlin, April 7, 1963; Louis Joughlin to file, April 9, 1963, in AAUPP; and author's interview with G. Ray Kerciu, April 24, 2003.

49. *JCL*, April 6, 7, and 10, 1963; *JDN*, April 6, 1963; Truss Jr. to Joughlin, April 7, 1963; and Joughlin to file, April 9, 1963; James W. Silver to Bill and Betty Silver, April 8, 1963, in BSP; undated news release, in UF. Later disagreement emerged over whether Noyes had *ordered* their removal, but an AP dispatch said that he had. See also James W. Silver to Betty and Bill Silver, April 11, 1963, in BSP.

50. *JDN*, April 6, 1963; *JCL*, April 6, 7, 8, and 10, 1963; *Miss.*, April 9, 1963; *MCA*, April 9 and 11, 1963.

51. *Miss.* and *JCL*, April 10, 1963; *MCA*, April 11, 1963.

52. *Miss.*, April 9 and 11, 1963; James R. Horton to J. D. Williams, no date [received May 8, 1963]; Rex L. Tucker to Williams, April 11, 1963; H. N. Eason to Williams, May 23, 1963; and Ed C. Sturdivant and Newton James to Williams, April 10, 1963, in UF; *RU* 3, no. 5 (Easter 1963).

53. *JCL*, April 11 and 18, 1963; J. D. Williams to H. N. Eason, May 27, 1963; and Williams to James R. Horton, June 6, 1963, in UF; *SSN*, May 1963; James W. Silver to Betty and Bill Silver, April 11, 1963, in BSP; *JCL*, April 20, 1963; *Miss.*, April 19, 1963.

54. Command report for March 1–April 30, 1963, in RG 319; Joseph A. Califano Jr. to J. Harold Flannery, June 6, 1963, in RG 319; Report to the Committee on Racial Discrimination, American Association of Law Schools, no date [after November 1963], in UF (hereinafter referred to as Report to AALS); *Miss.*, May 8, 1963.

55. James H. Meredith, "I Can't Fight Alone," *Look*, April 9, 1963, 70ff.; transcript of *Meet the Press*, May 26, 1963 (vol. 7, no. 26); speech by Meredith, June 2, 1963; and address by Meredith, July 5, 1963, in JHMP; *Miss.*, May 3 and 10, 1963; James W. Silver to Bill and Betty Silver, June 10, 1963, in BSP. *Look* paid Meredith $7,695 for his article. See T. George Norris to Meredith, February 14, 1963, JHMP. In Washington, he met briefly with Robert Kennedy; for a picture of them, see *JDN*, May 27, 1963.

56. *JA*, June 1, 1963; *New Orleans States-Item*, May 27, 1963; Meredith, "I Can't Fight Alone," 70; *Miss.*, May 3 and 10, 1963; *Meet the Press*, May 26, 1963.

57. *Meet the Press*, May 26, 1963; Meredith, "I Can't Fight Alone," 70.

58. *Meet the Press*, May 26, 1963; Meredith to Robert B. Ellis, August 6, 1962, in UF; Meredith to Ellis, April 11, 1963; and Ellis to Meredith, April 11, 1963, in JHMP.

59. *JDN*, April 24, 1963; *Miss.*, April 25, 1963; University of Mississippi Campus Senate Resolution no. 16, April 23, 1963, in UF.

60. Williams to IHL Board, May 16, 1963; and Petition to U.S. District Court, *Meredith v. Fair*, May 16, 1963, in UF. Also in *Meredith v. Fair* case file.

61. Motion for Preliminary Injunction, *Meredith v. Fair*, May 28, 1963.

62. Minutes, IHL Board, May 24, 1963, in Records of the IHL Board, Jackson, Miss.

63. *JCL* and *JDN*, May 29, 1963; *NYT*, June 3 and 6, 1963; *Miss.*, September 24, 1963; Cleve McDowell to Meredith, October 15 and 22, and December 11, 1962; McDowell to Admissions Office, Laws School, University of Mississippi, October 24, 1962; and McDowell to Constance Baker Motley, October 24, 1962, in JHMP; McDowell, Application for Law School, February 8, 1963; John H. Fox Jr. to Robert J. Farley, May 3, 1963, in IHLP; Farley to E. R. Jobe, May 11, 1963; [J. D. Williams?], memorandum to file, May 18, 1963; Fox to Williams, May 22, 1963; Fox to Farley, May 22, 1963, in UF.

64. *NOTP*, *JDN*, and *JCL*, June 4, 1963.

65. Motion for Construction of Injunctive Order, *Meredith v. Fair* [*McDowell v. Tubb*], May 25, 1963, in UF; *JCL*, *NOTP*, and *JDN*, June 4 and 5, 1963.

66. *JDN*, *NYT*, and *JCL*, June 5, 1963; *NOTP*, June 9 and 16, 1963; David Sansing interview with Verner Holmes and E. R. Jobe, in Verner Holmes Papers, ASCUM.

67. J. D. Williams to faculty, staff, and students of the Summer Session, June 3, 1963, in UF; *BN*, *JDN*, and *NYT*, June 5, 1963.

68. *NYT*, June 6, 1963.

69. *MCA*, June 6, 1963; *NYT*, June 6 and 7, 1963; *BN*, June 5, 1963; command report for June 1–30, 1963, in RG 319.

70. *JCL*, June 12, 1963; command report for June 1–30, 1963, in RG 319; Meredith, *Three Years*, 304 and 305.

71. James W. Silver to Bill and Betty Silver, June 12, 1963, in BSP; Meredith, *Three Years*, 304–5. For a copy of the statement with the two sentences scratched out, see MSSCP.

72. Meredith, *Three Years*, 305–6.

73. COUSAFOX to War Room, June 13, 1963, in RG 319; Scheips, "Role of the Army," 243–48 and 251; Meredith, *Three Years*, 302–3. Scheips's cost estimate for the army did not include personnel costs that would have been paid under normal circumstances, and he estimated the total cost for the federal government at $5 million.

74. Dean Love to Meredith, June 17, 1963, in JHMP; Love, report on conference with James H. Meredith, June 17, 1963; Lee H. Burford to Williams, June 6, 1963; and Williams to Burford, June 17, 1963, in UF; command report for June 1–30, 1963, in RG 319.

75. Resolution, Mississippi State Sovereignty Commission, June 20, 1963, in MSSCP; *JCL*, July 10, 1963.

76. Command reports for March 1–31 and April 1–30, 1963, in RG 319; Henry M. Miller to Meredith, February 1, 1963, and Ruby Hurley to Meredith, February 19, 1963, in JHMP; *NOTP*, April 15, 1963.

77. Speech by Meredith, June 2, 1963, in JHMP. The typed text is in all-capital letters and contains numerous typographical errors, so the quotations have been corrected.

78. Address by Meredith, July 5, 1963, in JHMP.

79. Ibid.

80. Ibid.

81. Ibid.; *JCL*, July 6, 1963.

82. *JCL* and *Chicago Tribune*, July 6, 1963.

83. *JCL*, July 7 and 9, 1963; Meredith to Arthur B. Spingarn, July 17, 1963; Stephen Gill Spottswood to Meredith, July 26, 1963; and Spingarn to Meredith, July 31, 1963, in JHMP.

84. Address by Meredith, July 5, 1963, in JHMP; *JCL*, July 6, 1963.

85. *JCL*, July 6 and 7, 1963.

86. C. E. Noyes to J. D. Williams, July 25, 1963, in UF.

87. *JCL*, August 18, 1963; Meredith, *Three Years*, 322; Commencement Security Plan, October 9, 1963, in UF.

88. See the references in note 87, above.

89. SAC Memphis to Director FBI (#2793) and SAC New Orleans (#2795), August 16, 1963; SAC New Orleans to Director FBI (#2796) and SAC Memphis (#2797), August 16, 1963, in FBI Files.

90. William P. Fidler to J. D. Williams, telegram, July 10, 1963; C. E. Noyes to Fidler, July 11, 1963; Charles Page to Williams, telegram, August 14, 1963; Mr. and Mrs. W. R. White to

Williams, telegram, August 16, 1963; James W. Conger to Williams and IHL Board, August 15, 1963, in UF.

91. *JCL*, August 13 and 16, 1963; resolution of the State Building Commission, August 14, 1963, in UF.

92. "A Report Prepared for the Board of Trustees, Institutions of Higher Learning of the State of Mississippi," August 14, 1963, in MSSCP; *NOTP*, August 16 and 19, 1963; *JDN*, August 15, 1963; *JCL*, August 16 and 17, 1963; Minutes, IHL Board, August 15, 1963.

93. *JCL*, *NOTP*, *JDN*, August 19, 1963; Meredith, *Three Years*, 324–27; Barrett, *Integration*, 221–22.

94. *JDN* and *JCL*, August 19, 1963.

95. *NOTP*, August 19, 1963; Meredith, *Three Years*, 326–28.

96. Meredith, *Three Years*, 322.

Chapter Twenty-one

1. *MPS*, October 10, 1962; Gunnar Myrdal, *An American Dilemma: The Negro Problem and Modern Democracy* (New York: Harper and Row, 1944), lxxv–lxxvi ("A White Man's Problem").

2. *MPS*, October 10, 1962; Myrdal, *An American Dilemma*, lxxv–lxxvi. For a more detailed, fully documented, discussion of the controversy in 1962 and 1963, see Charles W. Eagles, " 'The Fight for Men's Minds': The Aftermath of the Ole Miss Riot of 1962," *Journal of Mississippi History* (forthcoming). Below will be essential sources and location of quotations.

3. Copies of a later typescript of Mounger's remarks on October 1 are in the Verner Holmes Papers, ASCUM.

4. *JCL*, *MPS*, and *MCA*, October 3, 1962; *JST* and *OE*, October 4, 1962. Reports of the number of participants varied from 127 to 135.

5. *JCL*, October 2, 3, and 4, 1962; U.S. Congress, 87th Cong., 2nd sess., *Congressional Record* 108, no. 16 (October 1, 1962): 21426–511, passim; two statements issued by the Department of Justice on October 1, 1962, in Robert F. Kennedy Papers, John F. Kennedy Presidential Library, Boston, Mass.

6. Carl M. Brauer, *John F. Kennedy and the Second Reconstruction* (New York: Columbia University Press, 1977), 199–203.

7. *MCA*, October 8, 1962; *JDN*, October 4, 1962; *JCL*, October 2, 3, and 6, 1962.

8. *Baltimore Sun*, October 3, 1962; *JCL*, October 6 and 31, 1962; *JDN*, October 18 and 30, 1962.

9. *Pascagoula Chronicle*, October 9, November 14 and 30, and December 17, 18, 19, 20, and 21, 1962. Harkey reprinted the series as a pamphlet. See *Pascagoula Chronicle*, April 2, 1963. For a similar analysis by Scripps-Howard reporter Richard Starnes, see *KNS*, October 4, 1962. For his editorials Harkey won a public service award from Sigma Delta Chi. The journalism group also recognized other journalists for their coverage of the Ole Miss riot:

Peter Goldman of *Newsweek* for his reporting, Paul F. Conrad of the *Denver Post* for his editorial cartoon, and KWTV of Oklahoma City for its reporting. See *WP*, April 11, 1963.

10. Brauer, *Kennedy and the Second Reconstruction*, 198; George B. Leonard, T. George Harris, and Christopher S. Wren, "How a Secret Deal Prevented a Massacre at Ole Miss," *Look*, December 31, 1962; J. D. Williams to George Harris, December 18, 1962, in UF; *MS*, December 21, 1962; *MCA* and *MEJ*, December 19, 1962; "Where White Is Black," *The Economist*, January 12, 1963, 11; Silver to Sanford Higginbotham at al., January 16, 1963, in JWSP. On the press coverage, see [Albin Krebs], "'Kill the Reporters!,'" *Newsweek*, October 15, 1962, 100–101; Robert Wright Hooker, "Race and the News Media in Mississippi, 1962–1964" (M.A. thesis, Vanderbilt University, 1971); and Robin Belinda Street, "A Case Study in Crisis Public Relations: The Meredith Crisis at the University of Mississippi" (M.A. thesis, University of Mississippi, 1985); Gene Roberts and Hank Klibanoff, *The Race Beat: The Press, the Civil Rights Struggle, and the Awakening of a Nation* (New York: Knopf, 2006), 270–300; author's interview with Albin Krebs, November 7, 1998. On the extreme right, *The Dan Smoot Report* declared, "John F. Kennedy and Robert Kennedy are fully accountable for the blood that has been shed—and may be shed—in Mississippi." *The Dan Smoot Report*, October 8, 1962, copy in JWSP.

11. *JDN*, October 2 and 3, 1962; *JCL*, October 3, 1962; Hugh Clegg, "Someone Jumped the Gun" (unpublished manuscript), 246–49. The FBI's investigation can be followed in its files on the Meredith case and in RG 527. For the official report of the Mississippi State Highway Patrol and reports by individual patrolmen, see MSSCP-USM. The Justice Department's investigation is in USMP. Army units' after-action reports are summarized in "Appendix A: Oxford Lessons and Recommendations," in Paul J. Scheips, "The Role of the Army in the Oxford, Mississippi, Incident, 1962–1963," Histories Division, Office of the Chief of Military History, Department of the Army, June 24, 1965, 256–80. For "Operation Ole Miss" and "Oxford: A Warning for Americans," see ASCUM.

12. See the GLICP; *Pascagoula Chronicle*, April 26, 1963; and *WP* and *JCL*, April 25, 1963.

13. Sims Associates to State Sovereignty Commission, December 10, 1962, in MSSCP; *JDN*, March 29, 1963; *Miss.*, April 23, 1962; Yasuhiro Katagiri, *The Mississippi State Sovereignty Commission: Civil Rights and States' Rights* (Jackson: University Press of Mississippi, 2001), 120–21. For the documentary, see MDAH.

14. *JCL*, October 1, 1962; *Curtis Publishing Co. v. Butts*, 388 U.S. 130 (1967). Before he was indicted, Walker sued an AP reporter for filing a "completely false, unfounded, and malicious report" of his activities during the riot; he later filed lawsuits against the AP and a number of newspapers that carried the AP story. After Walker won a case in Texas, the U.S. Supreme Court in 1967 ruled against him because he was a public figure involved in a public controversy that required immediate news coverage and because "nothing" in the AP story "gives the slightest hint of a severe departure from accepted publishing standards." The Walker case was decided with a case involving allegations in *The Saturday Evening Post* that University of Georgia football coach Wally Butts "fixed" a game against the University of Alabama. Butts also lost his case. In the Walker and Butts cases, the Supreme Court extended its earlier ruling in *New York Times v. Sullivan*, 376 U.S. 254 (1957). In a similar but

unrelated case, Col. T. B. Birdsong and fourteen other highway patrolmen sued the Curtis Publishing Company for $1 million in damages as a result of a *Saturday Evening Post* article that referred to unnamed patrolmen as "those bastards" and attributed to them a "sizeable portion of the blame" for the disturbance in Oxford. Malcolm Montgomery, Ross Barnett's former law partner, filed the case in federal court in northern Alabama. On appeal, the Fifth Circuit Court of Appeals threw out the case. See Robert K. Massie, "What Next in Mississippi," *Saturday Evening Post*, November 10, 1962, 18–23, quotation on 19, and the case file for *Birdsong v. Curtis Publishing Co.*, in RG 21.

15. Charge to the Lafayette County Grand Jury by Judge W. M. O'Barr, November 12, 1962, in JWSP; indictment of James P. McShane, and *instanter capias* (order for immediate arrest), Circuit Court, Lafayette County, Miss., Special November Term, 1962; complaint, *Cyril T. Faneca, Jr. v. United States of America et al.*, U.S. District Court for the Southern District of Mississippi, Biloxi Division, November 1, 1962, in RG 21; declaration, *Virgil Norton v. James P. McShane, Nicholas Katzenbach, John Doar, and William Tucker*, Circuit Court of Lafayette County, February 4, 1963; *Norton et al. v. McShane et al.*, 33 F.R.D. 131; *Norton et al. v. McShane et al.*, 332 F. 2d 855 and 380 U.S. 981; *U.S. v. Faneca, Jr.*, 332 F. 2d 872; and *Faneca v. U.S.*, 380 U.S. 971; final report, Lafayette County, Miss., Grand Jury, November 16, 1962, in RG 527. Newspapers reported Niglia's indictment, but the records of the Lafayette County Circuit Court contain no record of it because it records indictments only *after* they have been served. The National Archives in Atlanta, Georgia, contains most of the case file for the Faneca lawsuit and some of the documents in the Norton case.

16. *JDN*, January 16 and 22, and June 4 and 6, 1963; *NOTP*, January 10 and 16, 1962; *WP*, June 8, 1963; *JCL*, January 16 and July 2 and 3, 1963; *U.S. v. Barnett and Johnson*, 346 F. 2d 99; Frank T. Read and Lucy S. McGough, *Let Them Be Judged: The Judicial Integration of the Deep South* (Metuchen, N.J.: Scarecrow, 1978), 254–65.

17. *The University of Mississippi and the Meredith Case* (University of Mississippi, November 15, 1962), 14 and 19; *JDN*, October 5, 1962; *MS*, October 17, 1962; *MCA*, November 1 and 10, 1962; W. Alton Bryant, "Mississippi Students," November 8, 1962, in UF.

18. Henry King Stanford, "Statement on Mississippi Case, 1962," November 27, 1962, in Minutes of the Commission on Colleges, *Proceedings of SACS*, November 26–29, 1962, 169–74; *JCL*, October 6 and November 16, 1962; Robert M. Sullivan to Samuel D. Thurman, December 11, 1962; Minutes of the Executive Committee, December 27, 1962, in AALSP.

19. William T. Doherty, "Confrontation at Ole Miss: A Southern Political Barbecue, 1962," *North Dakota Quarterly* 41 (Winter 1973): 5–36. For examples of other historians' assessments, see Taylor Branch, *Parting the Waters: America in the King Years, 1954–1963* (New York: Simon and Schuster, 1988), 633–72; John Dittmer, *Local People: The Struggle for Civil Rights in Mississippi* (Urbana: University of Illinois Press, 1994), 138–42; and Nick Bryant, *The Bystander: John F. Kennedy and the Struggle for Black Equality* (New York: Basic Books, 2006), 329–56.

20. Kirk K. Bast, "'As Different as Heaven and Hell': The Desegregation of Clemson College," *Proceedings of the South Carolina Historical Association* (1994), 38–44; E. Culpepper Clark, *The Schoolhouse Door: Segregation's Last Stand at the University of Alabama* (New York: Oxford University Press, 1993).

21. Dittmer, *Local People*, 142 and 157; Erle Johnston, *Mississippi's Defiant Years, 1953–1973: An Interpretive Documentary with Personal Experiences* (Forest, Miss.: Lake Harbor, 1990), 234–35.

22. "Alma Mater," words and music by Michael McWhinney and Jerry Powell, © 1963, 1964 by Alley Music Corp. and Trio Music Company, copyright renewed, international copyright secured, all rights reserved, used by permission; "Oxford Town," by Bob Dylan, © 1963, renewed 1991 Special Rider Music, all rights reserved, international copyright secured, reprinted by permission. "Alma Mater" parodied the 1958 hit "We'll Have These Moments to Remember."

23. In the days of Archie Manning (1968–70), the Rebels won two-thirds of their games.

24. For the recent history, see David G. Sansing, *The University of Mississippi: A Sesquicentennial History* (Jackson: University Press of Mississippi, 1999), 314–52.

25. *OE*, August 10, 1961, May 17 and 24, June 28, August 9, and September 13, 1962; U.S. Census Bureau, *1970 Census of Population: Characteristics of Population, Mississippi* (Washington, D.C.: GPO, 1973), 12; U.S. Census Bureau, *1990 Census of Population: General Population Characteristics, Mississippi* (Washington, D.C.: GPO, 1992), 13; U.S. Census Bureau, *2000 Census of Population and Housing: Summary Population and Housing Characteristics, Mississippi* (Washington, D.C.: GPO, 2002), 36. The 1970 census mistakenly reported Oxford's population as 13,846 because it included the university; it corrected the error in the next census report.

26. Author's interviews with Will Campbell, November 12, 1994, and September 12, 1997, and William Murphy, June 21, 1991. On Billy Barton, see *Miss.*, April 24, 1998; and *NOTP*, February 27, 1972.

27. Sansing, *The University*, 312; James W. Silver, *Running Scared: Silver in Mississippi* (Jackson: University Press of Mississippi, 1984), 96 and 183–205. See also James W. Silver, "Mississippi: The Closed Society," *Journal of Southern History* 30 (1964): 3–34.

28. Author's interviews with Robert Ellis, July 19, 1995, Frank Moak, July 17, 1995, and Katherine Rea, June 25, 1998; *OE*, May 9, 1968; *Dallas Morning News*, May 23, 1977; *NYT*, November 2, 1993.

29. Erle Johnston, *Mississippi's Defiant Years*, 222–28; Earl Black, *Southern Governors and Civil Rights: Racial Segregation as a Campaign Issue in the Second Reconstruction* (Cambridge: Harvard University Press, 1976), 181–83 and 208–11.

30. Jack Bass, *Unlikely Heroes* (New York: Simon and Schuster, 1981), 177 and 303; Johnston, *Mississippi's Defiant Years*, 369; Constance Baker Motley, *Equal Justice under Law* (New York: Farrar, Straus and Giroux, 1998), 212; author's interview with Charles Clark, January 3, 1992.

31. Author's interviews with James Meredith, May 13–16, 1996. See also Lois Romano, "The Long, Long Journey of James Meredith," *WP*, November 3, 1989; Glenn R. Simpson, "The Enigma of James Meredith," *Roll Call*, October 8, 1990, 12–14; John Ed Bradley, "The Man Who Would Be King," *Esquire*, December 1992; and Paul Hendrickson, *Sons of Mississippi: A Story of Race and Its Legacy* (New York: Knopf, 2003).

32. For black students and race relations at the university after 1963, see Sansing, *The University*; Nadine Cohodas, *The Band Played Dixie: Race and Liberal Conscience at Ole Miss* (New York: Free Press, 1997); various issues of the *DM*, especially October 1, 1992, and February 15, 1996; and *Oxford Town*, February 13–19, 1997. Reuben Anderson later served on the Mississippi Supreme Court.

33. Cohodas, *The Band Played Dixie*, 122–23; Sansing, *The University*, 311.

34. Anthony W. James, "A Demand for Racial Equality: The 1970 Black Student Protest at the University of Mississippi," *Journal of Mississippi History* 57 (1995): 97–120. In the early 1970s the university also chartered the first black fraternity and sorority. The university also became more comfortable with the civil rights movement by hosting symposia on the history of the movement in 1985, the media and the movement in 1987, and the law and the movement in 1989. In 1992 the university hired its first black head coach, Rob Evans, for the basketball team. See Sansing, *The University*, and Cohodas, *The Band Played Dixie*. In the background was a lawsuit filed in 1975 by Jake Ayers that challenged the equity of state funding of higher education for blacks and whites. Though the case did not pertain to Ole Miss in particular, litigation in *Ayers v. Allain*, later *Ayers v. Fordice*, lasted for more than twenty years.

35. See Cohodas, *The Band Played Dixie*; and Sansing, *The University*.

36. Sansing, *The University*, 340; flyer for Organizational Meeting, January 18[, 1996]; and Robert C. Khayat to John T. Edge, February 16, 1996, Civil Rights Commemoration Foundation to Robert C. Khayat, June 4, 1996, in private papers of John T. Edge; *Oxford Town*, February 19, 1997. For another discussion of the controversy over the civil rights memorial, see Robert E. Luckett, "Ole Miss and Racial Reconciliation: From James Silver to the Meredith Monument," paper delivered at the annual meeting of the Southern Historical Association in New Orleans, Louisiana, October 11, 2008 (copy in author's possession).

37. "Civil Rights Memorial Timeline: Highlights," no date [spring 2005?]; and Gerald W. Walton to Don L. Fruge, October 30, 1997, both in Edge Papers. The effort had various names: Civil Rights Memorial, Civil Rights Commemoration Foundation, and the Civil Rights Commemoration Initiative.

38. *DM*, February 27 and March 21, 1997.

39. "Call for Proposals for a Work of Art to Commemorate Mississippi's Role in Civil Rights," no date [2001], in private papers of Susan Glisson. The Edge Papers and the Glisson Papers document the fund-raising efforts.

40. "Call for Proposals," in Glisson Papers.

41. *DM*, January 8 and February 21 and 25, 2000.

42. The university's public relations office contains clippings from *USA Today*, the *Denver Post*, the *New York Post*, the *Los Angeles Times*, and *Jet*, as well as Mississippi newspapers.

43. *DM*, October 2, 2001, and February 4, 2002; Terry Adkins, proposal (statement, vita, narrative, drawings), April 27, 2002, in Glisson Papers; "Civil Rights Memorial Timeline: Highlights," in Edge Papers; Minutes, IHL Board, July 18, 2002, in Records of the IHL Board, Jackson, Miss.

44. L. Lesley Beeman Jr. to Terry Adkins, July 25, 2002, in Glisson Papers; Robert C. Khayat to John T. Edge, October 11, 2005, in Edge Papers.

45. See, for example, *DM*, September 5 and 24, and October 2, 2002.

46. *DM*, October 4, 2004.

47. *DM*, October 5, 2005.

48. *DM*, October 5 and 6, 2005.

49. *DM*, October 6, 10, 12, 13, 17, 18, and 28, 2005; *JCL*, November 4, 2005.

50. *DM*, October 2, 2006; Paul Hendrickson, *Sons of Mississippi: A Story of Race and Its Legacy* (New York: Knopf, 2003), 303–5.

51. James Meredith, *Three Years in Mississippi* (Bloomington: Indiana University Press, 1966), 4–5.

Essay on Sources

The story of Ole Miss, race, and James Meredith rests on wide and deep research in a variety of sources. A full bibliography would involve a cumbersome recitation of information contained in the notes and would not differentiate adequately among the many sources. Instead of a lengthy list, the following discussion highlights the major, unusual, and crucial sources in several broad categories: archival materials and manuscripts, newspapers, books, and oral histories.

The Archives and Special Collections at the University of Mississippi library contains several important manuscript collections. No earlier researcher had access to the extensive files of the J. D. Williams administration, previously stored unprocessed in various places at the university but now residing in the University Archives along with the smaller collection of Williams's personal papers. Cited as the University Files, the administration's papers contain newspaper clippings, university-generated documents, internal communications, and correspondence with alumni, political leaders, and others. Special Collections houses the voluminous personal papers of James Meredith that he gave to the university in 1997. Though they are far more extensive in covering his later life, the papers also provide indispensable documentation of Meredith's experiences up to and through 1963. Among many other holdings, Special Collections includes the important papers of two university professors, James W. Silver and Russell H. Barrett. Also at the university are the helpful files in the College of Liberal Arts. Other useful collections include the Will Campbell and Paul B. Johnson papers at the University of Southern Mississippi, the Walter Sillers papers at Delta State University, and the university presidents' papers and the Hodding Carter papers at Mississippi State University. Especially significant in the Carter papers are the added files of James Robertshaw, Carter's lawyer in the lawsuit brought by Edwin Walker.

Requested for the first time under the Freedom of Information Act, two major federal sources became available, but only after years of waiting. The FBI files on "the integration of the University of Mississippi by James Meredith" fill three file drawers. Though redactions for privacy sometimes limit their value, they contain hundreds of internal memos and reports, transcripts from scores of interviews, thousands of labeled newspaper clippings, and copies of many other relevant documents, such as court decisions. Filling another file drawer, the U.S. Marshals Service files provide extensive coverage of the marshals' involvement in 1962–63, especially their frequent reports on Meredith's activities and on-campus events. FOIA requests also obtained myriad documents from other parts of the Department of Justice and the U.S. Army. In Record Group 319 at the National Archives at College Park, Maryland, the documentary collection compiled by Paul J. Scheips for his Center for

Military History account of the army's involvement in Oxford contains the army's logs of events at the university, in addition to many other documents from scattered sources. The National Archives Southeast Region in Atlanta, Georgia, holds the *Meredith v. Fair* case file, the files for other federal cases arising from Mississippi, and the files of the U.S. Marshals Service, Northern District of Mississippi, Oxford Division. Among the many resources at the John F. Kennedy Presidential Library, the papers of Burke Marshall were the most important. More than one collection or record group often contains copies of the same document; the materials in RG 527, however, contain no deletions.

In Jackson, Mississippi, the state's Department of Archives and History has digitized the incomparable but incomplete files of the Mississippi State Sovereignty Commission. The archives also have transcripts of dozens of oral histories and many videos, including news film. The State Records Center holds the confidential files of the General Legislative Investigating Committee, but a director of its successor, the Performance Evaluation of Expenditure Review Committee, allowed access to the relevant records. The papers of the Institutions of Higher Learning at the Records Center were a disappointment because nearly all that related to Meredith were routinely destroyed in the 1980s. No records from the administration of Ross Barnett apparently survive.

At the national office in Washington, the papers of the American Association of University Professors yielded vital information on a range of controversies at the University of Mississippi. The files of the Southern Association of Colleges and Schools in Decatur, Georgia, also contain pertinent materials, especially for background. The papers of the Association of American Law Schools, archived at the University of Illinois, help with specific topics related to the law school.

Three individuals granted access to their important private papers: Alvin Kershaw of Louisville, Kentucky; James William Silver of San Francisco; and William P. Murphy of Chapel Hill, North Carolina.

Essential information came from perusing long runs of several newspapers: the *Jackson Clarion-Ledger*, the *Jackson State Times*, the *Jackson Advocate*, the *Greenville Delta Democrat Times*, the *Meridian Star*, the *Oxford Eagle*, the University of Mississippi's *Mississippian*, and the *Southern School News*, published monthly by the Southern Education Reporting Service in Nashville, Tennessee. Extensive but more selective reading of the *New York Times*, the *Memphis Commercial Appeal*, the *New Orleans Times-Picayune*, and the *Jackson Daily News* also proved enlightening. Many other newspaper sources were derived from the extensive clipping collections of the FBI, the U.S. Marshals Service, the University of Mississippi, and the Southern Education Reporting Service, the last compiled in the invaluable "Facts on Film" microfilm series.

Among many published works, several books provide basic background: David G. Sansing's *The University of Mississippi: A Sesquicentennial History* (Jackson: University Press of Mississippi, 1999); John Dittmer's *Local People: The Struggle for Civil Rights in Mississippi* (Urbana: University of Illinois, 1994); and James Meredith's *Three Years in Mississippi* (Bloomington: Indiana University Press, 1965). Unpublished, book-length manuscripts by Hugh Clegg ("Someone Jumped the Gun," in this author's possession) and by Paul J. Scheips ("The Role of the Army in the Oxford, Mississippi, Incident, 1962–1963") helped fill out the story.

Innumerable oral histories supplemented the documentary record and the published works. The John F. Kennedy Presidential Library, the University of Southern Mississippi's Center for Oral History, the Mississippi Department of Archives and History, and the Department of Special Collections at the University of Mississippi contain hundreds of pertinent oral histories. A variety of depositions and sworn testimonies appear in the files of the General Legislative Investigating Committee and of *Meredith v. Fair*, and the files of the FBI and the U.S. Marshals Service include hundreds of interviews and signed statements by witnesses and participants. Among the many personal and telephone interviews I conducted for *The Price of Defiance*, the following stand out as noteworthy: Jacqueline Schnur, M. B. Mayfield, Ollie Lee McEwen, Murray Patton, Willie B. Tankersley, Albin Krebs, Sadie O. Jones and Charles Dubra (nephew), Paul D. King, Clennon King (nephew), Mary Alice Lee, Stokes V. Robertson, Charles Dunagin, James L. Robertson, James L. McDowell, Will Campbell, Alvin Kershaw, John E. Cameron, William M. Ellis, James William Silver, Elizabeth Silver, E. Wilburn Hooker Jr., William P. Murphy, Charles Haywood, James H. Meredith, A. B. Lewis, Robert B. Ellis, Katherine Rea, Charles Clark, Edwin Walker, William J. Simmons, John C. McLaurin, C. B. (Buddie) Newman, Frank Barber, Verner S. Holmes, Curtis Wilkie, Clare Marquette, William Willis, G. Ray Kerciu, Arvid A. Sather, and Henry Gallagher. Oral histories are cited only when they provide vital information unavailable from other sources.

Acknowledgments

The three people listed on the dedication page are the most important and deserve my thanks first. In addition to being my three best friends and making everything worthwhile, they provided smart and wise counsel. From the beginning years ago, Brenda provided indispensable support of all kinds: she read every part of the manuscript multiple times and offered invaluable criticisms, vital suggestions, and essential encouragement. Our sons, Daniel and Benjamin, listened to countless stories, asked good questions, and offered astute advice. For example, when Benjamin first heard the quotation from Langston Hughes, he immediately insisted that I use the entire passage as a frontispiece.

Between Brenda's initial and final readings, I benefited from commentaries offered on a much longer manuscript by other knowledgeable and skilled scholars. As he has done so often, Gaines M. Foster read the manuscript as it emerged in pieces, guided its development, and improved it immeasurably. Enthusiastic about the project from the beginning, David G. Sansing brought his knowledge of the university's history to bear on an early draft and saved me from errors. As a vice chancellor, Gerald W. Walton made the crucial university files available for the first time, and later his careful reading of the manuscript as an English professor and a university veteran corrected the writing and clarified details. John Dittmer and David J. Garrow, two award-winning authorities on the history of the civil rights movement, generously applied their expertise to the manuscript with significant effects, and each on many other occasions gave sensible advice and necessary support. Keri Bradford Anderson used her editorial skill and her familiarity with the Mississippi movement to improve the manuscript in myriad ways. Though a Civil War historian, Paul C. Anderson commented wisely on my work from the perspective of an accomplished writer. As a nineteenth-century urban historian, Jeffrey S. Adler may have had limited knowledge of the subject, but his comprehensive, incisive critique proved indispensable. Two readers for the University of North Carolina Press, Charles C. Bolton and Robert J. Norrell, offered thoughtful assessments; Chuck was particularly capable on substance, while Jeff identified several important structural problems. Bradley G. Bond, Dana B. Brammer, and John R. Neff helped, often on short notice, by evaluating parts of the longer work. Each reader strengthened the manuscript, often by encouraging concisions and excisions, or what I came to call "dewriting." To each I owe a great debt because their work improved the book immeasurably.

During the research and writing, I received assistance from many others at the university and elsewhere. Dana Brammer, Jean C. Brammer, John R. Bradley, Al E. Moreton, and numerous other longtime residents of Oxford helped by explaining many aspects of the town, the university, and their histories. Thomas G. Dyer's comments at the 1995 meeting of the Southern Historical Association spurred work on Part One, especially the third chapter. Editors John B. Boles and Kenneth G. McCarty facilitated publication of longer versions of chapter 7 in the *Journal of Southern History* and parts of chapters 10 and 21 in the *Journal of Mississippi History*.

So many archivists and librarians helped with the research that they cannot be thanked individually, but the assistance of a few must be acknowledged: Anne Webster, Nancy Bounds, Walter Crook, and the late Dwight Harris at the Mississippi Department of Archives and History; Mattie Sink and Michael Ballard at Mississippi State University; Mary Evelyn Tomlin at the National Archives in Morrow, Georgia; and, at the University of Mississippi's J. D. Williams Library, reference librarians John D. Cloy and Royce Kurtz, Laura B. Love in the microfilm section, Martha Swan and her staff in Interlibrary Loan, and Thomas C. Verich, Jennifer Ford, and especially Leigh McWhite, in the Archives and Special Collections. Two individuals who are not archivists provided vital access to document collections—Jordan Kurland in Washington at the American Association of University Professors national office and John Turcotte in Jackson at the legislature's Performance Evaluation and Expenditure Review Committee, successor to the General Legislative Investigating Committee. With the latter, W. F. Minor's intercession proved essential, as has his knowledge, guidance, and wisdom over the years.

Though they are missed for many other reasons, I regret that five people who were important in my life and who were very interested in my work will not have a chance to read this book because of their deaths. My mother, Alice C. Eagles, always asked about my progress and hoped to see the finished product. George B. Tindall, my mentor, who himself long ago taught for one year at the University of Mississippi, read several draft chapters and offered encouragement. Winthrop D. Jordan, my colleague for more than twenty years and an authority on American race relations, hoped to read about the history of our employer. With a new concern for Mississippi and southern race relations, Johnny Williams, who was much more than an accountant and administrator, commented on several chapters and always wanted to know more. Joseph A. Herzenberg, a veteran of civil rights activism in Mississippi during the 1960s, read several chapters with his usual interest and perceptiveness.

Several years ago David Perry did me a great favor by introducing me to Chuck Grench, and they convinced me to work with the University of North Carolina Press. From our first discussions, Chuck has been enthusiastic about this book. As an exemplary editor, he has offered the best mixture of patience, direction, and encouragement. Katy O'Brien, his assistant and Gus's mother, has been similarly friendly, helpful, and efficient. Paula Wald and others at the press have also been professional and cooperative in every way. I am especially grateful for the thorough and precise, yet kind, copyediting provided by John Wilson.

Every day, many of my colleagues and coworkers have made my professional life easy and pleasant. For more than a decade Betty Harness especially has made the History Department an unusually good place to work, and she has been ably assisted by Michelle Palmertree, Marie Baker, Susan Nicholas, and Nikki Bourgeois. The last have been first: every morning Barbara Walker and Tim Miller have given my day in Bishop Hall a happy and orderly start. To each of them I am grateful.

Index

Adkins, Terry, 438–40
Alcorn A&M College, 55, 68, 72, 76, 81–88
Alexander, Paul G., 264, 292
"Alma Mater" (song), 431–32
American Association of University Professors (AAUP): and William P. Murphy, 195, 196; on student discipline, 376, 380, 393–94; and Kerciu, 411; and possible expulsion of Meredith, 422; after riot, 430
American Civil Liberties Union (ACLU): and Clennon King, 95–96; and William P. Murphy, 190, 192, 195; and William L. Higgs, 401
American Council on Education, 430
Anderson, Reuben, 435, 540 (n. 32)
Armstrong, Louis, 56, 57
Association of American Law Schools (AALS), 430; and William P. Murphy, 196, 197
Attala County, Miss., history of, 202

Baldwin, James, 397, 529 (n. 80)
Ball, Coolidge, 435
Barbour, William, 310
Barnett, Ross R., 112, 115, 173, 175, 178, 223, 263, 276, 277, 279, 282, 300, 405, 431; and Billy Barton, 182–88; and William P. Murphy, 194–95; background of, 281–82; speaks on statewide radio and television, 282–83, 355–56, 416; proclamation of interposition, 283, 290; popular support for, 283–84, 289, 291, 307–8, 337, 427; prepares resistance to courts, 285–86; participates in telephone negotiations, 288, 290, 291–92, 313, 314–16, 319–20, 324–25, 327, 331–32, 335–36, 339, 342–43, 365–66, 368; and IHL Board, 288–89, 293–94, 315–17; appears before legislature, 290–91, 293; and contempt charges, 291, 292, 309–12, 328–29, 334, 429; denies Meredith's first attempt to register in Oxford, 301–5; proclamation protecting state employees from contempt charges, 309; prevents Meredith's second attempt to register in Jackson, 315–18; misses Meredith's third attempt to register in Oxford, 321, 323; calls off fourth attempt to register Meredith in Oxford, 325–27; and contempt charges, 329, 409, 429; speaks at football game in Jackson before riot, 336–37; and SACS, 338; dispatches delegation to Oxford, 344; refuses to surrender, 366; and football game in Jackson after riot, 374; and Cleve McDowell, 415–16; on denying Meredith degree, 422–23; and controversy over riot, 425–26, 428, 430
Barnett-Kennedy telephone negotiations. *See* Kennedy-Barnett telephone negotiations
Barrett, Russell, 3, 405, 433; and Meredith, 388, 390, 406–7; criticizes student discipline, 394
Barrett, St. John, 328; and first attempt to register Meredith in Oxford, 302–4; testifies on contempt charges against university leaders, 305–7

91, 92; and James W. Silver, 148; defends university, 162; replies to Hooker-White charges, 166–68; before riot, 345, 347, 348, 350

Clemson University, 398, 431

Cohodas, Nadine, 3

Coleman, J. P., 100, 110, 155, 242, 291, 309, 421; and Medgar Evers's application to law school, 73, 75–76, 77; and Clennon King, 91–94; on Alvin Kershaw, 127, 133; supports James Silver, 156; testifies at hearing on contempt charges against state officials and university leaders, 306; named to U.S. Fifth Circuit Court of Appeals, 434

Collins, E. K., 292, 320

Colonel Rebel (mascot), 20, 23, 334, 374, 435

Committee of Nine, 380, 382, 388, 390, 399, 525 (n. 36), 530 (n. 8)

Communism, fears of, 62, 66, 126, 143, 144, 145–46, 147, 148, 149, 150, 160–80, 192, 278, 319, 324, 337, 381, 416

Confederacy, 58, 66, 153, 157, 324, 451 (n. 44)

Confederate flag, 20, 58, 309, 317, 333, 337, 350, 351, 359, 363, 371, 372, 374, 410–11, 436, 450 (n. 39)

Confederate monument, 17, 58, 359, 360, 361, 362, 364, 368, 436

Congressional delegation, Mississippi (except Frank Smith), 284, 324, 343–44, 426

Congress of Racial Equality (CORE), 90, 235

Cottrell, David, 77, 92

Cox, A. Eugene, 119–20, 499 (n. 10)

Cox, Archibald, 274

Cuba, 277, 361, 426

Curtis, Chester, 310–11

Dale, Malcolm, 182, 185

Dantin, Maurice, 67, 123

DeVane, Dozier A., 263, 271, 272, 496 (n. 24). See also *Meredith v. Fair*

"Dixie" (song), 13, 20, 179, 333, 337, 374, 436

Dixiecrat Party, university students and, 33–34, 144, 147

Dixie Week, 13, 23, 58

Doar, John, 346, 359, 366, 416, 422; at hearing on contempt charges against state officials and university leaders, 309–12; at Meredith's second attempt to register in Jackson, 315–18; at Meredith's third attempt to register in Oxford, 321–23; and Meredith's aborted fourth attempt to register in Oxford, 325–27; at contempt hearings, 328, 334; escorts Meredith to campus, 350, 352; with Meredith on campus, 371, 385, 400

Doherty, William T., 158, 430–31

Dolan, Joseph A., 346–49

Doyle, William, 3–4, 501 (n. 32), 506 (n. 58), 514 (n. 31), 515 (n. 44), 518 (n. 67), 519 (n. 75), 520 (n. 82)

Du Bois, W. E. B., 91, 220, 420, 463 (n. 27)

Dubra, Charles Herbert Thomas, 70–72

Dylan, Bob, 432

East, P. D., 181–83, 185, 187

Eastland, James O., 74–75, 127, 163, 428

Edge, John T., 436–40

Edgeworth, Homer, 264, 300

Ellington, Duke, 56–57

Ellis, Robert B., 59, 239, 346, 413, 433, 507 (n. 61); and Clennon King, 89, 90–91, 92; and Meredith's application, 201, 221–36 passim; testifies in *Meredith v. Fair*, 250–51, 252–54, 258, 259; at first attempt to register Meredith in Oxford, 303–4; testifies at hearing on contempt charges against state officials and university leaders, 309–10; absent at Meredith's second attempt to register in Jackson, 316; registers Meredith, 371; on Meredith's return, 395; and Dewey Greene, 400–401

Ellis, W. M. "Chubby," 137, 165–66

Elmore, Joe Earl, 125–26, 134

Hilbun, Benjamin F., 160; racial attitudes of, 29; and segregated sports, 105, 106, 110; and William Buchanan, 132

Hill, Stanley, 438

Hills, Charles, 66, 132, 237, 291, 338, 398, 427

Hines, Tom S., 92

Holmes, Hamilton, 3, 221

Holmes, Verner, 258–59, 302, 369–70

Hood, James, 431

Hooker, Edwin Wilbur, 116, 133, 164–65, 168, 181, 190. *See also* Hooker-White charges

Hooker-White charges, 165, 169–70, 479 (n. 22); university reply to, 166–68; IHL's disposition of, 168–69, 170; against William P. Murphy, 190–91

Howard, Frank, 405, 407

Howard, T. R. M., 73

Hunter, Charlayne, 3, 221

Hutcheson, Joseph, 310, 311, 328, 329

Institutions of Higher Learning, Board of Trustees (IHL), 27, 35, 68, 69, 404; and Charles Dubra's application, 72; and Medgar Ever's application, 73, 76–78; creation of, 76–77; sets university entrance requirements, 77–78; and Clennon King, 83, 85, 87, 88, 90, 91; and restrictions on university speakers, 117, 153; on Kershaw controversy, 124, 126–28; and James Silver, 156–57; and Hooker-White charges, 165, 168–69, 170; and William P. Murphy, 193–94, 195, 196, 197; response to Meredith's application, 222, 224; members summoned, 241; prohibited from interfering with Meredith, 283; considers options, 285–86; activities after court order, 288–89; hears Barnett, 293–94; directions to Meredith and Barnett, 301–2; at hearing on contempt charges, 309–12; and Meredith's second attempt to register in Jackson, 315–17; trustees go to university campus during

riot, 369–70; and Taylor Robertson case, 382; and Cleve McDowell's application, 414–15; and controversy over Meredith's statement after Evers's murder, 418, 421–24; and CRCI project, 438

Interposition, 100, 127, 191, 192, 284, 290, 291

Iona College, 105–6, 438

Ivy, James E. ("Blind Jim"), 43–48

Jackson State College, 24, 52, 106–7, 254, 255; Meredith at, 214–19, 230–31, 301

Jackson (Miss.) State Times, 82, 83, 85–86; and Billy Barton, 184–85

Jaquith, William Lawrence, 94–95, 96–97

Jeffreys, Joseph, 163–64

Jobe, E. R., 170, 222, 224, 241, 288, 302, 421; and early black applicants, 69, 73, 75; and Clennon King, 85, 89, 91; testifies at hearing on contempt charges, 309–10

Joffrion, A. Emile, 123, 126, 135

Johnson, Paul B., 285–86, 290, 325, 510 (n.43); at Meredith's first attempt to register in Oxford, 301, 303; blocks Meredith's third attempt to register in Oxford, 321, 323; participates in telephone negotiations, 324–25; and Meredith's aborted fourth attempt to register in Oxford, 325–27; speaks to legislature, 327–28; and contempt charges, 334, 409, 429; goes to campus during riot, 366; and controversy over riot, 426; subsequent political career, 431, 434

Jones, Albert, 185, 187, 188

Katzenbach, Nicholas, 287, 338, 344, 374; at Lyceum during riot, 348–70 passim; speaks to university students, 375; on student discipline, 380–81

Kennard, Clyde, 221, 226, 227, 264

Kennedy, John F., 405; and South and civil rights, 277–80; praises L. Q. C. Lamar, 278, 358; and Meredith case, 280–82; confers with Robert Kennedy, 329, 334–35;

participates in telephone negotiations, 335–36, 365–66, 368; issues proclamation and executive order, 339, 340; telegraphs Barnett, 343; addresses nation, 357–58; consults advisers, 365, 366, 367–68; on Meredith's return, 395; and controversy over riot, 425, 426, 430

Kennedy, Robert F., 235, 277, 279, 348, 352, 355, 356, 357, 367, 405; participates in telephone negotiations, 288, 290, 291–92, 300–301, 313, 314–16, 319–20, 324–25, 327, 331–32, 335–36, 338, 339, 342–43; meets at Pentagon, 329; confers with president, 329, 324–25, 365, 367–68; sends representatives to Oxford, 344; criticizes student discipline, 393; and controversy over riot, 430; speaks at university, 435

Kennedy administration: and civil rights, 279–80; and Meredith case, 280–81; plans for enforcement of court order, 286–88, 291

Kennedy-Barnett telephone negotiations (including conversations by their representatives), 288, 290, 291–92, 300–301, 313, 314–16, 319–20, 321, 324–25, 327, 331–32, 335–36, 338, 339, 501 (n. 37)

Kerciu, Ray, 407, 409–11, 421

Kershaw, Alvin, 121–35 passim

Khayat, Robert C., 436–41

Kilpatrick, James J., 189, 191, 334, 511 (n. 50)

King, Clennon, 165, 190, 191, 221, 227, 264, 400; background, 80–81; and controversy at Alcorn A&M College, 81–88; applies to university, 88–93; sent to Mississippi State Hospital, 94–95, 96–97; Meredith and, 212

King, Martin Luther, Jr., 86, 90, 95, 279, 291, 431

King, Morton B., 131, 138

Knobles, Craig, 386–87, 388, 394

Krebs, Albin, 60–68, 161, 459 (n. 29), 482 (n. 59)

Ku Klux Klan, 58, 330, 345, 434, 436

Lamar, L. Q. C., 278, 358

Leathers, Robert C., 69

Lewis, A. B., 222, 233, 239, 303, 389. See also *Meredith v. Fair*

Lewis, John, 441

Little Rock school crisis, 57, 174, 175, 179, 268, 278, 341, 426

Look (magazine), 427–28

Lord, Walter, 3

Lost Cause, 17–20, 24, 58

Love, L. L., 166, 168, 183, 258, 284, 347, 357, 417, 421, 433; and Ernest McEwen Jr., 54–55; and student discipline, 376–77, 378, 393

Lowman, Myers, 171–73, 174

Lucy, Autherine, 2, 91, 130

Lumpkin, Sam, 289, 324

Mabry, Malcolm, 162–63, 164

Malone, Vivian, 431

Marquette, Clare, 90, 371–72, 405

Marshall, Burke, 226, 280, 286–88, 305, 306, 309, 338; enters Meredith case, 280–81; relationship with Tom Watkins, 280–81; participates in telephone negotiations, 290, 291–92, 300–301, 315–16, 321, 324–25, 346, 347; at hearing on contempt charges, 328–29; and controversy over riot, 426

Marshall, Thurgood, 179, 225, 228

Mathews, Joseph J., 157–58

Mayfield, M. B., 49–54, 58, 59

McCain, William D., 174; racial attitudes of, 29

McDowell, Cleve: applies to university law school, 414; lawsuit to enter university, 414–15; enrolled at university, 416; expelled from university, 435

McDowell, Jimmie, 107–9, 111–12, 113

McEwen, Ernest, Jr.: as university employee, 54, 59; as student at Alcorn A&M, 55; and strike at Alcorn A&M, 83, 84, 86

McGill, Ralph, 181, 182, 185, 469 (n. 8)

McGowan, M. M.: and Clennon King, 95; and Billy Barton, 187; supports Barnett, 337–38

McKenzie, Hamer, 148–49, 160–61

McLaurin, John, 9, 192, 292–93, 320, 344, 354–55, 415

McLeod, J. R., 252

McNamara, Robert, 329–30

McShane, James P., 281, 286, 287, 292, 295, 371, 372, 429; at first attempt to register Meredith in Oxford, 302–4; at Meredith's second attempt to register in Jackson, 315–18; at Meredith's third attempt to register in Oxford, 321–23; and Meredith's aborted fourth attempt to register in Oxford, 325–27; testifies at U.S. Fifth Circuit Court of Appeals hearing on contempt charges, 328; during riot, 341, 348, 350, 356, 357

Media: and race, 11, 101, 106, 130, 170, 287, 299, 323, 326, 328, 330, 333, 346, 352, 358, 370, 416, 426, 430; state radio and television support racial orthodoxy, 100, 105, 178–80, 333; Meredith and, 226–27, 237, 248, 271, 295–96, 371, 374, 388–89, 397, 412–13, 416–17, 418–19, 421; Barnett speaks on radio and television, 282–83, 355–56, 416; university treatment of, 294, 398–99, 421, 509 (n. 37); at Meredith's second attempt to register in Jackson, 315, 317; university radio station (WCBH), 320, 346, 347, 376; at Meredith's aborted fourth attempt to register in Oxford, 325–27; Edwin Walker uses, 331, 334; President Kennedy addresses nation, 338, 342, 357–58; agitate defiance, 346; and crowd attacks, 354, 366; and assault on Gordon Yoder, 354, 516 (n. 49); and debate over riot, 425–28, 431–32; Sigma Delta Chi awards, 536–37 (n. 9)

Meredith, James H., 1–5, 282, 430, 439, 522–23 (n. 17); objectives, 24–25, 231–32;

applies to university, 201, 218–19, 221–36 passim; family and youth, 202–8; education, 205, 208–15; gains racial awareness, 206–17 passim; in air force, 208–18; marriage, 210; in Japan, 210–13; at Jackson State College, 214–19, 230–31; registers to vote, 217, 264, 265, 292, 300; political activity, 217–19; and MIAS, 218; involvement in NAACP, 218, 248; representation by NAACP, 224–36 passim; and press, 226–27, 237, 248, 271, 295–96, 371, 374, 375, 388–89, 392, 397, 412–13, 416–17, 418–19, 421; and Freedom Rides, 237, 248; gives deposition, 241–44; testifies in *Meredith v. Fair*, 244–46, 248–50; meets with McShane, 287; in seclusion, 295–96; convicted in voter registration case, 300; first attempt to register in Oxford, 302–5; second attempt to register in Jackson, 315–18; third attempt to register in Oxford, 321–23; aborted fourth attempt to register in Oxford, 325–27; testifies at hearing on contempt charges, 334; before and during riot, 345; goes to Baxter Hall on campus, 349, 350; registers at university, 371; daily life on campus, 373, 374, 379–90, 403–4, 406–9; leaves campus on weekends, 374; charged with traffic violation in Kosciusko, 391; decision about returning for spring semester, 392–93, 395–96, 397–98; meets with Chancellor Williams, 399–400; and local black community, 408; applies for university family housing, 413–15; reacts to Medgar Evers's murder, 416–18; speaks to NAACP meetings, 418–21; graduation, 421–24; after 1963, 434–35, 436; statue of, 440; quoted, 441–43. See also *Meredith v. Fair*

Meredith, Joseph, 438, 441

Meredith, Moses Arthur "Cap," 203–8, 209, 227, 247, 423

Meredith, Roxie Marie Patterson, 203–8, 209, 227, 247, 423

Motley, Constance Baker, 243, 263, 276, 308, 328, 329, 439, 492 (n. 13); advises Meredith, 227–30, 232–35, 270–71, 295, 391, 395; files suit in *Meredith v. Fair*, 236–37; on Meredith's return, 395; named federal judge, 434. *See also Meredith v. Fair*

Mounger, William H., 308, 426

Murphy, Harry S., 20–21, 68, 313, 459 (n. 29)

Murphy, William P., 95–96, 188–98, 433

Myrdal, Gunnar, 41, 150, 425, 443

National Association for the Advancement of Colored People (NAACP): and Legal Defense and Educational Fund (LDF), 2, 29, 31, 63, 68, 70, 118, 177, 180, 269, 278, 308, 395, 400, 408, 410, 414; and Charles Dubra, 71–72; and Medgar Evers, 72–78; and Clennon King, 81–91 passim, 95; white criticism of, 100, 104, 122, 125, 126–27, 130, 189, 192, 275, 289, 291, 315, 319, 378, 384, 403, 421; and Alvin Kershaw, 121–38 passim; assists Meredith, 218, 224–36 passim; criticizes Barnett, 308; Meredith speaks to, 418–21. *See also* Marshall, Thurgood; *Meredith v. Fair*; Motley, Constance Baker

National Student Association (NSA), 33, 34–35

"Negro," mispronunciation of: on WLBT, 179; by Dugas Shands, 248, 492 (n. 13), 493 (n. 33); by Charles Clark, 257–58; by Tally Riddell, 494 (n. 69)

Newman, C. B. "Buddie," 106, 133, 344, 355

Niglia, Dominic, 379–80, 429

Noyes, Charles, 410–11, 421

Ogden, Florence Sillers, 122, 173

Old South, 16, 24, 55, 58, 154, 155

"Ole Miss," origin of term, 17–18. *See also* University of Mississippi

Ole Miss Coloring Book, 404–5

Otis, Jesse R., 82–83, 85

"Oxford Town" (song), 432

Owen, Robert, 305–6

Parchman State Penitentiary, 36–39, 435–36

Parker, Mack Charles, 2, 11, 49, 111

Patriotic American Youth, 162, 176, 337, 387, 411

Patterson, Joseph T., 90, 91, 178, 252, 262, 263, 267, 275, 276, 285, 291, 306; participates in telephone negotiations, 291–92, 300–301; advises Barnett, 342; rebuts Katzenbach to students, 375–78

Patterson, Robert B. "Tut," 57, 99, 109, 161–62, 163, 165

Pickering, Charles W., 437

Pittman, Paul, 39, 184, 499 (n. 10)

Porter, L. B., 66, 292, 300

Providence Farm, 119–21, 165

Purser, Stuart R., 49–53

Putnam, Carleton, 173–74

Randall, George M. "Buck," 362

Rankin, John, 66

Rea, Katherine, 257, 258

Rebel Resistance, 383–84

Rebel Underground, 468 (n. 56); on unwritten law or rule, 115; on Jimmie Robertson, 176–77; promotes resistance to Meredith, 379, 382, 392, 394; criticizes university administration, 394; attacks Sidna Brower, 395, 405–6; and James Silver, 406; on Kerciu controversy, 411

Reconstruction, 27, 154, 239, 269, 278, 339

Redmond, William, 408

Regional Council of Negro Leadership, 2, 73

Reis, Harold F., 344, 349

Religion and race, 29, 50, 61, 65, 75, 88, 165, 167, 171–72, 180, 207–8, 216, 299–300, 409; Oxford clergy during crisis, 284–85, 324, 344–45. *See also* Religious Emphasis Week; *individual clergy*

Religious Emphasis Week (REW), 117–18, 119, 121–35 passim, 162, 168

302, 304, 320–21, 332, 400; in riot, 354–64 passim; harassment of Meredith, 371, 372–73, 376–77, 381, 386–87, 391, 393, 394, 404–5, 408–9, 412; friendly toward Meredith, 386–87. See also *Mississippian*; *individual students*

Tatum, Burnes, 348, 350
Taylor, Maxwell, 329, 338
Temple, William, 387, 388, 394
Thompson, Allen, 216–17, 235, 499 (n. 21)
Thompson, Roger, 408
Thorn, Roman Lee, Jr., 164
Till, Emmett, 2, 49, 118, 120, 124
Topp, Mildred, 405, 406, 532 (n. 35)
Tougaloo College, 2, 69, 225, 232
Trotter, William Chamberlain, 46, 163, 165, 166
Tubb, Thomas J., 288, 369–70, 421
Tureaud, A. P., 75, 76
Turner, R. Gerald, 432, 436
Tuttle, Elbert P., 255, 261, 262–63, 272, 309–12, 328, 329. See also *Meredith v. Fair*

United Daughters of the Confederacy, 17, 410
U.S. Army: plans, 286–87; mobilizes units in Memphis, 330, 338, 339, 340–41; uses black soldiers, 341, 348, 352, 353, 375; deploys to Oxford, 365, 368; arrives on campus, 369; with Meredith, 372–94 passim, 399–417 passim; Pfc. Dominic Niglia fires weapon, 379–80
U.S. Border Patrol, 341. *See also* U.S. Marshals
U.S. Bureau of Prisons, 341. *See also* U.S. Marshals
U.S. Department of Justice, 224, 225, 226, 280, 286, 291, 296, 300, 308–9, 321, 342, 344, 373, 378, 379, 380, 385; enters *Meredith v. Fair* as amicus, 274–75. See also *Meredith v. Fair*
U.S. District Court, Southern District of Mississippi. See *Meredith v. Fair*

U.S. Fifth Circuit Court of Appeals. See *Meredith v. Fair*
U.S. Marshals, 279, 281, 286–87, 295–96, 405, 439; move to Memphis, 330, 338; deploy to university and Lyceum, 340–54 passim; during riot, 354–70 passim; protect Meredith on campus, 371–96 passim, 399–424 passim; controversy over, 425–26
U.S. Supreme Court, 60, 63, 68, 70, 74, 124, 168, 170–71, 180, 190, 239, 267–68, 270, 272, 273–76, 281, 429, 519 (n. 73), 537 (n. 14)
University Greys, 17
University of Mississippi: social culture of, 9–10, 13–14; image and reputation, 11–12, 19–20, 21–22, 222–23; academic life at, 12–13, 14–15; history of, 15–21, 68–69; nickname (Ole Miss), 17–18; first Negro student at, 20–21; importance in state, 22–24; racial controversies before 1954, 31–40; black employment, 42–43; early black applicants, 68–70; response to Meredith's application, 221–36; official report on riot, 429–30
Unwritten law or rule (segregated athletics): creation of, 103–5; effects on university, 105–6, 107, 108, 111–12, 113; critics of, 106, 107–8, 109, 110–11, 112, 113–15, 176; supporters of, 106, 110, 115; effects on Mississippi State College, 108–11, 112, 114–15; broken by Mississippi State basketball team, 409

Vance, Cyrus, 286–87, 329–30, 338, 365
Vaught, John, 11, 102, 113, 139, 383, 526 (n. 49)
Voter registration case against Meredith, 264; appeal to Judge Wisdom, 265; case revived, 292; Meredith convicted in, 300

Walker, Edwin A., 405; speaks in Jackson, 174–75, 176; rallies forces for Oxford, 331,

334; in Oxford, 345–46; during riot, 360–62, 368–69; in legal battles after riot, 428–29, 433–34, 518–19 (n. 73), 537–38 (n. 14)

Walker, Robert, 435

Wallace, George C., 179, 409

Washington, Booker T., 80–81, 86, 88, 220, 420

Watkins, Tom, 306, 332; relationship with Burke Marshall, 280–81; participates in telephone negotiations, 300–301, 321, 324–25, 335–36, 338, 342–43, 346; advises Barnett, 341, 415

Weathersby, Pauline, 69

White, Hillery Edwin, 110, 124, 168, 181, 190; on *Brown* decision, 75; criticism of J. D. Williams, 137–38; background, 164–65. *See also* Hooker-White charges

White, Hugh L., 38, 70, 133, 153, 308, 421

Wiesenburg, Karl, 282, 291, 293, 327, 427

Wiggins, Marvin, 36–38

Wilds, Murphey C., 285, 344–45

Wilkins, Roy, 95, 225, 395, 420

Williams, Ben, 435

Williams, John Bell, 110, 127, 144, 163, 174, 175, 226, 239, 380

Williams, John D., 139, 146, 158, 160, 161, 183, 186, 404, 405, 411; and university development, 21; racial attitudes of, 26, 27–29; personal background of, 26–28; attempts to modernize university, 30–31; and racial controversies before 1954, 31–40; on Albin Krebs, 64, 66; and early black applicants, 68–70; and Clennon King, 97–98; on segregated sports, 103,

104, 106; on Alvin Kershaw, 122, 123, 127, 128, 129–30; and Morton King, 131; on compromise, 137–38; replies to Hooker-White charges, 166, 167, 168; and William P. Murphy, 192–96; and Meredith's application, 222–23; testifies in *Meredith v. Fair*, 259; prepares for Meredith, 284; absent from Meredith's first attempt to register in Oxford, 303; tries to calm students, 320; before riot, 345, 347, 350–51; and student discipline, 376–77, 380, 381–82, 393, 394; treatment of media, 398–99; meets with Meredith, 399–400; on departing professors, 403; and housing for Meredith family, 413–14; and Cleve McDowell, 414–16; on Meredith's statement after Evers's murder, 417; on awarding Meredith degree, 423, 424; on *Look* article, 428; end of career, 432

William Winter Institute for Racial Reconciliation, 437

Willis, A. W., 395, 397

Willis, William H., 380, 417. *See also* Committee of Nine

Winter, William F., 148, 156, 193, 437, 439, 441, 531 (n. 17)

Wisdom, John Minor, 220, 255, 256–57, 261, 262, 265–67, 269, 274, 291, 323. See also *Meredith v. Fair*

Wroten, Joseph, 264, 284, 291, 293, 327

Yarbrough, George, 131–32, 133, 292, 344, 354–55, 357; orders patrol to leave campus, 355

Yoder, Gordon, 354